'This new edition is a welcome presence in the market for textbook introductions to Western political thought. It is clear, comprehensive and broad – the kind of book that covers all the bases. It is a reliable one-stop-shop of Western political ideas that any student of the subject will be able to access.'

– **Graeme Garrard**, *Cardiff University, UK*

'This textbook provides students with a comprehensive introduction to a wide range of attempts to solve the perennial problems that characterise Western political thought. In synthesising the responses of a multitude of figures, from Ancient Greece to the turn to the post-modern, it gives an excellent introduction to how the canon of political theory can provide answers to the questions of where power lies, how it should be exercised, and where it can be resisted. Its value to students lies not only in its clear presentation of established figures in the discipline but also in its highlighting of the distinct contributions to this tradition that are made by neglected figures such as Du Bois, Douglass, Fanon and Goldman.'

– **Ben Turner**, *University of Kent, UK*

'John Morrow's *History of Western Political Thought* is astonishing in its breadth and admirable in its accessibility. Morrow is a talented writer and thinker who makes it easy to understand complicated arguments while still honouring the complexity and multiplicity of what we call Western political thought.'

– **Susan McWilliams**, *Pomona College, USA*

'In this clearly written and expertly presented history of Western political thought, John Morrow departs from the standard chronological treatment of "big thinkers" and instead highlights key themes. The volume also makes an effort to recognise how certain ideas were applied in ways that excluded large sections of society, and Morrow includes consideration of several thinkers – often overlooked – who played important roles in challenging inherited ideas about female or racial inferiority. The book also features an interesting consideration of theories of revolution, resistance and civil disobedience.'

– **Miriam Bankovsky**, *La Trobe University, Australia*

'Finally, a text for political thought that is attentive to the history of political thought, lays out the core ideas and arguments of Western political thought with formidable philosophic clarity and is mercifully free from the jargon of much contemporary political philosophy. My students love the plain language explanations of the political ideas and arguments that circle around them in public discourse.'

– **Lindsey MacDonald**, *University of Canterbury, New Zealand*

HISTORY OF WESTERN POLITICAL THOUGHT

THIRD EDITION

JOHN MORROW

This edition published 2019 by
RED GLOBE PRESS

Previous editions published under the imprint PALGRAVE

Red Globe Press in the UK is an imprint of Springer Nature Limited, registered in England, company number 785998, of 4 Crinan Street, London N1 9XW.

Red Globe Press® is a registered trademark in the United States, the United Kingdom, Europe and other countries.

ISBN 978-1-352-00594-3 hardback
ISBN 978-1-352-00572-1 paperback

This book is printed on paper suitable for recycling and made from fully managed and sustained forest sources. Logging, pulping and manufacturing processes are expected to conform to the environmental regulations of the country of origin.

A catalogue record for this book is available from the British Library.

A catalog record for this book is available from the Library of Congress.

CONTENTS

PREFACE TO THE THIRD EDITION

In preparing this edition I have pruned the text extensively to eradicate circumlocutions which survived earlier revisions. The material on contemporary themes which formed the general conclusion of the second edition has been revised and incorporated in the concluding sections of the substantive chapters. Additions to the third chapter on black emancipation and feminist thought have made it necessary to divide it into two chapters, one focusing on individual freedom and the other on social theories of liberty. In order to broaden the scope of the book and give a more complete sense of historical political thought in the Western tradition I have introduced discussions of thinkers' ideas on international relations where these align with the themes of the book. This edition concludes with an epilogue outlining 'post-modern' and 'post-colonial' reactions to the histories of Western political thought that form the subject matter of the book.

Steven Kennedy suggested that I consider a third edition of this book a few years ago but I did not begin to put my mind to it until after his retirement from Palgrave, now Red Globe Press. I am grateful for his encouragement and for that of Lloyd Langman who has succeeded him. Three referees provided full, generous and very helpful reports on an earlier draft of the revised text. I am most grateful to my wife Diana Morrow for reviewing new material. My executive assistant, Susan McDowell-Watt, has provided valuable assistance with the typescript.

John Morrow, University of Auckland,
New Zealand

LIST OF 'THINKER' BOXES

INTRODUCTION

This book is intended to provide a succinct but comprehensive treatment of thinkers, issues and debates that have been of central importance in the Western tradition of political thought. Many introductions to this subject survey the ideas of an extensive number of 'great thinkers' who are taken to represent the highpoints of a tradition jestingly referred to as extending 'from Plato to Nato'. This approach provides a chronologically coherent way of outlining the ideas of particular thinkers and allows for a consideration of the biographical and historical background in which their works were produced. At the same time, however, it makes it difficult to include considerations of a range of less commonly noted but historically significant political thinkers, and inhibits identification of thematic patterns in the history of political thought.

In order to overcome these difficulties this book is organised around themes that extend across wide tracts of European history. These themes highlight questions about politics that have played an important ongoing role in Western political thinking and identify continuities and changes in the ways in which they have been posed and answered over long periods of time.

Changing economic and social structures, varying forms of political organisation, religious beliefs and ways of viewing the human world mean that it would be anachronistic to treat Western political thinking as a homogeneous whole. At the same time, however, Western political thinkers have been aware of at least aspects of their past and have often formulated their ideas by reference to the ideas of their predecessors. These considerations explain why it makes sense to talk of patterns of change and continuity, and they also explain why this book makes only passing reference to non-Western political thought. For the most part, Western political thinkers have not reflected on systematic statements about politics developed in other cultures.

Periodisation

The two and a half thousand-years' span of European history with which this book deals is conventionally divided into a number of periods. This periodisation does not encapsulate absolutely discrete historical entities, but it is useful in capturing broad stages of Western development and the sets of intellectual, religious and political beliefs that correspond to them. The first thousand years, that is, from about 500 BC until 500 AD, is referred to as the 'ancient' period. During this millennium Western political thought focused on the city states of Greece, and on the Roman Republic and the Empire that succeeded it. There were some similarities between the governments of the Greek city states and that which emerged during the history of the Roman Republic, and thinkers who reflected on the experience of the latter were aware of the ideas of their Greek predecessors. For most of this period political thinking focused on pre-Christian societies, but in late antiquity it had to come to grips with the growing influence of Christian ideas in the Roman Empire.

The medieval period extends from the sixth century to the late fifteenth century. Medieval political thought reflected the Christian basis of Western culture at this time, the erosion of the authority of the Holy Roman Empire, the emergence of the complex system of economic, political and social organisation known as 'feudalism', and the appearance towards the end of the period of increasingly unified 'nation states'. These states dominated the political history of the early-modern period, which extended from the early sixteenth to the late eighteenth century. For the two centuries following the beginning of the Reformation in Germany in 1517 the division of Western Christendom into 'Protestant' and Roman Catholic communities had a major impact on political thought. These developments overlapped with the reappearance, particularly in Italy, of forms of government that focused on city states, and the recovery of philosophical works from the ancient world. Sometimes these writings promoted political ideas that ran counter to lessons derived from the Christian tradition. The influence of the latter was also blunted to some degree in the seventeenth century by the burgeoning interest in scientific investigation, and in the eighteenth century by the stress placed on human reason by the 'enlightenment' movements in a number of European countries. Taken together, these developments prepared the ground for the more secular perspectives on politics advanced by a number of 'modern' writers in the nineteenth and early twentieth centuries.

In the modern period political theory not only became increasingly, although not exclusively, secular in orientation, but it also focused on issues that were distinctive to the recent experience of Western societies and the other countries of the world that were influenced by them. Unprecedented developments in the economic life of these societies, conventionally categorised as the first 'industrial revolution', and the democratisation of social and political relationships, had a marked impact on the way that people thought about politics. The modern period witnessed the appearance of a wide range of complex political theories, elements of which were incorporated into the political ideologies attached to the perceived interests of distinct groups or classes within society. Thus while the political thinking of the modern world exhibited some continuity with that of earlier periods, it was also marked by the appearance of theories of mass politics, and those promoting deliberate, revolutionary change.

The focus of the book

For the most part, this book focuses on ideas of *rule* and sets these within the framework of the *state*. Central to this conception of politics is a series of questions concerning the purposes of political authority, the persons who should possess it and the ways in which it should be exercised. Western political thinking has been largely concerned with the internal dimensions of politics rather than with what is now called 'international relations' and this imbalance is reflected in the ideas discussed in this book. However, a number of chapters consider historical writers' ideas on war and interstate relations where these provide interesting insights that relate to the book's organisational themes. It thus provides discussions of the international political thought of Plato, Aristotle, Cicero, Polybius, Aquinas, Machiavelli, Grotius, Hobbes, Pufendorf, Rousseau, Kant, Burke, Hegel, J. S. Mill, T. H. Green, Marx and Lenin.

As is made apparent throughout this book, political thinking has always had a strongly prescriptive tendency. It almost invariably gives rise to arguments that favour certain political institutions, ideas and practices, and question alternatives to them. The themes explored in the following chapters identify sets of prescriptions relating to the purpose and nature of political rule and the structures within which it takes place. Part I of the book examines a number of responses to the question: to what ends should political authority be directed? In Parts II and III the focus shifts to arguments about *who* should exercise supreme authority and *how* such authority should be exercised. Finally, Part IV examines theories that justify resistance to political superiors and those that promote revolutionary challenges both to rulers and to the systems of government in which they are located.

The treatment of these themes is divided between a number of chapters exploring distinct sets of answers to the general questions posed in Parts I–IV. Although the positions discussed in each chapter exhibit fundamental similarities, they vary significantly. These variations can be explained by reference to the particular contexts in which the theories in question were produced, and to the common tendency for writers to use the ideas of their predecessors as starting points from which to develop new approaches to issues that have been considered by them. Each of the chapters follows a roughly chronological line of development and their historical scope reflects the richness of the material available and the persistence of a particular theme over time. Major thinkers appear in a number of chapters, with their ideas being considered alongside a range of ideas produced by historically significant but less prominent writers. Thus while this book presents a series of accounts of the ideas of those who are conventionally seen as 'great names' it also considers the arguments of thinkers who fall outside this august company but were significant in their own times.

As we shall see, writers' contributions to the history of Western political thought have been influenced strongly by their understanding of the problems facing their own societies, by their perception of the strengths and weaknesses of other treatments of them, and by presuppositions about human nature and social life grounded in fundamental religious or meta-ethical assumptions. Recent scholarly studies of the history of political thought have stressed the importance of these contextual and situational factors. They have warned of the need to avoid anachronism and to treat the past in a way that takes account of its distinctive character. The past, it has been said, is a foreign country: they do things differently there. While recognising the force of these strictures, one must also bear in mind that historical thinkers have rarely adhered to them. They have often formulated their ideas by drawing on, or reacting against, the arguments of their predecessors, and they have tended to treat the past as a treasure trove from which they can draw for their own purposes.

Western political thinking: A brief overview

The earliest systematic statements of political theory to survive in a relatively complete form were produced in the fourth century BC by the Greek writer Plato and his pupil Aristotle. These works focus on the type of state that was common in the Greek world in that period: the *polis,* or 'city state'. The *polis* was not merely an administrative unit, nor even just the source of protection or material well-being. For the Greeks the *polis* was, quite literally, a way of life. It provided the focal point of a complex web of artistic, economic, intellectual, moral, political and religious aspirations, embracing and reflecting the culture of the community, and providing the framework within which individuals realised their aspirations.

While ancient political theories focused on the *polis,* or in the case of the Roman writer Cicero, on the more extensive type of republican regime that emerged in the second and first centuries before Christ, medieval political theorists had to come to grips with an environment that contained a range of political institutions. Although these writers knew about the *polis* and from the thirteenth century had access to fairly complete versions of ancient political writings, they discussed empires and kingdoms as well as city states. They also explored the relationship between political institutions and ideas, and Christian conceptions of human life. For example, St Augustine of Hippo, writing in the fifth century AD, was highly critical of Greek and Roman assumptions about the ultimate value of political institutions and drew a sharp distinction between 'earthly cities' (such as the Roman Empire) and the 'heavenly city', which embraced the destiny of Christians. In the late medieval period, however, the growing interest in Aristotle encouraged a reassessment of the classical heritage. A number of writers, of whom the most important was the thirteenth-century philosopher and theologian St Thomas Aquinas, identified a close and positive relationship between political institutions and the realisation of Christian values. Much of Aquinas' theory focused on kingdoms rather than empires or city states. He sought to relate the exercise of political authority to humans' need to be subjected to systems of political regulation that embody fundamental principles derived from divine governance of the universe. In developing this position, Aquinas drew upon many of the details of Aristotle's political and moral philosophy, but he insisted that claims about the importance of the state must be set within a Christian framework.

The appearance of a number of rich and powerful city states in late medieval and early-modern Italy prompted political thinkers to focus anew on the problems encountered in this form of political organisation. The major issues facing these states, stability and survival, raised questions about the value systems of republics, as well as their internal organisation and external relations. The most original and influential thinker to emerge in this context was Niccoló Machiavelli, who produced a number of important works. Machiavelli drew on the classical past, and particularly the example of the Roman Republic, to develop a specification for a popular republican state. A striking feature of Machiavelli's work is that he treated politics in relation to the requirements of a distinctly political morality, and was openly critical of the effect of Christian ideas on political practice. These issues played an important role in his account of republics, and also in his treatment of the problems faced by single rulers, or 'princes'.

Chronology: Ancient and Medieval Periods c.400 BC–1500 AD

Year of Death	Thinkers	Works	Contemporary events	
BC				
d. 399	Socrates	No writings	431–404:	The Great Peloponnesian War.
	Protagoras		404–403:	Rule of the Thirty Tyrants at Athens.
	Democritus			
d. 347	Plato	*Republic* (c.380)	333:	Defeat of Greek forces by Alexander the Great.
		Laws (unfinished)		
d. 322	Aristotle	*Ethics*		
		Politics		
d. 264	Zeno	No writings		
*d. c.*125	Polybius	*The Histories* (c.146)	146:	Greek states fall under Roman control.
			133:	Gracchian land reforms attempted at Rome.
			123:	Second attempt at Gracchian land reform.
			88–82:	Civil war in Rome.
d. 43	Cicero	*The Republic*	63:	Cicero consul.
		The Laws	44:	Assassination of Julius Caesar.
			31–14 *AD*:	Rule of Augustus, end of Roman Republic.

Year of Death	Thinkers	Works	Contemporary events	
AD				
d. 397	Ambrose	*De Officiis Ministrorum* (386)	306–337:	Rule of Constantine the Great.
			312:	Constantine's conversion to Christianity.
d. 430	Augustine	*The City of God* (413–427)	410:	Sack of Rome by Alaric.
d. 496	Gelasius	*Address* (494)		
d. 565	Justinian I	*Digest* (533) *Institutes* (533)	527–565:	Rule of Justinian I.
			c.1000:	Venice established as a major naval and trading port.
			1066:	Norman conquest of England.
d. 1085	Gregory VII	*Decree Against Lay Investitures* (1075)		
d. 1180	John of Salisbury	*Polycraticus* (1159)	1075–1122:	The Investiture Controversy.
			1215:	Magna Carta.
			c.1240:	Latin texts of Aristotle's writings circulated in the West.
d. 1268	Bracton, Henry	*Of the Laws and Customs of England* (1268)		
d. 1274	Aquinas	*Summa Theologiae* (c.1266–73)		
d. 1342	Marsilius of Padua	*Defender of the Peace* (1324)		
d. 1349	William of Ockham	*A Short Discourse* (1346)		
d. 1357	Bartolus of Sassoferrato	*Tract on City Government*		
*d. c.*1430	Pizan, Christine de	*Book of the Body Politic* (1604)		
			1337–1453:	The Hundred Years War.
			1450–1550:	Renaissance in Italy.
			1494–5:	French Invasion of Italy.
			1517:	Start of the Protestant Reformation.

Chronology: Early-modern Period, *c.*1500–1800 AD

Year of Death	Thinkers	Works	Contemporary events	
d. 1520	de Seyssel, Claude	*The Monarchy of France* (1519)	1512:	Restoration of Medici at Florence.
d. 1527	Machiavelli, Niccoló	*The Prince* (1513) *The Discourses* (1513–19)	1527:	Florentine Republic re-established.

Year of Death	Thinkers	Works	Contemporary events	
d. 1540	Guicciardini, Francesco	*Dialogue on the Government of Florence* (1523)		
d. 1546	Luther, Martin	*On Secular Authority* (1523)	1517:	Protestant Reformation begins.
		Against the Murderous Thieving Hordes of Peasants (1525)	1524–5:	The Peasants' War in Germany.
d. 1560	Melanchthon, Philippe	*Philosophiae Moralis Epitome* (1550)		
d. 1564	Calvin, John	*Institutes of Christian Religion* (1559)	1536:	Calvin at Geneva.
d. 1572	Knox, John	*Letter to the Commonalty* (1558)	1562–98:	French Wars of Religion.
d. 1590	Hotman, François	*Francogallia* (1573)	1572:	Massacre of St. Bartholomew.
d. 1605	Beza, Theodore	*The Right of Magistrates* (1574)		
d. 1596	Bodin, Jean	*Six Books of the Commonwealth* (1576)		
d. 1600	Hooker, Richard	*Laws of Ecclesiastical Polity* (1593–7)		
d. 1623	Mornay, Philippe du Plessis	*Vindiciae Contra Tyrannos* (1579)	1625:	Charles I, King of England; beginning of his troubles with parliament.
d. 1617	Suarez, Francisco	*Tractatus de Legibus ac Deo Legislatore* (1611)		
d. 1645	Grotius, Hugo	*The Law of War and Peace* (1625)		
d. 1653	Filmer, Sir Robert	*Patriarcha* (1632–42)	1642–6, 1648:	Civil War in England.
d. c.1663	Overton, Richard	*An Appeal to the People* (1647)	1649:	Execution of Charles I.
d. 1679	Hobbes, Thomas	*Leviathan* (1651)	1649–60:	English Commonwealth.
d. 1677	Harrington, James	*Oceana* (1656)	1660:	Restoration of Charles II.
d. 1674	Pufendorf, Samuel	*The Law of Nature and of Nations* (1672)		
d. 1704	Locke, John	*Two Treatise of Government* (1689)	1688:	Glorious Revolution in England.
d. 1704	Bossuet, Jaques	*Politics Drawn from the Very Words of Holy Scripture* (1709)		
d. 1776	Hume, David	*Essays Moral and Political* (1741, 1742)		

Year of Death	Thinkers	Works	Contemporary events	
d. 1755	Montesquieu, Charles	*The Spirit of the Laws* (1748)		
d. 1771	Helvetius, Claude	*De L'Esprit* (1758)		
d. 1778	Rousseau, Jean-Jacques	*Discourses* (1749–55)	1775–83:	American Revolutionary War.
		Social Contract (1762)		
d. 1794	Beccaria, Ceasar	*On Crimes and Punishments* (1764)		
d. 1780	Blackstone, William	*Commentaries on the Laws of England* (c.1769)		
d. 1784	Diderot, Denis	*The Encyclopaedia* (1776) (with others)		
d. 1832	Bentham, Jeremy	*Fragment on Government* (1776)		
		Introduction to the Principles of Morals and Legislation (1789)		
d. 1836	Madison, James	*The Federalist* (1787–8)		
d. 1836	Sièyes, Abbé	*What is the Third Estate?* (1789)	1789:	French Revolution.
d. 1796	Burke, Edmund	*Reflections on the Revolution in France* (1791)		
		Appeal from the New to the Old Whigs (1792)	1793:	Execution of Louis XVI of France.
d. 1809	Paine, Thomas	*Rights of Man* (1791, 1792)		
d. 1797	Wollstonecraft, Mary	*A Vindication of the Rights of Men* (1791)		
		A Vindication of the Rights of Women (1792)	1793–4:	The Reign of Terror.
d. 1832	Godwin, William	*An Enquiry Concerning Political Justice* (1793)	1795–99:	The Directory in France.
d. 1797	Babeuf, Francois	*Tribune of the People* (1795)	1799–1804	Consulate in France.
d. 1821	de Maistre, Joseph	*Considerations on France* (1796)		
d. 1804	Kant, Immanuel	*Metaphysics of Morals* (1797)		

Machiavelli's works were produced at a time (around 1500) when many city states were falling prey to larger, more powerful nation states. From the early sixteenth century the focus of Western political thinking shifted finally and irrevocably to this form of state, but it did so against a backdrop of bitter religious controversy engendered by the Protestant Reformation and Catholic reactions to it. The six-teenth and seventeenth centuries were marked by new and important departures in political theory. On one hand, a number of important early-modern writers argued for systems of 'absolute sovereignty', which gave rulers more or less complete control over their subjects. On the other hand, these developments were resisted by those who were concerned about the effect that theories of absolute sovereignty would have on subjects' fulfilment of their religious obligations.

Absolutism developed in response to uncertainties about the relationship between subjects and rulers in the new nation states. These uncertainties resulted from concern about the bearing that traditional ('customary') systems of regula-tion and those derived from divine command ('natural law') would have on laws formulated by the person or persons who held supreme power in the state (the 'sov-ereign'). It was argued that productive forms of political organisation should be subject to the unquestioned authority of an absolute ruler. Early formulations of this theory incorporated ideas derived from medieval political theory. For example, the important late-sixteenth-century French writer Jean Bodin remained attached to ideas of natural law, and attempted to reconcile an absolute sovereign with the conventional constitutional structure of the French state. In contrast, his seven-teenth-century English successor, Thomas Hobbes, regarded these ideas as a major source of intellectual and practical confusion and sought to construct a 'scientific' account of politics. Hobbes dismissed past political thinking and was particularly critical of the influence of Aristotle. He wished to provide his readers with a clear and incontestable understanding of politics that would allow them to see that their safety and welfare could only be secured by an absolute sovereign. Theories of abso-lute sovereignty deprived subjects of the right to challenge the actions of rulers, thus rejecting the ambivalently formulated, but tenaciously held, idea that the exercise of political authority should be subject to constraint.

But while Bodin and Hobbes caused these ideas to be seriously challenged, they did not drive them from the field. To the contrary, the development of early-modern theories of absolute government prompted a restatement and refinement of tradi-tional arguments that pushed them in new, and potentially radical, directions. The turmoil that accompanied the emergence of a number of early-modern states was caused at least in part by the breakdown of a unified view of Christianity during the Reformation. From the late sixteenth century until the end of the next cen-tury, theories of absolute government were challenged by a number of writers who argued that they conflicted with humanity's fundamental obligations to God. An important result of these concerns was the development of a vigorous tradition of resistance theory. In their attempt to justify resistance to unjust rulers, some writers resuscitated traditional political ideas, such as those which held that rulers should be subject to legally defined constraints or to those embodied in systems of regulation (the 'laws of nature') derived from God that were binding because of his supreme authority over his creation.

Some statements of these positions, like that advanced by Hobbes' young con-temporary, John Locke, placed great weight on the assumption that all human beings are endowed with 'natural rights' that have important implications for the ways in which political authority is structured and exercised. In both the mid-seventeenth and the late eighteenth centuries, ideas of natural rights played a significant role in arguments about the distribution of political power. For example, natural rights the-ory was used to justify the revolutions in Britain's North American colonies in the 1770s and in France after 1789. In this period the radical Anglo-American thinker Thomas Paine developed a theory of thorough-going democracy that was based on natural rights. Although Paine and some of his contemporaries appealed to sup-posedly universal ideas about the 'rights of men' these rights were not extended to include women. From the early 1790s, however, a number of women writers resisted arbitrary exclusion from social and political rights, likening their condition to that of slaves. From the 1840s, the position of millions of African-American subjects of the United States who were actually enslaved was the focus of works of black writers who appealed to ideas of the rights of man that had underwritten the foundation of the Republic.

The assumption that democracy was necessary to promote the interests of *all* members of the community was given a distinctive cast by socialist thinkers. Socialists focus on the connection between popular control of political institutions and the elimination of inegalitarian and oppressive consequences of the development of modern capitalist economies. It should be noted, however, that socialists' understanding of these problems varies greatly. While some theorists have looked to a democratised state to regulate economic activity to produce general benefits, others – most notably those influenced by the writings of the nineteenth-century founders of modern communism, Karl Marx and Friedrich Engels – maintain that capitalism is incompatible with true democracy and promoted a revolutionary transformation that will destroy capitalism and the forms of political organisation that support it.

Chronology: Modern Period, *c.*1800–

Year of Death	Thinkers	Works	Contemporary Events	
d. 1858	Owen, Robert	*A New View of Society* (1813)		
d. 1830	Constant, Benjamin	*Principles of Politics Applicable to All*	1804–14:	Napoleon I Emperor of France.
		Representative Governments (1815)	1815:	Defeat of Napoleon at Waterloo.
d. 1848	Chateaubriand, François	*Monarchy According to the Charter* (1816)	1815:	Restoration of French monarch and many other rulers deposed during the revolutionary period.
d. 1831	Hegel, G. W. F.	*Elements of the Philosophy of Right* (1821)		
d. 1836	Mill, James	*Essay on Government* (1820)		
d. 1848	Wheeler, Anna	*Appeal* (1825)		
d. 1833	Thompson, William	*Appeal* (1825)		
d. 1834	Coleridge, S. T.	*Church and State* (1831)		
d. 1859	de Tocqueville, Alexis	*Democracy in America* (1835)		
d. 1881	Carlyle, Thomas	*Chartism* (1839)	1848:	Revolutions in various European countries; establishment of Second French Republic.
		Latter Day Pamphlets (1850)		
d. 1895	Douglass, Frederick	Speeches and essays *c.* 1840–		

Year of Death	Thinkers	Works	Contemporary Events	
d. 1858	Taylor, Harriet	*Enfranchisement of Women* (1851)		
d. 1862	Thoreau, Henry	*Civil Disobedience* (1849)	1861–5:	American Civil War; end of slavery in the US, 1865.
d. 1865	Proudhon, J.-P	*What is Property?* (1840)		
		Poverty of Philosophy (1846)		
		Federation (1863)		
d. 1873	Mill, John Stuart	*On Liberty* (1859)		
		Representative Government (1861)		
		On the Subjection of Women (1869)	1870:	Paris Commune; establishment of Third French Republic.
d. 1876	Bakunin, Michael	*Statism and Anarchy* (1873)		
d. 1882	Green, T. H.	*Lectures on the Principles of Political Obligation* (1882)		
d. 1883 d. 1895	Marx, Karl and Engels, Friedrich	*The German Ideology* (1845–47)		
		The Communist Manifesto (1848)		
	Marx	*Capital* (1867–83)		
d. 1933	Zetkin, Clara	*Various articles and speeches* 1880–		
d. 1900	Nietzsche, Friedrich	*Beyond Good and Evil* (1886)		
		The Genealogy of Morals (1887)		
d. 1900	Sidgwick, Henry	*Elements of Politics* (1891)	1914–18:	First World War.
d. 1938	Kautsky, Karl	*The Class Struggle* (1892)	1917:	Revolution in Russia.
d. 1947	Webb, Sidney	*Industrial Democracy* (1897)	1922:	Mussolini becomes dictator of Italy.
d. 1921	Kropotkin, Peter	*Mutual Aid* (1897)	1927:	Consolidation of Stalin's position in Russia's Communist Party.
d. 1923	Bosanquet, Bernard	*Philosophical Theory of the State* (1899)	1918:	Abdication of German Emperor; creation of German Republic.
d. 1932	Bernstein, Eduard	*Evolutionary Socialism* (1899)	1919:	Adoption of Weimar Constitution by German Republic.

Year of Death	Thinkers	Works	Contemporary Events	
d. 1920	Luxemburg, Rosa	*Revolution* (1899)	1933:	Hitler becomes Chancellor of Germany.
d. 1952	Maurras, Charles	*Enquiry into Monarchy* (1900)	1927:	Mao Tse-tung joins Communist Party.
d. 1923	Pareto, Vilfredo	*Socialist Systems* (1902)	1933:	Stalinist purge of Communist Party.
d. 1940	Goldman, Emma	*Anarchism* (1910)	1935–39:	Civil War in Spain.
d. 1929	Hobhouse, L. T.	*Liberalism* (1911)	1937:	Japanese invasion of China.
d. 1924	Lenin, Vladimir	*The State and Revolution* (1917)		
d. 1963	Du Bois, W. E. B.	*The Souls of Black People* (1903) *Darkwater* (1920) *Black Reconstruction in America* (1934)		
d. 1920	Weber, Max	*Various essays* (*c.*1919)		
d. 1938	Bukharin, Nikolai	*ABC of Communism* (1921)		
d. 1941	Mosca, Gaetano	*The Ruling Class* (1923)	1945:	Fall of fascist regime in Italy and Third Reich in Germany.
d. 1945	Hitler, Adolf	*Mein Kampf* (1925)	1947:	Independence of India.
d. 1953	Stalin, Joseph	*Problems of Leninism* (1925)		
d. 1940	Trotsky, Leon	*The Permanent Revolution* (1928)	1939–45:	Second World War.
d. 1945	Mussolini, Benito	'The Doctrine of Fascism' (1930)	1949:	Creation of People's Republic of China.
d. 1948	Gandhi, M.	*Nonviolent Resistance* (1935)	1950:	Korean War.
d. 1973	Kelsen, Hans	*General Theory of Law and State* (1945)		
d. 1937	Gramsci, Antonio	*Prison Note-books* (1947)	*c.*1950:	Civil Rights movements in The US.
d. 1992	Hayek, F. A.	*The Constitution of Liberty* (1960)		
d. 1961	Fanon, Frantz	*The Wretched of the Earth* (1961)		
d. 1968	King, Martin Luther	*A Letter from Birmingham Jail* (1963)		
d. 1976	Mao Tse-tung	*Numerous essays*		
b. 1921	Rawls, John	*A Theory of Justice* (1971)		
b. 1938	Nozick, Robert	*Anarchy, State and Utopia* (1974)		

The movement towards democracy in the nineteenth century prompted a variety of responses. Some writers (for example, Edmund Burke and Joseph de Maistre in the late eighteenth and early nineteenth centuries) upheld the claims of traditional, monarchical forms of government. Others questioned the moral and practical desirability of introducing democracy in the conditions prevailing in contemporary society. For writers such as John Stuart Mill, democratic government seemed likely to produce a morally and culturally stultifying 'tyranny of the majority', expressed in legal forms and through mass 'public opinion'. In response, Mill stressed the role that individual freedom would play in insulating those whose intelligence and originality would contribute to social and moral progress from the morally and intellectually stultifying impact of mass opinion. Mill also favoured systems of government that gave a prominent role to enlightened elites in preparing the way for democracy.

While Mill thought that democracy posed a threat to individual freedom and to human progress, a number of nineteenth- and twentieth-century writers rejected democracy because it conflicted with their ideas about the need for authority in human life. For them, authority was necessary to sustain social and political order, and to compensate for the intellectual and moral failings of ordinary members of the population. In the past, the principle of state authority had been embedded in monarchs, but in the modern world it was necessary to identify new elites who could provide leadership in cultures that could no longer sustain traditional forms of government. Some conceptions of elite rule co-existed with political systems that were formally democratic, but others, such as fascism and national socialism, looked to new authority structures that were appropriate for mass societies. Aspects of fascism and national socialism bear a passing resemblance to traditional conceptions of authoritarian monarchical government, but they were underwritten by ideas that were a product of the democratic and modern cultures they rejected.

Themes

This book opens with a consideration of the *ends* of politics, that is, it examines a range of responses to the question: what is the primary goal of political institutions and particularly of the state? Consideration of this question allows us to explore views about the values that are fundamental to political life. Although accounts of the ends of politics vary greatly, almost all political theorists identify the state with the definition and maintenance of *order*. They argue that regardless of the specific purposes the state fulfils, its authoritative position is necessary to ensure that human affairs are coordinated and regulated effectively.

Having surveyed these ideas, the remaining chapters in Part I examine theories that specify the particular values that are to be realised by political institutions. While some theorists argue that politics should provide the means to foster human *virtue*, others have as their primary concern the protection and/or promotion of individual *freedom* or *happiness*, and use these objectives to evaluate particular political forms and modes of political conduct.

Part II deals with arguments about the *location* of political power. It addresses a range of answers to the question: who should rule? Consideration of this issue raises the question whether claims concerning the ends of politics have any implications for the distribution of political power within the community. The chapters in Part II examine arguments about the desirability of placing power in the hands of a *single person*, a *restricted group*, or the *whole community*. Many treatments of these themes are framed in terms of preference for monarchy, aristocracy or democracy. However, ideas of single-person rule, and rule by a restricted group, are not confined to the types of government that are captured in conventional images of monarchy and aristocracy; they extend to include modern conceptions of dictatorship and elite rule.

Claims about *who* rules are conceptually distinct from those that specify the *ways* in which political power should be exercised. Approaches to this issue are addressed in Part III. The general question considered there is: how should power be exercised if it is to promote the ends of politics? Many treatments of this issue are underwritten by the assumption that even those who are ideally suited to exercise power (and are therefore entitled to do so) may not always act in ways that promote the purposes for which political authority exists. Having recognised this possibility, a number of political theorists have sought to identify normative and/or institutional means of evaluating, and where necessary regulating, the exercise of political power. Three theories that address this issue are discussed in Part III. Various thinkers have relied on ideas of natural law and natural rights, while others have placed their trust in constitutional arrangements that prevent officeholders from acting unilaterally. In addition, it has been argued that those who exercise political power must do so within systems of legal regulation that are beyond their control. These regulations provide a framework that prevents governors from acting contrary to the purposes for which government exists. All these accounts stress the need to constrain rulers, and may thus be contrasted with those that regard supreme governors (or sovereigns) as the source of law, and rely on them to impose systems of self-regulation that are consistent with their responsibilities to those whom they rule.

Finally, Part IV examines a number of theories that deal with responses to the persistent misuse of political power by rulers. These theories address the question: to what extent, and in what ways, may the exercise and possession of political authority be challenged by those who are subjected to it? Answers to this question are divided into two categories. Those in the first category, discussed in the context of resistance to unjust rulers and theories of civil disobedience, present a challenge to particular lines of conduct, or to particular aspects of public policy; they do not question the general legitimacy of a particular form of government. Resistance and civil disobedience are meant to ensure that political authority is exercised in ways that support the values identified with particular political systems. These theories may be contrasted with theories of revolution (whether conducted by violent or non-violent means) since they seek to destroy inherently unjust forms of government and replace them with alternatives that will promote human flourishing. The chapters in Part IV of this book examine medieval and early-modern theories of resistance, various important anarchist and socialist statements of revolutionary political theory, and theories of civil disobedience and non-violent resistance developed by a range of nineteenth- and twentieth-century thinkers. The book concludes with an epilogue discussing 'post-modern' and 'post-colonial' reactions to the major narratives of the history of Western political thought.

PART

I

THE ENDS OF POLITICS

Throughout the history of Western political thought there has been a focus on establishing criteria for evaluating the moral legitimacy of institutions and the actions of those who control them. It is generally assumed that humans' obligations to obey political superiors are closely tied to rulers' perceived legitimacy. When political theorists seek to explain and justify the exercise of political authority and the institutions in which it is embodied, they do so by reference to accounts of the 'ends' of politics, that is to fundamental purposes that can only be realised, or approached, through political means.

The following four chapters deal with a range of historically important theories that give pride of place to order, virtue, freedom and happiness as goals of politics. These themes have been central to the interests of political theorists over long periods of time, and they are sufficiently general to embrace a range of significant secondary values. This point can be illustrated by considering alternative values such as 'justice' or 'equality'. 'Justice' rests on a conception of

rightness that can be related to the general order of society, to individual freedom, or to the requirement that just institutions foster the well-being or happiness of those who are subjected to them. Similarly, the idea of equality (the equal recognition of the claims and interests of all members of society) has been considered important because it promotes happiness, secures freedom and is necessary to the pursuit of human perfection or virtue.

Part I opens with an examination of a range of accounts of the relationship between politics and order. These theories specify how order should be achieved and identify the central features of a desirable order. The subsequent chapters – dealing with virtue, freedom, social freedom and happiness – examine ideas concerning ends of politics that go beyond the attainment of order. While the focus is primarily on how these ideas apply *within* communities, the discussion also explores examples of how they have been applied to a consideration of the relationship *between* states.

POLITICS AND ORDER

1

Political theorists have produced three general sets of arguments about the relationship between order and politics. Order has been related to the need for coercive regulatory agencies to repress behaviour that threatens the stability of society and jeopardises beneficial human interaction. It has also been treated in more positive terms as a basis from which human beings can reap the material, moral and psychological benefits of cooperation. Most of these theories treat political authority as a key requirement for identifying and maintaining beneficial order. However, an important rival tradition of Marxist and anarchist thought calls the state into question and argues that it is necessary only because deep-seated oppression and exploitation disrupts naturally harmonious social relationships. Marxists and anarchists believe that once the social and economic structures of society have been transformed, a beneficial order based upon voluntary cooperation will emerge. This condition will be social, but it will not be political because it will lack both the state and the forms of coercive regulation that are central to politics.

This chapter opens with an examination of aspects of Greek and Roman political theory presented by Democritus, Protagoras, Plato, Aristotle and Cicero. The focus of ancient political theory was the *polis* or city state. Classical thinkers believed that a properly regulated *polis* formed an order that was directed towards the common good of its members and enabled them to cooperate in the pursuit of ideals that were fundamental to humanity. Although ancient writers recognised that the state played a regulatory and, where necessary, repressive role, their political thought emphasised the positive potentialities of politics.

The late-medieval writings of St Thomas Aquinas show how aspects of Greek and Roman political thought were incorporated within a Christian framework, and in the transition from the medieval to the early modern worlds, Machiavelli and other Renaissance writers drew upon classical models when formulating largely positive statements about the appropriate type of order for city states. Aquinas' and Machiavelli's perspectives differed from those which emphasised the repressive role of the state. A strong statement of this position appeared in the writings of St Augustine, an early medieval writer whose influence can be seen in the political ideas of Protestant reformers such as Martin Luther and John Calvin at the beginning of the early modern period. In the late sixteenth and seventeenth centuries prolonged and violent political turmoil in France and England prompted a number of important thinkers to clarify the relationship between politics and order, and to stress the need for a unified agency or 'sovereign' that was not subject to any authority within the state. This perspective on order will be discussed here by referring to the writings of Jean Bodin, Hugo Grotius and Thomas Hobbes.

Since these accounts insist on the need for a single source of authority in the state, they are sometimes seen as actually or potentially authoritarian. It is important to note, however, that Bodin and his successors were making a point about the *logic* of government, not promoting the harsh and repressive attitude towards the exercise of power that characterises conventional accounts of authoritarian rule. Authoritarianism reflects an aversion to popular government, a contempt for the intellectual and moral qualities of the bulk of the population, and a fixation with personal leadership that is not part of sovereignty theory. This strongly repressive conception of order can be seen in the writings of a range of nineteenth- and twentieth-century theorists, including Thomas Carlyle, Charles Maurras, Benito Mussolini and Adolf Hitler. Other modern thinkers advanced more positive accounts of politics that reflect earlier assumptions about order and cooperation. A range of such writers, from Rousseau in the mid-eighteenth century to the late-nineteenth-century liberal thinker T. H. Green, will be discussed in the penultimate section of this chapter. The chapter concludes with a brief preliminary discussion of Marxist and anarchist writers who identify a positive conception of order with a non-political condition.

Cooperative order in ancient political theory: Protagoras, Democritus, Plato and Aristotle

The earliest surviving statements of Greek political theory come from Athenian writers in the fourth and fifth centuries BC when Athens possessed a democratic structure in which all free, native-born, male adults participated in the political life of the community. As can be seen in the accounts of Protagoras' political ideas in Plato's *Protagoras*, and in surviving fragments of Democritus' writings champions of democratic politics in Athens related individual well-being to opportunities for cooperation. Protagoras argued that a shared sense of respect (*aidos*) and justice (*dike*) made it possible to compensate for individual weaknesses by cooperating with one another (Plato, 1991, pp. 13–14). Since these qualities were possessed by *all* human beings they provided the basis of a democratic order that was sustained by and fostered the distinctive attributes of its members (Farrar, 1992, p. 23).

Protagoras (born *c.* 485 BC)

Born in Thrace, Protagoras was a successful teacher of rhetoric. He travelled widely throughout the Greek world. He is said to have been a student of Democritus, but this claim is controversial. Protagoras' political ideas are presented in the dialogue by Plato that bears his name.

Key reading: Havelock, 1964; Kierstead, 2018.

Like Protagoras, Democritus traced the origin of the state to the need for protection or security. Initially, this goal was achieved by individuals acting on the basis of simple rules directed against those whose selfish conduct was a threat to them all:

> If a thing does injury contrary to right
>
> it is needful to kill it.
>
> This covers all cases.
>
> If a man do so
>
> he shall increase the portion in which he partakes of right and security in any [social] order (Havelock, 1964, p. 128).

From this exclusively negative conception of order emerged a growing appreciation that enforcement of basic rules promoted a sense of 'community', or shared interest, that was eventually embodied in the democratic *polis*. Both Democritus and Protagoras believed that participation in the political life of the state fostered fruitful cooperation across the community and helped to legitimate it in the eyes of its members. The *polis* thus enjoyed the support of individuals whose excellence gave them a leading role in it and of the citizens who attended popular assemblies.

Democritus (*c.* 460–380 BC)

Like Protagoras, Democritus was a native of Thrace. An important scientific and political thinker, his ethical and political ideas are preserved in a number of fragmentary statements.

Key reading: Havelock, 1964.

The idea that the *polis* promoted the satisfaction of fundamental human needs was endorsed by Plato, but he argued that a legitimate political order must have a hierarchical structure. Plato deduced this requirement from a principle of division of labour manifest in all human societies. In order to satisfy their basic needs, human beings cooperate with one another by engaging in specialised production and exchanging goods and services. These arrangements reflect what Plato took to be a primary fact about human beings, that is, they possess differing natural capacities, which equip them to fulfil only *some* of the functions required to supply their basic material needs. By restricting themselves to these functions, and by exchanging the products of their activity with others, individuals can satisfy their needs in the most efficient way. Plato claimed that the division of labour applies to political as well as to social functions and insisted that only limited sections of the population possess the necessary attributes to participate in the political life of the state. Plato's ideal state has a hierarchical structure based upon two distinct and exclusive classes: the 'producers', who engage in economic activity, and the 'guardians'. The latter are subdivided into two groups: the 'auxiliaries', who perform military and executive functions, and the 'guardians proper', who rule. Ruling functions are the sole preserve of the guardians because only they possess the necessary intellectual and moral qualities to exercise political power.

Plato saw his ideal republic as an order that integrates humans with their fellows and makes the realisation of individual and collective aspirations interdependent. However, his insistence on a strict and exclusive division of functions means that most of the population are excluded from the political order, or at least experience it only as a form of external regulation. The type of order necessary to secure social cooperation does not therefore extend to *political* cooperation between all members of the community. This implication is reinforced by Plato's insistence that an erosion of the strict separation of functions would corrupt the ideal republic and inaugurate a slide towards dissolution and anarchy, that is, towards chronic disorder.

Although Plato appeared to subjugate individual aspirations to the requirements of what he took to be a just political order, his ideal republic actually rests upon assumptions about individual psychology. The allocation of duties reflect what Plato regarded as the full range of distinctive individual attributes, and by this means he was able to claim that individuals realise their own nature by taking their rightful place in the *polis* (Farrar, 1992, pp. 30–31). In other words, Plato thought that hierarchical order satisfies the needs of the *polis* and its members.

Plato (427–347 BC)

Plato was born into the upper classes of Athens. He was a follower of Socrates, an influential teacher who was the principal figure in Plato's philosophic dialogues (cf. p.). In the 380s BC Plato founded the Academy, an institution dedicated to providing an appropriate, philosophically based education for young members of the Athenian upper classes. Impressed with the power wielded by Dionysius II, the ruler of Syracuse in Sicily, Plato made visits to that city in 367–366 and 361–360 BC, hoping to encourage him to perfect his rule by uniting power and knowledge. This hope was not realised. Dionysius' interest in philosophy was not as strong or as single-minded as Plato had hoped, and on both occasions his visits ended in periods of more or less overt detention.

Plato's perceptions of the failings of Athenian democracy played a significant role in framing his political thought. Thus in *Gorgias* he provided a trenchant critique of the role that rhetoric played in democratic regimes, providing unscrupulous demagogues with the means of gaining undue influence by pandering to the prejudices and passions of the population at large. In *The Republic* Plato argues the case for disinterested expert rule grounded in the knowledge of absolute and unqualified moral truth that gave rulers (the 'guardians') access to the knowledge of goodness itself. Other sections of the population are precluded from any role in politics. The rulers' moral qualities and their strictly controlled way of life are designed to ensure that they dedicate themselves and their expertise to the good of the state. Plato was as hostile to tyranny as he was to the irrationality and lawlessness of democracy. The dangers of unregulated power are recognised in *The Laws*, which was unfinished at the time of Plato's death. In this work Plato analysed the main features of a less demanding state than that outlined in *The Republic*, one that provides a political role for ordinary citizens, gives priority to the law as a stable and just basis for the community, and recognises a role for men of wisdom as protectors of the law.

Plato numbered Aristotle among his pupils in the Academy. He was one of the first of a long line of thinkers to be exposed to ideas that have attracted admirers and critics throughout the history of Western political philosophy.

Key reading: Cross and Woozley, 1971; Kraut, 1992; Reeve, 1988; White, 1979.

While Plato's analysis in *The Republic* focused on an ideal state, his pupil Aristotle examined the relationship between different forms of political order and the differing socio-economic bases of various communities (see p. 49). Aristotle thought that in some circumstances a strictly exclusive, hierarchical order may be appropriate, but he was far less sanguine than Plato about securing general acceptance of this form of rule. Aristotle's focus on identifying the best practical form of government was closely related to empirical considerations. He argued that in states with a mixture of classes, 'polity' is the most appropriate form of government. Polity gives weighted recognition to various claims, thus reducing the risk of revolution and chronic disorder. It also minimises the risk of misuse of power by combining elements of aristocratic, oligarchic and democratic forms of government (see p. 172).

Despite the differences between Plato's and Aristotle's conceptions of order, they both emphasised its positive role and sought to identify political structures that would satisfy this fundamental goal of politics. Their general position on this question was endorsed by a Roman successor, Marcus Tullius Cicero (see p. 206). In *Of the Republic* (*c.* 54 BC) Cicero distinguished the state (or 'commonwealth') from 'any collection of human beings brought together in any sort of way', and defined it as 'an assemblage of people in large numbers associated in an agreement with respect to justice and a partnership for the common good' (Cicero, 1970, p. 65). For Cicero, as for his Greek predecessors, the order created through political means and embodied in the state is of fundamental significance because it produces a form of common life that is central to human fulfilment.

Negative and positive conceptions of order in medieval political theory: St Augustine and St Thomas Aquinas

Christians originally rejected classical ideas of the ultimate significance of political life because their aspirations were focused on the world to come. Nevertheless, they still had to face the issue of how they should relate to the political institutions with which they came into contact. During the course of the first four centuries of the Christian era, consideration of this problem gave rise to two distinct perspectives on order. The strongly positive view of the possibilities of a Christianised Roman Empire adopted by some thinkers (Markus, 1991, pp. 94–102) was challenged by a powerful counter argument that ascribed a largely negative and repressive role to all political institutions.

From about 390 AD St Augustine of Hippo reacted sharply against the Christian version of the Greco-Roman perspective on politics and order which he had originally endorsed. This change is attributable to two developments. In the first place, following his ordination in 391 AD, Augustine's views were transformed by St Paul's account of the indelible and deep-seated implications of the sinful nature of humanity since the fall. Augustine believed that depravity and conflict are ineradicable features of human life and while they can be tempered to some degree, they will not be overcome until humanity is finally 'saved' by reabsorption into the timeless realm of God.

St Augustine (354–430 AD)

Born into a middle-class family from Thagaste in Roman North Africa, Augustine was educated in Carthage and Rome. He subsequently taught rhetoric in Milan. Following his baptism in 387 AD, Augustine returned to Africa. He was ordained priest in 391 and consecrated bishop of Hippo in 395. His political ideas were presented in the *City of God* (413–427), a wide-ranging work dealing with the relationship between paganism and Christianity in the context of the late Roman Empire.

Augustine saw the state as an institution that was necessary to deal with the implications of humanity's fall from a state of grace to one where sin was inevitable. But while he allowed that political institutions were capable of furnishing the benefits of peace, order and a type of justice to both Christians and pagans, he insisted that they were not positively connected to ultimate moral values. In this respect, Augustine's perception of political life differed significantly from that of many of his Roman and Greek predecessors.

Key reading: Deane, 1963; Markus, 1970; Markus, 1991.

The political bearing of these theological insights was driven home to Augustine by contemporary developments within the Roman Empire. From 406 AD the western provinces of Rome were subjected to a series of attacks by the Goths, which culminated in the sack of Rome in 410 AD. These events sparked dissension among the population over the increasing importance of Christianity within the Empire. Pagans claimed that Rome was being punished for neglecting its traditional gods, while Christians' alarm at the fragility of what they saw as a God-ordained imperial order prompted them to re-examine the relationship between their faith and political institutions. This issue was explored by Augustine in *City of God*.

Augustine's mature views on the political order can be divided into discrete but related parts. He drew a sharp distinction between the divinely endorsed 'natural' order and the order of human existence that was marked indelibly by the implications of human sinfulness. While the natural order was rational and unchanging, the human world was subject constantly to acts of wilfulness that clashed with Christian values (Markus, 1991, pp. 109–12). As Augustine argued that government is, and can only ever be, a human product, he rejected orthodox aspirations for a Christian commonwealth. States necessarily reflect the very variable moral quality of their members and can never embody true justice. They are associations of 'a multitude of rational beings united by a common agreement on the objects of their love' (Augustine, 1972, p. 890). Augustine stressed the sinful nature of humanity, and he assumed that no earthly community can be based on the love of God, nor can it be regarded as part of the natural order that leads to God.

This conception of political order underwrites Augustine's theory of the 'two cities': the 'city of God' and the 'earthly city'. He saw these as distinct entities, each distinguished by the 'object of its love'. The city of God is timeless, does not correspond with any earthly realm, and provides a positive framework for the realisation of the supreme end for humanity. This city is co-terminus with the 'earthly city', a term that Augustine applied to all political entities, including, of course, the Roman Empire. But while Augustine insisted that the earthly city is not part of the order that leads to God, he argued that as Christians must, of necessity, spend their allotted time in the world, it is of some limited and passing benefit to them. Although Augustine regarded politics as unnatural he thought social life was ordained by God and that Christians should not withdraw from the company of their fellows. Because of sin, however, even the minimal degree of order necessary to ensure sociability required the controlling and guiding influence of the state. Political institutions constrain sin to some extent by punishing sinful behaviour, and membership of the earthly city helps to secure the enjoyment of what Augustine called 'temporal things'. Above all, states can ensure a degree of peace and security, which is a prerequisite of social existence. The earthly city thus contributes indirectly to the realisation of Christian values, even though it is not positively related to the city of God:

> that part [of the Heavenly City] … which is on pilgrimage in this condition of mortality … needs make use of this peace … until this mortal state, for which this kind of peace is essential, passes away. And therefore, it leads what we may call a life of captivity in this earthly city as in a foreign land, although it has already received the promise of redemption (ibid., p. 877).

Although the order maintained by the earthly city is negative in the sense that it focuses on the repression of conflict and the other disruptive consequences of sin, Augustine stressed that it is essential for members of both cities and insisted that Christians must 'not hesitate to obey the laws of the earthly city by which those things which are designed for the support of this mortal life are regulated …' (ibid., p. 877). Obedience is even due to cruel and tyrannical rulers as they produce a modicum of order and their harsh and arbitrary rule, a consequence of the sin of the tyrant, forms part of God's providence. Thus while Augustine divorced political order from the natural order that leads to God, he gave it an important auxiliary role.

Augustine's circumscribed validation of political order was very influential in the medieval period and beyond. In the late medieval period, however, an alternative to the Augustinian position developed that incorporated aspects of the classical tradition that provided a markedly positive view of the potentialities of political order. This development is associated particularly with the Italian monk known to us as St Thomas Aquinas (see p. 47). Aquinas' endorsement of the Aristotelian claim that humans are by nature political animals was particularly significant.

Aquinas regarded government as a means of positively enhancing sociability: 'The fellowship of society being ... natural and necessary to man, it follows with equal necessity that there must be some principle of government within society'. Government is necessary to provide an 'ordered unity' among groups of human beings so as to ensure that 'in addition to the motives of interest proper to each individual there must be some principle productive of the good of the many' (Aquinas, 1959, p. 5). A central point about Aquinas' understanding of government's role in fostering effective cooperation, was reflected in his observation that government would be necessary even if the Fall had never occurred:

> because man is naturally a social animal ... men would have lived in society, even in a state of innocence. Now there could be no social life for many persons living together unless one of their number were set in authority to care for the common good (ibid., p. 105).

As a Christian, Aquinas could not accept the idea that human fulfilment takes place within the state, but he believed, nevertheless, that the order created by politics is directly related to the cosmic order that leads to God.

Aquinas' positive conception of political order was echoed in a number of important late medieval and early modern political works. Many of these theories were closely related to the theological perspective that underlay Aquinas' philosophy. For example, the late medieval Italian thinker Marsilius of Padua stressed the cooperative features of an order enjoyed within appropriately structured city states linking their promotion of peace and security with citizens' responsibilities as Christians. The city state also provided the focal point for Niccoló Machiavelli's writings, but he related political order to a conception of human fulfilment that focused on this world rather than the world to come. Thus unlike Marsilius, Machiavelli insisted that 'popular' republics under the control of all adult male citizens rested on values that are largely independent of, and in some ways hostile to, notions of politics that relate it to divine providence.

In addition to developing an account of a system of order created within a popular republic, Machiavelli also analysed 'princely' government, or rule by a single person. In this context, however, he stressed the need for the prince to maintain his supremacy over the state and to ensure that he is the sole active force in an order where the rest of the population is essentially passive. For example, Machiavelli advised princes that it is better to be feared by their subjects than to rely on their love:

> whether men bear affection depends on themselves, but whether they are afraid will depend on what the ruler does. A wise ruler should rely on what is under his own control, not on what is under the control of others (Machiavelli, 1988, pp. 60–61).

By emphasising the negative rather than the positive aspects of single-person rule, Machiavelli advanced a conception of the ends of politics that is similar to those produced by a number of important early modern thinkers. The Frenchman Jean Bodin, the Dutchman Hugo Grotius and his English contemporary Thomas

Hobbes developed theories of sovereignty that gave a new and distinctive emphasis to the state's repressive role and identified the need for an order created and maintained by a 'sovereign' who was the sole supreme authority within the state.

Order and sovereignty in early modern political theory: Bodin, Grotius and Hobbes

Jean Bodin's most important work, *The Six Books of the Commonwealth*, was produced in the midst of the series of civil wars that broke out in 1562 and continued for the next 30 years. In these wars, fought between a significant minority of French Protestants (the Huguenots) and the Roman Catholic majority, the French crown often aligned itself with the latter. From 1571 Bodin was closely associated with the King's younger brother, the Duke of Alençon, who led a group called the *politiques* who were committed to the toleration of Protestantism. In an environment where armed fanatics roamed at will, however, toleration would have to have been enforced, and for much of the late sixteenth century the French crown was unable or unwilling to do so. Its failure was, of course, largely a product of inadequate political will and restricted military capability, but these were in turn related to the prevailing understanding of the nature and extent of sovereign power, and of the purposes for which it existed. Bodin was particularly concerned with appeals to 'customary law' (regulations based on customary practice), and with claims that certain officials and grandees could legitimately resist the crown. He also insisted that it is rulers' responsibility to maintain a general beneficial order within their states and that that is impossible if there is more than one source of human authority in it. Bodin's overriding concern is signalled in the title of the first chapter of his book ('The Final End of the Well-ordered Commonwealth') and in the sentence with which it opens: 'A commonwealth may be defined as the rightly ordered government of a number of families, and of those things which are their common concern, by a sovereign power' (Bodin, n.d., p. 1).

One of Bodin's arguments depends on a parallel between the family and the state. In common with many of his contemporaries, Bodin sees the state as an extended form of the 'natural' patriarchal order created through the historically and biblically sanctified authority exercised by fathers over their families (Schochet, 1975). The state, like the family, will only be unified and beneficial if it is subject to a single source of supreme power. Although Bodin subscribed to the commonly held view that human beings were under a system of natural law that specified God's intentions for them (see pp. 199ff) he identified a need for regulations to cover matters upon which the laws of nature are silent and which can only be decided by a human authority that determines what is in the best interest of the community and removes causes of dissension among its members. Bodin ascribed this role to the sovereign and identified a number of exclusively held sovereign 'attributes', or powers necessary for the maintenance of a 'commonwealth' or state.

Given the circumstances in which he wrote, it is not surprising that Bodin gave precedence to the harmful effects of disorder, going so far as to imply that governmental oppression is likely to be far less damaging than conflict produced by insubordination within a weak or non-existent order. (Bodin, n.d., p. 14). At the same time, however, he was fully aware of the dangers arising from the misuse of political power, and stressed that legitimate sovereigns are subject to natural law and answerable to God. He also argued that a wise ruler will seek the advice and assistance of officials, corporate bodies and representative 'estates'. These measures buttress sovereignty by facilitating the 'right ordering' of the commonwealth and since they are self-imposed they do not compromise the sovereign's supremacy (ibid., pp. 79, 106–07).

Hugo Grotius (1583–1645)

Grotius, a Dutch jurist and philosopher, served in the Dutch administration but was imprisoned when his patron Oldenbarnevelt fell from power. After escaping from prison Grotius entered the Swedish service, serving as Swedish ambassador to Paris from 1634. He wrote important works on natural law, including *Of the Law of War and Peace* (1625). In common with a number of early modern thinkers, Grotius argued that humans' possession of natural rights meant that legitimate governments derived from the consent of those who were subject to them; in some circumstances, however, consent might give rise to states in which all political power lay in the hands of a single, 'absolute' sovereign.

Key reading: Haakonssen, 1985; Tuck, 1993.

The idea that order will be jeopardised by subjects' challenges to their sovereign's right to rule found its most thoroughgoing statement in the political theory of Thomas Hobbes in the mid-seventeenth century, but important features of his analysis were foreshadowed in Hugo Grotius' *The Law of War and Peace* (see pp. 174–75). Both these writers employ the idea of the 'state of nature', a device that played an important role in seventeenth- and eighteenth-century modern political thought. State of nature theory is an analytical rather than an historical tool. It uses the idea of a 'natural' condition where there is no state, to identify the shortcomings of a stateless existence, gain an understanding of the benefits of subjection to political authority and specify the requirements of an effective political order. State of nature theory thus uses the non-political to better understand the political realm.

Grotius argued that since individuals possess 'natural rights' that are not the product of social recognition or political enactment, legitimate government must derive from the consent of the natural beings who make themselves subject to it. These rights consist of the power to prevent other individuals interfering with life, liberty and body, and to claim material goods that are required to sustain life. Grotius thought that even in the 'state of nature', however, humans who were mindful of their obligations to God would not recklessly neglect their duty of 'sociality', that is, the 'care in maintaining society in a manner conformable to the light of human understanding' that 'is the foundation of right properly called' (Grotius, 1738, p. xvii). If human beings acted strictly in accordance with their rights, government would be unnecessary but in practice this ideal of *moral* order was inevitably undermined by malicious or ignorant behaviour that infringes natural rights and gives rise to conflict. Consequently, Grotius identified a need for a *political* order regulated by a sovereign who promulgates and enforces laws preventing individuals from pursuing their rights improperly and hence immorally.

While Grotius thought that sovereigny was necessary to remove humans from risks arising in the state of nature, he thought that the laws of nature and the principle of sociality were suffuciently robust to sustain a relatively safe international order. In *The Laws of War and Peace* Grotius developed a theory of 'the law of nations' based on a universally recognised drive for self-preservation, and a weak sense of sociability that discourages wanton injury and prompts reciprocity where this does not compromise self-preservation (Tuck, 1993, p. 174). The order created by the law of nations is a product of 'expediency' or rational self-interest, but Grotius also thinks it reflects the operation of a moral principle. It relies on sovereigns' consent and corresponds with a sense of justice arising from their Christian faith and subjection to God. Grotius believed that these obligations made the law of nations a generally effective guide for rulers in their interactions with others, even though it was not enforced by a human superior.

> [L]aw, even without a sanction, is not entirely void of effect. For justice brings peace of conscience, while injustice causes torment and anguish, such as Plato describes, in the breast of tyrants. Justice is approved, and injustice condemned, by common agreement of good men. But, most important of all; in God injustice finds an enemy, justice a protector. He reserves His judgements for the life after this, yet in such a way that He often causes their effects to become manifest even in this life, as history teaches by numerous examples (Brown et al., 2002, p. 330).

Grotius thought that in practice the requirements of natural law and the law of nations were identified through a fluid combination of rational enquiry and reflection on the practices of human kind. He thus regarded the law of nations as already existing and enjoying the general concurrence of rulers, rather than being a visionary project:

> just as the laws of each state have in view the advantage of that state, so by mutual consent it has become possible that certain laws should originate as between all states, or a great many states; and it is apparent that the laws thus originating had in view the advantage, not of particular states, but of the great society of states. And that is what is called the law of nations, whenever we distinguish that term from the law of nature (ibid., p. 329).

Since adherence to these laws is based on the mutual consent of those who are bound by them, it does not infringe sovereigns' prerogatives.

Unlike Grotius, Hobbes did not trace conflict in the state to the *improper* exercise of rights. To the contrary, he argued that it is a necessary consequence of individuals acting on the basis of their rights in the absence of an overarching authority (Haakonssen, 1985, pp. 239–41). In the *Leviathan*, Hobbes produced an account of politics that was coloured by his experiences of the English Civil War and the events leading up to it. He made direct reference to contemporary disorders, particularly those arising from political claims derived from religious doctrines, and those that gave an independent political role to persons or institution other than the sovereign. The first of these objections applied as much to proponents of conventional ecclesiastical power as to radical sectarians; the second was directed at the pretensions of over-mighty aristocratic subjects of the crown and those who claimed that the English parliament had an independent representative role. As Hobbes put it:

> If there had not first been an opinion received of the greatest part of England that these powers were divided between the King and the Lords and the House of Commons, the people had never been divided and fallen into this civil war; first between those that disagreed in politics; and after between the dissenters about the liberty of religion (Hobbes, 1960, p. 119).

These points of reference are important, but we must also bear in mind that Hobbes' *Leviathan* was presented as a generally valid, 'scientific' account of politics.

Hobbes' distinctive understanding of the state of nature and political alternatives to it reflects deep scepticism about the possibility of arriving at any elaborate and generally accepted account of moral truth (Tuck, 1984, pp. 104–05). This insight explains the range and intractability of the religious opinions that so exercised his contemporaries; it also shows why attempts to use these as the basis of politics were bound to produce conflict.

Thomas Hobbes (1588–1679)

After studying at Oxford Hobbes was tutor to William Cavendish, son of the first Earl of Devonshire, later becoming his secretary and tutor to his son. He moved to Paris in 1640 because he feared that his defence of the king in *The Elements of Law* would attract the hostility of parliament. Hobbes remained in Paris throughout the English civil wars, returning to England in 1651 when *Leviathan* had begun to attract sharp criticism from royalist exiles in France. He lived undisturbed in England during the Commonwealth and Oliver Cromwell's Protectorate, and was received at the court of King Charles II (whom Hobbes had tutored in Paris) at his restoration to the English throne in 1660. Hobbes remained on good terms with the King despite ongoing royalist hostility to his political philosophy.

Hobbes' most famous political work, *Leviathan*, built upon positions first advanced in *The Elements of Law* and *De Cive* (1642) to advance an unequivocal defence of absolute government. He argued that political communities that lacked a clear, single, unchallenged and unchallengeable source of political authority were unable to provide the degree of security necessary for beneficial human interaction. They tended inevitably to a condition where mutual suspicion made cooperation or even forbearance impossible, and where everyone was constantly fearful of their fellows, and frequently victims of the violence engendered by the sense of chronic uncertainty. Hobbes described this condition as a 'state of war' and sought to persuade his readers that its impact on human well-being was infinitely more damaging than that ever suffered at the hands of absolute rulers. He argued that viable political communities are created by their 'sovereigns', that is, by rulers whose right to frame and maintain systems of law are not open to question or scrutiny by their subjects. Attempts to curb the power of rulers – by appeals to tradition, the word of God, the rights of all or some of the subjects – comprised sovereignty and threatened to expose subjects to the horrors of the 'state of war'.

Although Hobbes' presentation of his case was coloured by conditions prevailing in England before and during the civil wars, he saw himself as furnishing an account of the nature and role of government and of subjects' obligations to obey their sovereigns that was valid universally. This claim was not accepted by many of his earlier readers. Hobbes' preference was for monarchy, but his theory of absolute sovereignty applied to all forms of government. As a result, his view offended those who supported monarchy for traditional reasons, while his rejection of mixed government and his refusal to countenance any notion of limited government clashed with the views of those who challenged royal power in the civil war period. Hobbes was also suspected of harbouring atheistic tendencies and of basing his political thinking on materialistic views of the natural and human worlds.

But while Hobbes' works were rarely popular, he is often regarded as the most significant English political thinker. His account of the sovereign as the source of law was important in nineteenth- and twentieth-century jurisprudence and the rigour of his treatment of other key issues in political philosophy has provided an ongoing challenge to his successors.

Key reading: Baumgold, 1988; Dietz, 1990; Skinner, 1996; Tuck, 1989.

Hobbes' scepticism allowed for only a very minimal (and he thought irrefutable) assumption about human aspirations. He argued that because human knowledge of the afterlife is uncertain and death puts an end to all human hopes, we can safely assume that people will agree that death is an evil that is to be avoided for as long as possible. If that is the case, it follows that avoidance of death is a 'right' that is generally recognised as a legitimate goal of all human beings. If individuals agree that it is right for human beings to preserve themselves, they will also recognise that it is right for them to do what *they* think is necessary to secure this end. This right precludes gratuitous damage to others since this is not necessary for self-preservation but as there are no authoritative agencies in the state of nature and no rules of conduct beyond the rights of nature, individuals must themselves judge what actions are necessary for their self-preservation (Hobbes, 1960, p. 84).

These three minimal rights (to self-preservation, to whatever is necessary for self-preservation, and to decide what is so necessary) are the only certain points in a moral world beset by scepticism. In these circumstances, private judgements on how self-preservation can be best secured mean that the state of nature is necessarily a 'state of war' and human life in it is chronically insecure, deprived and unutterably miserable:

> [D]uring the time men live without a common power to keep them all in awe, they are in that condition which is called war, and such a war, as is of every man against everyman .... In such condition, there is no place for industry, because the fruit thereof is uncertain: and consequently no culture of the earth; no navigation, nor use of the commodities that may be imported by sea; no commodious building; no instruments of moving and removing, such things as require much force; no knowledge of the face of the earth; no account of time; no arts; no letters; no society; and, which is worst of all, continual fear and danger of violent death; and the life of man, solitary, poor, nasty, brutish, and short (ibid., p. 82).

Hobbes' writings are sprinkled with grimly witty asides on human nature, but it should be noted that his analysis of the state of nature is not premised on human depravity. Even if people are moderate in their ambitions and generally good natured, a rational assessment of how they can best preserve their lives will inevitably propel them towards a state of war. In sharp contrast to the position advanced by Grotius, Hobbes argued that it is the exercise of rights that leads to conflict, not their abuse or disregard of the rights of others. Hobbes thought that this outcome is unavoidable because each individual has a right to judge the conduct of others and to respond in ways they think are necessary for their safety. Because natural individuals are roughly equal in the state of nature, Hobbes thought that they will be sanguine about their capacity to take what they want from others, and painfully aware of other's ability to take from them. Under these conditions

> there is no way for any man to secure himself, so reasonable, as anticipation; that is, by force, or wiles, to master the persons of all men he can, so long, till he see no other power great enough to endanger him: and this is no more than his own conservation require, and is generally allowed (ibid., p. 81).

Hobbes thus argued that the unavoidably subjective and relativistic nature of people's moral beliefs makes it impossible to rely on them to produce beneficial human interaction. Elaborate moral and religious ideas, conceptions of virtue and so on, cannot provide a reliable basis for human life since they vary so greatly. But neither can those very minimal and uncontentious moral ideas that Hobbes derived from his basic axiom concerning widespread agreement on the desirability of sustaining human life. Indeed, in the state of nature the exercise of rights produces bitter conflict and misery, not peace and beneficial order. These evils can only be avoided if humans abandon their right to private judgement and place themselves under a sovereign endowed with the unquestionable right to lay down and enforce rules of human conduct. Since humans often try to influence other peoples' behaviour by public pronouncements, the sovereign also has the right to decide what opinions are propagated publicly.

Hobbes' sovereign was an 'artificial' creature (one created by human beings rather than being found in nature) whose power establishes a system of certainty and peace to replace the uncertainty and discord of the state of nature. Effective human communities are beneficial orders created and maintained by a sovereign who acts 'in those things which concern the Common Peace and Safetie' and to whom individuals 'submit their wills, every one to his will, and their judgements, to his judgement' (ibid., p. 112). The sovereign's law specifies justice and injustice and all rights are determined by legal definition and enforced through its power. Hobbes insisted that the terms 'justice' and 'injustice' only have meaning in the commonwealth where the radical subjectivity and precarious enforcement of the state of nature are replaced by an order in which sovereigns specify and uphold regulations that govern the lives of their subjects and make peace and prosperity possible.

Because the state is fundamental to human well-being and is created by the voluntary actions of those who become the subjects of it, Hobbes insisted that individuals are obliged to retain their place within this order and can be justly punished for failing to do so. Significantly, he believed that the risks of a return to the state of nature is far more to be feared than subjection to any conceivable sovereign. Hobbes thought that those who complain about the exercise of sovereign power failed to consider that

> the state of man can never be without some incommodity or other; and that the greatest [incommodity] that in any form of government can possibly happen to the people in general, is scarce sensible in respect of the miseries and horrible calamities, that accompany a civil war, or that dissolute condition of masterless men, without subjection to laws, and a coercive power to tie their hands from rapine and revenge (ibid., p. 120).

In other words, the need for order is a fundamental requirement of human life, one that can only be satisfied by political institutions that replace private judgement with the authoritative and binding power of a sovereign.

Despite Hobbes' insistence on the unquestionable supremacy of the sovereign, it is a mistake to identify his conception of order with the systems of authoritarian and totalitarian rule that played such a devastating role in the twentieth century. The reason for this is that, although Hobbes thought that sovereigns should possess supreme coercive power, he saw no need for them to intrude into all aspects of the lives of their subjects. Moreover, the rationale of sovereignty means that individual subjects need not obey sovereigns whose acts or failures to act threaten their fundamental safety (see p. 261).

Hobbes' assumption that individuals in the state of nature are entitled to do *anything* that *they* think is necessary to ensure their preservation, applied to sovereigns in what was, in effect, an international state of nature: 'in all times, kings, and persons of sovereign authority, because of their independency, are in continual jealousies, and in the state and posture of gladiators' (Hobbes, 1960, p. 83). The international state of nature is both an apolitical and an amoral condition in which the behaviour of sovereigns is rightfully determined by their subjective judgements. In such a condition there can be no ideas of justice or injustice since, as we have seen, Hobbes thought these depended on specification and enforcement. An important consequence of this view was that it was not possible to distinguish just from unjust wars.

Despite this apparently bleak characterisation of the international environment, Hobbes did not argue for a transnational sovereign. Such a step would cut across his ideas about internal order by abolishing rulers' sovereign power and dissolving subjects' obligations to obey them. In any case, Hobbes seemed to think that such a step was unnecessary because parallels between internal and external states of nature were formal rather than substantive. In practice, external threats to sovereigns are limited in number, and they are by no means as exposed to the aggression of other state actors as individuals in the state of nature. Paradoxically, the material inequalities of sovereigns' powers means that the more powerful can feel far more secure than individuals in the state of nature, and the weaker are likely to be far less sanguine about their capacity to challenge them. Thus the conditions of 'diffidence' and equality of hope that make the internal state of nature such a lethally insecure environment do not apply to anywhere near the same extent in international relations. Finally, while war might pose a threat to the survival of *some* individual members of *some* states, the dangers are far more remote than those facing all individuals in the state of nature and far less likely to materialise as a fatal threat to particular subjects. The gladiatorial stance of sovereigns and other warlike symptoms of their rule – 'forts, garrisons, and guns upon the frontiers of their kingdoms; and continual spies upon their neighbours' (ibid.) – reflected their determination to use the resources of the commonwealth for the defence of its member and Hobbes noted that they were generally succesful in doing so. Because 'they uphold thereby, the industry of their subjects; there does not follow from it, that misery, which accompanies the liberty of particular men' (ibid.).

Nevertheless, to the extent that war has an adverse impact on the well-being of subjects by threatening their lives directly, or disrupting trade upon which their prosperity depends (Boucher, 1998, pp. 160–61), sovereigns have an interest in forging agreements with other rulers that make it less likely. In this respect, the external logic of sovereignty corresponds with its internal manifestations. In both cases, sovereigns have a rational obligation to protect their subjects and facilitate 'commodious living'. Significantly, Hobbes' cursory remarks on how sovereigns' obligations under the laws of nature were reflected in their dealings with other sovereigns are firmly linked to his understanding of their role in establishing and maintaining order within the state. Thus when he noted that 'there are certain natural Laws, whose exercise ceaseth not even in the time of war itself' he explained by way of example that he could not 'understand what drunkenness, or cruelty (i.e., revenge which respects not the future good) can advance towards peace, or the preservation of any man' (Hobbes, 1983, p. 73).

Cooperation and order in modern political theory: Rousseau, Kant and Green

In *The Social Contract* the Franco-Swiss philosopher Jean-Jacques Rousseau was sharply critical of Hobbes' claim that political order derived from the unquestioned power of sovereigns. Rousseau was one among a number of highly significant eighteenth- and nineteenth-century thinkers who stressed the role that voluntary cooperation and shared moral values played in sustaining political orders that opened up possibilities for human development that were frustrated in the state of nature and by political systems that favoured the sectional interests of some of their members. Rousseau sought to overcome these challenges by identifying a form of political association that respected the personal interests of its members while furthering a new and distinctly cooperative interest that members of a well-ordered community share with each other. Rousseau argued that while the particular wills of individuals are directed towards their interests, legitimate political communities generate a 'general will' that promotes the common interest of their members.

The idea of the general will is central to Rousseau's cooperative conception of political order. For Rousseau the primary issue in politics is to identify and maintain a form of order that will allow human beings to reap the benefits of interdependence while avoiding domination and manipulation. Rousseau believed that human interdependence makes order a necessity; the choice is between an order that serves the interests of only some sections of the population, and one that promotes cooperation and the common interests that emerge from it. Rousseau argued that an appropriate order can only be created by a process of 'contract', or agreement, between free beings. By renouncing their natural, pre-political, freedom individuals can create

> a form of association which defends and protects with all common forces the person and property of every associate, and by means of which each one while uniting with all, nevertheless obeys only himself and remains as free as before.... [T]his act of association produces a moral and collective body (Rousseau, 1987, p. 148).

Rousseau argued that the order made possible by legitimate political institutions opened up the prospect of a new form of human existence: the pursuit of shared values means that humans can be both *individual* and *social* beings. The transformative implications of political order are also apparent in the contrast that Rousseau's German successors drew between the potentialities of a regulated environment and the limitations of a situation where people seem to be free to follow their own inclinations. For example, the late-eighteenth-century philosopher Immanuel Kant wrote that while human beings are obliged to interact with their fellows in order to satisfy their needs,

> their inclinations make it impossible for them to exist side by side for long in a state of wild freedom. But once enclosed within a precinct like that of civil union, the same inclinations have the most beneficial effect. ... All the culture and art which adorn mankind and the finest social order man creates are fruits of his unsociability. For it is compelled by its own nature to discipline itself, and thus, by enforced art, to develop completely the germs which nature implanted (Kant, 1971, p. 46).

If human beings were naturally social, political order would be unnecessary, but since they are not, their inclinations prompt them to establish a rational legal order to satisfy their needs, and to ensure that they perform their moral duty to act justly. Kant distinguished a union 'of many individuals for some common end which they all *share*' from one in which they 'all *ought to share*'. He identified the latter with systems of 'public right' which are the subject matter of politics (ibid., p. 73). By cooperating to create and maintain public right, individuals minimise the risk of unjustly infringing one another's freedom.

> ### Jean-Jacques Rousseau (1712–78)
>
> A native of the Swiss city-state of Geneva, Rousseau's philosophical reputation developed after he moved to France in 1742. Although closely associated with leading figures of the French Enlightenment, Rousseau was sceptical of the assumptions about human progression to which many of these writers subscribed. Rousseau's works are wide-ranging, dealing with issues in the arts, education, science, literature and philosophy. His most important political writings are *Discourse upon the Origin and Foundation of Equality Among Mankind* (1755) and *The Social Contract* (1762).
>
> In the first of these works, Rousseau explored the moral and political implications of the growing interdependence of human beings as they might emerge from a condition of primitive, pre-social, unself-conscious isolation into increasingly developed and sophisticated social conditions. Rousseau's analysis of the advantages and hazards of the growth of 'civilisation' is multi-dimensional. It addresses the impact of economic advancement, the significance of the recognition of property rights, human beings' unsettling tendency to acquire a sense of self from their perception of how they appears in the eyes of others, and the political implications of these developments. In this account Rousseau highlighted the danger that the potential benefits of social life might be lost through the corruption of human nature and the onset of oppressive dependence, exploitation and antagonism. In the *Social Contract* he considered the political implications of the paradox of progression and corruption, identifying the requirements of a system of government that will allow human beings to reap the benefits of sociability while still retaining their independence. This account identifies the transformative possibilities opened up by active membership of a properly ordered political community. Rousseau's claim that legitimate forms of government express the 'general will' of the community appealed to a range of later thinkers (Hegel, Marx, T. H. Green and Lenin among them) with diverse views on the nature and purpose of the state.
>
> *Key reading:* Cullen, 1993; Hont, 2015; Masters, 1968; Shklar, 1969; Whatmore, 2015.

The creation of a political order thus makes it possible for humanity to pursue what Kant took to be its moral mission. While he gave due weight to the coercive dimensions of systems of public law, Kant's perspective on order is a generally positive one. The same point can be made about some of his successors. Thus in early-nineteenth-century Germany, G. W. F. Hegel (see p. 82) developed an elaborate account of the modern state that stresses the extent to which it provides a moral, psychological and political framework for realising the conceptions of personal and collective well-being that are characteristic of the modern world. Hegel argued that the 'essence of the modern state is that the universal should be linked with the complete freedom of particularity and the well-being of individuals' (Hegel, 1991, p. 283). That is, it forms an order that expresses humans' conceptions of both the individual ('particular') and social ('universal') dimensions of their lives and integrates these into a harmonious whole (see p. 84).

Aspects of both Kant's and Hegel's political philosophy played an important role in the thought of the late-nineteenth-century British writer T. H. Green. In stating his position, Green focused explicitly on what he regarded as the inadequacies of Hobbes' position. He rejected Hobbes' account of sovereignty on the grounds that it only explained the sovereign's possession of 'powers' not the rights that legitimated them, and misconstrued rights as purely individual attributes. (Green, 1986, pp. 44–45). For Green, in contrast, rights rest on *social* recognition of their role in ensuring that individuals are able to contribute freely to the common good they share with their fellows. In a clear reference to Hobbes' position, Green insisted on the common nature of the good and the need for rights to be recognised by all members of the community:

> Until the object generally sought as good comes to be a state of mind or character of which the attainment, or approach to attainment, by each is itself a contribution to its attainment by every one else, social life must continue to be one of war (ibid., p. 279).

T. H. Green (1836–82)

Sometimes viewed as the first professional political philosopher in England, Green made a career as a teacher at Oxford University. He reformulated liberal values and their political implications to take account of the importance of the interpersonal conditions of moral autonomy. Green's most important political work, *Lectures on the Principles of Political Obligation,* appeared posthumously, but he exerted a profound influence over those who came into contact with him at Oxford.

A critic of ideas that identified liberalism with individualism and with hostility to government action, Green drew on Rousseau and Hegel to argue for a positive view of freedom in which the state was seen as an agency that reflected the moral consciousness of the community and used its power to remove barriers to 'free' action. That is, to action through which individuals developed their moral capacity by contributing freely to the pursuit of objectives that they shared with other members of the community.

Key reading: Francis and Morrow, 1994; Morrow, 2017; Nicholson, 1990; Vincent and Plant, 1984.

Green thus argued that the obedience rendered to the political superiors who create and maintain beneficial order results from a widely held perception that sovereigns embody the general will of political communities and uphold systems of rights that promote a common good that is recognised by their members (ibid., p. 68). Sovereignty was as important to Green as it had been to Bodin and Hobbes, but he understood it in relation to the role it plays in creating a political order that is valued by those who belong to it. Consequently,

> [i]t is more true to say that law, as the system of rules by which rights are maintained, is the expression of a general will than that the general will is the sovereign. The sovereign, being a person or persons by whom in the last resort laws are imposed and enforced in the long run and on the whole, is an agent of the general will – contributes to realise that will (ibid., p. 75).

Rousseau, Kant, Hegel and Green all ascribed a central role to the state in defining and maintaining an order that will enable human beings to realise the potentialities for cooperation that they regard as fundamental to human well-being. Unlike thinkers who focused on the repressive and regulatory role of the state, these writers related order to the necessarily social dimension of human life, and treated political authority as a reflection of shared interests rather than being responsible for creating them. This conception of politics is epitomised in Green's claim that 'will not force is the basis of the state', and in his related argument that those with a developed sense of moral and social responsibility regard law as a guide and coordinator of human actions rather than a coercive force (ibid., p. 89ff).

Green's theory of political authority rested on the moral force he ascribed to the idea of the common good and the related claim that modern nation states provided a focus for realising it. He argued that this idea was fundamental to all forms of social interaction and to the legitimation of all social and political institutions. Over time, however, ideas of the common good had undergone qualitative developments that enhanced the understanding of what counted as a good. They had also been extended to include members of communities who had been illegitimately excluded from them. Thus the advent of Christianity had given rise to a deeper understanding of the good than that which had underwritten the Greek *polis* and extended its scope to include those (most notably slaves and women) who had not been regarded as members of it. It had also, however, introduced an idea of universal brotherhood which challenged the Greeks' distinction between themselves and the 'Barbarian' outsiders and extended potentially to all humanity (Green, 1986, pp. 263–73).

While sovereigns possessed the power and the legitimacy to act effectively against those who infringed the rights of members of their political communities, their writ did not extend into the international arena. Even here, however, the interactions of sovereigns were subject to the moral law (ibid., p. 264) that placed them under an obligation to enhance the common good. Green applied this imperative to the justification of war and the loss of life that unavoidably resulted from it. Deaths in war always involved wrong since they illegitimately curtailed individuals' right to free life. They might be justified, however, when the loss of life was necessary to prevent more significant damage to the common good. Green thus allowed that a purely defensive war to protect the political freedom of a state might be justified but noted that even when the claim was genuine, the killing resulting from war involves wrongdoing on the part of those who have wrongly precipitated it. Green thought few if any of the European powers were free of the moral taint of unlawful killing in war. Many wars resulted from dynastic ambitions of princes that were entirely removed from, and usually in conflict with, the real interests of their subjects. The same was true of wars fought to gain or hold colonial possessions, or to advance claims to the territory of third parties. In other cases, the unjust treatment of members of a political community, whether on allegedly religious or other grounds, promoted sympathy from migrants established in foreign countries, and other external sympathisers, that fuelled international tensions, prompted interference and encouraged them to look for assistance from other states (ibid., pp. 131–32).

Green regarded unjust wars and the adverse international implications of the systematic infringement of rights within states as demonstrating a general principle: serious inter-state conflict occurs where there is some moral deficiency in the internal organisation of the political and/or social relations of some or all of the protagonists. Hegel had suggested that patriotism or 'national feeling' made war more likely (see p.) but Green denied that this was necessarily so. Patriotism reflected the need for ideas of universal solidarity to be given a particular focus if they were to direct human action effectively. It did not necessarily generate antagonism towards the members of other political communities and would not do so if states really provided the framework for a moral order directed to the pursuit of the common good (ibid., p. 134). Indeed, Green argued that the closer states came to maintaining such an order internally, the less likely external conflict would be:

> There is nothing in the nature of the state that, given a multiplicity
> of states, should make the gain of one the loss of the other. The more

perfectly each one of them attains its proper object of giving free scope to the capacities of all persons living on a certain range of territory, the easier it is for others to do so; and in proportion as they all do so the danger of conflict disappears (ibid., p. 130).

In common with many other mid-nineteenth-century liberal internationalists, Green saw free trade within and between states as a particularly powerful means of forging common trans-state interests and raising awareness that they were compromised by international conflict (Bell, 2016, p. 239). Initially, this perception may derive from a self-interested view of personal loss through the disruption of trade, but Green argued that this could provide the basis for the development of a disinterested attachment to ideas of mutual respect for the rights of others and for the common good constituted by it (Green, 1986, pp. 136–37). Green thought that a just international order could emerge from a community of states committed to the liberal values of free trade, anti-militarism and the eradication of feudal influences in society and politics. As the internal moral development of states removed many of the deep-seated causes of international conflict, there was no reason why they should not look to systems of arbitration, or even an international court, to ensure that disputes did not give rise to war (ibid., pp. 134, 137).

Although there was no sovereign-like figure in inter-state relations, Green nevertheless thought moral law could promote the pursuit of the common good in this sphere, giving rise to an international order that rested on the same ethical considerations that made it the core of the rightly ordered state. This line of argument corresponds with his insistence that citizens' practical commitment to the common good was often not reliant on legal regulations and was only rarely due to the state's exercise of coercive power. If 'will not force *is* the basis of the state' there is no reason why it might not also be the basis of an international moral order produced by sovereigns' voluntary subscription to mechanisms that gave practical effect to the analogy between moral law and positive law (ibid., pp. 264–65).

Order, authoritarianism and totalitarianism in modern political theory: Carlyle, Maurras, Mussolini and Hitler

The theories discussed in this section focus on an alleged incompatibility between the requirements of order and democratic or 'popular' government. Arguments of this kind became increasingly important in the nineteenth and twentieth centuries as western states moved towards democracy. Early examples of an overtly authoritarian perspective on order can be seen in the writings of Thomas Carlyle and Charles Maurras. Carlyle and Maurras were influential men of letters rather than systematic political philosophers, but their widely circulated writings contained lengthy and significant treatments of political themes.

Thomas Carlyle (1795–1881)

Born and educated in Scotland, Carlyle was one of the leading literary figures of the Victorian period. A non-traditional critic of democracy and parliamentary government, Carlyle urged his contemporaries to accept the need for new forms of elite leadership. His political ideas are advanced in *Chartism* (1839), *Past and Present* (1843), *Latter Day Pamphlets* (1850) and elsewhere in his voluminous literary output.

Key reading: Morrow, 2006; Vanden Bossche, 1991.

Carlyle's political ideas were produced in response to the intellectual and spiritual uncertainties, and the resultant disorders, that he thought characterised English life in the 1820s and 1830s. Foremost among Carlyle's concerns was the credence given to theories of government that minimised the guiding and regulating role of the state, and their tendency to look to the advance towards democracy to solve the 'condition of England question'. In Carlyle's view, endorsement of a minimal state and working-class demands for full political rights are closely related: in the absence of effective elite leadership, the mass of the population are driven to find alternatives to what has, in effect, become a system of 'non-government'. Democracy is the epitome of this tendency because it places political control in the hands of those most in need of guidance and regulation. Carlyle did not deny that people have 'natural rights', but he gave a distinctive and authoritarian meaning to this idea. Their fundamental right is to appropriate leadership, 'the right of the ignorant man to be guided by the wiser, to be, gently or forcibly, held in the true course' (Carlyle, 1980, p. 189). Carlyle insisted that the general population has to be *governed*; that is, it needs to be placed under the control of the more able few. He attributed the disorderly condition of the working classes to an intuitive realisation of this necessity, and to their understandable yet futile attempts to find an alternative to a system that institutionalises elite self-interest and dereliction of duty. He assumed that if genuine elites took up a governing role the working classes' awareness of the need for direction will ensure their willing conformity to an appropriately structured hierarchical order.

In response to the weaknesses that he perceived in contemporary political culture, Carlyle placed increasing emphasis on the 'heroic' dimensions of effective political leadership. He argued that in times of rapid and destabilising change, society needs to be under the control of a 'heroic' statesman whose claim to pre-eminence is recognised by the general population. In his later writings (dating from the 1840s) Carlyle applauded powerful and decisive rulers such as Oliver Cromwell and Frederick the Great of Prussia, and implied that a determination to subjugate the population is a significant indicator of political greatness. He nevertheless retained the belief that political authority exists for the intellectual, material and moral benefit of the ruled.

Like Carlyle, the French writer Charles Maurras waged war on the liberal and democratic assumptions that were prevalent in modern European culture. Maurras's primary targets were the ideas of individual autonomy and equality espoused by radical republicans in France. In response, Maurras reiterated conventional right-wing ideas that had first been formulated by Joseph de Maistre in the late eighteenth and early nineteenth centuries (see p. 122). Maurras insisted that inequality and dependence are inescapable features of the human condition, and he argued that they require human relationships to be ordered hierarchically. Republican ideas of liberty, equality and fraternity thus flew in the face of the requirements of nature, and give rise to moral and practical anarchy. 'Revolutionary legality has broken up the family, revolutionary centralism has killed community life, the elective system has bloated the state and burst it asunder' (Maurras, 1971b, p. 254). Maurras believed that these insidious ideas had become so ingrained in the mass mind of European societies that it was almost impossible even to 'propagate the notion of order' (Maurras, 1971b, p. 256).

Maurras's original preference was for the restoration of absolute monarchy (see p. 143), but towards the end of his life he threw his support behind Marshall Pétain, the leader of the regime established in the southern part of France following the defeat of the Third French Republic by the Germans in 1940. Thus while aspects of Maurras's conception of order harked back to Maistre, others looked forward to political ideas that became commonplace in the fascist and national socialist movements that emerged in Italy and Germany in the 1920s.

These movements were virulently anti-liberal and anti-democratic, and sought to establish entirely new systems of overtly authoritarian order. This point was made

Charles Maurras (1868–1952)

Maurras was a journalist, literary figure and central player in the right-wing movement *Action Française*. His love for the monarchy and the French Catholic Church was matched by his unremitting hatred of democracy, republicanism and individualism. In common with a number of right-wing contemporaries in France and national socialist and fascists movements elsewhere in Europe, Maurras's political thought contained a strong thread of anti-Semitism.

Key reading: McClelland, 1996.

quite explicit in the definitive statement of fascist doctrine written jointly by the political head of the Italian movement, Benito Mussolini, and by the academic philosopher Giovanni Gentile. In this essay Mussolini and Gentile warned that, 'One does not go backwards. The Fascist doctrine has not chosen Maistre as its prophet. Monarchical absolutism is a thing of the past' (Mussolini, 1935, p. 25). Although fascists rejected the nineteenth-century tradition of liberal democracy, they conceived of the state as an 'organised, centralized, authoritarian democracy' that would mould the population into a system of order that was 'collectivist' and 'spiritual' rather than 'individualistic' and 'materialist' (ibid., p. 24). Mussolini and Gentile's rejection of these features of modern democratic political culture is clear enough, but their positive statements on the goals of the fascist state are expressed as broad-ranging, vague generalities that conjure up a vision of radical national revitalisation that would recapture the heroism of the Roman Empire for the modern Italian state.

Benito Mussolini (1883–1945)

Originally a left-wing journalist, in the years after the First World War Mussolini led the Italian Fascist Party in their successful attempt to gain control of the government formally headed by the King of Italy. Mussolini took the title of 'Il Duce' and was dictator of Italy. His role in Italian politics reflects his contempt for liberal democracy and constitutional government and his preference for a form of authoritarian single-person rule representing the will of the nation and giving effect to it.

Key reading: Brooker, 1991.

Redefinition of the relationship between the state and its members was central to this vision. Gentile and Mussolini rejected any idea that the state is an instrument that merely serves the interests of individuals or groups. To the contrary, the process of national renewal necessitates the realisation of the primacy of the state itself: it is an 'absolute before which individuals and groups are relative' (ibid., p. 25). Its primary purpose is to impose order through the efforts of an authoritative leader: 'Empire calls for discipline, co-ordination of forces, duty and sacrifice' (ibid., p. 30). These qualities had ossified under liberal democracy, and the proponents of Italian fascism made the recreation of order the prime objective of their political practice and a prominent theme in their political thinking.

While Italian fascism assumed a national political and cultural focus, the key theme of German national socialism was 'race'. National socialist thought and practice was ambiguous about whether the state or the party was the embodiment of its world view (*weltanschauung*), but its ideologists made it clear that political institutions were to be regarded as the handmaidens of race. Thus Adolf Hitler claimed that '[i]n the state [national socialism] sees on principle only a means to an end and construes its end as the preservation of the racial existence of man' (Hitler, 1969, p. 348). Alfred Rosenberg, the leading formal ideologist of the national socialist movement, made much the same point (Rosenberg, 1971, p. 192). However, since the national socialists insisted that controlled breeding, territorial expansion and the elimination and/or subjugation of allegedly 'inferior' racial groups was necessary to preserve the interests of the 'master race', authoritarian political institutions were of central importance. The alleged 'master race' was superior to all others, but its members varied in their capacities to such an extent that the vast majority of them had to be placed under the control of 'creative minds' with the insight and determination needed to protect the interests of their race. These individuals must control the state and impose 'disciplined obedience' on the masses. The hierarchy of racial groups could only be maintained if the principle of hierarchy structured the political life of the 'master race' (see p. 126).

Order without politics: Anarchism and Marxism

In concluding our consideration of theories that stress states' roles in forging beneficial order, it is useful to highlight the distinctive and pervasive character of this position by glancing at a significant rival tradition (see p. 87ff). Anarchists and Marxists were bitter opponents in the history of modern revolutionary socialism (see pp. 273–76), but held similar views of the relationship between politics and order. Like Rousseau's successors, anarchists and Marxists believed individual well-being to be materially, morally and psychologically dependent upon cooperation, and they sought to identify and promote an order in which these aspirations could be satisfied. They argued, however, that cooperative order is an exclusively *social* phenomenon, and regarded all political institutions, and particularly the state, as incompatible with it.

Anarchists and Marxists offered a variety of explanations for the existence of the state, all of which point to its fundamental illegitimacy. 'Social' anarchists and Marxists believed that the exploitative and antisocial implications of private property create tensions that can only be constrained by political authority, but they denied that such authority is a neutral force. To the contrary, the inequalities arising from the exploitation of labour are reflected in the domination of the state by those who control the material resources of society. While individualistic anarchists were not generally opposed to private property, both they and social anarchists launched radical critiques of all ideas of imposed authority, including those associated with conventional expressions of religion, with all forms of political direction and with conventional ideas of law.

The various targets of anarchist criticism were neatly summarised by Emma Goldman:

> Religion, the dominion of the human mind; Property, the dominion
> of human needs; and Government, the dominion of human conduct,
> represent the stronghold of man's enslavement and all the horrors it
> entails (Goldman, 1911, p. 59).

Goldman characterised anarchism as 'the philosophy of a new social order' (ibid., p. 56) and contrasted its natural basis with the artificial and counterproductive impositions of government. Government created a tenuous order 'derived through submission and maintained by terror', while anarchism held out the prospect of a 'true social harmony' that grew 'naturally out of solidarity of interests' (ibid., p. 65).

> **Emma Goldman (1869–1940)**
>
> Born in Lithuania (then part of the Russian Empire) and educated in Prussia, Goldman lived in St Petersburg until 1885, when she moved to the United States. She was active in socialist and anarchist politics and was imprisoned in 1917 for her part in an anti-conscription campaign. Upon her release from prison in 1919, Goldman was deported to Russia. She quickly became disillusioned with the course of the revolution, and in 1921 she left Russia to spend the rest of her life in exile in various European states. A number of Goldman's anarchist writings were published in 1910 under the title *Anarchism and Other Essays*.
>
> *Key reading:* Shulman, 1971.

Features of anarchism and Marxism will be examined more closely in subsequent chapters. At this stage, however, it is useful to consider briefly aspects of the relationship between these theories and state-focused ideas of order. First, there is a sense in which anarchists and Marxists see the state in terms that echo aspects of Hobbes' theory. Given the implications of private property and other sources of coercion, there *is* a need for a coercive state to mitigate the destructive competition and human misery that constantly threatens capitalist societies. Secondly, given the inequalities and exploitation that make the state necessary, anarchists and Marxists believed that the idea that individuals can create political structures that reflect their shared interests is illusory. These inequalities are merely embedded in the political order. In any case, the whole idea of the social contract is flawed because it assumes that individuals can be something other than social beings. Far from creating the basis of a viable social order, the creation of the state negates it. As the Russian anarchist Michael Bakunin put it, 'there is no room in this theory for society, only for the State … society is totally absorbed by the State' (Bakunin, 1973, p. 137). Finally, Marxists and many anarchists offered a backhanded endorsement of Hegel's conception of the state, but they insisted that it merely sustains an uneasy balance between intractably conflicting interests rather than resolving them. Paradoxically, Hegel's elevated idea of the political order was necessary only because of the irresolvable tensions within its underlying social structure.

Conclusion

The writers discussed in this chapter believed that the identification and maintenance of an appropriate order was a precondition for worthwhile forms of human existence. Except in the case of anarchists and Marxists, the coercive and persuasive capacities of the state were thought to be essential for the creation of order. Order was usually related to human benefit, but in some cases the need for it was seen as a requirement imposed upon humanity in fulfilment of its obligations to God, or as being necessary for the realisation of goals that are fundamental to human beings. The latter of these positions played an important role in the ancient world, while the former has been central to a long tradition of Christian political thinking.

The claim that the state is necessary to produce order gives rise to related ideas about the *form* the state should take. That is, it is argued that only certain types of political organisation are able to create and maintain a morally appropriate order. In many cases, a focus upon order resulted in the rejection of popular government and the promotion of hierarchical political and social structures. As a modern scholar has remarked of seventeenth-century political thought, 'order theory was a statement of the immutably hierarchical nature of the political world' (Burgess, 1992, p. 134). The need for the state was justified by the wilfulness of ordinary human beings and their inability to subject themselves voluntarily to effective forms of regulation. It should be noted, however, that order was not necessarily seen as incompatible with popular government. Both Bodin and Hobbes thought that democratic institutions are capable of producing order provided they are the sole source of law, and Rousseau and his successors identified legitimate political order with egalitarian rather than hierarchical principles.

Finally, it is useful to distinguish 'negative' conceptions of order from those with a 'positive' orientation. As we have seen, Augustine, Hobbes and modern proponents of authoritarian government treat political order as a means of repressing wrongdoing and/or compensating for the moral and intellectual shortcomings of large sections of the population. In contrast Plato's, Aristotle's, Aquinas', Rousseau's, Hegel's and Green's approach is far more positive, relating particular forms of order to maintaining cooperative conditions in which human beings can pursue other fundamental values.

Within Western political thinking, the state has usually been seen as the focal point of well-ordered and mutually productive social relationships. As noted above, anarchism, and in a more limited sense Marxism, are significant exceptions to this pattern. Writers in these traditions look beyond the state to situations where people form voluntary orders that do not need the support of political institutions and the systems of coercive regulation that they produce and sustain. It is true, of course, that for much of the history of Western political thought, authority has been centred in trans-national institutions such as empires but as far as the issue of order is concerned, imperial governments operate in ways that do not differ fundamentally from those employed by nation states. It is worth noting, however, that current claims concerning the emergence of 'global' society raise important questions about order as a goal of political institutions and actors. The tendency towards 'globalisation' involves forms of interaction, interdependency and direction which do not merely go beyond the state but threaten to bypass it. 'Global society' is a complex system which is beyond the control of any state and lacks any institution that is comparable with the ideas of sovereignty that feature so prominently in early modern and modern political theory. Contemporary states must seek to create and maintain viable and beneficial orders in contexts that are determined by the uncertain outcome of global forces to which they must respond.

POLITICS AND VIRTUE

2

This chapter focuses on the ideas of a number of important thinkers who saw politics as centrally concerned with the promotion of human goodness or virtue. While the focus on virtue did not mean that other ends are ignored, values such as freedom or happiness were treated in relation to the pursuit of virtue: that is, they were valued because of their connection with moral goodness. The chapter opens with a discussion of Plato's and Aristotle's views on politics and virtue. Both these thinkers examined the relationship between virtue and distinctive possibilities associated with membership of the city state or *polis*. In late medieval political thought the focus of the discussion extended to include nation states, and in the early modern period it was influenced by Protestant challenges to the authority of the Roman Catholic church. One consequence of the turbulence produced by these bitter religiously inspired political disputes was the rejection of 'virtue politics' by a number of important seventeenth- and eighteenth-century political thinkers. However, as will be shown in the last section of this chapter, the late-eighteenth-century German philosopher Immanuel Kant and a group of late-nineteenth-century English writers revived this way of thinking. Because Kant's idea of moral goodness applied to all human beings it gave rise to ideas about international right as well as to systems of political right that applied within states.

Politics and virtue in ancient political theory: Plato and Aristotle

Plato (see p. 23) was born in 428–427 BC, shortly after the start of the great Peloponnesian War that pitched Athens, which had grown into a semi-imperial regional power, against Sparta and its allies and dependants. By the time of his death in 348/47 BC Plato had witnessed Athens' defeat by Sparta in 404 BC, and the temporary overthrow of its democratic government. Although neither slaves, resident aliens nor women possessed political rights in Athens, its political culture was relatively liberal and open. Free adult males exercised a range of political rights and were entitled to play a role in the public life of the city.

The rise of Athens as a regional power transformed the character, direction and scale of political activity in the city, and during Plato's life the impact of this transformation was aggravated by the experience of war, defeat and revolution. The instincts that Plato brought to bear on these developments were generally conservative. One indication of this orientation was his initial enthusiasm when rule by 'the many' (the *demos*) was replaced by a dictatorship of 30 men identified with the long-established, well-to-do Athenian families from which Plato came. This coup, which took place in 404 BC, was short-lived, and so too was Plato's endorsement of it. But although 'the thirty's' cruelty, illegality and self-interest led Plato to withdraw his support for them, his initial approval of the overthrow of popular government in Athens reflected a deep-seated disenchantment with contemporary democratic politics and the moral attitudes that underwrote it.

Plato's views on the moral basis of political corruption are apparent in his critical treatment of two sets of relative newcomers in Athenian politics: the 'sophists', specialised, professional teachers, epitomised in the figure of Gorgias, after whom one of Plato's dialogues is named; and the 'demagogues', ambitious politicians, often from the *nouveau riche*. The sophists prided themselves on imparting skills of a general, non-specialised nature to those who wished to make their mark upon the public life of their city. In Plato's works Gorgias and his colleagues are closely identified with the art of rhetoric, and with a moral viewpoint that may be described as 'relativistic'. Moral relativists argue that conceptions of justice reflect the requirements of particular groups of people and are not immutable, universally applicable ideas. Since there are a variety of such groups, one must accept that basic behavioural norms will vary from place to place and from time to time. As we shall see, this view was anathema to Plato since it implied that moral standards are merely a matter of expediency and may quite accurately (and perhaps more honestly) be specified in the language of self-interest or power.

Plato was highly critical of the impact of moral relativism and rhetoric on the theory and practice of Athenian democracy and was alarmed at the way demagogues ingratiated themselves with the least enlightened and most numerous members of the citizen body by pandering to their partial and narrow conception of their own self-interest. In the *Gorgias*, Plato likened political oratory to the 'false art' of cookery:

> [it] pays no regard to the welfare of its object, but catches fools with the bait of ephemeral pleasure and tricks them into holding it in the highest esteem ... Now I call this sort of thing pandering and I declare that it is dishonourable ... because it makes pleasure its aim instead of good, and I maintain that it is merely a knack and not an art because it has no rational account to give of the nature of the various things that it offers (Plato, 1960, p. 46).

Orators debase the populace (in much the way that an unscrupulous medical attendant debases a self-indulgent patient) and hasten the ruin of the state. This corrupting process was made possible by the politically effective but morally debilitating potentialities of rhetoric. Rhetoric persuades; it induces belief rather than conviction founded on reason, and helps unscrupulous demagogues to flatter the ignorant by appealing to false ideas of self-interest that undermine attachment to fundamental moral truths. Plato thought it significant that demagogues were more popular with the ordinary people than were true statesmen committed to the pursuit of truth and distinguished by their moral virtue.

Plato's critical reaction to sophists and demagogues provided the basis for general statements on appropriate political structures and behaviours that were intended to re-establish the connection between politics and virtue. He thought the consequences of divorcing politics from virtue could be seen in the instability, moral dissolution and political unscrupulousness that disfigured contemporary politics. In many of his political works, most notably in the *Republic,* Plato painted a vivid picture of a corrupt state. Drawing an analogy between a grossly self-indulgent individual and a *polis* that has become obsessed with material luxuries, he portrayed this state as bloated and unhealthy (Plato, 1970, p. 107). It cannot rest content with a particular level of overindulgence, but is driven by forces (which parallel the psychological restlessness of the greedy individual) to seek ever new and often contradictory means of gratification. These debasing drives generated ruthless competition within the state and struggles for resources that prompted conflict with other states. It is important to note, however, that although Plato believed that the weaknesses of what he called contemptuously 'the luxurious state' have a *moral* source (its members' lack of internal regulation or self-constraint) he stipulated that they can only be cured by a radical course of *political* treatment.

That virtue is the end of politics is an axiom, a fundamental principle, of Plato's political thought: the *polis* was a cooperative order directed towards the realisation of goodness and the attainment of human perfection. Moral rules subject the appetitive and irrational aspects of human nature to its rational elements and thus ensure that virtuous individuals have well-balanced souls. This conception reflects Plato's attachment to a traditional ideal of the *polis,* but his views on its implications necessitated a radical restructuring of political institutions and rejection of the democratic values of Athenian political culture.

The *Republic* opens with a discussion of the nature of justice (or right), a value that both Plato and the other participants in the dialogue took to be central to political life and the defining characteristic of the state. Having refuted definitions of justice as 'telling the truth and paying one's debts' (on the ground that these practices may actually be harmful), and 'giving every person their due' (because this would imply that it is just to harm evil doers and thus lower them further in the scale of human excellence), Plato addressed variations on the theme that justice is merely a cover for the pursuit of self-interest. The first book of the *Republic* closes with refined versions of the self-interest argument. It is claimed that justice is merely a way of dealing with problems produced by the unrestrained pursuit of a natural inclination to self-interest. According to this view, justice is a general term describing systems of regulation that are necessary to counteract individuals' natural tendency to pursue the benefits that accrue from unpunished wrongdoing.

Neither these arguments nor the question of how justice should be defined are confronted in the first book of the *Republic*, which Plato concluded with a challenge:

> Prove to us ... not only that justice is superior to injustice, but that, irrespective of whether gods or men know it or not, one is good and the other evil because of what it inevitably does to its possessor (ibid., p. 99).

In responding to this challenge, Plato sought to establish a clear and comprehensive definition of 'justice', show its superiority to injustice, and finally explain why its practice is intrinsically beneficial to humanity. In the course of developing these arguments, he made it clear that justice is the key value in politics. To be a just member of a just state is the highest form of virtue to which human beings can aspire; it is so high in fact that politics becomes identified with the pursuit of perfection.

The close link between politics and human virtue is signalled in the opening passages of the second book of the *Republic*. Plato argued that since justice in the individual is so difficult to determine, he will begin by trying to identify it on a large scale, that is, in the state. This approach is presented as a way of compensating for cognitive myopia – we shall be able to see justice more clearly in the state because it appears there 'writ large' – but it also foreshadows Plato's conclusion that justice in the state and justice in the soul are analogous. Before arriving at this conclusion, Plato traversed an extensive terrain. He developed an account of the growth and corruption of a political community; he then identified the structural and behavioural requirements of an ideal city, and specified the personal attributes necessary to perform the range of functions essential to the survival of a well-ordered and hence just state. It is important to note that the political and social structure of the ideal state is premised on the idea that functions must be matched with and restricted to distinct capacities. While intellectual and moral potentialities can be fostered through education and training, Plato assumed that different human beings possess differing innate capacities; these may be developed, but they cannot be created.

Plato subscribed to the conventional idea that individuals achieve fulfilment as members of a *polis*. He argued, however, that as human beings have markedly different capacities, the structure of the ideal state must reflect this fact. A key requirement is that political power must be placed in the hands of a 'guardian' class that consists of people with highly developed moral and intellectual qualities. This group occupies the supreme place in a fixed and exclusive hierarchy and monop-olises political power. The guardians' total control of the state is justified by the overwhelming superiority of their grasp of the key attribute of governors: the knowl-edge of what is good for the state. This knowledge is a consequence of the guardians' acquaintance with the 'form' of goodness, that is, with goodness itself as an unqual-ified value that informs to a greater or lesser extent the world of ordinary thought and experiences (ibid., pp. 236–43). Individuals' capacity to grasp the forms is a consequence of distinct innate capacities that have to be nurtured and refined by a rigorous process of education, and verified through selection procedures that are blind to class, parentage or gender.

An unusual feature of Plato's position is that he argued that biological differences between men and women are irrelevant to fitness to rule. The main 'natural' differ-ence between the sexes centres on their role in the reproductive process, and Plato argued that it is not possible to infer from this that women are necessarily unfit for membership of the guardian class. He reiterated this argument in a later account of a second-best state in the *Laws* (ibid., pp. 201–10). In light of the deep-seated misog-yny in Athenian life, and the practice and political theory of subsequent Western societies, Plato's focus on *relevant* differences in settling questions of membership of the state has rightly been described as 'extraordinary' (Okin, 1992, pp. 36–38).

Since Plato considered the inferior capacities of women to be a consequence of education and social conditioning, it is understandable that he insists that women be exposed to the same system of education and testing as men. This regime is both intellectual and moral: it is designed to give guardians access to the form goodness, and endow them with the fortitude and strength of character necessary to draw the human world into closer correspondence with it. The effectiveness of the educa-tional and selective processes are reinforced by strict specifications concerning the guardians' way of life. They should not possess private property, nor should they enter into familial or marital relationships that will distract them from the sin-gle-minded pursuit of virtue (Plato, 1970, pp. 161–65, 211–23). This last stipulation means that women are freed from their traditional roles within the family and are thus able to take their full place within the state.

Plato's ideal state is based upon fundamental human needs, and its organisation takes account of natural attributes. It is harmonious, orderly and stable and since it is a perfect state, it must embody justice in its highest and most complete form. Plato argues that the perfect justice of the ideal state is a consequence of its distinguishing features: courage (the distinctive virtue of the auxiliaries); wisdom (embodied in the guardians); and discipline (which is infused throughout the whole). A society that upholds these virtues and assigns corresponding duties to the appropriately quali-fied people is just (Plato, 1970, p. 182). The same principle applies to individuals. The just individual's soul will be well-ordered; its elements will perform their proper function, and will exhibit a sense of due proportion. The elements in question are 'spirit', which produces bravery, and 'reason', which produces wisdom when it sub-ordinates appetite and spirit to it. The soul is just when these three elements work in harmony to produce a condition of overall balance that parallels that which char-acterises the just state. In contrast, injustice in the soul is analogous to injustice in the state. In both cases the constituent elements encroach on each other's functions, producing confusion, disorder and disharmony (ibid., p. 197).

The structure of Plato's ideal state is justified on the grounds that it is perfect in itself and makes it possible for its members to be morally good. However, because Plato thought that individuals have differing levels of natural capacities, the practice of virtue will take on a variety of forms: some will rule, others will fulfil necessary but subordinate roles within the state. Despite these differences the relationship between politics and virtue depends on satisfaction of a single general condition: namely that appetite – the cause of disorder in the luxurious state – is subject to the governance of reason.

The analogy that Plato drew between the unjust soul, the unjust state and an unhealthy organism signals his response to the question why justice should be preferred to injustice. The unjust person is racked by contradictory tensions. The just person, by contrast, enjoys a psychic harmony that is a consequence of the healthy, natural balance of his or her soul. This outcome exemplifies Plato's belief that moral goodness is closely related to beauty. Beauty involves harmony, due proportion and satisfying order. These values played an important role in Plato's political thought by underpinning the idea that moral rules reflect absolute values. Like beauty, moral goodness (or the practice of virtue) is infinitely satisfying because it reflects a disposition that is marked by a harmonious interrelationship of parts. It thus stands in stark contrast to the driven and discordant condition of those who seek satisfaction in bodily pleasures or immoral aspirations. As Plato put it, 'Virtue is a kind of mental health or beauty or fitness, and vice a kind of illness or deformity or weakness' (ibid., p. 198). To Plato and the other participants in the dialogue, the attractions of virtue make the preference for justice over injustice self-evident.

Since virtue (or the attainment of justice) is the goal of human life, it must necessarily play a central role in politics. One reason for this is that for Plato, as for other Greeks, the state is the all-embracing focus of human life. However, Plato's belief that there is a direct parallel between justice in the state and justice in the individual adds a distinctive element to this conventional view, one that makes a particular form of politics integral to the pursuit of virtue. Platonic politics are a precondition for the perfection of human nature, with justice in the state and justice in the individual being mutually reinforcing.

Plato's ideal state was a radical alternative to the 'luxurious' state, and (by inference) to contemporary city states which exhibited many of its characteristics. It was distinguished by rationality, self-control, moderation, and the subordination of material appetite to the dictates of morality and of selfish aspirations to the good of the community. This ethos had important implications for Plato's limited treatment of the ideal state's engagement with other states. The tensions that undermined social cohesion and a sense of common purpose in the luxurious state were sometimes the precursors of bloody civil conflicts (*statis*). They also often generated tense and violent relations with neighbouring states, as corrupt and self-indulgent communities sought to satisfy spiralling demands for material goods by plundering their neighbours, and factions recruited accomplices from other states to help them settle internal scores. These parallels between justice in the individual, justice in the state and justice between states, prompted an approach to international relations that was largely defensive and negative, assuming that interstate interaction was undesirable and would be unnecessary once the malign internal causes of it have been addressed.

Plato's Guardians were expected to control population growth to ensure their community was not subject to pressures that jeopardised its stability. They were also responsible for constraining the demand for material goods within natural and reasonable limits. Plato thought that extensive engagements with other states arose from erroneous views of human needs that exposed ideal states to corrupting influences which threatened their moral integrity. For these reasons, he specified that an ideal state should be self-sufficient, and its contact with the outside world minimal. While Plato allowed that it may occasionally be necessary to seize the territory of other states to maintain a balance between the population and resources, this rational necessity was very different from the dependence-driven tendencies to interference and expansion which resulted from insatiable avarice and self-indulgence.

But while ideal states could generally commit to isolationism, they were unlikely to be placed in an international environment where all states shared this commitment. As a result, Plato gave some consideration to how Guardians were to interact with neighbouring non-ideal states when that became necessary. In addressing this question, he advanced a position that reflected ideas on the role of identity and '*nomos*' in international politics that were common in contemporary Greece and were an important theme in the historian Thucydides' work on the Peloponnesian War (Thucydides, 1968). *Nomos* referred to 'law' in a formal sense but also extended to a range of customary practice associated with the *polei* of 'Hellas', the geographically, culturally, ethnically and linguistically defined area that was distinguished sharply in this period from non-Greek speaking 'Barbarian' kingdoms and empires beyond its boundaries.

The overwhelming sense of justice, stability and order that characterised Plato's ideal state was made possible by the collective identity instilled in its members, and the commitment to the interests of the whole that resulted from this. While Plato clearly did not think that these qualities could be replicated outside the tightly controlled environment of an ideal state, he believed that the shared identity arising from Greek ethnicity might provide the basis for a limited, but nevertheless valuable, sense of common interest. Plato's presentation of this position rested on the conventional distinction between Greeks and Barbarians. He argued that if the Greeks wished to minimise the risk of being defeated and enslaved by non-Greeks, they should avoid acting in ways which impeded their capacity to respond collectively to external threats. For this reason, Plato promoted practices which provided a normative basis for war between Greek states and might thus be seen as a counter to the highly destructive ethos which had led Thucydides to draw a parallel between savage class conflict within Greek states and wars of annihilation between them. Plato thus urged the Greeks to subscribe to protocols prohibiting the enslavement of Greeks by Greeks, and outlawing forms of symbolic and practical retaliation (setting up captured arms as trophies in their temples, devastating territory and burning houses) which provoked further violence and perpetuated antagonisms.

These constraints were underwritten by the special relationships which Plato, in common with many of his contemporaries, thought should exist between Greeks. Although they belonged to different political communities, they were, nevertheless, linked by 'ties of blood and kinship'. Unlike the 'external' relations which existed between Greeks and non-Greeks, these 'internal' ties made it possible for antagonisms to be confined to 'conflicts' rather than escalating into 'wars'. 'War' was a product of what Plato termed 'natural' enmity. By contrast, 'conflict' involved the use of force to bring members of a community (in this case the community of the Greeks) to their senses. It involved discipline rather than the forms of punitive destruction unleashed by warfare (Plato, 1994, pp. 186–89; 469a–471b).

The perspective on interstate relations in the *Republic* appeared also in the less than ideal state (Magnesia) that Plato discussed in the *Laws*. 'Magnesia' had to be fully prepared to ward off external threats, and to this end the state maintained an elaborate system of military organisation and regularly conducted realistic and deadly war games. These measures would ensure the state was prepared to defend itself and make aggression less likely by demonstrating formidable military capacity. Moreover, since the state lived off its own resources and did not engage in foreign trade, it was possible to minimise the threat to Magnesian values posed by the presence of foreigners. Plato noted, however, that this strategy might damage the state's reputation with its neighbours and weaken its hand in dealing with them. He therefore rejected the idea that Magnesia should be a closed state but insisted that it should impose strict controls which restricted foreign travel to those on official duty, including sanctioned 'observers' sent to learn from virtuous individuals abroad and in their carefully circumscribed visits to Magnesia (Plato, 1980, pp. 499–505).

Plato's conception of international relations thus reflects concerns (hostility to materialism, the importance of self-sufficiency and the possibility of forging a sense of community based on identity) that played a central role in his argument about the structural and ethical basis of the ideal state. Inter-state relations were to be circumscribed so as to eliminate ideas and practices that posed a threat to political structures and practices he thought essential to the pursuit of virtue in both ideal and less than ideal states.

Central aspects of Plato's account of the relationship between politics and virtue were challenged by Aristotle. Aristotle considered a life of contemplation to be the pathway to the highest virtue, but he qualified the rigour of this specification with the comment that such a way of life is unattainable for most human beings. Consequently, he offered an account of the ends of politics that relate it to the pursuit of a significant, if less than complete, ideal of human well-being. The *polis* is a focus of human virtue, but in Aristotle's theory this entails a view of the individual and the state that differs markedly from that prescribed for the members of Plato's ideal state.

Aristotle (384–322 BC)

A native of Stagira in northern Greece, Aristotle attended Plato's Academy from 367 to 347. Between 342 and 336 he was tutor to the son of Philip II, King of Macedonia, later known as Alexander the Great. In 336 Aristotle returned to Athens, remaining there until 323 as head of his own school, the Lyceum. Aristotle's intellectual interests were extensive, embracing biology, physics, logic and poetics, as well as moral and political philosophy. His major political work, *The Politics*, was published from lecture notes after his death. It bears the stamp of extensive research undertaken by Aristotle and his pupils at the Lyceum into different systems of government and political practice in the Greek world and beyond. It also reflects a belief that questions about ultimate values can be addressed by reference to the world of human experience and not, as in Plato's theory, to a world of perfection with which human affairs should be brought into correspondence.

In *The Politics* Aristotle treats the city state (or *polis*) as the supreme form of human association, one that incorporates more restricted associations such as the family and village and makes it possible for human beings to pursue the 'good life'. This condition is one that allows humans to realise their potential, and, while there are certain material preconditions of the good life, its distinctive and valuable features relate to the development and exercise of a range of moral and intellectual virtues by members of the community. In its more complete manifestations the good life requires that humans share in the public life of the community as citizen and officeholders. Since Aristotle thought that sharing was only possible between equals, he argued that the intellectual, material and moral characteristics of the population of a given community should determine who is qualified to be a citizen and to hold office. Aristotle's sympathies tended towards the claims of the 'few who are best' and points to forms of government that are essentially aristocratic. In some circumstances, however, democracy would be justified and, in any case, he recognised that there was something to be said for giving 'the many' a limited role in the political life of the community. For Aristotle, as for the Greeks in general, 'the many' embraced free males but excluded women and slaves.

Aristotle's moral and political ideas were very influential in the late medieval period when Aquinas incorporated aspects of them into an account of the state that reflected Christian values. His broad-ranging conception of the moral purpose of the state continued to be an object of interest to political thinkers in the early modern and modern periods.

Key reading: Johnson, 1980; Keyt, 1991; Mulgan, 1977.

In *Nicomachean Ethics* Aristotle identified political science – the science of the *polis* – with the realisation of 'human good' (Aristotle, 1975, p. 1094a). Since the *polis* is the most all-embracing of human communities, one that is directed to the good of all the members of the community, Aristotle claimed that it exists for the sake of the 'good life' of its members. He regarded this condition as the main end of human life and adopted a 'teleological' approach to politics that considers it in relation to the ends to which it is directed and the necessity for humans to cultivate and exercise two types of virtue, the 'intellectual' and the 'ethical'. The first of these embraces both 'practical wisdom' (which directs humans to ethical ends and the means appropriate to achieve them), and 'wisdom' as such, which involves the contemplation of unchanging objects of perfection. While a life of pure contemplation is 'too high' for human beings, Aristotle believed that 'wisdom' plays an important but not complete role in the good life. Such a life is, however, closely related to the pursuit of ethical virtues, and politics is central to their cultivation.

The virtues in question are courage, justice (honesty in business matters), magnificence (generosity to one's friends and one's city), magnanimity (ambition based on an accurate estimation of one's value to the community), good temper, friendliness and temperance (self-control of physical desires). Aristotle's list of ethical virtues has a clubbish air that contrasts sharply with the austerity of Plato's ideals, and reflects the values of the well-educated, well-established members of the Athenian upper middle class with which he identified (Wood and Wood, 1978, pp. 214–23). One should bear in mind, however, that these virtues are related to the type of political community familiar to Greeks. Seen from this point of view, the practice of ethical virtue is inseparable from membership of the *polis*.

The close relationship between politics and the good life is underlined by Aristotle's account of the *polis* as a 'community' in which its members share. In the first book of his *Politics* Aristotle distinguished three forms of association: the family, the neighbourhood or village and the *polis*. The first two of these associations differ from the *polis* because life in them is limited or incomplete. Although these associations make important contributions to the 'good life', this end can only be realised in a complete, self-sufficient community. The *polis* is

> an association which may be said to have reached the height of full self-sufficiency; or rather ... we may say that while it *grows* for the sake of mere life,... it *exists* ... for the sake of a good life (Aristotle, 1958, pp. 4–5).

The *polis* is the supreme form of association; it regulates the others and its end is the supreme end for its members. It is a cooperative order through which they practice virtue and thus enjoy the 'good life' and is so fundamental to human well-being that it could be described as 'natural'. Aristotle believed that 'natural' things are endowed with supreme value because they have realised their innate potentialities and have thereby attained their end. For human beings, the end is the perfection of their capacity for virtue, and since the state is central to this process it is not merely a matter of convention, as the sophists claimed. It follows that the *polis* is natural and man is, as Aristotle said, by nature a political animal (ibid., p. 6).

In Aristotle's theory, friendship and 'justice' are central features of the state. The former encapsulates the idea of a shared existence while the latter combines considerations of 'what is due to one' with what one deserves. That is, it refers to a 'distributive' idea of justice. This principle relates individuals' shares in and contribution to a community to their attributes and capacity; it specifies that 'equals should be treated equally', and this, of course, requires the determination of relevant capacities. When this principle is applied to the *polis* it raises questions about the relationship between the range of capacities possessed by its different members and the pursuit of the ethical goals that constitute the end of the community. Because the *polis* is a form of common existence, however, Aristotle thought there are limits to the differences that can exist between its members. A crucial consideration is that they must have enough in common to be able to share in the life of the community.

One important consequence of this stipulation is that the proportion of a given population that can be full members of a *polis* (or 'citizens' as Aristotle calls them) will vary. Where all are literally equal, then all may be citizens, but where there are significant differences in wealth, education, function or outlook, distributive justice requires that citizenship is limited to duly qualified sections of the population. Aristotle believed that women and slaves were precluded from citizenship because their 'natural inferiority' meant they cannot be the equals of free males, and consequently they cannot be members of the state. As functionally important members of the family, slaves and women contribute to the good life, but they do so under the direction of their putative superiors. They are 'instruments', as Aristotle put it, and thus cannot *share* in the good life or aspire to the level of virtue that membership of the *polis* makes possible (ibid., pp. 36–38; Okin, 1992, pp. 78–79). This line of argument points to the conclusion that true virtue only exists in states where citizenship is restricted to those who really are equals in virtue. Aristotle made this point when he contrasted a 'true' state with a political association that is really no more than a 'mere alliance' to provide mutual defence and promote economic activity (Aristotle, 1958, pp. 118–19).

At times, however, Aristotle appears to have taken a less restrictive position. By recognising that most societies have a mixed socio-economic, intellectual and moral composition, and allowing varying types and levels of political participation to those who are not equals in the strict sense, he recognised the limited but significant capacity for virtue possessed by free-born males (see p. 144). Without attaining the status of a true state, some political associations may thus transcend a 'mere alliance' and assume some of the characteristics of a *polis*; that is, they become associations devoted 'to the end of encouraging goodness' (ibid., p. 118). Of course, if one can identify the basis for a fundamental form of equality that encompasses all human beings, then it becomes possible to see a properly ordered political community as a means of promoting the moral goodness of *all* its members. It was a long time before this consideration was applied to women's political status, but in some medieval political theory, ideas derived from Christianity played a significant role in undermining the moral, if not the political, implications of the distinctions upon which Aristotle depended.

Aristotle not only eschewed the narrowly defined functionalism of Plato's account of ideal and less than ideal states, he also treated international relations as a positive aspect of a well-developed political community, rather than a necessary evil. He assumed that true states must have a political life that extends beyond their boundaries and that just as members of a *polis* share a way of life with one another, the *polis* shares an external life with other states. These relationships had limited objectives that could be specified in treaties rather than requiring a shared view of the good life and satisfying the ethical requirements identified with the *polis*. It did not follow from this, however, that Aristotle thought that the relationships between states were not subject to *nomos*. To the contrary, he thought that the conduct of war should be governed by a conception of justice which applied also to the conduct of individuals. For example, Aristotle had reservations about the moral rationalisation of the enslavement of those defeated in battle; this was only just where victors were manifestly superior to them. Thus while the Greeks' assumption that Barbarians were their inferiors by nature might seem to justify the enslavement of non-Greeks, it made it correspondingly more difficult to do so if the captives were Greeks. Aristotle noted that his contemporaries were sometimes squeamish about describing Greek prisoners of war as slaves, even when they were treated as such (Aristotle, 1958, pp. 18–19).

This line of argument was extended to produce what is, in effect, an embryonic theory of just war. War necessarily results in the subjugation of the defeated, and is only justified to the extent that those who become subject to the control of others have refused to render obedience to their superiors. This argument served to justify aggression on behalf of the Greek states against non-Greeks but it made aggression against other Greeks problematic. Insights into Aristotle's views on this question emerge from his association of international violence with tyranny, and from his criticism of Sparta, whose highly militarised political culture bore more than a passing resemblance to Plato's less than ideal state.

Aristotle observed that tyrants often embarked on aggressive foreign policies and were quick to resort to armed force to keep their subjects occupied and give an air of plausibility to claims to absolute power (ibid., p. 287). Since tyranny was inherently unjust, however, the strategies adopted to maintain it were also morally reprehensible. The case of Sparta was rather different. Here the whole political culture was directed towards warfare and, paradoxically, the Spartans' success on the international stage proved fatal to their state. The Spartans were, quite literally, unable to cope with peace: they collapsed as soon as they acquired an empire. They 'did not use the leisure which peace brought; and they had never accustomed themselves to any discipline other and better than that of war' (ibid., p. 97).

The fate of Sparta reflected the fundamental inadequacy of this state's conception of political community. Aristotle thought the idea that political life should be based on aggressive external engagement was an 'extreme' one; that is, it rested on a one-sided and hence unbalanced conception of the state. Security, or necessary expansion, were only means to an end. They could not constitute the good life, and should not determine the internal structure of the state, or provide the normative basis of it. If, as in the case of Sparta, these means become ends, they undermine the self-sufficiency that is characteristic of a well-developed political community. In seeking endlessly to enlarge the state, the Spartans' demonstrated that they saw the good life in quantitative terms, assumed a bigger state is a better state, and thus implicitly rejected the true view that the material prerequisites of the good life are instrumental and finite. When expansion became an end in itself, it encouraged the indiscriminate and harsh treatment of others, regardless of their claims to consideration. It was thus unjust in itself, and, moreover, it contributed to an external environment where the claims of justice are systematically ignored.

Virtue, politics and Christianity: Aquinas, Machiavelli, Luther, Calvin and Radical Protestantism

Although there are significant differences between Plato's and Aristotle's understanding of the nature and implications of virtue, they both believed it to be intimately related to politics. Their view may be contrasted with the Judeo-Christian tradition's suspicions of humanly created institutions, its reliance on God to produce a truly just society, and its tendency to regard life in the state as at best a form of exile from the promised land. Augustine's rejection of Greco-Roman conceptions of the naturalness of the state, and the divorce between politics and the pursuit of ultimate values that was implied by it, represented an attitude towards politics that was common in early medieval European thought (see p. 21). This view probably related to a general problem (faced both by the Jewish people and by Christians in the Roman Empire) of how the faithful should respond to demands placed upon them by theologically questionable, or at least diverse, political units. It was thus no accident that when the Augustinian position was challenged in the late medieval period, the Christian state had become the predominant form of political organisation in Western Europe (Copleston, 1975, p. 238). This challenge was made by Christian thinkers who attempted to redefine the relationship between their faith and the recently rediscovered formulations of the political ideas of a number of 'pagan' Greek thinkers. In the late twelfth and early thirteenth centuries St Thomas Aquinas produced accounts of the political implications of these developments that were of ongoing importance in the history of political thought.

St Thomas Aquinas (c. 1225–74)

Aquinas, a native of Sicily and a member of the Dominican Order, was educated in Naples, Paris and Cologne. He taught at Cologne before returning to Italy, where from 1259 to 1268 he wrote the first part of his major work, *Summa Theologiae*; the second part, which was never completed, was written in Paris between 1269 and 1274. Aquinas' political thought was part of a large-scale system of Christian ethics that was informed by his appreciation of Aristotle's writings. In addition to the *Summa,* Aquinas also wrote a treatise *On Princely Government* and commentaries on Aristotle's ethics and politics.

Although Aquinas was committed to the conventional Christian idea that human perfection was not possible on earth, he nevertheless regarded social life and political institutions as being of great moral significance. A well-ordered state provided a framework in which its members might enjoy peace and security, provide mutual support and act justly towards one another. Human beings were under an obligation to live in conformity with 'laws of nature' which reflected God's intentions for them. Human law was a system of regulation that applied the requirements of natural law to specific situations and utilised the power of the state to uphold these requirements. Natural law thus provided the basis for human law and the standard against which its form and administration was to be measured. While this view of law emphasised the moral significance of the state, it also imposed significant moral constraints on the conduct of rulers towards their own subjects and members of other political communities. The tradition of natural law thinking in which Aquinas has played a leading role was important in medieval, early modern and modern political thought and continues to have an impact on contemporary discussions of human rights.

Aquinas stressed the advantages that might flow from monarchy but in common with Aristotle he also thought that in some circumstances monarchical states might be strengthened by arrangements that gave complementary political roles to elites and to the broader population. These ideas are associated with theories of 'mixed government'.

Key reading: Copleston, 1975; Finnis, 1998.

Although he thought that Greek philosophy could not be regarded as an adequate statement of the human condition because it was not informed by the fruits of Christian revelation, Aquinas insisted that Christianity was in harmony with the high point of philosophy found in Greek writings, and thus completed the understanding of the human condition for which the Greeks had striven. An important consequence of this view was that Aquinas restored the close connection between virtue and politics found in Greco-Roman thought but extended membership of the state to virtually the whole of the population.

Unlike Aristotle, Aquinas did not think that a genuine political community needs to be made up of equal beings. In his view inequality is natural to humanity, as is the need for regulation by the 'more wise'. But neither inequality nor subordination detracts from the dignity of human beings: all are God's creatures and even the wisest are subject to God's direction and control (Aquinas, 1959, p. 103). Aquinas distinguished between political subordination and servile subjection, a penal condition resulting from sin. He argued that only the latter excludes individuals from membership of the state, or from participation in the 'good life'. As a Christian thinker, Aquinas did not regard the good life as an ultimate end for humanity; this consists in the reconciliation of God and man through the latter's attainment of the 'beatific vision of God in heaven' (Copleston, 1975, p. 200). He argued, however, that political life is natural, and consequently that states can make a significant and positive contribution to the realisation of ultimate values. By linking the 'good life' to humanity's infinite end, Aquinas elevated the status of politics and gave it a strongly positive role in promoting virtue and the pursuit of perfection. This point was made quite clear in his discussion of the duties of a king: 'because the aim of a good life on this earth is blessedness in heaven, it is the king's duty to promote the welfare of the community in such a way that it leads fittingly to the happiness of heaven' (Aquinas, 1959, p. 79).

Aquinas insisted that the state is not merely a damage-limitation mechanism made necessary by man's fall from grace. Even if human beings were free from sin, they would still be in need of direction and guidance in their pursuit of the common good (ibid., p. 105). Political institutions maintain peace, ensure an adequate supply and distribution of the material necessities of the good life, and promote cooperative behaviour that maximises the benefits of social life (ibid., pp. 3–9). Aquinas maintained that social and political life is a significant stage in a continuum of human perfectibility: the 'beatific vision' forms *the* end, but it incorporates goals attainable though political means rather than displacing them.

Thus for Aquinas, political authority was an important aspect of a system of cosmic order and guidance directed to the realisation of Christian values. This approach was endorsed widely by late medieval and early modern political thinkers but did not go completely unquestioned. The most historically significant challenge to the identification of politics with Christian virtue was produced by Niccoló Machiavelli, a citizen and servant of the republic of Florence. Machiavelli's understanding of politics was underwritten by a sharp distinction between *virtú*, a morally neutral concept referring to qualities necessary to preserve states, and the conventional or 'classical' 'virtues' that were overtly antagonistic to Christian influences in politics.

The Prince deals with the security of a single ruler, while the *Discourses* are concerned with the practice and maintenance of popular republican regimes, but both works are premised on the assumption that politics is a sphere of human endeavour with its own distinctive standards. The tension between this view and conventional conceptions of virtue is nicely illustrated by Machiavelli's suggestion that it is dangerous for princes to act generously. Giving to others is only truly virtuous when it is done for its own sake and is exemplified by anonymous donations to those in need. Because princes should commit their resources to enhancing the security of their kingdoms and direct material favours to this end, they are committed to an instrumental approach to giving that is incompatible with true generosity.

> [I]f generosity is practised in such a way that you will be considered generous, it will harm you. If it is practised virtuously, and as it should be, it will not be known about, and you will not avoid acquiring a bad reputation for the opposite vice. Therefore, if one wants to keep up a reputation for being generous, one must spend lavishly and ostentatiously. The inevitable outcome of acting in such ways is that the ruler will consume all his resources ... and if he wants to continue to be thought generous, he will eventually be compelled to become rapacious, to tax the people very heavily, and raise money by all possible means. Thus, he will begin to be hated by his subjects and, because he is impoverished, he will be held in little regard (Machiavelli, 1988, p. 56).

Niccoló Machiavelli (1469–1527)

A citizen of the city-state of Florence, Machiavelli studied law and then embarked on a career in the city government. He held a number of administrative and diplomat roles in the Florentine government and was responsible at one time for aspects of military policy. Machiavelli's political career came to an end in 1512 when the republican government of the city was overthrown by the Medici. His most famous political writings, *The Prince* (1513) and *The Discourses* (1513–19), were not published until after his death.

The Discourses considered the nature and benefits of republican systems of government, the characteristics required of citizens of such regimes, and the means of ensuring their survival. *The Prince*, which was dedicated to Lozenzo de Medici, focused on principalities, or states ruled by a single person. Machiavelli's stated purpose was to show princes what approach to politics they needed to adopt if they were to retain control of their state and prevent it falling victim to conquerers, to usurpers, or to proponents of popular government. His work was directed particularly to 'new' princes, rulers who had recently acquired control of their principality by force of arms and who did not therefore have the aura of long-established tradition, or the habitual obedience of the people, to aid them. Machiavelli's analysis of examples drawn from practical politics provided the basis for an exploration of the nature of princely government, the relationships between princes and other rulers and between princes and their subjects. In both of these works, Machiavelli dwelt at length on the implications of the military requirements of effective government and he also advanced a conception of political morality that distinguished this field of human activity from others. The latter of these themes signalled Machiavelli's rejection of many of the assumptions underlying medieval political thinking.

Bold and at times paradoxical statement of these ideas made 'Machivellianism' a byword for cynical opportunism among contemporary and later readers. At the same time, however, his account of the distinctive nature of politics and his sympathetic appreciation of the spirit and practice of republican government made him an influential figure in early modern political thought in Italy, America and Britain, and an object of great interest to historians of the political thought of this period.

Key reading: Donaldson, 1988; Skinner, 1981.

Although Machiavelli's writings added a new and discordant element to political thinking in early modern Europe, the link between politics and virtue received a new lease of life at the hands of various thinkers who played important roles in the Protestant Reformation which began in Germany in the last decade of his life.

Martin Luther, the 'father of the Reformation', identified politics with magistracy, and restricted its scope to maintaining public order and supporting a church based on scriptural principles. Like Augustine, Luther justified coercive authority by referring to the depravity of most human beings, and he ascribed a negative rather than a positive status to the political framework in which this was set. In *On Governmental Authority* (1523) Luther distinguished between those who belong to the 'kingdom of God' and those who belong to the 'kingdom of the world', arguing that since all human beings are naturally 'sinful and wicked, God through the law puts them all under restraint so that they dare not wilfully implement their wickedness in actual deeds'. Among the few who are true Christians, the government of Christ produces righteousness, but the rest of humanity must be subjected to earthly government to ensure 'external peace and [to] prevent evil deeds' (Hillerbrand, 1968, pp. 47, 48). A broadening of this view can be seen in the ideas of Luther's German contemporary, Philip Melanchthon. In Melanchthon's *Philosophical and Moral Epistle* (1530) the state is identified not merely with the good life, but with the 'eternal good'. This end is fostered positively through the efforts of government to 'maintain, cherish and organize the religious life of the community' (Allen, 1951, p. 33). Although Melanchthon's statement of this position was undeveloped, it foreshadowed the fuller account of the relationship between politics and virtue produced by the great French Protestant reformer Jean Calvin.

In his *Institutes* Calvin made it clear that he was advancing an alternative to what he regarded as two erroneous positions, one of which may reflect his reading of Machiavelli's distinction between the *virtú* of a prince and the virtues of a Christian. In addition, Calvin was responding to anarchic tendencies within contemporary radical Protestantism arising from claims that those in receipt of the divine spirit have no need to subject themselves to political authorities (Calvin, 1950, vol. 2, pp. 1485–86). Although Calvin was as much concerned with maintaining order as Luther, he offered a more positive account of the role of political institutions. In response to claims that princes are morally autonomous or that government is unnecessary for true Christians, Calvin argued that although human beings are subject to two forms of government – the 'spiritual' and the political or 'civil' – these are not at variance with one another. God's kingdom 'yet to come' does not deprive political authorities of their moral significance. To the contrary, since it is God's will that humans live as 'pilgrims' on earth, and since political institutions play an essential role in their journey, they are of great moral importance (ibid., p. 1487). For Calvin, no less than for Augustine, these institutions perform important controlling functions, particularly with respect to the ungodly mass of humanity. He argued, however, that even the 'children of God' required the preparatory discipline of human law in order to ensure that they will be 'partially broken in by bearing the yoke of righteousness' (ibid., vol. 1, p. 359). The fact that Calvin described law by reference to 'righteousness' points to a positive connection between politics and Christian virtue: while government prevents 'tumults', it also establishes and maintains conditions in which humans may live 'holily, honourably, and temperately' (ibid., p. 847). For Calvin, therefore, politics is directly connected to the pursuit of virtue. All political authority comes from God and is necessary to train humanity in those parts of an all-embracing system of virtue that relate to life on earth. Government exists for the sake of Christian virtue and would be necessary even in a community made up of the 'godly'.

Jean Calvin (1509–64)

A native of France, Calvin was a leader of the Protestant Reformation in Geneva, which city he sought to turn into a model reformed community, a 'Protestant Rome'. His political ideas were presented in *Institutes of the Christian Religion* (1536). Calvin's influence was particularly marked among his Protestant compatriots, known as the 'Huguenots', and among religious reformers in Scotland.

Key reading: Hopfl, 1982, 1991; Skinner, 1978.

Because Calvin's ideas were formulated with the backsliding and 'ungodly' population of contemporary Geneva in mind, he laid great stress upon the corrective and disciplinary role of political institutions. These concerns played an important role in subsequent accounts of politics formulated by writers in the Protestant tradition. Some Protestant thinkers looked to conventional political institutions to provide Christian leadership, but others promoted religious leadership over political authority. For example, the early-sixteenth-century German writer Michael Sattler urged contemporaries to form communities under the guidance of 'shepherds' charged with ensuring that 'the name of God is praised and honoured among us, and the mouths of blasphemers are stopped'. Regulation of this kind differs from conventional politics in both its aim and its method of enforcement: it aims at the direct pursuit of Christian virtue by maintaining the spiritual integrity of the community. Sattler argued that the most appropriate form of discipline within a Christian community is the threat of expulsion from it, and he distinguished this form of enforcement from those employed by the existing government: 'Worldly people are armed with spikes and iron, but Christians are armed with the armour of God – with truth, with justice, with peace, faith, and salvation, and with the word of God' (Sattler, 1991, p. 178).

In the post-Reformation period, Christian conceptions of virtue were sometimes given a radical political bearing. Thus the English republican writer Algernon Sidney defined virtue as 'the dictate of reason, or the remains of divine light, by which men are made benevolent and beneficial to each other', and he argued that those who possess reason should not be subject to laws to which they have not given their consent. Those who lack virtue, however, have no claim to political liberty and should be subject to regulation by the rational and virtuous (Scott, 1988, p. 39).

On occasion, heightened expectation of a millenarian transformation of the human condition led radical Protestant writers to entertain the hope that regenerated human beings could form political communities that were legitimated by their pursuit of Christian virtue. The overthrow of a religiously unacceptable monarchy and the military successes of the 'godly' in mid-seventeenth-century-England were taken as signs that God had ordained that his 'saints' would have a special and privileged role to play in the process of salvation. A number of writers formulated a conception of the potentialities of a 'godly commonwealth' in which the 'chosen' would ensure that citizens' aspirations and duties correspond to radicalised Christian perceptions of perfection. The godly commonwealth would thus fuse virtue and the requirements of political life so as to realise the ultimate expectation of the reign of God upon earth (Wootton, 1994, p. 436). Ideas of a godly commonwealth must be distinguished from various seventeenth-century manifestations of utopian thinking that argued for strict forms of regulation designed to impose godly standards on recalcitrant and weak human beings. The purpose of these arrangements was not so much the promotion of virtue as the elimination of wickedness through institutional constraints and mechanisms that would eliminate sources of temptation (Davis, 1994, p. 343).

The belief that politics could, and indeed should, be made to correspond to the complete realisation of Christian notions of human perfectibility was a product of the distinctive combination of radicalised theological doctrines and the breakdown of established patterns of political and social authority in parts of early modern Europe. The experience of the dangerously disruptive implications of 'virtue politics' in the mid-seventeenth century was to have a significant impact on other, contrary, ideas about the ends of politics in Western political thought (see pp. 283–84). But while the seventeenth century saw the end of significant attempts to implement godly commonwealths, it did not mark the termination of the tradition of virtue politics. This perspective continued to be espoused by radical Protestants who were the ideological and theological descendants of early modern sectarians, and its specifically Christian elements were restated by 'Christian socialists' in the nineteenth and twentieth centuries. The most theoretically sophisticated modern formulations of virtue politics were produced in late eighteenth-century Germany by Immanuel Kant and by T. H. Green and other British idealists towards the end of the following century.

Virtue, perfection and freedom: Kant and the British idealists

Kant's understanding of the moral basis of politics derives from the ideas that motivation is central to morality and the distinguishing characteristic of moral actions is that they spring from a 'reverence' for moral law (Kant, 1972, p. 65). Humanity comprises a 'kingdom of ends', a 'systematic union of different rational beings under common law'. They all stand 'under the *law* that each of them should treat himself and all others, *never merely as a means*, but always *at the same time as an end in himself*' (ibid., p. 95). The idea that humans should be treated as *ends* not *means* precludes them being regarded as mere instruments for the attainment of other ends. This view of morality makes freedom a condition for the pursuit of virtue: if people are to act morally, they must will the good for its own sake, not because of any benefit it will bring them, or in reaction to the coercive influence of other human beings or institutions.

Immanuel Kant (1724–1804)

Born in Konigsberg in East Prussia, where he remained all his life, Kant was an academic philosopher whose work spanned a wide variety of fields. The most renowned philosopher of his day, Kant's emphasis on individual moral autonomy laid the basis for a conception of politics that, because it required a break with the past, was in general accord with the revolutionary events that occurred in North America and Europe in the latter part of his life. At the same time, however, he regarded free action as being valuable in relation to the moral perfection of humanity and as necessary to ensure that individuals respected the moral integrity of their fellows. These ideas have been influential in nineteenth- and twentieth-century liberal thought, especially in the writings of T. H. Green and John Rawls. Kant's political works include *The Metaphysical Elements of Justice* (1797) and *Perpetual Peace: A Philosophical Sketch* (1796).

Key reading: Murphy, 1970; Reiss, 1971; Williams, 1992.

But while freedom is central to Kant's conception of right action, he did not regard it as a sufficient condition for morality or for the pursuit of perfection. The goal of human action, the 'essential end', is the development of humanity's distinctive moral and physical capacities marked by a progression from 'bondage to instinct to rational control – in a word, from the tutelage of nature to the state of freedom. ... This consists in nothing less than progress towards perfection' (Kant, 1975, p. 60). Virtue is thus to be understood in relation to perfection; freedom is valuable because of the role it plays in the practice and development of people's capacity for virtue (Rosen, 1993a, pp. 188–89).

This conditional understanding of freedom provided the basis of Kant's conception of the relationship between politics and virtue. At first sight, the fact that political authority imposes rules upon individuals seems to make it antagonistic to the growth of virtue. Although Kant acknowledged the force of this objection, he resisted the conclusion that virtue and politics are antithetical. Thus while he distinguished 'juridical' from 'ethical' legislation, and argued that only the latter is strictly moral because it operates 'internally' upon conscience rather than externally upon behaviour, Kant argued that government may make important contributions to human perfection. Provided juridical legislation is a product of a political system based upon the consent of subjects and directed towards their common interests, it creates conditions that foster moral action. Government constrains instinctive behaviour and makes it easier for reason and morality to become the basis of human conduct.

Thus while politics is a matter of practical necessity, it is also conducive to the pursuit of perfection. Kant stressed that its benefits are not merely derived from the constraint imposed upon 'wild freedom'. To the contrary, he argued that the 'veneer of morality' produced by juridical legislation fosters the growth of true morality:

> each individual believes of himself that he would by all means maintain the sanctity of the concept of right and obey it faithfully, if only he could be certain that all the others would do likewise, and the government in part guarantees this for him; thus a great step is taken *towards* morality (although this is still not the same as a moral step), towards a state where the concept of duty is recognised for its own sake, irrespective of any possible gain in return (Kant, 1971, p. 121, note).

From this perspective, states' coercive actions inhibit obstructions to rational freedom and hence also to the practice of virtue and the pursuit of perfection (Murphy, 1970, p. 94).

The underlying principles of Kant's philosophy are universalistic and thus have implications for relationships that extend beyond particular communities and cultures (Orend, 2000, p. 25). Kant explored some of these implications in essays on 'perpetual' peace. He noted that in eighteenth-century Europe, peace was frequently disrupted by bloody and costly conflicts prompted by the territorial ambitions of 'enlightened' despots who saw it as their duty to increase the size and power of their kingdoms (Beale, 2006, p. 506). Kant made a barbed reference to this false conception of the 'true glory of a state' by linking it to a satirical image of the peace of a graveyard and pointing out that in this context conventional peace treaties merely signalled short-lived suspensions of hostilities (Kant, 1996, p. 317). By contrast, Kant's proposals were intended to lay the basis for peace in the true sense, creating a system of 'international right' which was similar to, but by no means identical with, the 'political right' that secured individual members of states the freedom necessary for their pursuit of moral goodness. Kant also promoted a system of 'cosmopolitan right' applying to individuals considered solely as members of humanity. These expressions of right form an integrated system reliant on the maintenance of each of its components (Kleingeld, 2006, p. 480).

Although Kant thought that actual states varied in their capacity to define and maintain systems of political right, he assumed that in Europe at least they had made worthwhile progress in pursuit of this objective. The situation with respect to the relations between states was very different. The international environment, without settled enforceable laws or executive and judicial authorities, was characterised by systemic rather than passing conflict and by an all-pervasive sense of insecurity. In these circumstances states were prompted to make pre-emptive strikes against perceived threats and encouraged to gain permanent control of those who seemed likely to threaten them. These measures, however, provide only a temporary respite because an enlarged state presents a heightened threat to its neighbours and they respond by seeking to restore the *status quo*. Moreover, international relations did not satisfy the requirement that legitimate coercion derived from consent, so sovereigns' use of force is 'devoid of justice'. It disrupts systems of political right, violating the freedom of members of settled civil societies and hindering the state's educative influence on subjects' moral development (Kant, 1971, p. 49). Kant's response to this situation was to urge states to abandon 'a lawless state of savagery' and enter 'a federation of peoples in which every state, even the smallest, could expect to derive its security and rights not from its own power or its own legal judgement, but solely from this great federation ... from a united power and the law-governed decisions of a united will' (Kant, 1971, p. 47).

Kant's essay 'Perpetual Peace: A Philosophical Sketch' (1795) mimicked eighteenth-century treaty documents in being presented in series of 'preliminary articles' and 'definitive articles', the former addressing particular causes of conflict while the latter seek to secure a permanent basis for amicable relations in the future (Kant, 1996, pp. 322, 325, 328). Kant's treaty statements were designed to eliminate war, not merely (as was the case with conventional diplomatic exchanges) to gain a temporary breathing space on terms that set the stage for further conflict.

The Preliminary Articles address practices which lay the seeds of ongoing conflict or facilitate militaristic political cultures, and usually also involve a violation of political right. They thus prohibit secret treaty clauses of aggressive intent, territorial expansion, interference in the internal affairs of other states and gratuitous brutality, all of which make future conflict highly likely. Standing armies and access to loans to purchase war materials are also outlawed since they put states on a permanent war footing and predispose rulers to utilise these expensive resources. Kant thought that territorial expansion and forced regime change are morally objectionable because they ignore citizens' rights to determine how they are to be governed, and that the very idea of mercenary and standing armies was contrary to the ideal of human dignity embodied in public right. He draws a parallel between the forced transfer of subjects from one state to another, and the assumptions underlying the common eighteenth-century practice of rulers turning their subjects into mercenaries and selling their services to other rulers. 'The hiring out of troops of one state to another against an enemy not common to both' entails that 'the subjects are thereby used and used up as things to be managed at one's discretion'. Kant condemned standing armies on similar grounds: 'being hired to kill or to be killed seems to involve a use of human beings as mere machines and tools in the hands of another (the state), and this cannot well be reconciled with the right of humanity in our own person' (ibid., p. 318).

Kant's definitive articles facilitate the universal adoption of republican forms of government as a necessary postive condition for perpetual peace. His views on this point rest on the assumptions that ordinary citizens have no interest in making war because the costs fall on them and they receive no compensatory benefit. It is only under republican constitutions that 'the people' as a whole have a direct and determining role in deciding questions of war and peace (ibid., pp. 323–24). Republics are identified with ideas of human dignity and autonomy, which are incompatible with the instrumental and directive culture of militaristic monarchies. The definitive articles also promote multi-lateral agreements which resemble those through which political right is established. Each state

> for the sake of its security, can and ought to require the others to enter with it into a constitution similar to a civil constitution, in which each can be assured of its right. This would be a *league of nations*, which, however, need not be a state of nations (ibid., pp. 325–26).

Kant's language points to a process – a '*federalising* of free states' – rather than an emphatic act of creation. He thus proposes a 'league', a vehicle of cooperation which is far looser than a 'federation' or 'international state' (Kleingeld, 2006, p. 483). The league's role is to ensure that its members respect the preliminary articles of the treaty, not to establish a general system of public law with the coercive apparatus necessary to uphold it. Kant distinguished the league from an international state, arguing that the latter would require a uniform system of legitimate rule that would supplant the systems of political right maintained by its component parts. In so doing, it would form an entirely new political unit that would cease to be an *inter-national* state and become a single nation: 'we have to consider the right of *nations* in relation to one another insofar as they comprise different states and are not fused into a single state' (Kant, 1996, p. 326).

The third definitive article points to a potentially universal system of 'cosmopolitian' right which harmonises the relationship of all rational beings and presupposes that 'the community of nations of the earth has now gone so far that a violation of right on *one* place of the earth is felt in *all*' (Kant, 1996, p. 330; Wood, 2006, p. 357). At this stage, however, cosmopolitan right is restricted to 'hospitality': that is, 'the right of a foreigner not to be treated with hostility because he has arrived on the land of another' (Kant, 1996, p. 329). Cosmopolitan right is important for stateless persons or refugees, as well as for shipwrecked mariners and others who find themselves thrown into direct contact with members of other societies and seek access to their territory and resources. Under cosmopolitan right, individuals may seek such access and should not be subject to mistreatment while making their appeal. They must, however, accept the decision of those who legally occupy the territory on whether they remain in it. This requirement springs from a corresponding principle of 'inhospitality' prohibiting visitors from demanding rights over the possessions and lives of their hosts. Kant applies this principle to Europeans' relationship with indigenous peoples, arguing that claims to their territory are without any basis in justice, being wholly derived from superior powers of compulsion (Kant, 1996, p. 329). They represent practices characteristic of a state of war, a condition that is devoid of right and necessarily antithetical to the values that will advance the cause of peace.

Kant's political thought is connected directly to that of the final group of exponents of virtue politics discussed in this chapter. The writers in question are conventionally referred to as the 'British idealists', a label that signals their attachment to ideas that were current in late-eighteenth- and early-nineteenth-century Germany. The most important thinker in this group was T. H. Green, a highly influential figure at Oxford University in the 1870s and early 1880s (see p. 33). The political affiliations of the British idealists were largely liberal, but they sought to reformulate liberalism into a 'positive' rather than a 'negative' doctrine. In the past, liberals had successfully attacked institutions and practices that protected the exclusive interests of privileged sections of the community, but the idealists thought that the time had come to give liberal ideas a more positive aspect. Traditional liberal notions of freedom must be refined to take account of the social context of human action, and to recognise that liberty requires a capacity to act, and not merely the absence of constraints. These modifications would allow liberals to promote an active state that would use its power to enforce acceptable standards of industrial safety and municipal hygiene, eliminate misuses of property and promote the education of the population. These measures were justified on the ground that a deprived, unhealthy and ignorant population is not free in any meaningful sense, not free, that is, to act as moral, autonomous beings (Green, 1986, pp. 196–212).

Although autonomy was important for the British idealists, they stressed that liberty itself is not an absolute value. Particular liberties have to be related to the 'common good', that is, a non-exclusive, moral good that individuals share with all other members of the community (Bosanquet, 1899, pp. 118–54; Green, 1986, pp. 25–26). A community that recognises the common good and seeks to attain it through the action of individuals, social groups and the state, is pursuing the 'good life'. The idealists derived this notion from Aristotle's writings, but they imbued it with Platonic overtones of perfection. Green stressed, for example, that the state and other social and political institutions exist for the sake of goodness and he related this directly to the perfection of the individuals who comprise it: 'To speak of any progress or improvement or development of a nation or society or mankind, except as relative to some greater worth of persons, is to use words without meaning' (Green, 1986, p. 256).

This stipulation drew attention to the idealists' belief that virtue is a personal quality. They insisted, however, that political institutions can play an important role in promoting human perfection. Of course, since this end involves the self-willed pursuit of goodness, the state's role is indirect rather than direct. In idealist political thought the relationship between the state and virtue has a number of dimensions. First, as the experience of 'classical' liberalism shows, political authority can be exercised in an essentially 'negative' way; that is, it can be used to destroy class privilege buttressed by the misapplication of political power. By contrast, states which embody the moral aspirations of the whole community can use their power and influence to ensure that institutionalised impediments to the realisation of the common good are eliminated. Secondly, as indicated above, the state can act in a more positive fashion, extending opportunities for the development and practice of virtue to all its members. In addition, however, there is an important further sense in which the idealist perception of politics is intimately and necessarily linked to virtue. For these writers, the perfection of individuals is brought about by their active and conscious realisation of the 'common good'. Consequently, to the extent that the state embodies the common consciousness of its members – something the idealists thought became far more probable and less haphazard when it took on a democratic character – then politics is central to the practice of virtue.

Kant's theory applies to 'all rational beings', but in keeping with a tradition that can be traced back to Aristotle he excluded women from this category (Okin, 1992, p. 6). Green, however, implicitly rejected this assumption, arguing that while there are significant differences between men and woman, these relate to their education and social roles, not to rationality or moral worth. In the course of a discussion that made direct reference to the shortcomings of the moral ideas of the ancient Greeks, Green argued that all human beings must be recognised as having an equal right to develop their moral personalities. He insisted that modern society must recognise 'the proper and equal sacredness of all women as self-determining and self-respecting persons' (Green, 1986, p. 281), a sentiment that was carried through to his practical involvement in educational initiatives directed at the needs of women (Anderson, 1991).

Conclusion

Many historically significant Western writers regarded membership of a political community as essential to the pursuit of moral objectives that are fundamental to human well-being. This idea lay behind Plato's and Aristotle's conception of the *polis* and played a central role in Christian political thinking. The most developed statement of the last of these views, one that was directly connected to aspects of ancient political thought, was presented by Aquinas, but it also appeared in the writings of Calvin and other Protestant thinkers in the early modern period.

Claims about the positive relationship between politics and virtue give rise to specifications of institutional forms that foster virtue. Many of the theorists discussed in this chapter assumed the need for systems of regulation that place the more rational and virtuous members of the population in positions of authority.

This requirement is reflected in a long tradition of political thinking that promoted various forms of hierarchy, but it is important to note that the thinkers who made these claims justified political hierarchy on the ground that it is necessary to promote virtuous conduct on the part of all, or in some case most, members of the community. Government exists for the good of the governed, and the major task for political thinkers is to identify forms of rule that will facilitate the attainment of this goal. Since the realisation of this objective will be threatened by rulers who use power for corrupt purposes, it is important to establish barriers to misrule (see pp. 235ff).

During the second half of the nineteenth century and most of the century which followed, the emergence of largely secular conceptions of human well-being, and an increasing scepticism about moral objectivity, prompted a retreat from ideas about the ends of politics that rested on claims about what God intends for humanity. In the last few decades of the twentieth century, however, religious ideas have had more prominence with the re-emergence of Christian fundamentalism in the United States and elsewhere in the west, and with promotion of the political role of religion in a number of predominantly Islamic countries (see pp.). In addition to these modern survivors of traditional approaches, some writers have focused on the need for liberal-democratic regimes to be underpinned by a culture that depends on the virtues of their citizenry, and have attempted to identify attitudes and qualities that are conducive to the growth and maintenance of such a culture (Glaston, 1992, p. 1; Macedo, 1992).

3 POLITICS AND FREEDOM

The theories discussed in this chapter are drawn from the early modern and modern world because it was only in these periods that arguments about freedom assumed a central place in the history of political thought. For ancient and medieval thinkers freedom was a secondary value relating to conceptions of the good life, or to the requirements of religious notions of virtue. This chapter begins with a consideration of the markedly political notion of freedom that was central to the classical republican tradition of Renaissance Italy. Classical republicans, the most important of whom was Niccoló Machiavelli, considered freedom in relation to needs of the state, rather than seeing it as an attribute that belonged to individuals. Machiavelli's understanding of freedom differed from that of both John Locke and Thomas Paine because both of these writers regarded individual freedom as 'natural': it is a right possessed by individuals that sets limits to the exercise of political authority. The chapter concludes with a consideration of two sets of critical arguments about the very partial application of this idea in late eighteenth- and nineteenth-century Europe and North America. The first concerned the exclusion of women from the exercise of political rights that were seen by writers such as Paine as necessary to protect a universal right to freedom. The second set of arguments focused on the complete denial of this right to African-Americans in the southern United States while slavery persisted, and its very incomplete recognition thereafter.

Freedom and politics in the classical republican tradition: Marsilius, Bartolus and Machiavelli

Classical republicanism grew out of the political experiences of the late-medieval and early-modern city states of Italy but it drew on ideas derived from the ancient world and had a significant impact on seventeenth- and eighteenth-century Anglo-American political thought. The Italian city states occupied territory that had formed the core of the Roman Republic and were the locus of the renaissance, or rebirth, of classical learning in the fourteenth and fifteenth centuries. Classical republicanism is often identified with Machiavelli, but his account of political liberty was preceded by those produced by Marsilius of Padua and Bartolus of Sassaferrato in the first half of the fourteenth century.

The classical republican idea of freedom is similar in its general bearing to that of the Romans. Unlike theorists who focus on the liberty of the individual, classical republicans treated individual freedom in relation to the freedom of the state. A state is free when it is independent of external control by other states or rulers, and is ruled by its citizens, rather than a 'prince' (Skinner, 1978, vol. i, pp. 157–8). Liberty is thus the distinguishing characteristic of an independent republic. Both Marsilius and Bartolus rejected Aquinas' claim that monarchy is a generally applicable ideal (see p. 132) and argued that small, self-contained entities are best served by republican forms of government founded, as Bartolus put it, 'on the body of the people' (ibid., p. 53). They thought these states are less liable to be plagued by the bitter factionalism which marks other regimes and poses a constant threat to peace, tranquillity and public well-being. Marsilius followed Aristotle in describing the state as a community of freemen: 'every citizen must be free and not undergo another's despotism, that is, slavish dominion' (Marsilius, 1956, vol. ii, p. 47). However, while these writers gave freedom a prominent place in their accounts of politics, their ultimate justification of popular government reflected the belief that peace and tranquillity are preconditions for the realisation of a Christian conception of virtue.

The connection between political freedom and Christian aspirations was rejected by Machiavelli. Moreover, while he endorsed some of the central features of the classical republican tradition, his work marked a departure from important aspects of it. Like his predecessors, Machiavelli identified liberty with independence and self-government, and he stressed the role that free citizens play in maintaining the external and internal integrity of the state. He was, however, highly sceptical of the prospects of peace and tranquillity in human life and did not give moral primacy to them. In addition, he rejected the idea that a unified citizen body is a necessary or even a desirable feature of republics.

The key to Machiavelli's conception of political freedom lies in his idea of *virtù*. This term has a range of meanings, but it refers in general to those active qualities that are necessary for the maintenance of a state. In free states, or republics, citizens must possess a high level of personal commitment to their city, they must have the will and capacity to defend it against external enemies, and they must also be willing and able to play an active and wary role in its internal affairs. Their life and loyalty must focus on the state and they must be free of obligations to self-interested individuals or factions that might compromise it. In other words, the kind of *virtù* that is appropriate to republican government preserves both its external freedom and its internal system of self-government. *Virtù* and liberty have a symbiotic relationship: freedom engenders *virtù*, and *virtù* ensures the state remains free.

An important consequence of Machiavelli's understanding of the implications of republican *virtù* was that he thought it made a degree of disorder (or 'tumult') both unavoidable and beneficial. *Virtù* requires *active* dedication to the good of the state, and since different sections of the community will take differing views of this, republics must necessarily be in a condition of tense equilibrium produced by the pull of different conceptions of how the public good might best be served. Machiavelli thought that the tumultuous condition of popular republics is a sign of health. It indicates that citizens are practising the *virtù* upon which the liberty of the state depends (Machiavelli, 1975, vol. i, p. 218).

This argument, which Machiavelli illustrated with glowing references to the productive tensions that marked the heyday of the Roman Republic (ibid., pp. 218–73), signalled a break with the view that liberty is conducive to internal peace. It also meant that Machiavelli had abandoned the instrumental view of liberty that appeared in the writings of Bartolus and Marsilius: liberty, republicanism and *virtù* are so inseparably entwined that one can hardly say that one value is subsidiary to the others. This feature of Machiavelli's theory is related to his explicit rejection of the conventional idea that *virtù* and virtue are synonymous, and to his reservations about the political value of Christian, as opposed to pagan, religion (ibid., pp. 240–50). Machiavelli's arguments point to the need for a distinctive standard of *political* morality, that is, for rules of conduct that relate to the requirements of different kinds of state rather than to universal standards external to politics. In his book on principalities Machiavelli urged princes to ignore the dictates of conventional morality and to do whatever was necessary to keep the populace under control (Machiavelli, 1988, pp. 55–71). In republics, however, political morality requires the cultivation of *virtús* that are closely related to liberty; only a free and active population can maintain a free state. Since republican regimes require citizens to strive to maintain their common political life and the distinctive morality that is integral to it, Machiavelli thought that they were glorious *human* achievements.

Politics and 'natural' liberty: Locke, Paine, J. S. Mill

For the classical republicans, liberty was an inherently political concept; it related to the needs of the state and its implications for individuals were discussed in these terms. This perspective on freedom is quite distinct from that which attributes liberty to pre-political or 'natural' human beings, and then seeks to understand what happens when they come together to form political societies. One approach to this problem has been considered in an earlier discussion of aspects of Hobbes' political thought. For Hobbes the creation of political society requires the renunciation of natural liberty and the establishment of a sovereign whom all should obey (see pp. 210ff).

Hobbes' claim that nothing was worse than the state of nature was questioned by many of his contemporaries and successors. Samuel Pufendorf, for example, thought that human beings could create forms of government that would save them from the hazards of the state of nature without requiring submission to an absolute sovereign (see pp. 213ff). The same general point was made by the late-seventeenth-century English writer John Locke. While many of the central features of his political thought – particularly his understanding of the state of nature and of the factors that would both motivate people to leave this condition and justify their doing so – had been current in European political thought for more than a century, Locke's position was novel in the sense that he made individual freedom a necessary feature of political relationships. Before Locke, natural liberty was discussed in terms of the creation of political authority, but he insisted that individuals retain some rights even in a political or 'civil' condition (Tuck, 1979).

John Locke (1632–1704)

Locke, a fellow of Christ Church, Oxford, was a philosopher and physician. He was a close associate of the Earl of Shaftesbury whose involvement in political manoeuvres and plots against Charles II and his brother (later James II) forced Locke into exile in Holland. Locke's most famous political work, *Two Treatise of Government*, was written in exile some time during the early 1680s. It was revised and published in 1689 to justify James' ejection from the throne as a result of the 'Glorious Revolution' of 1688–89.

Locke argued that political power was entrusted to rulers and that legitimate government was based on consent. Government was created to enhance individuals' capacity to give effect to laws of nature that stipulated God's intentions for humankind and provided the normative basis for social and political life. When rulers acted in ways that were contrary to this requirement they violated their trust, impugned their legitimacy and weakened their claim to the obedience of their subjects. In extreme cases subjects may have a duty to resist unjust rulers.

Aspects of Locke's political theory – his understanding of the laws of nature, the view that government was based on the consent of the governed, the right to resist unjust rule and to reconstitute the political community – played a significant role in eighteenth-century political thinking and in revolutionary movements in the United States, France, Ireland and South America.

Key reading: Dunn, 1984b; Grant, 1987.

Although Locke's position may be usefully contrasted with Hobbes', the target of his major political work, *The Two Treatise of Government* (1689), was Sir Robert Filmer, the author of *Patriarcha*. Filmer argued that political power is derived directly from the patriarchal (or fatherly) supremacy conferred by God upon Adam, the first father. From the time of God's grant to Adam there has been no 'state of nature', or any natural liberty, because all humans were born in subjection to their natural fathers and patriarchal monarchs (see pp. 215–16).

Locke's *First Treatise* presents a detailed refutation of Filmer's universal patriarchalism and a defence of the natural liberty of humankind; the *Second Treatise* explores the political implications of this. Like many of his contemporaries, Locke used the idea of a state of nature to identify the social implications of human nature, to establish a rationale for the state which responded to them, and to specify the key features of legitimate political authority. He argued that human beings in the state of nature are endowed by God with natural liberty so that they can take responsibility for themselves and thus act in conformity with their creator's intentions as stipulated in the 'laws of nature'. While natural individuals are thus free from subjection to other human beings they are in a condition of 'liberty not licence': 'The natural liberty of man is to be free from any superior power on earth, and not to be under the will or legislative authority of man, but to have only the Law of Nature for his rule' (Locke, 1967, p. 301). The laws of nature specify that human beings must preserve themselves, assist in the preservation of others and uphold the laws of nature by judging and punishing those who breach them (ibid., p. 289). However, while Locke denied there is such a thing as patriarchal authority even within the family – children are subject to 'parental' power, exercised equally by both parents and terminating when they become adults – he subsequently restored the dominion of men over women by claiming they had superior strength and ability and restricted political rights to them (Okin, 1992, pp. 200–1).

Locke's state of nature is far less forbidding than Hobbes'. He argued that any violence suffered by individuals will be less damaging to them (and far less inhibiting to their fulfilment of their obligations to God) than the dangers posed by a Leviathan or by an all-powerful Filmerian patriarch. However, while a state of natural liberty is far from being a dire one, Locke acknowledged that this condition entails certain 'inconveniences', due more to ignorance and partiality than to ill-will. These failings are particularly significant in an environment where each individual is responsible for interpreting, applying and enforcing natural law. Consequently, Locke argued that the state of nature will be marred by accidental injustice. He implied, moreover, that since human beings are under a general injunction to understand the law of nature and to uphold it to the greatest possible extent, they must improve upon the state of nature if they can find a way of doing so. Membership of the state fulfils this requirement because it opens up the possibility of establishing certain and impartial systems of judgement and enforcement in place of the precarious arrangements that exist in the state of nature.

Since human beings are naturally free, however, any curtailment of their liberty must involve *consent*; in other words they must *agree* to forego their natural liberty and place themselves under the control of a political superior: 'Men being ... by nature, all free, equal and independent, no one can be put out of this estate, and subjected to the political power of another, without his own *consent*' (ibid., p. 348). This process is relatively straightforward in a situation where people actually come together to form a political society, but it becomes problematic if applied to a pre-existing state. Locke addressed this problem formally by means of the idea of 'tacit consent', which involves identification of conditions that, if satisfied, signify consent. Thus when adults choose to live in a country they consent tacitly to accept its political system and obey the sovereign.

For Hobbes, there is a sharp qualitative difference between the state of nature and political society, but in Locke's theory natural liberty casts a permanent shadow over the state. Individuals in the state of nature are under an obligation to adhere to the laws of nature; their natural liberty is designed to make them responsible for fulfilling this obligation. In political society this obligation persists; by consenting to obey legitimate political authorities individuals are, in effect, voluntarily assuming responsibility for arrangements that will uphold the laws of nature more effectively and committing themselves to live by them. In so doing, they are making a conscientious attempt to fulfil the ends for which God created them. Moreover, since humans' fundamental obligation under the law of nature persist within the state, they have a responsibility not to tolerate forms of government or exercises of political power that seriously compromise this obligation. This feature of Locke's theory provides the basis for stipulating institutional requirements of legitimate government, and for a theory of justified resistance to flagrantly unjust sovereigns (see pp. 318ff). Membership of political society *suspends* natural liberty rather than *abolishing* it; it always remains in the background. If the purposes for which it exists and the purposes for which it is suspended are not satisfied, human beings must take up their natural liberty and resume responsibility for identifying and maintaining the laws of nature.

For Locke, therefore, the legitimacy of government depends on its willingness to give effective legal form to the implications of the law of nature and avoid acting in ways that threaten the 'life, liberty and estates' of those who are subject to it. Locke believed that while these requirements are incompatible with the type of arbitrary rule that he associated with Hobbes' Leviathan or with a Filmerian patriarch, they can be satisfied by monarchical, aristocratic or democratic systems of government. Towards the close of the eighteenth century, however, arguments concerning natural liberty were used to promote republican government and to delegitimate monarchy and aristocracy on the ground that they were incompatible with individuals' natural right to liberty. The most notorious and long-remembered statement of this position was advanced by the Anglo-American writer Thomas Paine.

Paine's conception of republican government is based on a particular understanding of the relationship between natural liberty and political society. In the first part of his *Rights of Man,* he distinguished 'natural' from 'civil' rights (Paine, 1976, p. 90). Paine's natural individuals possess a range of rights of action and opinion (including religious faith) whose free exercise is subject only to the condition that it does not injure the natural rights of others; they also have a right to prevent interference in the exercise of their rights. Governments are created when individuals pool their rights of judgement and enforcement to ensure that these functions are better performed; they thus become matters of 'civil right', subject to public control. Paine insisted, however, that members of a legitimate political community retain the right to untrammelled exercise of the natural rights that have not been ceded to the state. Paine's account of the foundation of government on pre-existing natural rights thus points to a fundamental continuity between the liberty enjoyed by individuals in a pre-political condition and that which is recognised and protected within a legitimate political society.

Although natural freedom is a central value for writers such as Locke and Paine, its political implications are not straightforward. At one level, political institutions ensure that liberty, which is necessary for the well-being of individuals, is made secure from infringement by other individuals. At the same time, however, both Locke and Paine argued that individual freedom places constraints upon the exercise of political authority. Seen from this point of view, freedom is not so much an end of politics as something that determines its scope.

A similar element of ambiguity is apparent in John Stuart Mill's account of the relationship between politics and freedom. Aspects of Mill's political thought will be discussed in other chapters of this book, but it should be noted here that his essay

Thomas Paine (1737–1809)

Born and raised in England, Paine emigrated to Philadelphia where he made a name for himself as a supporter of the American cause during the revolutionary war. He held a number of political appointments in the United States before returning to Europe in 1787 to promote a single-span, pierless iron bridge that he had designed. Following the publication of *The Rights of Man* (two parts: 1790, 1791), a radically antimonarchical work, Paine fled to France to escape prosecution. He was active in French politics, narrowly escaping execution during the Terror.

In *Common Sense* (1776), a work that attracted widespread attention in America and Britain, Paine provided a justification for American independence that involved a systematic critique of the practice and principles of hereditary government. He pursued this line of argument with even greater effect in *The Rights of Man*, the most widely circulated radical contribution to the debate over the relative merits of what Paine called 'old' (hereditary monarchy) and 'new' systems of government (representative democracy) that took place in Britain as the revolution progressed across the channel in France. In Paine's view, the purpose of government was to take care of a very limited range of functions that could not be adequately performed by individuals themselves or though voluntary social interaction. Individuals were endowed with a range of natural rights, and provided that these were upheld, they were capable of pursuing most of their legitimate interests, either singly or by cooperating with others. Individuals created government to exercise those few rights (of adjudication and protection) that required concentrated and organised power. Paine argued that the principles and practices of hereditary monarchy were directly contrary to these requirements. By contrast, representative democracy ensured that officeholders were attached to the interests of the community.

Paine came from a very humble background and prided himself on being self-educated. His works were written in straightforward, rhetorically effective, direct prose and were laced with pithy epigrams. As a result, they enjoyed a huge circulation among the lower classes in the 1790s and remained popular with proponents of radical political reform throughout the nineteenth century.

Key reading: Claeys, 1989b; Dyck, 1988.

On Liberty (1859) is often regarded as a seminal discussion of the topic. In this work Mill provided an emphatic defence of individual liberty:

> [T]he sole end for which mankind are warranted, individually or collectively, in interfering with the liberty of action of any of their number, is self-protection. That the only purpose for which power can be rightfully exercised over any member of a civilised community, against his will, is to prevent harm to others (Mill, 1983, pp. 72–3).

This statement precludes restrictions on individuals' freedom on the basis of paternalistic claims to superior knowledge of what is good for them . In *On the Subjection of Women* (1869) Mill applied aspects of this line of argument to counter a range of assumptions concerning the inferiority of women that were used to justify their legal and social subjection to males, and to exclude them from a range of rights. He argued that even if the assumptions of current inferiority were well-grounded, this did not justify gross infringements of the liberty of women; without liberty, women, like slaves, lacked the opportunity to develop their intellects or to contribute to general progression.

Mill thought that freedom is a good in itself, but more consistently and significantly he argued that it is necessary both for the development of the moral and intellectual character of individuals and for the progressive advancement of communities. Although insisting that the principle of liberty applies to all adult members of reasonably 'civilised' communities, Mill's interest in freedom was closely related to his belief that genius and originality, qualities found in only some members of the population, are of crucial importance to the progress of humanity. He was thus concerned to protect those who were capable of identifying new and potentially valuable ideas and modes of life from the conformist tendencies that were gaining strength in emerging democratic cultures: freedom was necessary to ensure experimentation and to make it possible for exceptional individuals to 'point the way forward' to their fellows (Thomas, 1985, p. 108).

These remarks on the relationship between freedom and progression assumed that a threshold level of 'civilisation' had been reached in Western societies. Where low levels of general civilisation made it inappropriate to apply the liberty principle Mill allowed that elites had a paternalistic duty to educate and 'civilize' those who would eventually be in a situation to enhance progression through the exercise of freedom. He thus argued that British control of India and the West Indies was justified, provided that these soceieties were below the civilisation threshold *and* the imperial power really did actively assist the intellectual and moral development of those subject to it. This line of argument entailed that once the society in question had reached the requisite level, imperial control was unnecessary and unjustified. It also meant, however, that where the attitudes and conduct of the imperial power mitigated against the 'civilisation' of indigenous peoples, its rule became tyrannical and illegitimate. Mill's later criticism of imperial rule in India and the West Indies and his censure of European settlers in Australia and New Zealand for their brutal and exploitative treatment of indigenous populations was entirely consistent with these qualifications. Such treatment, which was often justified by assumptions about fundamental racial inferiority that Mill rejected, inhibited the development of indigenous populations rather than fostering it (Smits, 2008, pp. 11–12).

Although Mill identified a sphere of liberty that deliniated an area where an individual's freedom of action should be protected from legally sanctioned and socially endorsed interference, he did not regard the principle of liberty as a warrant for indifference towards others, or for reducing the scope of government to the protection of individuals. To the contrary, Mill applied the notion of 'harm' to society as well as to individuals, and he allowed that government may use its regulatory capacities to ensure that individuals do not harm social interests, either through their actions, or by failing to contribute to the fulfilment of social functions (Collini, 1977, p. 345). As Mill put it in his discussion of what is 'due to society':

> living in society makes it indispensable that each should be bound to observe a certain line of conduct towards the rest. This conduct consists, first, in not injuring the interests of one another; or rather certain interests, which, either by express legal provision or by tacit understanding ought to be considered as rights; and secondly, in each person's bearing his share ... of the labours and sacrifices incurred for defending the society or its members from injury and molestation (Mill, 1983, p. 132).

> ### John Stuart Mill (1806–73)
>
> The most important British political thinker since Hobbes, John Stuart Mill was the son of James Mill, Jeremy Bentham's closest disciple. He is credited with having shorn 'Benthamism' of much of its crassness while remaining committed to an essentially utilitarian approach to politics. Mill wrote important works on logic, political economy, moral and political philoosophy, and an extensive range of essays addressing current issues in economics, social policy and politics. He was a member of the British parliament from 1865 to 1868.
>
> In *On Liberty* (1859), Mill argued that interference with others, whether by individuals, the concerted forces of social opinion, or the agents of government, was only justified in cases where their actions were likely to inflict positive harm on others. Mill's position on this issue was strongly opposed to prevailing paternalistic argument and sentiment since it precluded interference that was justified on the grounds that it was necessary for the good of the person or persons concerned. His argument reflected a series of assumptions about the value of self-reliance, the social and individual advantages of liberty of thought, action and expression, and the threat to social progression that was posed by those who sought to eliminate or even curb challenges to prevailing ways of thinking about religion and personal and public morality.
>
> *Considerations on Representative Government* (1861) presented Mill's views on the impact of various political arrangements on the progressive civilisation of humanity. He emphasised the need to tailor democratic institutions so that they would provide opportunities for individual and social development while minimising the risks arising from the limited educational level of the majority of the population in even the most 'advanced' societies of Western Europe.
>
> *Key reading:* Capaldi, 2017; Collini, 1977; Francis and Morrow, 1994; Ten, 1999; Thomas, 1985.

A number of features of Mill's doctrine of liberty are particularly significant in relation to the idea of freedom as an end of politics. In the first place, he argued that freedom places limits on the action of government: it may not impose upon the sphere of liberty. Secondly, the preservation of liberty requires mechanisms of legal constraint that will protect individuals in the exercise of their individual liberty. Thirdly, since Mill related individual freedom to human progress, there is a sense in which he treated liberty as an instrumental value. Fourthly, Mill insisted that liberty must be enjoyed by *all* sections of the adult population and, consequently, he played an active role in promoting emancipation campaigns in support of African-Americans in the United States and women across the Western world.

Gender and freedom: Olympe de Gouges, Mary Wollstonecraft, William Thompson and Anna Wheeler, and Harriet Taylor

Although Plato had suggested in the *Republic* that there was nothing in women's nature to prevent them undergoing training for the Guardian class, until relatively recently, Western political thinking has been dominated by male writers and has followed Aristotle in regarding women as naturally and irredeemably inferior to men (Hall, 2016). For centuries this alleged inferiority was used to justify women's exclusion from political office, voting and exercising other political rights. It also placed them in a position of subordination to men that extended across a full range of social and familial rights and functions. In a later chapter we will review the implications of a strong feminist reaction against these long-standing views for contemporary theories of democratic government (see below). Here the discussion focuses on earlier challenges to ideas about female inferiority by considering the works of a number of late eighteenth- and nineteenth-century writers who argued that freedom was a universally applicable end of politics, not one that applied only to men.

In the late medieval period Christine de Pisan had defended the right of the mother of the infant king of France to rule on his behalf by arguing that women were capable of acquiring the capstone virtue that Aquinas called 'prudence'. This quality, which Christine characterised as 'the mother and guide of all virtues', brought the other virtues (courage, mercy, wisdom and so on) into an appropriate alignment with the requirements of political rule. Christine argued that since women were capable of being prudent in this special sense they were capable of assuming political office, acting as the advisors of princes and educating future rulers. Christine's work was usually marked by expressions of calm, pious rationality but she occasionally offered ironic commentary on male claims. Thus when considering why women were not allowed to plead in court she suggests a gendered division of labour that is not altogether flattering to legal masculinity: 'God gave men strong, powerful bodies to stride about and to speak boldly, which explains why it is men who learn the law and maintain the rule of justice.' (Pisan, 1982, p. 20) Although neither Christine's work, nor that of the late seventeenth-century English writer Mary Astell, who upbraided the poet and radical politician John Milton with the question '*If all men are born free*, how is it that all Women are born slaves?' made an emphatic case for full *political* rights for women (Wilson, 2016), they fired well-directed early shots in a campaign that was later taken up by female contemporaries of Thomas Paine and French promoters of the 'rights of men and citizens'.

Olympe de Gouges's *The Rights of Women* (1791) posed a version of Astell's question in a pamphlet that mimicked the structure of the 'The Declaration of the Rights of Men and Citizens' issued by the French National Assembly two years earlier (Zizek, 2016). She asked the beneficiaries of this declaration what gave them the right to 'oppress my sex? Your strength? Your talents? Observe the creator in his wisdom; survey nature in all its grandeur, which you seem to want to emulate, and offer me, if you dare, an example of the tyrannical empire … .' (de Gouges, 2011, p. 30). De Gouges compared the situation of women in revolutionary France with that of slaves in Africa who had been released from physical bondage but not given access to the political and economic rights needed to take advantage of their purely nominal freedom (ibid., p. 36). These rights were necessary if the sexual, social and political subjection of women under the ancient regime was to give way to a situation where they could forge a new role for themselves as 'female citizens', that is, true partners in a republic of free and equal beings (ibid., p. 31).

Olympe de Gouges (1748–1793)

Having established a reputation as an author and playwright in the 1780s, de Gouges became a revolutionary patriot during the revolution but was executed in 1793 for allegedly royalist sympathies. Her *Les Droits de la femme* [*The Rights of Women*] (1793) attacked the framers of the 1791 constitution for excluding women from any political role in the new state. From the 1980s feminist writers have come to see de Gouges's pamphlet as an important contribution to revolutionary feminism.

Key reading: Cole, 2011; Zizek, 2016.

De Gouges justified her demand for female emancipation by referring to the rights and interests of women and to the effect that their emancipation would have on the moral tone of the republic. Mary Wollstonecraft, her English contemporary, advanced a similar line of argument, although she does not appear to have known of de Gouges' work. Wollstonecraft's critique of women's servile position in contemporary social and political culture involved an implicit rejection of Paine's endorsement of the biblical warrant for female subjection (Paine, 1976, p. 89). In her *Vindication of the Rights of Men* (1790) Wollstonecraft pointed to the divergence between the structure and practice of British government and what she referred to as the 'rights of humanity' (Wollstonecraft, 1790, p. 2). Two years later, in the *Vindication of the Rights of Women,* she related contemporary claims about the moral and intellectual weakness of women to the inferior yet covertly powerful position in which they were placed. Lacking formal rights, their influence was exerted through corrupt and debasing means that were more appropriate to the *mores* of a harem than a free and supposedly civilised society. In common with de Gouges, Wollstonecraft challenged constitutional reformers in France and England to extend the logic of the rights of man to the rest of humanity:

> If the abstract rights of man will bear discussion and explanation, those of women, by a parity of reasoning, will not shrink from the same test ... .
> Consider ... whether, when men contend for their freedom, and to be allowed to judge for themselves respecting their own happiness, it be not inconsistent and unjust to subjugate women, even though you firmly believe that you are acting in the manner best calculated to promote their happiness? Who made man the exclusive judge, if woman partake with him in the gift of reason? (Wollstonecraft, 1995, pp. 68–9).

She subsequently argued that the recognition of women's natural rights justified their exercise of political rights as well: 'women ought to have representatives, instead of being arbitrarily governed without having any direct share allowed them in the deliberations of government' (ibid., p. 237). Wollstonecraft presented the emancipation of women as a source of universal benefit: 'let women share the rights, and she will emulate the virtues of man' (Wollstonecraft, 1983, p. 319). In these circumstances, men and women would be capable of forming partnerships that would enrich not only their lives, but also those of their husbands, of the children for whom they were responsible, and the wider society to which they belonged.

Mary Wollstonecraft (1759–1797)

Wollstonecraft, who was the author of a wide range of educational, literary, religious and political works, was associated with the dissenting Protestants who played an important role in the intellectual life of late-eighteenth-century England. Wollstonecraft's first major political work, *A Vindication of the Rights of Men* (1790), was written in response to Edmund Burke's *Reflections on the Revolution in France.* Her *A Vindication of the Rights of Women* (1792) had a broader cultural focus, but it nonetheless included the claim that women should have political and civil rights and elect representatives of their own.

Key reading: Coole, 1988; Lokke, 2016; Okin, 1992.

Astell's, de Gouges's and Wollstonecraft's metaphorical references to women as slaves reflected their sense of how deep-seated was the gendered source of female subordination. A particularly forceful and more nearly literal form of this line of argument appeared in a work written by William Thompson and Anna Wheeler in 1825. Their nominal target was James Mill, who had argued that women did not need to possess political rights to protect their interests since these were 'included in' those of their husbands or fathers, and would thus benefit from the protection afforded by their capacity to oversee the actions of governors (see below, p.). Paradoxically, Thompson and Wheeler's powerful evocation of marriage as a literal form of slavery meant that women's interests *were* forcibly included in those of their husbands. They argued, however, that in one respect at least, the position of married women was worse than that of a slave because they had agreed to assume this position rather than having it imposed upon them as a consequence of capture or birth.

> Woman is then compelled, in marriage ... by the positive, cruel, partial, and cowardly enactments of law, by the terrors of superstition, by the mockery of a pretended vow of obedience, and to crown all, by the force of an unrelenting, unreasoning, unfeeling, public opinion, to be the literal unequivocal slave of the man who may be styled her husband. ... I say emphatically the slave; for a slave is a person whose actions and earnings, instead of being under his own control, liable only to equal laws, to public opinion, and to his own calculations, ... are under the arbitrary control of any other human being ... . This is the essence of slavery, and what distinguishes it from freedom. (Thompson and Wheeler, 1970, pp. 66–67)

Thompson and Wheeler's argument was also distinctive because they obliquely suggested the sexual origins of male domination through repeated reference to the 'rod of iron' through which they exerted their despotic authority in the domestic sphere (Jose, 2016, p. 61). But while Thompson and Wheeler stressed that male domination was deep-seated, they thought it could be dispelled by removing the legal basis of female enslavement in the family. In order to secure this objective, and to ensure that they retained their liberty, women must possess the political rights claimed for men by writers such as Paine. These rights provided the only security for equal civil and criminal laws. If women's liberty was ensured they would then be in a position to contribute to the development of society through 'the expansion of the mind, of the intellectual powers, and of the sympathies of benevolence' (Thompson and Wheeler, 1993, p. 169).

J. S. Mill's views on female emancipation were inspired by those of Harriet Taylor, his companion and then his wife. In an essay published in 1850 Taylor applauded the female suffrage movement in the United States because it involved a plea *by* women for political rights as well a plea *for* these rights. It thus demonstrated a practical commitment to free agency as well as promoting an objective that was critical to the emancipation of women. Drawing a parallel with the position of slaves, Taylor argued (in a way that echoed Frederick Douglass' position; see p.) that exclusion of women from the franchise was inconsistent with the fundamental principles of US government. It also ran counter to the arguments employed in contemporary movements for 'universal' suffrage in Britain (Taylor, 1993, pp. 4–6). Since government had long since ceased to be a matter of superior force, male domination of the political sphere could not be justified by reference to relative physical strength (ibid., pp. 7–10). Taylor also rejected contemporary commonplaces that upheld a rigid distinction between a private (female) sphere and a public (male) one. This distinction imposed an arbitrary and improper limitation on women's range of action and on their capacity to utilise their abilities fully: 'The proper sphere for all human beings is the largest and highest which they are able to attain to. What that is, cannot be ascertained, without complete liberty of choice' (ibid., p. 11). Even if women were inferior to men – and Taylor thought that any inferiority was due largely to social expectations and environmental conditions – that was no reason for maintaining systems of social and political subordination that prevented them from developing their characters and contributing to the 'moral regeneration' of humanity.

Black emancipation: Frederick Douglass and W. E. B. Du Bois

Slavery poses the most extreme challenge to freedom. Slaves' entire existence is reliant on the will of their 'owners' and their status as the property of other human beings is reflected in the arbitrary and cruel treatment to which they are exposed. Slavery existed in the ancient world and was, as we have seen, discussed by Aristotle (see above p. 49). Europeans continued to enslave one another in the medieval and early modern periods and made extensive use of slaves in their colonies. They also engaged in a cruel and extensive trade in slaves from the west coast of Africa to plantation colonies in the Americas and the Caribbean. The French Revolution dealt slavery a fatal blow in Europe and ended the practice in France's overseas territories, but Napoleon re-introduced it in French colonies growing sugarcane in 1802. The British outlawed the slave trade throughout their Empire in 1807 but did not abolish slavery until 1833. After this time, the southern United States provided the most striking and widely debated example of the systematic enslavement of blacks by whites. In these states approximately three million men, women and children of African-American descent were subject to the arbitrary control of white owners whose rights over them were supported by a raft of laws passed by southern legislatures. Although slavery was outlawed in the northern states of the Union, the claims of southern owners were recognised in the federal government's Fugitive Slave Act of 1850. This act allowed southern slave owners to recover slaves who had escaped to states where slavery was outlawed.

The persistence of slavery in the United States attracted widespread critical comment from secular and Christian abolitionists in Great Britain and North America. Even before J. S. Mill became sceptical of the developmental justification for European imperialism (see above, p. 106), he portrayed the slave system as a grotesque caricature of paternalism that often gave rise to the arbitrary and brutal mistreatment of blacks at the hands of their legal owners. Mill rejected claims about the 'natural' and inevitable inferiority of blacks, denying that alleged demonstrations of present incapacity justified that assumption, or the forms of control and exploitation that perpetuated it. Slavery represented a gross, counterproductive violation of freedom that could never be justified by reference to the developmental interests of those subjected to it (Mill, 1850, p. 30). In common with other white anti-slavery advocates, Mill promoted the abolition of slavery in the United States and the recognition of blacks as free and equal members of American society. By the middle of the nineteenth century a number of African-American writers in the United States had made a mark in abolitionist circles and some black intellectuals continued to play an active role in promoting the freedom of black Americans after the formal abolition of slavery in 1867. The discussion here will focus on the ideas of Frederick Douglass and W. E. B. Du Bois.

Douglass described the abolition campaign as 'the great struggle ... between slavery and freedom' and attacked the assumptions of racial inferiority that were advanced to justify whites' ownership of blacks in the southern states (Douglass, 2000, p. 346). The complete and unlimited nature of this control was reflected in the indignities and cruelties which slave owners were permitted to inflict upon 'their' slaves. Claims about the racial sources of blacks' alleged inferiority to whites meant they were not recognised as having 'natural rights' or as being entitled to exercise the civil rights that depended on them. These arguments involved an implicit rejection of Paine's belief that all human beings come into the world with a complete and unqualified set of natural rights (see above, p.). Rather than serving as a means of protecting the freedom of African-Americans, the laws of the southern states and the federal recognition of the rights of slave holders over 'fugitive' slaves were instrumental in subjecting them to the absolute and arbitrary control of their white owners.

Frederick Douglass (1818–95)

Douglass was born into slavery in Maryland and remained a slave, working in various manual occupations, until he escaped to New York City in 1838. From 1841 he played a leading role in the abolitionist movement in the northern United States, applying to it his self-taught skills as a journalist and public speaker. Douglass also wrote three autobiographies, which included accounts of his experiences as a slave and conveyed his ideas on equal rights for blacks and the recognition of black culture. He campaigned for the cause during an extensive tour of England, Ireland and Scotland in 1845–46. Prior to the Civil War he was an active supporter of Abraham Lincoln and was deeply disappointed not to receive a commission in the federal army. After the war Douglass continued his journalism and public speaking and he also held a number of government appointments. He was the first African-American to serve as a US marshal, and he also held a senior diplomatic appointment to Haiti.

Despite his high public profile, Douglass continued to suffer the race-based affronts that marked the lives of African-Americans in the post-slavery era. He argued that such discrimination was inconsistent with the founding principles of the republic and with natural law and stressed the importance of the contributions that Africans had made to the development of human civilisation.

Key reading: Andrews, 1996; Blight, 2018; McFeely, 1991.

In powerful speeches and journalistic writings, Douglass challenged the anti-abolitionists' starting point by appealing to ideas which echoed those of traditional Western natural law thinking. As we shall see, natural law theorists argue that political authority and human law are subordinated to the requirements of a legal order that derives its legitimacy from God (see p.). Douglass' approach was distinctive, however, because he thought that access to natural law could be gained through the interaction of reason, emotion and experience rather than reason alone. This approach broadened the perceptual basis of the natural law and heightened the imperative force of the conclusions drawn from it (Lloyd, 2016, pp. 12–13). It promoted a sense of common humanity that had been obscured by prejudice, oppressive laws and customs, and superstition. It stripped these veils away and enjoined attitudes and conduct that assisted the preservation and flourishing of all human beings, without distinctions of race, religion or nationality. For Douglass, as for Aquinas, natural law was the legitimating basis of all systems of human law. This idea underpinned his criticism of a US Supreme Court decision upholding slave owners' rights. Douglass pointed to a 'higher court' to which its judgements were subordinated and in which the universal right to liberty was 'self-evident'.

> The voices of nature, of conscience, of reason and of revelation, proclaim it as the right of all rights, the foundation of all trust, and of all responsibility. … The sun in the sky is not more palpable to the sight

than man's right to liberty is to the moral vision. ... To decide against this right ... is to decide against God. It is an open rebellion against God's government. (Douglass, 2000, p. 348)

Although the American republic had been founded on the right to liberty, Douglass argued that racial prejudice, reinforced in some cases by the baleful influence of the churches, had vitiated its origins by denying this right to three million of its subjects. In a speech to a predominantly white audience on 4 July 1852, Douglass pointedly told his listeners that this day was 'the birthday of *your* National Independence, and of *your* political freedom' (Douglass, 2013, p. 25, emphasis added):

> I am not included within the pale of this glorious anniversary! Your high independence only reveals the immeasurable distance between us. The blessings in which you, this day, rejoice, are not enjoyed in common. The rich inheritance of justice, liberty, prosperity and independence, bequeathed by your fathers, is shared by you, not by me. ... This Fourth of July is yours, not mine. You may rejoice, I must mourn (ibid., p. 25, 30, emphasis added).

He mourned both the exclusion of his fellow African-Americans from membership of the political community and the Republic's practical denial of the ideals of freedom and equality upon which it was founded.

Douglass' response to the Fugitive Slave Act brought his claims about the anti-republican implications of slavery into sharp relief. This act was incompatible with the ideas of freedom that supposedly underwrote the foundation of the United States. It meant that those who were committed to uphold the laws and constitutions of the republic were necessarily committed also to use the powers of the federal government to punish slaves who had escaped from the southern states, and to thus uphold property claims that were incompatible with original republican ideas of liberty (ibid., p. 22).

In the wake of the formal abolition of slavery, Douglass argued for the 'reconstruction' of the United States on a basis which corresponded with the founding ideals of the Republic and with any 'plain reading' of its original constitution (ibid., pp. 39–40). 'The Constitution, as well as the Declaration of Independence ... give us a platform broad enough, and strong enough, to support the most comprehensive plans for the freedom and elevation of all the people in this country, without regard to color, class, or clime' (Douglass, 2000, p. 350). The Republic's commitment to 'justice' and 'liberty' (ibid., p. 353) would not be realised until blacks possessed the vote and had full access to the protection of the law, and state legislatures were deprived of the right to pass laws that discriminated against them (ibid., p. 578). In addition, however, Douglass argued that complete liberation would not occur until blacks were able to shake off the impact of prejudice that was so deeply ingrained that whites only acknowledged their achievements by denying their race. This 'metamorphosing power' implies that if admirable blacks are 'not exactly white' they 'ought to be'. Whites where only able to acknowledge blacks' achievements by treating them as individualised exceptions to a pattern of predominant inferiority: 'race, as such, is destitute of the subjective original elemental condition of a high self-originating and self-sustaining civilisation' (Douglass, 2000, pp. 583–84). In order to free blacks of these debilitating misconceptions, Douglass promoted programmes of public education by institutions run by and for blacks that would recover the historic achievements of African and Egyptian cultures and draw on the recent experience of liberated blacks in the West Indies. These programmes would 'develop manhood, ... build up manly character among the colored people' and 'teach them the true idea of manly independence and self-respect' (ibid., p. 385).

Although Du Bois's writings appeared long after the Civil War, they showed as clearly as Douglass' that formal emancipation had not brought substantive freedom to blacks in the United States. In a series of works that appeared from the 1880s Du Bois considered the question of the development of members of black communities in modern America in light of their past as slaves, and their ongoing subjection to systemic and pervasive discrimination. Du Bois urged African-Americans not to deny the reality of race, far less to understate the past achievements and potentialities of their own, but rather to develop the distinctive capabilities they could bring to the progression of 'civilisation and humanity' in the national community to which they rightly belonged (Du Bois 1986, p. 825). Thus in *The Souls of Black Folk* (1903) Du Bois argued that the goal of African-Americans was not to 'Africanise America' or to 'bleach' their 'Negro soul[s] in a flood of white Americanism' but 'simply to make it possible for a man to be both a Negro and an American, without being cursed and spit upon by his fellows, without having the doors of Opportunity closed roughly in his face' (Du Bois [1903], 1989, p. 5).

William Edward Burghardt Du Bois (1868–1963)

Du Bois, who was born into a family of free blacks in rural Massachusetts, is commonly regarded as the outstanding African-American intellectual of his generation. He was educated at Fisk University, a college for blacks founded in Nashville after the Civil War, Harvard University and the University of Berlin. His initial interests were in philosophy but at Harvard his focus shifted to history and the study of social problems. His Harvard dissertation, *The Suppression of the African Slave-Trade to the United States* (1895), was the first book published in Harvard's Historical Studies series. In 1896 Du Bois worked at the University of Pennsylvania on an empirically based study of the lives of poor blacks in Philadelphia, which explored the impact of historical and environmental factors on their impoverished way of life. He provided further accounts of the ongoing social and psychological impact of slavery and of subsequent discrimination in *The Souls of Black Folk* (1903), a book that drew on historical, sociological, biographical and fictional sources. Du Bois argued that the failure to extend meaningful freedom and economic opportunities to former slaves and their descendants was fundamentally unjust and deprived American society of important contributions to its progressive development.

Having taught at Atlanta University for a number of years, Du Bois took up a more overtly activist role as director of research and publication with the fledgling National Association for the Advancement of Colored People and as long-serving editor of its *Crisis* magazine. This publication played a role in promoting the upsurge of African-American arts and letters, known as the Harlem Renaissance. Du Bois was also a key influence in the emergence of Pan-Africanism and was an important figure in its international promotion. From about 1910 he became increasingly committed to socialism and from the mid-1920s, after a visit to the Soviet Union, began to identify with the communist movement. Du Bois's left-wing politics gave a new direction to the political and intellectual controversies which marked his career and resulted in his unsuccessful indictment as an unregistered agent of a foreign power during the politically motived judicial harassment of 'unAmerican' activists in the late 1940s and early 1950s. In the closing years of his life Du Bois joined the Communist Party of the United States, renounced his US citizenship and accepted an invitation to live in recently liberated Ghana.

Key reading: Gooding-Williams, 2009; Lloyd, 2016; Reed, 1997.

Prior to the Civil War, blacks saw emancipation as 'the key to a promised land of sweeter beauty than ever stretched before the eyes of wearied Israelites' (ibid., p. 7). These dreams were not realised when emancipation came. To the contrary, Du Bois thought that the condition of freed slaves was the most piteous sight among all the destruction and sorrow of the end of the Civil War. Without a 'cent of money, … an inch of land, … a mouthful of victuals – not even ownership of the rags on his back', the condition of the freed slave was 'a mockery of freedom' (ibid., p. 120). Four decades after emancipation, former slaves were still no more than 'half-free serfs'. Neither emancipation itself, nor the subsequent granting of the vote, nor the struggle for higher educational attainment by some blacks, had produced significant advances towards the realisation of African-Americans' aspirations. To the contrary, their physical freedom and personal security were precarious, they were sunk in poverty and they had not overcome the disruptive and demoralising impact on family life of two centuries of slavery. In the decades after the war the dire situation of blacks in the South was compounded by an economic system that exposed former slaves to exploitation by merchants and landlords, by the practical negation of their rights to protection under the law, and successful moves by some states to deprive them of political rights. These developments were accompanied by a growing estrangement of whites and blacks. Appeals to shared superiority as members of the white race had given the white working classes an elevated social standing and provided psychological compensation for their exploitation by white capitalists. Racially-based appeals to the working classes also created a divisive cross-class political alliance of workers and capitalists which was directed against black workers in the economic sphere and against blacks from other classes in society and politics (Du Bois [1935], 1966, pp. 700–1).

These developments, and the reinforcement of ideas of black inferiority in discriminatory applications of the law, reduced black offenders in the South to a situation of practical slavery through exploitation by white labour contractors. They undermined the sense of 'common humanity and a common destiny' on which the progress of American culture depended (Du Bois, 1989, p. 150). Du Bois's sense of the impact of blacks' exclusion from the benefits of American citizenship, and of their ongoing exposure to racially-derived prejudices that cast them beyond the pale of 'common humanity', were captured in a comment that echoed Rousseau's views on the flawed consciousness of those whose sense of self was driven by competitive reference to how others saw them (see below p.). It was as if African-Americans were cursed with a 'double-consciousness', a 'sense of always looking at one's self through the eyes of others, of measuring one's soul by the tape of a world that looks on in amused contempt and pity' (ibid., p. 5).

Although Du Bois thought that post-war economic relationships played a significant role in turning ex-slaves into serfs, he sharply resisted the approach to economic improvement promoted by Booker T. Washington, an influential black orator, publicist and organiser. Washington headed a movement that urged ambitious sections of the black community to sacrifice political and civil rights, and aspirations for higher education, in order to focus on succeeding in business and acquiring property. Du Bois did not think this trade-off would really produce widespread economic benefits and he emphatically rejected the idea that the reconciliation of the black and white members of the community should be achieved by subjecting the former to 'industrial slavery and civic death' (Du Bois, 1989, p. 47). Such an outcome was radically incompatible with the ideas of equality and freedom upon which the United States had been founded (ibid., p. 50). In its place, Du Bois promoted an integration of 'work, culture and liberty' that subordinated the pursuit of wealth to the self-directed utilisation of the potentialities of African-Americans to advance what he described as the 'greater ideals of the American Republic'. As suggested above, he did not see this process in terms of the assimilation of African-Americans to white culture. Rather, it required that the distinctive qualities and historical and cultural experiences of both races were brought to bear on the community's progressive development (ibid., pp. 9–11).

Conclusion

In *Darkwater* Du Bois echoed references to the 'enslavement' of women that had appeared in earlier works promoting female liberation, arguing that the progressive development of states committed to universal freedom required the full emancipation of women as well as of the members of former slave communities. Du Bois position reflected the fact that as many Western societies edged towards democracy in the second half of the nineteenth century the ongoing social and political subordination of women throughout Europe, and the refusal to give substantive recognition to African-Americans' claims for equal rights, remained a substantial barrier to the realisation of the idea that freedom was a fundamental end of politics. In both of these cases, moreover, subordination was justified implicitly and explicitly by biologically based assumptions that blacks and women were unfitted by nature to exercise the rights to free life that Locke, Paine and some of his British and French contemporaries thought was the defining feature of just, well-ordered political communities. As we shall see in later chapters, these concerns did not disappear in the twentieth century when democracy had become the norm in the Western world.

FREEDOM, POLITICS AND SOCIABILITY

4

Although Mill recognised society had interests that might be harmed by some exercises of individual liberty he treated what belonged to individuals and what belonged to society as falling within separate spheres. In this respect his conception of liberty differed significantly from those developed by an important group of late eighteenth-, nineteenth- and twentieth-century political theorists who claimed that freedom was the product of the interaction between individual and social impulses. These thinkers sought to identify political and social structures that maximised the individual and social benefits of this distinctive idea of freedom and they also considered the implications of their theories for the relationship between states. The origins of this tradition can be seen in the writings of Jean-Jacques Rousseau and developed versions of it were presented by G. W. F. Hegel and T. H. Green. These writers argued that the modern constitutional state provided new and significant opportunities for human freedom. This line of argument was rejected by Marxists and by anarchists who sought to develop stateless modes of social organisation.

Freedom, sociability and the state: Rousseau, Hegel and Green

Although Rousseau treated the natural condition as one of complete freedom, he laid the groundwork for later accounts of the relationship between freedom, sociability and the political characteristics of the modern state. In his *Discourse on the Inequality of Mankind* Rousseau traced the impact of the growth of sociability and related improvements in agriculture and technology to natural liberty. Rousseau warned, however, that these putative benefits may be purchased at a terrible cost: the *Discourse* concludes with an account of a contractual process by which the rich, powerful but insecure members of the population trick their fellows into establishing a state that reinforces existing inequalities and exacerbates the oppression of the poor by the rich. In the final analysis, servitude becomes universal: the rich give power into the hands of a despot in order to secure their property and to ensure the continued subjection of the mass of the population.

> Here is the final stage of inequality, and the extreme point that closes the circle and touches the point from which we started. Here all private individuals become equals again, because they are nothing. And since subjects no longer have any law other than the master's will, nor the master any rule other than his own passions, the notions of good and the principles of justice vanish (Rousseau, 1987, p. 79).

This outcome is tragic because it epitomises the corruption of a process that may, in other circumstances, be generally beneficial. Sociability erodes the radical independence of natural human beings, but it may replace this either with domination and servility, or with a form of interdependence that preserves the physical, intellectual and moral integrity of members of the community created by it. The second of these possibilities holds out the hope that natural freedom may be transformed into a qualitatively different kind of liberty that allows human beings to reap the unalloyed benefits of sociability. Liberty of this kind is 'civil' or political, and it can exist only in a state that avoids bad faith, delusion and the reinforcement of pre-political inequalities.

These requirements were examined in Rousseau's most important political work, *The Social Contract*. It opens with a striking statement of the dilemma of liberty in 'civilized' societies:

> Man is born free, and everywhere he is in chains. He who believes himself the master of the others does not escape being more of a slave than they. How did this change take place? I have no idea. What can render it legitimate? I believe I can answer this question (ibid., p. 141).

In common with the theorists discussed earlier, Rousseau used the idea of a contract to explain the process through which individuals agree to curtail their natural liberty and place themselves under the command of a political superior. For Rousseau, however, this process necessitates the complete renunciation of claims based upon natural rights and their recreation as rights recognised and protected by the state. At the point of renunciation, individuals return to the equality of the initial stages of the state of nature; the recreation of rights signals that they are now in a new environment where claims must be considered in relation to the 'common interest' they have created by forming political society. As members of the state, they exchange their *natural* liberty for *political* freedom, for a form of liberty that both reflects and facilitates their interdependence.

> At once, in place of the individual person of each contracting party, this act of association produces a moral and collective body composed of as many members as there are voices in the assembly, which receives from this same act its unity, its common *self*, its life and its will (ibid., p. 148).

The range of individuals' interests has been enlarged by the common concerns they share with their fellow citizens. These concerns are the focus of political relationships based on freedom and equality, not determined by natural inequalities that existed in a pre-political condition. For Rousseau, however, the transformative implications of the social contract do not apply to women. In a line of argument that is radically inconsistent with his overarching view of the possibilities of human transformation, Rousseau claimed that women were destined to remain in a condition of 'natural' subservience that precluded them from enjoying the right to political freedom which men secured through the social contract (Okin, 1992, pp. 144–45).

When pursuing common or general interests, citizens act in response to a 'general will' directed towards shared interests that are different from (but do not necessarily preclude) private interests. When Rousseau stipulated that people in the state are as 'free' as they were before, he does not mean they are free in the same way. To the contrary, political freedom focuses on people's pursuit of their shared aspirations. This requirement has important implications for the structure of the state and for the ways in which power is exercised. The point to note here, however, is that Rousseau thought that political life involves a distinctive conception of freedom. Members of the state abandon natural liberty and independence, but they have the opportunity to take on the morally and intellectually challenging mantle of interdependence and political freedom. Thus while Rousseau started with a consideration of natural liberty, he concluded by identifying a new form of freedom that is qualitatively different from that enjoyed by individuals in a natural condition. This view of freedom played an important role in subsequent political thought.

Rousseau thought that securing beneficial interdependence in the international environment was infinitely more challenging than within political communities.

He compared it unfavourably with the natural condition of humankind, likening sovereigns to the jealous and insecure personalities who stalked what contemporaries were pleased to call 'civilized society'. While individuals in the state of nature have very limited material aspirations, there are no natural limits to the size of states or to what they accumulate and consume. Consequently, their behaviour is invariably greedy and vicious. In common with individuals who have emerged from the state of nature, the rulers of states are given to comparative judgements because their viability and vulnerability depends on their strengths relative to those of their neighbours. As a result, they engage in competitive and oppressive behaviours to confirm and feed their sense of self-worth and to overawe others (Rousseau, 2005b, p. 67). Moreover, because civil societies transcend the limitations of the state of nature, interstate conflicts are quite different from the limited, spasmodic and inconsequential outbursts of violence which occur between natural beings. As a result, the international environment oscillates between a 'state of war' – a condition of declared, targeted, enmity directed at the destruction of its object – and 'waging war', that is, engagement in 'long-term continuous hostilities' (ibid., p. 71). Thus for Rousseau, relationships within the international environment resemble those of the 'uncivil' societies depicted in the *Discourse on Inequality* rather than those of the original natural condition. Sovereigns are obsessed with the need to expand their dominions wherever they see an opportunity to do so and are indifferent to considerations of public utility and justice.

Although Rousseau concluded that peaceful co-existence was impossible in an environment dominated by corrupt states, he allowed that this goal might be pursued with some prospect of success if the states concerned satisfied the requirements of legitimacy which he had advanced in *The Social Contract*. Rousseau offered two different possibilities. The first of these depended on his ideas about scale, self-sufficiency and class outlined in that work and dealt with in more detail in the *Discourse on Political Economy* (1755). In these works Rousseau argued that sharp inequalities of wealth eroded a sense of common interest, making it more likely that political power would be used to further the particular interests of sections of the community rather than the common good of all its members. Similarly, he maintained that states which embraced extensive, and thus economically and socially diverse populations, were far less likely to sustain legitimate governments than those with smaller populations and more confined territories (Rousseau, 1987, pp. 124, 167–68, 170). These economic and geo-political considerations suggested that beneficial community, and true citizenship, were most likely to flourish in small states with homogenous populations and a strong sense of distinctive national identity. By limiting their material aspirations, citizens avoided generating the disparities of wealth that gave rise to oppression and malign dependence, minimised the community's reliance on resources controlled by its neighbours, and greatly reduce the need for contact with them. As a result, they would have little reason for engaging in conflict, and would run little risk of being drawn into it by accident (ibid., pp. 130–31, 169–72; Fidler, 1999, pp. 128–30).

As noted earlier, the antagonistic features of the interaction of corrupt states may be compared with the condition of malign asocial sociability that Rousseau depicted in the *Discourse on Inequality*. A similar parallel occurs with his claim that peace may be secured by reducing the interdependence of legitimate political communities. But while this line of argument might show how conflict could be minimised, it implies that international relations can only be made tolerable if states recreate a natural condition that is devoid of positive moral significance or progressive possibilities. It presupposes that the mitigation of the state of war requires disintegration and indifference rather than integration, interdependence and the assumption of a sense of shared responsibility.

This conclusion is quite at odds with Rousseau's position on the internal implications of human freedom, and perhaps in recognition of that he explored a second, more positive, model that mitigated conflict by confederating well-ordered states rather than separating them (Fidler, 1999, pp. 132–33). The scope of the confederation was limited, however, and looked more like a defensive alliance that would assist legitimate political states to resist the unwanted attentions of corrupt and predatory international actors than an integrated moral system with scope for developing a significant sense of international community.

Rousseau's ideas were of great interest to a number of significant political theorists, among whom were G. W. F. Hegel. Because Hegel's *Elements of the Philosophy of Right* contains statements such as 'the real is the rational' and the 'state is the realisation of freedom', it has been easy for critics to dismiss him as an apologist for absolute, despotic government. The fact that Hegel was (by virtue of his professorial position) an employee of the Prussian government has sometimes been used to support this interpretation. In fact, however, Hegel was a firm supporter of the constitutional and legal reforms undertaken in Prussia in the second decade of the nineteenth century (Wood, 1991, pp. ix–x). He believed that only a liberalised, constitutional state can be identified with freedom. In other words, only a *modern* (as opposed to an ancient, feudal, absolute or indeed revolutionary) state is capable of embodying true freedom. It was Hegel's purpose to show what freedom means in the modern world, and to identify the political implications of this idea. Only in this special sense can the 'state' be described as the realisation of freedom.

Georg Wilhelm Friedrich Hegel (1770–1831)

Hegel, a German academic philosopher, synthesised important but 'one-sided' conceptions of a range of reflections on human experience that had emerged in the course of the history of Western philosophy. He wrote on aesthetics, logic and the philosophies of history, mind and science, as well as on political philosophy. His major political work, *The Elements of the Philosophy of Right* (1821), is often known in English as *The Philosophy of Right*.

Hegel's political writings focus on the 'State' and present an understanding of the distinctive features of modern social and political life that was derived from close study of political and economic developments in the most 'advanced' states of the period, France and Great Britain. The modern state was not an ideal (in the Platonic sense) but it represented the latest and most complete attempt thus far to create political institutions that protected the freedom of individuals while recognising that individual life and consciousness was forged in interaction with cultural and social forces that were independent of particular individuals. In a manner that echoed Aristotle's idea of the *polis*, Hegel's 'state' incorporated other social forms, bringing them together in a complex, dynamic whole that integrated aspects of human experience and made rational freedom possible. *The Elements of the Philosophy of Right* thus discusses the family, 'civil society' (incorporating economic markets, a distinctly modern phenomena and agencies of collective responsibility which had been inherited from the past), as well as government.

This account of the modern state includes many references to the history of Western political philosophy, with Plato, Aristotle and Rousseau being especially prominent. Hegel's political philosophy was important for a range of later thinkers, including Bakunin, Marx, T. H. Green and modern 'communitarians'.

Key reading: Avineri, 1972; Wood, 1991.

Since Hegel believed human thought to be a reflection of human consciousness upon human experience, he insisted that philosophy cannot leap ahead of its time. Because its role is to understand what *is*, the question 'what is the idea of freedom?' must focus on what 'freedom' entails in the modern world. Hegel, however, did not merely reproduce ordinary accounts of freedom. Rather, he sought to identify a conception of 'rational freedom' based upon a philosophical analysis of human aspirations and their institutional manifestations.

Rational freedom harmonises limited or 'abstract' claims promoting the unimpeded pursuit of individual preferences with the demands and possibilities of social and political life. People are not free when they isolate themselves from others and follow their own arbitrary impulses. To the contrary, individuals act freely when they consciously integrate their aspirations and actions with those of other members of their community (ibid., pp. xiv–xvii). In this way, individuals act 'universally' because they move beyond dependence on external forces which they cannot avoid but seem entirely detached from, and often apparently hostile to, their aspirations and interests. 'Only in this freedom is the will completely *with itself* ... because it has reference to nothing but itself, so that every relationship of *dependence* on something *other* than itself is thereby eliminated'. Universality thus removes significant limitations on human action and opens up possibilities that are not available in the restricted condition of isolated, non-integrated individuals: the will 'is *universal,* because all limitation and particular individuality ... are superseded within it' (Hegel, 1991, p. 54). An important implication of this position is that social life, or as Hegel's German contemporaries put it, the 'sphere of duties', is far from being a barrier to human freedom. Freedom will be more complete when people's perceptions of social life and the institutions that embody them contribute to individuality (to a socially integrated sense of selfhood) rather than being seen as, and to some degree actually constituting, a barrier to the full exercise of individual liberty.

Human life must constitute what Hegel called a 'concrete universal'. A concrete universal avoids 'abstract particularity', a perspective that views individuals as atoms that can only be brought together (as in Hobbes' *Leviathan*) in mechanical, and to some degree mutually frustrating, combinations. It provides for the subjective freedom of the individual (thus eliminating 'abstract' or one-sided universality, which sees the individual *only* as a member of a collectivity, as in Plato's *Republic*), and also recognises and embodies shared needs. It thus provides individuals with the opportunity to formulate and pursue goals that reflect their particularity while also giving scope for cooperative social action. In short, the 'concrete universal' abolishes neither the individual nor society but beneficially combines them.

In the *Philosophy of Right* Hegel presented an account of the modern state as a concrete universal. This does not imply that it cannot be improved upon, merely that the modern state was the most complete embodiment of rational freedom known to Hegel. In this state, freedom is 'actual'; that is, there is scope for individual liberty, but its exercise is harmonised with a collective good that is both genuine and capable of being recognised by its members (ibid., pp. 288–89). Modern freedom has three dimensions: 'abstract' or personal freedom; conscience or 'subjective morality'; and 'ethical' or social life. In the first case, individuals think of themselves as *persons, indeterminate choosers'* (Wood, 1991, p. xiv), who see the world as a place where they can exercise freedom in the simple arbitrary sense. Hegel described this conception as the basis of 'abstract right', which protects rights through legal institutions regardless of the use to which they are put. Adult human beings also evaluate their conduct by reference to universal values present in the sphere of conscience or subjective morality that provide an inwardly valid standard. In order to be effective, however, this standard must be recognised and protected by the social institutions that collectively form what Hegel called 'ethical life'. Ethical life is the third dimension of freedom, one that is necessary because of the incompleteness and instability of both abstract right and morality:

> The sphere of [abstract] right and that of morality cannot exist independently ...; they must have the ethical as their support and foundation. For right lacks the moment of subjectivity, which in turn belongs solely to morality, so that neither of the two moments has any independent actuality (Hegel, 1991, p. 186).

Ethical life contributes to freedom by maintaining institutions whose value is recognised by individuals. Hegel grouped these institutions under three headings: the family, 'civil society', and the 'police and the corporation'. The family meets needs that arise from ties of blood; it is based on love. This aspect of human life contributes to rational freedom, but its basis *is natural* rather than *rational*. Individuals do not choose their families, and while family membership may be a necessary condition of rational freedom, it is not a sufficient one. The reason for this is that the identity of individual family members merges with that of their respective families, and over time a family disintegrates into a plurality of families. Family life thus fails to recognise fully the particularity of its members, and it is also an unstable condition.

Hegel identified one significant exception to his general claim about the limitations of family life. He argued that the 'vocation' of females 'consists essentially only in the marital relationship' and justified this position by referring to what he took to be the distinctive cast of the female mind. He thus claimed that although 'women may have insights ... taste, and delicacy ... they do not possess the ideal' of freedom. Consequently, 'when women are in charge of government, the state is in danger, for their actions are based not on the demands of universality but on contingent inclination and opinion' (ibid., p. 207). This characterisation is a consequence of restricting female fulfilment to the family sphere, and excluding them from 'civil society', the sphere through which citizenship is mediated. It seems to follow (although Hegel does not make the point) that if women were brought up to play a role in civil society they would develop intellectual and moral dispositions that would allow them to take a full role in the political life of the community.

Hegel argued that individual identity is recovered in 'civil society'. In part this term refers to a modern 'market' society that recognises and protects a realm of private activity where individuals pursue their own conception of their interests. Unlike many modern writers, however, Hegel did not think that civil society is reducible to self-interest. To the contrary, he insisted that it has social dimensions that are not merely accidental consequences of the 'invisible hand' of market exchanges (Wood, 1991, p. xx). Civil society has a duty to educate potential members and a collective responsibility to prevent morally debilitating poverty ('pauperism') because this is incompatible with its ethos. Moreover, Hegel argued that since individuals within civil society identify with trade and professional associations, they are not purely free-floating and isolated. Although these institutions give a social dimension to economic pursuits, however, Hegel did not think they could prevent occasional yet damaging economic crises. For this reason, the play of market forces must be set in a framework of general regulation carried out by public authorities performing what Hegel termed 'police functions' (Hegel, 1991, pp. 260–70).

Thus while civil society provides invaluable scope for some expressions of freedom, it is not a final, self-contained model for rational freedom. Modern society requires a political state to resolve the tensions produced in civil society and also to provide a focus of identification that is inherently and completely, rather than partially and to some degree accidentally, social. In his account of the political dimensions of the modern state, Hegel sought to identify the rational dimensions of a constitutional monarchy. In a state of this kind, the monarch personifies subjective freedom, and its representative assemblies ('estates') represent distinct groups within civil society. Since they are elected by their constituent members, estates provide a vehicle for the expression of their free subjectivity. Finally, the modern state must have a professional civil service dedicated to the universal or common interests of the community (ibid., pp. 282–359). These details relate closely to Hegel's interest in the reform movement in contemporary Prussia. It is important to recall, however, that this 'political state' (essentially the machinery of government) is only one aspect of the modern state. This entity embraces the whole community and is thus a complex web of ideas, individuals and institutions that together constitute rational freedom and make it possible.

Writers who approach politics from the perspective of natural liberty treat the state as an important but limited agency that reconciles aspects of natural freedom with the requirements of social life. This view played a role in Rousseau's theory, and Hegel was thus critical of Rousseau's attempt to derive the general will from individual wills, and to deduce the state from a contractual arrangement that must necessarily be based on the 'arbitrary will and opinions' of natural individuals (ibid., p. 277). In response to the limitations of Rousseau's theory, Hegel argued that rational freedom can only incorporate viable aspects of the concern with individual freedom if politics is understood in relation to a particular type of society. This society needs government, but its distinctive features cannot be explained solely by reference to the implications of coercive social coordination of natural liberty. Hegel's multi-layered conception of freedom underwrote a political theory that encapsulated all the salient features of the modern state and produced a theory of community rather than just a theory of government. It also underpinned a distinctive view of international relations that involved an implicit critique of Rousseau's international theory and an explicit critique of Kant's.

Hegel draws a clear parallel between the conditions of freedom for individuals and for states. Just as individuals rely on the recognition of other free beings if their freedom is to become real, so too does the freedom of the state require recognition by other independent states:

> The state has a primary and absolute entitlement to be a sovereign and independent power *in the eyes of others*, i.e. *to be recognised* by them. ... [T]he legitimacy of a state, and more precisely ... of the power of its sovereign, is a purely *internal* matter (one state should not interfere in the internal affairs of another). On the other hand, it is equally essential that this legitimacy should be *supplemented* by recognition on the part of other states. But this recognition requires a guarantee that the state will likewise recognise those other states which are supposed to recognise it, i.e. that it will respect their independence ... (ibid., pp. 366–67).

States are thus embedded in an international community (albeit a very limited one) in a way that parallels individuals' integration in the far more complex interdependencies of civil society and the state. From Hegel's perspective, Rousseau's attempt to mitigate the asocial civilisation of the modern international environment by expecting states to retreat into something akin to the natural condition of humankind would be a regressive and self-defeating step.

The relationships between sovereigns take the form of interactions based on agreements and thus resemble the contractual arrangements that structure the interactions of individuals in civil society. They differ from these, however, in being far less complex than the relationships that develop within the highly interdependent life of civil society and they are not subject to adjudication and enforcement by a constituted power. They are only an *'obligation'*, something which *'should be observed'* but remains dependent on the active concurrence of sovereigns concerned (ibid., pp. 368, 367). In this environment the prospect of disagreement ending in war is always and necessarily present. Hegel argued that Kant's attempt to put a permanent end to war by federating the states of Europe would deny sovereigns the individuality necessary to free membership of a political community (see p.). His scheme does not abolish conflict but merely displaces the point at which it occurs: 'the state is an individual, and negation is an essential component of individuality. Thus, even if a number of states join together as a family, this league, in its individuality, must generate opposition and create an enemy' (Hegel, 1991, p. 362). Moreover, Hegel argued, since the league requires an agreement between states, it must continue to rely on the wills of the particular sovereigns who are party to it (ibid., p. 368). Kant's position was thus held to be wrong in principle and could not be applied effectively or consistently in practice.

When sovereigns act on the international stage they do so in order to further the welfare of their state, and their recognition by others arises from an understanding of their role in relation to it. Their actions are not directed at a universal interest beyond the state, but at its specific requirements. Since these requirements are aspects of a concrete whole Hegel rejects the claims of those who present the pursuit of the state's interests as being somehow opposed to morality. 'The immediate existence … of the state as the ethical substance, i.e. its right, is directly embodied not in abstract but in concrete existence … and only this concrete existence, rather than any of those many universal thoughts which are held to be moral commandments, can be the principle of its action and behaviour' (ibid., p. 370). Hegel's target here is Kant's idea of cosmopolitanism as a principle of international law and other theories which implicitly discount the ethical purpose of the state (see p.).

Since sovereigns are committed to the welfare of their states and there is no sovereign to resolve disputes between them, war is an unavoidable, but by no means an ever-present, feature of the international environment (Hegel, 1991, p. 369). Hegel regards the particular grounds of war as being indeterminate since only the sovereign can decide when disputes with other states need to be settled by war, or whether the danger of injury is sufficient to warrant pre-emptive action. At the same time, however, he noted that the shared experiences and values of European states have a significant bearing on how they responded to the actions and perceived intentions of their neighbours. 'The European nations … form a family with respect to the universal principle of their legislation, customs, and culture, … so that their conduct in terms of international law is modified accordingly in a situation which is otherwise dominated by the mutual infliction of evils' (ibid., p. 371). This idea of a shared international culture, which is similar to Burke's (see p.), has implications for states' approach to war. In particular, it encourages them to see peace (not annihilation) as the outcome of war, to respect ambassadors and not use war as an occasion to attack the internal public and private institutions and interests of their enemies (Hegel, 1991, p. 370).

Hegel insisted that while citizens have a duty to take an active role in war and if necessary to lose their lives, they should not be seen as acting to protect the lives and property of individuals since these are necessarily compromised by war. Rather, the individuals' responsibility in war relates to the ethical necessity for maintaining the independence and sovereignty of the state. In fighting for the state they recognise that their individuality relies on the freedom of the state through which their freedom is affirmed. In this sense, the sacrifice of individuals in war gives expression to their realisation that selfhood depends upon integration in the state. Hegel's consideration of international relations from the standpoint of the state, and in relation to its role in providing a concrete affirmation of the freedom of its members, is thus entirely consistent with the strongly state-centric character of his political thinking.

Hegel's political theory has had a mixed reception. Aspects of it were of great, although critical, interest to Marx and other German radicals, but he was also identified with extreme reactionary conservatism, and praised and blamed for that (Wood, 1991, p. viii). His views on international conflict and war were also criticised sharply during the First World War on the grounds that they contributed to the intellectual underpinning of a militaristic culture in pre-war Germany (see p). It can be argued that these reactions rest on serious misunderstandings of Hegel's political philosophy. They certainly give insufficient weight to those features of it that proved attractive to nineteenth-century liberal thinkers such as T. H. Green and his followers, and to contemporary political theorists (see p. 71).

Like Hegel, Green thought that freedom involves the integration of individuality and sociability and drew attention to the embodiment of these values in the ideas and institutions of modern constitutional states. He argued that state action can contribute to freedom by protecting rights, or claims to free action. States lay down rules that are backed by coercive sanctions but may also serve as guides which citizens follow freely. Properly framed legislation may extend citizens' scope for free actions by removing obstacles to it arising from the improper use of economic, social or political power, from ignorance, poor environmental conditions, and historically ingrained habits of subservience. These measures contribute to what Green called a 'positive' conception of freedom – 'a positive power or capacity of doing or enjoying something worth doing or enjoying, and that, too, something we do or enjoy in common with others' (Green, 1986, p. 199; Morrow, 2017) – which is compatible with the underlying thrust of liberal politics.

Social freedom and the critique of state theory: Marx

Hegel's political theory did not have a marked impact on the English-speaking world until almost half a century after his death, but it was the subject of immediate critical scrutiny from radical German thinkers. These writers gave serious consideration to Hegel's attempt to reconcile free individuality with sociability but were highly critical of his attachment to constitutional and liberal-economic values. In terms of the subsequent history of Western political thought, the most significant response to Hegel was produced by the revolutionary socialist Karl Marx and his associate Friedrich Engels.

Like Hegel, Marx thought that a complete conception of freedom must take account of the social dimensions of human personality. In Marx's view, however, the philosopher of right failed to understand the true basis of human consciousness, individuality and sociability. He argued that an adequate understanding of the state must start from a clear conception of the basis of human existence, namely the social conditions under which humanity produces the material necessities of life. Marx claimed that human beings cannot be free unless they produce freely; that is, under circumstances in which their activities are directed to fulfilling their fundamental needs through cooperative interactions that reflect their intrinsically social nature.

Although Marx's presentation of this argument is exceedingly complex (and contentious), the implications he drew from it are relatively clear. They derive from his claims about the necessarily oppressive nature of private property. Marx thought that capitalists' control of labour and its fruits involved the 'alienation', or loss, of forms of activity that were fundamental to humanity and to sociability. Alienation involves a fatal diminution of humanity's capacity to exercise its distinctive attributes, including free will: 'the activity of the worker is not his own spontaneous activity. It belongs to another, it is a loss of self' (Marx, 1975, p. 327).

As we have seen, Hegel was aware of the potentially damaging implications of economic inequality and looked to the state to overcome these. Marx argued, however, that the state cannot achieve this worthy end because its structure and ethos are products of, and reflect the inequalities attendant upon the intrusion of *private* property into the realm of *social* production. These inequalities give rise to class antagonisms, and there can be no genuine sense of community, no universal or general interest in a society divided along class lines. Nor can the state be seen as a disinterested force valiantly struggling to resolve class tensions or limit their impact on freedom. To the contrary, the modern state, like all the states that preceded it, is merely a reflection of the interests of the dominant class. Although it may present itself as an embodiment of the general interest, the state's conduct reflects (in a more or less subtle form) the oppressive tendencies embedded in what Marx called the 'social relations of production'. The state, Marx wrote, 'is nothing more than the form of organisation which the bourgeois necessarily adopt for internal and external purposes' (Marx and Engels, 1968, p. 59).

Marx's conclusion was that the realisation of freedom must await the overthrow of political institutions and of the systems of economic exploitation and inequality that underpin them. True and universal freedom requires a social system that is both 'communistic' (meaning that productive resources are collectively rather than privately held) and stateless. Marxists believe that freedom can only be attained when private property and the state have been destroyed. This general position was endorsed by a number of other revolutionary socialists who viewed communism through an anarchist lens. For these writers, however, Marx and Engels' ideas posed at least as much of a threat to the realisation of human freedom as Hegel's (see below p.).

Freedom and anarchy: Godwin, Proudhon, Bakunin, Kropotkin, Stirner, Warren and Tucker

If we think of the state as a core aspect of politics, then anarchism points to the termination of politics as this is usually understood. Anarchists' rejection of the state hinges on a belief that it is necessarily antithetical to liberty and to human well-being. All anarchists regard freedom as a fundamental value but they take differing views on the implications that should be drawn from this insight. Some anarchists promote a social conception of freedom that seeks to avoid the authoritarian implications of Marxist forms of revolutionary socialism, while others focus on the autonomy of the individual and regard the demands of the state as a threat to it.

This latter line of argument was first formulated systematically in William Godwin's *Enquiry Concerning Political Justice* (1794). Godwin's political ideas are marked by a concern with rational independence, and a suspicion of many of the features of the political and religious establishment of Georgian England. Political justice depends on people's capacity to take an impartial view of their interests and those of their fellows, and to act in ways that maximise human happiness: 'by justice I understand that impartial treatment of every man in matters that relate to his happiness, which is measured solely by a consideration of the properties of the receiver, and the capacity of him that bestows' (Godwin, 1969, vol. i, p. 126). Political justice is a product of 'rational benevolence', of a rationally guided intention to take account of the happiness of others. Godwin argued that freedom is crucial to benevolence because resort to coercion displaces rational deliberation and rational assent with calculations based on fear. Consequently, he rejected a wide variety of attitudes, practices and institutions that he regarded as hostile to the exercise and development of rational humans' faculties. Many of these coercive influences were identified with the monarchical and aristocratic culture of eighteenth-century Europe, but Godwin's critique of the state is a general one. States work through systems of law that blindly predetermine how actions should be evaluated and responded to. Moreover, since the final sanction of law is coercion not reason, Godwin argued that governments can neither respect reason nor – however good their intentions – create an environment where it becomes the basis of human conduct. Godwin looked forward to the replacement of the state by small and intimate communities where individuals would be subject only to the rational and non-coercive influences of their neighbours' arguments (Godwin, 1969, vol. ii, pp. 191–212).

William Godwin (1756–1836)

The philosopher and novelist William Godwin had a contemporary reputation as a proponent of extreme rationalism in ethics and politics. He is widely credited with having produced the first modern and systematic account of the anarchist position in his celebrated *Enquiry Concerning Political Justice* (1793). This work, which created a sensation when it first appeared, presented a systematic critique of the role that coercion played in even the most civilised states and called into question all forms of non-rational authority, including those exercised within political communities.

Key reading: Philp, 1986.

Godwin's practical political prescriptions are very cautious. For example, although he admitted that revolutions may be necessary to free society from tyranny, he was not sanguine about their capacity to promote human and social progression: they rely upon violence and create situations where rational deliberation is virtually impossible (ibid., pp. 272–73). Nineteenth-century anarchists often treated Godwin as an important figure in the development of anarchist thought, but those who adopted a revolutionary socialist version of this doctrine abandoned his practical caution and rejected his tendency to treat social influences as a threat to the autonomy of individuals. The most important accounts of social anarchism were produced by the French writer P.-J. Proudhon and two Russian thinkers, Michael Bakunin and Peter Kropotkin.

Proudhon maintained that since authority and liberty are inescapable, mutually dependent facts of human existence, it is necessary to identify forms of social and political organisation that balance authority by liberty so as to maximise the scope of the latter. He argued that only anarchy, a system in which 'social order arises from nothing but transactions and exchanges', can satisfy this requirement (Proudhon, 1979, pp. 6–7, 11). Anarchy was to be created through a contractual process recognising the autonomy of the participants and giving rise to a 'federation' rather than a centralised state:

> What is essential to and characteristic of the federal contract ... is that in this system the contracting parties ... not only undertake bilateral and communicative obligations, but in making the pact reserve for themselves more rights, more liberty, more authority, more property than they abandon (ibid., p. 39).

Central government would be replaced by an agency directed by local authorities and citizens themselves. Federation 'consists in ruling every people, at any given moment, by decreasing the sway of authority and central power to the point permitted by the level of consciousness and morality' (ibid., p. 49). Proudhon contrasted the order created through anarchy with the liberty-sapping chaos of a centralised state: 'what you call unity and centralisation is nothing but perpetual chaos, serving as a basis for endless tyranny; it is the advancing of the chaotic condition of social forces as an argument for despotism – a despotism which is really the cause of chaos' (Proudhon, 1923, p. 246).

Pierre-Joseph Proudhon (1809–65)

Brought up in humble circumstances in the Jura region of south-central France, Proudhon began his adult life in the printing trade. While working as a printer he continued his education, and by the 1840s had gained a reputation as an important radical thinker. At first his ideas were admired by Marx, but Proudhon's subsequent development of an anarchist position that rejected capitalism while still allowing forms of private property made him a target of Marxist criticism. In common with other anarchists, Proudhon looked to a federal model to coordinate large-scale human interaction while avoiding the liberty-destroying and counterproductive resort to political authority and the state. His most important political writings are *What is Property?* (1840), *Philosophy of Poverty* (1846), *The Idea of the Revolution of the Nineteenth Century* (1851) and *Federation* (1863).

Key reading: Avrich, 1988; Woodcock, 1965.

For Proudhon, as for many other anarchists, the preservation of liberty required economic as well as political change. Proudhon regarded the principle of federation as a key element in this process. He described capitalism as a system of 'financial feudalism' and argued that it must be replaced by an 'agro-industrial federation' that would organise public services and regulate the economic condition of the individuals and associations that were contractual members of it (Proudhon, 1979, pp. 70–71). Large-scale industrial enterprises would be controlled by working men's associations that must resist the temptation to infringe on the autonomy of their members: 'the best association is one into which, thanks to a better organisation, liberty enters most and devotion least' (Proudhon, 1923, p. 98).

In Proudhon's account of anarchism, federation is the key to forms of social solidarity that do not undermine individual freedom. A stress upon combining liberty and solidarity is also a central theme in socialist conceptions of anarchism. In Michael Bakunin's case this point was made by reference to the conditions of human consciousness. Bakunin drew upon Hegel's theory in seeing human self-consciousness as a product of interaction. Consequently, he thought that *individual freedom* can only be understood in the context of a *free society*:

> Being free … means being acknowledged, considered and treated as such by [another person] and by all [others] around him … [T]he liberty of any individual is nothing more or less than the reflection of his humanity and his human rights in the awareness of all free men – his brothers, his equals (Bakunin, 1973, p. 147).

This doctrine combined two of the slogans of the French revolutionaries – 'liberty' and 'fraternity' – and implied the third: 'equality'. Like other social anarchists, Bakunin thought the inequalities produced by capitalism were incompatible with both freedom and fraternity. Social control of resources would recognise the inherently cooperative nature of human life and ensure that they do not become the means through which some individuals deprive their fellows of liberty. Bakunin insisted that authority of any kind is incompatible with human freedom and also with free sociability.

> ### Michael Bakunin (1814–76)
>
> The son of a member of the Russian gentry, Bakunin spent the greater part of his adult life in various European countries propagating anarchism and engaging in fruitless revolutionary conspiracies. His view of the revolutionary potential of the peasantry was influential in parts of Italy and Spain. Bakunin was highly critical of the statist tradition of Western political thinking and of the liberty-renouncing implications of social contract theory. He also denounced the reliance on revolutionary elites that featured in many forms of nineteenth-century socialism, including that identified with Karl Marx. He engaged in a bitter dispute with Marx on revolutionary tactics and struggled with him for control of the First International, an organisation of European socialists. Bakunin condemned what he saw as the authoritarian implications of Marx's theory of revolutionary change and later treated his whole philosophy as a pseudo-science that threatened to stifle the spontaneity of the working classes. His political ideas were presented in a range of pamphlets; his most developed statement, *Statism and Anarchy* (1873), an extended critique of Marxism, was published a year after his expulsion from the International.
>
> *Key reading:* Avrich, 1988; Crowder, 1991.

Bakunin conceived of anarchy as a new social order where the only restrictions on human freedom come from moral and intellectual influences. Externally imposed authorities are to be swept away and replaced by the self-recognised, self-imposed authority of science and of the natural laws that underlie human interaction. In a true society people are

> *compelled not by the will or oppression of other men, nor by the repression of the State and legislation, which are necessarily represented and imple-mented by men* and would make them slaves in their turn, *but by the actual organisation of the social environment, so constituted that while leaving each man to enjoy the utmost possible liberty it gives no one the power to set himself above others or to dominate them, except through the natural influence of his own intellectual or moral qualities,* which must never be allowed either to convert itself into a right or to be backed by any kind of political institution (ibid., pp. 152–53).

These conditions can be satisfied if human life is focused on small-scale organ-isations, reflecting the natural sociability of limited sections of the population. Autonomous communities should be linked by a system of federation that facilitates cooperative activity. Federalism thus produces the same benefits for communities as anarchism does for individuals.

Bakunin's rejection of the state rests upon the idea that social life is natural and does not have to be sustained by the intrusive oversight of government. For anarchists, the state's unnecessary curtailment of freedom damages sociability. This line of argument is clearly at odds with mainstream political thinking. Although the history of Western political thought presents a range of accounts of the ends of politics, there is general agreement that the state is an unavoidable and important feature of human existence. Towards the end of the nineteenth century this belief was reaffirmed by writers who reflected on the political implications of theories of natural selection. Thus T. H. Huxley (who thought of himself as a follower of Charles Darwin) argued that states ensure that the 'struggle for existence' is directed towards the benefit of the community (Huxley, n.d., pp. 339–40). Huxley's argument implies a challenge to anarchism because it makes the state essential and justifies it by reference to a fashionable scientific theory. This challenge was taken up by Peter Kropotkin, a leading late-nineteenth-century exponent of social anarchism.

Peter Kropotkin (1842–1921)

Born into a well-connected noble family, Kropotkin served in the Russian imperial college of pages and in the Imperial Army. He subsequently acquired a significant reputation as a geographer and a mild-mannered but effective theorist of revolutionary anarchism. Kropotkin was imprisoned in both France and his native Russia before spending much of his later life in exile in London. He regarded anarchism as a scientifically grounded theory of society and the state, a doctrine that was expounded most comprehensively in a series of articles that were published in book form as *Mutual Aid* in 1897. In common with a number of other nineteenth-century anarchists, Kropotkin linked the state to systems of privilege and exploitation that disrupted cooperation and frustrated mutual aid. Anarchism thus involved an end of the state, capitalism and private property; it looked to a stateless future where needs would be meet through spontaneous cooperation of autonomous human beings.

Key reading: Avrich, 1988; Cahm, 1989; Crowder, 1991.

In *Mutual Aid* Kropotkin surveyed a wide range of historical and scientific data that he thought lent support to an anarchist conception of the cooperative and social basis of human life. An examination of both the natural and human world led Kropotkin to reject Huxley's understanding of the struggle for existence. He argued that species that survive and develop are distinguished by their capacity for 'mutual aid'. Kropotkin acknowledged that struggle plays a role in this process, but he claimed that it takes place *against* external forces, not *between* members of the same species. Natural selection reinforces cooperative behaviour within species and groups, eliminating antisocial tendencies, and giving rise to patterns of evolutionary development and systems of social ethics that prioritise cooperation and discourage conflict.

Kropotkin's explanation of the mechanics of human and social development leaves no room for the state. Humans are naturally sociable and any progress they have made has followed an evolutionary pattern that can be explained by the principle of mutual aid. For Kropotkin, the state is an aberration in human history, one that appeared relatively late in the day (Kropotkin, n.d., pp. 216–22). In making this point, Kropotkin extolled the virtues of the guild system of medieval Europe, arguing that it provided a sophisticated exemplification of the principle of mutual aid. Significantly, the rise of the modern state involved the destruction of guild society. In place of cooperative self-regulation, the state directed from the top, and sought to justify its position by adopting a range of theories that make the existence of political authority a precondition of social life (ibid., pp. 226–27). Kropotkin argued that the state is a standing contradiction of the mutual aid principle and is fundamentally antisocial. It is based on sectional and class domination, and despite its elaborate ideological trappings, it has been unable to deliver the security and prosperity it promises. In place of harmony, justice, peace and progress the state has generated conflict, injustice and stagnation. For Kropotkin, the regressive effects of political authority are epitomised by the state's reliance on law – a system of imposed, insensitive and impersonal regulation – and by the brutality of penal practices that are a logical consequence of its reliance on repression as a tool of social control (Kropotkin, 1971, pp. 338–72).

In common with other revolutionary anarchists, Kropotkin believed that the breakdown of the modern capitalist state would provide an opportunity for reconstituting a genuine society based on natural principles. He also endorsed the common anarchist view that the revolutionary process must not be perverted by substituting the authority of revolutionary government or 'state socialism' for the capitalist state. For Kropotkin, anarchism should be based on a federation of decentralised territorial 'communes', or voluntary associations, which would embody *all* social interests. Unlike Proudhon and Bakunin, Kropotkin thought that the organisational principle of these communes should be 'collectivism' rather than 'mutualism'. That is, the commune itself should own all productive resources, rather than these being under the mutual control of those engaged in particular forms of production. The community would be responsible for allocating goods on the basis of *need* rather than *contribution.* Kropotkin maintained that these arrangements would most accurately reflect the natural principle of mutual aid: voluntary association means that all members of the community can exercise and develop their capacities for 'free initiative, free action, free association'. Collectivism recognises the fundamentally mutual and integrated character of social existence. The goal is to foster 'the most complete development of *individuality* combined with the highest development of voluntary association in all aspects, in all possible degrees, for all imaginable aims' (Kropotkin, 1970, pp. 127, 123).

In the late nineteenth and early twentieth centuries social anarchists' views on how their revolutionary socialist programme was to be advanced clashed with those advanced by followers of Karl Marx (see pp. 273–76). From its inception social anarchism also faced challenges from proponents of a strongly individualistic strands of anarchism. The potential for conflict between social and individualistic anarchism was clearly signalled by Max Stirner in *The Ego and Its Own*. Like Marx, Stirner was a radical critic of Hegel, but he rejected all social conceptions of freedom including those associated with revolutionary socialism. In *The Ego and Its Own* Stirner drew a distinction between 'political liberalism', a theory that upholds personal equality as a goal and promotes a 'rational' democratic state, and 'social liberalism' or communism. Political liberalism subjects individuals to a rational state, while socialism subjects them to 'society': according to the latter '*no one* must *have,* as according to political liberalism *no one was to give orders*; as in that case the *State* alone obtained the command, so now *society* alone obtains the possessions' and will make individuals work for it (Stirner, 1995, p. 105).

Max Stirner (1806–56)

Born Johann Caspar Schmidt in Bayreuth, Stirner had an undistinguished career as a student at the universities of Berlin, Erlangen and Konigsberg. While working as a teacher in Berlin in the early 1840s, Stirner was associated with 'the free', a group of radical Hegelians whose meetings were attended by Friedrich Engels. His major political work, *The Ego and its Own,* was published in 1844 to widespread critical comment. It provided a radical critique of a wide range of political, social, moral and religious ideas, practices and putative obligations that imposed on what he called the 'ego', rejecting the conservative and liberal state and the alternatives to them promoted by radical democrats and revolutionary socialists.

Key reading: Carroll, 1974; Leopold, 1995; Paterson, 1971.

This line of criticism was a consequence of Stirner's wish to uphold the integrity of what he called the 'ego', understood not as a set of desires or a conventionally selfish individual, but as an empty potentiality that fills itself by taking whatever the world offers. Stirner shared his radical contemporaries' distaste for religion, monarchy and fatherland, but he went far beyond them and rejected all ideals on the grounds that they impose external standards upon the ego and seek to recruit it for alien causes. In Stirner's account, the ego is ensnared by moral, religious and political ideas that are merely devious and self-serving representations of other people's aspirations. Because these impositions are adopted by individuals as *their* cause, they are especially tenacious. Like the 'spooks' that haunt the minds of those 'possessed' by supernatural spirits, these ideas are products of the imagination that return to control and terrify their creators. As Stirner put it:

> Man your head is haunted; you have wheels in your head! You imagine great things, and depict to yourself a whole world of gods that has an existence for you, a spirit realm to which you suppose yourself to be called, an ideal that beckons to you. You have a fixed idea! … [a]n idea that has subjected the man to itself (ibid., p. 43).

Since Stirner wrote in a context that was influenced by Hegel's political philosophy and by radical extensions of this general position, it is not surprising that one of the spooks he wished to lay to rest was the state. His anarchism was, however, unusual in rejecting not only political authority, but *all* ideas and practices that claim the individual's allegiance and respect. Community, 'humanity', love, property and religion are all hostile to the ego. Once people understand this, these 'spooks' will be banished; the ego will regain its purity and can set about realising its self-formulated purposes. These purposes often require interaction with other egos, but Stirner distinguished these instrumental exchanges from conventional and radical conceptions of sociability. When egos cooperate they do so from their own points of view, and on the basis of their own conception of their own interest; they do not act on the belief that they are contributing to causes that are not their own or to 'common interests'.

Having rejected all bases for human action resting on extra-individual claims, Stirner was left with an environment made up of morally and psychologically self-contained beings. His theory thus embodies a radically individualistic form of anarchism. Paradoxically, however, it does not preclude certain forms of domination. To the contrary, Stirner thought that some individuals may choose to place themselves under the absolute control of others. In doing so, however, they yield to superior power or attraction, not because they believe that other individuals have a claim upon their loyalty (ibid., p. 150). In this, as in other Stirnerian relationships, there is no meeting of minds: each party relates to the other from its own point of view. Even if large-scale cooperation or subjection were to appear in a Stirnerian world it would not provide the basis for the state because free individuals lack any of the psychological and moral features necessary for social and political relationships.

This chilling conclusion reflects a belief that even liberty can acquire the status of an idol to which the ego is sacrificed. Stirner's extremism is unusual, but the sorts of reservation that he expressed about the damaging implications of social integration are a feature of individualistic anarchism. For example, the mid-nineteenth-century American writer Josiah Warren defined liberty as the 'sovereignty of the individual', and argued that this is incompatible with social arrangements that imply anything more than a trivial degree of combination: 'The only ground upon which man can know liberty, is that of DISCONNECTION, DISUNION, INDIVIDUALITY' (Warren, 1970, p. 322). The state is necessary only because human beings become interdependent and develop 'united' interests. Warren's solution to this problem was to make government unnecessary by urging individuals to be self-subsistent and independent:

If governments originate in combined interests, and if government and liberty cannot exist together, then the solution to our problem demands that there be NO COMBINED INTERESTS TO MANAGE … [A]LL INTEREST AND RESPONSIBILITIES MUST BE ENTIRELY INDIVIDUALIZED, before the legitimate liberty of mankind can be restored – before each can be sovereign of his own without violating the sovereignty of others (ibid., pp. 325, 329).

Warren's views on the tension between liberty and sociability, and his attempt to dissolve this by reducing interdependence, are echoed in the writings of his American follower, Benjamin Tucker. Tucker contrasted the benefits of competitive exchanges between free individuals with the tendency for collective action to become enshrined in monopolies that favour some sections of the population over others (Tucker, 1970, p. 175). Anarchism undercuts the basis of monopolies in land, capital and professional services because it withdraws from them the support of the state and throws these areas of life open to the invigorating breezes of individualised competition. This principle can also be applied to individual protection. There is no need for this function to be monopolised by the state; indeed, many dangers result from such an arrangement. Tucker therefore looked to voluntary associations for self-defence or to commercial agencies to provide protection for individuals without requiring the subservience of authoritative institutions that undermine individual freedom (ibid., p. 181).

Conclusion

In contemporary political theory the contrast between Mill's conception of freedom and that of Rousseau, Hegel and Green has been mirrored in a debate between 'liberals' and 'communitarians'. This debate developed in reaction to the ideas of John Rawls and Robert Nozick, two of the most important American political thinkers of the late twentieth century. Rawls developed an argument in support of institutions that gave effect to the idea of 'justice as fairness'. These institutions have to satisfy two principles: each person should have an equal right to the most extensive liberty that is compatible with a similar liberty being enjoyed by others; and social and economic inequalities are only justified when they produce the greatest benefit to the least advantaged, and are attached to offices and positions that are open to all by virtue of equality of opportunity. Rawls maintains that the first of these principles has priority over the second, and that 'liberty can be restricted only for the sake of liberty' (Rawls, 1973, p. 302). The emphasis on liberty appears in an even more uncompromising form in Nozick's work. He starts with a conception of human beings as bearers of inviolable 'natural' rights, and argues that these leave very limited room for legitimate governmental action (Nozick, 1974).

Both Rawls and Nozick thought that it is important for individuals to have the opportunity to formulate and pursue their own goals, subject, of course, to the proviso that they recognise a like freedom on the part of others. Although this general line of argument has played an important role in the history of Western political thought, there is, as we have seen in this chapter, an alternative position that anchors freedom to the social dimensions of human personality and stresses the implications of *social* membership for individual action (see pp. 84ff). In contemporary political thought this 'communitarian' position was restated in reaction to Rawls' and Nozick's work. Despite the differences in their accounts of the *source* of individual rights – Nozick regards them as being fundamental, while Rawls derives them from a contractual process – both writers have been portrayed by their communitarian critics as proponents of 'primacy-of-right theories' (Taylor, 1992, p. 30). These theories may thus be seen as modern expressions of the idea that individual freedom sets limits to the scope of politics, and that it has important implications for the ways in which political power can be exercised (see p. 74).

In contrast, modern communitarianism relies on a *social* conception of freedom that has affinities with that found in the theories of Rousseau, Hegel and the British idealists (see pp. 86–90). The parallel with Hegel's position has been made quite explicit in the work of the Canadian philosopher Charles Taylor (Avineri and de-Shalit, 1992, p. 2). Like Hegel, communitarians believe that ethical principles are embedded in social ideas and institutions. They argue, moreover, that societies must be seen as *communities,* as pre-existing structures of institutions, sympathies and ideas, not as contractually based aggregations of individuals. Communitarians contrast the notion of what Michael Sandel calls the 'unencumbered self' of modern liberalism with the 'embedded self' that is produced by membership of a community. They argue that liberal theory rests upon a conception of the 'unencumbered self' that fails to recognise that people's conception of themselves is a consequence of their location within a community.

In Taylor's formulation, communities are thought to possess common cultures, and integration within a culture is a precondition for any meaningful conception of moral autonomy. Taylor contrasts his view with that implied by primacy-of-right theories that assume that individuals can develop their distinctly human attributes 'outside of society or outside a certain sort of society' (Taylor, 1992, p. 35). In Sandel's writings, arguments about the empirical falseness of the liberal view of personality are related closely to claims concerning the intrinsic benefits of conceptions of social and political life embedded in distinctive communities. These conceptions point to ideas of individual flourishing that are set in the context of a common good. Sandel claims that membership of a community in which 'moral ties' are 'antecedent to choice ... engage the identity as well as the interests of the participants, and so implicate its members in a citizenship more thorough-going than the unencumbered self can know' (Sandel, 1992, p. 19). For Michael Walzer, the very idea of a state requires the idea of the common good: 'states don't only preside over a piece of territory and a random collection of individuals; they are also the political expression of a common life' (Walzer, 1992, p. 78).

It is important to note that the communitarians' opponents do not necessarily accept the implications that are imputed to them. Will Kymlicka, for example, has argued that liberalism can retain its integrity without denying the importance of collective endeavours. He claims that communitarians have failed to distinguish 'collective action' from 'political action' and have consequently ignored the extent to which liberal values uphold rights that protect the former against the latter. For example, freedom of speech and association (two of Mill's fundamental liberties) are rights ascribed to *individuals,* but they are essential if they are to formulate and pursue *collective* goals (Kymlicka, 1992, p. 175). According to this view (which unconsciously echoes Thomas Paine's position – see pp. 64ff) community reflects natural social interaction and does not need, and in fact may well be hindered by, political prescriptions that distort 'normal processes' of voluntary cooperation.

In addition to arguing that liberal conceptions of politics do not preclude communal values, proponents of the liberal position have argued that communitarianism is conservative and morally relativistic: it overemphasises existing values and attachments, and denies the validity of universal standards. Michael Sandel's appeal to the idea of 'civic republicanism' has been questioned on both these grounds. For Sandel, civic republicanism is 'implicit within our [the United States] tradition'. As Amy Gutmann asks, however, would one want to revive those aspects of the tradition that 'excluded women and minorities, and repressed most significant deviations from white, Protestant morality in the name of the common good?' (Gutmann, 1992, p. 132).

POLITICS, HAPPINESS AND WELFARE

5

This chapter discusses a number of theories starting from the assumption that the primary purpose of politics is to promote human interests, happiness or welfare. They regard government as an agency with a distinctive and general responsibility for ensuring that those who are subject to it enjoy as many of life's advantages as possible. While some of these theorists argue that this responsibility entails an active and positive role for government in, for example, distributing material goods, that is not a necessary feature of this perspective. In other cases, it is argued that government's role is to guarantee a framework of human interaction in which individuals can pursue their own conception of their own best interests.

At first sight it may appear that the claim that happiness or welfare are the ends of politics is self-evident and cannot provide the basis for a distinctive approach to the subject. This judgement is, however, questionable. While we may accept the close and direct relationship between government activity and the advancement of the welfare of the general population, the earlier chapters demonstrate that a range of other views of the ends of politics have been prominent in the history of political thought. Even if one leaves aside theories that subjugate any plausible conception of individual and social welfare to impersonal ends such as the good of the race, or the attainment of a distant goal such as that held out by Marxists, it is apparent that many political thinkers relate happiness or welfare to other, apparently fundamental values and understand them in their terms.

The accounts of the ends of politics discussed in this chapter are distinctive because they make human well-being the starting point of political analysis. In the theories discussed here, human interests, human happiness or general welfare are regarded as *primary* political values that provide criteria for evaluating political institutions and action. Since this perspective on politics is a distinctly modern one, this chapter focuses largely on eighteenth- and nineteenth-century writers. It begins with a brief sketch of the form of Christian utilitarianism developed by the late-eighteenth-century English philosopher William Paley. Other early European proponents of utilitarian theories, such as the Abbé Saint-Pierre, also discussed ideas of human happiness in relation to Christian belief. In its developed forms, however, the doctrine became fundamentally secular and based on what was claimed to be a 'scientific' approach to politics. This development is traced through the writings of David Hume in Scotland, Claude Helvetius in France and his Italian contemporary Cesare Beccaria to Jeremy Bentham, who is usually regarded as the most significant exponent of 'utilitarianism'. Bentham's position was modified by his English successors, John Stuart Mill and Henry Sidgwick. Mill and Sidgwick accepted the general premise of utilitarianism – that political institutions must promote the 'greatest happiness of the greatest number' – but they subjected Bentham's account of this doctrine to significant revisions. The chapter concludes with a brief discussion of the diffusion of a utilitarian perspective on politics in late-nineteenth- and early-twentieth-century political theory.

Early utilitarianism: Paley, Saint-Pierre, Hume, Helvetius and Beccaria

In the early modern period Protestant and Catholic political thinkers grounded utilitarian ideas in Christian frameworks. One of the most influential figures in this tradition was William Paley, an Anglican clergyman and university teacher whose

The Principles of Moral and Political Philosophy was a standard late-eighteenth- and early-nineteenth-century political text. Paley maintained that God's intentions for humanity could be identified by the tendency of actions to 'promote or diminish general happiness' (Paley, 1803, vol. i, p. 69). He defined happiness as a condition in which the 'aggregate of pleasure exceeds that of pain' (ibid., p. 22) and argued that individuals and governments can act in conformity to God's will by identifying actions that tend to promote general happiness and aligning human conduct with this standard. But while Paley thought that *actions* should be judged by their tendency, he maintained that *actors* (or 'agents') should be judged by their 'design' or intention in acting. Paley's identification of a utilitarian standard of judgement is thus part of a theory of virtue, although he believed that God promotes virtue through utilitarian means. He thus defined virtue as '*the doing good* to mankind, in obedience to the will of God, and for the sake of everlasting happiness':

> It seems most agreeable to our conceptions of justice, and is constant enough to the language of scripture, to suppose, that there are prepared for us rewards and punishments of all possible degrees, from the most exalted happiness down to extreme misery (ibid., pp. 50–51).

Rewards or sanctions applied by God thus reinforce human attempts to encourage individuals to maximise the happiness of their fellows.

Earlier in the century a French Catholic priest, Abbé Saint-Pierre, stressed the role played by supernatural sanctions in encouraging individuals to overcome their narrowly selfish aspirations and to act in ways that contribute to the happiness of their fellows. The goal of political rule was to promote 'the diminution or cessation of evils and of sorrows, and the multiplication and augmentation of goods and pleasures' (Keohane, 1980, p. 365). He urged governors to educate their subjects so that they acquired a true understanding of their interests and learnt to regulate their passions by reason. The educational role of the state should be supplemented by a machine-like system of government that encouraged subjects to act in ways that contributed to the happiness of the public and discourage those that harm it. Saint-Pierre argued that

> it is necessary to assume that in society the interests of individuals will incessantly and strongly conflict with the public interest and often come to dominate and ruin society unless the Legislator arranges laws and regulations so that particular individuals cannot advance their selfish interest except by procuring the interests of others at the same time.... [T]he penalty necessarily attached to the infringement of the law ... [must be] sufficiently inevitable that no citizen is ever tempted to resist the law (ibid., p. 372).

The regulatory influence of the law is crucial to Saint-Pierre's scheme. Individual freedom should only be allowed when it can be shown to advance the general happiness of the population: 'Liberty should be augmented when it makes for good, license repressed when it leads to evil' (ibid., p. 365).

Although Christian versions of utilitarianism continued to be important in the late eighteenth and early nineteenth centuries, this period witnessed the development of a quite distinctive tradition of utilitarianism that was marked by growing scepticism about the role of religion in political theory and a desire to arrive at a scientific understanding of politics. The noted Scottish philosopher David Hume

> ### David Hume (1711–76)
>
> Hume was educated at the University of Edinburgh. After toying with the law, he was employed as a private tutor, in the British diplomatic service in Paris, in an administrative role in the British Army, and as an Under Secretary of State in London. He found a settled and congenial appointment as Keeper of the Advocates' Library in Edinburgh. A leading figure in the Scottish Enlightenment, Hume gained a degree of notoriety because of his sceptical views of Christianity. His works, on various aspects of philosophy, economics, social and political theory and history, received widespread notice in Britain and continental Europe. His most important political writings appeared in *Essays, Moral and Political*, first published in 1741. In these essays Hume advanced a theory of justice that did not rely on the religiously grounded assumptions that had played such a role in earlier political thinking, and nor did it relate political legitimacy to the origin of government, or the distribution of political power in a given community. Hume's work marked a significant shift in the focus of Western political thinking and has continued to have a marked impact on modern political philosophy.
>
> *Key reading:* Haakonssen, 1993; Miller, 1981; Whelan, 1985.

gave an important impetus to this development. According to Hume, accounts of politics that are premised on Christianity are conceptually incoherent and empirically untenable. He argued that politics should focus on the satisfaction of interests valued by members of a particular community, and he described justice as an 'artificial' virtue that specifies modes of conduct that are conducive to the realisation of these interests (see pp. 226–27). In making this case, Hume maintained that the purpose of government is to promote the 'utility of the public' and he argued that the best way of doing so is for it to formulate and uphold rules of justice that reflect a community's experience of how its interests can best be realised.

Hume's approach to politics was endorsed by a number of his contemporaries and successors, but while they accepted his argument that the ends of politics could be described by reference to the realisation of interests, they thought that *all* actions and institutions should be subject to continual scrutiny using means-end calculations to gauge their consequences. These writers rejected Hume's argument that the most useful practices and institutions emerge as a consequence of human experience, and are upheld by habit and authority (Miller, 1981, p. 191). An important consequence of this move was that while Hume stressed the role of justice in giving stability to human interaction and depreciated rapid change, other utilitarians promoted radical political reform as a means of ensuring that political power is consciously used to maximise utility.

Jeremy Bentham does not seem to have known of Saint-Pierre's writings, but he acknowledged a direct debt to both Hume and Claude Helvetius, the author of *De l'Esprit* (1758). Helvetius equated moral order with an underlying structure of rationality that enables humans to identify scientifically valid notions of right and wrong. The moral order focuses on *this* world, not on the world to come; it legitimates immediate enjoyment, and it integrates individual and social needs in such a way that the maximisation of individual pleasure promotes social utility. For Helvetius, morality consisted not merely in adherence to the rules of justice, as it had for Hume, but in the *direct* pursuit of what he called 'the interest of the public', that is, 'of the greatest number' (Halévy, 1972, p. 19). Helvetius believed human action to be governed by self-interest, and he emphasised that the interests of the public have to be brought into harmony with those of individuals by social and educational influences, including those supplied by government:

> Moralists declaim continuously against the badness of men, but this shows how little they understand of the matter. Men are not bad; they are merely subject to their own interests. The lamentations of the moralists will certainly not change this motive power of human nature. The thing to complain of is not the badness of men but the ignorance of legislators, who have always put the interest of individuals into opposition with the general interest (Horowitz, 1954, p. 77).

Helvetius was no less insistent than Saint-Pierre that the main role of government is to identify and maintain systems of law that cause the interests of individuals and those of the public to correspond. The interests of the public are those of the *general* population, not particular classes or groups.

Utilitarians' definition of good governments as those which promote the interests of all members of the community has had important implications for ideas about the penal role of law. Punishment, which necessarily involves pain for those who are subject to it, is only justified to the extent that it effectively discourages wrongdoers from future action which is detrimental to the general good. The Italian philosopher Cesare Beccaria made an important early contribution to a utilitarian theory of punishment. Beccaria's *On Crimes and Punishments* was first published in the author's native Italian in 1764 and translated into both English and French shortly thereafter. In this work Beccaria attempted to solve the problem of promoting an identity of interests by a minute analysis of the motivational requirements of a utility-maximising system of penal law. While he did not deny the importance of Christianity, Beccaria restricted his analysis to the province of political thought and action:

> It is for theologians to chart the boundaries of the just and the unjust, insofar as the intrinsic good or evil of an action is concerned; but it is for the student of law and the state to establish the relationship between political justice and injustice, that is to say, between what is socially useful and what is harmful (Beccaria, 1995, p. 5).

From this point of view, the definition of what is 'criminal' depends on a consideration of 'harm to society', and the purpose of punishment is to prevent such harm and deter future offending (ibid., p. 24).

Beccaria's influence on later developments in utilitarian thinking are most apparent in his impact on Bentham. Bentham adopted Beccaria's critical or 'censorious' stance towards existing legal codes and practices, and sought to reduce legal prescriptions to a series of clear and unequivocal statements that would allow individuals to understand their obligations. Bentham also followed Beccaria in rejecting the practice of allowing judges to interpret law. Judge-made law undermines the function of legal codes because it means that the specification of criminal action takes place *after* the fact. Proper systems of law should identify prohibited actions and should specify an appropriate penalty so that those who are tempted to behave wrongly can take account of the consequences they may face when deciding how they will act. In such a system the role of the judge is merely to determine when the law has been broken and to apply the appropriate penalty or 'sanction' (ibid., pp. 14–15).

Benthamite utilitarianism: Bentham, J. S. Mill and Sidgwick

Although Bentham was impressed with Beccaria's account of law and its implications for systems of punishment, aspects of his theory differ significantly from those of his predecessor. Unlike Beccaria, Bentham rejected conventional ideas such as natural law and the contractual basis of government. He also ignored Beccaria's attempts to limit the pursuit of utility by assumptions about the dignity of humankind (Hart, 1982, pp. 49–51). For Bentham utility was an unqualified end of

Jeremy Bentham (1748–1832)

After undergoing legal training, Bentham's private fortune made it possible for him to devote his life to projects aimed at legal, penal and political reform. Recognised as the founder of the English school of 'utilitarian' political and moral philosophy, Bentham's political ideas were expounded in *A Fragment on Government* (1776), *An Introduction to the Principles of Morals and Legislation* (1789) and a range of other works, many of which remained incomplete and unpublished on his death.

Bentham's principle of utility specified that government existed to further the 'greatest happiness of the greatest number' and took the maximisation of pleasurable sensations and the minimisation of painful ones as the criteria of 'happiness'. His statement of this position and its implications was not reliant on the religious assumptions that had played such an important role in earlier political thinking. It pointed beyond conventional notions of class, and disregarded qualitative distinctions between types of pleasure or the merits of those who might experience them. Government was obliged to consider the interests of the whole community, not the interests of groups within it, particularly not the interests of those who exercised political, administrative and judicial authority. In his political and legal writings (he also wrote on economics, education, criminal justice, morals and psychology), Bentham explored the implications of these ideas for systems of law and for administrative and constitutional structures. The purpose of law was to prohibit actions that were contrary to the interests of the community as Bentham perceived them, and to apply sanctions that would discourage wrongdoing. Administrative and constitutional structures should maximise the expertise that was brought to bear on matters of public concern, while guarding against the misuse of power by rulers and officials.

Although Bentham was originally intrigued by the idea that an enlightened despot might be an appropriate agent of utilitarian reform, he later thought that democratic institutions were necessary to ensure that government was not subject to the 'sinister interests' of rulers, officials and elites. In the early decades of the nineteenth century, Bentham was at the centre of a group of radical political reformers known as the 'Benthamites'. This group included James and John Stuart Mill. Bentham's constitutional ideas attracted the attention of a number of contemporary radical reformers in continental Europe and in Latin America and versions of utilitarianism have played an important ongoing role in nineteenth- and twentieth-century moral, political and legal philosophy.

Key reading: Hart, 1982; Hume, 1993; Lyons, 1973; Rosen, 1993.

politics. Moreover, while Beccaria defined utility by reference to the *equal* maximisation of the happiness of each person within a given society, Bentham understood it in aggregative terms: the principle of utility stipulates that human action should be evaluated by reference to the 'greatest happiness of the greatest number'.

Bentham's career as a philosopher grew out of his concern with the deficiencies of English law and legal thought. This interest continued throughout his life and gave rise to a staggeringly large body of writings on the topic; it also led, naturally enough, to a consideration of political thinking and political practice. Since law operates within and on the basis of a framework that is established and maintained by government and specified in legislation, the two areas are closely related. From early in his career Bentham argued that both government and the legal system should be evaluated by direct reference to the standard of 'utility'.

Bentham first applied himself to what he regarded as the dangerous absurdities of the English Common Law. His initial target was Sir William Blackstone, a noted jurist and author of the widely read *Commentaries on the Common Law of England* (1765–69). Bentham claimed that Blackstone epitomised the deafness to the 'voice of reason and utility' that characterised English law. In *A Fragment on Government* Bentham attacked the methodological and verbal obscurities of English law, rejected its penchant for conflating description and justification, and deplored its reliance on ideas such as 'precedence', which endow the past with unquestioned authority. *A Fragment* invited Bentham's contemporaries to 'break loose from the trammels of authority and ancestor worship in the field of law' and to ground legal reasoning and legal practice on the principle of utility (Bentham, 1967, p. 103).

In *An Introduction to the Principles of Morals and Legislation* (1789) Bentham wrote that 'utility' is

> *that principle* which states the greatest happiness of all those whose interest is in question, as being the right and proper, and only right and proper and universally desirable, end of human action: of human action in every situation, and in particular in that of a functionary or set of functionaries exercising the powers of Government (ibid., p. 125, n.1).

In order to give precise content to this formula, Bentham insisted that the idea of happiness should be specified in terms of maximising pleasure and minimising pain. He saw this stipulation as corresponding with the 'springs' or originating impulses of human action: 'Nature', Bentham wrote, 'has placed mankind under the governance of two sovereign masters, *pain* and *pleasure*. It is for them alone to point out what we ought to do, as well as to determine what we shall do' (ibid., p. 125). Bentham thought that by characterising happiness in this way he had identified a simple, empirically quantifiable reference point for private individuals and legislators (Lyons, 1973, pp. 32–34). This reference point did not depend on theology or supernatural sanctions. Moreover, since it made no attempt to distinguish pleasures except in terms of intensity and duration, it was inherently non-elitist in its implications: pleasures and pains are sensations experienced *by all* human beings and are not dependent upon intellectual enlightenment or the example or leadership of elites.

Bentham's theory of human behaviour was based on a general assumption concerning egotism, but he saw utility as the basis of both individual and social life. At times he pointed towards a natural harmony of interests. More often, however, he argued that the purpose of government is to harmonise, or at least to integrate, the personal interests of individuals with those of their fellows. It is significant that the title of one of Bentham's most important published works linked 'morals' and 'legislation'. Utility is seen as both a moral and a political principle: it is intended to guide both private individuals and those who exercise power over others.

In his accounts of the 'greatest happiness principle' Bentham sought to establish a clear, incontrovertible standard for evaluating the conduct of governors and the institutional mechanisms through which they operate. This standard relates to the identifiable interests of the individuals who make up the community, not to the requirements of an omnipotent God or to particular individuals or classes. Consequently, one of Bentham's primary political concerns was to discredit systems of government that pursue 'sinister' interests in disregard to those of the community as a whole. He maintained that happiness is the end that all individuals can be expected to value above all others, and that the purpose of politics is to give reality to this aspiration by ensuring that the maximisation of happiness is pursued in the most effective manner possible:

> An action ... may be said to be conformable to the principle of utility ... when the tendency it has to augment the happiness of the community is greater than any it has to diminish it ... A measure of government ... may be said to be conformable ... to the principle of utility, when in like manner the tendency it has to augment the happiness of the community is greater than any which it has to diminish it (Bentham, 1967, p. 127).

Although pains and pleasures are 'real' they are not necessarily easy to determine or quantify. For example, Bentham acknowledged that the same stimuli may have differing effects on different individuals. However, he did not think that these variations impose an insuperable barrier to the application of the principle of utility. He argued that since it is relatively easy to determine what causes pain to most human beings, government can specify actions that should be prohibited to protect the innocent and ensure the effective punishment of those who inflict pain on their fellows. The *Introduction* presented a detailed analysis of the relationship between modes of punishment and the maximisation of utility. This aspect of Bentham's work was related to his long-standing interest in penal reform, an interest that gave rise to concrete proposals for constructing and regulating penal institutions.

However, while Bentham believed that an effective penal system is necessary to discourage individuals from causing pain to their fellows, he believed that the role of government is far more limited when it comes to the promotion of pleasure. Since individuals are the best judges of what gives them pleasure, it is incumbent upon government to leave them as much freedom as is consistent with the avoidance of harm to others. On the one hand, then, by means of its protective and penal activities, government should prevent people causing pain to others, while on the other hand it should leave individuals to identify and pursue those things that give them pleasure provided that they do not do so in ways that inflict pain on others.

Although Bentham tended to stress the negative and protective role of government, he allowed that utility may require a more positive role for it and identified four goals that should be secured by a sound, utility-sensitive constitution: the provision of subsistence, abundance, security and equality (ibid., p. 196). Bentham thought that to a considerable degree the first three of these objectives could be satisfied by maintaining conditions favourable to the operation of a free market. In most circumstances the market provides an effective mechanism for encouraging individuals to undertake productive labour, and it allows them to benefit from their efforts. The fact that free markets recognise the right to private property ensures that people will be secure in their possessions. Bentham warned that any attempt to impose equality will limit the effectiveness of the market, and if it is achieved by periodic redistribution it will threaten security of property and thus produce uncertainty, which is a form of pain. He insisted, however, that extreme inequality inhibits the maximisation of happiness because the increase of pleasure derived by the rich for a given increase in income is far lower than that experienced by the poor. Great inequality is also objectionable because it augments the power of the rich over the poor. This consideration was an important one for Bentham, for while he believed that government *can* serve the cause of utility, he argued that it will not do so if it is under the control of particular classes or individuals. He was thus left with the problem of balancing the benefits derived from a system of free exchange with those produced by the very different principle of equality. For the most part, he was prepared to leave the market to produce a generally beneficial balance, but he also identified a role for government in this process. Government can help ensure subsistence by controlling the price of basic food stuffs such as bread. It could also promote employment and productivity by boosting the money supply. Since these measures help to reduce extreme poverty, they also make a modest contribution to softening the grossest inequalities without undermining the generally beneficial role of a free market (Bentham, 1952–54, vol. iii, pp. 257–58).

These economic applications of the principle of utility were formulated in writings that were not published until long after Bentham's death, and friends who knew of his thoughts on these matters disagreed with them. However, these policy proposals provide a valuable illustration of Bentham's approach. Having identified human happiness as the starting point of political analysis, and having specified this in terms of maximisation of pleasure and minimisation of pain, Bentham was able to take an instrumental view of other ideas and values. He thus rejected natural right theory, and what he regarded as the mischievous and confusing formulations of the Common Law. These doctrines lack the clarity of the principle of utility and tend, if anything, to buttress claims that will impede its realisation. He also refused to be tied down by the principle of *laissez-faire,* that is, the idea that it is desirable for government to restrict itself to performing a narrow range of regulatory and protective functions. Bentham rejected a dogmatic attachment to this doctrine: 'I have never', he wrote,

> nor ever shall have, any horror ... of the hand of government in economic matters ... The interference of government, as often as ... any the smallest balance on the side of advantage is the result, is an event I witness with altogether as much satisfaction as I should its forbearance, and with much more than I should its negligence (ibid., pp. 257–58).

At the same time, however, he argued that personal freedom is generally conducive to human happiness, and he gave both the political and the economic dimensions of this an important but derivative and secondary role in his theory. Equality is treated in a similarly flexible but far more restricted way. While freedom and equality were thus important for Bentham, he believed their role has to be determined by reference to the master principle of politics, the idea of the greatest happiness of the greatest number. These values could serve the cause of utility; they are not themselves of ultimate value and politics cannot be explained by reference to them.

The implications of Bentham's principle of utility were far reaching. In addition to promoting legal and penal reform, he also considered radical changes to political representation and government administration to ensure that the distribution and exercise of political power were consistent with its requirements. In the latter part of his life Bentham looked to democratic representation to check the actions of legislators. He also argued that strict accountability should be built into the structure of public bureaucracy, and that the operation of government should be subjected to the checking influence of public opinion and a free press. The purpose of all these measures was to ensure that the exercise of political power would be directed towards the greatest happiness of the greatest number, not to the private 'sinister' interests of elites (Hume, 1993; Rosen, 1993b; Schofield, 1993).

These strictures applied as much to government's external responsibilities as to its internal management of the affairs of the community. Saint-Pierre had already drawn this connection when framing his scheme for 'perpetual peace' in the early years of the eighteenth century. He argued that persistent international conflict compromised programmes of internal reform, noting that if rulers had a true view of the extent of their responsibilities and the difficulty of fulfilling them, they would not seek to add to their burdens by expanding their territories. They would, he claimed, be 'as ardent in restricting their States and their Rights as they are [now] eager to expand both of them' (Rousseau, 2005b, p. 77). Saint-Pierre thought that a radical change in the practice of European international relations was essential to the advancement of public utility. The key problem was the lack of a common system of public law supported by effective mechanisms for adjudicating disputes and punishing wrongdoing.

> Such is the Constitution of Europe, that the Sovereigns are not sure of Justice in Affairs ... without resolving to be at immense Charge of Armaments by Sea and Land; ... They have agreed upon no Laws that might serve either to fix the Bounds of the Territories of each State, or to render the Commerce between their People convenient, safe, equal, universal and perpetual: They have pitched upon no Arbiters or Interpreters of the Laws of their Society, and so long as they shall remain without Society, they can find no Remedy for their Misfortunes (Saint-Pierre, 1714, p. 9).

Saint-Pierre's response to this utility-frustrating situation was to propose the adoption of a framework of international cooperation that would eliminate conflict between states and inaugurate 'perpetual peace'. This framework involved a confederation of states, or a 'European republic' governed by a permanent assembly (the 'Diet') of representatives of the sovereigns. The Diet was to be created by a treaty by which the sovereigns renounced the use of force against their European neighbours. It would settle dynastic and territorial disputes by arbitration and be empowered to use force against recalcitrant European states and their external enemies. Once guaranteed the security provided by the European republic, rulers would be free to focus their resources and attention on enhancing the happiness of their subjects. They would encourage the arts and sciences, stimulate commerce and promote general prosperity (ibid., pp. 79–82).

Although Bentham did not have direct knowledge of Saint-Pierre's writings he may have known of his scheme of perpetual peace via Rousseau's discussion of it (Rousseau, 2005b). The elimination of war certainly played an important role in his views on the implications of the principle of utility for international relations. Bentham's approach, however, was more broad ranging than that of his predecessor. In *Principles of International Law* (1789) he took a systematic look at the implications of the principle of utility for international relations, basing his analysis on a strict analogy between government's internal and external responsibilities: 'the end that a disinterested legislator upon international law would propose to himself, would ... be the greatest happiness of all the nations taken together.' The object would be to 'prevent international offences' and 'encourage the practice of positively useful actions' (Bentham, 1843a, p. 538). In the absence of effective mechanisms of international arbitration, however, this meant that sovereigns would need to balance the pain caused to members of a foreign nation against the benefit that their external actions secured for their own subjects. Bentham noted that such a calculation might justify war, a position that was entirely consistent with the assumption that security was a precondition of happiness (ibid., pp. 538–39; Hoogensen, 2005). In addition, however, sovereigns also had a positive obligation to assist others if the diminution of the happiness of their subjects was offset by enhanced benefit accruing to others through their action.

But while there were circumstances in which rulers might be justified in going to war, Bentham regarded armed conflict as generally inimical to utility: 'The happiest of mankind are sufferers by war; and the wisest nay, even the least wise, are wise enough to ascribe the chief of their sufferings to that cause' (Bentham, 1843a, p. 546). In response to this situation Bentham proposed 'A Plan for an Universal and Perpetual Peace' directed towards three related objectives: 'simplicity of government, national frugality and peace' (ibid., p. 546). This essay focused primarily on the relationship between Britain and France but Bentham thought that if lasting peace was established between these bitter rivals, the tranquillity of Europe would soon follow. He identified a range of causes of internal conflict – alliances, trade agreements and restrictions on international trade, overseas possessions, unnecessary levels of armaments – and argued that it was not in Great Britain's interest to continue to support these expensive and risky practices. He argued that colonies were rarely if ever a source of profit to the mother country and that possession of them made conflict with other European powers far more likely. Measures of trade protection provided only the most temporary relief to a nation's traders and manufacturers, while for developed countries the costs of war always outweighed the benefits. Finally, Bentham identified secrecy as a common source of international tension and as a means of concealing the real beneficiaries of otherwise harmful treaties and military and colonial ventures. Bentham proposed that France and Britain agree to submit their disputes to arbitration and did not think it necessary for the 'common court of judicature' to have coercive powers: 'Establish a common tribunal, the necessity for war no longer follows from difference of opinion. Just or unjust, the decision of the arbiters will save the credit, the honour of the contending party' (ibid., p. 552).

Over the course of his long career Bentham's views on questions such as whether colonisation could be justified varied, although for the most part his statements reflected the application of the principle of utility to distinctive issues in particular circumstances (Scholfield, 2006, pp. 201–20). At times he thought that properly organised settler colonies in unoccupied territory may advance utility by relieving population pressure in European countries, but remained generally sceptical about the financial benefit of colonies and the risks imposed by them. Late in his career Bentham provided the Spanish people with a series of financial calculations showing that they gained no benefit from their colonies and encouraging them to grant them independence (Bentham, 1995). At this time he also argued that colonisation provided scope for members of government to enrich themselves at the expense of the rest of the community and thus provided opportunities for a whole range of 'sinister interests' which corrupted constitutional mechanisms and frustrated attempts to align the interests of governmental elites with those of the rest of the community (Scholfield, 2006, pp. 211–20). These criticisms were not reserved for Spanish colonies. Unlike some later utilitarians who became enthusiastic imperialists, Bentham castigated British rule across the globe as involving the 'denial of justice, oppression, extortion, corruptive influence, despotism' and dismissed the 'pretence of protection' that was used to justify it (Bentham, 1995, p. 153; Pitts, 2003, pp. 206–20).

Bentham's statement of the principle of utility enjoyed a wide circulation in a number of European countries and made an impact on newly independent states in South America (Dinwiddy, 1993). Bentham's account of the relationship between happiness and politics was also of ongoing significance for nineteenth-century political thinking. Some responses were hostile. A number of writers objected to the radically secular nature of Bentham's theory (ibid.). Others, for example Samuel Taylor Coleridge and Thomas Carlyle, criticised Bentham for producing a mechanical, degraded and de-spiritualised conception of human nature and social relationships. Carlyle actually rejected happiness as a goal but even some of his less puritanical contemporaries were uneasy about the way Bentham formulated his case. The most important sympathetic statement of this view appeared in an essay which John Stuart Mill regarded as a defence of utilitarianism.

Mill's father, James, was a close associate of Bentham and in his early life the younger Mill was an ardent proponent of 'Benthamism'. While John Stuart Mill's general admiration for Bentham never waned, he thought that aspects of Bentham's political philosophy needed to be restated in a way that took some account of the criticisms levelled by Coleridge, Carlyle and others. In *Utilitarianism* (1861) Mill argued that while Bentham had performed a valuable service in pushing human happiness to the forefront of the political agenda, the idea of what happiness meant, and what it implied, needed further refinement. In place of Bentham's essentially quantitative understanding of pleasure, Mill argued that an account of the greatest happiness principle needed to recognise the existence of 'higher' and 'lower' pleasures:

> It is quite compatible with the principle of utility to recognise the fact, that some kinds of pleasure are more desirable and more valuable than others. It would be absurd that while, in estimating all other things, quality is considered as well as quantity, the estimation of pleasures should be supposed to depend on quality alone (Mill, 1983, p. 7).

Mill placed particular emphasis on a *qualitative* notion of pleasure, and he claimed that the superiority of 'higher' pleasures can only be determined by those who are exposed to a range of pleasures (ibid., p. 10). An important consequence of this modification was that it tended to erode the universally objective features of Bentham's theory. Mill's views on what constituted a source of higher pleasure also had important implications for his reformulation of utilitarianism. Mill included among the higher pleasures those connected to 'altruism', or a disinterested concern with the well-being of others, and thus displaced Bentham's assumption concerning egotism. He also attached great weight to pleasures derived from the cultivation of aesthetic sensibilities and intellectual faculties. These modifications to classical utilitarianism have the effect of elevating the role of elite judgement in determining questions of utility since, unlike other members of the population, they are able to appreciate the pleasures derived from artistic and intellectual experiences as well as those coming from more commonplace sources of happiness.

In addition to introducing a qualitative dimension to calculations of 'greatest happiness', Mill made other significant additions to classical utilitarianism. In a review of an essay by James Mill, T. B. Macaulay chastised him for building a theory of government without reference to its history: 'We have here an elaborate treatise on Government, from which, but for two or three passing allusions, it would not appear that the author was aware that any governments actually existed among men' (Lively and Rees, 1984, p. 101). John Stuart Mill responded to Macaulay's criticisms by relating the idea of utility to the particular circumstances of given societies. He argued that the pursuit of happiness cannot, and ought not to be, divorced from considerations that will promote human progress within a particular social and political context. This stipulation means that the question of utility has to take account of the prospects of future happiness that progress will produce, and it implies that the long-term prospects of improvement might often take priority over short-term considerations, particularly in cases where the latter is based largely on lower pleasures. Thus while Mill still regarded happiness as the goal of politics, he insisted that political issues should be discussed in relation to the role that progress plays in extending the scope and the quality of human happiness.

One consequence of this view was that Mill developed a complex response to demands for 'popular' or democratic forms of government (see p. 159). It also led him to argue that it is improper for society to interfere with individuals' liberty except in cases where they interfere with the liberty of others (see pp. 67ff). This principle is spelt out in one of Mill's most famous works, *On Liberty*. Mill's argument in this work is related to his reformulation of utilitarianism because liberty is held to be essential to the progress of humankind: it is upon such progress that the increase in human happiness (as Mill understood it) depends.

During the latter part of the nineteenth century the process of revising Benthamite utilitarianism was continued by Henry Sidgwick. Sidgwick's political thought was developed in quite conscious opposition to the ideas of virtue and perfection that appeared in T. H. Green's political philosophy (see pp. 59–60). Green and his followers admired Mill's attempt to refine utilitarianism, and they were encouraged to see that he had moved away from the merely quantitative idea of pleasure that they identified with Bentham (Green, 1986, pp. 24, 313, 360–61). At the same time, however, they thought that the fact that aspects of Mill's arguments were not compatible with Bentham's formulations pointed to fatal weaknesses in utilitarian moral and political philosophy. In addition to confronting Green's criticisms, Sidgwick also tackled other contemporaries who held that liberty is the primary focus of political thinking.

Henry Sidgwick (1838–1900)

An academic philosopher who taught at Cambridge University, Sidgwick defended utilitarianism against T. H. Green's critique, but presented a version of it that eschewed many of the radical implications drawn from Benthamite formulations of the doctrine. His most important political work was *Elements of Politics* (1891).

Key reading: Schneewind, 1977.

Sidgwick regarded utilitarianism as the most systematic and scientific statement of ethical theory, one that had a long and respectable pedigree. He rejected Green's claim that perfection is the goal of human endeavour and the end of government on the grounds that it was dogmatic and philosophically incoherent. In Sidgwick's view, utilitarianism embodies the common sense of humanity in a rational form. He claimed a

> general – if not universal – assent for the principle that the true standard and criterion by which right legislation is to be distinguished from wrong is conduciveness to the general 'good' or 'welfare'. And probably the majority of persons would agree to interpret the 'good' or 'welfare' of the community to mean, in the last analysis, the happiness of the individual human beings who compose the community; provided that we take into account not only the human beings who are actually living but those who are to live hereafter (Sidgwick, 1891, p. 34).

Sidgwick linked utility to 'common opinion', and claimed that prevailing conceptions of government reflected a general endorsement of utilitarian aspirations and values. For this reason Sidgwick was far less critical of existing institutions than

Bentham had been and directed his critical attention to current political argument and practice.

For example, Sidgwick considered contemporary claims that liberty is sacred and that the action of government should be restricted to preventing individuals harming one another. These statements were more extreme than those of J. S. Mill because his principle of liberty does not preclude government action in pursuit of public objectives (see p. 67). In response to this line of argument, Sidgwick contended that both 'paternalistic' and 'socialistic' interferences with liberty might sometimes be justified because the psychological and sociological assumptions upon which a utilitarian defence of individual liberty rests are not always soundly based. 'Paternalistic' legislation, that is, government action directed towards the good of the individual whose liberty is interfered with, may be necessary because individuals are not always the best judges of their own interests. This is clearly so with respect to children, but it might also apply, for example, to people's capacity to judge the services offered by professional practitioners. Sidgwick was, however, wary of this form of interference, insisting that the central principle to be kept in mind is that paternalism can only be justified where there is empirical proof that individuals cannot be trusted to look after their own interests (ibid., pp. 40–61).

'Socialistic' interference – for the good of society – deals with cases where the pursuit of individual interests does not maximise general welfare (ibid., pp. 137–40). In presenting an example of this type of interference Sidgwick echoed Hume's argument that government is necessary to provide services ('public goods') that cannot be reliably produced through individual effort; he also discussed the right of the state to control property when the public good requires it (ibid., pp. 144–47). He insisted, however, that these measures are not 'collectivistic'; that is, they are not related to doctrines promoting the redistribution of wealth within society. Although such measures may be justified in some circumstances, Sidgwick argued that under existing conditions they would be detrimental to the pursuit of utility because would undermine the benefits produced by individual liberty (ibid., pp. 151–60).

The diffusion of utilitarianism: Socialism and welfare

Sidgwick's writings mark the effective conclusion of nineteenth-century attempts to use Bentham's formulation of utilitarianism as the basis for large-scale, systematic political theorising. Rather than being overcome by other accounts of the ends of politics, however, utilitarianism was diffused into a number of different political theories. This tendency was apparent to some degree in Sidgwick's generally conservative, status-quo-oriented reformulation of what had begun as an overtly provocative challenge to existing thought and practice. It also reflected the extent to which a secular, human-centred, want-regarding approach had come to form the mainstream of Western political thinking. Henceforth theories that took virtue, order or freedom as their starting point had to present themselves as more plausible alternatives to an approach towards politics that had received its most systematic and influential formulation in the tortured prose of Jeremy Bentham.

While Sidgwick reconciled utilitarianism with conservative politics, other late-nineteenth- and early-twentieth-century writers adapted it to causes that sustained its radical credentials. In this period non-Marxist socialists were among the most important absorbers of at least the spirit of Benthamite political thinking. From its origins in the early nineteenth century, socialist thinking had sharply contrasted the misery produced in a competitive capitalist society with the potentialities for general well-being of social and political structures that fulfilled the promise held out by the revolutionary ideal of 'liberty, equality and fraternity'. Since socialists supposed that humans possessed an inherent tendency for sociability, their understanding of happiness went beyond the minimalist, hedonistic formulation favoured by Bentham. They tended to adopt the position on the integration of individual and social values that lay at the heart of Helvetius' theory (Horowitz, 1954, p. 192).

In addition, many socialists adhered to a qualitative conception of utility that resembled aspects of J. S. Mill's reformulation of Bentham's doctrine. For example, Beatrice Webb described Bentham as the 'intellectual god-father' of her husband Sidney, an important figure in the history of British socialism. She argued, however, that while she and her husband thought that action should be judged in terms of its utilitarian consequences, they took a broad view of what this involved:

> There is no other sanction we care to accept but results, though we should be inclined to give, perhaps, a wider meaning to results. For instance, the formation of a noble character, the increase of intellectual faculty, stimulus to sense of beauty, sense of conduct, even sense of humour, are all ends that we should regard as 'sanctioning' action; quite apart from whether they produce happiness of one or all, or none (Webb, 1948, p. 210).

Socialist views on how human well-being can be maximised vary considerably, but they generally tend to place particular emphasis on the role of government in eliminating poverty and eroding those degrees of social and economic inequality that are inconsistent with human happiness. As the noted English socialist G. D. H. Cole put it, 'The reason – the only valid reason – for being a Socialist is the desire, the impassioned will, to seek the greatest happiness and well-being of the greatest number' (Cole, 1935, p. 16).

Conclusion

In 1978 the British philosopher Stuart Hampshire described utilitarianism as having been 'a bold, innovative, even a subversive doctrine, with a record of successful social criticism behind it' (Hampshire, 1978, p. 1) but argued that it had become narrow and obstructive. This criticism reflected the tendency of contemporary philosophers to focus on the 'ethical', rather than the more 'political' dimensions of utility. One sign of that were vigorous disputes over the viability of 'action' as opposed to 'rule' applications of the doctrine. While some writers argued that utilitarians should act on the basis of *rules* that tend to maximise happiness, others adhere to formulations that are close to Bentham's idea that good *actions* are those that directly promote utilitarian outcomes (Barrow, 1991, pp. 107–23). These disputes often arise in the course of discussions of the implications of utility that consider its function in establishing a 'code of personal conduct' that guides individuals in the stance they should take on issues of public debate such as war, punishment or abortion. The focus of these discussions differs from those reflecting utilitarianism's historical role as a *public* doctrine, designed (as Bentham intended) to guide legislators and citizens in their attempts to find the best solutions to problems of public or political conduct (Goodin, 1995, pp. 7–10). This approach relates to what has been called 'institutional utilitarianism', a subset of rule utilitarianism which identifies and upholds rules and practices that maximise the happiness of political societies. These rules may involve large-scale specifications of public policy and they may also be invoked to support particular political structures and forms of organisation. It has thus been argued, for example, that democracy can be justified on the grounds that an analysis of democratic societies shows that they have a good record for maximising the happiness of their members (Mulgan, 2007, pp. 164–65).

PART

II

THE LOCATION OF POLITICAL AUTHORITY: WHO SHOULD RULE?

In Part I we considered a number of historically important accounts of the purpose of government. In this part we examine a range of responses to the question: 'Who should rule?' Consideration of this matter prompts concerns about the structure of political authority and the qualities required by those who exercise it. Since political authority involves the capacity to coerce human beings, to specify goals and the means of their attainment, to maintain systems of order, and to infringe individual liberty, it is understandable that many political thinkers have given considerable thought to determining how such authority should be allocated. It should be noted, however, that views of *who* should hold political authority are distinct from questions about *how far* that authority should extend. It is important, for example, to guard against the tendency to suppose that monarchy must be absolute

while democracy is necessarily limited in what it can demand of those subject to it. The fact that a particular person or persons hold political power does not necessarily imply anything about the way in which it is used, although, as we shall see, some theorists identify certain forms of government with the advancement of particular interests.

The tenacity of the theme of this part of the book is reflected in the framework adopted for it. Aristotle classified types of government by reference to the location of political authority, and distinguished between the rule of the 'one', the 'few' and the 'many'. This framework is similar in some respects to that which distinguishes between 'monarchy', 'aristocracy' and 'democracy', but it has the advantage of extending the discussion beyond the range of types that are usually associated with these forms of government.

RULE BY A SINGLE PERSON

6

The prevalence of democracy in the modern world should not blind us to the fact that the idea of single-person rule has had a dominant place in the history of Western political thought. Indeed, the modern preference for popular government is an exception in a tradition of political thinking that has generally been hostile to democracy. While this hostility has been a common feature of defences of monarchy, that is, rule by a single person who is endowed with the sanctity and trappings of 'kingship', it has been shared to some degree by those promoting non-monarchical conceptions of rule by 'the one'. In particular, proponents of single-person rule share a common belief that rulers should provide a sense of unity and direction in the state. They also assume that it is possible to identify a person who possesses the distinct and relevant attributes that are necessary to attain these ends.

This chapter discusses ancient, early-modern and modern accounts of government by 'the one'. It also examines modern, non-monarchical accounts of single-person rule. Some of these theories treat the ruler as the only really significant political actor in the state, but others focus on the need for single-person rule to be set in a framework where other actors also play important political roles.

Single-person rule in the ancient world: Plato, Aristotle and Cicero

Although Plato's *Republic* dealt primarily with rule by a very restricted class, it also contains brief but significant references to single-person rule. Plato's account of this theme deals with both pure and corrupt rule by 'the one' and represents an early, historically important, treatment of the subject. In discussing the forceful objection that, whatever its merits, an ideal state could never be brought into existence, Plato suggested that single-person rule may provide a solution to the apparently intractable problem of expecting a system of philosophic rule to emerge from an environment dominated by an unruly and irrational populace subject to corrupting influence of self-interested members of the upper classes.

Plato identified two escapes from this dilemma. One option is for a philosophic recluse to take advantage of a chance occurrence to take control of the state and compel the community to listen to him. Another possibility is that an existing head of government, or his heir, may be inspired by philosophy to embark upon a programme of radical reconstruction. In short, philosophers must become kings, or a king must become a philosopher (Plato, 1970, pp. 259–65). While pointing to the potentialities of philosophic kingship, however, Plato also discussed the threat posed by tyranny, a corrupt and harmful form of single-person rule which is even further removed from the ideal of philosophic rule than democracy.

In democratic regimes, the lawlessness and chronic instability that arise from unbridled popular liberty are exacerbated by the common people's determination to misuse their political influence to plunder the rich, and the latter's attempts to resist these depredations by seizing control of the state. The ordinary people respond to this threat by placing military power in the hands of a popular champion. At first he and the population are in a relationship of symbiotic debasement – he flatters and indulges them, they admire and reward him – but once he gains a position of dominance the state is gripped by a new kind of lawlessness. Rather than being subjected to the whims of a fickle and debauched populace, government is now under the control of an arbitrary and cruel individual.

Plato characterised tyranny as a form of 'patricide' – the offspring of the populace, the tyrant, ends up using violence against his 'parents' – and portrayed the tyrannical character as a criminal type. While philosophers prepare themselves for rule by remaining detached from the intellectually and morally debasing influences of a corrupt society, the tyrant climbs to a position of unregulated supremacy by first immersing himself in this society and then outdoing the population in baseness. The servant of a corrupt master turns the latter into his slave by the consistent and single-minded cultivation and exercise of many of the same character traits (ibid., pp. 324–49).

The contrast between a corrupt and a good form of single-person rule reappears in Aristotle's writings. In the *Politics* Aristotle defined kingship as a form of rule that is directed to the common good. In contrast, tyrants govern in their own interest, ignoring any legal constraints on their conduct (Aristotle, 1958, pp. 131, 160–80). This point is important because, like Plato, Aristotle considered rule according 'to law' to be preferable to personal rule by *ordinary* human beings, because it avoids the caprice and partiality to which all such people are naturally inclined (ibid., pp. 171–72; Mulgan, 1977, pp. 83–85; see pp. 221–22). The corollary of this argument is, however, that completely enlightened people can rule without law. There is no danger of them acting corruptly, and since they are not bound by law they can react sensitively and appropriately to the requirements of a particular situation.

Aristotle's views on the appropriateness of rule by the one rest on his belief that the distribution of political power should reflect the relative merits of different sections of the population. While it is thus unjust for political equality to be maintained among those who are unequal in knowledge and virtue, single-person rule will be just if a given individual really is markedly superior to the rest of the population. Significantly, however, Aristotle's discussion of single-person rule is overshadowed by scepticism about such marked superiority, and by doubts over its acceptability to the rest of the population. He observed that those who truly merit supremacy will be like gods among men while those who lack virtue and wisdom usually show a marked reluctance to acknowledge these qualities in others (Aristotle, 1958, pp. 135–59, 204, 237–41).

Like Plato and Aristotle, the Roman writer Cicero distinguished between 'corrupt' and 'good' forms of single-person rule and expressed a guarded preference for kingship as the best type of simple constitution (Wood, 1988, p. 146). However, he thought that the benefits of monarchy – understood as a system that provides a sense of unity and direction and acknowledges the marked superiority of an individual – can be reaped without its dangers if it comprises merely one element of a 'mixed' constitution (see p.). Cicero's model for this type of government was derived from the political experience of pre-imperial Rome. In this case, however, monarchy was embodied in the office of consulate rather than being the determining principle of the constitution (ibid., pp. 165–66).

Medieval ideas of monarchy – early theories of kingship: Thomas Aquinas and Christine de Pizan

In the medieval period, theories of single-person rule rested upon ideas of kingship. While Christianity gave medieval conceptions of monarchy a distinctive character, they cannot be divorced from other traditions. Early Christian accounts of monarchy (dating from the sixth century) developed in a context where imperial power had begun to lapse and the Roman Empire had fragmented into a number of largely autonomous political units whose governance reflected earlier 'Barbarian' (non-Roman and non-Christian) ideas. Moreover, towards the end of the medieval period – that is, from the thirteenth century – accounts of rule by the one were often framed within the context of Aristotle's writings. For example, medieval writers repeated observations that had appeared in classical statements on the evils of tyranny, and also endorsed Aristotle's views on the relationship between monarchy and the personal virtues of the monarch.

Early examples of a Christian idea of kingship appeared in the legal code issued under the authority of the Emperor Justinian in the first half of the sixth century. The key point of this theory, one that distinguishes it from earlier 'Barbarian' accounts which made kingship a matter of election or choice, is that the powers of rulers are held to be divinely instituted and divinely ordained; the power and authority of kings is a gift of God, and the source of their powers is symbolised by anointment (Ullmann, 1975, p. 48; Nelson, 1991, p. 218). This conception of 'descending' power has a number of important implications. In the first place, while it means that kings have no *right* to their power – one cannot have the right to receive a gift – it gives them a unique standing in relation to the conduct of human affairs, and can thus be used to discredit claims that monarchs are subordinate to religious authorities: their power comes directly from God. Moreover, while the power of single rulers was independent of choices made by their subjects, this theory made it clear that kings have distinctive, divinely ordained responsibilities for them. In many medieval writings the various sections of the population are presented as members of the king's household, a point that reinforces the idea that monarchy embodies a paternal or 'patrimonial' conception of government. This image of kingship is captured in a poem written by Archbishop Wulfstan of York in the tenth century:

> For the Christian king
>
> It is very fitting
>
> That he be in the place of a father
>
> For the Christian people.
>
> And in watching over and warding them
>
> Be Christ's representative … (Nelson, 1991, p. 240).

Monarchical power is not only paternal, it is also intensely personal: the king keeps 'faith' with his leading subjects and they with him. Moreover, while kingship is seen as a direct grant from God, this model of rule stresses consensus and 'faithfulness' rather than coercion.

Medieval conceptions of kingship place great stress on the distinctive personal qualities of rulers, particularly their responsibility to be both the model for, and sustainer of, virtue. They also reflect a belief that the primary role of the ruler is to ensure peace, and that he is endowed with supreme moral authority. The latter of these ideas was challenged by medieval proponents of papal power who wished to secure ultimate moral authority for the Church. From the late thirteenth century, however, those who upheld temporal rulers' moral supremacy were able to fortify their position by drawing on the recently rediscovered political works of Aristotle.

Aquinas, for example, accepted Aristotle's arguments about the importance of political rule in sustaining mutually beneficial social life. He believed that as God made human beings dependent upon their fellows and tied their perfection to the cultivation of a range of social virtues, humans needed to be directed by a 'general ruling force' that harmonises their interactions to ensure they can live together in the 'unity of peace'. This requirement is satisfied to some degree by all legitimate forms of government, but Aquinas (following Aristotle) argued that rule by a single person is capable of producing the greatest benefit for those subject to it (Aquinas, 1959, pp. 11, 107). Because monarchy places power in one person's hands it can provide unified direction for society and thus avoids the internal dissension and factionalism that often occurs in collective forms of rule. Moreover, Aquinas argued that government by a single person corresponds to a 'natural principle'. In the same way as the heart rules the body, reason rules the soul, bees are ruled by a single bee, and the whole universe is ruled by one God, 'the best form of government in human society is that which is exercised by one person.' This argument by analogy is buttressed by the fruits of human experience. Properly conducted monarchies have proved to be stable and generally beneficial, but where power is shared, society is frequently torn with dissension (ibid., pp. 13, 17–19).

Aquinas' reference to the benefits of monarchical rule reflects the widely held ancient and medieval distinction between kingship and tyranny. Earlier medieval thinkers stressed that tyrannical conduct impugns the moral authority of a ruler. As we shall see in a later chapter, this point could provide the grounds for disobeying, or even resisting, rulers who have become tyrannical (see pp. 237ff). In his treatment of tyranny Aquinas endorsed the conventional view that good rulers serve the common good while tyrants ignore the interests of the community and look to their own private interest. Aquinas claimed, however, that the impact of the improper exercise of monarchical power is unlikely to be as harmful as the corruption of an aristocratic form of government. Aristocratic corruption is invariably accompanied by violent factionalism, which, because of the number of parties or families involved, destroys social peace. Except in very extreme cases, the corruption of monarchy tends to bear on particular individuals, not on the entire community. Aquinas deployed this line of argument to support his general preference for monarchy, but he did not attempt to conceal the evil involved in the tyrannical exercise of monarchical power. To the contrary, he adopted Aristotle's views on the incompatibility of tyranny and virtue. Lacking virtue themselves, tyrants are jealous of the virtue of any of their subjects, and they try to prevent them combining with one another since this will pose a threat to their continued dominance. Moreover, tyrants often sow discord among their subjects so that, fearing one another, they cannot unite against the tyrant. As a result, tyranny undermines the very idea of government. Instead of preserving peace and fostering virtue, it generates strife and debases the population (Aquinas, 1959, p. 19).

Aquinas' treatment of the evils of tyranny – it essentially involves exercises of power in ways that are incompatible with the true function of government – gives a special weight to the virtue of the ruler. The importance that medieval writers ascribed to princely virtue appears very clearly in an extensive body of literature presented as 'mirrors of princes'. Works in this genre were designed to encourage princes to acquire and practice the ideal princely virtues that were portrayed in them. Thus in *The Book of the Body Politic* (1406), Christine de Pizan laid great stress on the duties that princes owe to both God and their subjects, and urged them to follow the biblical example of the good shepherd (Pizan, 1994, p. 16). Princes should exemplify the virtues of love, generosity, human pity, mercy and good nature, and eschew the vices of lechery, bad temper and cruelty (ibid., pp. 23–30, 53–54). Christine likened the sovereign to the 'head' of the political community (the body politic) and treated princely virtue as a precondition for a virtuous state: 'in order to govern the body of the public polity well, it is necessary for the head to be healthy, that is virtuous. Because if it is ill, the whole body will feel it' (ibid., p. 5). Although virtues are universal in the sense that they should be cultivated by all members of the community, Christine made it clear that the distinctive position occupied by the prince means that his practice of virtue differs from that of other members of the body politic: 'the thing that is appropriate for the prince is not appropriate for the simple knight or the noble, and likewise the opposite' (ibid., p. 58).

Christine de Pizan (*c.* 1364–*c.* 1430)

Born in Venice but brought up in France where her father was a court physician, Christine de Pizan is regarded as France's first woman of letters. She wrote a number of works, the best known of which were intended to further the education of women, and was closely engaged with contemporary French politics. Her major political work, *The Book of the Body Politic* (*c.* 1404), was written to guide the 14-year-old heir to the throne during a crisis over succession arrangements.

Key reading: Christine de Pizan, 1994; Adams, 2014.

In the medieval period the stress upon monarchical virtue underwrote theories of government that gave rulers extensive, indeed virtually unlimited, power (Dunbabin, 1991, pp. 483–92). It should be noted, however, that kings' rights were set in a context in which rulers were expected to consult with their subjects, to maintain faith with them and to be ever mindful that while human law might be in their hands, they were always subject to natural law and to the control of God, the direct source of the power of legitimate rulers.

Monarchy in early-modern political theory: Bodin, Hobbes, Filmer and Bossuet

In the later medieval period, the conception of kingship sketched above was combined with ideas that modified the impact of royal supremacy. Increasing weight was given to customary law and to the need for princes to take advice or 'counsel' when exercising a law-making role. The implications of claims concerning 'natural rights' to property, and the need for these to be recognised in a cooperative approach to taxation, strengthened the representative role of estates. These developments were reinforced by the idea that since government relates to the needs of the governed, it could be said to reflect their consent. They thus provided seeds that later grew into theories that challenged the ideas of descending power and monarchical supremacy (ibid., pp. 501–19).

One response to these developments was the formulation of early-modern sovereignty theory. In its essential assumptions, sovereignty theory does not concern itself with who rules. What matters is that there is a sovereign capable of imposing order in human society (see pp. 24ff, 210ff). This point emerges very clearly in Hobbes' writings. While expressing a preference for single-person rule on the (not very plausible) ground that a ruler's appetite for rapacity is likely to be less damaging than the demands of a collective sovereign, Hobbes took a generally cool and detached attitude to the question of whether the one, the few, or the many should rule.

Hobbes' French predecessor, Jean Bodin, also gave a relatively even-handed account of various forms of government, stressing (in line with medieval precedents) that sovereigns are subject to the laws of nature and are charged with furthering the common good (Bodin, n.d., pp. 51–52). Bodin maintained, however, that monarchy is likely to be more stable than either aristocratic or democratic forms of government; the former has a tendency for factionalism, while the latter, because it incorporates the entire population, suffers from their ignorance, passion and gullibility (ibid., pp. 190–200). Bodin's treatment of sovereignty often echoed medieval theories of kingship. An example of this tendency appeared in his attempt to connect sovereignty with the rule of fathers over their families, a strategy that played a central role in Sir Robert Filmer's account of patriarchal monarchy (ibid., pp. 6–17). Between 1630 and 1652 this otherwise obscure English country gentleman produced a trenchant and single-minded defence of monarchy that played an important role in subsequent early-modern thinking on this form of government.

Filmer's political writings were produced in the context of the challenges to single-person rule that occurred before and during the English Civil War. In *Patriarcha* (a work significantly subtitled 'A Defence of the Natural Power of Kings Against the Unnatural Liberty of the People') Filmer made it clear, however, that his arguments were directed not only against proponents of popular government in his own society, but also at thinkers who ascribed natural liberty to human beings and claimed that this entitled them to choose their own form of government (Filmer, 1949, p. 53). In response to this 'plausible and dangerous opinion', Filmer made a case for absolute monarchy. He argued that only this form of government conforms to God's expressed will as conveyed through the Scriptures and reflected in the history of human society (see below pp. 215–16).

Sir Robert Filmer (1588–1653)

Filmer, a country gentleman from Kent, upheld the absolute power of the English crown, and was a virulent critic of what he saw as the dangerous pretensions of Charles I's opponents before and during the English Civil War. During the war he was imprisoned briefly by the parliamentarians and suffered financially as a result of his adherence to the royalist cause. Filmer's principal political work, *Patriarcha*, was written before the Civil War, but was not published until 1680, when it was brought into service to resist attempts to exclude the Catholic Duke of York (subsequently James II) from succession to the English crown.

Filmer treated society and government as natural features of human life, ones that originated in the extension of the principles of family relationships to larger groupings of human beings. He argued that the Biblical account of Adam and Eve was a perpetually binding declaration of God's intention that families and more extensive social groupings should always be subject to the complete, unquestioned control of the eldest males and that this principle was most fully captured in systems of absolute monarchy. By means of these arguments, Filmer sought to present absolute monarchy as the only legitimate form of government and to show that challenges to monarchs, including claims to share in exercising political power, or to judge their conduct, were without foundation.

Appeals to political patriarchal principles were likely to carry weight in a society where male domination was prevalent. It is a measure of the significance of Filmer's work that it prompted Locke to produce a lengthy refutation of it. In conservative circles his work survived Locke's critique and continued to have an appeal until late in the eighteenth century.

Key reading: Cuttica, 2016; Laslett, 1949; Schochet, 1975.

Although he rejected natural liberty, Filmer offered a naturalistic defence of single-person rule that took the biblical account of the creation as the benchmark of what is natural because it is the clearest statement of God's intentions for humanity.

He argued that when God granted the whole world to Adam, he prescribed a divinely ordained model of human government. Adam's dominion over his offspring showed that God intended human beings to be subject to a single ruler. From this starting point, Filmer argued that patriarchal rule, the rule of the eldest male over his family and the rule of descendants of the first father over multitudes of families, is the only legitimate form of political authority. By dividing the world between his sons, Noah created a number of kingdoms in place of the single one that he had inherited from the descendants of Adam, but these states were themselves governed in conformity with the patriarchal principle. In a detailed analysis of post-biblical history, Filmer sought to establish that this principle lies behind *all* legitimate and beneficial systems of government in the ancient and modern worlds (Filmer, 1949, pp. 53–60).

For Filmer, the Scriptures provided proof-positive of the rightness of monarchy: God has taught us 'by natural instinct, signified to us by the Creation and confirmed by His own example, the excellency of monarchy'. This conclusion is confirmed by the fruits of human experience: 'the best order, the greatest strength, the most stability and easiest government are to be found in monarchy, and in no other form of government'. It is also buttressed by the lack of any convincing evidence of alternatives, either in God's expressed intentions or in the experience of humankind. Indeed, much of the burden of Filmer's case for monarchy rests on arguments concerning the biblical illegitimacy, conceptual incoherence and practical dangers of all other forms of rule. Thus in his discussion of the period when the ancient Hebrews lacked a king, Filmer commented that, 'where every man doth what he pleaseth, it may be truly said, there is no government'. Similarly, in his examination of Aristotle's account of types of government, Filmer focused critically on his classifications of aristocracy and democracy. He claimed that monarchy is the only good form of government of which a coherent account can be given, and summoned up the past to confirm his judgement: if 'godliness and honesty' are taken to be the ends of government, then the histories of ancient Rome, Venice and the Low Countries show that these ends can be fulfilled only where political authority is placed in one person's hands (ibid., pp. 84, 86, 189, 196–99).

The Scriptures, history and philosophy therefore concurred in identifying monarchy as *the* form of government; they also established that rule by a single person must conform to a hereditary pattern of transmission. Filmer claimed that legitimate authority descends through the line of the eldest male, a stricture that not only identifies female subordination as God-ordained, but also means that women's inferiority to patriarchs in the family and the state is perpetual. In Filmer's model all humans are born into natural subordination, and while some exercise patriarchal authority as heads of families, only a very few assume complete superiority by inheriting political authority from their fathers. This conception of familial and political power strikes a sharply discordant note in modern Western ears, but to Filmer's contemporaries it corresponded with much of the imagery, language and legal forms of their society (Schochet, 1975). Moreover, his strictures on popular government, and jeremiads on aristocratic interference with monarchical power, and the hazards of mixed government, go a long way towards explaining why Filmer's work found a receptive audience among those who had experienced the turmoil of the Civil War.

Filmer's use of a literal interpretation of the Bible to justify absolute monarchy found an independent parallel in Jacques Bossuet's *Politics drawn from the Very Words of Holy Scripture*. This work, which was commenced before the publication of Filmer's *Patriarcha* but was not published until 1709, was part of a tradition of French political thinking that went back to Bodin. Bossuet utilised the Bible in support of paternal forms of government and claimed that these conform to a divinely ordained model. Unlike Filmer, Bossuet allowed that legitimate governments of this sort can be formed either on the basis of the consent of subjects, or by conquest that was subsequently legitimised by the approval of the conquered subjects. In both cases, however, consent merely confirms the natural pattern of paternal government:

> Men ... saw the image of a kingdom in the union of several families under the leadership of a common father, and ... having found gentleness in that life, brought themselves easily to create societies of families under kings who took the place of fathers.

Bossuet argued that monarchy is the most ancient, common and hence the most natural form of government and he identified it with a number of distinct and unique advantages. It is least likely to suffer from divisions and most conducive to unity, and it is also particularly appropriate when it comes to satisfying the military requirements of the state. Moreover, hereditary (as opposed to elective) monarchy reinforces these advantages. It establishes a natural pattern of perpetuation, encourages the king to care for his state as a patrimony to be transmitted to his male heir, and endows rulers with the dignity that derives from an office that is beyond the reach of contention (Bossuet, 1990, pp. 44, 47–48, 49–51).

As we shall see, the absolutist aspects of Filmer's and Bossuet's positions parallel Hobbes' theory in important respects, but their emphatic and exclusive preference for monarchy harks back to medieval political thinking (see pp. 118–20). In this respect it is significant that in the opening chapter of *Patriarcha,* Filmer portrayed the idea of natural liberty as a 'new' opinion, one that had acquired currency only within the last century. Like medieval thinkers, Filmer identified a divine source for monarchy, and like them he endowed it with a paternal aura. He also related monarchy to the good of the community, understood, as we have seen, in terms of 'holiness and peace' (Filmer, 1949, pp. 53, 103). However, these aspects of Filmer's thought must be placed alongside others that mark a departure from medieval patterns. In the first place, Filmer's patriarchal imagery has more to do with power and constraint than with fatherly affection. When the eighth-century-ruler Alfred the Great of England wished to identify the common strand in his relationship with his subjects, he referred to the love he felt for them all (Nelson, 1991, p. 239). In contrast, the subjects of Filmer's patriarchal ruler are more likely to be identified by the fact that they all owe unquestioning obedience to the king's commands. Secondly, in Filmer's theory, medieval ideas of royal supremacy as a partnership give way to a stress on the unrestrained and all-embracing power of the monarch. Finally, medieval thinkers regarded the power of kings as a direct, unmediated *gift* from God. Filmer, however, thought that kings possess supreme power as a *right* derived from the natural law of patriarchal inheritance; power comes originally from God, but its transmission is mediated through human generation and rulers have a right to it. As we shall see in a subsequent chapter, this point has important implications for subjects' capacity to respond to bad government (see pp. 215–17).

Monarchy in eighteenth- and nineteenth-century political thought: Absolutists, romantics, Maistre and Maurras

Following the 'Glorious Revolution' of 1688–89 the British monarchy developed in a mixed rather than an absolutist direction, and so in some ways Filmer's arguments were overtaken by events. However, aspects of his theory had an impact in the modern period with echoes being heard in late-eighteenth-century accounts of monarchy (Gunn, 1983, p. 171). They can also be seen in the political attitudes of romantically inclined young aristocrats in the 1840s (Francis and Morrow, 1994, p. 175). For the most part however, these Filmerian survivals were peripheral to mainstream political thinking in England. This point can be illustrated by reference to two of the most significant British political thinkers of the eighteenth century: David Hume and Edmund Burke. While the former allowed that monarchy could be an admirable form of government, he rested this judgement on the assumption that the king would govern in a regular and law-bound manner rather than arbitrarily. Provided these conditions were satisfied, Hume thought there was little in principle wrong with absolute monarchy (Hume, 1987, pp. 51–53, 94; Miller, 1981, pp. 145–48). Burke, in contrast, treated monarchy as an aspect of a broadly based aristocratic political culture. Burke's monarch infused warmth and civility into politics, but except in symbolic terms, or as part of a representative structure in which the aristocratic and wealthy have a dominant influence, did not stand at the centre of politics (see pp. 131–33).

On the European continent, ideas of monarchy were closely connected to absolute conceptions of sovereignty. In eighteenth-century France, monarchy was sometimes presented in neo-Filmerian hues, but it was also discussed in terms that he would have deplored. Thus while Denis Diderot (a key figure in the French Enlightenment) allowed that kingly authority was a 'gift of heaven', he traced its legitimate origins to the consent of the governed expressed through a contractual arrangement, and criticised the hereditary transmission of political offices (Diderot, 1992, pp. 7–11, 90–91, 200–201; Rowen, 1980, pp. 133–34). In the German states, some accounts of monarchy utilised notions of natural liberty against which Filmer had railed. It was claimed that having once possessed natural freedom, individuals sought to protect their interests by exchanging freedom for the benefits provided by an enlightened, absolute ruler (Krieger, 1972, pp. 50–71).

In the wake of the French Revolution a number of French and German romantic writers produced accounts of monarchy that responded both to popular republican government and to the enlightened despotism of the eighteenth century. The romantic regeneration of monarchy rested upon a critique of eighteenth-century theories of monarchy that identified a paradoxical connection between the underlying basis of monarchical absolutism and the harsh systems of popular government that had displaced it during the 1790s. It also focused on the spiritually impoverished character of eighteenth-century conceptions of monarchy. Romantics claimed that eighteenth-century political thinkers presented a mechanical conception of the state. Having based their theory on isolated individuals who possessed natural liberty, these writers adopted a narrowly instrumental account of the relationship between rulers and their subjects. Theories of absolute monarchy thus shared common ground with revolutionary doctrines, and could not offer an effective alternative to them because they deprived monarchy of aesthetic and poetic qualities that appealed to the affection and loyalty of ordinary people (Beiser, 1992, pp. 236–39; Morrow, 2011, pp. 55–56; Müller, 1955, p. 153).

In place of these dangerous and uninspiring doctrines, the German Romantics sought to reaffirm ideas of community and interdependence and to identify a distinctive role for monarchy that recaptured many of the images of medieval kingship. They thus stressed that political authority should be endowed with an aura of aesthetically satisfying, psychologically reassuring familial warmth, and they argued that a paternal conception of monarchy would best satisfy these requirements. This feature of romantic political thought is particularly marked in the writings of Novalis, but it appears also in those of Frederick Schlegel. Novalis pictured an idealised royal family made up of a young, pure and devoted couple as the symbol of true monarchy based on faith and love (Beiser, 1992, pp. 264, 272; Novalis, 1996). Schlegel also maintained that monarchs can only be effective if they are presented as objects of veneration (Schlegel, 1964, pp. 122–24). Although German political Romantics paid considerable attention to the aura of monarchy, they claimed that this must be underwritten by constitutional arrangements that endow the monarch with a distinctive and supreme set of political functions. He must be the symbolic and effective centre of a cohesive, organic community, not merely the most powerful force in what Novalis tellingly described as the 'factory state' of eighteenth-century absolutism (Novalis, 1996, p. 45).

One of the key points of romantic conceptions of monarchy is the demand that it must conform to deep-seated human needs. In this respect, romantic political thought has a naturalistic frame of reference, but related this to the historical experiences of a community rather than to the original creative power of God. The idea that monarchy is natural to certain political communities also played an important role in the writings of Joseph de Maistre, a contemporary of the German Romantics. Maistre, however, buttressed his account of monarchy with a general defence of the need for authority in human relationships that was similar in some respects to the position advanced by Filmer. Like Filmer, Maistre argued that hereditary monarchy produces a range of practical benefits that count in its favour and tell against alternatives, particularly those that involve popular rule. For example, in an echo of Bossuet's position, he claimed that hereditary monarchy settles questions of succession and thus puts supreme power beyond the reach of ambition. Single-person rule also provides unity and stability by concentrating power in one pair of hands. Moreover, since Maistre endorsed commonly held assumptions about the partiality and wilfulness of the mass of the population, he thought it important for power to be placed in the hands of a person whose upbringing and lack of private interests minimised the risks involved in any form of human rule. Finally, Maistre argued that the unquestioned supremacy of a single person allows for a degree of relative equality among members of a political community; none could aspire to supremacy and none would feel slighted by, or envious of, the relatively minor distinctions that exist between subjects of an all-powerful monarch (Maistre, 1965, p. 27).

Joseph de Maistre (1753–1821)

Born into a noble family in the Kingdom of Sardinia, Maistre served as a legal official and later as ambassador of the government-in-exile at the Russian imperial court in St Petersburg. In 1817 Maistre returned to Europe, but rapidly became disillusioned with the monarchs whose restoration he had long awaited. Maistre's standing as a critic of the revolution and its ideological basis matches, if it does not surpass, that of Edmund Burke. His major political writings are *Considerations on France* (1796) and *Study of Sovereignty* (first published in 1884).

Key reading: Lebrun, 1988; Wilson, 2011.

While there is no indication that Maistre was ever well-disposed to the changes that occurred in France from 1789, his defence of monarchy was based on experiences of a republican system of government that had become internally authoritarian and externally aggressive. Maistre was a shrewd observer of the bloody course of political events in France, and as a subject of the King of Savoy he suffered great personal hardship when the revolutionary armies invaded his native country. One effect of this experience was to sharpen the belief that monarchy produces real benefits for those who are subject to it. He argued that since monarchy is a system of rule that recognises a natural principle of subordination, it is able to make the exercise of supreme power relatively benign and generally beneficial (ibid., pp. 68–69, 113–19).

By contrast, those who attempt to put ideas of natural liberty into effect were quickly driven to set up systems of rule that are necessarily oppressive because they conflict with natural principles of social and political organisation. In the French context, this development allowed self-interested and rapacious elites to wield unbridled and cruelly exercised power from behind a facade of popular government, legitimated by Rousseau's idea of the 'general will' (see pp. 31–32).

Although Maistre wished to see the Bourbons restored to the French throne, his conception of monarchy was not that of the enlightened absolutism of the eighteenth century. The same general point may be made of the last significant defence of monarchy in Western political thought. This account was produced by Charles Maurras, a prominent figure in French right-wing politics in the late nineteenth and early twentieth centuries (see p. 37). Like Maistre, Maurras argued that a properly constituted monarchy is far less oppressive than republican forms of government, and like Maistre also, his views on this issue were closely related to the historical tradition and recent experiences of France. Maurras did not presume to make universally applicable statements about forms of government, but he thought that sociability and hierarchy are prevailing features of *all* forms of human life.

Maurras's motto was 'Authority at the top, liberty below'. He argued that these two conditions can be satisfied by monarchy because it takes a national focus and only utilises supreme power directly for national purposes. In this respect it is quite different from republicanism, a system of government in which electoral processes and the demands of parliament made local and private interests directly and intrusively subject to the power of central government (Maurras, 1971a, pp. 220–21). Thus for Maurras a free republic was, paradoxically, more harmful to liberty than other forms of government. 'Liberty is a right under the republic, but only a right: under the sovereignty of the royal throne, liberties will relate to actual practice – certain, real, tangible, matters of fact.' In democratic regimes government is the temporary but all-effective slave of those who control a majority in parliament; under monarchy it is a disinterested source of authority and control. A monarchical state thus protects liberties in general rather than subjecting them to the control of sectional interests who attain their freedom at the expense of the rest of the population (ibid., pp. 230, 220–21, 231, 225).

These advantages could presumably be produced by any form of single-person rule, but Maurras identified them particularly with the French monarchy. The benefits of rule by a single person were enhanced by the long-established ties that bound the French people to their historical royal family. Like Edmund Burke, Maurras regarded historical experience as a form of 'second nature'; it is so ingrained in the psyche of members of the community that it forms the mental and emotional furniture of their minds. From this perspective, the connection between the French people and their royal family reinforced the natural character of the traditional social and political hierarchy (ibid., pp. 235–36). When writing of the French royal family (known in modern times as the 'House of Bourbon'), Maurras referred to it by an ancient designation as the 'House of Capet' (ibid., p. 237). This archaic language reflects his tendency to think of monarchy in medieval rather than modern terms, a point that is underlined by the contrast he drew between the leniency of traditional royal rule and the intrusively centralising aspirations of late-seventeenth- and early-eighteenth-century monarchs.

Despite Maurras's close self-identification with the exiled Bourbons, his ideas were not endorsed by the royalist mainstream and he became disillusioned at the prospects of restoring traditional monarchy. In the later stages of his life, Maurras supported Marshall Pétain, the head of the 'Vichy' regime established in the southern part of France by the triumphant ruler of the German Reich. At that time Pétain seemed the only hope of saving the historical and authoritarian France to which Maurras was committed. This shift in allegiance was spurred by desperation, but in some respects it was a fittingly delusional end to monarchical thinking in the Western tradition. Monarchy persists in a number of European countries and lingers fitfully in some former colonies. However, while crowned heads play symbolic roles within these states, they can hardly be said to rule.

Presidents and dictators in modern political theory: Weber, Hitler

---

Adolf Hitler (1889–1945)

Hitler, the leader of the National Socialist movement in Germany, wielded complete power as *Fuehrer* from 1933 until the collapse of his regime at the end of the Second World War. His political ideas (Hitler can hardly be said to have advanced a political philosophy) were propagated in *Mein Kampf* (My Struggle) (1925).

Key reading: Brooker, 1991.

When the imperial German monarchy collapsed at the end of the First World War Germany became a democratic federation. In some quarters this move was thought to pose challenges that could only be met by incorporating an element of single-person rule within the new republican regime. Thus in 'The President of the Reich' (1919), the eminent economist and sociologist Max Weber made a case for a popularly elected president to counteract the fragmenting tendencies resulting from the power of state governments in the federation and the impact of proportional representation on the German national assembly or *Reichstag*. Under the existing constitutional arrangements parliament alone was not a sufficient guarantee for democratic rule: 'today … all constitutional proposals have succumbed to crude blind faith in the infallibility and omnipotence of the majority – of the majority in parliament, that is, not the majority of the people' (Weber, 1994, p. 307). In these circumstances, it was necessary for the will of the people to be embodied in a president who was elected by them, rather than being chosen by the majority in parliament. It was, Weber argued, '*essential* for us to create a *head of state* resting *unquestionably on the will of the whole people,* without the intercession of intermediaries' (ibid., p. 304). He claimed that:

> A popularly elected president, as the head of the executive, of official patronage, and as the possessor of a delaying veto and the power to dissolve parliament and to consult the people, is the palladium of genuine democracy, which does not mean impotent self-abandonment to cliques but subordination to leaders one has chosen for oneself (ibid., p. 308).

The perceived need for personal leadership in modern, non-monarchical states that Weber identified has been found in other forms of contemporary political thinking. Thus in the theories of 'third world democracy' that are discussed in a later chapter, claims about the pivotal role of single-party government in guiding societies away from the trammels of colonial rule frequently include references to the need for these parties to be led by strong, charismatic figures who through their role in struggles for independence epitomise the aspirations of the community forged through the liberation processes (see pp. 158–60). In other settings, theocratic regimes that are legitimated by commitment to Islamic values may reserve a special place in the political system for a figure whose claims to supreme influence is based upon religious authority (see p. 298). While these regimes place a particular emphasis on leadership by individuals, they do not necessarily see this as an alternative to systems of government in which the population at large participate. In this respect, they differ significantly from the forms of modern dictatorship that played such a devastating role in the twentieth century.

Unlike the dictators of republican Rome, who were installed in power in order to stave off crises, most modern dictators aim for lifetime tenure of office and seek to determine who will succeed them. While these rulers have supremacy in the state, they are often identified with a movement and/or mass party, or with a segment of an existing elite, most commonly the military. Historically, the most important example of this form of rule occurred in Germany between 1932 and 1945 under Adolf Hitler, head of state and leader of the National Socialist Party. This case is particularly significant because, while many effective dictators have had to operate within and justify themselves by reference to systems of government that are nominally based on a non-dictatorial principle, Hitler's domination of German politics was set in a state that was overtly based on personal leadership. In contrast, Hitler's Italian contemporary, Benito Mussolini, held the title of chief of government in Italy, but the fascist regime over which he presided was set within the framework of a constitutional monarchy. Similarly, many South American dictators have been presidents of their republics, or have headed supposedly stop-gap administrations that are dominated by the military but connected to republican constitutions by incorporating a few non-military figures.

While Weber saw a leader chosen by the people as essential to the maintenance of democratic government, the conception of single-person rule that emerged in Germany in the early 1930s was premised upon the intractable difficulties produced by parliamentary democracy. Of course, some theories of monarchy rely heavily on judgements concerning the ills of popular government, but the case of modern dictatorship is rather different. These regimes invariably developed in reaction to practical experience of modern, parliamentary democracy, and their rationale is closely bound up with this experience. In particular, theories of modern dictatorship involve a two-pronged attack on democratic government, one directed at parliamentarianism, the other reflecting a general contempt for ordinary citizens. These themes are clearly apparent in Hitler's *Mein Kampf.* In this work, written before Hitler came to power, observations on the decadence of parliamentary politics and the insipid, self-interested character of conventional politicians, are invariably coupled with references to what Hitler called the 'unshakeable stupidity of the voting citizenry'. These criticisms are directed particularly at the politics of the pre-war Austro-Hungarian constitutional monarchy and the post-war Weimar Republic in Germany (Hitler, 1969, pp. 339–40).

Hitler promoted a conception of government based on the personal responsibility of the leader and the total obedience of the rest of the community to him. The *fuehrerprinzip* ('leadership principle') determines how supreme power should be located, but it was also a general principle of social and political organisation that required all levels of society to be subject to the oversight of subordinate leaders who regulate distinct spheres of political, social or economic activity (Brooker, 1985, p. 60). Neither the supreme leader nor his subordinates owe their position to success in conventional electoral competitions. In response to the question 'Does anyone believe that the progress of this world springs from the mind of majorities and not from the brains of individuals?' Hitler stressed the primacy of struggle in elite selection and depreciated the bravery and sagacity of ordinary citizens (Hitler, 1969, pp. 465–66, 78–81).

The *fuehrerprinzip* involves a commitment to a radical elitism that makes the position of the *Fuehrer* a consequence of proven capacity to further the interests of the German race. This aspect of Nazi ideology reflects a lurking animus towards the existing upper classes and the intelligentsia. Elitism of this kind signalled the non-traditional nature of Hitler's conception of single-person rule, a feature of his political thinking that was also apparent in his understanding of the relationship between the leader and the masses. Although he rejected conventional notions of democratic representation, Hitler claimed to have identified a 'truly Germanic democracy' in which the leader is elected by the masses but then assumes full, perpetual personal responsibility for the state. He insisted, however, that the 'genius' of the leader is not actually discovered through the electoral process. To the contrary, those capable of assuming supreme power establish a direct relationship with the population through the force of their personality conveyed through public performances. As a result of his interaction with the masses at public meetings, the putative leader transforms 'philosophy' into a 'tightly organised political community of faith and struggle, unified in spirit and will'. This transformation can only be brought about by the spoken word, 'the power which has always started rolling the greatest religious and political avalanches in history' (ibid., 1969, pp. 392, 83, 346, 98). Elections confirm mass recognition and play no further role after the leader has secured control of the state.

This account of the leader's succession to power illustrates one of the distinctive features of modern dictatorship. Although this form of rule is a product of the reaction against the experience of modern parliamentary democracy, it nevertheless incorporates aspects of modern political culture. While the relationship between the leader and the people is held to be a 'Germanic' one based on 'faith, honour and care' (Brooker, 1985, p. 56; Neumann, 1944, p. 342), these echoes of medieval kingship do not bridge the gap between monarchical and dictatorial conceptions of single-person rule. The leader's legitimacy springs from his role in relation to 'the race', not to universal values. Moreover, he elevates himself to a dominant position in the minds of the population and is then elevated to a position of unquestioned and unquestionable supremacy through the modern (but self-terminating) mechanism of mass election.

Conclusion

While it would be seriously misleading to conflate monarchical, theocratic and dictatorial theories of government, these accounts of the way in which power should be allocated share certain common and distinctive features. In the first place, they all assume that ability and/or virtue of a kind required by rulers is found only in a few individuals. A corollary of this claim is an underlying assumption of the general political incapacity of the vast bulk of humanity. Furthermore, proponents of single-person rule assume that the unity of a community must be created by and symbolised in a single, personal head of state. An organic conception of the state is not the sole preserve of those who endorse rule by a single person, but theories of this kind give the organic analogy a peculiarly literal interpretation. Like the human organism, the state must have a head who controls and directs the actions of its members. Finally, it seems clear that these conceptions of government are more usually related to a belief that the state exists for the purposes of virtue or order, rather than having freedom or individual happiness as its end.

THE RULE OF THE FEW

7

In the previous chapter it was noted that some accounts of monarchy set that form of single-person rule in the context of a system of social and political authority in which the 'aristocracy' plays an important role. This conception of aristocracy is considered in some detail in the present chapter. However, Aristotle's characterisation of aristocracy as 'the rule of the few who are the best' points to a form of government which is not part of monarchy and does not require that aristocrats are of 'noble' birth. Aristocracy in this sense played an important role in ancient political thought, and had some currency in the nineteenth and twentieth centuries.

Arguments in favour of allocating exclusive or supreme power to the few generally rest on assumptions about the limited moral and/or intellectual capacity of ordinary members of the population. It is claimed that the attributes necessary to ensure good and effective rule are restricted to relatively narrow sections of the population, and that only those who possess them should play a leading role in government. The attributes in question are moral and intellectual, although in some cases they also relate to cultural values that are acquired through membership of hereditary elites. Hereditary claims to rule are the hallmark of conventional conceptions of aristocracy as an essential component of monarchy. Whether the claims of an elite are hereditary or based on alleged moral and intellectual pre-eminence, rule by the few is only legitimate when it benefits the whole community, not just those who rule.

This chapter presents accounts of the more or less pure forms of elite rule promoted by Plato and Aristotle. In these theories the stress is upon moral and intellectual excellence, although in Aristotle's case notions of cultural superiority also play a role. Classical accounts of rule by the few can be contrasted with the more conventional accounts of aristocracy developed by medieval, early-modern and modern theorists. Although these theorists often referred to classical sources, many of them emphasised the hereditary basis of aristocratic government. Discussions of aristocracy usually focus on its internal benefits but in the late eighteenth century the Anglo-Irish writer Edmund Burke also claimed that shared aristocratic values had been the basis of a beneficial European international order. The chapter concludes with a discussion of modern, non-aristocratic ideas produced by writers who promoted rule by cultural, intellectual and/or party elites.

The rule of the few in ancient political theory: Plato and Aristotle

Plato's guardians clearly exemplify rule by the few: even though they comprise a small section of the total population of the state, they exercise complete control over the ideal republic. Members of this class are distinguished by their knowledge of and their attachment to ultimate goodness. Their selection, training and intensive and prolonged education are designed to ensure that the state is ruled by its 'best' citizens, those with the intellectual, moral and temperamental qualities necessary to determine the good and pursue it single-mindedly. Plato's ideal state was just in a double sense. It is right and just that the most rational element rules the less rational, and where this happens political power will be exercised for the good of the whole community. The advantages of rule by the few are highlighted by Plato's frequent pejorative references to popular rule. Democracies are dominated by the least rational members of the population, and disfigured by their inevitable tendency to produce a narrowly selfish form of class rule that ends up in chaos or tyranny (see pp. 20–21).

In the *Republic* Plato did not offer an overt defence of pure aristocracy but a number of aspects of his account point to the advantages of collective rather than single-person rule. One of the perils lurking below the surface of the ideal state is the corruption of those who wield supreme power. If the guardians really possess the qualities that Plato ascribed to them, corruption would seem to be impossible. However, he was not overly sanguine about this outcome and suggests that collective elite rule is a way of establishing a series of checks carried out *by* members of the guardian class *upon* each other. Perhaps as a way of lessening the potentially insidious features of this system, Plato stressed that the guardians form a special kind of 'family', something that is made easier by their lack of natural familial relationships and their communal way of life (Plato, 1970, pp. 220–22). An advantage of family feeling among the guardians is that Plato thought that it would encourage a unified commitment to the ethos of this class, a means of assurance and support that would not be available to a single ruler, however wise and good he might be.

Although Plato's guardians form an 'aristocracy' in Aristotle's sense of the term, 'meritocracy' is perhaps a more appropriate designation of this class since their right to rule is deliberately stripped of any of the conventional connotations of aristocracy. Their status is strictly 'achieved' rather than 'ascribed'. Plato was vague about many of the details, but the general thrust of his argument is that the guardians should be drawn from all classes, and that their children will not become guardians if they fail to come up to scratch. Moreover, rulers have no mundane privileges as a consequence of their position in the state. To the contrary, they do not possess property or enjoy conventional family life. In response to a criticism that rulers living under these conditions will not be happy, Plato upholds his ascetic ideal by retorting that the state does not exist for the benefit of its rulers; their way of life is justified by the need to avoid private interests that may corrupt them or distract their attention from the pursuit of goodness. In any case, goodness entails a degree of ultimate satisfaction that cannot be equated with the alluring but, according to Plato, debasing creature comforts that are usually associated with 'happiness' (ibid., pp. 163–65).

The strict asceticism that Plato saw as part of rule by the few in the *Republic* is modified in *The Laws*, where he dealt with a second-best state designed to cope with a lack of supreme virtue among rulers. This state is to be structured and regulated by a system of law that will compensate for the deficiencies of its members. However, in order to apply these laws and ensure that they are subject to periodic revision, Plato set up an elaborate system of judicial and reviewing councils. Some of these bodies are to be filled by members of the ordinary population; others will be staffed by the more virtuous members of the community. Plato thought that the political structure laid down in *The Laws* would avoid the dangers of democracy on the one hand and monarchy on the other by combining aristocratic and democratic elements. The former would result from a system of open election, the latter from the use of a mechanism known as the 'lot'. The Greeks' understanding of the implications of selection through election differed significantly from that associated with modern systems of democratic government. For the Greeks, election favoured the upper classes because it meant that judgements of worth and social prestige could play a role in selection procedures. In contrast the lot, essentially a blind draw, or lottery, identified officeholders through a process of chance. Its outcomes were not influenced by the particular qualities of candidates; indeed, the laws of probability would ensure that the numerically superior lower classes would dominate assemblies or offices selected by this method. The fact that Plato included a system of election within his second-best state provided for the incorporation of an aristocratic element in the constitution. However, since all citizens would be eligible for office, the system was based upon a meritocratic, rather than a hereditary, conception of aristocracy (Klosko, 1986, pp. 211–25; Plato, 1980, pp. 223–45).

Aristotle's *Politics* presents an account of rule by the few that embraces some of the features conventionally associated with 'aristocracy'. Aristocracy exists where the best men rule in the common interest, but Aristotle assumed that in other than ideal states the best will be only a small section of the population and noted that in these 'so-called aristocracies', their claims are based on relative rather than absolute virtue. These aristocrats, or 'nobles' as Aristotle often called them, are markedly superior to other members of the community but have not attained true virtue. One consequence of their imperfect virtue is that while they play a central role in the state, their power is not absolute and is placed within a variety of mixed constitutional forms. These arrangements combine virtue with wealth, numbers, free status or some combination of these, thus acknowledging the limited degree of virtue among even 'the best', and the consequent need to recognise the weight of other claims derived from wealth, freedom or numbers. In addition, since 'the best' are only relatively so, it is important to guard against the corrupt use of power and the appearance of 'oligarchy', a system of rule in which the few, usually economically dominant, rule in their own interest rather than in the interest of the whole community (Aristotle, 1958, pp. 117, 131–32, 204–205).

Setting a pattern that was to be common in subsequent treatments of aristocracy, Aristotle assumed that the virtues of 'so-called' aristocrats are related to their unassuming possession of wealth, to education and to their cultural and intellectual milieu. This assumption corresponds to the treatment of virtue in Aristotle's *Ethics*. Although he identified the contemplative life with true virtue, he made it clear that this end is too exalted for most human beings, and concentrated instead on a range of virtues appropriate to ordinary social and political life. The moral virtues include 'courage' (especially as applied to military action), 'justice' (honesty in business dealings), 'liberality' (generosity to one's friends and the *polis*), 'magnanimity' (a proper sense of self-worth), 'good temper' and 'temperance' (Aristotle, 1975, pp. 115aff; Mulgan, 1977, p. 4). These qualities are commonly identified with aristocratic culture.

In addition to the imperfect but nevertheless beneficial form of so-called aristocracy, Aristotle discussed an ideal form. In a genuine aristocracy, political power is assigned to the truly virtuous, who rule in the common interest and are treated as belonging to an aristocratic community. That is, Aristotle equated the citizen body with those who are both absolutely and relatively fit to rule – they are both virtuous and equal in virtue with their fellow citizens – and consigned those whose birth (slaves), gender (women) or occupations (agricultural, commercial, unskilled) was incompatible with moral virtue to an underclass who are necessary for the realisation of the ends of the state but are not true members of it. By dividing the aristocratic citizen body into those who fight (the young) and those who rule, however, Aristotle undermined his stipulation that the state is ideally a union of equals, sharing the function of ruling and being ruled. Whatever the coherence of this distinction, it means that within the context of an aristocratic community Aristotle's conception of an ideal state entailed rule by all *full* members of the community who were, nevertheless, a small minority of the total population. As with Aristotle's account of so-called aristocracy, his treatment of its ideal form incorporates prejudices based on age, birth, gender and class that are conventionally associated with aristocratic rule (Aristotle, 1958, pp. 279–306).

Medieval and early-modern conceptions of aristocracy: Aquinas, Machiavelli and Harrington

Aristotle's discussion of an aristocracy in mixed government had an important influence on subsequent political thought. For example, the Roman thinker Cicero identified an aristocratic component within the republican constitution of Rome, assigning this role to the senatorial class to whom he ascribed many of the cultural and intellectual qualities that Aristotle associated with so-called aristocracies. For medieval writers, however, government by the few was only one element in a broader conception of essentially monarchical rule (see pp. 114–17). In early medieval Europe, kings were held to have been endowed with supreme power by God, but this power formed the basis of a complex web of interactions and responsibilities, the most immediately important of which were those embodying the 'faith' that bound a king to his closest and most important subjects. These people were the king's servants, and their proximity to the throne, together with their economic, cultural and military importance, gave them a distinctive role in the state. They formed what was, in effect, an aristocratic class within a mixed government.

In practical terms the relationship between the king and his most powerful subjects was a consequence of the emergence of feudalism in European states, but with the rediscovery of Aristotle's writings in the thirteenth century these relationships could be described in ways that consciously echoed the political theory of the ancients. Thus Aquinas argued that the danger of tyranny is greater in pure aristocracy than in monarchy because, when a number of people rule, conflict is more likely, and this often tempts members of the ruling group to utilise political power for their own selfish purposes. He credited mixed government with forestalling this threat and the less immediate one presented by monarchy. This solution recalls Aristotle's most practical form of government, but it fuses monarchy, aristocracy and democracy rather than democracy and oligarchy. Aristocratic power – that is, 'government by the best elements, in which a few hold office according to virtue' – is justified by the social dominance, wealth and moral attributes of its members. Like the monarch, aristocrats derive their legitimacy from their virtues, and while these are not as exalted as those expected of good kings, they are nevertheless significant. 'The best form of constitution ... results from a judicious admixture of the *kingdom,* in that there is one person at the head of it; of *aristocracy* in that many participate in government according to virtue; and of *democracy* or popular rule, in that rulers may be elected from the people and the whole population has the right of electing its rulers' (Aquinas, 1959, p. 149). The fact that members of the aristocracy are usually wealthy and that their position is based on birth provides a further link between medieval conceptions of the role of the few and that found in Aristotle's writings.

The idea that aristocracy should sit within the framework of monarchy to provide mixed government persisted into the early-modern period. During that time, however, some thinkers saw aristocracy as a key element in a republic. This perspective on the political role of the virtuous few is most closely identified with the city states of Renaissance Italy, but it was echoed in seventeenth-century English and eighteenth-century American political thought.

In the second half of the fifteenth century a number of Florentine writers drew upon an idealised, indeed in some ways mythical, picture of the republican *and* aristocratic constitution of Venice in order to assert claims to influence by wealthy Florentines who resented the dominant power wielded by the semi-princely house of Medici. Harking back to classical discussions, these writers ascribed to 'the few' the role of guardians of the state, who would fill important offices on behalf of the population and thus use their virtues in the service of the common good (Pocock, 1975, pp. 100–103, 185–86). In this case the few are closely integrated with the life of the city state. Machiavelli emphasised this point by observing that while aristocracies of this kind are consistent with long-lived but territorially non-aggressive republics, the existence of landed aristocracies or 'gentry' is generally fatal to all forms of republic (Machiavelli, 1975, vol. i, pp. 220–22, 335).

James Harrington (1611–77)

Harrington, an attendant to Charles I in 1647, was involved in republican politics in the years of the Cromwellian protectorate. His major political work, *Oceana* (1656), has been seen as an important contribution to the anglicisation of civic republican ideas derived from Renaissance Italy. He thus applied ideas of natural aristocracy to an English context and considered the impact of the decline of feudal landholdings on the distribution of political power within the community.

Key reading: Davis, 1981; Harrington, 1992.

Partly as a result of the influence of Italian models, ideas of aristocratic republicanism were used in seventeenth-century England and eighteenth-century America when alternatives were being sought for discredited conceptions of monarchical government. In these settings, the focus was on 'natural' aristocracy; that is, claims to rule were based on a general recognition of natural superiority. Since monarchy was no longer acceptable, neither was the hereditary determination of elite status. Leaders are still required, but these should be selected by the people, whose role is to recognise the capacities of 'natural aristocrats' and to defer to them. These leaders possess extensive property, education and leisure, but such attributes are not qualifications for office; to the contrary, they are entitled to aristocratic standing because of their 'natural superiority of talent' (Pocock, 1975, pp. 414, 515–17). Thus the mid-seventeenth-century English writer James Harrington described the nobility of his ideal state of 'Oceana' as having

> nothing else but their education and their leisure for the public, furnished by their ease and competent riches, and their intrinsic value which, according as it comes to hold weight in the judgement or suffrage of the people, is their only way to honour and preferment (Harrington, 1992, p. 141).

Hereditary aristocracy in modern political theory: Burke, Coleridge, Chateaubriand and Constant

While 'the few' played a central role in early-modern conceptions of republican government, they were also important in late-eighteenth- and early-nineteenth-century accounts of constitutional monarchy. This form of government is not 'aristocratic' in any strict sense because sovereignty is lodged either in the monarch or in the 'king in parliament', that is, in the king in association with representative bodies. The distinctive character of this position is highlighted by Edmund Burke's strictures on the 'despotism of aristocracy' (Burke, 1834, vol. i, p. 130). Like some other late-eighteenth- and early-nineteenth-century writers, Burke treated aristocracy as a necessary feature of constitutional monarchy, not as a form of pure government.

Edmund Burke (1729–97)

Burke, a native of Ireland, made a career in English politics as an intellectual man-of-business for a leading faction of the Whig Party. He played an important role in parliament and in a number of administrations from the mid-1760s until the 1790s. Burke was a famous orator and published many of his speeches. He also wrote a number of important political pamphlets, including *Reflections on the Revolution in France* (1791), a work that attacked French revolutionaries and their English sympathisers and resulted in a breach between Burke and leading members of his party. Although Burke did not deny that humans may once have had natural rights he argued that these claims had no force in long-established communities such as Britain and France. In political society, rights derived from law, a system of regulation that had evolved out of a long series of only very partially reflective practice. Like other customs of which it formed a part, it related closely and productively with the distinctive social, cultural and religious character of the community. Burke argued that appeals to natural rights and attempts to use them as the basis for constructing new systems of political authority neglected the experience of past generations, threatened the stability of the community and deprived its members of the benefits of social life. When applied to Britain and France, this perspective gave rise to a conservative theory of politics that gave priority to established institutions and to the role of traditional, largely aristocratic, elites.

Key reading: Dwan and Insole, 2012; Garnett, 2018; Hampsher-Monk, 1987.

Burke claimed that the aristocracy made two distinct but related contributions to constitutional monarchy. In the first place, because hereditary aristocrats have been among the richest members of their society and are particularly well-endowed with landed wealth, they exert an important influence in societies where wealth and political power are closely correlated. Secondly, and more importantly, it was claimed that the influence ascribed to members of this class was justified because of the critical role they played in a generally beneficial, but hierarchical social and political culture shaped by sharp material inequalities that prevailed in late-eighteenth- and early-nineteenth-century European states. Before they were disrupted by the French Revolution, these governments had ensured stability, provided general security of property and encouraged commerce and material progression. It was argued that they could play a similar role in the post-revolutionary world when monarchies were re-established in a number of European states.

Burke's response to the Revolution indicates that among the significant advantages of an aristocratic political culture was its capacity to insulate government from the direct influence of an invariably ignorant and often blindly and destructively self-interested populace and from threats posed by dangerously ambitious adventurers from other social classes. In addition to these merely negative advantages, however, Burke ascribed a number of important positive attributes to aristocracy. To some extent these have to do with ability and probity, with what might be called 'political virtue', but Burke's defence of the predominant social and political influence of 'the few' extended beyond an exclusively meritocratic standpoint.

The breadth of Burke's conception of the benefits of aristocratic government is apparent in his treatment of the hereditary basis of European aristocracy. He claimed that because aristocratic influence and wealth are transmitted through genealogical inheritance the social and political structure is endowed with a 'natural' aspect. Moreover, by connecting the past with the future, the hereditary principle provides the community with a sense of historical and cultural identity. Human beings are not alone in the world but face its adversities clothed in a reassuring 'cloak of custom'. In addition to these symbolic but psychologically valuable consequences of hereditary aristocracy, Burke claimed that the connection between aristocracy and large, stable landholdings encourages respect for property of all kinds, with the holdings of the aristocracy forming 'ramparts' that protect other forms of property within the state (Burke, 1969, p. 140). Finally, Burke associated aristocracy with 'manners', that is, with ideas of 'civility', a system of cultural ethics that modifies the generally beneficial but potentially disruptive pursuit of economic self-interest. Aristocratic influence thus complements that of religion. Both religion and aristocracy embody values that safeguard society without preventing progression built on the inheritance of the past (Pocock, 1985, pp. 193–212). At the same time, however, the cultural ethics of aristocracy provide society with less immediately practical but nevertheless significant benefits. In Burke's writings, as in those of the German Romantics, monarchs are endowed with an aura of warmth and grace that underwrites their political position (see p. 139). This concern with tone is also applied to the aristocracy. As Burke put it, 'nobility is a graceful ornament to the civil society. It is the Corinthian capital of polished society' (Burke, 1969, p. 245).

In his last political work, *Letters on a Regicide Peace*, Burke portrayed pre-revolutionary Europe as a community of states, a 'commonwealth', whose international relations were underpinned by a common monarcho-aristocratic culture. This culture, apparent in the 'similitude … of religion, laws and manners and local establishments', made Europe 'virtually one state having the same basis of general law, with some diversity of provincial custom' (Burke, 1834, II, p. 299). Burke's characterisation qualified earlier statements of national particularity and gave prominence to Roman law as a common source of the public and private law of European monarchies (Hampsher-Monk, 2014, pp. xxxv–xvi). It was not, however, inconsistent with it. Pan-European culture transcended and infused distinct national histories and languages without abolishing them. Burke claimed that shared culture even made differences of religious profession relatively insignificant: 'The nations of Europe have had the very same Christian religion, agreeing in the fundamental parts, varying a little in the ceremonies and in the subordinate doctrines' (Burke, 1834, II, p. 299).

Burke's reference to 'similitude … of manners' was particularly important for the relationship between rulers. He used this term to refer to values that beneficially underpinned social interaction by moderating the impact of animal passions, material self-interest and physical necessity by softer sensibilities derived from fine arts, belle letters, religion and other 'civilising' tendencies in 'advanced' societies. In *Reflections* Burke stressed the role that manners played in easing and smoothing the relationship between classes in the state, thereby ensuring that the competitive severities of commercial society did not undermine a sense of common identity and shared interest in sharply unequal societies. In the *Letters* he also argued that the cultural and social values shared by social and governmental elites of eighteenth-century European states meant that they pursued their interests on a basis of trust and mutual understanding. This ethos made diplomacy possible, limited strategic ambitions to objectives that did not threaten the survival of other international actors, and concluded wars on terms that were consistent with the idea of Europe as a 'commonwealth'. Burke identified a number of central features of the revolutionaries' programme that were fatal to the monarcho-aristocratic culture of the commonwealth of Europe directly. They advanced the 'regicidal' principle of popular sovereignty which entailed that by 'a fixed law of nature, and a fundamental right of man, … all government, not being a democracy is an usurpation. That all kings … are usurpers; and for being kings may and ought to be put to death, with their wives, families, and adherents.' They established 'Jacobinism', that is, the forced redistribution of the estates of lawful proprietors, as the basis of society, and atheism as the basis of the state. They introduced a counter-culture of revolutionary manners that reflected their 'determined hostility to the human race' (Burke, 1834, II, p. 296).

Burke had focused primarily on the domestic dimensions of this challenge in the *Reflections*. In *Letters on a Regicide Peace* he considered the threat that Jacobinism posed to the international relations of Europe. Having initially precipitated a civil war at home, the Jacobins were embarking on a civil war against the powers of Europe collectively and, indeed, all humanity: 'the faction in France … assumed a form, … adopted a body of principles and maxims, and … regularly and systematically acted on them, by which she virtually … put herself in a posture, which was itself a declaration of war against mankind' (ibid., p. 303). Burke denounced the original revolutionaries and their successors as 'the evil spirit that possesses the body of France' and attributed to them diabolical powers that were infinitely more of a threat to the rest of Europe than monarchical France had ever been (ibid., pp. 305–06). These powers reflected the supernatural energy of 'desolating activity' (ibid., p. 306) and their unprecedented aggression: 'It is a war between the partisans of ancient, civil, moral, and political order of Europe, against a sect of fanatical atheists which means to change them all. It is not France extending a foreign empire over other nations: it is a sect aiming at universal empire, and beginning with the conquest of France' (ibid., p. 307). This sect was conducting a war of annihilation that was fundamentally different from the limited conflicts which characterised the interstate relations of the eighteenth-century European 'commonwealth'.

While Burke treated the influence of aristocracy and religion as parts of the same political and social culture, an interesting and influential alternative position was developed by a younger contemporary, the poet and philosopher Samuel Taylor Coleridge. Like Burke, Coleridge placed weight upon the moderating influences of the non-material aspects of aristocracy – the 'delicate superstition of ancestry' may to some degree 'counteract the grosser superstition of wealth' – but he argued that in a well-balanced state political influence derived from both ancestry and wealth must be subjected to humanising influences embodied in philosophical and clerical elites, or a 'clerisy'. The 'clerisy' are an independent section of society made up of clergymen of the Church of England and members of other professions educated in the universities. They are charged with fostering intellectual and moral values and ensuring that these are brought to bear on those who exercise political and social power (Coleridge, 1990, pp. 62, 172–95).

The basis of Coleridge's conception of 'clerisy' lay in his distinctive understanding of the intellectual requirements of Christianity, but this approach to politics has appeared in a number of forms in the history of political thought. As we shall see, J. S. Mill stressed the importance of secular elites in democratic societies. The idea of the clerisy also has a parallel in Islamic political thought. For example, in the reform of the Iranian state that was embodied in the constitution of 1906–7, religious leaders were assigned a corrective and monitorial role over those who held political office. In light of Coleridge's insistence that a clerisy is necessary to infuse human values into the political system, it is interesting to note that in Iran those who derived their moral authority from their knowledge of divine law (*sharia*) were seen as having a special responsibility for the matters of social justice specified in that body of law (Akhavi, 1990, pp. 15–16).

Burke's account of the role of aristocracy was produced in response to what he saw as the desecration of aristocratic monarchy by the French revolutionaries. Similar accounts of the role of the aristocracy appeared in the works of post-revolutionary writers in France. These theorists accepted many of the consequences of the revolution and attempted to forge a new image of constitutional monarchy for the post-revolutionary age. Thus both François Chateaubriand, a conservative but non-reactionary figure in restoration politics, and the liberal writer Benjamin Constant justified the retention of an aristocratic element in the restored monarchy after 1815.

Chateaubriand was intensely critical of the pseudo-aristocracy created by the Emperor Napoleon and argued that the restoration of the Bourbons required the restoration of a genuine aristocracy in France. It was necessary, he argued, to re-establish '*aristocratic families*' as 'barriers and safeguards of the throne'. Such families would provide a setting in which to place a monarch who symbolised

> that tradition of ancient honour, that delicacy of sentiment, that contempt of fortune, that generous spirit, that faith, that fidelity which we so much need, and which are the most distinctive virtues of a *gentleman*, and the most necessary ornaments of a state (Chateaubriand, 1816, p. 231).

In addition, however, Chateaubriand stressed that the influence and wealth of an aristocracy must be embodied in the chamber of peers if it is to balance the democratic influences represented in the elected chamber of deputies (ibid., p. 30). For Chateaubriand, therefore, aristocracy was an essential part of a new form of constitutional monarchy.

This view was endorsed from a liberal perspective by Benjamin Constant, who argued that a hereditary aristocracy with its own chamber in parliament is necessary to sustain a constitutional monarchy. An aristocracy of this kind makes *hereditary* monarchy less extraordinary. Hereditary pre-eminence ensures that a group within the population has high social status and that its members are wise and virtuous. Constant saw these qualities as underwriting a beneficial system of government that combines traditional notions of hereditary rule with the modern demand that states are based on the principle of popular sovereignty. Moreover, since hereditary aristocracy is independent of both the crown and the people, it forms an intermediary between the monarch and a popularly elected assembly, one that is capable of safeguarding the interests and rights of both these other elements in the constitution (Constant, 1988, pp. 198–99).

These justifications of aristocracy, like those of Burke and contemporary English writers such as Coleridge, mark the effective termination of conventional aristocracy as an important theme in Western political thought. Indeed, even in Burke's statements there are discordant elements that point forward to other conceptions of rule by the few. For example, in a pamphlet defending his acceptance of a pension from the crown in the face of criticism from the Duke of Bedford, the aged and ailing Burke emphasised the importance of meritocracy as a basis for high office. He remarked that able men of business like himself were responsible for maintaining the structure 'which alone' made Bedford 'his superior'. Elsewhere, Burke included within a 'true natural aristocracy' not only the nobility, but also leading judges, intellectuals and the most successful and respectable members of the business community. People with these qualifications 'form in nature, as she operates in the common modification of society, the leading, guiding, and government part' (Burke, 1834, vol, ii, p. 265, vol. i, p. 525). Neither of these remarks is enough to detach Burke from conventional aristocratic conceptions of politics, but the lurking animus implied by the first, and the generalised meritocracy conveyed by the second, point towards a non-aristocratic view of government by the few.

Non-hereditary elites in modern political thought: J. S. Mill, Nietzsche, Mosca, Pareto, Blanqui and Lenin

Conventional aristocracy has persisted in parts of the modern world, but like monarchy it has long ceased to be an object of interest for political theorists. The main reason for this is that since about the middle of the nineteenth century the general tendency of Western political development has been towards representative democracy, or the rule of 'the many'. Although this development has given the population at large an important *formal* role in politics, it has not always been accompanied by an abandonment of arguments concerning the effective dominance of the few. To the contrary, the spread of democratic government has seen the development of a distinctive body of political thinking that deals with the role of elites *within* systems that are ostensibly democratic. These arguments must be distinguished from conventional accounts of aristocracy that are set in a monarchical context, and place a great deal of emphasis on ideas of heredity and tradition. In contrast, elite theory stresses merit and demonstrable political ability rather than the inherited social qualities that are ascribed to conventional aristocracies.

One important account of the relationship between elite rule and emerging democracy appeared in John Stuart Mill's writings. Mill's understanding of human progression led him to adopt a wary attitude towards democratic rule; he thought that under prevailing conditions, systems of mass politics would accentuate the conformist tendencies that were already apparent in modern society. At its most extreme, these tendencies would produce a 'tyranny of the majority', but even their more restrained manifestations would discourage the intellectual and moral experimentation to which Mill attributed the progress of civilisation. In response to these threats to progression, Mill assigned a general educational role to an intellectual elite within society. Its purpose was to equip the masses for intellectual and moral development. In addition, however, he insisted that the administration of the state must be left in the hands of the enlightened and expert few, and he promoted an electoral system that would ensure that the checking and regulatory institutions of representative government would have an elite bias. This last goal was to be achieved by a franchise that gave all sane adults at least one vote, while endowing those who satisfied certain educational, professional and occupational qualifications with a number of votes. The purpose of this allocation was to allow the mass of the population to gain experience in fulfilling a political role while ensuring that they were unable to bring the weight of numbers to bear in a way that undermined Mill's educational and progressive conception of the state (Mill, 1983, pp. 284–86). Since the elites' influence and political experience were held to have an educational role, Mill's unequal distribution of electoral influence was to be a long-term, but still temporary, feature of modern politics. Provided that the bulk of the population were sufficiently enlightened, Mill thought that representative democracy was the ideally best form of government (see p. 136).

Mill's position was a somewhat uneasy one. On the one hand he thought that democracy was inevitable, but on the other his concern with human progression led him to place emphasis on elite intellectual leadership in the foreseeable future to curb the impact of democratic politics. The fact remains, however, that Mill thought that in some circumstances elite rule should give way to democracy. In this respect his position differed from that of the late-nineteenth-century German philosopher Friedrich Nietzsche, who regarded democracy as a moral and practical disaster that at best served to prepare the ground for a new and quite distinctive political system based on the pre-eminence of an essentially aristocratic elite group.

Nietzsche's conception of aristocracy emerged out of a wide-ranging assault on values such as pity and the depreciation of individual self-affirmation that he identified with Christian morality and humanism, liberalism and socialism. These movements were modern surrogates for ossified religious faiths, sharing with them ideas of fundamental equality framed in terms of universal moral laws that Nietzsche took to be embodiments of the 'herd instinct' of ordinary human beings. In place of ideas that he regarded as corrupt, self-serving and debilitating, Nietzsche promoted an alternative morality that would direct human beings to take personal responsibility for realising their 'wills'. Nietzsche's conception of 'will' is essentially active: it is a personal force directed to the single-minded, relentless pursuit of the satisfaction of its own desires for pleasure or joy by attempting to mould the world to its purposes. 'It is *not* the satisfaction of the will that causes pleasure ... but rather the will's forward thrust and again and again becoming master over that which stands in its way' (Nietzsche, 1968, p. 370). These aspects of Nietzsche's theory resemble parts of Stirner's work, with which he may have been familiar (Carrol, 1974; Leopold, 1995, pp. xi–xii). However, Nietzsche thought that only *some* human beings are capable of conforming to this conception of morality; these were the *Ubermensch,* supermen who transcend the ordinary human condition to enjoy a supreme form of cultural existence.

Wilhelm Friedrich Nieztsche (1844–1900)

Born in the Prussian province of Saxony, Nietzsche was an academic philosopher whose work was devoted to a critique of the moral basis of modern Western cultures. His ideas on elite leadership and the 'will to power' proved amenable to adoption by later fascist and national socialist thinkers. Of his works, *Beyond Good and Evil* (1886) and *The Genealogy of Morals* (1887) have the closest bearing on political theory.

Key reading: Ansell-Pearson, 1994.

The only positive prospect that Nietzsche associated with liberal democracy was the possibility that its levelling and enervating tendencies would clear the ground for the emergence of a new aristocratic class of supermen who would seize control and subject the population (Detwiler, 1990, pp. 173–74). In all other respects, Nietzsche's position entailed a radical aristocratic critique of the cultural, moral and political structures of both democratic and more authoritarian forms of mass state (Ansell-Pearson, 1994, pp. 151–52). 'Every heightening of the type "man" ... has been the work of an aristocratic society – and thus it always will be; a society which believes in a long ladder of rank order and value differences in men, which needs slavery in some sense' (Nietzsche, 1967, p. 199). This is not just a matter of conventional subservience since Nietzsche stressed the need for what he called 'the pathos of distance'; that is, he believed that the length of the social hierarchy encourages 'that other more mysterious pathos, that longing for ever greater distances within the soul itself, the evolving of ever higher, rarer, more spacious, more widely arched, more comprehensive states – in short: the heightening of the type "man," the continued "self-mastery of man"' (ibid., p. 199). The complete subordination of the masses is essential to this 'mysterious pathos'. Nietzsche thus promoted a system of elite rule in which the population is effectively sacrificed to the interests of an aristocratic cast that is free of the humanitarian delusions of service that he claimed had sapped the will of conventional European aristocracy:

> the essential nature of a good and healthy aristocracy is that it does *not* feel it is a function (whether of royalty or of the community) but its meaning, its highest justification. Therefore, it accepts with a clear conscience the sacrifice of an enormous number of men who must *for the sake of the aristocracy* be suppressed and reduced to incomplete human beings, to slaves, to tools (ibid., p. 200).

For Nietzsche, therefore, aristocracy is a mutually exclusive alternative to other forms of government because it necessitates rule by an elite in its own interest. This position not only contrasts with Mill's views on the guiding and enlightening function of elite rule, but is also radically at odds with other contemporary strands of European political thinking that regarded elitism as an inevitable and persistent feature of democratic politics.

In the late nineteenth and early twentieth centuries the Italian thinkers Gaetano Mosca and Vifredo Pareto, and the former's German disciple, Robert Michels, developed descriptive, 'scientific' accounts showing that all systems of social and political regulation are elitist (Parry, 1970, pp. 30–63). As Mosca put it,

> In all societies … two classes of people appear – a class that rules and a class that is ruled. The first class, always the less numerous, performs all political functions, monopolises power and enjoys the advantages that power brings, whereas the second, the more numerous class, is directed and controlled by the first (Mosca, 1939, p. 50).

The experience of representative democracy in late-nineteenth- and early-twentieth-century Europe, and a desire to prove their general case by showing that even these regimes conformed to the general elitist pattern, led Mosca, Pareto and Michels to pay a great deal of attention to the rule of the few in putatively democratic environments. They thought that their theory of elite rule was an empirical one reflecting the fact that, whatever the constitutional formalities of a society, elites always *do* rule. As Pareto put it, an elite 'exists in all societies and governs them even in cases where the regime in appearances is highly democratic' (Pareto, 1966, p. 155). This position differs from many of those discussed earlier because these writers stressed the normative claim that elites *should* rule.

Democratic societies, even the most self-consciously democratic organisations such as working-class parties (the object of Michels' attention), are effectively subject to the rule of the few. Elites are not seen as uniform cohesive entities; indeed, both Mosca and Pareto identified elite strata (Bottomore, 1966, pp. 9–10). They are, however, thought to possess a number of common qualities that explain their controlling position, and they are endowed with organisational capacities, political skills and a clear sense of purpose. Moreover, their power is cumulative – its sources are strengthened by the possession of power – and self-perpetuating. Mosca and Michels stressed the organisational capacity of the elite and observed that its restricted size and frequent interaction between its members makes it easier for elites to organise effectively than the masses. Pareto's account focuses on the distribution of psychological character traits within a given population. In democratic systems these organisational or psychological characteristics allow members of the elite to manipulate a supposedly all-powerful mass made up of a large and diverse number of unimaginative, poorly organised and not clearly directed individuals (Mosca, 1939, pp. 247, 411–12).

These judgements on the relative superiority of elites provided the basis for the preferences for particular forms of elite rule that lurk behind the scientific form of both Mosca's and Pareto's theories. Thus Pareto was dismayed at the decadent and corrupting effects of rule by those with highly developed political intelligence but little grasp of large moral aspirations or ideas. Writing in the wake of the First World War, he identified an increasing tendency for newly rich members of society (the 'plutocracy') to enter into manipulative alliances with the 'masses' to produce a form of 'demagogic plutocracy'. This alliance, directed against the well-established propertied classes, was the predominant feature of modern parliamentary government:

> The modern parliamentary system, to all intents and purposes, is the effective instrument of demagogic plutocracy. Through elections and through political transactions in parliament, considerable scope is given

to the activities of individuals who are well endowed with instincts of combination. Indeed it now seems clear that the modern parliamentary system is to a great extent bound up with the fate of plutocracy (Pareto, 1966, p. 315).

Subsequently Pareto looked to the Italian dictator Mussolini as a heroic representative of solidarity, order and discipline who would renovate the moral basis of Italian society. In contrast, Mosca's preferences were those of a liberal-conservative (Parry, 1970, pp. 41, 47). In his later writings he bemoaned the tendency for the political elites who had emerged under democracy to manipulate the population by pandering to tawdry moral standards. However, as universal suffrage had now become irreversible, it was too late to restrict the vote to the middle classes, who could have provided an intellectually and morally sound source of stimulation for, and replenishment of, the elite. As an alternative, Mosca redefined the idea of the ruling class. He appealed to what was, in effect, an extra-political elite, to restore the moral tone of social and political life by assuming an educational rather than a degenerative role in its interaction with the masses. Writing in the years of political and moral crisis that followed the conclusion of the First World War, Mosca urged the ruling class to 'gain a clear conception of its rights and duties ... Then only will it learn to appraise the conduct of its leaders soundly, and so gradually regain in the eyes of the masses the prestige that it has in large part lost'. He appealed to enlightened members of the middle class to 'make up a small moral and intellectual aristocracy, which keeps humanity from rotting in the slough of selfishness and material appetites' (Mosca, 1939, p. 493). In this formulation, Mosca's ruling class has become an intermediary body that stands between political leaders and masses: its influence is exercised through moral and cultural means rather than through its possession of political office. Democratic politics involves the masses on the one hand and political leaders on the other, but since the latter are unable to provide moral and intellectual leadership this will have to be supplied through an elite whose impact on politics is indirect.

Assertions of the woeful incapability of the 'masses' are a common feature of arguments that ascribe a dominant political role to 'the few'. The few must rule because the many are either incapable of exercising political authority, or do so in a morally reprehensible manner. A different version of this view of the relationship between elites and masses has been used to justify the role of an elite or 'vanguard' party in galvanising the masses into effective revolutionary action (Parry, 1970, pp. 55–56). The idea of a conspiratorial elite party can be found in the writings of a number of nineteenth-century French writers and is associated in this period particularly with Auguste Blanqui (1805–81). In the relatively brief periods of his adult life when he was not in prison, Blanqui operated on the revolutionary fringes of nineteenth-century French politics. Although he thought that 'the people' would play a crucial role in the revolutionary process, their oppressed and listless condition meant that they would have to be spurred into action by a group of intellectuals whose revolutionary commitments distanced them from the class structure of contemporary society. This elite would forge an alliance with the masses that was based on a strict division of labour. It formed a closed, conspiratorial body that would be secured against infiltration by the authorities while it worked to organise the masses and direct their action. The revolutionary elite would not consult the people, and nor would it take them into its confidence: like the general staff of an army it directed the troops from above. Blanqui adhered to a vision of a radically libertarian and egalitarian future, but he insisted that the pursuit of this goal necessitated the temporary subjugation of those who would finally enjoy the fruits of social and political transformation (Bernstein, 1972, pp. 62–64).

Blanqui's idea of a revolutionary elite came to fruition in the history of twentieth-century revolutionary Marxism. The key thinker in this tradition was not Marx himself, but V. I. Lenin, the leading figure in early-twentieth-century Russian revolutionary communism. In *What is to be Done?* Lenin argued against spontaneous mass risings on the ground that they would produce aimless destruction rather than concerted and effective revolutionary action. He maintained that under pre-revolutionary conditions, and especially within the context of an autocratic police state, the masses lack the unity and informed sense of direction that will make it an effective revolutionary force. Even under more favourable circumstances, the most that could be hoped for is the growth of a 'trade union consciousness', but that would blunt its revolutionary capacities. Although Lenin thought these capacities are latent within the bulk of the population, he believed that they need to be fostered and channelled by a trained, politically conscious, tightly knit and centrally directed elite organisation (see p. 335).

In Lenin's version of revolutionary elitism, the members of the vanguard are distinguished by their attachment to and knowledge of a Marxist theory of revolutionary transformation. However, the basic assumptions of his theory – the formlessness of the masses, and the need for them to be given shape, unity and a sense of direction by an elite – are common to all forms of elitism. It is true, of course, that Lenin's conception of elite rule is directed to the attainment of an end that will make it redundant. As in Mill's case, however, this is a distant goal. For Lenin and his successors, the overthrow of autocracy marks only the first stage of revolution; it is also necessary to create the economic, political and social conditions necessary for the transition to a communistic society.

Vladimir Ilyich Lenin (1870–1924)

Lenin was leader of the Bolshevik Party at the time of the (second) Russian Revolution in October 1917. His revolutionary tactics played an important part in that event and in the subsequent development of the Soviet Union. Lenin's application of Marxist ideas to the Russian situation laid the basis for a form of state socialism that was built upon the dominance of the Communist Party, and justified its position by reference to the tenets of 'Marxist-Leninism'. *What is to be Done?* (1905) and *The State and Revolution* (1917) are among the most important works in Lenin's vast output. His political writings dealt with a range of issues concerning the role of a vanguard party in a revolutionary situation and the way in which this elite might utilise the power of the state to establish the conditions for the emergence of communism. Lenin was highly critical of anarchists and of other reformist and revolutionary socialists, engaging with them in sharp polemics, fiercely contested political struggles and bloody civil war.

Key reading: Harding, 1992; McLellan, 1979.

The transition to communism requires the abandonment of forms of elite rule and the creation of a genuinely democratic system of government. In common with other Marxists, Lenin adopted a view of the democratic credentials of modern society that corresponded with Mosca's and Pareto's observations about their elitist character. Unlike these writers, however, Lenin did not regard elitism as inevitable. In formulating his conception of 'people's democracy' Lenin thought he had produced a theory that rested on a full understanding of the requirements of democratic government and the implications of it. His position built upon a long tradition of democratic thinking, but, as we shall see in the next chapter, Lenin tailored this to his understanding of the prospects for human liberation held out by Marxism.

Conclusion

Since modern elite theorists based claims to rule upon the politically significant personal qualities of limited members of the community, they shared some common ground with Plato and Aristotle. However, significant variations existed within this general pattern. For Lenin the qualities in question were largely intellectual and ideological. In this respect at least, his position was similar to that of Plato, Mill and Nietzsche. While other elite theorists tended to relate elite status to membership of a particular class, they did not argue for forms of class rule. Rather they assumed that people occupying certain positions in the social structure enjoy the educational advantages and ways of life that will make it possible for them to play a prominent role in politics. Elite status is personal, but it is accepted that elites usually come from particular classes.

In contrast, theories of hereditary aristocracy involve a notion of class rule. Although only particular members of the aristocracy occupy leading state offices, the class itself is given a privileged political and social position and provides social and cultural as well as political leadership. This class is hereditary, membership of it is legally defined and entry to it is strictly controlled. While hereditary aristocracies have sometimes existed within republics (as, for example, in Rome and Venice) they are found more usually in hereditary monarchies. In these cases, aristocracy is one reflection of ideas about the location of political power that rest upon the claim that appropriate ability and status should be determined according to the principle of hereditary transmission.

8 THE RULE OF THE MANY

Because democracy of one kind or another is a feature of the modern world, it is easy to overlook the fact that arguments about the positive political significance of 'the many' have had a chequered career. Both Plato and Aristotle associated democracy with lawless and unstable rule and many of their successors endorsed the unfavourable connotations they attached to this form of government. Despite this persistent hostility, the history of Western political thought includes a series of significant counter-arguments concerning the just and beneficial nature of democratic (or 'popular') government. In arguing their case, proponents of rule by the many seek to show that exclusive claims made on behalf of the 'one' and the 'few' are incompatible with the effective pursuit of the ends of politics. But while arguments in favour of popular rule have often made a case for giving the many a significant formal role in politics, they have not always promoted exclusive control of the state by 'the people'.

This chapter opens with a consideration of Protagoras', Democritus' and Aristotle's views on democracy in the Greek world. The second section of the chapter examines a tradition of popular republicanism in Renaissance Italy that built upon insights derived from ancient political theory. The third and fourth sections discuss theories of popular government in seventeenth-century England and late eighteenth-century America and France. These arguments were advanced in revolutionary contexts. When democracy became the goal of popular reform movements in the nineteenth century it promoted wide-ranging discussions of its merits, possibilities and dangers among both liberal and socialist thinkers. These arguments provide the focus for the fifth and sixth sections of this chapter. The last part of the chapter considers twentieth-century critiques of aspects of Western democracy produced by Marxist thinkers and by those promoting the independence and development of post-colonial states. The chapter concludes with a brief survey of some contemporary reactions to liberal-democracy from feminist writers and from proponents of 'participatory' and 'deliberative' democracy.

'The many' in ancient Greek political theory: Protagoras, Democritus and Aristotle

Although democratic government in Athens was occasionally challenged by those who wished to introduce government by 'the few', its longevity suggests that it was generally accepted by most of the population. Indeed, evidence from Greek drama – produced for popular rather than elite consumption – and from documents such as the funeral speech given by the popular leader Pericles during the war with Sparta convey a sense of pride in Athenian democracy. Unfortunately, however, the most developed surviving statements of Greek political ideas were written by people such as Plato and Aristotle, whose attitude towards Athenian democracy was either openly hostile or at best extremely sceptical (Jones, 1957, pp. 41–42; Sinclair, 1988, pp. 202–203). Positive accounts of democracy in Athens have survived only in fragmentary and/or second-hand statements of the ideas of Protagoras and Democritus.

These writers identified democracy with the realisation of both personal and collective interests and with respect for the autonomy of individual citizens (Farrar, 1992, p. 22). They believed that it fostered a harmonious form of political life that was buttressed by respect for traditional values, and set popular participation within the context of elite leadership. This feature of Athenian democracy was emphasised by Democritus in his account of the formation of the democratic *polis* under the guidance of Solon (594–593 BC). At that time, according to Democritus, the dominant nobility showed 'compassion' for the many by giving them a political role. He argued that this gift created consensus within the community, and laid the basis for Athens' subsequent prosperity by ensuring that it avoided the inter-factional and interclass strife that plagued many of its neighbours. Democritus did not, however, rest his case for the democratic state on this basis alone. He also identified democracy with freedom and argued that by participating in the state individuals are able to reconcile their personal aspirations with those they share with other members of their community. Citizens are thus full members of an institution that is widely recognised as the focal point of a truly human existence (Havelock, 1964, pp. 142–43).

Protagoras' conception of democracy also rests on the idea that this form of government is intrinsically and universally beneficial. He argued that *all* human beings (or at least, all male adults) are endowed naturally with 'respect' and a sense of justice that entitles them to play a role in the *polis*:

> [W]hen there is a question about how to do well in carpentry or any other expertise, everyone, including the Athenians thinks it right that only a few should give advice, and won't put up with advice from anyone else … but when it comes to consideration of how to do well in running the city, which must proceed entirely through justice and soundness of mind, they are right to accept advice from anyone, since it is incumbent on everyone to share in that sort of excellence, or else there can be no city at all (Plato, 1991, p. 15).

Citizens' participation in the political life of the state reinforces their original endowment of respect and justice and thus recognised that excellence was not the exclusive preserve of aristocrats (Farrar, 1992, p. 24). Protagoras and Democritus, however, still left a place for aristocrats within the democratic *polis*. Like the natural aristocracy of early-modern political thought, these figures provide leadership by assuming the burden of important offices, but they are chosen by the people and are subject to periodic scrutiny by them (Havelock, 1964, pp. 146–53). Significantly, both leaders and their fellow citizens are seen as part of a democratic culture the members of which possess the political virtue necessary to sustain the state (Kierstead, 2018, p. 18).

Despite reservations about Plato's ideal republic, Aristotle's ideal aristocratic state bears important similarities to it. By excluding all but the truly virtuous from membership of the political community he creates a system of government that is not significantly different from the egalitarian elite of Plato's guardians (see pp. 149–50). However, while this state represents Aristotle's ideal, his *Politics* contains extensive discussions of worthy but less than ideal states, including those with a democratic element.

In his formal classification of constitutions, Aristotle identified two types of rule by the many. 'Polity' is a 'good' constitution because the many rule in the common interest; democracy is a corrupt variant, because they rule in their own exclusive interest. He noted that 'rule by the many' usually means rule by the poor (Aristotle, 1958, pp. 110–16). Given Aristotle's understanding of the political implications of distributive justice, and given that the populations of most societies are unlikely to be strictly equal, there is a sense in which rule by the many will always be suspect: democrats wrongly believe that 'equality in one respect – for instance, that of free birth – means equality all round' (ibid., p. 136). This claim is unjust because it rests on a single criterion and ignores other relevant and significant inequalities. The implications of this line of argument is that 'polity' will only be just when all are equal in a number of significant respects.

Aristotle's detailed treatment of democracy identifies five sub-types. The least unjust gives some recognition to the claims of wealth and refinement. From here we descend through three increasingly unjust types to an extremely unjust form. Each stage in the descent is marked by the abandonment of moderating influences – property, the law, and a mixture of rural and urban populations – leaving a state in which the urban poor, supported through taxes imposed on other classes, exercise direct control in a system of grossly self-interested, unrestrained rule that is analogous in its arbitrary, lawless characteristics to the worst form of tyranny (ibid., pp. 167–69; Mulgan, 1977, p. 74).

This dire picture of mass indulgence matches that of Plato, but Aristotle was prepared to allow that 'the many' may have *some* claim to a political role. While ordinary people are individually inferior to 'the few', they may *collectively* possess a degree of wisdom that is greater than that found in a few superior individuals. Aristotle used the analogy of a shared feast to which many contribute in support of this argument, and he also referred to the role ascribed to the Athenian public in judging theatrical performances. In addition, he argued that there is a difference between the expertise required to *produce* something, and the practical experience needed to *judge* whether it works well (Aristotle, 1958, pp. 123–27; Mulgan, 1977, p. 105). For example, a shoemaker's expertise is required to produce shoes but only those who wear them can tell whether they are a good fit. When applied in a political context this analogy suggests that those who feel the effect of political actions may well be the most appropriate judges of them.

These concessions to democracy relate to Aristotle's later suggestion that in many circumstances 'polity' will be the most practicable form of government. In this formulation the term 'polity' no longer refers to a good form of rule by the many, but is applied to systems that successfully mix 'democratic' and 'oligarchic' elements so as to moderate their vices. The many are thus given a judging role (as in Democritus' theory and also to some degree in Athenian practice), but executive functions are left in the hands of the more able, subject, of course, to the scrutiny of the population at large. Another possibility is that while some offices are filled by 'lot', others are filled by election (Aristotle, 1958, pp. 176–78, 180–84), an arrangement that allows considerations of capacity and prestige to play a role in selecting key officers of the state (Jones, 1957, p. 49). These procedures contrast with the exclusion of the populace from the political institutions of Plato's ideal state, but they are similar in important respects to the 'second best' state sketched in *The Laws*. The laws of this state provide for popular elections, but arrange the electoral system in such a way as to ensure that the distinctive attributes of 'the few' are recognised (see p. 230).

An important benefit of giving limited recognition to the claims of the many is that it satisfies the idea of distributive justice: it acknowledges that they have *some* worth and make a significant contribution to the state. In addition, 'polity' also tempers the dangers of democratic and oligarchic domination of the state. It should be noted, however, that because Aristotle regarded 'polity' as a merely practicable rather than a desirable state, his account of the political significance of 'the many' has an instrumental and mundane air. It thus differs from the positions taken by both Protagoras and Democritus. These thinkers based the claims of the many on generalised moral attributes and argued that democracy generates not only safety, but a distinctly human way of life. Respect and justice in Protagoras' account, and compassion and consensus in that of Democritus, harmonise individual and collective aspirations and make the democratic *polis* an admirable form of government.

'The many' in early-modern political theory: Classical republicans, radical Protestants and Levellers

Themes that appeared in ancient accounts of the rule of the many resurfaced in the first half of the thirteenth century. At that time a number of Italian city states began to incorporate male householders within political systems formerly dominated by nobles. At first these states looked to Roman models, but following the appearance of a Latin translation of Aristotle's *Politics* in the middle of the thirteenth century, Greek ideas came to play an important role in justifying systems of popular government (Skinner, 1992, p. 59).

Defenders of the Italian republics emphasised independence from external control and the need for the state to be governed by the free citizenry rather than by restricted groups or over-mighty individuals. The second of these goals was to be achieved by a variety of measures that subjected officials to the scrutiny of 'the many', and through a conception of active, participatory citizenship that ensured the state was directed towards common rather than to particular ends. In Machiavelli's political writings these two forms of freedom are related by his claim that the external liberty of the state is most likely to be maintained by a militia made up of free citizens (Machiavelli, 1975, vol. i, pp. 266–67, 310–11, 361–67). Internally, the free citizens ensure that the republic is not corrupted by the self-interest of particular classes; externally, they bring the same sense of general commitment to defending the state against foreign enemies.

Given the hostile monarchical and imperial environment in which it arose, it is not surprising that classical republican thought focused on preserving republics in face of these threats. It also associated other important goals with independent popular republics. Political freedom was conducive to glory as well as safety and provided the many with opportunities to develop and exercise their talents for the good of the community. Service in the militia and participation in the political life of the republic thus serve to reconcile communal and personal aspirations. The active citizen develops his capacities through participation in the life of the state, and in so doing contributes to the maintenance and glory of the republic. In serving the state's interest ordinary citizens can thus enhance their own capacities and attain fame, honour and glory.

One of the central assumptions of popular republicanism is that the loyalty of the many can be relied upon because they have the largest stake in the common interest and will seek to protect and advance it. However, popular government is also justified on other grounds. For example, Marsilius of Padua argued that loyalty and obedience are relatively easy to secure in popular republics because citizens think of the law as something they have created and imposed upon themselves. In an echo of an argument common in classical political theory, he also claimed that ordinary members of the population are best equipped to evaluate officeholders' attachment to the common good, and can be relied on to see through the self-interested proposals advanced in the cause of a faction (Marsilius, 1956, vol. ii, pp. 46–47).

The most significant seventeenth-century developments in democratic political thought took place within 'Leveller' circles in the late 1640s during the English Revolution. The term 'Leveller' is used by historians to describe a group of publicists and activists with connections in the victorious parliamentary army. Following the defeat of the Royalist forces in 1647, members of the army debated the conduct of the parliamentary leadership and the basis upon which the state should now be 'settled'. Many of the Levellers' demands raised matters of particular concern to the army's rank and file, but they also promoted measures of economic, legal and religious reform. Some of them also took up the cause of parliamentary representation, attacking electoral corruption, and at times raising fundamental questions about the basis, distribution and use of political power (Wootton, 1994).

The idea that government is authorised by the people plays an important role in Richard Overton's *An Appeal from the Commons to the Free People* (1647). As the title of this work suggests, Overton believed that individuals retain a residual right to free action, even within a civil condition. Overton grounded this right upon 'reason', a faculty that is only fully developed in God, but which is possessed to a significant degree by all sane adults. 'Right reason' is 'the firm and sure foundation of all just laws and governments'. Governments are just when they act in accordance with reason, and when their actions are of a kind to which rational human beings will consent: 'all just human powers are but betrusted, conferred, and conveyed by joint and common consent; for to every individual in nature is given an individual propriety by nature, not to be invaded or usurped by any' (Woodhouse, 1951, pp. 324, 327).

In the *Appeal,* Overton was largely concerned with establishing the grounds for challenging unjust government and with urging rulers and elected officials to recognise that they derived their authority from the consent of rational beings. At times however, some of the Levellers utilised the idea of a fundamental (rather than a conventional or historical) basis for government to argue for the inclusion of the adult male population within the electoral process. The most well-known example of this line of argument occurred in a debate held at Putney on 28–29 October 1647 in the 'General Council of the Army', a body made up of commanding officers and regimental representatives of the parliamentary army. The council was convened to consider a printed paper, *The Case of the Army Stated*, but when it met this document was superseded by another, subsequently published as *An Agreement of the People.* Among a variety of demands, the *Agreement* stipulated that the right to elect parliamentary representatives should be vested in every adult male (Tuck, 1993, p. 247). This demand alarmed some senior officers, but their objections to it provoked a defence of the electoral role of 'the many'. A system of popular election was justified by referring to the 'birthright' of every 'Englishman' and the sacrifices made by the common people in the Parliamentary cause. In addition, one of the participants in the debate, Colonel Rainborough, identified a relationship between human reason, consent and just government that was similar to that advanced by Overton. Unlike Overton, however, Rainborough extended the idea of consent to include participation in the process through which law is created, and he buttressed this by a reference, designed to refute arguments that connect electoral rights with 'fixed' (material) possessions. All have an interest in the law since all must be regulated by it; all are endowed with reason, and therefore all should play a role in selecting those who make the law (Woodhouse, 1951, pp. 53, 61, 56).

At a later stage in the debate Rainborough argued that recognition of the electoral claims of the many is necessary to avoid 'enslavement' of the population (ibid., p. 67). It is not clear, however, whether he thought that their exclusion would produce unjust laws, or whether the mere fact that the many lack political rights entails enslavement. In a subsequent discussion of the franchise, the Levellers' demands were modified to exclude those who receive poor relief, or who are servants under the exclusive control of a particular employer. This concession, a response to the hostility aroused by the more radical position advanced by Rainborough, was in keeping with a central presupposition of early-modern political thinking. The franchise will not protect the freedom of servants and paupers whose lives are constrained by economic dependence; to the contrary, it will extend the influence of those upon whom they depend. Even allowing for this concession, however, it seems clear that at times the Levellers promoted a significant electoral role for the many. While there is no question that the many will *rule,* they are to be assigned an important role in the process through which legislators are chosen and their actions scrutinised. Some formulations of the Leveller position thus rest on ideas of popular sovereignty, consent and the significance of human reason, which came to play an important role in subsequent democratic accounts of the location of political power.

Popular government in the age of the American and French revolutions: Madison, Sièyes, Condorcet and Paine

In seventeenth-century England the demand for universal male suffrage was a radical proposal, but it did not depart from the conventional idea that 'the many' was only one part of an essentially aristocratic political system. This way of thinking persisted in the eighteenth century. It was common among English writers who extolled the virtues of a mixed constitution containing 'monarchic', 'aristocratic' and 'democratic' elements, and it also attracted the admiring attention of foreign writers such as Baron Montesquieu (Montesquieu, 1949, vol. ii, pp. 151–62). In the last third of the eighteenth century, however, a series of political crises, the first occurring in Britain's North American colonies and the second in France and other European countries, produced new and historically significant restatements of the political importance of 'the many'.

Britain's North American colonies rejected hereditary monarchy and aristocracy and established republican forms of government. The most striking feature of this process was an extension of the idea of popular participation to include significant elements of popular *rule*, particularly at the local level. These developments involved a clear rejection of the claim that 'the many' was 'virtually' represented by a restricted section of the population who possessed electoral rights, and an even smaller proportion who sat in representative assemblies and filled important public offices. Although some white males were excluded from the franchise, the American political nation was, by contemporary standards at least, very extensive and the range of positions filled by election very wide (Wood, 1992, pp. 91–92). In the years following the war with Britain, and particularly in 1787 when a new constitution was being discussed, the implications of popular government were the subject of extensive debate.

'Anti-federalist' writers who promoted a confederation that located power within the states themselves, rather than in a central federation, claimed that voting and office holding are necessary to promote the distinctive and private interests of the variety of individuals within the political community. People enter political society to promote their *own* good, and the only way to ensure this is to endow them with political rights. These rights provide opportunities to choose representatives and officeholders whose interests are the same as theirs. An important feature of this position is that it abandons the classical republican idea of a *unitary* public interest, and adopts a *pluralistic* conception of government: since electors have a variety of interests they need to be represented by a range of different individuals who constitute a representative cross-section of the population. Thus while 'the many' are entitled to have their interests reflected in the distribution of legislative and other offices, their diversity means they have ceased to exist as a coherent, unified political grouping. From this point of view, it is significant that one of the most important anti-federalist writers talked not of 'the many', but of a range of narrowly defined sectional interests: 'professional men, merchants, traders, farmers, mechanics etc' (ibid., p. 101). Since 'the many' do not exist as a distinct and unified interest, popular government does not pose a threat to particular sections of society.

The extent and consequences of this fragmentation of the political community, and the related denial of the political significance of a 'common interest', were questioned by those promoting a federal constitution. Contributors to the *Federalist Papers* argued that despite the fragmenting effect of 'interest' politics, 'the many' share an interest in undermining the property rights of the few. Consequently they argued for a federal system of government on the grounds that its extended scale would weaken the immediate political influence of the ordinary members of the population. A leading 'federalist', James Madison, argued that it is necessary to 'filter' the narrow interests of local communities and interest groups through a more extensive electoral process so that the better educated will tend to be elected to federal offices. These people possess 'a knowledge of the interests and feelings of the people'; they do not merely reflect the aspirations of a range of narrowly self-interested groups (Hamilton et al., 1942, pp. 45–46, 169).

James Madison (1751–1817)

Madison, a leading figure in revolutionary politics in America, was later Secretary of State and President of the United States (1809–17). Together with Alexander Hamilton and John Jay, he was author of *The Federalist* (1787–88), a work that sought to integrate the ordinary population in the new American republic while limiting the risk that it would use its electoral power to pursue its own interests at the cost of that of the community at large.

Key reading: Hampsher-Monk, 1992; Wood, 1992; Zuckert, 2017.

Madison made it clear that he believed there *was* a public interest, not merely a variety of individual or sectional interests: 'the public good, the *real* welfare of the great body of the people is the supreme object to be pursued' (ibid., p. 234). In its general bearing, Madison's position echoed earlier ideas concerning 'natural aristocracy' within a system of popular government (see p. 154). He relied, however, less upon the capacity of the many to pursue the common good by recognising the *virtú* of their natural' superiors, than on socio-political mechanisms that avoid narrow sectionalism. Despite the self-interest of the bulk of the population, Madison thought it possible to produce a disinterested and informed elite at the federal level.

While most of those involved in the early stages of the French Revolution aimed to establish a constitutional monarchy rather than a republic, the series of events that began with the calling of the Estates General in Paris in the summer of 1789 had important implications for the development and spread of ideas of popular government. The revolution itself involved a degree of popular participation in public affairs that was quite foreign to large, long-established European states (Fontana, 1992, pp. 107–10). As in the United States, abolition of hereditary aristocracy and commitment to fundamental human equality eroded formal class distinctions and merged 'the many' into 'the people'. As the Abbé Sièyes put it, 'There was once a time when the Third Estate was in bondage and the nobility was everything. Now the Third Estate is everything and nobility is only a word' (Sièyes, 1963, p. 145).

This change was signalled quite clearly in a declaration issued by the National Assembly in Paris. The *Declaration of the Rights of Man and of Citizens* treats 'men' and 'citizens' as virtually synonymous: 'Men are born, and always continue, free and equal in respect of their rights … The end of all political associations, is the preservation of the natural and imprescribable rights of man.' The *Declaration* identifies law with the 'will of the community', and stipulates that the rights that individuals possess in a political condition include 'a right to concur, either personally, or by their representatives, in its formation' (Ritchie, 1894, pp. 291, 292). In the formulation advanced by the Marquis de Condorcet, a leading philosopher of the period, this right derives from people's natural liberty: 'no citizen can be obliged to obey laws to which he has not contributed as much as any other citizen, either directly, or by an equal right to elect representatives and to be elected' (Baker, 1975, p. 268). There were varying views on qualifications for citizenship. For example, when Sièyes spoke of the 'Third Estate' he meant the propertied classes rather than the entire population (Sièyes, 1963, pp. 13–14). Drawing a distinction between 'active' and 'passive' citizenship, he argued that only those who satisfy a tax-based qualification should vote, and that eligibility for election should be determined by a property qualification. In contrast, Condorcet promoted universal male suffrage.

In common with proponents of popular government in the United States, their counterparts in France had to confront the possibility that political incorporation of 'the many' might unleash the rapacious tendencies that had been associated with democracy since ancient times. Despite his support for universal suffrage, Condorcet remained apprehensive about the urban masses' ignorance and capacity for destruction and insisted that general enlightenment promoted by public institutions would be necessary to ensure that the potentialities opened up by the Revolution were realised (Baker, 1975, p. 269). Sièyes' views on the extent of the 'political nation' were more limited than those of Condorcet. He still thought it necessary, however, to 'filter' the influence of ordinary voters through a system of indirect election. Sièyes also envisaged an elaborate range of additional precautions against the empowerment of what might be merely a transient, self-interested and reckless majority, including annual replacement of parts of the assembly and division of this body into separate sections that would consider legislation independently (Sièyes, 1963, pp. 20–21).

The quality of the majority produced by popular election was of crucial importance to Sièyes because he thought it should express the 'general will' of the community directed towards its common interests. If this was achieved, the majority could thus be regarded as 'the *nation*' (ibid., pp. 151, 154, 163–64). Sièyes understood the general will as an aggregate of individual wills, but his strictures against transitory, and in a sense unrepresentative, majorities implied that popular electoral participation would not necessarily produce a true expression of the nation's common interest. This point became perfectly clear in Saint-Just's attitude towards 'the many'. Louis-Antoine Saint-Just, a leading member of the Committee of Public Safety during the Terror, looked to popular elections to produce an 'elective aristocracy'. Once in power, this body should give the people what was good for them rather than what they seemed to want (Hampson, 1991, pp. 42–46, 105–106). As we shall see, this conception of the relationship between popular politics, the 'general will' and elite domination came to play a central role in Marxist ideas of post-revolutionary democracy (see pp. 155–56).

Perplexity about the perils of popular politics and the relationship between leaders and followers in a new, representative environment does not appear to have played a significant role in the thinking of Thomas Paine. One reason for this is that Paine regarded the American Revolution as an exemplar of non-destructive radical political change. Moreover, Paine discounted the excesses of the French Revolution as a regrettable but understandable consequence of previous repression and the reactionary stance to it of the upper classes in France and other European countries. He believed that 'society' possesses a natural cohesion and that the main threat to beneficial social interaction comes from oppressive and unjust government, particularly monarchy and hereditary aristocracy (Paine, 1976, pp. 193–206).

Paine maintained that natural and beneficial interdependence, reciprocal interests and a natural tendency to social living create bonds between human beings that will survive the destruction of the state. In support of this claim, he referred to the experience of the American colonies after the authority of the British crown had been rejected and before the creation of a 'new' republican government. Paine applied the word 'new' to a distinctively modern form of popular 'representative' government that first appeared in North America. Unlike classical democracy, which involves *direct* rule by the people and is only viable in geographically limited city states, representative government is suitable for large and populous states. Its key feature is the 'delegation of power for the common benefit of society' through the popular election and frequent recall of members of a legislative body who are truly representatives of the people (ibid., pp. 185–87, 193, 197).

Paine's understanding of the benefits of representative government emerged from a series of trenchant contrasts between 'new' and 'old' governments but it also had clear implications for federalist attempts to contain popular politics. He identified 'new' governments with rationality, sensitivity to the real interests of society and a diffusion of knowledge throughout the community. By contrast, hereditary, 'old' governments had been established by usurpation or conquest. They systematically disregard popular interests, and make no attempt to develop or harness the intelligence of the community. The hereditary principle gives supreme power to those who have no proven capacity for ruling, and who lack knowledge of, or sympathy for, the interests of the general population. Such unjust and irrational superiority can only be maintained by coercion and by promoting the ignorance and incredulity of the ordinary people. Representative government, however, draws upon *all* the talents of the community; it 'concentrates knowledge necessary to the interest of the parts, and of the whole'. It casts aside the mysteries in which monarchy is shrouded and 'diffuses such a body of knowledge throughout a nation, on the subject of government, as to explode ignorance and preclude imposition'. For Paine, inclusion of the whole population in the political system was thus a matter of both justice and great practical benefit: it would make government the *servant* of society; it would prevent imposition by narrow sectional interests, and create a climate of openness and informed sensitivity that would promote the interests of individuals and society (ibid., pp. 198–206, 203, 206).

Democracy in nineteenth-century political theory: James Mill, Constant, Tocqueville, J. S. Mill, Taylor, Green and Hobhouse

The practical impulse given to popular government by the French Revolution was initially short-lived. By the close of the 1790s France had adopted a constitution in which representative institutions served as a facade for military dictatorship, and after 1815 the restoration of monarchical regimes throughout Europe signalled a widespread reaction against the political claims of 'the many'. Despite these early setbacks, the nineteenth century witnessed the creation of representative regimes in many European states. By the middle of the century a number of important writers had begun to argue that the advent of 'democracy' (a term that was beginning to lose the unfavourable connotations that had attached to the rule of the many since ancient times) was inevitable. There was a feeling that deep-seated socio-economic changes meant that while the establishment of democratic government could be delayed, it could not be postponed indefinitely (Maier, 1992, pp. 126–27). But while these developments were seen as inevitable, they did not meet with universal approval. As we have seen, some theorists identified a tendency for the few to dominate even within the context of ostensibly popular systems of government (see p. 162). It remains true, however, that in the nineteenth century arguments about the merits of popular government assumed a volume and importance not previously attained in the history of political thought.

In the early decades of the nineteenth century the adoption of 'universal' male suffrage was frequently seen as an antidote to the deficiencies and injustices of aristocratic politics. This perspective loomed large in Thomas Paine's writings, and continued to have currency among those who lived to see (and to deplore) the restorations of 1815. In England, for example, William Cobbett, the self-proclaimed 'People's Friend', argued for an extension of voting rights on the ground that the corruption of traditional elites meant that it was necessary for the people to protect their own rights and defend their own interests (Cobbett, n.d., pp. 5, 12–13). His contemporary, William Hazlitt, took a similar line, but also stressed, as Paine had done, that a system of popular representation was necessary to ensure that government would embody the 'wisdom of the community' rather than the narrow, self-seeking attitudes of the aristocratic classes (Hazlitt, 1819, p. 318). The idea that popular representation would check the misuse of power by sectional interests played a particularly important role in the justification of democracy advanced by James Mill, the utilitarian disciple of Jeremy Bentham.

James Mill (1773–1836)

Born in Scotland, Mill embarked on a literary career in England, where he enjoyed the friendship and patronage of Jeremy Bentham. His *Essay on Government* (1820) was widely regarded as a Benthamite blueprint. In this work Mill presented a rationale for manhood suffrage by reference to the need to align the interests of officeholders with those of the rest of the community and thus to prevent the misuse of political power by those whose duty it was to promote the 'greatest happiness of the greatest number'.

Key reading: Macpherson, 1977; Thomas, 1979.

In his *Essay on Government* Mill took it for granted that in large and populous states the people cannot exercise power themselves; they can, however, effectively safeguard their interests by choosing representatives who will 'check' the actions of government. Popular representation provides 'security' against privileged minorities' misuse of political power to further their own 'sinister' interests at the cost of the interests of the rest of the community (Mill, 1984, pp. 72–73). Mill argued, however, that effective representation, and hence effective security against 'bad government', does not necessarily require a full-blown system of representative democracy. Those whose interests are 'included in', or covered by, the interests of other people – children, women with husbands or fathers, and young adult males – will be adequately protected even if they do not have the right to vote (ibid., pp. 78–80). The same happy outcome will result from a property-based franchise that embraces the majority of the population. Mill simple-mindedly assumed that the majority's interest in exploiting the minority would not be sufficiently strong to overbalance the general benefits of 'good government' (ibid., pp. 81–82). In countries such as England, this arrangement would produce the further benefit of curbing the irrationality of lower-class voters: the majority would be dominated by the middle classes whose moderation and rational good sense would guide and direct them (ibid., pp. 93–95).

These arguments allowed Mill to restrict popular participation but still ensure that government would not be biased by 'sinister interests'. A similar position was advanced by his French contemporary, Benjamin Constant (Constant, 1988, pp. 206–09). Constant, however, produced a more sophisticated theory incorporating bedrock concerns with justice and the rights of individuals. As individual liberty was a fundamental requirement of modern society, Constant worried that popular sovereignty might come to mean that government could do anything. He therefore argued that a commitment to *limited* government must become enshrined in 'public opinion' and supported by a balance of powers lodged in distinctive constitutional bodies (ibid., pp. 183–85).

Constant's reservations on this issue resurfaced in a sharper and more developed form in the writings of Alexis de Tocqueville and John Stuart Mill. These thinkers challenged James Mill's and Jeremy Bentham's complacent endorsement of majority rule and also expressed doubts about the sort of 'public opinion' that was beginning to emerge within the democratic, egalitarian societies of the modern world. Tocqueville's views on democracy were framed by his observations of American society in the early 1830s but were written with an eye to developments within European states.

Alexis de Tocqueville (1805–59)

Tocqueville was a French politician and historian. His place in the history of political thought is largely a consequence of *Democracy in America* (1835–40), a work that resulted from a tour of the United States during which he was struck by the tendency towards conformity in American society and reflected on the political implications of this tendency and its likely consequences for moral and intellectual development. Tocqueville's observations and arguments on the social and cultural characteristics of a society with an egalitarian ethos and no hereditary elite had an important impact on John Stuart Mill's understanding of democracy in modern societies.

Key reading: Atanassow, 2017; Balot and Tong, 2018; Drolet, 2003; Siedentop, 1994.

According to Tocqueville, the adoption of popular government is an inevitable consequence of the growing democratisation of modern societies. These developments are admirable in many ways: democratic government promotes the welfare of the mass of the population and it also engenders a spirit of self-reliance, and respect for what are, in effect, self-made and self-imposed laws. However, the benefits of democracy are offset to some degree by undesirable features. Popular election provides no guarantee that capable people will attain public office, and the pressure exerted by the relatively poor majority results in marked increases in public expenditure. For Tocqueville, Paine's claim that representative government would be just, rational and cheap had proved to be unduly optimistic. Furthermore, Tocqueville had serious doubts about the adverse impact of democratic cultural values on political democracy (Tocqueville, 1945, vol. i, pp. 48–56, 206–58).

Democratic societies subscribed to deep-seated ideas of equality that were beneficial in some respects but might have injurious effects on intellectual standards and social cohesion. For example, Tocqueville observed that priority was given to views of ordinary members of the American population, and ideas of intellectual authority, or leadership by enlightened elites, were largely ignored. At the same time, the ethos of social egalitarianism fostered a strident individualism that had isolated people from one another. Tocqueville argued that the absence of social or intellectual authorities creates a vacuum that is filled by a generally ill-informed public opinion. All are equal, but since they are mentally isolated from their fellows, they cannot withstand a body of public opinion that reflects the combined prejudices of a majority of their equals, and they see no reason why they should seek to do so (Lively, 1965, pp. 87–88; Tocqueville, 1945, vol. ii, pp. 104–07). Thus while democratic citizens have shaken off traditional yokes, they have assumed new, self-imposed ones that sap intellectual vigour and impede moral and cultural progression. These tendencies are apparent in democratic attitudes towards government. Paradoxically, the apparently anarchic impulses of modern democracy are counteracted by social forces for conformity and dependence that encourage the growth of a centralised and paternalistic state. In eighteenth-century Europe a state of this kind had been imposed upon a population who were bereft of political rights; in democratic America the majority has imposed it upon itself and the rest of the community (Tocqueville, 1945, vol. i, pp. 267–78; vol. ii, pp. 99–104, 304–48).

Tocqueville's depiction of democracy in America had a salutary effect on English attitudes towards popular government and the democratisation of social relationships. For example, in *On Liberty* John Stuart Mill alluded to the United States when warning his readers that the end of aristocracy does not necessarily mean the end of tyranny (Mill, 1983, pp. 67–68). 'Popular government' invariably means majority rule and there is no reason why this body should be any more sensitive to individual liberty than traditional rulers have been (ibid., p. 75). Mill addressed some of the more strictly political implications of the argument of *On Liberty* in *On Representative Government*.

In this work Mill argued that representative democracy is the 'ideally best' form of government because it allows for both the most effective protection for individuals, 'self-protection', and for the exercise and development of a range of capacities that will make individuals dignified, self-reliant, yet self-consciously and freely attached to the interests of the community (ibid., pp. 208–18). Mill denied, however, that the franchise is a right: voting for legislators and government officials might prompt the exercise of power over others and no one can claim the right to this. Rather, political rights are a privilege that should extend only to those who will use them properly. Mill believed that most ordinary members of the population in contemporary Europe and North America lacked the rationality and self-control to resist temptations to use their power tyrannically. Consequently, he proposed a modified form of representative democracy that would yield practical and educational benefits while avoiding the dangers inherent in prematurely adopting an ideally best form of government. When considering representation in mid-nineteenth-century Britain, Mill suggested that the professional governing elite should be subject to the scrutiny of an elected chamber chosen through a system of 'plural voting': everyone would have one vote, but those satisfying academic, professional and property requirements should be given additional votes. This system allowed the least developed members of the community to protect themselves, and to experience the developmental benefits of political participation without being in a position to impose their unenlightened and self-serving demands on the rest of the population (ibid., pp. 284–90). These provisions applied to women as well as to men (see pp. 67–68).

In the latter part of the nineteenth century, Mill's idea that the exercise of political rights would serve the dual function of protecting individuals and facilitating the development of admirable character traits, was incorporated within a framework where sociability was a primary value. Democracy thus became an important component of the new conception of political community that was developed by the British idealists (see p. 45). T. H. Green, for example, regarded popular government as a way of eliminating 'bias by private interests' and making the state the vehicle of the common good. In addition, he argued that the recognised connection between law and the conscious pursuit of the common good is strengthened if the population has a direct, or even an indirect, role in the processes through which laws are made (Green, 1986, pp. 93, 96–97).

The importance of democracy for the idealist conception of the state was stressed by Green's successors. Bernard Bosanquet regarded democratic representation as an important modern development that provides a way of canvassing and expressing conceptions of the common good arising from the diverse experiences of members of the community. These conceptions need to be interpreted and put into effect by elected officials and by professional public servants, but democracy prevents expert rule from developing into elite domination by ensuring that officials are ultimately responsible to the citizenry at large (Nicholson, 1990, pp. 214–15). It also gives concrete expression to the positive relationship between government and the realisation of the moral aspirations of the community. It is natural that citizens are wary of government when it is in the hands of particular classes, but once a state becomes democratic these suspicions become groundless: government now reflects aspirations for the realisation of the common good that are embedded in the ideas and practices of the whole community (Ritchie, 1902, p. 74).

L. T. Hobhouse (1864–1929)

Educated at Oxford, Hobhouse taught at that university and was later the first professor of sociology at the University of London. In addition to undertaking academic work, Hobhouse was a prominent journalist and was closely associated with the liberal *Manchester Guardian.* Like T. H. Green, by whom he was influenced, Hobhouse sought to formulate a new but still liberal conception of an active democratic state. His principal statement of this position was *Liberalism* (1911).

Key reading: Collini, 1979; Simhony and Weinstein, 2001.

This conception of democracy was endorsed by a range of influential late-nineteenth- and early-twentieth-century liberal thinkers, although some of them felt a sense of unease about the practical realities of contemporary democratic politics. L. T. Hobhouse, a late-nineteenth-century proponent of the new liberalism inaugurated by Green, considered representative democracy to be both unique and valuable: it provides a way of giving 'recognition of the duties of government and the rights of the people'; it protects 'personal freedom and (the) equal consideration of all classes' and expresses 'a growing sense of social solidarity', upon which the modern state rests' (Hobhouse, 1990, pp. 188–89). He noted, however, that although Britain had become increasingly democratic in its internal politics, it continued to impose its will on a large empire. Imperialist sentiment fostered through the manipulation of public opinion by newspaper owners and the more general impact of demagogic political leaders seemed to Hobhouse to be depriving popular government of its moral standing and threatened European peace (Hobhouse, 1909).

Socialism and democracy: Babeuf, Owen, Marx, Webb and Bernstein

Many of the themes of nineteenth-century socialism – liberty, the end of class government and the revival of a true sense of community – were similar to 'advanced' liberal ideas, but socialists' understanding of the economic dimensions of oppression led them to use 'democracy' to refer to a system of general equality, and to regard popular government as an instrument for reconstituting social and economic relationships. An important consequence was that many socialists were critical of what they saw as the liberals' formal, restricted and purely political understanding of democracy.

An early example of this line of argument appeared in the speech by Francois-Noel ('Gracchus') Babeuf when he and his fellow conspirators were on trial before the High Court of Vendome in 1796. Their conspiracy, described as 'the last episode of the French Revolution' (Bax, 1911), was also the first act in the development of modern socialism. Babeuf argued that the narrow franchise of the 1795 constitution and the dominant legislative role ascribed to the five-member 'Directory', undermined the imperfect but significant gains of the revolution. The principles of liberty and equality and the commitment of French society to the welfare of all its members implied by them were now virtually abandoned. As Babeuf put it, 'the Revolution is not yet at an end, since the wealthy have diverted its fruits, including political power, to their own exclusive use, while the poor in their toil and misery lead a life of actual slavery and count for nothing in the State' (Babeuf, 1972, pp. 44, 47). Babeuf's conspiracy aimed to remedy these defects by creating a 'republic of equals' in which political authority was vested in the hands of 'the people' and applied to satisfying their just and egalitarian social and economic demands.

Babeuf's ideas attracted the sympathetic attention of Bronterre O'Brien, a leading figure in English socialism in the 1830s and 1840s (Plummer, 1971, p. 60). O'Brien, together with followers of Robert Owen and other socialists associated with the 'Chartist' campaign for universal (male) suffrage, argued that legal and political equality and justice are worthless while significant economic and social oppression persist (Claeys, 1989a, p. 83). O'Brien called for a general democratisation of human relations that extended beyond parliamentary institutions. Socialists more generally stressed the importance of popular participation in a range of small-scale political and social institutions (community councils, cooperatives and trades unions); rejected the competitive, selfish and sectional ethos of conventional parliamentary politics; and promoted general moral improvement as a way of developing people's social capacities and sympathies.

Robert Owen's socialism focused on small communities as the basic unit of government, and thus contrasted with the position taken by those who wished to democratise and socialise the state. For example, in the 1840s the French social democrat Louis Blanc argued that state capital should be used to fund autonomous enterprises controlled by directors elected by the workers themselves. A system of 'workers' democracy' was to be inaugurated by a popularly elected government committed to the interests of all the members of the community rather than particular classes. A similar aspiration motivated Blanc's contemporary Auguste Blanqui, but he developed a conception of revolutionary politics that harked back to Babeuf. Having set the revolution in train, an elite would institute a 'dictatorship of true republicans' (Lichtheim, 1968, p. 67) responsible for dispossessing the rich and creating an egalitarian society. For Blanqui this dictatorship was a necessary, albeit temporary, means of realising the goals that lay at the heart of the tradition of radical democracy that had been inherited from the French Revolution (see p. 88).

The Blanquist conception of dictatorship was revived by Lenin when he sought to create a rationale for a 'people's democracy', a form of government that would bridge the gap between the revolutionary overthrow of the Tsarist state in Russia and the emergence of a state-less condition Marx called 'communism' (see p. 100). The fact that 'people's democracy' could be presented as a legitimate development of Marx's political ideas reflected the ambiguities of his treatment of popular government. Marx made it clear that without a fundamental transformation of the socio-economic structure, the liberating claims made for conventional representative democracy were purely formal. He saw 'bourgeois government' as merely the latest expression of a state that furthers the interests of the dominant class within society. Democratic representation does not alter the character of this state but merely conceals its true nature: universal suffrage is a mechanism for determining 'once in three or six years what members of the ruling class should misrepresent the people in Parliament' (Marx and Engels, 1973, vol. ii, p. 221).

In the *Manifesto of the Communist Party* (1848) Marx and Engels claimed that a successful proletarian revolution would raise 'the proletariat to the position of ruling class', a measure they identified with triumph in 'the battle of democracy' (Marx, 1973, p. 86). Later, in his reflections on the Paris Commune of 1870–71, Marx presented the 'commune' – government by relatively small, locally based committees of popularly elected representatives – as a valuable alternative to the sham democracy of 'bourgeois' representative government. The commune would give back to the community 'the State power which claimed to be the embodiment of that unity independent of, and superior to, the nation itself, from which it was but a parasitic excrescence' (Marx and Engels, 1973, vol. ii, p. 221). Communal government provided a way for 'the people' to direct their collective action towards the transformation of economic and social relationships. Marx noted, however, that the peculiar context of the Paris Commune – a revolutionary civil war – severely limited its general applicability as a model of socialist politics. In other situations, Marx regarded conventional democracy as a way of developing the consciousness and organisational capacities of the working class so that they could become a revolutionary force capable of seizing control of the state and inaugurating a 'dictatorship of the proletariat'.

This dictatorship would be like other forms of government in that it would act in the interests of a particular class, but it would differ fundamentally from them because the class in question would represent the interests of humanity. Having overthrown the bourgeoisie, it would use state power to destroy the social, economic and political vestiges of bourgeois rule, thus preparing the ground for its own demise and for the end of class government. Since the state was a class instrument, the attainment of full equality and freedom under communism would make it redundant; the state would 'wither away', leaving a genuine community of cooperating human beings who would collectively organise their affairs.

The limited scope of Marx's political (as opposed to his historical, economic and social) theory posed problems for his successors (Dunn, 1984, p. 21). In the late nineteenth century a number of socialists adopted more conventional conceptions of democracy than that proposed by Marx. Many important English socialists presented socialism as an extension of what they saw as a tradition of democratic reform. Thus Sidney Webb, a leading member of the reformist Fabian Socialist Society, described socialism as the 'economic side of the democratic ideal' that had emerged as the dominant feature of nineteenth-century political developments (Webb, 1889, p. 35). The advent of democracy meant that the state was no longer under the control of what the Benthamites had called 'sinister interests'; it was now a conscious agent of the common good and could be used to harness the economic resources of society to the requirements of the community. While Webb thought that efficient government would only be possible if administration was placed in the hands of expert elites, he insisted that representative institutions were necessary to guard against 'sinister interests'. This principle was applied to both central and local government.

Eduard Bernstein (1850–1932)

Bernstein was an early member of the Marxist German Social Democratic Party and subsequently developed a theory of gradual, non-revolutionary political and social transformation that orthodox Marxists branded as 'revisionist'. Bernstein had first-hand experience of late-nineteenth-century British socialism and drew upon this to present an alternative path to socialism that did not require class war or violent revolution. This position was advanced in *Evolutionary Socialism* (1898), a work that has been seen as an important influence in the development of contemporary European social democracy.

Key reading: Tudor and Tudor, 1988.

Webb also applauded the appearance of a combination of expertise and popular responsibility in organisations such as trades unions. His description of these developments in terms of 'industrial democracy' (ibid., pp. 30–36) attracted the favourable attention of the German social democratic writer Eduard Bernstein. Bernstein described trades unions as 'the democratic element in industry. Their tendency is to destroy the absolutism of capital, and to procure for the worker a direct influence in the management of an industry' (Bernstein, 1972, p. 139). Unlike Webb, who was largely untouched by Marx's ideas, Bernstein developed a theory of 'social democracy' that would overcome perceived inadequacies in Marxist accounts of the transition of socialism.

According to Marx, the 'political sovereignty' of the 'class party of the workers' was an essential condition for the attainment of socialism. Bernstein observed, however, that even in advanced capitalist societies the workers did not form a homogenous mass. Consequently, if government 'by the people' was to be anything other than a temporary outburst of aimless and destructive terror like that which appeared in the French Revolution, it was necessary to identify a system that would embrace the interests of the whole community. Democracy and socialism would come together as different manifestations of a desire to place the interests of the community above those of classes who monopolised its economic and political resources.

Bernstein defined democracy as 'an absence of class government, as the indication of a social condition where a political privilege belongs to no one class as opposed to the whole community'. In both its political and economic manifestations, socialism involved an idea of 'universal citizenship' not class dictatorship; it should really be seen as an extension of the concern for 'free personality' that had inspired liberals but had only been partially understood by them. Conventional democratic institutions embodied the political aspects of this tradition. Socialists should build upon the assumption of political power by the community, utilising the state as a vehicle for pursuing the material and social interests of the community. Bernstein regarded socialism as an expression of the 'principle of association' and the democratic state as a way of realising the political aspects of this principle and then pursuing its social and economic dimensions (ibid., pp. 96, 142).

Socialism, democracy and black emancipation: Du Bois's platonic Fabianism

In an earlier chapter we considered W. E. B. Du Bois's witheringly critical reaction to the ongoing curtailment of the liberty of black Americans after the abolition of slavery in 1863. In the face of attempts by the Southern states to deprive blacks of the political rights secured by the fifteenth amendment of 1870 – 'The right of citizens of the United States to vote shall not be denied or abridged by the United States or any State on account of race, color, or previous conditions of servitude' – Du Bois insisted that voting rights were a necessary means of self-defence for members of the black community. Advancing a position that he thought applied to the North, the South and indeed, to all modern, market societies, he explicitly rejected arguments (like those of J. S. Mill) that justified the paternalistic curtailment of the political rights of 'partially undeveloped people'.

> [I]n any land, in any country under modern free competition, to lay any class of weak and despised people, be they white, black, or blue, at the political mercy of their stronger, richer, and more resourceful fellows, is a temptation which human nature seldom has withstood and seldom will withstand (Du Bois, 1920, pp. 143, 144).

Significantly, Du Bois did not think this argument precluded members of these communities who possessed superior education, expertise and moral qualities from providing leadership to their fellows. Indeed, he thought that the widespread enhancement of blacks' capacity for self-development, and hence for contributing to the progression of modern society, depended upon them taking on these responsibilities. In one of his essays, Du Bois appealed to Platonic precedents when arguing the need to develop a leading cadre of black college graduates who had undergone a rigorous and highly intellectual education. He also advanced a view of the natural stratification of well-ordered societies that echoed a central theme of Plato's *Republic* (Du Bois, 1920, p. 69 and see above). Unlike many of his contemporaries, however, Du Bois did not see hierarchy in racial terms and he promoted an ethos of distributed rather than centralised leadership: college graduates 'should be made a missionary of culture to an untaught people' while the trained blacksmith should exemplify 'a free workman amongst serfs' (ibid., p. 70). In addition, however, he believed that the exercise of power should be subject to the democratically-fostered expression of popular aspirations and interests.

When exploring this conception of democracy in *Darkwater* (1920) Du Bois echoed Aristotle's point that the population as a whole are the best judges of the impact of the decisions of officeholders (see above, p. 144). He also argued, however, in a way that mirrored Thomas Paine's theory of 'representative government', that democracy injected all the knowledge and intelligence of the community into government decision-making. In so doing, it ensures that the just claims of all citizens are met:

> So soon as a nation discovers that it holds in the heads and hearts of its individual citizens the vast mine of knowledge, out of which it may build a just government, then more and more it calls those citizens to select their rulers and to judge the justice of their acts (Du Bois, 1920, p. 143).

Du Bois invoked this position to support the anti-paternalist position that he had earlier justified by reference to the unavoidable partiality of members of competitive social orders. He applied it specifically to the situation of his fellow African-Americans and to women. Du Bois argued that in both cases, the inclusion of hitherto excluded 'voices from within the veil' (the subtitle of *Darkwater*) would protect their interests more effectively and enhance the overall quality of American democracy. Society would only capture the full benefits of democracy when government was informed by knowledge arising from all the various groups subject to it.

The same general principles applied to the organisation of economic activity. Du Bois decried the economic and social inefficiency of production and distribution in modern capitalist societies and argued for a combination of elite leadership and mass participation in the industrial sphere which paralleled the position he had advanced on purely political democracy. He criticised the ongoing domination of powerful individuals and oligarchies in the economic affairs of the community and, in language which echoed Beatrice and Sidney Webb's, he promoted 'industrial democracy'. In common with British Fabians, he saw the 'public democratic ownership' of utilities and economically critical monopolies, and the redistribution of some of the profits consumed by capitalists, as important early stages in bringing it about (Reed, 1997). Characteristically, Du Bois tied these proposals to an appeal to 'human brotherhood' that underwrote his attack on public and private racism in the post-civil war period, seeing a connection between this and the Russian revolutionaries' appeal to the idea of 'comradeship' (Du Bois, 1920, pp. 157–58).

Non-liberal theories of democracy in the twentieth century: 'People's' and 'Third World' democracy

In the twentieth century prevailing patterns of democratic thinking in Western societies were 'liberal-democratic'. Democracy was justified on the grounds that it combined liberal concerns with individual freedom with the protective, developmental and social benefits that were expected to flow from rule for and by the many. These liberal conceptions of democracy were challenged by two rival traditions. The first of these theories, variously known as 'people's', 'proletarian' or 'communist' democracy, grew out of an attempt to fill the gaps left by Marx's account of post-revolutionary politics; the second, 'Third World' or 'developmental democracy', has been important in a number of newly independent former colonies.

People's democracy built upon aspects of the Blanquist and Marxist traditions, but was a direct consequence of Lenin's understanding of what was necessary to further the revolutionary process after the Bolsheviks seized power in October 1917 (Harding, 1992, pp. 161–77). As we have seen, Marx's theory of 'true democracy' was extremely sketchy; in addition, however, the situation confronting Lenin was problematic in Marxist terms. Having seized control of the state, Lenin's conspiratorial elite was faced with the problem of pursuing the elusive goal of communism in a society that lacked the economic, social and political characteristics that Marx identified with an advanced stage of capitalist development. Imperial Russia was autocratic rather than bourgeois, and possessed neither a developed economy nor an extensive class-conscious proletariat.

In response to these difficulties, Lenin formulated a new conception of democracy in which a class-conscious party elite used political power to create the conditions necessary for embarking on the path to true communism. The party assumed responsibility for eliminating internal opposition, developing an economic basis that would match the technical and productive achievements of advanced capitalism and create a class-conscious proletariat that would carry the revolution to its end. These herculean labours were to be directed by a unified elite party that was able, by virtue of its knowledge of Marxism and a ruthless commitment to the true interests of the proletariat, to discern and implement the 'real will' of the people (Lenin, 1971, pp. 303, 322–23, 326–32, 371, 534–38).

In the hands of Joseph Stalin, Lenin's successor at the head of the Communist Party, this model was transformed from a dictatorship of the class-conscious proletariat into the virtual dictatorship of an individual, a step that many commentators see as an inevitable consequence of an authoritarian theory of leadership. It is important to note, however, that at least in its formal structures and in its rationale, Lenin's conception of a people's democracy incorporated ideas that are only explicable in relation to less contentious accounts of popular government. In the first place, although party membership was far from universal, the party itself operated on the basis of 'intra-party democracy'. That is, party positions were to be formulated after full and free discussions among all its members, and once they had been adopted by the party they were binding on all its members. Secondly, while people's democracy did not allow for competition *between* parties, the policy of the party and the appointment of those holding representative and other positions were legitimated by electoral processes based on universal suffrage. Given the 'revolutionary vanguard' role that Lenin ascribed to elites, however, it is not surprising that these elements of democratic practice were set in a framework where party elites played a central role (see pp. 141–42). For example, intra-party democracy was set in a framework of 'democratic centralism' in which leadership flowed downwards and responsibility flowed upwards; in addition, candidates for election were nominated by the party (White et al., 1982, pp. 222–25).

It is clear that features of people's democracy have facilitated elite manipulation and, given a certain combination of circumstances, the most oppressive tyranny. It is at least arguable, however, that while people's democracy is incompatible with liberal democracy, its distinctive features reflect values that have played a role in the history of democratic thinking. People's democracy takes a collectivist rather than an individualistic focus; it adopts an 'objective' rather than a 'subjective' conception of interests, and it incorporates a strongly positive understanding of freedom. None of these considerations justify people's democracy, but they may explain why it must be regarded as incorporating at least some aspects of democratic conceptions of rule.

Much the same point may be made about Third World democracy. During the colonial period democratic ideas played an important role in independence movements. They provided the basis for appeals to liberal elites within colonising powers, and to indigenous populations. However, leading figures in anti-colonial movements argued that 'liberal' Western notions of democracy could not be adopted by their societies. These theories clashed with indigenous values and did not address the developmental imperatives (in education, public health, economics and nation building) facing countries emerging from long periods of colonial domination. Third World democracy was presented as a system of democratic rule that embodied values appropriate to non-Western societies and also matched their needs.

Third World democracy has a number of components. First, it rests upon the recovery of indigenous values. An important example of this approach grew out of the 'Negritude Movement', a name given to a group of African writers who were active in the period immediately before and after the Second World War. In conscious opposition to the derogatory stereotypes that were prevalent in colonialist culture, these writers promoted a pride in blackness and upheld the continued relevance of traditional practices and ideas derived from pre-colonial village and tribal cultures. An idealised image of the past was to serve as the basis for reconstructing post-colonial society, with the years of colonisation being seen as a period of slumber that had no positive bearing on the liberated state (Nursey-Bray, 1983, p. 97).

In theories of Third World democracy, traditional values underwrite a novel conception of a democratic *society*, of which a democratic *state* was only one element. They also promoted economic structures that spurned the individualistic ethos of free market capitalism and were intended to foster the development of community resources for community purposes. These structures incorporated ideas identified with harmonious, pre-colonial village communities that were free of class divisions and in which authority was structured by kinship and age and was marked by cooperation based upon and reinforced by traditional values. In these circumstances there was no place for either the individualism of Western capitalism, or the class-structured society that provided the focus of Marxist analysis and practice (Macpherson, 1965, p. 30).

The political counterpart to this social pattern is the 'consensual community', held together and directed by decision-making processes that involve consultation and agreement rather than the imposition of majority views on the minority. Because villages and tribes in the modern world are grouped together in extensive and often artificial nation-states, however, post-colonial societies have had to establish systems of central coordination and decision-making that were not part of the pre-colonial condition. In Third World democracy a national consensus is forged and expressed through a single ruling party, whose position is endorsed through mass election. The party becomes a focus of unity, one that cuts across ethnic, religious and tribal lines (Nursey-Bray, 1983, pp. 104–06).

Like people's democracy, this distinctive form of post-colonial rule has often descended into single-person or elite tyranny, but it retains theoretical justifications and institutional features that connect it to aspects of the Western democratic tradition. Third World democracy is collectivist rather than individualistic; it rests on a positive rather than a negative conception of liberty – promoting liberation and development among the oppressed and deprived – and it advances a substantive rather than a purely formal notion of equality: it presupposes that a democratic community is a community of economic, social and political equals (Macpherson, 1965, p. 33). Moreover it is premised, like people's democracy, on the idea that the community has a single, unified, true interest: only when this exists can the 'real will' of the community be embodied in a single party.

The recent history of post-colonial societies forms fertile ground for deep scepticism about the legitimacy and viability of Third World democracy. However, the system has worked tolerably well in some countries at some times. In any case, the attempt to create a political role for the many in societies that lack the cultural, economic and social values found in long-established Western states reflects a more widespread concern about the appropriateness of Western democracy in non-Western countries. This issue plays an important role in the political practice of states such as Singapore, and it also lies behind assessments of the authenticity of democracy in large and relatively long-established post-colonial states such as India (Khilnani, 1992, p. 205).

Conclusion

Having long been regarded as a marginal and highly unsatisfactory alternative to monarchy and aristocracy, democracy now occupies the centre of the political stage. The reasons for this development are complex, but an important clue to its theoretical significance can be found in the connection that both Tocqueville and John Stuart Mill made between the democratisation of nineteenth-century society and the spread of democratic forms of government. The first of these developments eroded ideas of natural superiority and subordination, prompted the disappearance of legally enshrined status distinctions, and thus created conditions that made democracy more likely. An earlier, although less overt, statement of this position is implied in Paine's arguments about the need for government to correspond to a social structure made up of individuals who possess equal claims to consideration and protection. In Paine's case these claims were based upon natural rights, but this alone is not sufficient to justify claims to political equality. It is possible to assume, as earlier writers had done, that these rights would be adequately protected by non-democratic forms of government. For this reason, an important part of the historical case for democracy has involved attempts to show that the interests of individuals will not be satisfactorily served unless they are endowed with political rights. Many historical arguments in favour of democracy thus focus on the inadequacy of monarchical and aristocratic alternatives. Within contemporary Western democracies, however, attention is now focused on identifying forms of democratic practice that will overcome what are seen as limitations on the effective exercise of political rights by those whose formal possession of them is unquestioned.

Although late-eighteenth- and nineteenth-century women proponents of female emancipation thought this objective required a transformation of the gender-based perceptions that underwrote the sexual, social and political subordination of women in Western societies, they, like their male counterparts, placed particular emphasis on the role that political rights played in securing other forms of freedom. The relationship between personal and political subordination has been a focus of ongoing attention in the history of political thought and has been prominent in contemporary feminist critiques of Western liberal democracy. Since the 1960s a range of feminist philosophers have argued that gendered power relations which have their origin in personal relationships have perpetuated the systemic bias against women that has become integral to the Western tradition of political thinking and persists in expressions of it that seem most sensitive to the claims of individual liberty. In particular, it is argued that the liberal distinction between a 'public' political sphere, which is subject to scrutiny and control by the state, and a 'private' sphere of voluntary actions between autonomous beings, conceals the reality of the persistent influence of patriarchal power (Millett, 1970; Siltanen and Stanworth, 1984, pp. 185–208). One of the tasks of contemporary liberal feminist political theory has been to expose the ways in which male domination of the private sphere undermines the credibility of modern democracy by impinging on women's effective exercise of their political rights. Two aspects of this line of argument are discussed here. The first concerns the impact of private constraints upon political participation, while the other raises questions about the gender requirements of authentic democratic political practice.

Private constraints on female participation are associated with inequality in the family. Feminist writers argue that the unequal division of domestic labour increases the relative costs of political activity for women. Further, it is claimed that women's inferior earning capacity and the structure of power within the family discourage women from participating politically because their perception of their political effectiveness (their sense of 'political efficacy') is lower than that of men. The impact of these inequalities is exacerbated by the norms that govern politics. It has been observed, for example, that even at the local community level, participatory occasions tend to be structured according to male values and biased towards the more effective participation of men (Mansbridge, 1980, pp. 105–07).

In response to these problems, feminist writers argue that the attainment of true political equality requires a reduction in the cost of participation borne by women (through the provision of services that meet their needs and the sharing of domestic responsibilities), as well as the adoption of institutional strategies such as women's cauci that preclude male domination and facilitate the development of a stronger sense of political efficacy in women. These measures are intended to make female participation more likely and more effective, to erode the male-dominated power structure, and to contribute to the development of the skills and sense of efficacy that are necessary for future participation in other areas of politics. In addition to the measures outlined above, some feminists argue that since the public and private spheres are not as distinct as conventional liberal theory implies, it is necessary to adopt political practices that take account of this. An important implication of this position is that private experiences – as conveyed, for example, through 'personal disclosure' – are relevant to political contexts. Further, it is argued that if political action is to advance the liberation of women, then it is necessary to conduct it in ways that promote 'prefigurative forms' of attitude, behaviour and language that are consistent with this goal and discourage those that are not (Phillips, 1991, pp. 113–14).

These strategies are designed to make liberal democracy live up to its name; to ensure, in other words, that political equality is not merely formal but also substantive. Without the elimination of deep-seated forms of domination along gender lines, 'the rule of the many' will remain, at best, 'the rule of the many who are male'. As long as this situation continues to prevail, the universalistic claims made for democracy, the insistence that all should be treated equally, that differences should be ignored and that everybody should be subjected to the same rules applied in the same manner, will merely serve to perpetuate male domination of both public and private spheres.

Feminist critiques of liberal democracy are part of a broader concern about the extent to which it delivers on its promise to give effect to the interests of the many. Some of these arguments have been been shaped by ongoing concerns about the role of elites in democratic political processes. From the 1940s, a number of influential studies of Western democracies pointed to features of the relationship between political elites (actual and aspiring officeholders) and powerful interest groups that compromised democratic decision-making at both local and national levels (Sartori, 1965; Schumpeter, 1954, pp. 269–96). Political elites' desire to win and retain public office encourages them to be particularly responsive to agendas promoted by well-organised interest groups and to pay little attention to the often hidden preferences of the overwhelming majority of largely passive citizens who merely respond to options placed before them at elections. This model of democratic practice, one that reflects the pluralistic and interest-driven character of modern, economically developed and complex societies, emerged from empirical studies of democratic processes and gained normative credence from the tendency for ordinary voters to limit their participation to limited instrumental engagements that are consistent with the image of the 'unencumbered-self' reflected in mainstream liberal thinking (see p. 96). It has also sometimes been claimed that democracies avoid extremism and instability if their day-to-day operations are not subject to high levels of popular involvement (Macpherson, 1977, pp. 77–92).

From the 1960s both the empirical and normative claims made on behalf of the elite model were challenged. Some of these challenges came from 'New Left' student groups active in Europe and the United States in the second half of the decade and from feminists. They argued that low levels of voter engagement were not a sign of satisfaction with democratic outcomes but a rational response to powerlessness. In fact, the structures of conventional democratic politics and the impact of highly inequitable access to rare but politically significant resources such as education, money and time have meant that the egalitarian implications of universal political equality (enshrined in equal voting rights, open access to office, freedom of assembly, expression and organisation) were largely formal rather than substantive.

In response to the alleged shortcomings of conventional Western democracies, proponents of 'participatory democracy' proposed a range of strategies to lower barriers to ordinary citizens' participation in decision-making processes. As noted above, some of these initiatives are designed to facilitate participation by women. Others are more general. They include a focus on neighbourhood and workplace politics, both on the grounds that decisions made at this level had an immediate impact on issues that were of concern to ordinary citizens, and because limited resources could be used more effectively at this level; an identification of new agendas (such as environmentalism) that have an important potential impact on the quality of life and are not already constrained by dominant elites; and measures to forge coalitions of interests that had not previously had a voice in the decision-making processes.

Participatory democracy is intended to improve the sensitivity of political processes and thus ensure that outcomes reflect the 'real' interests of the population at large. In some cases, these interests are seen in terms of an erosion of economic disparities and the provision of enhanced educational, medical and social services to poorer sections of Western societies. Some proponents of participatory democracy also aim to transform the ethos and practice of democratic politics. Thus one of the advantages claimed for increased participation is that it will promote citizens' sense of political efficacy and encourage future participation. In this respect, and in its focus on giving substance to political rights that might otherwise be largely formal, participatory democracy upholds an ideal of active citizenship that echoes classical republicanism and also plays a role in Rousseau's, Green's and Hobhouse's political thought. For writers in this tradition, active membership of the state requires the cultivation and practice of such politically relevant moral virtues as autonomy, the willingness to sacrifice selfish interests and an active concern with the common good. Thus in some accounts of participatory democracy, the benefits associated with enhanced political engagement reflect ideas about the close link between politics and virtue (Macpherson, 1976, pp. 93–115; Pateman, 1970, pp. 1–21).

The classical republican overtones of some statements of participatory democracy connect it with the idea of the embedded self discussed by proponents of modern communitarianism (see p. 96). This point is made obliquely in one of Michael Sandel's critiques of the liberal position entitled 'The Procedural Republic and the Unencumbered Self' (Sandel, 1992). It also finds an echo in critiques of pluralistic democracy advanced by proponents of 'deliberative democracy'. The focus here is not just on participation, but on the quality of participation by those who are affected by collective decision-making. As the use of the term 'deliberation' implies, this view of democracy concentrates on discussion and debate of important issues, not on voting. Rather than seeing politics as a competition between competing interests, it sees it as a deliberative processes involving rational exchanges between citizens and advances an ideal of a democratic community that sees these processes as being fundamental to it (Cohen, 1989, p. 21). The aim of these exchanges is to produce agreement and, if possible, consensus on issues of public policy. The stress on rational exchange is part of a more general commitment to the idea that those who engage in genuine deliberation must be prepared to move beyond a narrow view of self-interest to make appeals that are endorsed by others and might be accepted by third parties (Gutmann and Thompson, 1996, pp. 2–3). On this view, deliberative democracy is designed to have an impact on decision-making *and* on the perceptions of members of the community: it is 'expected both to produce policies that reflect public views and to encourage citizens ... to refine and enlarge their views of what policies should be pursued' (Ferejohn, 2000, p. 76). While the deliberative approach to democracy is related to attempts to make democratic politics more participatory, it is also associated closely with the focus on identity in feminism and other expressions of modern political thinking (see p. 182). Deliberative requirements make it possible for a range of participants to bring to decision-making processes perspectives and concerns which reflect the identities that they share with others.

Deliberative democracy's concern with the quality of decision-making by the many evokes a theme that goes back to Plato's arguments about the importance of expertise in politics and his assumptions that most of the population lack the philsophical insight and self-control necessary to exercise political power in the pursuit of ultimate values (see pp. 113–14). An interesting treatment of these matters appeared in the writings of Hannah Arendt, a significant figure in American intellectual life in the second half of the twentieth century. Arendt contrasted Plato's position with that of Socrates, attributing to the latter the exemplary promotion of the idea of 'thinker-citizens' whose interactions with their fellows was designed to encourage them to be more philosophical in their approach to politics (Lederman, 2016, pp. 487–88). Socratic dialogue was the key to realising this objective through the open examination of opinions by participants who are treated as equals. Arendt saw politics as a product of the interaction of thought and action, and believed that in a Socratic framework this produced 'equalisation' among the participants. It thus made possible an authentic form of democracy in which 'no one rules and no one is being ruled' (ibid., p. 489). While Plato had thought that justice would be realised where kings were philosophers or philosophers kings, Arendt looked to Socrates' example to frame a model of democratic interaction which ensured that citizens would be more philosophical.

PART

III

THE EXERCISE OF POLITICAL AUTHORITY

Having considered a number of historically significant accounts of the ends of politics and the location of political power, we now examine statements about how such power should be exercised. These theories explore the appropriate means for determining the propriety of rulers' conduct, and the extent to which their actions should be subject to either *normative* or *institutional* constraints. Normative constraints specify standards to which rulers should conform and to which subjects may appeal, while institutional constraints are formed by mechanisms that regulate the way in which power is exercised. These issues play an important role in accounts of legitimate political practice. They also provide the basis for challenges to political authority that are discussed in the final part of this book.

Part III opens with a chapter examining theories of natural law and natural rights. These theories reflect a common belief that the exercise of political power within and beyond the state should conform to objective standards that are beyond the reach of those whose behaviour is regulated by them. The second chapter in this section examines a number of theories of 'mixed government'

that stipulate that power should be distributed between a number of institutions to ensure that rulers cannot abuse their position and, more positively, that they act in the interests of the community as a whole. The viability of mixed government has been questioned by a number of thinkers who have argued that order can only be attained in states presided over by an all-powerful, unquestionable ruler, an absolute sovereign. This approach has given rise to the absolutist theories of government discussed in Chapter 11.

Part III concludes with an examination of claims about the need for those who hold political power to be subject to legal constraints. In addition to dealing with a range of arguments concerning the rule of law, Chapter 12 outlines an important strand within this tradition that claims the exercise of political power must be set within a framework of rules that conform to the requirements of justice. These theories imply that the approaches taken by all the thinkers discussed in earlier chapters are inadequate, but they focus particularly on the dangers posed by theories of absolute government and the related idea that laws are commands.

THE SANCTIONS OF 'NATURE'   9

In order to understand the regulatory role of appeals to 'nature', it is necessary to distinguish theories that rely on the idea of 'natural law', or 'the law(s) of nature', from those that focus on 'natural rights'. Theories of natural law identify expectations and norms that are not themselves the product of human intention or human will. These norms legitimate human action and justify the exercise of political authority (Finnis, 1980, p. 23). Natural law is held to be 'natural' in two related senses. In the first place, it is so fundamental to human life that its binding force is a matter of moral necessity rather than choice. Secondly, and as a consequence of this, it is claimed that adherence to natural law is supremely appropriate for human beings.

Natural law theories often depend on the assumption that God has a direct authoritative role in human life. Natural law is thus seen as a system of rules that tell human beings how they must act if they are to achieve the ends to which God directs them. These laws are said to be 'rational' because they are appropriate means to attain specified ends; they are also rational in the sense that human beings discover them by the use of their reason. However, some writers also relate the rationality of natural law to its role in meeting fundamental human needs. This point can be illustrated by a comment made by the Dutch writer Hugo Grotius (1583–1645). Grotius was a devout Christian, but he thought that natural law would be binding even if 'there is no God, or he takes no care of human affairs', because it embodies rational precepts that are necessary for social existence (Grotius, 1738, p. xix).

All the writers discussed in this chapter believed that natural law has important implications for evaluating rulers' conduct and determining the fundamental rightness of humanly contrived rules that regulate social and political life. It thus provides a framework prohibiting the use of political power for certain purposes and promoting it in others. This framework specifies the relationship between *natural* and *positive* law, that is, between laws that are not due to human enactment and those that are laid down (or 'posited') by human beings and enforced through human agency. Human law is necessary because the laws of nature are general rather than specific, and lack the element of physical compulsion that is required to induce selfish human beings to act rationally (Finnis, 1980, pp. 28–29). Natural law theorists insist that human law is only legitimate if it is compatible with the general purposes specified by natural law.

While natural law is a *framework* of legitimate action, 'natural rights' (or 'human rights' as they are often referred to in contemporary political theory) are *entitlements* that individuals claim against other individuals and governments and belong to them by virtue of their humanity. Unlike legal rights, natural rights are not created by the state and apply in the state of nature as well as in political society. Legitimate governments recognise these rights and take account of them when framing positive law. Since natural rights are ascribed to human beings, they are frequently associated with an individualistic approach to politics. That is, they identify claims to free action by right holders that others are obliged to respect.

Liberty is an 'active' right that may be contrasted with 'passive' rights arising from other people's obligation not to interfere with the legitimate free actions of others. Passive rights specify the *duties* of others (including rulers) rather than the *liberty* of the right holder. The difference between these types of rights can be illustrated by comparing property rights with the right to charitable assistance. Private property rests on an active conception of rights and includes recognised and enforceable claims to use and dispose of things we own. In contrast, rights to charitable assistance are passive. They take the form of a claim *against* other individuals that obliges them to act charitably in specific circumstances (Tuck, 1979, pp. 7–15).

The distinction between active and passive rights underlies some important political implications derived from theories of natural rights on the one hand, and natural law, on the other. Nevertheless, the thinkers discussed in this chapter all maintained that an appeal to nature provides criteria for evaluating the conduct of rulers. They argued that if rulers ignore the injunctions of natural law, or fail to recognise their subjects' natural rights, they misuse the power vested in them. Since they are acting in ways that are incompatible with the ends of politics, the legitimacy of their rule is called into question and in some cases subjects might be entitled to resist them (see p.).

In what follows, examples of these approaches to politics will be drawn from a number of influential figures in the history of Western political thought. We shall begin by examining the role played by the idea of the 'natural' in ancient political theory and then trace the development and application of natural law thinking in the ancient, medieval and early-modern periods. Discussions of Aquinas' and Pufendorf's work illustrate how natural law was applied to regulating rulers' interaction with other sovereigns and providing criteria for 'just war'. Aspects of the European tradition of natural law underwrote radical theories of natural rights which emerged during the revolutionary decades of the late eighteenth century. The chapter concludes with a discussion of human rights in contemporary political theory.

The 'natural' in ancient political theory: Plato, Aristotle and Cicero

Plato's and Aristotle's views on the regulatory force of nature were framed in reaction to contemporary claims about the purely conventional character of law and the *polis*. In Plato's *Republic* Thrasymachus argues that since it is 'natural' for the strong to dominate the weak, the regulative actions of rulers are often merely a cover for the pursuit of their self-interest. Where they really do protect the weak from the strong they are unnatural. By contrast, Plato thought his ideal state was natural because it promoted the satisfaction of fundamental human needs by adopting a structure that mirrored the distinctive natural endowments of the various classes within the community. This claim was illustrated by a parallel between the well-ordered state and the well-ordered 'soul':

> we agreed that a city was just when its three natural constituents were each doing their job, and it was disciplined and brave and wise in virtue of certain other states and dispositions of those constituents ... Well, then, ... we shall expect the individual to have the same three constituents in his character and to be affected similarly, if we are to be justified in attributing the same virtues to him (ibid., pp. 185–86).

A just state is thus 'natural' because it corresponds to fundamental human attributes and satisfies basic material, social and psychological needs. Both the structure of the ideal state and the conduct of true rulers (directed towards the creation and maintenance of a just and stable state) satisfy these requirements. In contrast, the behaviour of rulers in unjust states reflects a corruption of the soul and produces instability, 'injustice, indiscipline, cowardice, ignorance and vice of all kinds' (ibid., p. 197).

Like Plato, Aristotle resisted contemporary claims about the purely conventional nature of justice, law and the state. In the *Nicomachean Ethics* he distinguished between the 'natural' – that which 'everywhere has the same force and does not exist by peoples' thinking this or that' – and the purely 'legal' (Aristotle, 1975, 1134b). Thus some things (adultery, murder and theft) are always wrong and their prohibition is not subject to the discretion of rulers. In addition to this understanding of nature as a source of universal standards, Aristotle also relates the natural to the distinctive 'good' or end of an object. According to this view, that which is more fully developed is more 'natural' because it has achieved its potential, or realised its 'essential' qualities.

Aristotle's 'teleological' conception of nature (one that is framed in terms of an object's end or *telos*) plays a central role in his account of human development and of the political dimensions of this process. Since he believed that membership of a *polis* is necessary to the 'good life' he regarded the state as a natural institution. Although the family and the neighbourhood appear first in human experience, they cannot offer the same scope for virtuous conduct as the state. Man is, as Aristotle put it, 'by nature a political animal'; that is, a being whose potentialities can only be developed fully within the *polis* (see p. 47). This teleological treatment of the *polis* implies that nature provides a criterion for evaluating political structures and behaviours. Aristotle thus distinguished 'right' from 'wrong' constitutions by examining whether power is exercised for the good of the community, or merely for the good of those who wield it (see p. 169). Right constitutions accord with the requirements of nature because they provide a political framework within which citizens can realise their potentialities. In contrast, unjust forms of government pervert the state from its true and natural role.

Although the idea of nature played a role in aspects of Plato's and Aristotle's political thinking, they did not present it in a distinctive and systematic form. A more developed account appears in the works of the Roman writer Marcus Tullius Cicero, who built upon a tradition that derived from the stoic school in Athens. Members of this school (originating in about 300 BC) argued that the universe is governed by 'right reason' which pervades all things and is identical to the supreme god, Zeus. As the stoic writer Chrysippus put it, reason is 'the ruler over all the acts both of gods and men … For all beings that are social by nature, it directs what must be done and forbids what must not be done' (Sigmund, 1971, p. 21).

Marcus Tullius Cicero (106–43 BC)

Born into a lower division of the Roman nobility, Cicero trained as a lawyer in Rome and Athens. He became a leading figure in Roman legal circles and built a political career upon this success. In 63 BC he served as consul, the most important office in Roman politics. Cicero was deeply committed to the traditional republic, in which the aristocracy had a leading role. The closing years of his life were overshadowed by events that signalled the final collapse of this system. Cicero's major political writings are *The Laws* (c. 50 BC) and *The Republic* (c. 54 BC), titles that reflect his attachment to the tradition of classical political philosophy that originated in Athens.

Key reading: Wood, 1988.

Like Plato's, Cicero's political ideas were formulated against a background of social and political dissolution. He utilised a theory of natural law to combat what he saw as rampant and destructive self-interest among his contemporaries, and to defend the traditional structure and practice of Roman politics. Cicero thought that the principles of natural law were reflected in key features of the Roman constitution and he reacted sharply to the corruption of an admirable system of government by the malign interaction of unscrupulous members of the Roman elite and the propertyless masses.

Cicero maintained that 'right reason in agreement with nature', which is 'universal in application, unchanging and everlasting', forms the basis of 'true law' (Cicero, 1970, p. 211). Law thus has a divine origin and is made accessible to human beings through reason: 'just as that divine mind is the supreme Law, so, when [reason] is perfected in man, [that also is Law]' (ibid., p. 383). Human law (whether of a customary or positive kind) is legitimate only insofar as it conforms with the fundamental principles of natural law. In an echo of Aristotle's language, Cicero defined justice as a 'mental disposition which gives everyman his desert while preserving the common interest' (Wood, 1988, p. 74). Its 'first principles ... proceed from nature' and serve both right and utility. Since the 'common interest' embraces the legitimate claims of all members of the state, there can be no conflict between the *real* interests of individuals and those of their fellows. The state is 'an association in justice', regulated by objective criteria enshrined in natural law (Cicero, 1970, p. 77). In concrete terms, the law of nature enjoins human beings to refrain from wilfully injuring one another, respect both public and private property, keep their promises, and act generously (Wood, 1988, p. 76).

Adherence to natural law is of universal benefit; those who ignore it act unnaturally, unjustly and contrary to their own real interests. These stipulations apply to rulers as well as to all other human beings. Cicero, in common with Plato and Aristotle, condemned the use of public authority for private purposes: such activity is the hallmark of the tyrant, one who governs through force and fear because his actions have no basis in justice and no hold upon the moral consciousness of his unfortunate subjects. There is, Cicero claimed,

> no creature more vile or horrible than a tyrant, or More hateful to the gods and men ...; for though he bears a human form, yet he surpasses the most monstrous of the wild beasts in the cruelty of his nature. For how could the name of human being rightly be given to a creature who desires no community of justice, no partnership in human life with his fellow-citizens – aye, even with any part of the human race (ibid., p. 156).

This remark refers to Tarquin the Proud, a notoriously bloody despot, but his grossly illegitimate use of political power – epitomised by his disregard of 'partnership' or 'community of justice' with his fellows – is merely an extreme example of a form of rule that is inhuman because it is unnatural. The self-interested use of power by the masses was no more acceptable than that of a despot. Cicero was thus highly critical of attempts to institute 'agrarian laws', which deprive the rich of their property. Laws of this kind undoubtedly offended Cicero's pro-aristocratic sensibilities, but he also condemned them because they were contrary to the natural law that obliges rulers to protect the property of their subjects.

Cicero's responses to the injustice of the despotic Tarquin, and to the rapacity of the propertyless masses at Rome, reflect the impact of natural law thinking upon his understanding of the requirements of political justice. They also explain his reservation about the practical dangers of rule by the 'one' or the 'many', and his preference for the form of mixed government that he identified with the Roman Republic (see pp. 190–93).

Medieval conceptions of natural law: St Thomas Aquinas

During the medieval period Cicero's ideas provided an important point of reference for political theorists who developed a sophisticated body of natural law theory. From the late twelfth century medieval natural law thinking was also influenced by the rediscovery of Aristotle's writings on this subject. In place of the ancients' appeal to gods presided over by a supreme god, medieval thinkers looked to a single source of divine authority. Their understanding of God's authoritative relationship to human beings was derived from Christian revelation and from the body of theology that had been deduced from this by the early leaders (or 'fathers') of the Church. Medieval natural law theory involved a series of attempts to work out the implications of divine leadership for the conduct of human affairs in a situation where the focus of attention was shifting from a transnational empire to a multitude of nation states. St Thomas Aquinas is generally considered to have provided the most sophisticated and influential medieval account of natural law, one that brought a distinctive orientation to bear on its implications for the exercise of political power. An important aspect of this approach was his attempt to integrate ideas about the naturalness of the state that were derived from ancient, pre-Christian political thought, with a body of theology that built upon the fruits of Christian revelation.

Aquinas' treatment of natural law begins with a general definition of law as 'a rule or measure of action in virtue of which one is led to perform certain actions and restrained from the performance of others' (Aquinas, 1959, p. 109). Rules of this kind are directed towards the common good of the community, and are framed and enforced by the person or persons responsible for fostering it. Since 'reason' (or more fully, 'right reason') is the faculty that directs action to its appropriate end, one can say that law is 'nothing else than a rational ordering of things which concern the common good; promulgated by whoever is charged with the care of the community' (ibid., p. 113). Ultimately this responsibility lies with God, the creator and governor of his entire creation, but in the human world, and especially in less extensive communities such as the state, it lies with the ruler.

In line with his view of God's supreme position, Aquinas argued that systems of legitimate law derive from 'eternal law', that is, a set of rules formulated by God to direct the actions of *all* of his creation.

> Just as in the mind of every artist there already exists the idea of what he will create by his art, so in the mind of every ruler there must already exist an ideal of order with respect to what shall be done by those subject to his rule. ... Accordingly, the eternal law is nothing other than the ideal of divine wisdom considered as directing all actions and movements (ibid., pp. 119–21).

While eternal law forms the core of all legitimate or true systems of law, those which specifically direct human beings may be subdivided into distinct types. In his discussion of this topic in *Summa Theologica*, Aquinas identified three such categories of law: divine law, natural law and human law. These terms differentiate the immediate *sources* of law, not those whom it directs. All these forms of law direct human beings to their 'end', but they are derived from a number of sources, and focus on different aspects of human experience.

Unlike many earlier Christian exponents of natural law theory, Aquinas went to some pains to differentiate natural law from divine law. While the former relates to the 'natural' qualities of humanity, the latter is necessary because the destiny of human beings lies in their attainment of 'eternal blessedness', a condition that extends far beyond the limitations imposed by their natural faculties. Since it is necessary for humans to be placed under a system of law that is incapable of error and addresses both their external activities and those 'hidden interior actions of the soul' that are an important aspect of human perfectibility, they must be subject to divine as well as to natural law. Divine law is necessarily all-encompassing; it supplements the variable products of human reason with the fruits of revelation and the teachings of the Church. In contrast, human and natural law are limited in scope, the latter by its very nature, the former because of its unavoidable concern with the external rather than the internal side of human action. Human law thus embraces only those aspects of life that can be known to human beings and regulated by them (ibid., p. 117).

Aquinas argued that natural law is derived from and closely related to humans' natural faculties and inclinations. Rational reflection upon these inclinations enables them to understand the implications of eternal law for their natural existence. Because humans share in divine reason to some degree, they can acquire both 'a natural inclination to such actions and ends as are fitting' and an understanding of the substance of natural law. Hence 'the natural law is nothing else than the participation of the eternal law in rational creatures' (ibid., p. 115). Aquinas identified three major 'precepts' (or general rules) of natural law, each of which corresponds to a natural inclination. The inclination towards *preservation* gives rise to precepts enjoining the preservation of human life and prohibiting its wilful destruction; the inclination towards *procreation* produces precepts governing sexual relationships and the care of children, while that promoting a positive concern for the *good of humanity* produces an inclination to live in society (since this is necessary to human well-being) as well as ensuring that social life produces the benefits of which it is capable (ibid., p. 123).

When the general precepts of natural law are subjected to rational reflection directed towards the good of particular communities, they form the basis of legitimate or 'true' human law. 'Human reason' proceeds 'from the precepts of the natural law, as though from certain common and indemonstrable principles, to other more particular dispositions ... [which are] called human laws' (ibid., p. 115). Both the specification of human law and its enforcement are necessary to provide the discipline required for a virtuous life, particularly in respect of those things which are directly dependent upon social life. Although human law is not merely a copy of natural law, Aquinas maintained that it is validated morally by it (Finnis, 1980, p. 28). The detailed specifications of legitimate human law relate to natural law in one of two ways. They are either 'conclusions' drawn from its precepts – for example, a law against murder is a conclusion drawn from the precept prohibiting harm to other human beings – or they are applications of a general requirement to a particular instance. Human laws thus specify penalties 'in determination of' the natural law requiring that those who transgress should be punished (Aquinas, 1959, p. 129). These distinctions identify the relationship between human and natural law, and they also address more specific queries concerning the extent to which particular human laws can be derived from natural law. The first of these issues is important if positive law is to be seen as legitimate, while the second deals with problems posed by the variety of human laws. In either case the relationship between human law, natural law and eternal law provides a criterion for distinguishing 'just' from 'unjust' laws and defining standards of probity to which the acts of rulers should conform.

The fact that true human laws are just does not preclude the possibility that they will take various forms. Human laws are formulated to promote the welfare of particular communities: they must differ in their details according both to the circumstances of the community in question and the characteristics of those whose lives they regulate. The crucial point is that any variations must accord with the general purposes specified by natural law and embodied in its secondary, or derivative, precepts. Laws that benefit only those who hold political office, or narrow the idea of the common good by imposing unfair burdens on some members of the community, are contrary to natural law and necessarily involve the illegitimate exercise of political power. The same holds true of laws that fly in the face of divine law, such as those enforcing idolatry. Human law simply cannot address the positive, internal requirements of divine law since these relate to the conscience, but some uses of political authority might be illegitimate because they are clearly contrary to the expressed will of God (ibid., p. 137).

In the same way that eternal law embodies the will of God, human law is the will of the human lawgiver or ruler. Because rulers create and enforce human law they cannot be subject to its constraining force. However, just rulers will subject themselves to what Aquinas called the 'directive power' of human law because they are under an overriding moral obligation to further the common good and just laws are important means to this end. Because rulers *are* the immediate source of human law, however, they may amend it when this becomes necessary, and they may also dispense with it in particular cases. As with all legitimate exercises of power, however, acts of dispensation are not arbitrary. Good rulers are guided by a sincere and impartial concern for the common good, not by self-interest, and they act in conformity with the precepts of natural law (ibid., pp. 137–39, 143).

Aquinas' account of the relationship between natural and human laws provides a criterion for evaluating the former and specifying the general but overriding concerns that determine the ways in which political power should be exercised. For example, in common with a number of his predecessors, Aquinas identified tyrannical rule with a wanton disregard for natural law, one that gives rise to unjust actions on the part of rulers and their agents, and to systems of regulation that are perversions of the very idea of law (ibid., pp. 55–61). He also deployed natural law theory to delegitimise some uses of political authority. For example, Aquinas argued that private property is in accordance with natural law because it is necessary for peaceful and generally productive social interaction. This means that rulers are under an obligation to recognise these rights. Consequently, subjects can only be taxed without their consent in cases of emergency, and can only be forced to give up their property to others when a general obligation to provide charitable assistance comes into play (ibid., p. 171).

The regulatory force of natural law applies to external as well as internal relations. Aquinas argued that while it is illegitimate for rulers to wilfully attack other states, there were circumstances in which war was justified. This argument is framed in response to scripturally supported claims that Christians should not actively resist evil or even defend themselves, and that war is always sinful because it is 'contrary to peace'. Aquinas responded to these claims by citing Augustine's dictum that wars were just 'when a nation or a state is … punished for having failed to make amends for wrong done, or to restore what has been taken unjustly' (ibid., p. 159). War may thus be seen a continuation beyond the bounds of the state of the responsibilities that rulers exercise under natural law within the state. In the same way that the prince is '"an avenger to execute wrath upon him that doth evil"' so too is he charged with the 'duty of defending the state, with weapons of war, against external enemies' (ibid.). When they make legitimate declarations of war, rulers are acting for the common good, both in the defence of the right of their subjects and in punishing those who are guilty of serious breaches of natural law.

Aquinas' stress on rulers' responsibilities allows him to counter biblical injunctions prohibiting forceful resistance to evil by private persons and to treat those who actually 'take up the sword' as acting in response to the commands of a legitimate superior. Both these commands, and actions in fulfilment of them, must be motivated by a 'right intention', that is, an intention to punish those who deserve it, and/or provide restitution for those who have suffered through their wrongdoing. This stipulation rules out wars launched for territorial gain or booty and delegitimises wars motivated by ideas of princely reputation and glory (ibid., pp. 37–39).

For Aquinas, as for Augustine, the overarching objective of just war is the restoration of peace, a goal which mirrors the general purpose of legitimate rule within the state: '"For the true followers of God, even wars are peaceful, not being made for greed or out of cruelty, but from desire of peace, to restrain the evil and assist the good"' (ibid., pp. 159–61). This stipulation has important implications for the conduct of war, as well as for the ruler's motivation in waging it. It confirms the prohibition of wanton cruelty in war that is implied by the insistence on appropriate motivation, and when combined with the punitive and restorative rationales for just war it points to the need for inter-state violence to be proportionate to legitimate cause and be consistent with its ultimate objective.

Aquinas thus thought that rulers' obligations to uphold natural law within their state finds an external parallel in their duty to actively resist the unjust actions of other rulers and their subjects. Since, however, they have no legislative power over external actors, they are only able to deal with significant wrongdoing by non-subjects through violent executive action. Aquinas' criteria of just war – legitimate authorisation, just cause and rightful intention – are related closely to natural law specifications of legitimate authority that he applied in his account of political rule within the state. Rulers who ignore these conditions undermine their authority in the same way as tyrants do.

Although Aquinas refers to Augustine as an authority in his discussion of just war, his predecessor had at times seen just war as a benefit for those who were the object of it: Christians will wage war, 'in a spirit of benevolence; their aim will be to serve the defeated more easily by securing a peaceful society that is pious and just. For if defeat deprives the beaten side of the freedom to act wickedly, it benefits them' (Augustine, 2001, p. 38). In place of this passive, or at least diffident image, Aquinas' theory of just war promoted rulers' positive duty under natural law to defend their subjects (Aquinas, 1959, p. 83). Moreover, for Aquinas as for Aristotle, ideas of common good extend beyond the limits of particular states, and the requirements of natural law that relate to them provide the basis for transnational ideas of political society. The stipulation that only legitimate rulers can authorise war prohibits private vengeance against external wrongdoers and affirms that punitive action beyond the state is an expression of common interests and shared values. The idea that 'common well-being ... is the object of justice' thus applies to both externally and internally focused exercises of political authority (ibid., p. 165).

Natural rights in early-modern political theory: Suàrez, Grotius, Hobbes and Pufendorf

When 'natural freedom' became an important theme in early-modern political theory, it was often treated in a conventional natural law framework that was similar in most respects to that developed by Aquinas. For example, the influential Spanish writer Francesco Suàrez (1547–1617) argued that if humans had not fallen from grace they would not have been subjected to coercive authority. Even in this situation however, they would be directed or guided by other human beings and they were, in any case, subject to divine jurisdiction as specified by both divine and natural law (Suàrez, 1856–78, vol. iii, p. 417). While Suárez remained deeply committed to Roman Catholicism, the approach to natural freedom advanced in his writings formed the starting point for theories of politics that became increasingly divorced from the theological underpinnings of Christianity.

An important stage in the secularisation of natural rights theory can be discerned in Hugo Grotius' and Samuel Pufendorf's writings. Although Grotius continued to regard natural law as a product of divine wisdom enforced by divine command, he raised the possibility that it could be justified on the grounds of reason alone (see p. 167). Given the absence of human superiors in the state of nature, and given also the dependence of human beings upon the fruits of sociability, there is a logical necessity for effective systems of regulation that will make sociability viable. From this perspective, the 'law of nature' can be understood as a system of regulation that is necessary for social life, rather than one that derives its binding force from its divine source. For Grotius, sociability necessitates rights to natural liberty, promise keeping and respect for private property (Grotius, 1738, p. xvii; Haakonssen, 1985; Tuck, 1979, pp. 67–77). For Pufendorf, the law of nature stipulates natural equality – 'every man should esteem and treat another man as his equal by nature, or as much a man as himself' – and this facilitates reciprocity, rules out natural servitude and underwrites the impartial adjudication of wrongdoing (Pufendorf, 1934, pp. 330, 336–40).

Grotius believed, however, that even when sociability is sustained by the logical force of the laws of nature it is likely to be precarious. The reasons for this unproductive uncertainty are spelt out most graphically in Thomas Hobbes' account of the state of nature, but his is only one of a number of contemporary statements that point to the hazards of a natural condition and identify the state as a solution to them. For example, while Pufendorf traced the evils of the state of nature to depravity, ignorance and weakness, rather than to the implications of the legitimate pursuit of one's rights, the contrast he draws between this condition and civil society is at least as sharp as Hobbes': in a natural condition 'there is the rule of passion, war, fear, poverty, ugliness, solitude, barbarism, ignorance, savagery'. In contrast, membership of political society makes it possible for human beings to enjoy 'the rule of reason, peace, security, riches, beauty, society, refinement, knowledge, good will' (Pufendorf, 1927, p. 91).

Since Grotius and Pufendorf considered natural beings to be free, they insisted that the acquisition of political power must be based on consent (Tuck, 1993, p. 175). However, this condition applies only to the *original* creation of sovereign power. Once sovereignty comes into existence, those who were subject originally to the paternal power of their fathers assumed the obligations that had been entered into by them. This stipulation limits the consent requirement quite significantly, but in any case the fact that government is created by consent does not necessarily impose restraints upon the exercise of political power by sovereigns. The reason for this is that bearers of natural rights are free to place themselves under an absolute ruler, or even to become slaves. However, while Grotius and Pufendorf regarded the creation of an unlimited (even despotic) sovereign as a legitimate outcome of consent, they did not make it a necessary one. Subjects may renounce all their rights, but they can create a useful source of political authority by consenting to something less awesome than Hobbes' Leviathan. This possibility rests upon the principle of 'interpretative charity', which assumes that subjects retain some rights. That is, the contractual arrangement that creates sovereignty permits the contracting parties to set limits on the way in which sovereign power is exercised (Pufendorf, 1934, p. 1064; 1927, p. 131). These stipulations rely on the obligatory force of promises and are therefore products of the law of nature.

Unlike Hobbes, Pufendorf maintained that rights implied corresponding duties to respect the rights of others (Brown et al., 2001). These duties were given a decidedly positive direction by his idea of 'sociality':

> The laws of … sociality … [which] teach one how to conduct oneself to become a useful … member of society, are called natural laws. … On this basis it is evident that the fundamental natural law is: every man ought to do as much as he can to cultivate and preserve sociality. Since he who wills the end wills also the means …, it follows that all that necessarily and normally makes for sociality is understood to be prescribed by natural law (Pufendorf, 1991, pp. 35–36).

Sociality was threatened by external as well as by internal lawlessness, so sovereigns had a duty under natural law to resist threats to it that came from outside the state and were answerable to God for their performance of it.

Pufendorf's views on this responsibility reflected the pattern of international relations that emerged from the Treaty of Westphalia of 1648. It established what he took to be the fundamental requirement for a system of international law, namely, the recognition of European sovereigns as rightful rulers of their subjects and territories, and as moral equals to whom considerations of justice applied (Pufendorf, 1934, pp. 17a, 22a). The Treaty laid the basis for a generally pacific European landscape in which sovereigns maintained a balance of power through alliances, diplomacy and relatively limited bouts of corrective warfare (Tully, 1991, pp. xv, xx–i). Three features of Pufendorf's political thinking were well-aligned with this international system.

In the first place, Pufendorf identified the laws of nature with the promotion of sociality and thought that there was widespread understanding that they were subject to divine enforcement. Secondly, and as a consequence of that, he rejected Hobbes' assumption that individuals in a state of nature have the right to do anything that they think necessary to preserve their lives (see p. 28). Thirdly, since natural individuals were subject to moral constraints specified in the law of nature, states of nature were not, as Hobbes had argued, necessarily conditions of war. Pufendorf recognised that sociality was likely to be impaired by greedy and irrational behaviour but this meant that war disrupted peace in the state of nature, not that it was a condition of war.

The difference between Hobbes' and Pufendorf's characterisation of the state of nature is exemplified in the latter's utilisation of the idea of 'just war'. While Hobbes insisted that the state of nature is a non-moral environment where the terms 'just' and 'unjust' have no meaning (see above, p. 176) Pufendorf thought that as the laws of nature played a positive, if by no means consistent role in the international state of nature, it was possible to apply ideas of justice there and to distinguish just from unjust wars. Wars were justified morally when those who embarked on them acted to protect interests recognised by the laws of nature and conducted themselves in ways that were consistent with them. If diplomacy or arbitration failed, sovereigns had a duty to declare war on foreign powers, repel incursions on their territory, and recover property or reparations wrongfully withheld. Pufendorf's warning that 'good sense and humanity counsel us not to resort to arms when more evil than good is likely to overtake us and ours by the prosecution of our wrongs' (Pufendorf, 1991, p. 168) is consistent with his protective and reparative justifications for war. It suggests that obviously reckless declarations may not be just.

Pufendorf's account of the moral rationale of war corresponds with his understanding of the ends of the state and the role of natural law in promoting and sustaining sociality. By contrast, unjust wars are prompted by 'avarice and ambition, namely lust for wealth and lust for power' (ibid., p. 168). Sovereigns who are motivated by these considerations unjustly disrupt international peace and hazard the security of their subjects. They thus act contrary to natural law in a double sense. Their ambitions are unjust and their actions have an adverse impact on domestic and international sociality.

Finally, Pufendorf argued that the laws of nature have implications for the conduct of war. Pufendorf did not shrink from the harsh realities of international violence, observing that 'the most proper forms of action in war are force and terror', that participants rightly share an 'intention to inflict the last degree of suffering' on each other and that they are entitled to utilise fraud and deceit whenever they think it necessary. He insisted, nevertheless, that the moral prohibition of promise-breaking applies in war as well as in peace, and that savagery in warfare should not be gratuitous and unrelated to the grounds of just war: 'Humanity ... requires that so far as the momentum of warfare permits, we should inflict no more suffering on an enemy than defence or vindication of our right and its future assurance requires' (ibid., p. 169).

Natural law, natural rights and limited government: Locke

Although Locke thought it important to differentiate natural rights from natural law (Sigmund, 1971, p. 91), he insisted that they are closely related because the primary natural right, the right to complete freedom from control by other human beings, was conditioned by the laws of nature. As he put it in the *Second Treatise of Government*,

> [a]ll men are naturally in ... a *State of perfect Freedom* to order their actions, and dispose of their Possessions, and Persons as they think fit, within the bounds of the Law of Nature, without asking leave, or depending upon the Will of any Man (Locke, 1967, p. 287).

This state of 'perfect freedom' is related negatively to the law of nature. Thus Locke argued that as all individuals in the state of nature are equals, no one has the right to assume a position of supremacy without the consent of those who will become their subjects. He also, however, offered a positive justification for natural freedom, one that rests on his understanding of human beings' responsibilities to God, their acknowledged creator and master:

> For Men being all the Workmanship of one Omnipotent, and infinitely wise Maker; All the Servants of one Sovereign Master, sent into the World by his order and about his business, they are his Property, whose Workmanship they are, made to last during his, not one anothers' Pleasure. And being furnished with like Faculties, sharing all in one Community of Nature, there cannot be supposed any such *Subordination* among us, that may Authorize us to destroy one another, as if we were made for one anothers' uses, as the inferior ranks of Creatures are made for ours (ibid., p. 289).

Humans' responsibility to God provides the basis for a prioritised list of obligations. First, they should seek to secure their own preservation. Secondly, they should be actively concerned for the preservation of others when this does not conflict with self-preservation. Thirdly, they must avoid harming others, and finally, they should uphold the law of nature by punishing transgressors and extracting compensation from them (ibid., pp. 289–90).

In the state of nature the fulfilment of these obligations is problematic because of natural individuals' limited physical power and their tendency to judge partially and punish harshly (and thus unjustly) in cases that affect themselves. Locke argued, however, that these 'inconveniences' will be compounded if arbitrary, unlimited power is placed in the hands of governors. Indeed, those who lay claim to such power put themselves into a state of war with their fellows by posing an active threat to their preservation (ibid., pp. 293–94, 297). In direct contradiction to the position advanced by Grotius, Hobbes and Pufendorf, Locke argued that voluntary submission to an absolute ruler is a breach of the law of nature: it makes self-preservation, and the fulfilment of other obligations to God, dependent upon the will of another:

> *Freedom* from Absolute, Arbitrary Power, is so necessary to, and closely joyned with a Man's Preservation, that he cannot part with it, but by what forfeits his Preservation and Life together. For a Man, not having the Power of his own Life, *cannot*, by Compact, or his own Consent,

enslave himself to any one, nor put himself under the Absolute, Arbitrary Power of another, to take away his Life, when he pleases. No body can give more Power than he has himself; and he that cannot take away his own Life, cannot give another power over it (ibid., p. 302).

Locke denied that paternal power is absolute, and he would not allow that submission to a parent can provide the basis for subjection to an absolute sovereign. 'Paternal power' (which is more accurately termed 'parental power') is regulated by the laws of nature, and since it concerns the nurturing and education of children, it can only be exercised over those who have not attained adulthood. In any case, Locke drew a sharp distinction between 'paternal' power which operates within the family and the 'political' power possessed by the legitimate ruler of a state. Political power is created by the consent of free, rational beings and is directed through the agency of government to the good of the community. By providing 'established, settled known laws', 'known and indifferent judges' and power to back their right judgement (ibid., pp. 368–69), government alleviates the problems of determination, adjudication and just and effective punishment that occur in the state of nature. It thus makes an invaluable contribution to human preservation and in so doing provides those subject to it with a means of fulfilling their obligations under the law of nature.

> A Man … having in the State of Nature no Arbitrary Power over the Life, Liberty, or Possession of another, but only so much as the Law of Nature gave him for the preservation of himself, and the rest of Mankind; this is all he doth, or can give up to the Common-wealth, and by it to the *Legislative Power*, so that the Legislative can have no more than this. Their Power in the utmost Bounds of it, is *limited to the publick good* of the Society' (ibid., p. 375).

When rulers defy these stipulations, government is 'dissolved', a phrase that Locke used to show that it has lost its legitimacy. In these circumstances, rulers exercise despotic, not *political*, power. Consequently, they no longer have a claim upon the loyalty and obedience of their subjects. As we shall see, Locke argued that subjects of unlawful rulers have an obligation to cast off their authority and recreate a legitimate government (see pp. 248–52).

The radical application of natural rights in late-eighteenth-century political theory: Condorcet and Paine

In eighteenth-century Germany, Grotius' and Pufendorf's conception of pre-political beings consenting to trade their freedom for the security provided by an all-powerful monarch provided the basis for theories of absolute monarchy (Krieger, 1972, p. 67). Elsewhere, however, a more radical tradition of natural rights thinking echoed aspects of Locke's theory. Thomas Jefferson's 'Declaration of Independence' of 1775–76 appealed to 'inalienable rights' to 'life, liberty and the pursuit of happiness', while at an earlier stage in the contest between Britain and her North American colonies, James Otis, in *The Rights of the British Colonies Asserted and Proved* (1764), argued that the law-making powers of the British parliament were conditioned by a higher authority, variously described as 'the laws of nature and of nations, the voice of universal reason, and of God' (Sigmund, 1971, p. 112). However, the most politically far-reaching statements of the radical implications of natural right appeared during the European revolutions that followed the collapse of the *ancien régime* in France in 1789.

The 'Declaration of the Rights of Man and Citizens', issued by the French National Assembly in 1789, placed natural rights at the centre of the new system of government. The preamble to this document stated that 'ignorance, neglect, or contempt of human rights, are the sole causes of public misfortunes and corruptions of Government', while its second clause stipulated that 'the end of all political associations, is the preservation of the natural and imprescriptible rights of man; and these rights are liberty, property, security, and resistance to oppression' (Ritchie, 1902, p. 291). The 'Declaration' was prefixed to the French Constitution of 1791. Some writers saw this document as a significant but incomplete embodiment of the political implications of natural rights. For example, in his *Sketch for a Historical Picture of the Progress of the Human Mind* (1793) Antoine-Nicolas de Condorcet looked to future developments to produce a social and political structure that took full account of the expansive possibilities opened up by the recognition of universal human rights. For Condorcet, rights were related to the realisation of the potentialities of all human beings, and he thought this required universal suffrage, full equality between the sexes, the self-determination of colonial societies, freedom of thought and expression, and the assumption of social responsibility for education, welfare insurance and a measure of wealth redistribution (Condorcet, 1955, pp. 171–202).

The challenge to absolute monarchy in France was watched with great interest by radical writers in Great Britain who appealed to natural rights when developing sharp criticisms of traditional English government. The most widely circulated of these criticisms, *The Rights of Man*, was written by Thomas Paine, an Englishman who had played a prominent role in the American Revolution. Paine utilised a radical interpretation of biblical history to argue that the creation provided an egalitarian and libertarian model that had binding implications for the regulation of human affairs: 'Every history of the creation, and every traditionary account ... all agree in establishing one point, *the unity of man*; by which I mean, that all men are all of *one degree*, and consequently that all men are born equal, and with equal natural right.' Complete equality was enjoyed by succeeding generations as well as by the original human inhabitants of the world: 'every child born into the world must be considered as deriving its existence from God. The world is as new to him as it was to the first man that existed, and his natural right in it is of the same kind' (Paine, 1976, p. 88). Paine thus identified a direct relationship between each individual and God, and used this as a basis upon which to claim that all human beings possess identical, inviolable natural rights.

These rights – to intellectual and religious liberty, to pursue one's 'comfort and happiness' in any way that is 'not injurious to the natural rights of others', and to judge and to punish those who breach this condition – 'appertain to man in right of his existence'. They provide what Paine called the 'foundation' of 'civil rights', those rights 'which pertain to man in right of his being a member of society' (ibid., p. 90). For Paine, as for Locke, problems of jurisdiction and enforcement provided the motivation for creating political authority. As in Locke's theory, the exchange of natural for civil rights created a moral continuity of the natural and political condition:

> The natural rights which are not retained, are all those in which, though the right is perfect in the individual, the power to execute them is defective. They answer not to his purpose. A man, by natural right, has a right to judge in his own cause; and so far as the right of mind is concerned, he never surrenders it: but what availeth it him to judge, if he has not power to redress? He therefore deposits this right in the common stock of society, and takes the arm of society, of which he is a

part, in preference and in addition to his own. Society *grants* him nothing. Every man is a proprietor in society, and draws on the capital as a matter of right (ibid., pp. 90–91).

Because no one has a right to subject other human beings to their authority, government must be based on the consent of those who wish to place *some* of their natural rights in a collective agency. Paine insisted that individuals must retain full control over their religious and intellectual rights ('rights of mind') because they can be exercised perfectly well without the assistance of government and interference with them negates their value to right-holders. In addition to these historically significant limitations on the exercise of political power, Paine's conception of natural rights had other important implications. Like Locke's predecessors, Paine employed the idea of 'interpretative charity' to eliminate the possibility of a total surrender of rights to an absolute sovereign: 'Man did not enter into society to become *worse* than he was before, nor to have fewer rights than he had before, but to have those rights better secured' (ibid., p. 90). This stipulation explains why Paine thought that people should not give up their right to religious and intellectual freedom; it also underwrote his claim that as many tasks as possible should be left to voluntary social cooperation (see p. 66).

The idea of interpretative charity plays a particularly important role in Paine's critique of monarchical and aristocratic government. Paine thought that free individuals would never voluntarily place themselves under monarchy because they will then be worse off than they were in a state of nature. Monarchs lack information and expertise – they are selected on the basis of irrational, hereditary processes – and have no sympathy with the interests of their subjects. By contrast, 'new' governments – by which Paine meant representative democracy – are closely attached to the true feelings of the community and utilise its talents. If officeholders really represent the interests of their constituents and are selected on the basis of proven ability and probity, there will be a close fit between the interests and intelligence of society and the attributes, motivation and conduct of officeholders (see pp. 149–51). Under these conditions the exercise of political power contributes to the good of all the members of the community and will thus ensure that the purpose of civil society – to facilitate individuals' pursuit of their 'comfort and happiness' in accordance with their natural rights – will be fulfilled.

Although some radicals and socialists continued to appeal to natural rights until well into the nineteenth century (Claeys, 1989a), this period also saw a growing reaction against this way of thinking. As we have seen, a number of conservative thinkers rejected the individualistic focus of revolutionary appeals to natural rights. They argued in favour of the ideas of historical community on the grounds that they matched the facts of human development and provided the framework for psychologically satisfying and stable social and political systems. Among radical critics, however, it was not the individualistic cast of natural rights theories that was at issue, or the threat they posed to the established order, but rather their detrimental impact upon favoured programmes of political reform. A rhetorically powerful example of this approach was presented by Jeremy Bentham in his essay 'Anarchical Fallacies' (1824). Bentham claimed that rights are a product of government and that there can be no rights in a natural condition. He dismissed the contrary view as

mischievous nonsense: immediately a list of these pretended rights is given, and those are so expressed as to present to view legal rights. And of these rights, whatever they are, there is not it seems, any one of which any government *can*, upon any occasion whatever, abrogate the smallest particle (Bentham, 1843a, vol. ii, p. 501).

Bentham argued that rights should only be recognised in what is 'advantageous to society', as determined by reference to his principle of utility. He dismissed natural rights as dangerous fictions that ignored considerations of utility and imposed dysfunctional constraints on the use of political power to advance the 'greatest happiness of the greatest number'.

Nineteenth-century proponents of social freedom were no more enamoured of natural rights theory than Bentham and his followers. For Hegel, natural rights were identified with one-sided conceptions of abstract right that focused on the arbitrary choices of individuals and were not integrated into the systems of morality and social interdependence that are required if humans are to experience true freedom (see p. 83). The British idealists' stress on rights and social recognition ruled out conceptions of natural rights as fundamental pre-social attributes of individuals. T. H. Green noted that claims recognised in progressive modern states may have evolved from earlier, 'primitive' states of society but he insisted that neither their origin nor their transmission explained why they were recognised as rights. That depended on their perceived value in relation to the common good (Green, 1986, pp. 16–17).

Conclusion

Theories of natural law and natural rights identify normative constraints on the exercise of political power. Actions that fail to satisfy the requirements of natural law, or encroach upon natural rights, frustrate the purposes for which government exists and are therefore illegitimate. Although natural law theories frequently involve a 'passive' conception of rights, they give rise to a more positive conception of government than those that rest upon ideas of natural right. In many formulations, natural rights doctrines are strongly defensive. That is, they specify individual claims to free action and they prohibit exercises of political power that infringe natural rights. These features of natural rights theory are reflected in Locke's condemnation of arbitrary government, and in Paine's rejection of hereditary monarchy and aristocracy. Even where natural rights play an important defensive role, however, they may give rise to positive political outcomes. Thus while Paine insisted that legitimate forms of government must take account of individuals' natural rights, he also argued that these rights can only be adequately defended in systems of popular, representative government.

Bentham's and Green's criticisms of natural rights theory were part of a more general tendency for this way of thinking about politics to be pushed to the margins of nineteenth- and early-twentieth-century political thought. In recent years, however, natural rights theory has again become of interest to some contemporary political philosophers. These discussions sometimes engage with historical treatments. Thus in *Natural Law and Natural Rights*, the English philosopher John Finnis developed a modern restatement of natural law theory which includes extensive reflections on the significance of Aquinas' ideas (Finnis, 1980). In a very different vein, the American philosopher Robert Nozick has used a conception of natural rights which he derived from Locke to challenge a range of assumptions concerning the claims that states and other collective entities make on their members (see p. 95).

While Finnis' suggestion that 'human rights' can be treated as 'contemporary idiom for "natural rights"' is generally useful, there are significant differences in the way that these ideas are presented, and in some of the implications that are drawn from them (Finnis, 1980, p. 198). Unlike the natural rights of historical theory, human rights are not seen as expressions of God's will. Rather, these rights belong to individuals by virtue of their humanity (Gewirth, 1981, p. 119). Moreover, while both historical and contemporary theorists treat natural rights as fixed and universally valid, many of them think they may be subject to change – for example, new rights may emerge – and they seek to prioritise existing rights on the basis of circumstantial considerations. Some rights may have to give way to others, and not all human rights can be recognised in all situations (Pennock, 1981, p. 7). Moreover, contemporary thinking about human rights often looks beyond the bounds of the state, stressing the need to uphold these rights within the international community. Thus while human rights are accepted in principle as a basis for fundamental legal enactments within states, they are also recognised as a matter of international concern (Henkin, 1981, pp. 258–59).

In the latter case, questions arise about the content of human rights and the ways in which they can be upheld effectively. Apart from practical problems of enforcement in an international environment that recognises state sovereignty, the idea of human rights runs the risk of universalising standards that are only adhered to in certain (usually Western) cultures. One way round this difficulty is to restrict ideas of human rights to *political* contexts. This approach rests on the idea that despite wide cultural divergences, right claims made in response to torture, arbitrary imprisonment and censorship are genuinely universal (Ingram, 1994, pp. 199–200).

In other cases, however, it has been argued that rights claimed by sections of the population are as fundamental to their well-being as universal rights are for humanity as a whole. Three related sets of such claims have played a significant role in contemporary political thought. The first is associated with feminist critiques of the assumptions underpinning liberal democracies, the second has arisen in the context of a debate on the implications of multiculturalism in Western societies, while the third has an important bearing on the application of ideas of restorative justice to the indigenous populations of countries now dominated by migrants and their descendants.

Iris Marion Young and a number of other prominent feminist philosophers active in the 1980s and 1990s argued that the pursuit of gender equality in Western societies was impeded by pseudo-universal values embedded in liberal-democratic cultures. They argued that it is necessary to adopt structures and procedures that take account of the *special* (and neglected) interests and needs of sections of society (including, but not limited to, women) whose oppressed status is merely confirmed if they are treated *as if* they are already equal with others. This is because the universal ideal ignores differences in an arbitrary and unfair way. That is, it ignores some interests (those important to women) and promotes others (identified with men) while pretending that these interests are really universal ones.

In practical terms, special interests can be given recognition by granting special rights to members of disadvantaged groups. These rights are justified on the grounds that they are necessary to counteract and overcome the injustices and inequalities that are built into existing institutions and practices and that will be perpetuated if everybody is merely granted the same rights. Examples of these special rights include affirmative action and equal opportunity programmes, the provision of targeted facilities and services, and structuring political organisations so that they recognise the special rights accorded to some of their members (Young, 1990b).

Young's feminism was part of a broader agenda promoting what has become known as 'identity politics'. This approach rests on the assumption that group membership and the status of groups have a significant impact on how individuals conceive of their lives and frame their futures. An important aspect of this way of thinking is that group membership and the identity that flows from it must be regarded as a political, rather than merely a private matter. The interests of individuals as members of groups should be recognised in the political realm, protected, and in some cases furthered, by being assigned rights. In much the same way that Paine thought of rights as necessary to individual autonomy, they are also held to be necessary to groups and the embedded individuals whose identity is forged by membership of them. It is not therefore a matter of groups seeking toleration, or the mere right to exisit; rather, they have stronger claims that should be recognised in law and upheld by the state.

Issues of difference and identity have been at the heart of a vigorous debate in contemporary political theory on 'multiculturalism'. Will Kymlicka has been an important contributor to this debate, and especially to that part of it which concerns the role of ethnic and national minorities in modern nation states. These states have rarely been homogenous. Indeed, one of the early challenges facing European nation states was the perceived need to forge a sense of national identity which was often hostile to diversity, or at best indifferent to it. These attempts met with varying degrees of success and in the latter part of the twenieth century migrations have introduced a range of new groups into established nation-states. Some liberals would argue that the state should be neutral between ethnic and cultural groups, offering their members the same universal rights that are enjoyed by other citizens. Partly because members of these groups frequently suffer significant economic and social disadvantages, however, offers of this kind have not necessarily been greeted with enthusiasm. To the contrary, claims have been made to special rights by members of groups and their representatives, and issues concerning the status of groups have become prominent in contemporary political and philosophical debate.

Kymlicka's contribution starts from an allegedly liberal stand point since he relates group membership to individual consciousness. The life plans of group members, the individual projects of mainstream liberal theory, are inextricably tied up with the values to which the group and its members subscribe and the cultural practices to which they adhere. For this reason, Kymlicka argues that some groups should enjoy legal protection and special rights, including those of limited self-government. These rights do not apply, however, to *all* groups. Kymlicka makes a distinction between 'societal cultures' that form the basis for a distinct, embracing and historically enduring way of life for their members, and 'sub-cultures' and other 'life style choice' groups that do not meet these requirements (Kymlicka, 1995, pp. 18–19).

This distinction has been called into question by those who wish to extend special rights to a far wider range of groups with which individuals identify closely. The point at issue here is whether groups based on voluntary associational principles, or on other forms of identity, for example, gender or sexuality, also have claims to special recognition. In some cases, this requirement is not just a matter of recognising a range of identities and group rights because some claims arising from societal-cultural identity may curtail options for voluntary association and other focal points of identity, including those arising from gender and sexuality.

The third area where a reliance on universalistic notions of rights has been found wanting is where sections of the population of liberal democracies have claims that extend beyond those provided by the recognition of universal rights for protection against harm. Examples of such claims include indigenous peoples' attempts to redress the grievously detrimental impact of colonisation upon their educational and health status and life prospects, and to have rights to property, self-government or cultural recognition restored (Ivison, 1997, pp. 165–66). These claims sometimes appear to conflict with universalistic notions of human rights subscribed to by descendants of migrant groups in former settler colonies. Since, however, the history of these societies has been marked by the systematic and casual disregard of the rights of indigenous communities, the recognition of special claims is justified by reference to these injustices and inequalities, and to their ongoing accumulative impact on the cultural, economic and social well-being of indigenous peoples. Measures of redress adopted in Australia, Canada and New Zealand thus include special rights of access to targeted educational and health facilities and services, and the utilisation of mechanisms such as reserved seats and electoral quotas which help to ensure effective participation in political decision-making. In some cases, rights are assigned to groups rather than individuals in recognition of their distinctive socio-cultural significance for indigenous peoples. These responses are distinct from, but may be related to, government-mandated processes for investigating historical infringements of the rights of indigenous peoples. As unjustly treated parties, they are entitled to benefit from restorative measures that parallel those applied to other members of the community whose rights have been infringed.

MIXED GOVERNMENT, BALANCED CONSTITUTIONS AND THE SEPARATION OF POWERS

10

This chapter considers theories that identify distinctive constitutional arrangements that constrain rulers' wrong actions and facilitate their active pursuit of the good of the community. The theorists discussed here almost invariably assume that assigning exclusive power to particular individuals, groups or classes carries with it significant risk that power will be misused. The means chosen to manage this risk tend to be *institutional* rather than *normative* and focus primarily on mechanisms of government rather than promoting desirable standards of political behaviour. However, this point must not be pushed too far. As we shall see, it is common for theorists of mixed government, balanced constitutions and the separation of powers to connect these institutional arrangements to particular value systems that mould the attitudes and behaviours of officeholders.

Although these institutional restraint are frequently combined, it is important to distinguish them because they are sometimes offered as alternatives, and they involve differing approaches to the exercise of political power. A number of important political thinkers argue that mixed governments mitigate the risks of misuse of power that arise from pure constitutional forms by assigning specific, complementary roles and powers to institutions and/or offices that embody monarchical, aristocratic and democratic principles. Very often these offices are reserved for the members of different social groups or classes, and are portrayed as appropriate vehicles for utilising the virtues of the one, the few and the many.

It is sometimes said that these arrangements involve a 'sharing' of power (Fritz, 1954, p. 84), but it is perhaps more accurate to say that supreme power is created *through* the interaction of the various elements that participate in government. It is produced by the system rather than being located in, or shared by, its constituent elements. Most commonly, legislative (or law-making) functions are performed by the democratic and aristocratic elements, the latter being given a distinctive leadership role in this process; executive (or rule-implementing and governing) functions are reserved for the monarchical element. Taken together, this functional division gives rise to a balance of power that produces political stability and mitigates the risk of tyranny, self-interested high-handedness or self-interested lawlessness resulting from the corruption of pure constitutions.

However, systems of checks and balances reflect only some of the assumptions that underwrite theories of mixed government. The key idea in these systems is the separation of functionally distinct powers (typically of an executive, legislative and judicial kind) to ensure that the coercive influence of government can only be brought to bear if they act in concert. This arrangement requires neither a mixture of principles nor a mixture of social forces or classes. Consequently, separation of powers may be instituted in a democratic republic such as the United States. Thus while mixed government is an alternative to democracy, the separation of powers may be a feature of a democratic polity.

Finally, it is useful to distinguish between mixed constitutions and those that separate powers from what some ancient philosophers called 'moderate' constitutions, or governments of the 'middle-way'. Rather than seeking to mix pure elements or to separate functions, 'moderate' government relies on a compromise between pure forms of government which rests on the assumption that one class embodies the virtues of other sections of the population while being free of their vices. Significantly, this compromise does not utilise the interaction of elements or classes. Rather, it identifies a middle ground between them, one that may incorporate or acknowledge some democratic, oligarchic or monarchical features but does not derive these from interaction of the one, the few and the many. In constitutions of the 'middle-way' one favoured disinterested class plays a predominant role which tempers the tendencies to extremism that occur in pure forms of rule.

We shall look first at the treatment of these ideas by philosophers in ancient Greece and Rome, and then examine the adaptation made to them by early-modern writers. In some cases, these theories about the internal organisation of the state had direct implications for its role in international politics. The chapter concludes with a consideration of mixed government and the separation of powers in revolutionary and post-revolutionary America and France.

Mixed government in ancient political theory: Plato, Aristotle, Polybius and Cicero

Plato's *Republic* presents an argument for the most pure of pure governments. Subsequently, however, he acknowledged that the difficulties of establishing and maintaining a regime of this kind make it necessary to identify a good, but less than perfect, state in which no single class or individual will be endowed with absolute authority. This argument, put forward in *The Laws,* addresses the risk of locating supreme power in the hands of those who do not meet the rigorous standards required of true guardians. Plato's treatment of this issue reflects an awareness of the tendency for power to corrupt the character of those who possess it.

In *The Laws* Plato proposed two strategies for eliminating this danger. First, the constitution of 'Magnesia' limited the scope for human corruption by making the laws themselves, rather than officeholders, supreme (see pp. 46–47). Magnesia was to have a complete and elaborate system of 'constitutional' laws defining a range of offices and courts, and regulating the conduct of those who exercise political and judicial authority. These laws would provide a fixed framework that promotes good government and prevents the abuse of political power by officeholders. The sanctity of the law is reinforced by the symbolism adopted by the new state and is ensured by the 'guardians of the laws', whose primary task is to uphold the law and ensure strict adherence to it. These officials are elected by the population at large, who are divided into four classes based on property holding. The purpose of this arrangement is to allow all to vote, but to give greater weight to the more educated; it therefore conforms to what Plato described as a true understanding of 'equality': 'much' is granted to 'the great' and 'less to the less great' (Plato, 1980, p. 230). It also supports Plato's second strategy, that is, a compromise between monarchy and democracy which combines a system of mixed government with devices associated with a 'moderating' approach to the exercise of political power.

In addition to the moderating effect of the electoral system, aspects of mixed government are incorporated into a complex range of other political and judicial offices that have distinctive functions and are filled by different classes and age cohorts. These arrangements produce a mixture of elements and establish processes for checking and balancing particular exercises of power. For the most part, the constitution of Magnesia combines democratic and aristocratic-oligarchic elements, but an important institution, the 'nocturnal council', adds an element of Platonic kingship. This council (so named because it meets before dawn) is made up of priests of high distinction, the 10 senior guardians of the laws and the minister of education. Each of these people is attended by a protegé aged between 30 and 40 who undertakes research for the council. This role is important because the nocturnal council is charged with a range of legal, philosophical and didactic functions. It evaluates the soundness of the laws, drawing where necessary on external experiences; suggests amendments to them; and inculcates an understanding of the moral basis of the state among the general population (ibid., pp. 502, 512ff). It should be noted that the council does not have any governing role: it cannot *change* the laws (this power is reserved for the guardians of the law), nor does it wield executive or judicial power. It is an evaluative and reflective body whose impact depends on how the guardians of the laws respond to its recommendations.

Like Plato, Aristotle regarded mixed government as a practical rather than an ideal option. However, if one takes account of his recognition that many states have mixed populations, and his belief that there is something to be said for the claims of the one, the few and the many, there is a sense in which mixed government is not only prudent but just (see p. 195). It is prudent because it avoids the resentment of those excluded from power under pure forms of government, and it may be just because it acknowledges the distinctive, but not overriding, merits of various sections of the population and their capacity to contribute to the state.

Aristotle referred to this form of government as 'polity'. Having originally used this term to identify a constitution in which the many rightly hold power and exercise it for the common good, 'polity' was subsequently seen either as a form of government that mixes elements of democracy with oligarchy (tinged with aristocracy), or as one whose social composition gives it a moderate cast (see p. 143). Aristotle's version of mixed government includes various mechanisms that recognise the legitimate but not exclusive claims of the many who are poor and the few who are wealthy. Since the many have some capacity to discern whether power is being exercised properly, they judge the performance of officeholders at the end of their terms and also identify those who seem most likely to govern impartially. These arrangements are premised on a distinction between being qualified as an elector, and being qualified for office. The many elect, but they choose from among members of the population whose wealth and education endow them with the attributes required of officeholders (Aristotle, 1958, pp. 123–27). In addition, however, Aristotle also discussed a variety of electoral practices that produce mixed government by ensuring that the poor have a chance to occupy some offices, while others are restricted to members of the upper classes. The first of these outcomes can be realised through a 'lot' system, or random selection; the second is produced by election through a ballot. Unlike selection by lot, which rests on blind chance, election through ballot (whether open or secret) allows for merit to be taken into account; it also permits the direct or indirect influence of social factors such as deference. Similar results can be achieved by attaching a property qualification to some offices, but not to others (ibid., pp. 174–78).

These arrangements produce a form of rule that mixes elements of democracy with those of oligarchy in ways that satisfy the requirements of distributive justice. This is a good thing in itself, and since power is held justly it may also facilitate its proper exercise. Mixed government prevents one dominant class from abusing its position because it must rely to some extent on the approval of other classes. It also makes good government more likely by capitalising on the imperfect but valuable merits of the wealthy few and the numerous poor.

Finally, Aristotle suggested that the regulatory effects of mixed government may be enhanced if they are built upon a social structure dominated by the middle orders of society. It should be noted, however, that this 'moderate' form of government seems to be an alternative to conventional forms of mixed government. The fact that such a class is relatively large means that the numerical preponderance of the poor will be reduced (ibid., pp. 179–84). One effect of this arrangement is that Aristotle's second form of 'polity' involves an important shift in focus: its superiority depends on the distinctive attributes of the middle class, not on the superiority of a mixed constitution over other, pure, forms (Mulgan, 1977, p. 106). However, a mixture of principles may be an important addition to this system because it gives some recognition to the claims of other classes and thus avoids the reactive dangers that result from the exclusive possession of power by one class.

Aristotle argued that a large middle class will have a moderating effect on the exercise of political power because of the distinctive attributes of this group. Free of the arrogance of the rich and the feckless desperation of the poor, the middle class are more likely to act reasonably than either of the other classes. Moreover, since its members are comfortably off, they are neither obsessed by wealth nor forced by hardship and encouraged by envy to see political power as a means of enriching themselves at the expense of the public. This attitude corresponds to some degree with Aristotle's belief that the virtuous regard property merely as an instrument to the good life, and his condemnation of those who place a high value on the accumulation and display of riches.

In addition to capitalising on the political implications of the middle classes' measured attitude towards wealth, Aristotle argued that their social position and outlook reinforce their moderating influence. The rich, being used to getting their own way, tend to rule despotically, while the poor are habituated to servitude. Both these classes are thus ill-fitted to share rule and being ruled. When the rich have exclusive control of the state it takes on the appearance of a master-slave relationship, interrupted from time to time by outbursts of lawless rebellion by the poor. As there can be no friendship between these classes the state cannot be described as an association that exists for the good of all its members. A state dominated by the middle class will exhibit markedly different characteristics. Members of this class are self-assured without being arrogant, and being part of a similarly disposed group, they can form relationships of friendship that make them willing to share in rule and being ruled. The middle class also acts as a buffer between the rich and the poor, preventing them from despoiling and oppressing the other. It thus forms the basis of a government that, because it acts for the common good, is able to win the support of most of the population and avoid the instability and injustice that invariably accompanies revolutions. Aristotle thought that turmoils are a consequence of the illegitimate exercise of political power and assumed that this danger can be avoided if those who have a disposition and an incentive to rule justly play a central role in the state.

Aristotle's belief that both mixed and moderate constitutions provide a means of preventing bad government and promoting beneficial exercises of political power was shared by the later Greek thinker, Polybius (c. 200–118 BC). Polybius was primarily a historian, and rather than analysing the general benefits of mixed government, he used this idea to explain the longevity and success of the Roman Republic. Writing under the shadow of the Roman conquest of Greece in the early part of the second century BC, Polybius sought initially to explain to his compatriots why the Romans had succeeded in gaining control of the Mediterranean region. As his work progressed, however, he also offered assurance to the Romans themselves about the prospects and requirements of their continued pre-eminence.

Polybius (*c.* 200–118 BC)

Born in Arcadia in Western Greece, Polybius played a prominent role in the Achaean League when the Greek city-states were still independent of Rome. At the conclusion of the Third Macedonian War in 167 BC, he was among the thousand hostages sent to Italy. During a long period of exile Polybius became closely associated with the politician and general Scipio Africanus. He later acted as an intermediary between the Romans and the Achaean League and took an administrative role at Rome when the League was finally dissolved in 144 BC. His most important work was an extensive history of the Roman Republic.

Key reading: Fritz, 1954.

Polybius traced the success of the Roman Republic to its system of mixed government. Unlike pure constitutions, which undergo a natural process of growth and decay – from military despotism through kingship, tyranny, aristocracy, oligarchy, democracy and mob rule, ending in despotism (Polybius, 1979, pp. 307–09) – mixed government is able to combine 'all the virtues and distinctive features of the best government, so that no one principle should become preponderant, and thus be perverted into its kindred vices'. It ensures that the 'power of each element should be counterbalanced by the others, so that no one of them inclines or sinks unduly to the other side. In other words, the constitution … remain[s] for a long time in a state of equilibrium thanks to the principle of reciprocity or counteraction' (ibid., pp. 310–11). This arrangement had been achieved by Lycurgus when he established the Spartan constitution, but it was adopted by the Romans only after a long series of experiments and difficulties.

In Polybius' analysis, the constitution of the Roman Republic combines monarchical, aristocratic and democratic elements. The consuls, the senate and the people (both through the tribunes and in the assembly) exercise a considerable but incomplete range of powers. The constitution thus rests on the interdependence of elements that check the pursuit of sectional interests and ensure that political power is directed towards the good of the state (ibid., pp. 313–16). In addition to showing that this system avoided the misuse of power, Polybius also emphasised its effectiveness. The key point in this respect was the capacity to capitalise on the positive virtues of each of the pure forms of government. In Rome, the monarchical, aristocratic and popular elements not only exercised a jealous watch over one another, but they also demonstrated their particular commitment to the good of the state, especially in times of crisis:

> [W]henever some common external threat compels the three [elements] to unite and work together, the strength which the state then develops becomes quite extraordinary. No requirement is neglected, because all parties vie with one another to find ways of meeting the needs of the hour, and every decision taken is certain to be executed promptly, since all are cooperating in public and in private alike to carry through the business in hand (ibid., p. 317).

The mixed constitution of the Republic thus provided a check on the abuse of power, and also stimulated a sense of corporate spirit that built upon competitive sectional pride and was regulated by religious and social customs that made honesty a cardinal virtue. In these circumstances, a 'spirit of emulation and the ambition to perform deeds of gallantry' actively promoted the public good. In so doing, it endowed Rome with the commitment and power to maintain its territorial integrity and establish control over states that were far more extensive and populous (ibid., pp. 348–49; Fritz, 1954, pp. 84–85).

Polybius' account of the relationship between Rome's internal political structure and its international role focused on the sense of mutual insecurity that arose when states that were capable of effectively threatening one another came into close and unavoidable contact. His analysis implies that like nature, the international system abhors a vacuum, and he treated Roman expansionism as an inevitable consequence of this. Since Rome was surrounded by the Carthagians to the south and west, and the Greeks and Macedonians to the east, expansion was necessary for its survival. Having identified the structural features of the international environment, Polybius then focused his attention on explaining why Rome succeeded in subjugating its rivals and why its rivals succumbed. His explanation hinged on arguments about the distinctive features of the 'institutions' of the Roman Republic, a term that embraced both the constitution of the Roman state and its political culture (Polybius, 1979, pp. 153–57, 302–03).

Polybius attributed Rome's success to the traditional constitution of the Republic and to the fact that it had reached the highpoint of its development when it confronted its rivals for domination of the Greco-Roman world. In this respect, Rome had a distinct advantage over the Carthagians. The structure of their constitution was very similar to that of Rome but it was beginning to be corrupted by the undue influence of the democratic forces. By contrast, Rome's well-balanced mixed constitution mitigated the risks of pure forms and ensured that all elements of the community shared in it. The Republic was a 'public thing', at once the focal point of unity in the face of common danger and of a keen competitive spirit between parts of the state that was directed to the common good. As a result, it was capable of generating and sustaining the 'irresistible power' which underwrote its resilence in the face of adversity and its ruthless pursuit of advantage when victory was in sight (ibid., p. 317).

These traits were reinforced by cultural practices which Polybius saw as a product of more or less conscious design. He thought that the funeral rites of men who had achieved fame on the field of battle provided a powerful example of the alignment of personal and public values. The custom that required family mourners to wear the death masks of heroic ancestors ensured that

> the fame of those who have performed any noble deed is made immortal, and the renown of those who have served their country well becomes a matter of common knowledge and a heritage for posterity. But a more important consequence of the ceremony is that it inspires young men to endure the extremes of suffering for the common good, in the hope of winning the glory that waits upon the brave (ibid., p. 347).

Polybius adduced these examples to support a general claim concerning 'the pains taken by the Roman state to produce men who will endure anything to win a reputation for valour in their country' (ibid., p. 346). He contrasted the staying power of the Romans with the brilliant effervescence of Athens. While the Athenians' popular heroism and occasional examples of outstanding leadership produced stunning successes, they did not form a basis for its lasting domination of international politics. Because the Athenian constitution gave vent to natural inclinations rather than curbing and directing them, democratic Athens was unable to match the relentless consistency which distinguished the history of republican Rome (ibid., p. 339).

Polybius' treatment of the virtues of the Roman Republic focused on elements embodying the principles of monarchy, aristocracy and democracy rather than social classes or forces. However, his familiarity with conventional Greek modes of constitutional classification, together with his detailed knowledge of Roman history and politics, meant that his account implicitly assumed a link between elements and classes. In Rome the consuls and the senate (drawn from the upper echelons of society) had responsibilities that corresponded to ideas of kingship and aristocracy. Similarly 'the people', the democratic element in the constitution, comprised those who Aristotle had described as 'the many who are poor'.

Arguments about the importance of connections between constitutional elements and classes is a marked feature of the writings of Polybius' Roman successor, Cicero. His defence of mixed government focused on an ancient ideal of the Roman Republic that gave way to anarchy and military despotism in the century following the Gracchi's assault on the landholdings of the aristocracy in 133 BC. In his *Republic,* Cicero employed a musical analogy to describe a properly constituted state, that is, one in which the exercise of political power was directed towards the common good:

> [A]s ... perfect agreement and harmony is produced by the proportionate blending of unlike tones, so also is a State made harmonious by agreement among dissimilar elements, brought about by a fair and reasonable blending together of the upper, middle, and lower classes, just as if they were musical tones (Cicero, 1970, p. 183).

Although Cicero actually discussed the mixed constitution in relation to its beneficial effect on the relationship between 'the people' and the upper classes, this analogy is useful because it draws attention to the 'proportionate', 'fair and reasonable' blending of dissimilar elements. Cicero's formulation reflects his belief that if a mixed constitution is to ensure good government, it must take account of the differing weights to be ascribed to different elements, and not merely, as in Polybius' account, of the need to assign different functions to the elements. Cicero argued that the balance achieved by the Roman constitution in its heyday was a consequence of the prominent role ascribed to the senate, and hence also to the upper classes from which its members were drawn. The constitution of Republican Rome established an 'even balance of rights, duties and functions, so that the magistrates have enough power, the counsels of the eminent citizens enough influence, and the people enough liberty' (ibid., p. 169). Under this system

> the government was so administered by the senate that, though the people were free, few political acts were performed by them, practically everything being done by the authority of the senate and in accordance with its established customs, and that the consuls held a power which, though one of one year's duration, was truly regal in general character and in legal sanction (ibid., p. 167).

While the people were said to possess sovereign power (*potestas*) in the sense that government existed for the common benefit and was sanctioned by the entire population, authority (*auctoritas*), the influence that determined how power was to be exercised, resided with the upper classes: 'liberty has been granted in such a manner that the people were induced by many excellent provisions to yield to the authority of the nobles' (ibid., p. 487).

In the ideal state outlined in Cicero's *Laws,* these 'excellent provisions' reserved the most important offices for those who have been born into, or are acceptable to, the nobility. They also included a system of election that accords great influence to that class. The people voted by secret ballot (rather than by voice or a show of hands) as a 'safeguard to their liberty', but they were not prohibited from showing their ballots to members of the upper class if they wished: 'these ballots are to be shown and voluntarily exhibited to any of our best and most eminent citizens, so that the people may enjoy liberty also in this very privilege of honourably winning the favour of the aristocracy' (ibid., p. 505). The last part of this quotation is particularly important because it conveys Cicero's belief that the effectiveness of a mixed constitution depends not only on its formal stipulations, but also on its impact on the informal relationship between the people and the aristocracy. If voters are permitted to show their ballots to members of the nobility, this will foster deferential relationships – based on voluntary submission to the guidance offered by those one respects – between the most important classes in the state.

Cicero maintained that a mixed constitution with a strong aristocratic bias satisfies the requirements of proportionate justice. It also promotes relatively stable and good government by avoiding the risks of corruption posed by pure aristocracy and the dangers of excluding the people from a role in regulating the partnership of which they form a part. Cicero's statement of this case is reinforced by his belief that the provisions of natural law are closely reflected in the historical practice of the Roman state, being embodied either in its laws or in the 'customs of our ancestors' (ibid., p. 399). Since the nobility contains a large hereditary element (derived from what the early Romans called 'fathers of the state') who are responsible for and knowledgeable about custom, it follows that a constitution that gives aristocrats a leading position will help ensure that political power is exercised through desirable means for appropriate ends. However, because even aristocrats may stray from the path of custom and virtue, it is necessary to integrate them with the people by their joint involvement in elections, and to subject them to the regulatory influences of religion (Wood, 1988, p. 174). Moreover, the very fact that the people have some political influence makes it necessary for the nobility to take their interests into account: deference implies voluntary submission and mutual benefit. Although Cicero considered that the rich have a larger stake in the state than the poor (Cicero, 1970, p. 151), his definition of the state as a partnership and the literal meaning of the word 'republic' (*res publica*, the public thing) mean that power should be exercised in the interests of the entire community. In short, the mixed constitution is a means of ensuring that the exercise of political power conforms to the ends of the state.

Cicero's idea of justice had both positive and negative dimensions. It required that individuals and communities should not seek to harm others unless 'provoked' by unjust behaviour, and that they should respect others' property and rights. In addition, however, he argued that human beings were naturally sociable and interdependent. This meant they were under a positive obligation to offer assistance to one another if it did not impose unreasonable hardships on themselves (Cicero, 1991, pp. 9–10).

These specifications were applied to Rome's external relationships. Cicero argued that while the Republic remained true to its constitution, and more broadly to 'the ways of our ancestors' (*mos maiorum*), imperial expansion was just.

> As long as the empire of the Roman people was maintained through acts of kind service and not through injustices, wars were waged either on behalf of allies or about imperial rule; wars were ended with mercy or through necessity; the senate was a haven and refuge for kings, for peoples and for nations; moreover our magistrates and generals yearned to acquire the greatest praise from one thing alone, the fair and faithful defence of our provinces and of our allies. In this way we could truly have been titled a protectorate than an empire of the world (ibid., p. 72).

He contrasted this roseate condition with the disregard for the treaty rights of allies which had become common in the closing decades of the second century BCE:

> If this habit of lawlessness begins to spread and changes our rule from one of justice to one of force, so that those who up to the present have obeyed us willingly are held faithful by fear alone, then, though our own generation has perhaps been vigilant enough to be safe, yet I am anxious for our descendants, and for the permanent stability of our commonwealth, which might live on for ever if the principles and customs of our ancestors were maintained (Cicero, 1970, p. 217).

Cicero appealed to 'the law of human fellowship' to provide a normative structure that extended from political communities into the international environment. As in his political theory generally, however, this term was coloured by an attachment to the particular merits of Roman tradition and by Romano-centric presuppositions about that country's relationships with outsiders. It was also conditioned by the assumption that, although natural law applied to human beings in general, priority should always be given to the claims of one's country (Cicero, 1991, p. 160). When this doctrine was combined with assumptions that superiors had a right to rule their inferiors and that 'the wise and good and brave' have a right to seize resources and apply them more effectively to the common good, it provided a justification for Rome's imperial role. These presuppositions also played a role in Cicero's theory of just war.

Cicero argued that wars in defence of the 'honour' and 'safety' of a state, or to revenge wrongs against it, were just (Cicero, 1970, pp. 211–13). This specification was consistent with his more general account of justice since threats to a state's honour or safety might be seen as interfering with its legitimate interests. Once Rome acquired an empire, however, this formulation justified a resort to arms in defence of allies and clients: their safety was now one of Roman's legitimate concerns, and the Romans had an obligation to 'keep faith' with them (Cicero, 1991, p. 10).

In identifying 'honour' 'safety' and vengeance as grounds for declaring war, Cicero treated interstate violence as equivalent to individuals' right of self-defence and states' right to punish those who infringed the rights of their subjects. The overarching goal was to secure just peace: 'Wars ought to be undertaken for this purpose, that we may live in peace, without injustice'. This objective had important implications for the ways in which just wars were commenced and concluded. In the Roman tradition, wars were only just if declared by the process laid down in the 'fetial law'; this required a formal demand for restitution before war was declared, thus confirming the idea that just wars were waged to right a wrong and that where restitution was made a declaration of war was unnecessary and unjust (ibid., pp. 15–16). Moreover, since war was justified as a way of securing peace with justice, Cicero urged victors to show appropriate constraint and to only punish the vanquished when justice required it: 'once victory has been secured, those who were not cruel or savage in warfare should be spared' (ibid.). Similar considerations applied to the conduct of war. Cicero thus argued that combatants in wars who fought for the glory of the empire were obliged to show more restraint than when the question of survival was at stake.

Mixed constitutions in early-modern political theory: Marsilius, Guicciardini, Machiavelli and Harrington

As we have seen, medieval writers tended to focus on monarchical systems and even when they considered various elements of government, these were treated in relation to a single supreme figure. Thus while Christine de Pizan identified three estates that make up the body politic – the Prince and other princes, knights and nobles, and the common people – and stressed their interdependence, her theory is not one of mixed government because the prince is the ruling element in the state. Princes rule, nobles play a protective and supporting role, and the common people sustain the whole body (Pizan, 1994, pp. 4, 63–64, 90). When mixed government was discussed by most medieval writers they did little more than reiterate the position taken by Greek and Roman theorists and incorporate this within a monarchical framework. Aquinas' references to Aristotle's classification of constitutions thus stressed the supremacy of the one, the virtuous conduct of the few who hold office and the participation of the many, but they did so in order to urge princes to utilise the distinctive virtues of their subjects:

> the best ordering of power within a kingdom is obtained when there is one virtuous head who commands over all; and who has under him those who govern virtuously; and when, furthermore, all participate in such government, both because all are eligible, and because all partici-pate in the election of those who rule (Aquinas, 1959, p. 149).

Marsilius of Padua's work provides an important exception to this pattern. Marsilius subscribed to the conventional medieval idea that legitimate government serves the common good and that this can best be ensured through securing peace and unity in political communities. Unlike Aquinas, however, he thought that this is most likely to occur in a popular republic where the power residing with the people is exercised by councils or officials. The discretion of these groups or individuals is constrained by a system of checks that allows the people to ensure that officeholders act in the common interest (Skinner, 1978, vol. i, p. 64). A very similar position was advanced by Marsilius' contemporary, Bartolus, and a significant and novel varia-tion of it was produced by Juan de Segovia (1393–1458) in an argument that was originally formulated to support the final supremacy of councils of the Church over the Pope. Segovia likened rulers to the heads of corporate bodies such as colleges. These figures act as the *agents* for their corporation and their power can be checked by its members if it is not exercised for the common good (Black, 1992 pp. 177–78). In all these cases, the fact that those exercising power are dependent on the scrutiny of electors serves as a check upon them.

This check occurs within a pure system of democratic government, and is not, as in ancient political thought, a democratic element in mixed government. When Marsilius' successors revived this approach they often took Venice as their model. The Venetian Republic was of great interest to other Italians because its enjoyment of a long period of stability and prosperity contrasted markedly with the chequered experiences of many of its neighbours. Its success in avoiding the damaging effect of internal dissension was attributed to a mixture of monarchical, aristocratic and democratic elements exemplifying the doctrine laid down by Plato in his *Laws*. The beneficial effects of this arrangement were assisted by an elaborate system of ballot-ing, which minimised the risk that power would be utilised by factions rather than being directed to the common good (Skinner, 1978, vol. i, pp. 140–41). Renaissance writers regarded factional disputes as a major threat to the liberty of states because they left them vulnerable to the attack by over-mighty citizens and better-directed and more unified external rivals.

In the fifteenth and sixteenth centuries the Venetian example was widely dis-cussed in Florence, a strife-ridden city that had succumbed – with brief periods of respite from 1494 to 1512 and 1527–30 – to the princely domination of its most powerful family, the Medicis. Some writers urged the Florentines to inject a strong aristocratic element into their constitution. Thus Francesco Guicciardini

(1438–1540) argued that the Republic of Florence was weakened by a polarisation of the monarchical element – the *gofaloniere*, who was elected for life – and the democratic element, which dominated the popularly elected *Consiglio Grande*. The creation of a senate drawn from the upper classes would provide a means of balancing these two elements: it would act as a 'moderating force between tyranny and popular licence' and provide a way of keeping the most able and best qualified citizens happy. Restricting government to such people would ensure that power was placed in the most capable hands and also satisfy the ambition of those whom it would be dangerous to alienate (Guicciardini, 1994, p. 114). Although Guicciardini took Venice as his model, the role he ascribed to the senate echoed aspects of Cicero's account of the Roman Republic (Pocock, 1975, pp. 122–38).

The experience of the Roman Republic was put to a very different use by Machiavelli in his *Discourses*. In common with many of his contemporaries, Machiavelli identified good government and the proper exercise of political power with the preservation of internal and external liberty. He thought, however, that both aspects of liberty make it imperative that political rights are extended to the ordinary people and that they should exercise these rights vigorously (see p. 173). These requirements are set within a mixed rather than a pure constitution. In their prime, monarchy, aristocracy and democracy provide good government, but because they lack effective checking and balancing arrangements they invariably degenerate into tyranny, oligarchy or anarchy (Machiavelli, 1975, vol. i, pp. 212–14). Like Polybius, Machiavelli presented mixed government as a solution to this problem, one that will slow, if it cannot stop, the corruption that inevitably afflicts both the natural and the human worlds. In part, Machiavelli regarded a mixed constitution as a defensive device – 'if in one and the same state there was principality, aristocracy and democracy each would keep watch over the other' (ibid., p. 215) – but he also thought that it would produce positive benefits. Thus an extensive democratic element provides the state with a powerful citizens' militia that enables it to defend itself and to expand.

Rome's time of glory was short compared with the centuries of stability enjoyed by Sparta and Venice, but it is clear that Machiavelli regarded Rome as a model highly worthy of emulation. An expansionary republic provides scope for *virtú*, both in the commitment it requires of its citizens and because expansion is itself a form of *virtú*: it involves an attempt to bring aspects of a hostile environment under the control of a state and thus provides a way of contending with *fortuna*. For both these reasons, Machiavelli portrayed the expansionary republic as a glorious expression of active humanity (ibid., p. 226).

Machiavelli's treatment of expansionary republics focuses exclusively on the interests of the state and its members. The same general point applies to his views on princely *virtú* (see above, pp. 77–78). Princes were enjoined to exert as much control as possible over the external environment, acting in anticipation of perceived threats when it was prudent to do so. Expansion brought enhanced risk, however, making an established ruler a 'new' prince with respect to territories seized from neighbouring princes or republics. In the former case, Machiavelli thought that swift, targeted violence against elites and those connected with the displaced royal house would usually prove effective in removing potentially dangerous sources of resistance. If the new prince refrained from interfering with the property of the populace it was likely that they would shift their allegiance to him. Popular republics are far harder to absorb because their members are habituated to the invigorating benefits of freedom. Machiavelli observed that new princes would be well advised to lay waste these territories and then resettle them. They might also take positive advantage of the situation to give their pre-existing subjects booty from the newly conquered state. These are the only circumstances in which Machiavelli thought princes could safely ingratiate themselves with their subjects by acts of apparent generosity. In other cases, they depleted their resources, imposed burdens on some or all of their subjects and risked weakening their position by prompting resentment rather than gratitude (see p. 52).

Since all principalities and popular republics were driven to engage aggressively with their neighbours, glory and security were purchased at the cost of international instability. Machiavelli's political theory thus gives rise to an image of international relations in which interstate relations are governed by the principle of 'reason of state' (*raison d'etat*) and subject only to the considerations of political morality arising from the distinctive internal characteristics of participant states. Some of the requirements of a successful foreign policy are aligned with conduct which preserve states from corruption (Boucher, 1998, 138). Thus members of a citizen army (or militia) demonstrate the active commitment to the good of the commonwealth which is also expressed through political participation and their turbulent but invigorating contests with other sections of the community (see p. 145).

Given the dangerously competitive nature of the external environment, the survival of principalities and popular republics requires active engagement in international affairs through diplomatic and military means. This in turn necessitates close attention to what is going on beyond the boundaries of the state and to its military capabilities and resources. By contrast, *status quo* states such as Sparta or Venice need only adopt strong defensive positions that will discourage attacks and avoid appearing as a threat to their neighbours (Machiavelli, 1975, vol. i, p. 6). While the first of these requirements is relatively easy to satisfy, the unavoidable mutability of human affairs represented by the figure of *fortuna* makes appropriate self-containment very difficult. For that reason Machiavelli regards the Roman approach as being the safest and best option (ibid.).

Machivelli's references to the history of Roman, Sparta and Venice show that he regarded past experience as an important guide in external as well as in internal affairs. He also drew upon the experience of Italian states in support of a strong preference for militias over mercenaries, or troops provided by allies (auxiliaries). Militias owe their first allegiance to the commonwealth and each citizen-soldier has a personal interest in their public duty of defending it. By contrast, auxiliaries are beholden to their sovereign, not to the state in which they happen to be deployed. Mercenaries are singularly unreliable since they are liable to be swayed in their loyalty by offers of more lucrative employment and owe their first allegiance to their leaders. Issues of reliability and control also explain Machiavelli's apparently perverse injunction to avoid alliances with strong powers and seek to ally with the weaker ones. His line of reasoning here is based on the assumption that powerful allies will seek to subjugate their weaker allies to their ends. An alliance with weaker parties avoids this risk and might also provide opportunities to exploit them.

Unlike many other proponents of the mixed constitution Machiavelli did not present this form of government as a means of ensuring internal tranquillity. On the contrary, he argued that the class conflict that marked the history of the Roman Republic had actually been beneficial: 'in every republic there are two different dispositions, that of the populace, and that of the upper class and ... all legislation favourable to liberty is brought about by the clash between them' (ibid., p. 218). This clash was productive because the ordinary people had a distinct place in the political structure of the republic and were thus provided with an outlet for their collective energy. It also meant that they possessed a recognised bargaining tool that they could bring to bear if they thought that their interests were being ignored (ibid., p. 219). In sharp contrast to conventional accounts of the dangers of popular republics, Machiavelli regarded 'the people' as the true friends of liberty rather than a threat that had merely to be kept in check. They do not desire power (the aim of the rich), but freedom from oppression; they lack the sense of insecurity felt by those in a privileged but not impregnable position, and being poor they are less able to effect a rapid change even if they wish to (ibid., pp. 220–22). Unlike Cicero and other defenders of aristocratic republics, Machiavelli regarded the rich as the most significant threat to the liberty of the state because of their political ambition and their capacity to corrupt the poor. Aristocratic ambition either spurs the poor to seek vengeance for slights and oppression, or it encourages them to collaborate in the corruption of the state in order to win their share of the spoils of bad government (ibid., p. 222).

These dangers can be avoided if a strong and independent popular element is maintained in the constitution, one that counters the pretensions of the rich and prevents them from subverting government from its proper concern with the common good. Popular government is not incompatible with a degree of elite direction, but this must come from a 'natural aristocracy' rather than one distinguished solely by birth or riches. Since Machiavelli thought that the many are amenable to honest direction – although ignorant, the populace is 'capable of grasping the truth and readily yields when a man, worthy of confidence, lays the truth before it' (ibid., p. 219) – his position implies that prolonged mass discontent is a sign of elite corruption and/or ineptitude.

For Machiavelli, therefore, a mixed constitution ensures that political power is exercised for the good of the entire community and is essential if republics are to be preserved from corruption. Except in static and geographically secluded republics such as Venice, these goals can only be realised if the state has a strong and politically active popular basis. The people are not merely a threatening force that has to be bought off and controlled; to the contrary, they form an essential component of the state, one that possesses distinctive capacities that help ensure the proper exercise of power by those who hold office.

Guicciardini's admiration for the Venetian constitution was echoed by the seventeenth-century English republican writer James Harrington. In response to the collapse of monarchical government in England, Harrington argued for a return to the lessons of 'ancient prudence', that is, the approach to government exhibited in the uncorrupted form of the Roman Republic and surviving in the modern world in the constitution of Venice. Like his Italian predecessors, Harrington equated just government with the pursuit of the common good, and he stressed that this end could only be achieved by a system of rule that did not merely counteract self-interest, but channelled it in such a way that it would produce public benefit. Unless

> you can show such orders of government as, like those of God in nature, shall be able to constrain this or that creature to shake off that inclination which is more peculiar unto it and take up that which it regards the common good or interest, all this is to no more end than to persuade every man in a popular government not to carve himself of that which he desires most, but to be mannerly at the public table, and give the best from himself unto decency and the common interest (Harrington, 1992, p. 22).

'Decency' can only be ensured by a complex set of institutions that directed human action to the common good. Harrington argued that the state must be an 'equal commonwealth', by which he meant that property must be so dispersed among the population that its power is balanced, thus avoiding the class antagonism that afflicted the late Roman Republic. In particular, he stressed that there must be a balance of power between the few and the many, one that is maintained by a 'perpetual law establishing and preserving the balance of dominion, by such distribution that no one man or number of men within the compass of the few or aristocracy can come to overpower the whole people by their possession in lands' (ibid., p. 33).

In addition to preserving this socio-political balance, the state should also maintain a balanced arrangement of offices, or a balance of 'authority'. This quality is a 'good of the mind', a product of the 'heavenly treasures of virtue', as distinct from the 'earthly treasures of power' (ibid., p. 19). Given humans' tendency to favour their own interests, the practice of virtue must depend on fixed constitutional laws, not upon the wills of individuals. A properly ordered government forms an 'empire of laws, not men' (ibid., p. 8). Harrington's constitutional laws specify a complex system of balloting designed to purge electoral outcomes of self-interest (Davis, 1981). They also impose a rigid separation between three governing functions: the senate debates, the popular assembly 'determines' or decides, while the execution of laws rests with 'magistrates'. Harrington believed that Machiavelli had placed insufficient positive emphasis on the 'gentry' or nobility, but like his Italian predecessors he associated elite leadership with 'natural' rather than hereditary aristocracy: it forms a senate of *authority*, not *power* (Harrington, 1992, pp. 23, 15, 36).

Separation of powers in eighteenth-century and early-nineteenth-century political theory: Montesquieu, Madison, Sièyes and Constant

A significant (and overt) expression of dissent from Harrington's judgement on the Venetian Republic appeared in Montesquieu's *The Spirit of the Laws*, which was published to great acclaim in 1748. In this work Montesquieu bemoaned the position of the 'poor subjects' of the Italian republics. In these states,

> the same body of magistrates are possessed, as executors of the laws, of the whole power they have given themselves in [their capacity] ... of legislators. They may plunder the state by their general determinations; and as they have likewise the judiciary power in their hands, every private subject may be ruined by their particular decisions (Montesquieu, 1949, vol. i, p. 152).

This criticism rests on Montesquieu's belief that good government is incompatible with a unified source of power within the state, regardless of the way in which this power is constituted.

Charles-Louis de Secondat Montesquieu (1689–1755)

Having trained as a lawyer, Montesquieu served as a legal official in the royal administration in Bordeaux. He had wide scientific, literary and political interests and travelled throughout Europe. On a visit to England in 1729 he conducted a close study of English political institutions, some of the results of which appeared in his widely acclaimed *The Spirit of the Laws* (1748). He regarded the English constitution as exemplifying the role that a separation of legislative and executive powers plays in preserving the liberty of subjects and the rule of law.

Key reading: Richter, 1977.

Montesquieu's primary concern is with 'political liberty', that is, the 'right of doing whatever the laws permit' (ibid., p. 150). Political liberty exists only when each subject enjoys a 'tranquillity of mind arising from the opinion each person has of his own safety'. Consequently, 'when the legislative and executive powers are united in the same person, or in the same body of magistrates, there can be no liberty; because apprehensions may arise, lest the same monarch or senate should enact tyranni-cal laws, to execute them in a tyrannical manner' (ibid., pp. 151–52). In addition to stressing the importance of subjects' sense of security, Montesquieu also built requirements relating to efficiency into his account of properly constructed and regulated government. For example, he insisted that legislative bodies are incapable of effectively executing law and must be restricted to formulating it (ibid., p. 155).

These goals can only be attained if distinctive functions are reserved for dif-ferent institutions; they also necessitate a mixed social order of the kind promoted by other thinkers discussed in this chapter. Montesquieu identified three types of governmental power: the legislative or law-making power, the executive power as it applies to defence and external relations, and the executive in its internal and penal capacities. In free countries, those in which 'every man who is supposed to be a free agent is his own governor', legislative power 'should reside with the whole people' and be embodied in a representative assembly chosen by those whose attachment to a particular locale ensures an accurate representation of geographical and sectional interests (ibid., p. 154). Since members of the nobility have distinct interests and are likely to suffer at the hands of popular assemblies, they should form a sepa-rate assembly that cannot promote legislation but may reject that proposed by the elected chamber (ibid., p. 163). As noted above, the legislative body is ill-equipped to carry out executive functions. In any case, if it attempts to do so it will contravene the principle that the abusive exercise of power can only be avoided by separating functions. Consequently, the legislative arm of government must be restricted to formulating law, scrutinising the actions of the executive and levying taxes.

Separation of powers prevents the executive (lodged in the monarch) from for-mulating or determining legal enactments. Montesquieu thought, however, that the monarch should possess a veto:

> If the prince were to have a part in the legislature by the power of resolv-ing, liberty would be lost. But as it is necessary he should have a share in the legislature for the support of his own prerogative, this share must consist in the power of rejecting (ibid., pp. 159–60).

This stipulation highlights an important feature of Montesquieu's understanding of the conditions attached to the exercise of political power. While he insisted on a separation of powers to avoid legislative-executive tyranny, his account points to what in England was called the 'coordination of power', that is, an arrangement stipulating that one branch cannot act positively without the agreement or 'coordi-nation' of another (Hampsher-Monk, 1992, p. 238).

Aspects of Montesquieu's approach were reflected in the arguments advanced by various contributors to the *Federalist Papers* and were incorporated into the structure of the new American republic (see p. 176). The fact that this government was a pop-ular republic left no room for either a hereditary head of state or a hereditary aris-tocracy: all legislators and officeholders are chosen through systems of selection and election which reflect the state's popular basis. However, the assumption of popular sovereignty does not eliminate the threat of tyrannical misuses of power. To the con-trary, *Federalist* writers argued that it is still possible for officeholders to oppress the people and/or for some of the people to oppress others. The first of these threats can be avoided by an effective system of representation, but the second requires the sort of regulation that Montesquieu proposed. Separation *via* coordination means that members of legislative bodies can neither hold executive offices nor nominate others to them and that presidents should possess a qualified veto on legislation. Similarly, while it is necessary to separate legislative and judicial functions at the federal level and to ensure the judicial independence of the executive by appointing judges for life, these officials are nominated by the president and their appointments must be confirmed by the senate (Hamilton et al., 1942, pp. 256–60, 263–67).

Madison justified the federal system on the ground that it would ensure a degree of filtration, promoting popular election of the 'best'. It would thus ensure efficient government by incorporating an element of 'natural' aristocracy in a republican framework. In addition, while the direct and frequent re-election of members of the House of Representatives would give proper weight to the preferences of the people, the indirect election of senators by state legislatures and the imposition of a higher age and a longer residency qualification was meant to ensure that this part of the legislative branch would contain representatives of the most able sections of the population. The fact that the Senate's term was longer than that of the House would give a degree of stability to the legislative body and help ensure that it would contain people with an extensive fund of relevant experience.

The *Federalist*'s rationale for the constitutional structure of the new American republic reflected the importance these writers ascribed to imposing constraints on the exercise of power within the state. Good government requires institutions and offices that avoid tyranny yet allow the talents of the most able members of the population to be harnessed to popular government. In the absence of a formal monarchy or aristocracy, the form of government that emerged in the wake of the revolution could be described as 'unmixed'. At the same time, however, the complex interdependence of actors and institutions exercising separate aspects of functionally defined powers, and the infusion of social forces into the processes through which officials are chosen, replicated many of the features that characterise conventional accounts of mixed government.

The revulsion against the unchecked power of popular assemblies that occurred in France in the late 1790s provided Sièyes with the opportunity to produce a complex constitutional structure that echoed a number of features of Harrington's 'orders of government'. However, the dominant role ascribed to the 'first consul', and the fact that this position was occupied by Napoleon Bonaparte (who possessed an independent power base in the army), negated its effectiveness. The new constitution merely provided an elaborate screen for the real head of state, one that turned the representative chambers into his corrupt cyphers.

The Emperor Napoleon was forced into exile in 1814, but on his return to France the following year he agreed to adopt the role of a constitutional monarch. Shortly after the promulgation of a new constitution in April 1815, Benjamin Constant (who had had a hand in drafting this document) published a work entitled *Principles of Politics Applicable to All Representative Governments*. In addition to presenting an implicit endorsement of Bonaparte's new position, Constant's book provided a detailed general account of constitutional rule required by states that respected individual liberty and the rule of law.

Benjamin Constant (1767–1830)

A native of Switzerland, Constant was educated in Bavaria and Edinburgh. After serving at the court of Brunswick, Constant settled in Paris in 1795. He was actively engaged in French politics and supported the return of Napoleon as a constitutional monarch. His various political writings were brought together in a collection of volumes that began to appear in 1820. In these works he sought to combine aspects of the traditional government of France with electoral, judicial and administrative reforms that would absorb new elements in the state and ensure that its power protected liberty rather than threatening it.

Key reading: Constant, 1988.

Unlike his immediate predecessors in France and America, Constant looked to a constitutional monarchy to achieve these ends. His system incorporated an aristocracy, but in deference to contemporary developments in European political culture, it also recognised popular sovereignty and thus reflected a partial return to traditional notions of mixed government. Constant regarded monarchy as a 'neutral' power, an elevated and impartial element that maintains a balance between the representative power of public opinion located in an elected assembly, the executive power entrusted to nominated ministers, and the judicial power vested in the court system (ibid., p. 185). The Crown is assigned distinct functions – the right to dissolve the assembly when it threatens liberty, the nomination of ministers, the distribution of honours – but it also provides the state with an important psychological and symbolic element:

> It is … the masterpiece of political organisation, to have created, amidst those dissensions, without which no liberty is possible, an inviolable sphere of security, majesty, impartiality, which leaves those dissensions to develop without danger, provided they do not exceed certain limits, and which, as soon as some danger becomes evident, terminates it by legal constitutional means, without any trace of arbitrariness (ibid., p. 187).

The checking role of the monarch in relation to the popular assembly is reinforced by a separate chamber of hereditary legislators, the peers. In addition to providing a 'counterbalance' to the democratic forces located in the popular assembly, a hereditary chamber supports the monarch and reduces the distance between him and his subjects. This last point is underlined by reference to the naturally despotic aura of simple single-person rule in very recent French experience: 'the elements of the government of one man, without a hereditary class are: a single man who rules, soldiers who execute and a people that obeys' (ibid., p. 198). While supporting and softening monarchy, a hereditary chamber also plays an important quasi-judicial role in relation to the executive. The purely 'private' crimes of ministers – including those involving a clear violation of citizens' rights – should be dealt with through the court system, but their 'public' misdemeanours – dereliction of duty, disregard for due process, actions tending towards arbitrary rule – should be investigated by a special tribunal of peers. This stipulation rests on the belief that the issues at stake in these cases involve a trial between 'executive power' and the 'power of the people'. Consequently they have to be heard by those who are independent of each of these interests, but share a general connection with them (ibid., p. 234). The peers are an element in public opinion and thus have an interest in liberty. They also support the integrity of the constitutional structure upon which their own position depends. Moreover, their social position, upbringing and experience gives them a special insight into the interests of the state, one that will help them to make the fine judgements necessary to determine complex cases arising in a political environment where conduct is subject to a range of influences that cannot be adequately specified in fixed and relatively simple legal codes. Constant also thought that the delicacy of these cases and the need to avoid besmirching the office of a minister in the course of investigating the conduct of its present and temporary occupant, meant the peers' tact and 'mildness of manner' were also of considerable importance.

Finally, in order to give due weight to the principle of popular sovereignty, direct expression to prevailing public opinion, protection to the particular interests of ordinary members of the population, and prevent any tendency to despotic collusion on the part of the other powers in the state, legislative proposals must be discussed and approved by a popular, elected assembly. Electors must satisfy a modest property qualification and candidates also have to meet an age qualification. These conditions will ensure that electors possess 'the leisure indispensable for the acquisition of understanding and soundness of judgement', and that those elected by them include among their interests a 'love of order, justice and conservation' (ibid., pp. 214, 215).

Conclusion

Constant treated mixed government in relation to monarchical political systems. This application of the idea can be contrasted with the way that the doctrine was applied in the ancient world. Ancient political theory focused on identifying certain offices or institutions with monarchical, aristocratic and democratic qualities. These qualities were attached to the office or institution, not to membership of either hereditary or non-hereditary classes. In these theories, monarchy, aristocracy and democracy are primarily elements within the constitution.

Because mixed government has often been related to the requirements of hereditary monarchy, it became irrelevant as Western states have either abandoned monarchy or transformed it in such a way that the democratic element comprises the dominant force within the state. The case is quite different with separation of powers theories. As noted above, this doctrine focuses on functions, and does not allocate these to particular classes or legally defined sections of the population. Consequently, this approach to regulating the exercise of political power is quite compatible with democratic forms of government and has played an important role in the United States and in a number of other modern Western countries.

ABSOLUTE GOVERNMENT

11

Theories of absolute government often incorporate ideas derived from natural law theory that emphasise rulers' obligations to uphold natural law. They are distinctive, however, in stipulating that government will only be effective and conceptually coherent if sovereigns hold *all* the agencies of government in their hands, and are the unquestioned and unquestionable source of law. To the extent that natural law directs and constrains absolute sovereigns, it only does so because they impose these obligations upon themselves. Their actions may be subject to divine regulation, but they cannot be regulated, judged or punished by those over whom they rule.

Absolute government is underwritten by a sharp distinction between 'sovereigns' and 'subjects'. The former have the right to command, and the latter are under an obligation to obey. Subjects possess no moral or legal rights to challenge the sovereign's actions. Theorists of absolute government adopt a unitary view of sovereignty that precludes separation of powers and mixed government but while most of them believe that its crucial requirements – that sovereign power must be *absolute,* or finally determining for members of a particular state, and *unitary* – are most effective under monarchy, they allow that sovereign power may also be lodged in aristocratic or even democratic constitutions.

This chapter opens with an account of the equivocal role played by ideas of absolute government in medieval and early-modern political theory. We will then consider the theories of absolute sovereignty formulated by Jean Bodin in France, by Thomas Hobbes in England, and by the German writer Samuel Pufendorf. The fourth section of the chapter considers the distinctly monarchical theories of absolute government produced by Sir Robert Filmer and Jacques-Bénigne Bossuet. The concluding section examines the role played by ideas of absolute sovereignty in eighteenth- and early-nineteenth-century utilitarianism.

Monarchical supremacy and the beginnings of absolutism: Seyssel

The emergence of theories of absolute government in early-modern European political thought marked a significant shift from medieval ideas of monarchy. Medieval kings were supreme heads of state, but ruled within institutional and normative structures that constrained their actions and set law-making power within frameworks of customary practice. Monarchs were the central but by no means the only figures in legislative processes, and many of their subjects continued to rely on customary law to regulate their interactions with one another. These features of medieval monarchy are reflected in the writings of Claude de Seyssel but aspects of his account also provided the critical starting point for subsequent theories of absolute government.

Seyssel's *The Monarchy of France* (1519) utilised ideas of mixed or limited government, but assumed that power flowed downwards from the crown. While insisting upon royal supremacy, however, Seyssel placed great weight upon the fact that the monarch was part of a system containing advisors, 'parlements' (largely judicial rather than legislative bodies) and ecclesiastical institutions which constrained royal power (Seyssel, 1981, pp. 49–57). These constraints were more like the friction created by a flywheel than the countervailing forces produced by systems of checks

---

Claude de Seyssel (c. 1450–1520)

Seyssel, a native of Savoy in northern Italy, spent his adult life in the service of the French crown before retiring to his bishopric in Marseilles. His most important political work, *The Monarchy of France* (1519), forms an important element in the transition between medieval constitutionalism and early-modern absolutism in French political thought.

Key reading: Seyssel, 1981.

---

and balances. In a particularly apposite image Seyssel likened them to 'bridles' on the monarchy, thus highlighting the way constitutional structures harnessed the power of a strong and competent monarch to produce the maximum benefit for the kingdom, supported and guided weak rulers, and restrained the headstrong or wicked. However, this image of the bridled sovereign was shortly to be replaced by one that pictured the ruler as a 'coachman' solely responsible for directing the state. The bridle was now placed on the subjects and other political actors rather than the sovereign (Keohane, 1980).

This change in imagery reflected a shift in the contemporary understanding of the nature of sovereignty that had important implications for attempts to specify the conditions under which power should be exercised, the relationship between rulers and subjects, and their respective rights and duties. The theory of absolute government first developed by Jean Bodin in the late sixteenth century underwent further refinement at the hands of the far less conventional, mid-seventeenth-century English thinker Thomas Hobbes (Burgess, 2013, pp. 1, 19–20). Hobbes' theory was modified in important respects by Samuel Pufendorf in the latter part of the seventeenth century, and in this form absolute sovereignty played an important role in eighteenth-century political thinking. Although Hobbes' ideas were not generally popular they were reflected in 'command' theories of law developed by eighteenth- and early-nineteenth-century utilitarians (see p. 218–19).

Legislative supremacy and absolute government: Bodin

Bodin's experience of the debilitating effect of civil war in late-sixteenth-century France is important in understanding many of the details of his theory of absolute government. Interestingly, this theory was not a product of reactionary political or religious views since Bodin was, by contemporary standards at least, a proponent of moderate and generally tolerant solutions to the problems facing France. He supported extensive reform of the political and economic administration of the French state, and thought the crown should adopt a policy towards its Protestant subjects that favoured toleration rather than persecution (Franklin, 1992, pp. xxii–xxiii). Bodin insisted, however, that both these initiatives depended on the general acceptance of strong, unified government.

Bodin's theory was designed to undercut the position of Catholic magnates who claimed to have independent rights and privileges that allowed them to resist moves towards toleration. It also challenged Protestants' claims that the crown's unwillingness to protect them constituted royal tyranny and infringed their alleged right to resist the sovereign when their fundamental interests were threatened (see pp. 243ff). These pressing political concerns intersected with Bodin's interest in theoretical issues concerning the relationship between indivisible power and supreme authority in the state (Franklin, 1992, p. xxiii). Having originally adopted a less than absolute view of supremacy, Bodin subsequently developed a

Jean Bodin (1529/30–96)

Bodin, who was trained as a lawyer, became an official in the household of the Duke of Alençon in 1571. His early writings were on history and economics; he also wrote on witchcraft, ethics, natural philosophy and comparative religion. Bodin's major political work, *The Six Books of the Commonwealth* (1571), appeared during the French Wars of Religion which raged between political factions identifying with Roman Catholicism on the one hand, and Protestantism on the other.

In common with his noble patron, Bodin favoured religious toleration and thought that in the prevailing environment of sectarian distrust it would need to be enforced by a strong ruler. Bodin's concerns were reflected in the defence of absolute monarchy presented in *Six Books of the Commonwealth*. This form of government was one in which a single ruler (the sovereign) enjoyed unquestioned administrative, judicial and legislative supremacy. Bodin developed a definition of sovereign power, identified the scope of it and specified the range of powers that needed to be exercised by monarchs if they were to retain supremacy and fulfill their obligations to their subjects and to God. These powers, which Bodin treated as the 'marks' of sovereignty, might be delegated to others, but they were always exercised on behalf of sovereigns and belonged to them. They were a fundamental feature of sovereign power and were integral to the state; if they were alienated to individuals or institutions they compromised the supremacy of the sovereign and deprived the state of its capacity to ensure peace and stability. The marks of sovereignty included the right to declare war and make peace, to levy taxes and to serve as the final source of appeal. They were encompassed in the right to make laws that were binding on all subjects and to do so without seeking the consent of others.

While Bodin insisted that sovereignty must be absolute, he did not think that this type of government precluded traditional constraints on how sovereign powers were actually exercised. These constraints did not call the power of the sovereign into question nor did they imply that powers wielded by subjects were independent of the sovereign. Bodin placed great stress on sovereigns' moral obligations to use their powers for the good of the community and to regulate their conduct by the requirements of natural law.

Bodin's theory, which was particularly influential in France, was the first developed statement of a theory of absolute sovereignty; others were produced by his countryman Bossuet and by Filmer and Hobbes in England.

Key reading: Franklin, 1992, 1994; King, 1974; Lloyd, 2017.

fully-fledged account of absolute government. The reasoning behind this shift was both logical and practical: less than absolute power would negate sovereignty and leave the state prey to conflicting sources of authority that gave rise to anarchy and destruction rather than right order and general benefit.

In his *Six Books of the Commonwealth* Bodin defined sovereignty as 'the absolute and perpetual power of a commonwealth' (Bodin, 1992, p. 1). Perpetual power is irrevocable and has to be distinguished from power held by virtue of an office conferred by someone else, or under specified conditions. In each of these cases, the grantor of the office possesses the capacity to revoke the grant and so power cannot be said to be 'perpetual'. Absolute power is not subject to human regulation; it has 'no other condition than what is commanded by the law of God and of nature' (ibid., p. 8). Bodin made it clear that absolute power entails an untrammelled exercise of executive and legislative supremacy. A sovereign must not

> be subject in any way to the commands of someone else and must be able to give law to subjects and to suppress or repeal disadvantageous laws and to replace them with others – which cannot be done by someone who is subject to the laws or to persons having command over him (ibid., p. 11).

For Bodin, laws were expressions of the 'will' of sovereigns in the form of a command. They cannot be questioned by subjects and sovereigns are not obliged to institute any particular legal enactment or to restore ones that existed in the past. Sovereigns cannot be bound by customary law, by laws enacted by their predecessors, or even by laws they have promulgated. The first two types of law only acquire binding force when confirmed by the sovereign, in which case their legality is a consequence of an expression of his will. A sovereign's own laws cannot bind him precisely because they are an expression of his will:

> although one can receive law from someone else, it is impossible by nature to give one's self a law as it is to command one's self to do something that depends on one's own will. As the [Roman] law says ['*No obligation can exist that depends on the will of the person promising.*'] (ibid., p. 12).

Obligations are binding because they are upheld by someone other than those who are bound by them, and sovereigns are, by definition, subject to no other human being: if they were, they would not be sovereign.

In common with his predecessors, Bodin stressed the sovereign's obligation to uphold natural law, but he reserved the right of enforcement to God alone. As far as the sovereign is concerned, the binding force of natural law is moral and self-imposed. While Bodin clearly thought natural law to be important, he drew an unconventionally sharp distinction between positive and natural law. While the sovereign is under an overriding obligation to God to promulgate just positive laws and to administer them justly, Bodin regarded these laws as being made by the sovereign rather than being deductions from, or applications of, natural law. He also made it clear that the sovereign's law-making power does not depend on the consent of his subjects. Unlike medieval writers, who saw consent as completing the sovereign's legislative actions, Bodin insists that 'the main point of sovereign majesty and absolute power consists of giving the law to subjects in general without their consent' (ibid., p. 23). In addition to sovereigns' emphatic but completely independent obligations to natural law, they were also bound to adhere to certain 'fundamental laws'. In France these laws specified succession to the throne and regulated the monarch's control of his property, the 'royal domain'. Bodin believed that these laws cannot be seen as limiting sovereignty. Rather, sovereign power in a particular state is defined by reference to laws of this kind. Significantly, breaches of fundamental law cannot be challenged by subjects but are nullified at the death of a sovereign who has wrongfully ignored it (Franklin, 1994, p. 308).

The unquestionable right to create law was regarded by Bodin as one of the distinctive, exclusive and indivisible 'marks' or attributes of sovereignty. In discussing these marks Bodin went to great lengths to show that many political actors who exercise extensive and important powers do so only on the authority of their sovereign and forfeit them when this authority is withdrawn. Moreover, he argued that sovereigns cannot share sovereign attributes with their subjects:

> the notion of a sovereign (that is to say, of someone who is above all subjects) cannot apply to someone who has made a subject his companion. Just as God, the great sovereign, cannot make a God equal to Himself because He is infinite and by logical necessity ... two infinities cannot exist, so we can say that the prince, whom we have taken as the image of God, cannot make a subject equal to himself without annihilation of his power (Bodin, 1992, p. 50).

A consequence of these stipulations is that generalised law-making power must be regarded as *the* definitive mark of sovereignty: 'all other rights are comprehended in it' (ibid., p. 58). Bodin argued, however, that the generality of this power makes it necessary to specify other marks of sovereignty. Although a range of functions may be performed by important subjects, the sovereign's standing in relation to these functions is unique. For Bodin, the distinctive position of the sovereign is shown by his independent possession of these rights, by the absence of legitimate control over him by other human beings or institutions, and by the derivative and dependent way in which these rights are held and functions performed by subjects. Marks of sovereignty include the right to make war and peace, to appoint officeholders or confirm appointments made by others, to provide final judgement and pardons, and to issue currency and regulate weights and measures. These rights are diverse, but they are essential attributes of a sovereign because they are necessary for the safety, prosperity and justness of the state (ibid., pp. 59, 67, 71, 73, 78, 80–81).

In addition to these largely practical rights, a sovereign also has the right to 'fealty and liege homage', 'faith and homage' (ibid., p. 78). In language that reflects a growing tendency to semi-deify secular rulers, Bodin argued that a precise understanding of the status of the sovereign is necessary because, there being nothing 'greater on earth, after God, than sovereign princes', it is important that we 'respect and revere their majesty in complete obedience, and do them honour in our thoughts and in our speech. Contempt for one's sovereign prince is contempt toward God, of whom he is the earthly image' (ibid., p. 46). Like the other attributes of sovereignty, 'faith and homage' is not owed to non-sovereign figures (Bodin, n.d., p. 36).

Bodin's theory of sovereignty is open to criticism on the ground that it fails to distinguish between the *powers* of government – which he claimed should be indivisible – and the *need* for a coherent legal system to have a fundamental norm for conflict resolution. It also ignored the possibility that legislative and executive powers may be shared in ways that make sovereignty a function of their interaction (Franklin, 1992, pp. xx–xxi; King, 1974, pp. 271–73). Bearing in mind that Bodin believed that his account rested on the logic of sovereignty, these objections are well met. But in acknowledging that, one should not lose sight of the particular considerations that led him to believe that government must be absolute. In the first place, the traditional structure of government in early-modern states was based on a variety of imprecise and inadequately analysed arrangements of powers. The lack of clarity that marked these arrangements was exacerbated by the practice of referring to monarchs as if they were absolute sovereigns, even when their exercise of power was constrained by the need to secure the cooperation of other actors and institutions (Franklin, 1992, p. xviii).

This point is illustrated by Seyssel's claim that the three 'bridles' of religion, justice and inherited law 'regulate' the absolute power of the King (see p. 251). For Bodin, of course, power that is regulated by human agency cannot be absolute, but the suggestion that it may be points to the intellectual confusion that proved positively dangerous in the unsettled conditions existing in France in the mid to late sixteenth century. Moreover, Bodin's understandable concern with order, and his desire to eliminate conflicting sources of authority and systems of coordination that could not be relied upon to produce effective government, led him to emphasise the sovereign's unified command and to dismiss the claims of those who tried to justify their conduct by appealing to institutions and laws that seemed to give them immunity from the power of the crown.

Bodin's concern with unified command is apparent both in his statement that 'the government of all commonwealths ... rests on the right of command on one side, and the obligation to obey on the other' (Bodin, n.d., p. 9), and in his argument that the family provides a 'model' of a rightly ordered commonwealth (ibid., p. 12). This parallel trades on conventional patriarchal conceptions of familial authority and allows Bodin to emphasise the need for a unitary sovereign power by raising the spectre of divided authority in the family: 'No household can have more than one head ... [because] if there was more than one head there would be conflict of command and incessant family disturbances' (ibid., p. 10). Like members of a family, the diverse range of people who comprise a state can only form a unified and peaceful whole if they are furnished with a unifying element:

> a ship is no more than a load of timber unless there is a keel to hold together the ribs, the prow, the poop and the tiller. Similarly a commonwealth without sovereign power to unite all its several members ... is not a true commonwealth (ibid., p. 7).

Bodin believed that this unifying role can be fulfilled only if the powers of government are themselves unified. Consequently, he rejected theories of mixed government on the grounds that they are conceptually incoherent and practically divisive: if one examines so-called mixed constitutions it is evident that one group or element is really sovereign. However, since this is not clearly recognised by participants, the result is a form of political disorganisation that involves the 'corruption of a state ... continually agitated by the storms of civil sedition until sovereignty is wholly lodged in one form or another' (Bodin, 1992, p. 105).

Bodin was aware that systems of absolute government might facilitate the abuse of power by rulers, but he thought that this risk is one that human beings must accept if they wish to have a reasonable prospect of enjoying the benefits of good government. As he put it in the course of a discussion of the possible abuse of parental power: 'Anyone who wishes to abolish all those laws which were liable to give rise to difficulties would abolish all laws whatsoever' (Bodin, n.d., p. 14). Since the family is the model for a rightly ordered commonwealth, this dictum presumably applies to sovereign as well as to parental power.

One reason why Bodin was sanguine about the benefits of absolute government was that he thought sovereign power was subject to a range of moral constraints that were central to the idea of the state as a 'right order':

> It ... is not the rights and privileges which he enjoys which makes a man a citizen, but the mutual obligation between subject and sovereign, by which, in return for the faith and obedience rendered to him, the sovereign must do justice and give counsel, assistance, encouragement, and protection to the subject (ibid., pp. 20–21).

Subjects cannot enforce the performance of these duties, but Bodin believed that they will be taken seriously by any sovereign worthy of the faith and homage of his subjects. Moreover, sovereigns are subject to natural law and are more closely bound to it than their subjects. Bodin's frequent references to the quasi-divine status of sovereigns serves to encourage subjects to revere them. It also emphasises his view that, because sovereigns have this status, they have a special relationship with God and are even more strongly bound to fundamental moral codes than other human beings:

> every prince on earth is subject to [divine and natural law] … it is not in their power to contravene them unless they wish to be guilty of treason against God, and to war against Him beneath whose grandeur all the monarchs of this world should bear the yoke and bow the head in abject fear and reverence (Bodin, 1992, p. 13).

Although Bodin thought that tyrannical sovereigns cannot be resisted by their subjects, the language he used to describe them makes their dubious moral standing quite clear. 'Tyrannical monarchy is one in which the laws of nature are set at naught, free subjects oppressed as if they were slaves, and property treated as if it belonged to the tyrant' (Bodin, n.d., p. 57). The welfare of subjects is jeopardised and tyrants are deprived of peace or any sense of security: they 'constantly tremble for their lives and harbour a thousand suspicions, envies, rumours, jealousies, desires for revenge, and other passions that tyrannize the tyrant more cruelly than he could tyrannize his slaves with all the torments he might imagine' (Bodin, 1992, p. 121).

In Bodin's view, therefore, absolute power must be distinguished from tyranny. Moreover, he argued that a good sovereign will take measures to ensure that his rule is as just and efficient as possible. Many of these measures relate closely to the institutions that had been praised by earlier exponents of constitutionalism in France. Bodin urged rulers to maintain bodies of advisors and to take their advice seriously. They should utilise representative institutions such as 'estates' to provide them with advice, as well as an opportunity to reconsider and, if necessary, to revise their decisions if the interests of the state require it. Princes must also shun those who encourage them to exercise their power in inappropriate ways: 'those who uphold such opinions are even more dangerous than those who carry them out. They show the lion his claws and arm princes with a show of justice' (ibid., p. 39). As advisors and representative institutions have no right to impose their will on their sovereign they contribute to the proper exercise of power without undermining the principle of absolute government.

Bodin's account of absolute government in terms of the necessity for the unifying, ordering presence of a sovereign was developed by his successors in France. Thus his young contemporary Charles Loyseau produced a detailed analysis of the process through which the kings of France disposed of honours and offices. Central to this account was the argument that the sovereign is the sole source of all offices and honours, including titles of nobility: 'the definition of nobility is that it proceeds "from those possessing sovereign power"' (Loyseau, 1994, p. 92).

In France, Bodin's account of sovereignty and developments based upon it were authoritative throughout the *ancien régime*. Elsewhere in Europe, however, the theory of absolute government was formulated in very different terms. The most significant of these theories was produced by the English writer Thomas Hobbes in the mid-seventeenth century. Like Bodin, Hobbes regarded the creation and maintenance of order as the primary goal of politics and he thought that it could only be ensured by an absolute sovereign. Unlike Bodin's, however, Hobbes' account of absolute government did not rely on conventional notions of natural law, nor did it place any great reliance on the prescriptive force of Christianity.

Absolute sovereignty: Hobbes' Leviathan

The core idea in Hobbes' defence of absolute sovereignty is that it provides the only means of ensuring that citizens will enjoy the security required for self-preservation or any prospect of well-being. This security depends ultimately on the combined powers of individuals, but Hobbes made it clear that this is not solely a matter of numbers: 'be there never so great a multitude; yet if their actions be directed according to their particular judgements, and particular appetites, they can expect thereby no defence, no protection, neither against a common enemy, nor against the injuries of another'. Security required that the resources of the community were directed by a permanent, continuous 'common power' (Hobbes, 1960, p. 110). Hobbes' justification of absolute sovereignty rested ultimately on his understanding of the characteristics of the state of nature, but he suggested that even without resort to this worst-case scenario, we can identify common human traits that render unregulated and unenforced order fragile and short lived. Humans compete against one another for dignity and honour; they tend to prefer their private interests to those of the public; their reason prompts them to challenge established practices and to disagree with their fellows, a tendency that is exacerbated by their capacity to communicate their ideas to others, and by their desire to show off their superiority (ibid., p. 111). These traits all mean that beneficial human interaction has to be forged and maintained by a single directing force that will curb humans' disruptive tendencies. This force can only be provided by an absolute sovereign, the 'Leviathan', or that

> *mortal god*, to which we owe under the *immortal God*, our peace and defence. For by this authority, given him by every particular man in the commonwealth, he hath the use of so much power and strength conferred on him, that by terror thereof, he is enabled to form the wills of them all, to peace at home, and mutual aid against their enemies abroad. And in him consisteth the essence of the commonwealth; which, to define it, is *one person, of whose acts a great multitude, by mutual covenants one with another, have made themselves every one the author, to the end he may use the strength and means of them all, as he shall think expedient, for their peace and common defence* (ibid., p. 112).

Hobbes thought that the creation of legitimate sovereignty has an important impact on its distinctive characteristics. The transition from the state of nature to a 'civil' or political condition results from a contractual arrangement whereby individuals agree to forego their natural right to do anything they consider necessary for their preservation and create a sovereign power by 'gifting' their powers to a specified person or persons. Hobbes describes the sovereign as an 'actor' whose actions are 'authorised' by subjects and 'belong' to them. The fact that individuals 'authorise' the sovereign was important for Hobbes because it means that subjects are the 'authors' or originators of both the sovereign and his actions. Like lawyers who act for their clients, sovereigns act for their subjects and cannot have their actions set aside by them. The process through which sovereign power is created ensures that the sovereign possesses rights that enable him to act effectively to promote the 'common peace' and safety of those who have gifted him these powers. Hobbes identified two categories of 'rights of sovereigns'. First, he specified a number of negative rights that insulate sovereigns from challenges by their subjects. Subjects cannot attempt to change the form of government by which they are ruled, because to do so would involve a breach of their covenant with one another. It would also result in their being punished by the sovereign. Since the sovereign's actions 'belong to' the subjects, they would thus be punishing themselves and contradicting the protective rationale that led them to create sovereign power. The same considerations mean that sovereigns cannot be accused of treating their subjects unjustly:

> he that doth anything by authority from another, doth therein no injury to him by whose authority he acteth: but by this institution of a commonwealth, every particular man is author of all the sovereign doth: and consequently he that complaineth of injury from his sovereign, complaineth of that whereof he himself is author; and therefore ought not to accuse any man but himself; no nor himself of injury; because to do injury to one's self, is impossible (ibid., pp. 115–16).

Even if subjects act unanimously – thus eliminating any question of breaking the contractual agreement they have with each other – they still have no right to change the form of government because they have given all their powers to the sovereign as a 'free gift', and will thus be taking from him what is rightfully his (ibid., pp. 113–14). Moreover, since there is no contract between subjects and sovereigns, the former cannot require the latter to forfeit their powers on the ground that they may have breached conditions attached to the transfer of power from subject to sovereign: without a contract there can be no conditions, and without conditions there can be no breach of them.

By insulating the sovereign's exercise of power from the judgement and control of subjects, these stipulations ensure that the sovereign is the absolute ruler of the state. In addition, Hobbes identified a range of positive rights that facilitate the exercise of this power. Sovereigns are solely responsible for matters of war and external defence, determining property rights, for final legal judgments, apportioning punishment and reward and deciding honours and orders of precedence (ibid., pp. 116–18). Since Hobbes thought that dissension on religious matters was a primary cause of conflict, he also insisted on the sovereign's right to prescribe articles of public faith and practice. Unlike 'godly' rulers, however, Hobbes' sovereign is under no obligation to impose *particular* religious professions or behaviour on his subjects and cannot be censured for failing to do so (see above, pp. 54–55). In common with Bodin Hobbes insisted that sovereign rights are indivisible and non-transferable: they 'make the essence of sovereignty; … [they] are the marks, whereby a man may discern in what man, or assembly of men, the sovereign power is placed, and resideth' (Hobbes, 1960, p. 118). These rights are the marks of sovereignty because the sovereign's exclusive possession of them provides the only satisfactory guarantee of the peace and safety of the subjects. If these rights are divided, then so too is the state: 'unless this division precede, division into opposite armies can never happen' (ibid., p. 119).

In common with Bodin, Hobbes' thought of laws as giving effect to sovereigns' commands. They are the *sole* source of law in the state and are not subject to the laws they have created. Laws that appear to owe their binding force to custom are, in fact, binding because they have received the explicit or tacit endorsement of the sovereign and have thus become *his* laws (ibid., pp. 174–75). Like the laws of nature, the laws of the commonwealth promote peace and safety. Once commonwealths are created, however, the precepts of natural law are only binding on subjects if they are enshrined in civil law and enforced by sovereigns (ibid., p. 174). Civil law thus 'abridges' people's rights under the laws of nature; indeed, this is why the commonwealth is created. Subjects may retain a greater or lesser degree of personal liberty, but its extent will be defined by law, or, to be more precise, they have liberty 'where the law is silent' (ibid., p. 143).

Hobbes thus maintained that the exercise of sovereign power must not be limited by institutional constraints, by law, or by the oversight of those who are subject to it. Such limitations have the effect of dividing power and preventing the sovereign from bestowing unity and order on the state. Like Bodin, Hobbes maintained that the fixed and final resting place required by viable legal systems can only be achieved if all agencies and functions of government are placed in a single pair of hands. As in Bodin's case, however, this stipulation is not seen as a warrant for tyrannical government. Although subjects cannot challenge sovereigns' exercise of their powers, Hobbes allowed that individual subjects' obligations to their sovereign cease if he poses an immediate threat to their lives, or even to their fundamental interests, or if he is unable to protect them effectively (ibid., pp. 144–45). While the individuals concerned were still vulnerable to their former sovereign's coercive capacity, they were no longer obliged to suffer punishment or disadvantage in obedience to his commands. Hobbes stressed, however, that subjects had no right to resist collectively their sovereign's mistreatment of others because their safety was not threatened and the capacity for collective action of any kind was solely due to the strength and unity produced by sovereign power.

In addition, while the exercise of sovereign power is arbitrary in the sense that sovereigns' actions are neither regulated by law nor subject to the scrutiny of their subjects, Hobbes believed that it should accord with the rationale of government: political order is critically important because it provides a greater degree of protection for individuals than they could reasonably hope to attain either in the state of nature or in conditions of civil strife that resemble it. Significantly, Hobbes not only specified the *rights* of sovereigns but also their *duties*. These were all subsumed in one overriding obligation:

> The office of the sovereign ... consisteth in the end, for which he was trusted with the sovereign power, namely the procuration of *the safety of the people*; to which he is obliged by the law of nature, and to render an account thereof to God, the author of that law, and to none but him (ibid., p. 219).

The law of nature in question here is that which enjoins gratitude: '*that a man which receiveth benefit from another of mere grace, endeavour that he which giveth it, have no reasonable cause to repent him of his good will*' (ibid., p. 99). Having received sovereign power as a gift from those who become his subjects, the ruler should not act in ways that cause them to regret having bestowed this gift upon him. If he does misuse the gift there will be no basis for trust, voluntary assistance or reconciliation and members of the community will thus be deprived of the psychological underpinnings of secure and effective government and of its practical benefits (ibid., p. 99).

Hobbes argued that the sovereign's obligations under the laws of nature relate not only to 'bare preservation, but also all the other contentments of life' (ibid., p. 219). Sovereigns must protect their subjects, instruct them in their duties towards their rulers and to one another, formulate good laws and ensure that they retain all the rights of sovereignty. These obligations cannot be enforced by subjects, but since they are backed by the laws of nature their binding force is as strong as that which morally compels subjects to submit to a sovereign and to remain loyal and obedient to him. There is thus a symmetry between the logic of subjection and the logic of sovereignty: while it is rational for subjects to obey sovereigns and proper for them to do so, it is no less reasonable and proper for sovereigns to exercise their power in ways that correspond to the rationale and conditions determining their creation. Given his contemporaries' predilection for disobeying their sovereigns, however, Hobbes laid particular stress on obedience: 'Take away in any kind of state, the obedience, and consequently the concord of the people, and they shall not only not flourish, but in short time be dissolved' (ibid., p. 222). But while he clearly thought that *any* kind of sovereign power is better than none, he made it equally clear that obedience – and hence the attainment of both 'bare preservation' and 'contentments' – is far more likely to occur where the sovereign's exercise of absolute power makes a significant rather than a minimal contribution to the well-being of his subjects.

Hobbes' theory of sovereignty has been described as equating the state with a 'unified structure of will and power that incorporates and is independent of both rulers and the subjects' (Tully, 1991, p. xxxii). As subjects, subjects cannot lay a claim to sovereign power, but nor can the sovereign as sovereign divide his rights or alienate any of them; to do so would destroy both sovereignty and the state it defines and sustains. A similar conception of the state was advanced by Hobbes' contemporary, the German writer Samuel Pufendorf, but his account was designed to correct what he saw as unsatisfactory features of Hobbes' theory.

Natural law, sociability and absolute government: Pufendorf

Like Hobbes, Pufendorf equated ideas of shared sovereignty with confusion and disorder. He argued that an absolute sovereign is the only viable solution to the shortcomings of the state of nature and can be justified by an appeal to the laws of nature. As we have seen, however, Pufendorf derived these laws from the requirements of sociability rather than from the natural right to self-preservation (see p. 174–75). An important consequence of this qualification is that Pufendorf saw the state as a means of furthering the general purposes specified by the laws of nature and derived its legitimacy from this role: 'against those ills with which man in his baseness delights to threaten his own kind, the most efficient cure had to be sought from man himself, by men joining into states, and establishing sovereignty' (Pufendorf, 1934, p. 959). States foster productive human intercourse by punishing those whose disregard for natural law undermines the advantages of sociability; they provide stable, secure environments in which the impact of public and family education can be most effectively applied to recalcitrant human beings, and where they can benefit from the civilising effect of social life. As Pufendorf put it, 'it is the first fruit of civil society, that in it men may accustom themselves to lead an orderly life' (ibid., p. 956; Tully, 1991, p. xxxi).

Samuel Pufendorf (1632–94)

A Saxon by birth, Pufendorf spent a large part of his life in the service of the Swedish crown. He wrote extensive histories of Sweden and a number of other European states. His most important political work, *Of the Laws of Nature and of Men* (1672), was a major contribution to the early-modern statements of natural law, a doctrine that Pufendorf used to develop a strong theory of sovereignty that differed in a number of significant respects from that advanced by Hobbes.

Key reading: Tuck, 1993; Tully, 1991.

Paradoxically, Pufendorf rejected Hobbes' account of the formation of the state because he thought it yielded an insufficiently strong notion of sovereignty. He argued that Hobbes failed to realise that since the covenant between natural beings is mutual, it will become void if any one individual fails to obey the sovereign. In order to deal with this alleged problem, Pufendorf argued that the creation of political authority involves not merely one agreement and a gift, but two agreements and one decree (Pufendorf, 1991, pp. 135–37; Tully, 1991, p. xxxi). First, heads of families – the focus of sociability in the state of nature – create an association through a contractual agreement specifying that they will seek a common leader who will ensure their safety. Secondly, the members of this association (or a majority of it) issue a decree stipulating the form of government they think will secure this end. The government so established may be absolute in the conventional sense, or it may be constrained by fixed or fundamental laws. Finally, the association enters into an agreement with a person or persons upon whom they confer sovereign power. Pufendorf insisted that unlike the free gift that empowers Hobbes' sovereign, this agreement is *reciprocal*. The subjects undertake to obey the sovereign and to be cooperative and respectful towards him; the sovereign undertakes to be responsible for the safety of the state and to exercise power in accordance with any constraints specified in the decree. Having promised, each party is bound by the laws of nature to maintain the unified structure they have created. Since sociability will be precarious without safety, and since security is impossible without sovereignty, it can be said that 'supreme sovereignty came from God as the author of natural law'. Even though sovereign power is created by human beings 'the command of God to establish states manifests itself through the dictates of reason, by which men recognised that the order and peace which natural law considers as its end, cannot exist without civil society' (Pufendorf, 1934, p. 1001).

Unlike Hobbes, Pufendorf did not believe that a reciprocal process of sovereignty formation left the sovereign open to the scrutiny of his subjects. Nor did it provide the basis for rebellion. The sovereign's immunity can be traced to the rights that exist in a state of nature. Pufendorf maintained that since individuals in this condition lack the power to legislate or to punish, they cannot 'reclaim' these rights if they think the sovereign's conduct has nullified their agreement with him. Moreover, while the people form themselves into a union or association in their passage from the state of nature, this association does not possess supreme authority. To the contrary, authority of this kind only comes into being as a consequence of its agreement with the sovereign. Having never possessed supreme power, the people cannot be said to have delegated it to the sovereign and cannot, therefore, repossess it. Finally, since citizens are necessarily subject to their sovereign, there is no place in Pufendorf's theory for the idea that citizens share sovereignty and subjection with rulers (Tully, 1991, p. xxxiv).

Pufendorf thus insulated the sovereign from the authoritative censure of subjects by insisting that only the former possesses or has ever possessed *political* authority. As a consequence, his sovereign is no less absolute than Hobbes' and equally free from the binding force of civil law and liability to punishment at the hands of his subjects (Pufendorf, 1934, pp. 1055–56). However, while Pufendorf insisted on the supremacy of the sovereign, he allowed for two constraints on the exercise of sovereign power, neither of which can be traced to the political authority of subjects. In the first place, while individuals' natural right to self-defence may justify their resisting 'extreme and unjust' violence at the hands of their sovereign, this right is a product of natural law, not of *political* authority. Secondly, Pufendorf argued that 'sovereign authority' may appear in either an 'absolute' or a 'limited' form:

> Absolute authority is said to be held by a monarch who can wield it according to his own judgement, not by following the rule of fixed, standing statutes, but as the actual condition of affairs seems to require, and who uses his own judgement in protecting the security of his country as its circumstances require (Pufendorf, 1991, p. 147).

In contrast, limited sovereign authority exists when the power conferred on a sovereign is defined by fixed limits specified in the decree that identifies the form of government the association has decided to adopt. Where these stipulations exist, they form part of the reciprocal agreement by which sovereignty is created. These limitations are particularly appropriate in relation to monarchy because 'the judgement of a single man is liable to error and his will may tend towards evil' (ibid., p. 147). Since the sovereign has promised to assume a form of supremacy that is subject to these limitations, he is obliged by the laws of nature to rule according to these terms. In circumstances in which these limitations threaten the safety of the state, the sovereign can only act when authorised to do so by the people or its deputies. As is the case with the right to self-defence, these limitations were established prior to the creation of the state and do not rest, therefore, on the political authority of the subjects. Like Bodin's fundamental laws, they define the state without impugning the supremacy of the sovereign (see p.).

Absolute sovereignty and divine right monarchy: Filmer and Bossuet

While Hobbes and Pufendorf regarded an absolute sovereign as a rational necessity, they allowed that power of this kind could be located either in a single person or in a corporate body made up of the few or the many. Their theories of absolute sovereignty can thus be contrasted with those produced by two of their contemporaries in England and France: Sir Robert Filmer and Jacques-Bénigne Bossuet. These writers rejected the idea of natural freedom and denied that government is legitimated through a contract. They argued that the only appropriate form of government is one in which a monarch, endowed with power by divine right, exercises absolute control over his subjects. The use of the male pronoun is singularly appropriate in dealing with these writers since they considered the Bible to be the only legitimate source of political principles, and argued that according to the scriptures political authority must be patriarchal in both origin and form (see pp. 118–20). Although Filmer was critical of Hobbes' derivation of the state from a condition of natural freedom, he applauded his treatment of the rights of sovereignty because he saw it as a central element of any viable conception of the exercise of political power, one that 'no man, that I know, hath so amply or judiciously handled' (Filmer, 1949, p. 239). Filmer was equally impressed with Bodin's thoughts on this subject and quoted him with approval and at great length (ibid., pp. 304ff). From Filmer's point of view, Bodin was particularly important because he identified political authority with the power that fathers exercise over their families.

Filmer identified monarchy as the only legitimate form of government, and argued that monarchs have an unquestionable right to exercise complete control over their subjects. He claimed, for example, that there is no scriptural warrant for either democracy or mixed government, and argued that the weaknesses of these forms of government are clearly demonstrated by experience. Democracy has shown itself to be completely incompatible with order, or even with the semblance of good government, for the simple reason that 'the nature of all people is to desire liberty without restraint, which cannot be but where the wicked bear rule' (ibid., p. 89). Mixed government is hardly an improvement on this, because in such a case the exercise of sovereign power is subject to constraints imposed by 'the people', who must ultimately be in a position to judge their rulers in their individual capacities and according to their own consciences. Filmer's view on the temperament of the 'people' meant that he thought their role in mixed government would necessarily give rise to 'utter confusion, and anarchy' (ibid., p. 297).

For Filmer, ruling involves an exercise of will and this can only be effective if the sovereign's will is single and unified. His will cannot be restrained by a law of which he is the sole human source, interpreter and enforcer (ibid., pp. 96, 106). Like Bodin, Filmer stressed the general obligation of absolute rulers under the laws of nature and underlined the requirement by pointing to the implications of the patriarchal nature of political authority:

> As the Father over one family, so the King, as Father over many families, extends his care to preserve, feed, clothe, instruct and defend the whole commonwealth ... [A]ll the duties of a King are summed up in an universal fatherly care of his people (ibid., p. 63).

Sovereigns may appoint judges and advisors and call parliaments but Filmer insisted that as these officers and institutions are created by the sovereign they cannot be seen as imposing an external check on his absolute power. The sovereign's duties to his subjects cannot be enforced by them: sovereign power is ordained by God and is subject to his control alone.

Although Filmer's account of absolute government has a general bearing, his attack on what he saw as the novel and dangerous ideas of natural freedom and mixed monarchy was directed in the first instance at threats facing the English crown in the mid-seventeenth century. Bossuet's *Politics Drawn from the Very Words of Holy Scripture* had an even more specific focus in explaining and justifying what he considered to be the admirable system of government presided over by Louis XIV of France. Moreover, while Bossuet thought that this regime conformed to a divinely created and sanctioned model of absolute monarchy, he stressed the parallel between the monarch and God rather than concentrating (as Filmer had done) on the gift of power conferred on Adam by God and handed down by him to his successors. Bossuet's work employed language and imagery that was used by Louis XIV himself and by those who shared his conception of government.

Jacques-Bénigne Bossuet (1627–1704)

Although he was a bishop in the Catholic Church, Bossuet upheld the absolute power of the French crown against both its Protestant and Roman Catholic rivals. Bossuet served as tutor to the heir to the French crown in the early 1670s. His major political work, *Politics Drawn from the Very Words of Holy Scripture*, published posthumously in 1709, advanced a theory of patriarchal government that was similar in significant respects to that of Sir Robert Filmer.

Key reading: Keohane, 1980; Bossuet, 1990.

In an advisory memoir for his heir, Louis referred to the monarch as a 'human god'. Like a deity, the king was an active creator of order within his kingdom and ceaselessly vigilant of its affairs. Contemporary references to Louis as the 'Sun King' had less to do with the splendour of his person and court than with the life-giving and invigorating oversight ascribed to him. In a very real sense the king *is* the state; the government is merely an information-gathering machine that allows him to act in the best interests of his subjects (Keohane, 1980, pp. 245–49). Bossuet endorsed this conception of royal power, but he buttressed it with a detailed analysis of the political significance of Holy Scripture.

Although God created men as social beings, they can only benefit from this condition if they are subject to the constraining force of government. In contrast to earlier characterisations of governing institutions as the bridles of sovereigns (see above), Bossuet described them as a 'bridle of the passions' of humanity (Bossuet, 1990, p. 14). In order to fulfil this role and to produce union and security, all power must be in the hands of a figure who is endowed with the same authority over his subjects as God exercises over his whole creation:

> Majesty is the image of the greatness of God in a prince. … The power of God can be felt in a moment from one end of the world to the other: the royal power acts simultaneously throughout the kingdom. It holds the whole kingdom in position just as God holds the whole world. If God were to withdraw his hand, the entire world would return to nothing: if authority ceases in a kingdom, all lapses into confusion (ibid., p. 160).

Like Filmer, Bossuet maintained that absolute monarchy is the ideal form of government, but while he related this to a paternal pattern, he stressed that it is modelled on God himself. The precedent of Adam upon which Filmer placed such importance was ignored. God was the first and true king, one who had himself exercised paternal government of his subjects: 'God having placed in our parents, as being in some fashion the authors of our life, an image of the power by which he made everything, he also transmitted to them an image of the power which he has over his works' (ibid., p. 41). The image in question is both monarchical and absolute: 'without this absolute authority, he [the monarch] can neither do good nor suppress evil: his power must be such that no one can hope to escape him; and, in fine, the sole defence of individuals against the public power, must be their innocence', as determined by the prince (ibid., p. 81). This claim serves to undercut theories of government (promoted at that time by a number of Protestant thinkers) which held that the infringement of fundamental rights warrants defensive resistance on the part of subjects (see pp. 243ff). However, while Bossuet stressed that sovereigns are not accountable to human beings, he denied that this means that absolute government should be equated with *arbitrary* rule. To the contrary, absolute rulers must cherish the liberty of their subjects and protect their property. Bossuet thought that known and stable laws are an important feature of good government and while the formulation and administration of these laws is sovereigns' prerogative, they are under a strong moral and religious obligation to govern rationally and justly. He regarded the fear of God as the 'true counterweight to [human] power' and warned that God 'lives eternally; his anger is implacable, and always living; his power is invincible; he never forgets; he never yields; nothing can escape him' (ibid., p. 101).

Absolute sovereignty and utilitarianism: Saint-Pierre and Bentham

As we have seen, a number of eighteenth- and early-nineteenth-century thinkers sought to reformulate the conventional idea that government should ensure the happiness of subjects into a precise and scientific form that would make it a useful tool to gauge the effectiveness of various forms of government. This tool was meant to form the basis of ambitious programmes of administrative, legal and political reform (see pp. 95ff). An important aspect of these utilitarian statements of the ends of politics was that they were often married to conceptions of sovereignty that echoed early-modern theories of absolute government.

An early example of this form of utilitarianism appeared in the writings of the Abbé Saint-Pierre in the first half of the eighteenth century. As noted above, Saint-Pierre's statement of utilitarianism differs from Jeremy Bentham's later formulations because it retains a place for religious sanctions (see p. 97). Despite this, however, Saint-Pierre believed that human agency has an important role to play in curbing people's destructive passions and ensuring that their understanding of their own interests can be fitted into a harmonious system that will maximise both individual and general happiness. Saint-Pierre placed a premium on peace and order – 'charity, concord, and tranquillity are greater goods than truth' (Keohane, 1980, p. 369) – and argued that this can only be attained if power is held and exercised by an absolute ruler. A unified source of authority will secure peace and use its power to encourage human beings to form habits that will produce utility-maximising behaviour.

Saint-Pierre regarded divided authority as an impediment to good government, but he also stressed that the effective exercise of absolute power depends on the rationality of rulers and the machinery of government. While earlier exponents of absolute monarchy in France sought to combine absolute rule with self-imposed restraints drawn from conventional constitutional theory, Saint-Pierre maintained that effective government is necessarily despotic. Ideally, therefore, the state should be ruled by an enlightened despot, one who combines unbridled power with highly developed rationality, wide-ranging information, and expertise in ruling: 'when power is united to reason, it cannot be too great or too despotic for the greatest utility of society' (ibid., p. 370).

In addition to applying this idea to a traditional but enlightened monarch, Saint-Pierre suggested that the monarch should be placed within a system of government that does not depend on his personal qualities. This system was an administrative machine made up of laws and enforcement agencies that harmonise the interests of individuals so as to maximise public utility. It also includes mechanisms to ensure that officials identify their interests with those of society. If these goals are achieved, there is no need to be concerned with limiting the exercise of power because the actions of officeholders will necessarily be conducive to the public good (ibid., pp. 370–72).

The details of what has aptly been described as Saint-Pierre's vision of government as 'a perpetual motion machine' reflect the distinctly eccentric cast of the mind of its creator. Nevertheless, later – less bizarre – formulations of utilitarianism incorporate the concern with absolute sovereignty that forms a central element in Saint-Pierre's theory of government. Thus in his *Fragment on Government* Jeremy Bentham dismissed both natural rights and the Common Law of England on the ground that they impeded government's capacity to produce laws that maximise utility. According to Bentham, natural rights are part of an outmoded and essentially meaningless approach to politics that focuses attention on the origins of government and the basis of political obligation. For Bentham these are not important questions because government *exists* and subjects *are* in the habit of obeying their political superiors. The key issue is not the origin of political power, but the *tendency* of government (Francis, 1980). Good governments are those that promote the greatest happiness of the greatest number by framing laws that consistently prompt individuals to advance the cause of utility (Bentham, 1967, pp. 281–435).

If laws are to provide an effective stimulus to utility-maximising behaviour, they have to be formulated and enforced in ways that make them a rational and certain guide for human conduct, and an effective source of 'sanctions' (or punishments) that can be applied to those who infringe them. These requirements led Bentham to insist that laws must be clear and rational, so that they send unequivocal and consistent signals to those whose behaviour is regulated by them. Bentham therefore demanded that law be organised in a codified form, and was scathingly dismissive of what he saw as the arcane, impenetrable and ramshackle features that distinguish the Common Law of England. In addition, however, he argued that one of the major impediments to a clear, rational structure of law in England (and one of the primary causes of its practical and theoretical absurdity) is that it lacks any consistent and determinate source. English law at the time comprised an irrational and confusing mixture of parliamentary statutes, and variations on these formulated by judicial decisions based on precedent and judges' interpretations of the intention behind legislative enactments. These practices were a recipe for bewilderment; they failed to provide clear guidance on how individuals should behave. They also reflected a failure to grasp the nature of sovereignty and its implications. In common with Hobbes, Bentham argued that both the logic of law and its practical effectiveness required sovereigns who were the single, absolute and final source of authority in their states. The sovereign is a definitive person or persons to which subjects are habitually obedient. Only this view of sovereignty will ensure that the law becomes what it ought to be, that is, an instrument for promoting the greatest happiness of the greatest number.

In making this point Bentham was not suggesting that *any* exercise of law-making power is acceptable. To the contrary, his strictures on codification and his stipulation that utility is the *only* proper end of government clearly indicate that an absolute sovereign (which could be a person, a group or the entire population) is only *one* requirement of good government. At times he even suggested that he did not think it necessary for sovereign power to be unlimited and indivisible (Bentham, 1967, pp. 98–99). Nevertheless, he seemed to think that utility is most likely to be maximised if the sovereign is absolute: 'any limitation is in contradiction to the general happiness principle' (Bentham, 1843b, p. 119). Sovereigns should not be constrained by other powers (as in theories of mixed government), nor should they be subject to rules (like those embodied in natural law) that constitute an overarching authoritative structure to which the actions and enactments of legitimate rulers are required to conform. Like Bodin and Hobbes, Bentham thought that laws were to be seen as the commands of sovereigns, directed in his case to giving effect to the principle of utility.

Conclusion

The assumption lying at the root of theories of absolute government is that effective systems of rule require a final arbiter. This figure, the sovereign, possesses exclusive responsibility for creating and enforcing laws designed to sustain order and facilitate the pursuit of other goals. Historically, this theory has often been given a strongly monarchical cast. However, as both Bodin and Hobbes made clear, the logic of absolute sovereignty applies to all stable and effective forms of government. Early-modern sovereignty theory incorporates both natural law and natural rights, but these were not thought to impose political constraints on sovereign power. Natural rights explain the process through which sovereignty is created, but they do not play an authoritative role in regulating political power. Similarly, although natural law is held to be binding upon sovereigns, subjects are not entitled to police their sovereign's conduct. Sovereigns who act contrary to natural law will be judged and punished by God, not by the human beings who are subject to them.

While early-modern theories of absolute government pay a great deal of attention to subjects' obligations to obey their sovereign, modern exponents of this doctrine generally ignore this issue. Utilitarians take the existence of government for granted, and focus on its tendency, or effects. The Hobbesian conception of sovereignty was valuable to these writers because it identifies the key requirement of an effective system of government. Law is seen as a way of issuing clear, unequivocal instructions to members of the community so as to ensure that their actions correspond to the dictates of utility. As we shall see in the next chapter, the idea of law as a command, and the assumption that government has a responsibility for directing the actions of subjects, has been challenged by those who argue that the exercise of political power should be set within a framework that makes government the servant – not the master – of law.

12 THE RULE OF LAW AND RULE-BOUND ORDERS

Theories of absolute government broke with a long tradition of political thinking that stressed that the actions of governors should be restrained by systems of law. Law defined the nature of the environment in which rulers acted and the framework within which they exercised power. Both natural law and mixed constitutions served this general function, the first by identifying an objective standard to which human law has to conform, the second by stipulating arrangements of offices and/or powers that effectively regulate the conduct of specified political actors. But while there is some common ground between these ways of regulating the exercise of political power and those discussed in this chapter, the theories considered here are distinctive because they identify human law itself as the source of regulation.

The key idea here – that 'power ought to be exercised within institutionally determined limits' (Lloyd, 1994, p. 255) – is often expressed in terms of the 'rule of law'. That is, it is argued that political power must be exercised according to known, fixed rules, and that departures from these standards can be subject to legal challenge. These theories stress regularity and the importance of known conditions, and reject arbitrary or capricious exercises of power. Since the doctrine of the rule of law means that the law itself is supreme, it has a deeply ambivalent, and in some cases an openly hostile, relationship with theories of absolute government. These theories treat law as a product of sovereignty, not as something that regulates the way in which sovereign power is exercised.

A number of theories that give a prominent place to the regulatory and restraining role of human law are discussed in this chapter. We shall first examine Plato's and Aristotle's views on the need for law to counteract the 'passions' to which even good rulers are liable. Aristotle's views on this issue are particularly important because they played a direct role in medieval accounts of the relationship between rulers and the law. In the late medieval and early-modern periods this conception of law was often built up into theories of constitutional government that placed limits upon sovereign power and subjected it to legal constraints.

Bodin and Hobbes regarded these constraints as dangerous products of confused thinking and developed their theories of absolute sovereignty in opposition to it. Despite their efforts, conventional ideas of the rule of law continued to play a role in subsequent political thought. The most interesting developments focused on the *nature* of the laws that delineated the powers of rulers and the idea that a properly regulated state compromises a 'rule-bound order' rather than one created by the commands of rulers. An important formulation of this position appeared in the writings of the eighteenth-century Scottish philosopher David Hume. The need to exercise political authority through systems of law also played a significant role in eighteenth- and early-nineteenth-century French and German thought. In the twentieth century these theories provided inspiration for Friedrich A. Hayek's conception of a rule-bound order. Hayek sought to revive the idea of the rule of law in the face of the dangers posed by widespread acceptance of theories that identified law with the determinations of those occupying positions of political authority. His critique was applied both to totalitarian conceptions of government and also to what he regarded as the authoritarian tendencies of modern democratic regimes.

The rule of law in ancient political theory: Plato and Aristotle

The rule of law is essential to the survival of 'Magnesia', the less-than-perfect state that is the focus of Plato's attention in *The Laws*. In this work Plato identified regime maintenance as a primary role of law: 'legislation should be directed not to waging war or attaining complete virtue, but to safeguarding the interests of the established political system, whatever that is, so that it is never overthrown and remains permanently in force' (Plato, 1980, p. 172). However, since most systems of law and most commonplace accounts of justice are designed to protect the interests of the dominant group within the state they are inherently problematic. They do not produce stability because they are always being challenged by those whose interests are not protected by the existing legal structure, and they fail to satisfy the requirement that the state exists for the benefit of *all* its members. As Plato put it:

> our position is that this kind of arrangement is very far from being a genuine political system; we maintain that laws which are not established for the good of the whole state are bogus laws, and when they favour particular sections of the community, their authors are not citizens but party-men; and people who say those laws have a claim to be obeyed are wasting their breath (ibid., p. 173).

Conversely, however, good laws can provide some compensation for the absence of philosophical rulers by securing justice for all and thus removing grounds for seditious and destabilising behaviour. In order to do so, however, law must be impartial in its provisions, and removed from the control of those who may be tempted to use it as an instrument of particular interests. These requirements are reflected in Plato's specification that the regulations governing the allocation of offices and the conduct of officeholders in Magnesia must be subject to fixed provisions. In short, law must be sovereign:

> Where the law is subject to some other authority and has none of its own, the collapse of the state … is not far off; but if law is the master of government and government is its slave, then the situation is full of promise and men enjoy all the blessings that the gods shower on a state (ibid., p. 174).

The bulk of *The Laws* is devoted to identifying legal provisions that will ensure the state remains as free as possible from individual and class partiality. Plato thus insisted that when the state is formed it must be provided with an extensive body of law that will regulate all its most important political, legal, educational, social and economic activities. A central feature of these arrangements is the identification of a special group, the 'guardians of the laws', who are charged with preserving the fundamental structure of the state and ensuring that any extensions of the legal code conform to the principles upon which it was founded (ibid., p. 227).

Aristotle's statements on the rule of law form part of his treatment of rule by a single person, and as in Plato's *The Laws*, they rest on the belief that when political authority is placed in the hands of people who are unable to satisfy the rigorous requirements of Platonic guardianship, rulers must be subject to regulation. In his discussion Aristotle draws a distinction between an absolute ruler exercising 'regal' power, which is not circumscribed by law, and the leading figure in a 'political' constitution defined by law. In its pure and complete form, 'regal' government may capitalise on the intelligence and virtue of a superior human being. Aristotle recognised, however, that even those who are fit to be monarchs may be swayed by passions that cloud their judgement. This realisation means that a strong case can be made for a form of political monarchy that sets single-person rule within a framework of law. While the ruler is the supreme human figure in the state, the law itself is really sovereign.

The advantages of such an arrangement depend to a considerable degree upon the character of the law. Aristotle argued that good laws must provide a 'neutral authority'; that is, they should be reasonable and impartial (Aristotle, 1958, pp. 147, 173). Such an authority is essential if the exercise of political power is to provide justice for the state.

> He who commands that law should rule may … be regarded as commanding that God and reason alone should rule; he who commands that a man should rule adds the character of the beast. Appetite has that character; and high spirit too, perverts the holders of office, even when they are the best of men (ibid., p. 146).

While the exercise of political authority is usually regulated through what might be termed 'constitutional' laws, it is not possible for law to cover all cases. It deals with general matters and cannot specify what might be appropriate in certain cases, or in particular circumstances. Aristotle thus sought to combine the regularity and impartiality of law with a degree of personal initiative that allows rulers to depart from the strict letter of the law when equity, justice and good sense require it. He therefore concluded that

> the one best man must be law-giver, and there must be a body of laws.
> … [T]hese laws must not be sovereign where they fail to hit the mark – though they must be so in all other cases (ibid., p. 142).

This stipulation applies to both written and unwritten codes of law, but Aristotle suggested that it is especially appropriate with respect to 'unwritten custom' (ibid., p. 147). Aristotle did not explain why he ascribed a special status to customary law, but he might have thought that the fact that these laws have been passed down from generation to generation means that they are communal rather than personal products. They are thus more likely to be impartial than laws that come from a determinate personal source.

Aristotle's preference for customary law was echoed by Cicero, although, as we have seen, he tended to justify this by treating custom as an expression of natural law (see p. 191–92). It also played a role in medieval and early-modern conceptions of the relationship between rule and law that relied on Aristotle's distinction between 'regal' and 'political' forms of monarchy.

The rule of law in medieval and early-modern political theory: 'Bracton', Aquinas, Marsilius, Seyssel and Hooker

Because most medieval political thinking was premised on the superiority of monarchy, questions concerning legal constraints on rulers were necessarily framed by reference to the relationship between kings and law. Early medieval ideas of kingship drew upon Germanic conceptions that stressed the authority of customary law and the need for rulers' legislative innovations to be endorsed by representative mechanisms that signified their subjects' consent to these additions to, or departures from, customary law. This tradition was partially displaced by the ambiguous inheritance of Roman law doctrines that made the emperor the source of law (while stipulating that he should govern according to law), and by the role ascribed to natural law (Pennington, 1991, p. 426). It should be noted, however, that although the natural law provided an objective standard of 'right' law, it still left the problem of determining whether human law was consistent with it. Widely held beliefs that kingly rule was the best source of human law made it difficult to subject human rulers to law without challenging their sovereignty and undermining their capacity to ensure unity and order. The tensions between ideas of objective law, the need for rulers to uphold the law they had created, and the conceptual and practical dangers inherent in challenges to royal supremacy, meant that medieval political thought contained a number of strands that gave differing weights to each of these considerations. These theories could provide the basis for the development of either theories of absolute sovereignty, or constitutional theories that placed the exercise of sovereign power within a framework of legal constraints. Nevertheless, in medieval and in much early-modern thinking, there was a widely shared view that the exercise of political authority should be set within a normative framework, even when the responsibility for adhering to these standards was left to rulers themselves.

The dilemma posed by the interdependence of kingship and law was captured in a thirteenth-century English work:

> The king must not be under man but under God and under the law, because law makes the king. Let him therefore bestow upon the law what the law bestows upon him namely rule and power, for there is no [king] where will rules rather than [law] (Black, 1993, p. 153).

The unknown author of this work (conventionally but erroneously ascribed to Henry Bracton) solved this dilemma by arguing that when kings do not impose the 'bridle' of law upon themselves, their most important subjects ('earls' and 'barons') should impose it upon them. This idea is obviously related to later constitutional conceptions, especially those promoting 'mixed' constitutions. Whatever its future importance, however, this formulation did not shed a great deal of light on the relationship between the ruler and the law. In particular, it failed to recognise the possibility that kings may stand in a complex relationship to the law such that they are in some respects bound by it, and in other respects able to go beyond, or 'dispense' from it.

Some medieval thinkers discussed this possibility with the help of Aristotle's distinction between 'regal' and 'political' rule. It was claimed that while kings should normally act as if they are bound by the laws they create, there may be occasions when they should act in a regal manner. Most commonly it was allowed that when equity, mercy or dire necessity require it, the ruler may depart from the letter of the law. Significantly, it was claimed that these actions need not be seen as expressions of the 'will' of the monarch; they do not relate to his personal or partial interests, but rest upon impartial reason and gain their legitimacy from this. As Aquinas put it:

> [if] will ... is to have the authority of law, [it] must be regulated by reason when it commands. It is in this sense that we should understand the saying that the will of the prince has the power of law. In any other sense the will of the prince becomes an evil rather than law (Aquinas, 1959, p. 111).

In common with many other medieval thinkers, Aquinas noted that while legitimate rulers exercise both 'regal' and 'political' rule, they most commonly confine themselves to the latter and act within a framework where the content of law is not reliant on the will of the ruler. In the second decade of the thirteenth century, however, Laurentius Hispanus' claim that the 'will' of the prince 'is held to be reason' marked a step on the road to absolutism because it made 'will' the measure of reason and thus broke with the conventional idea that reason is the measure of legitimate will. Laurentius still related princely will to the good of the public, however, and endorsed other ideas that drew rulers back within the confines of law (Pennington, 1991, pp. 427–28).

A conception of royal supremacy in which ordinary exercises of power are subject to the constraining force of law was achieved by utilising a distinction between 'theocratic' and 'feudal' conceptions of kingship. Royal theocracy is unquestionable, but kings are also feudal overlords. As such, their relationships with their subjects are specified in a complex series of contractual arrangements that have all the force of law, and cannot be overridden by a declaration of will on the part of one of the parties (Ullmann, 1975, pp. 146–47). An important example of the application of these ideas occurred in England in 1215. In that year the major English barons utilised their feudal relationship with King John to force his acceptance of 'Magna Carta'. This document signalled the king's recognition of the rights of his subjects and his willingness to adopt mechanisms to protect them, but it did so without calling his supremacy into question.

The fact that one of the chapters of Magna Carta specified that certain forms of taxation could only be levied with the consent of the Great Council means that this document can be seen as marking an important stage in the development of ideas of constitutional government. Constitutional theories focus, however, on the relationship between different elements in the state, and only address the question of the relationship between law and political authority obliquely. In particular, theories of this kind do not necessarily deal with the question of whether political power should be subject to and confined by legal stipulations. In other words, while constitutional theories may specify *who* can make law, they do not necessarily relate law-making to a pre-existing body of rules.

In the late medieval period Marsilius of Padua drew upon Aristotle's ideas when presenting his case for the role of law in a just state:

> It is necessary to establish in the polity that without which civil judgements cannot be made with complete rightness … . Such a thing is the law. … Therefore, the establishment of law is necessary in the polity (Marsilius, 1956, vol. ii, p. 37).

Law is free from 'perverted emotions'; it often embodies the wisdom of past experience, and it gives government a degree of stability and peace because it reduces the risk of unjust and ignorant rule (ibid., pp. 38, 39–42). In making a case for the importance of law, however, Marsilius adopted the unusual step of advancing a strongly positivistic account of the source of human law, while maintaining that its content could be evaluated by an appeal to higher, non-legal norms (Canning, 1991, pp. 460–61). For the most part, late medieval-early modern thinkers tended to tread an uneasy path between upholding the legislative supremacy of rulers and assuming that law-making activity took place within a legal framework. This tendency appears quite clearly in Claude de Seyssel's analysis of the French monarchy (see p. 224). 'Concord' and 'unity' are only possible if subjects render complete obedience to the king, but the king himself is subject to the three 'bridles' of religion, justice and 'police'. Both justice and 'police' (dealing with social and economic order) rest on 'laws, ordinances and praiseworthy customs' (Seyssel, 1981, pp. 49–57). Bodin's definition of law in terms of the command of the sovereign was not endorsed by Seyssel or most of his contemporaries. In any case, even Bodin allowed that sovereigns' *private* transactions should be subject to legal provisions, and that they have no right to ignore those fundamental laws that define the extent of their state and their claim to rule it (see p. 254).

(see p. 254)

Marsilius of Padua (1275/80–1342/43)

Born and educated in Padua, where he trained as a physician, Marsilius subsequently practised medicine in Italy and taught at the arts faculty in Paris. His major political writing, *Defender of the Peace* (1324), which attacked the Papacy for the destabilising role that it had played in the affairs of Italy, was condemned as heretical, and Marsilius was forced to seek refuge in Bavaria. He played an important role in the republic established in Rome during Lewis of Bavaria's expedition to Italy in 1327–30. Marsilius advanced a picture of the state that related it to a conception of the good life echoing aspects of Aristotle's political theory, but he stressed both earthly happiness and the beneficial role that life in a political community might play for Christians whose eyes were fastened on heavenly salvation.

Key reading: Gerwith, 1956; Lewis, 1954.

Seyssel's contemporaries took a variety of views on how far the framework created by the triumvirate of pre-existing 'laws, ordinances and praiseworthy customs' related to political supremacy. For example, some writers thought that customary law (taken to embody the consent of the community) is supreme in republics but not in monarchies. Others argued that while custom is binding in private matters – those concerning 'contracts, wills, dues and obligations for landholding, inheritance practices' – the prerogative of the ruler might overrule it when the good of the public is at stake (Lloyd, 1994, pp. 267–69).

By the late medieval period the diversity of English customary law had largely given way to a more unified body of 'Common Law'. This law was held to be related to customary law because it emerged out of the practice of the community. It was, as a later writer put it, 'so framed and fitted to the nature and disposition of this people, as we may properly say it is conatural to the Nation, so as it cannot possibly be ruled by any other Law' (Pocock, 1957, p. 33). A special status was accorded to the Common Law and even the actions of the king were subject to it. For the late-sixteenth-century writer Richard Hooker:

> the best limited power is best, both for [kings] and for the people; the most limited is that which may deal in fewest things, the best that which in dealing is tied unto the soundest perfectest and most indifferent rule; which rule is the law. I mean not only the law of nature and of *God* but every national or municipal law consonant thereunto. Happier that people, whose law is their *King* in the greatest things than that whose *King* is himself their law (Hooker, 1989, p. 146).

Richard Hooker (1554–1600)

Hooker taught Hebrew, logic and theology in Oxford in the late 1570s and early 1580s. A Protestant critic of puritan influences in the Church of England, Hooker was the author of *Laws of Ecclesiastical Polity* (1593–97), often regarded as one of the most important early-modern defences of the English church and state.

Key reading: McGrade, 1989.

In early-modern, as in late medieval, political thought, the relationship between royal supremacy, unity and order, the status ascribed to natural law, and lingering notions of government by consent made it difficult to sustain both a strong conception of rule and an idea of law that was not reduced to the will of the sovereign. Bodin's tacit endorsement of some conventional wisdom concerning law's role in regulating the exercise of political power is testament both to the tenacity of these ideas, and to the complex and qualified ways in which they were formulated. The application of Thomas Hobbes' radical scepticism to the turmoil of the seventeenth century cut through these entanglements and produced an unalloyed statement of legislative sovereignty: rule had become the measure of law. However, the position Hobbes advanced coexisted with other theories (such as that produced by John Locke) that incorporated elements of late medieval-early modern thinking and conveyed ideas about the rule of law in traditional colours. Hobbes apart, this line of thinking was not challenged seriously until the middle of the eighteenth century, when the Scottish philosopher David Hume identified just political order with the determination and enforcement of distinctive general rules. While Hume thus insisted on the rule of law, he also developed a new and significant account of the *nature* of law.

Hume's rules of justice

Hume's political thinking reflected a growing scepticism about religious truth that was the hallmark of the reorientation of European intellectual culture known as the 'Enlightenment'. The term was first employed by the French writer Voltaire, but enlightenment thinking in France was only one manifestation of a general European movement that sought to base human thinking and human society on a new, scientific basis. Hume was also interested in explaining the true basis of political society to his contemporaries so that they would not be led astray by the dangerous and erroneous doctrines that had played such a powerful role in recent European and British history (Forbes, 1975, pp. 91–101).

Hume thought that a scientific approach to politics necessitated the abandonment of perspectives underwritten by what he described as 'two species of false religion', namely 'superstition' and 'enthusiasm'. These perspectives were not merely false (i.e., conceptually incoherent and empirically untenable), they were also detrimental to human well-being. 'Superstition', a consequence of humans' 'weakness, … melancholy, together with ignorance', was manifest in a desire to appease incomprehensible forces by resort to 'ceremonies, observances, mortification, sacrifices, presents'. It threw government into the hands of religious tyrants and produced 'endless contentions, persecutions, and religious wars' rather than productive order (Hume, 1994, pp. 46, 49).

'Enthusiasm' – a product of 'hope, pride, presumption, a warm imagination, together with ignorance' – was equally dangerous in giving rise to conflict which sprang from individual self-assertion. Enthusiasts believed that they, and they alone, had a special relationship with God and a duty to make the world corresponded to their privileged view of the requirements of Christian virtue. Hume thought that numerous exemplifications of the nature and consequences of enthusiasm could be seen in the history of the Protestant sectarians in the sixteenth and seventeenth centuries. Although the effects of these bouts of enthusiasm were relatively short-lived, they had demonstrated a dangerous 'contempt for the common rules of reason, morality, and prudence' that prompted 'the most cruel disorders in human society' (ibid., p. 48).

The ill-consequences of both superstition and enthusiasm resulted from a failure to develop a coherent account of the nature and purpose of government. For those in the grip of superstition, political authority could only be explained in occult terms; for religious enthusiasts, it was tailored to satisfy the alarming conceit of those whose self-ascribed sense of virtue placed a premium upon self-rule. Hume's reflections on the recent history of many European societies led him to the view that enthusiasts indulged these fantasies at the expense of the rest of the community. In a sense, however, this was not surprising since neither they, nor the devotees of superstition, were able to formulate a proper view of the ends of government. A coherent account of the state could not be produced by those who were in the grip of ignorance and incredulity.

The charges that Hume levelled against those in the grip of superstition and enthusiasm did not apply to other, less extreme, conceptions of politics. He argued, however, that these theories lacked philosophical coherence because they rested upon religious assumptions that could not stand up to rational scrutiny. In response to these inadequacies, Hume developed a theory of politics that was independent of Christianity and focused on the relationship between human interests, morality and political authority. There was a utilitarian dimension to Hume's thinking, but, as noted above, he did not think that the *direct* pursuit of happiness or pleasure could be an end of politics (see p. 109). Rather, politics was a means of promoting and protecting a 'public interest', which was made up of a combination of the interests held by members of a given society and specified by 'rules of justice' that were impartial in form, directed to the public good and enforced by government (Haakonssen, 1981, pp. 39–41).

The starting point of Hume's theory is a series of arguments suggesting that fundamental moral notions such as 'justice' are 'artificial', not 'natural'; they are, in fact, necessary to make social life viable and generally beneficial. Hume argued that social life is a means by which humans compensate for being unable to satisfy their basic needs adequately. Having compared the human condition with that of various animals, he ascribed to social life the attributes that enable humanity to match, and indeed excel over, other species:

> By society all his infirmities are compensated; and though in that situation his wants multiply every moment upon him, yet his abilities are still more augmented, and leave him in every respect more satisfied and happy than it is possible for him in his savage and solitary condition ever to become (Hume, 1962, p. 56).

An appreciation of the benefits of sociability encourages human beings to become aware of a correspondence between the general interest and their own interests. However, in order to ensure that the former is not undermined by a narrow and partial conception of the latter, humankind developed rules of justice that make social intercourse stable and generally beneficial. Formulation of these rules, and development of a sense of justice and injustice that make them binding upon members of a given society, are necessary if social life is to provide the means by which human beings can pursue their own interests.

Hume could discern no natural motive impelling human beings to pursue the public interest: it is too remote a goal for practical purposes, and will not overcome the general and natural partiality that most human beings feel for their own interests (ibid., pp. 52, 58–59). Justice thus arose as a result of 'education and human conventions' rather than being an intrinsic characteristic of human beings (ibid., p. 54). Hume made it clear, however, that the artificiality of justice does not in any way demean it. To the contrary,

> I make use of the word *natural* only as opposed to *artificial*. In another sense of the word, as no principle of the human mind is more natural than a sense of virtue, so no virtue is more natural than justice. Mankind is an inventive species; and where an invention is obvious and

absolutely necessary, it may as properly be said to be natural as anything which proceeds immediately from original principles, without the intervention of thought or reflection (ibid., pp. 54–55).

Hume traced the origin of ideas of justice to the problems produced by disputes over material possessions. Without fixed rules of property that specify what belongs to whom and prevent interference with others' possessions, social life would be virtually impossible. Justice thus originates in peoples' appreciation of the need for a general 'abstinence from the possessions of others'. This appreciation gives rise to an agreement about rules to realise this end and forms the basis of the ideas of justice and injustice (ibid., pp. 59–60). Hume regarded rules of justice as essentially negative. That is, they tell people what they ought not to do if their actions are to avoid damaging the public interest (Haakonssen, 1981, p. 39). Actions that conform to the laws of justice may well be subject to other forms of moral evaluation – for example, a just action may not be benevolent – but these considerations do not concern justice, and therefore fall outside the scope of what can be enforced through legal mechanisms. All laws

> are general, and regard alone some essential circumstances of the case, without taking into consideration the characters, situations, and connections of the person concerned, of any particular consequences which may result from the determination of these laws in any particular case which offers. ... It is sufficient if the whole plan or scheme be necessary to the support of civil society, and if the balance of good, in the main, do thereby preponderate much above that of evil (Hume, 1962, pp. 277–78).

Although adherence to just rules is to the general advantage of all members of society, people may tend on occasion to act unjustly in order to gain an immediate benefit. Rules of justice must therefore be enforced, and government is the means by which this can be done. By maintaining these rules, by settling disputes about what they entail, and by ensuring that public goods are provided for, government thus serves the interests of those it controls. Since, however, it is impossible for the whole population to directly and consistently equate their immediate interests with upholding the laws of justice, society must be under the regulation of those whose circumstances and situation ensure they have such an interest. 'These are the persons', Hume writes,

> whom we call civil magistrates, kings and their ministers, our governors and rulers, who, being indifferent persons to the greatest part of the state, have no interest, or but a remote one, in any act of injustice; and, being satisfied with their present condition and with their part in society, have an immediate interest in every execution of justice which is so necessary to the upholding of society (ibid., pp. 99–100).

Hume's view of the role of government as the upholder of laws of justice precludes the pursuit of constructive and particular interests that distinguishes the conduct of the devotees of superstition and enthusiasm. Rather than restricting themselves to maintaining a system of artificial rules, these people regarded government as mechanism for giving effect to natural sentiments (Whelan, 1985, p. 354).

While Hume thought that the particular principles upheld by government reflect the value system adhered to by a given society (Haakonssen, 1981, p. 43), he maintained that their general form promotes public benefit. When Hume applied this idea to contemporary society he sought to identify forms of legal regulation that would contribute to the growth of 'civilisation'. This term referred to the material, cultural and scientific capacities that produce higher levels of public utility than had been attained in less developed conditions. The essential requirement is that systems of law and political regulation should produce certainty and security; that is, they should conform to the general structure of rules of justice rather than being arbitrary and uncertain impositions. Hume thus identified the rise of what he called the 'arts and sciences' with governments based on systems of law that regulate the conduct of both subjects and rulers: 'from law arises security: From security curiosity: And from curiosity knowledge' (Hume, 1994, p. 63). The first stage in this process – the development of law as the regulator of social interaction – cannot take place under despotic or 'barbarous' monarchies 'where the people alone are restrained by the authority of the magistrates, and the magistrates are not restrained by any law or statute' (ibid., p. 63). Hume argued, however, that monarchies can adopt the legal practices that first appeared in republics and thereby provide an environment where civilisation is able to flourish. In 'civilised monarchy',

> the prince alone is unrestrained in the exercise of his authority. ... Every minister or magistrate, however eminent, must submit to the general laws, which govern the whole of society, and must exert the authority delegated to him after the manner, which is prescribed. The people depend on none but their sovereign, for the security of their property. He is so far removed from them, and is so much exempt from private jealousies or interests, that this dependence is scarcely felt. And thus a species of government arises, to which, in a high political rant, we may give the name of *Tyranny*, but which, by a just and prudent administration, may afford tolerable security to the people, and may answer most of the ends of political society (ibid., p. 69).

In other words, the rule of law incorporating rules of justice may exist within a variety of constitutional frameworks. The crucial issue is whether government is conducted on the basis of known, impartial and certain rules that provide security against other individuals and government itself. If these conditions are satisfied, people can be assured that political power is exercised in a way that is conducive to public benefit. Hume believed that constitutional regimes such as that which existed in England provide the best security against the misuse of political authority, but he thought that government can be absolute without being arbitrary. The fact that power is exercised through legal means is more important than the fact that it is in the hands of an absolute ruler.

The rule of law in eighteenth- and early-nineteenth-century French and German theory: Montesquieu, Constant and the *Rechtsstaat*

Hume's idea that detailed formulations of rules of justice reflect the value systems of particular societies means that legal structures will vary from place to place and time to time. A similar point was made by Hume's French contemporary, Baron de Montesquieu. Although Montesquieu adopted some aspects of conventional natural law theory, he stressed the distinctive features of systems of positive law: 'Law in general is human reason ...[and] the political and civil laws of each nation ought to be particular cases of the application of human reason'. These cases should take account of the nature and principles of different systems of government, the physical characteristics of the people, their history and even the geographical and climatic features of their country (Montesquieu, 1977, p. 177).

Starting from this presupposition, Montesquieu identified a range of fundamental laws addressing the form of government, the liberty of subjects in relation to the constitution ('political liberty') and their liberty as subjects. Political liberty exists where 'no one is compelled to do what is not made obligatory by law' and is most effectively secured by a system of constitutional checks that prevent, or at least minimise, the risk of misuse of political power (ibid., p. 244). While political liberty is a purely legal matter, the liberty of the subject rests on a broader basis made up of laws, 'manners, customs or received examples'. It consists in 'security, or the opinion that people have of their security' (Montesquieu, 1949, vol. i, p. 183). For Montesquieu, therefore, the rule of law is supported by public opinion and other non-legal constraints that ensure that the conduct of government is both reasonable and legal.

Important aspects of Montesquieu's general position were incorporated in the theory of constitutional monarchy developed by his successor Benjamin Constant (see p. 158). Constant stipulated that constitutional government give clear legal recognition of the liberty of the subject, and protect it through legal procedures that lie beyond the control of those holding political office. The goal is to establish a 'union of men under the empire of laws', an arrangement that precludes arbitrary applications of either political or judicial power (Constant, 1988, p. 292).

This ambition also lies behind the idea of a *Rechtsstaat* (the 'state of law'), which was developed by Constant's German contemporaries. Given the variety of forms of government that existed in early-nineteenth-century Germany, it is not surprising that this idea was not tied to any particular set of political institutions but applied to any form of government that acts upon *all* its citizens through general laws. Unlike the negative conception of law developed by Hume, the laws upheld by a *Rechtsstaat* are capable of being given a strongly positive bearing that promotes the pursuit of social goals by an active state (Krieger, 1972, p. 260). To the extent that this application of the idea of law produces regularity and uniformity it marks an improvement on the arbitrary conduct of despotic rulers. Its positive implications, however, meant that the *Rechtsstaat* was consistent with the idea of the *Kulturstaat*, that is, a state dedicated to the development of a particular way of life among its citizens. This shift was made possible by an absence of clear specifications of the generality of law in early-nineteenth-century accounts of the *Rechtsstaat*: they merely required that laws should be applied equally to all subjects. The limitations of this understanding of the rule of law was subject to sharp criticism in F. A. Hayek's writings.

Hayek's rules of justice

Hayek's work in political theory was closely related to his primary role as an economist. For example, many aspects of his political thought were influenced by his understanding of the type of order that emerges as a result of the free exchange of goods and services in a market economy. Hayek thought of himself as working in the tradition in which Hume played an important role, but his conception of rules was applied much more directly and overtly to developing strictures on the exercise of political power. Hayek's understanding of the rules of justice involved very restricted limits being set on legitimate political regulation, restrictions that went far beyond more conventional constitutional or rule-of-law doctrines. For Hayek the rule of law meant the rule of a *particular type* of law, not mere adherence to legally prescribed standards.

Friedrich von Hayek (1899–1992)

An Austrian by birth, Hayek taught economics in England, Germany and the United States and was awarded the Nobel Prize for his contributions in this discipline in 1974. His most important political writings are *The Road to Serfdom* and *The Constitution of Liberty* (1960). Hayek sought to restore what he saw as the long cherished truths of liberalism, both from socialists who had openly disavowed them, and from supposed liberals who had subverted them. He argued that meaningful ideas about individual freedom were incompatible with the expectation that modern states had an obligation to achieve 'social justice' for their members. For Hayek the idea of social justice was fundamentally incoherent since it implied that justice concerned outcomes rather than processes; it was also highly dangerous as a goal of political action and legal regulation because it meant that the actions of individuals would need to be constrained in order to achieve the outcomes promoted by its proponents.

However well-meaning proponents of social justice may originally have been, the pursuit of this false ideal set humankind along what Hayek called 'the road to serfdom'. This road led from the welfare state to the totalitarian regimes of the twentieth century because the logic of control was remorseless. In order to deal with the 'unintended consequences' of actions that resulted from individuals' pursuit of their preferences, states endlessly extended their interference in the lives of those subject to them. Hayek argued that individual liberty would only be respected in societies subject to the 'rule of law', that is, to settled regulations that provided a framework of human action but did not seek to direct it to predetermined outcomes. For Hayek, free markets were models of liberty-reflecting and beneficial systems of human action because exchanges taking place within them arose from individuals' perceptions of their needs and priorities and provided the most efficient way of satisfying their aspirations. They did so without resort to state-planning or coercion and were, indeed, compromised fatally when states adopted these practices.

Key reading: Barry, 1979; Kukathas, 1989.

Hayek's arguments on this point were developed in overt opposition to the 'constructionist rationalist' tradition that he identified with Hobbes and Bentham and with the command theory of law to which they subscribed. He also claimed, however, that their way of thinking about law had tainted the theory and practice of modern democratic politics. The key element of Hayek's critique of these traditions is that they rest on the erroneous assumption that order must be created through the commands of political superiors, whether these be monarchical sovereigns or popularly elected sovereign legislative chambers.

While Hayek did not doubt that some sort of order can be created and sustained through a command system of law, he rejected the possibility that it will be either efficient, generally beneficial or morally acceptable. Free individuals can respond quickly and reasonably sensitively to the emerging demands of their fellows, and to the unknowable consequences of the infinite number of transactions that take place in a complex society. An order created by commands simply cannot maximise the benefits of human interaction; when it attempts to do so it gives rise to unproductive uncertainty, inefficiency and arbitrary oppression. For Hayek the paradoxical nature of attempts to create order through the commands of a sovereign is shown by the tendency for such regimes to be as oppressive as Hobbes' 'Leviathan', and yet to reproduce many of the deprivations that characterise his 'state of war'. Hayek supported this claim by reference to the history of communist states in Russia and Eastern Europe. He also pointed, however, to the dangers lurking behind the more benign facade of Western welfare states committed to achieving 'just' distributions of economic benefits among their members. In pursuit of this idea, democratic regimes oppress their subjects to a greater or a lesser degree, impede technological and material development, and inhibit the processes of spontaneous experimentation which are the key to human progression.

These outcomes result from attempts to create and sustain a beneficial order through the actions of an all-powerful political figure. For an order created through commands to satisfy this requirement, it is necessary to presuppose either an impossibly extensive degree of knowledge on the part of the orderer, or endless regulation so as to channel and/or repress humans' expectations and control their behaviour. If one cannot *know* what humans want, then one must *make* them conform to a pattern that can be known. In short, a created order is utopian in aspiration and must be oppressive and unproductive in practice. Hayek's idea of a 'spontaneous' order was advanced as the only viable alternative to the forced, inefficient and endlessly oppressive model promoted by Hobbes, practised unconsciously by proponents of *Kulturstadten* and modern social democrats, and epitomised in the history of the 'command economies' of the communist states of Eastern Europe. Spontaneous orders are very different. They are unintended products of past action that make possible a wide range of individually willed and executed actions that are constrained by rules but are not directed by them to secure certain ends. Hayek developed this conception of a spontaneous order by direct reference to the series of expectation-driven and want-satisfying actions that characterise a pure market economy. But he believed that economies of this kind are only one example of a wide variety of maximally beneficial orders that are found throughout human life, and indeed in nature as well.

The political implications of this approach are explored most fully in Hayek's major work in political theory, *The Constitution of Liberty* (1960), and are restated in his later writings. The critical aspects of this work built upon Hayek's earlier exploration of rational constructionism, and particularly its totalitarian consequences, in *The Road to Serfdom* (1944). In *The Constitution of Liberty*, Hayek's belief that he was making a contribution to a long tradition in political thinking that focused on the need to subject political authority to the regulatory force of fixed law was signalled in epigrams drawn from a wide range of historical thinkers, including one taken from a work attributed to the medieval writer Henry Bracton (see p. 278). Significantly, this motto draws attention to the dangerous implications of unspecified obligations:

> that is an absolute villeinage from which an uncertain and indeterminate service is rendered, where it cannot be known in the evening what service is to be rendered in the morning, that is where a person is bound to whatever is enjoined to him (Hayek, 1960, p. 133).

Hayek argued that unlimited political authority produces a form of servitude in the modern state that is as harmful to freedom as that exercised by feudal lords over their 'villeins'. Liberty and the maximisation of individual choice and general well-being are only possible in political communities regulated by what Hayek called 'rules of law' or 'rules of just conduct'. These rules are 'normative'; they tell individuals what 'they ought and ought not to do' (Hayek, 1982, vol. i, p. 45) and some members of society may be forced to obey them when legal requirements conflict with their personal interests. Hayek insisted, however, that the need for such rules does not detract from the spontaneous character of the order created by them: 'its particular manifestation will always depend on many circumstances which the designer of these rules did not and could not know' (ibid., p. 46). The overall order is thus *facilitated* by rules of law rather than *created* directly by them. Moreover, Hayek argued that rules of law most productive of beneficial spontaneity are themselves the product of spontaneous order rather than legislative enactment. Unlike Hobbes 'Leviathan', who is empowered to create order, the government in Hayek's spontaneous order merely enforces, and in some cases 'improves' rules that have already shown themselves to be beneficial (ibid., p. 51).

The purpose of rules of justice is to delineate a private sphere where individuals are protected from coercion by other individuals or government. Hayek maintained that the range and content of this sphere can only be specified in general terms; a greater degree of specificity would itself be coercive. Consequently, he argues for general rules that govern

> the conditions under which objects or circumstances become part of the protected sphere of a person or persons. The acceptance of such rules enables each member of a society to shape the content of his protected sphere and all members to recognize what belongs to their sphere and what does not (Hayek, 1960, p. 140).

These rules have a negative cast that distinguishes them sharply from 'commands'. Commands are *directive*; they are addressed to particular individuals, and are intended to produce a state of affairs that is determined by the person issuing the command. In contrast, general rules are 'directed to unknown people, ... abstracted from all particular circumstances of time and place and refer only to such conditions as may occur anywhere at any time' (ibid., p. 150).

When acting in a framework made up of general rules, individuals must satisfy the largely negative conditions specified by them. Provided they do so, they are free to act as they choose. Since these rules inhibit the actions of others, they allow individuals to make assumptions that will inform their planning and action. As Hayek put it, general rules are 'instrumental, they are means put at his disposal, and they provide part of the data which, together with his knowledge of particular circumstances of time and place, he can use as the basis for his decisions' (ibid., p. 152). When people obey commands they pursue other people's ends, but when they act within the laws of justice they follow their own. For this reason, Hayek argued that the idea of law as a command is appropriate only in systems of regulation that are applied to administrators and government officials: it is necessary to direct the conduct of these individuals so that they can perform their assigned task. By the same token, however, when this model is applied to citizens at large, they are reduced to the status of unpaid servants of the state.

Hayek's conception of the rule of law has important implications for how government power should be exercised. Private individuals can only be coerced to enforce known law; such law must, of course, take the form of a general rule. As a consequence, except when it is applied to public servants, political power must be confined within the limits specified by just laws. Governments that use their coercive powers for other, more extensive, purposes are acting beyond the limits of their legitimate competence and are embarking on a path that is conceptually indistinguishable from that which leads to 'arbitrary tyranny' (ibid., p. 206). These steps are often justified by the erroneous and dangerous assumption that whatever government does is right and legal. Hayek believed that in the late nineteenth and early twentieth centuries a long and sound tradition based on ideas of the rule of law was undermined by conscious or unconscious proponents of a Hobbesian conception of law. The wide recognition accorded to legal positivism in British and American legal circles, the perversion of the *Rechtsstaat* into the *Kulturstaat* in late-nineteenth- and early-twentieth-century Germany, the imposition of communism in Russia and Eastern Europe, and the acceptance of ideas of distributive justice in Western democracies were all underwritten by rejection of a substantive notion of the rule of law.

Hayek denied that a command system of law can be self-limiting. It is not likely, for example, that the sovereign will create and maintain a system of minimal order while leaving space for spontaneous action by the subject. The reason for this is that command theory rests on the assumption that beneficial human arrangements are *due* to human intention; as we have seen, Hayek rejected this position. Many features of a spontaneous order are themselves the product of spontaneity. Command theory ignores this, and operates on the fatally flawed assumption that beneficial order is created through the foreknowledge of the orderer. As Hayek thought that foreknowledge was highly imperfect, systems of order relying on it produce inefficiency and oppression rather than general benefit.

Conclusion

Hayek set his notion of a law-bound order within a tradition that constrains political power within a legal framework. This tradition has a long pedigree in the history of Western political thought, but ancient and early-modern exponents of the idea of the rule of law did not attempt to provide strict specifications of legitimate law. Historical conceptions of the rule of law stress the importance of the consistency of human law, and the need for it to be applied in a regular and non-arbitrary manner. This perspective is consistent with the ideas of law advanced by natural law theorists but they thought that rulers should retain a considerable amount of discretion, and they did not restrict the directive scope of legitimate laws. Their main concern was to establish the principle that the exercise of political power must further the common good, not merely the particular good of rulers.

While Hayek endorsed this general view of the role of law, he built on Hume's argument about the artificial nature of ideas of justice to produce specifications of legitimate legal regulation that were tied to the requirements of the 'rules of justice'. Hayek's conception of these rules has significant implications for the scope of law and for the extent to which it can legitimately direct human conduct towards the pursuit of particular ends. This challenge is apparent in his trenchant critiques of the constructivist views of law found in utilitarian political theory and in the work of proponents of social freedom who look to the modern state to assist in the pursuit of the common good. Hayek regarded his rules of justice as exemplifying the principle that good laws serve the general interest of all members of society. In the past these interests were threatened by monarchs and aristocrats but they were also seen as at risk in modern democracies committed to conceptions of politics which treated law as a directive tool.

PART

IV

CHALLENGING POLITICAL AUTHORITY

The difficulties of maintaining legitimate rule, stability and order have been enduring preoccupations in the history of political thought. Constitutional safeguards may be circumvented through the corrupt application of human ingenuity, or they – and the legal system of which they form a part – may fail to produce substantive justice through the accidental or wilful myopia of lawmakers. Ignorance, or indifference to the divine sanctions which underwrite natural law, may also make this an ineffective means of regulating the conduct of governors. In response to these problems, a number of writers have developed theories to justify resistance to rulers who abuse their position. In addition to these defensive responses to the aberrant corruption of legitimate authority, there have also appeared a range of theories with overtly revolutionary implications. These theories promote the destruction of prevailing systems of government and the reconstitution of a just social order that maximises human well-being.

Concerted challenges to political authority usually focus on one or more of the following issues. First, they question whether political power has been acquired and exercised in accordance with formal or informal rules. Secondly, they consider whether these rules are consistent with widely shared beliefs about the qualities expected of rulers and the outcomes of the proper exercise of political power. Finally, it is frequently argued that acceptable relationships of subordination and superiority must be consented to by those who occupy subordinate positions (Beetham, 1991, pp. 16–19). Rules, beliefs and modes of consent are often culturally specific, but in some cases they may be seen as local applications of universally valid standards. For example, as noted above (see pp. 167ff), the legitimacy conferred on governments and/or rulers who uphold natural law reflects assumptions about the relationship between human enactments and universally binding rules that are not a matter of human determination.

Questions about the legitimacy of regimes and rulers are often linked to issues of 'political obligation'. Theories of political obligation consider the object of obligation ('to whom or what do I have political obligations?') and its extent, limit and justification (Horton, 1992, pp. 12–13). Ideas of legitimacy and political obligation both hinge on beliefs about the rightful forms, sources and purposes of political authority. While recognising this point, however, it is important to note that ideas of legitimacy are more closely tied to the exercise of political power than those arising from questions of political obligation. These obligations not only relate to obedience and rightful subjection but may extend to duties of a moral rather than a legal nature. Moreover, political obligation is often set in the context of a 'political community', an entity of which government is merely a part. An important implication of this wider relationship is that while political obligation often has to do with obedience to those in positions of political authority, this need not necessarily be the case. As we shall see in the chapters that follow, people's obligations to their political community may oblige them to disobey a particular law, or even seek to depose rulers, or to replace one system of government with a more acceptable alternative (ibid., pp. 166–67). In other words, issues of political obligation may undermine the legitimacy of a given form of rule and may compel subjects to seek more satisfactory alternatives to them.

The first chapter in Part IV examines a range of arguments that justify resistance to unjust rulers but do not challenge the legitimacy of the system of government in which they operate. In medieval and early-modern political thought, this approach gave rise to arguments that focused on how subjects should react to rulers who corrupt kingly government into 'tyranny'. Theories of *revolution* differ from theories of *resistance* because they promote the overthrow of a *system* of government, rather than seeking merely to regulate rulers' conduct, or in some cases, remove them from power. Some early-modern theories of resistance may imply revolutionary conclusions, but developed and overt theories of revolution are a feature of the modern world. They have played a prominent role in nineteenth- and early-twentieth-century conceptions of anarchism and socialism, and in anti-colonial movements in Africa and Asia. The final challenge to authority discussed here involves various forms of 'civil disobedience'. Some of these theories were developed by revolutionary movements for national independence, but they differ from more conventional theories of revolution in promoting non-violent processes of radical change.

RESISTING UNJUST RULERS 13

Resistance theories justify resistance by reference to the *rationale* of government, they specify the *conditions* under which it may take place, they stipulate the *form* it may take and they identify *the person or persons* entitled to undertake it. Over the course of the history of Western political thought, thinkers have also addressed the question 'who may resist?' Some writers restrict the right to limited sections of the population while others argue that in certain circumstances it is possessed by all or most members of a political community.

Considerations of these issues relate closely to ideas about the ends of government, the location of political authority and the exercise of political power. For most of those who regard order as the end of politics, resistance is necessarily problematic; much the same can be said of proponents of absolute sovereignty. However, since resistance may jeopardise the continued existence of the state, it is not surprising that even critics of absolutism tread very carefully on this issue. These writers, who are no more enamoured of anarchy than Hobbes or Filmer, often go to great lengths to show that resistance to unjust rulers may be necessary to strengthen the political order, thus making it an obligation in some circumstances. In these cases, theories of resistance imply a distinction between the larger purposes served by membership of a political community, the way that power is exercised within it, and the relationship between subjects and rulers.

Although resistance always has important political implications, it is useful to distinguish theories that see resistance as *extra-political* from those that locate it *within* the structure of the state. Many medieval theories fall into the first category because resistance is portrayed as a corrective device that is applied *to* politics. In contrast, some early-modern thinkers identified sources of resistance to the gross misconduct of rulers that were part of the structure *of* the state. These theories are often described as 'constitutional' because they assume that legitimate forms of government incorporate institutions and officeholders endowed with the right to curb the excesses of princes. Mechanisms of resistance are thus legal and political; they are *part* of the structure of the state rather than being external to it.

Resistance in medieval political theory: Aquinas, John of Salisbury, William of Ockham and Marsilius

In the early medieval period, Germanic ideas of kingship gave rise to a relatively straightforward and non-contentious understanding of appropriate responses to the abuse of political authority. Germanic kingship depended on popular acceptance, often expressed through acclamation and paying homage. In cases where a king acted in a clearly unjust manner this endorsement was withdrawn; he was deprived of his authority by the whole community or by a significant part of it, and a successor was nominated and acclaimed in his stead (Franklin, 1969b, p. 11). Later medieval ideas of Christian kingship, together with the growing complexity and sophistication of political society, meant that this approach was no longer appropriate. In particular, the stress on 'peace and union' as primary political goals, and identification of the state with the king, meant that resistance (carrying with it the risk of discord, bloodshed and 'tumults') was seen as highly problematic.

This point was underlined by the biblical injunctions to 'obey the powers that be' because they owe their position to divine choice and hold it through divine sanction. It was also buttressed by St Augustine's idea that depraved members of the earthly city should be subject to strict authority and liable to suffer injustice on account of their flawed characters and sinful conduct (see p. 28). In these cases, the legitimacy of rulers does not depend on the consent of their subjects. Rather, subjects are under a general obligation to obey those who have been placed in authority over them.

These conceptions of the source and function of political authority leave little or no room for legitimate resistance to princely injustice. At the same time, however, it was recognised that rulers may abuse their position to such an extent that they undermine the rationale of the state. The coexistence of these potentially incompatible ideas means that medieval arguments about resistance were marked by equivocation. Nevertheless, a number of influential writers cautiously endorsed resistance to unjust rulers, specified the circumstances in which such action may be undertaken, and identified those entitled to undertake it. These theories usually focus on the issue of how subjects should respond to 'tyranny', or the consistent, extreme and widespread misuse of political authority, typically involving contempt for the law and cruelty.

The medieval position is reflected in Aquinas' injunction that subjects have a general obligation to obey secular rulers. This obligation is emphasised by a parallel that Aquinas drew between rulers in human society and God's role in the government of the universe:

> In the same way as in the natural order created by God, the lower must remain beneath the direction of the higher, in human affairs inferiors are bound to obey their superiors according to the order established by natural and divine law (Aquinas, 1959, p. 177).

Aquinas stressed that this obligation is not incompatible with humans' religious obligations or with the idea of Christian liberty. Because human beings 'are freed by the grace of Christ from the defects of the soul, but not from those of the body' (ibid., p. 179), secular governors are necessary to regulate 'external' conduct. Aquinas insisted, however, that obedience to secular rulers is limited. For example, Christians are not obliged to obey human laws that conflict with God's commands, nor can their 'interior acts' be subject to regulation by other human beings. In addition, because all humans are 'equal in nature', rulers cannot presume to regulate them in the performance of natural functions such as reproduction (ibid., p. 177). Where rulers exceeded their legitimate authority in these matters, however, they should be met by 'passive disobedience' rather than resistance. That is, subjects should refuse to obey particular commands, but not make a direct attempt to correct a ruler's conduct, or to challenge his overall authority, and they remain liable to punishment at his hands. Aquinas likened passive disobedience to the conduct of 'holy martyrs who suffered death rather than obey the impious commands of tyrants' (ibid., p. 183). He allowed, however, that resistance may be justified in *some* circumstances.

Aquinas adopted the Greek view that tyrants place the private good of the ruler above the welfare of his subjects. Tyranny is thus contrary to the rationale of the state, and resistance to tyranny is not 'seditious' because it is the tyrant who has compromised the peace and safety of the community and those who resist injustice are merely reacting to the misuse of political authority. In the same way unjust laws are not proper laws, unjust rulers are not to be regarded as authentic sources of political authority. Their legitimacy is undermined because they act contrary to widely accepted beliefs about the nature of the common good.

The fact that Aquinas' discussion of resistance focuses on the problem of tyranny reflects his belief that the obligations imposed on human beings by natural law mean that authority is shared by both the king and other members of the community. In most circumstances this arrangement makes resistance difficult to justify, but the fact that the laws of a tyrant are not true laws because they are not directed towards the good of the community cuts through these complexities. Tyrants can be resisted on the same grounds that justify coercive protective action against any other kind of outlaw. As we shall see, a variation on this position plays an important role in early-modern resistance theories.

The medieval English philosopher known as 'John of Salisbury' justified resistance to tyrants and usurpers on the grounds these forms of rule were not authorised by the consent of those subject to them. This was true by definition of usurpers since they seize power by force of arms but it was no less true of tyrants. Since tyrannical rulers act unjustly in treating their subjects with undue severity, pursuing their own interests and neglecting those of the community, they have to depend on forced compliance extracted through cruel means, rather than on the consent of their subjects (John of Salisbury, 1990, pp. 49–50). John made it clear that both tyrants 'with title' and usurpers may legitimately be resisted and killed by their oppressed subjects: subjects are under no obligation to obey those who are systematically unjust, or those who lack entitlement to rule (ibid., p. 25). By ignoring the claims of justice, tyrants pervert a gift of power that has been bestowed upon them by God: 'As the image of the deity, the prince is to be loved, venerated and respected; the tyrant, an image of depravity, is for the most part even to be killed' (ibid., p. 191). It is important to note, however, that John thought that tyrannicides act as *agents of God* rather than as *members of a political community*. In other words, they are not subjects of those they slay; they stand outside the state (Lewis, 1954, vol. i, p. 249).

John of Salisbury (1115/20–80)

After studying in Paris, John served on the staff of the papacy and of two archbishops of Canterbury. He was Bishop of Chartres from 1176. In his most important political work, *Policraticus* (1159), John argued that subjects may resist and if necessary kill tyrants and usurpers.

Key reading: Nederman, 1990.

Unlike 'constitutional' resistance, which will be discussed below, the theory advanced by John of Salisbury is not, therefore, strictly speaking, a political one. Agents of God are not part of the political community and their relationship to it does not involve issues of political obligation. The private status of John's resisters, and the fact that they are authorised by God, reflects his belief that disregard for justice is blasphemous. Given this view, it is more accurate to speak of a *duty* of resistance derived from humans' obligations to God than a *right* of resistance belonging to subjects. As we shall see, one of the important developments in early-modern resistance theory was a move away from the idea that resistance is a religious duty with political implications, towards more political conceptions of rights to resist. These theories were developed in the sixteenth and seventeenth centuries, but aspects of them were foreshadowed in works by two medieval thinkers, William of Ockham and Marsilius of Padua.

William of Ockham (1280/85–1349)

William, who was a member of the Franciscan Order, taught in Oxford before a dispute with the pope in Avignon over elements of his writings encouraged him to seek the protection of Lewis of Bavaria. For most of the rest of his life he attacked what he saw as the pretensions of the papacy. A renowned logician and theologian, his major political work was *A Short Discourse on the Tyrannical Government of Things Divine and Human* (1346).

Key reading: William of Ockham, 1992.

William's *A Short Discourse on the Tyrannical Government of Things Divine and Human* focused on papal claims to temporal supremacy over the Holy Roman Emperor. It asserted the right of the latter to resist the spurious and unjust claims of the former. In arguing this case, however, William developed a conception of resistance that could be applied to other political relationships. He denied that any ruler has a claim to absolute power over his subjects because such a relationship is incompatible with Christian liberty. 'Christ's law' enjoins human freedom and specifies that subjection to human superiors can only be justified if it promotes their subjects' good (William of Ockham, 1992, pp. 25–28). William thought that in many cases sovereignty is created by human enactment, and he argued that this means that political power can be resisted by those who establish it. While sovereigns are entitled to exercise '*regular* superiority' over their subjects, gross breaches of justice provide grounds for reversing this relationship. That is, subjects can assume occasional supremacy over their (putative) superiors to ensure that power is exercised for the common good of the community (ibid., p. 112).

An important feature of William of Ockham's theory of resistance is that it recognises a popular basis for this right. In considering the appropriate response to imperial heresy, Ockham allowed that the right to *judge* in such a case lies with the pope because of his acknowledged spiritual supremacy. However, the *right* to punish a heretical emperor lies not with the Holy See, but with the electoral princes who collectively form the 'senate' of the Holy Roman Empire. If this body is negligent in supervising the correction of the emperor, the duty to punish devolves to 'the people' because they are the original source of imperial power and the power of imperial supervision (ibid., pp. 159–60). In this case at least, Ockham identified a *legal* and *constitutional* basis for popular resistance that makes it part of the structure of the state. This position is echoed in a far less equivocal form in Marsilius of Padua's *The Defender of the Peace* (1324).

Marsilius was unusual among medieval writers because he identified 'peace and order' with republics rather than monarchies (see p. 145). In Marsilius' republic the supreme ruler is subject to laws made by a popularly elected assembly (Marsilius, 1956, vol. ii, p. 45). This body has the right to regulate the conduct of the ruler and to correct, punish or depose him if he acts contrary to the law:

> since the ruler is a human being, he has understanding and appetite, which can receive other forms (than those of the law), like false opinion or perverted desire, or both, as a result of which he comes to do the contraries of the things determined by the law. Because of these actions, the ruler is rendered measurable by someone else who has the authority to measure or regulate him, or his unlawful actions, in accordance with the law (ibid., p. 87).

For Marsilius, conformity with law is the key requirement for legitimate political action and so the power of rulers must be curtailed when they ignore this stipulation.

Marsilius' formulation prefigured later resistance theories because it rests on the idea that illegal behaviour by rulers may be resisted through legal mechanisms that embody the principle of popular sovereignty. The people are thus both the *source* of law and (through their elected representatives) the *means* of judging and correcting unjust rulers. A feature of this type of theory is that it does not, strictly speaking, justify resistance to governors. Rather, it legitimates a reaction by one part of the government (the legislative) against another, the ruler. This process is analogous to the interaction of elements within a mixed constitution, a point that emerged quite clearly in early-modern theories of 'constitutional resistance'.

Resistance in early reformation political theory: Luther and Calvin

The Protestant Reformation raised questions about resistance to political authority because, both in supranational entities such as the Holy Roman Empire and unified states such as England, France and Scotland, the adoption or rejection of reformed religion was not universal. As a result, the religious views of sovereigns did not always coincide with those of all their subjects. When rulers sought to impose their conceptions of 'true' religion, questions were raised about whether subjects were entitled to resist measures that ran contrary to fervently held, religiously-based conceptions of justice. Two distinctive perspectives on resistance emerged from the political implications of the Reformation. The first position was largely religious in orientation. It concerned the way Protestants should respond to rulers who sought to impose unacceptable religious doctrines and practices upon them. These impositions clashed with people's perception of their obligations to God and led them to question the legitimacy of rulers who used their power in such a way. Consideration of this issue sometimes raised the separate question of whether obedience should be owed to heretical princes, that is, those who remained attached to Roman Catholicism and obedient to the pope. This question implied that adherence to a 'true' conception of Christianity was a necessary condition for political legitimacy.

In addition to these issues concerning the political implications of humans' obligations to God, the Reformation period also saw the emergence of a perspective on resistance that focused on rulers' conduct and subjects' responses to princes who acted unjustly. This line of enquiry eventually led to the formulation of theories of resistance that related obedience to membership of a true political community, and withheld legitimacy from regimes and rulers whose characteristics and actions were incompatible with it.

Approaches to these questions were influenced by the circumstances faced by different groups in various European states. In particular, they reflected their conception of the problems and possibilities facing reformers at critical stages in the process of reformation and counterreformation. An important issue was the degree of support that reformers enjoyed among elites and the general population. These contextual considerations help to explain why many statements on resistance were marked by a high degree of ambivalence, and were formulated in equivocal terms. Even allowing for this, however, a number of distinct positions can be identified. The first of these appears in the writings of Martin Luther and Jean Calvin, two of the 'fathers' of the Reformation; their ideas provide a benchmark against which later and more radical statements from Germany and France can be compared.

In *On Secular Authority* (1523) Luther confronted the threat posed to the Reformation by political authorities (in this case the emperor) by advancing a doctrine of toleration that rests on a distinction between the jurisdiction of secular and spiritual governments (Hopfl, 1991, p. xviii). The fact that Luther identified discrete spheres of authority rather than establishing a standard that relates to the power of rulers and the religious duties of subjects means he was able to reject imperial claims without undermining his general hostility to resistance. Luther's support for established political authorities and his emphasis on the need for regulation reflect his aversion to the chaotic potentialities of popular action. He believed that God had created secular authority to check anarchic tendencies in human society, and he regarded non-resistible sources of human authority as necessary to the attainment of this end. Like later proponents of absolute sovereignty, Luther stressed the personal nature of rule (ibid., p. xiv), and insisted that subjects are obliged to render complete obedience to their sovereigns. Both the argument of *On Secular Authority* and Luther's subsequent endorsement of the justification of resistance issued by the city of Madelburg in 1546 rest on a distinction between resistance by princes and semi-sovereign corporate entities against the emperor and popular resistance against princely and corporate authorities. As far as the ordinary population is concerned, questions about the rightful source of political authority and the way in which it should be used are subsumed by an overriding obligation to live an orderly existence by observing unquestioning obedience to 'the powers that be'.

Martin Luther (1483–1546)

Luther, a native of Saxony, studied and taught theology at the University of Wittenberg and took monastic orders. His public rejection of the theological basis of Catholicism in 1517 marked the beginning of the division of Western European Christians into Roman Catholics and Protestants. In the course of grappling with the political implications of this division, Luther wrote a number of political tracts, including *On Secular Authority* (1523).

Key reading: Hopfl, 1991.

Luther's hostility to popular resistance was given a new sense of urgency by the Peasants' Revolt of 1525, a movement that challenged the authority of Protestant princes and produced a number of emphatic rejections of Luther's doctrine. For example, the author of *To the Assembly of the Common Peasantry May 1525* argued that while political authority is necessary to regulate the impious and protect the pious – 'the torturing punishments of hell are never so terrible that they would drive us from evil if there were no temporal fears and punishments' (Anon, 1991, p. 105) – it is only legitimate if it is a genuinely *Christian* authority. Authority of this kind is possessed only by a ruler who 'truly protects brotherly love, zealously serves God, his lord, and paternally tends to the flock of Christ' (ibid., p. 106). This stipulation stresses both the spiritual and temporal interests of the community, and promotes the idea that legitimate rule is based on the concept of stewardship. It entails a rejection of claims to power based on spurious assumptions of superiority and exercised largely for the aggrandisement of rulers:

> All the popes, kings, etc. who puff themselves up in their own estimation above other pious poor Christians, claiming to be a better kind of human being – as if their lordship and authority to rule others was innate – do not want to recognise that they are God's stewards and officials. And they do not govern according to his commandments to maintain the common good and brotherly unity among us. God has established and ordained authority for this reason alone, and no

others. But rulers who want to be both lords for their own sake are all false rulers, and not worthy of the lowest office among Christians (ibid., pp. 107–108).

Faced with the corruption of political authority, subjects have a duty to engage in defensive resistance. They are entitled to depose ungodly tyrants who, by failing to acknowledge their obligations to their subjects, breach their obligations to God and thereby negate the moral basis of their political supremacy.

Luther's hostile response to these radical ideas of popular resistance was echoed by Jean Calvin. In his *Christian Institutes* (1559) Calvin built a strict doctrine of non-resistance upon his theory of the necessity for political authority. He stressed that as 'private men' subjects owe complete obedience to their rulers, regardless of the way in which power is used; only God has the right to punish those who abuse political authority. After citing many examples of divine punishment, Calvin enjoined princes to 'hear and be afraid', but he also issued a stern warning to subjects:

> As for us, ... let us take the greatest possible care never to hold in contempt, or trespass upon, the plenitude of authority of magistrates whose majesty it is for us to venerate ... even when it is exercised by individuals who are unworthy of it and do their best to defile it by their wickedness. And even if the punishment of unbridled tyranny is the Lord's vengeance, we are not to image, that it is we ourselves who have been called upon to inflict it (Calvin, 1991, p. 82).

At the same time, however, Calvin allowed that resistance may be appropriate in systems of government where popularly elected magistrates are duty-bound to restrain unjust rulers (ibid., p. 82). This concession is based on the assumption that since these magistrates are part of the structure of authority, rulers are not, strictly speaking, being resisted by their subjects. Moreover, resistance by popular magistrates does not call the legitimacy of government into question; it merely utilises one element of government to redress wrongs perpetrated by another and is essentially restorative.

Calvin's treatment of this issue illustrates the ambiguities of Reformation statements on resistance, but it also marks the beginning of a line of argument that embeds the justification of resistance in mixed government. To the extent that Calvin upheld the right of nominally subordinate magistrates to challenge their superiors, he laid the foundation for less-guarded theories of resistance produced by writers associated with his French followers, the 'Huguenots'.

Resistance theory in the late sixteenth century: Beza, Hotman and Mornay

The equivocation that marked Calvin's statements on resistance resulted from his unyielding adherence to the idea that political authority is divinely ordained and that even unjust rulers are often agents employed by God to punish his particularly unworthy subjects. Calvin's position also reflected widespread fears of the threat posed to the orderly reformation of society by radical, populist sectarians attempting to take the process of reformation, and the ongoing government of a reformed, 'Godly' society, into their own hands. In Calvin's native France, Protestants, or 'Huguenots', were a minority group, but they were led by members of the high nobility and harboured hopes that their faith might be tolerated by Catholic monarchs. These factors strengthened the hand of those urging caution and moderation in practice, and expressing a degree of theoretical ambiguity in advancing their political claims. From time to time, however, the pressure of events forced Huguenot thinkers to take a clear stand. The outbreak of military hostilities between Catholics and Protestants in 1562, the increasingly important role played by a violently anti-Huguenot faction led by the noble house of Guise, and traumatic events such as the St Bartholomew's Day Massacre of 1572 (when thousands of Protestants were murdered in Paris and the provinces) made it essential for the Huguenots to identify grounds for resisting a government that gave free rein to their violent opponents. Significantly, the French governments of this period were fortified both by religious ideas and by theories of absolute government. As we have seen, these theories place unquestioning obedience at the centre of the relationship between subjects and their sovereigns (see pp. 204ff). The rationale for this form of rule was thought to be so compelling that it overcame all the conventional qualms about legitimacy.

In the course of confronting these difficulties, a number of writers with Huguenot connections developed important resistance theories. These statements, which avoided the extreme popularism current within some of the German sects, gained a significant and lasting foothold in the history of political thought. Developments in France were paralleled by those in the still fraught, but less consistently and overwhelmingly hostile environments of contemporary England and Scotland. The work of various Huguenot writers is of particular importance, however, because they developed a distinctly *political* conception of resistance. Their theories focused increasingly on the relationship between human subjects and temporal rulers, and did not treat either sovereignty or subjection as consequences of prior obligations to God. Resistance comes to be seen as a response to a breach in a contractual relationship forged by human beings; it was a *right* that belongs to human beings by virtue of their role in creating political authority, not a *duty* owed by Christians to God. Questions of obedience were thus set within a framework of *political* obligation, and beliefs about the exercise of power considered in relation to people's understanding of the duties they owe to their political community.

Four main lines of argument can be identified within the complex and often hesitating process through which a fully fledged conception of resistance emerged. The first of these arguments draws on theories that treat resistance as a right of self-defence, one that is justified by an appeal to private-law conceptions of individual rights. The second builds upon the role ascribed in Lutheran theory to 'inferior magistrates', that is, to public officials who owe general obedience to a prince, but also exercise authority over ordinary members of the population. The role of inferior magistrates may be contrasted with ideas about 'ephoral' authority, which lay at the heart of the third line of argument. 'Ephors' (the term derives from the ancient Spartan constitution) are officials or assemblies that are constituted by the people rather than ordained by God for religious ends. The final argument utilises Catholic conceptions of natural law to formulate a contractual account of the state, and it makes this the basis of both obligation and resistance. These theories justify resistance on the grounds that the abuse of political authority implies a breach of faith that may be punished by correction or deposition of the sovereign by his putative subjects (Skinner, 1978, vol. ii, pp. 319–21).

The appeal to private law rests on the assumption that victims of illegal aggression by rulers are entitled to activate a right to self-defence that is more commonly evoked when individuals are attacked by their fellows. It was claimed, for example, that the actions of an emperor who exceeds his jurisdiction are those of a felonious private individual rather than a legitimate sovereign (ibid., pp. 197–201). Although this theory has radical implications for determining *who* may resist, the individualistic conclusions that can be derived from it were usually evaded by arguments showing that the agent of self-defence is not the individual, but an inferior official or a corporate body representing the entire community.

This line of argument was used by moderates associated with Luther – imperial aggression is to be resisted by princes who are normally subject to the emperor – but more radical versions of it were developed by Scottish and English writers. For example, in response to Queen Mary's persecution of English Protestants, Christopher Goodman came to the conclusion that it is 'lawful for the people, yea even it is their duty' to ensure that 'every rotten member' is cut off and that the law of God is imposed 'as well upon their own rulers and magistrates as upon others of their brethren' (ibid., p. 235). In Goodman's case, and in that of the leading Scottish Calvinist John Knox, this argument is supported by reference to a 'covenant' or agreement between God and his subjects. In this line of argument, resistance is seen as a *duty* owed to God, rather than a *right* possessed by human beings (ibid., p. 236). Lutherans and Calvinists thus look to established authorities, not private people, to undertake acts of resistance.

An advantage of this move is that it avoids the dangerous implications of private resistance and conforms with the privileged position conventionally accorded to the 'powers that be'. Resistance by inferior magistrates utilises God-ordained powers to punish those whose particular and extensive wrongdoing undermines their claims upon the loyalty of both their subjects and those magistrates who are usually subordinate to them. According to Luther's associate Martin Bucer, Christian magistrates are duty-bound to uphold God's expressed commands against ordinary subjects and recalcitrant superior magistrates (ibid., pp. 205–06). This argument was elaborated by John Knox, who drew a distinction between the 'person' and the 'office', and argued that resistance to the former does not undermine the authority of the latter. A significant point about Knox's use of this distinction is that it challenges the Augustinian idea that tyrants are ordained by God to punish sinners: it is now possible to claim that while the *office* of ruler is divinely ordained, occupants of this position who ignore God's intentions should be resisted (ibid., pp. 225–26).

In both its original and modified formulations, the role ascribed to inferior magistrates does not depart from the conventional idea that rulers of all degrees are ordained by God. This is also true of those theories that ascribe a central role to 'ephoral' authorities. Theories of this kind have provided a fertile soil for the development of accounts of resistance that rest on appeals to popular sovereignty, not on the idea of the divine ordination of sovereigns. A tentative and restricted statement of popularly elected assemblies' role in resisting rulers' unjust impositions was advanced by Calvin in the *Christian Institutes*. This theory was attractive to Calvin's Huguenot successors because it allowed them to appeal to non-Protestant elements in the French nobility who resented absolute tendencies in French government. The key figures in this development were François Hotman, Philippe Mornay and Theodore Beza.

François Hotman (1524–90)

Hotman was a French convert to Protestantism who lived in exile in Switzerland during the last third of his life. His best-known political work, *Francogallia* (1573), considered the question of how Christians should respond to tyrannical rulers.

Key reading: Franklin, 1969b.

In *Francogallia* (1573) Hotman presented an account of Biblical, European and French history that emphasises the role played by representative assemblies in curbing tyrannical monarchs. Hotman noted that reliance on assemblies limits the danger of destabilisation because it avoids a *direct* appeal to the general population. For example, he pointed out that the resort to armed force against Louis XI in the 'War of the Commonweal' of 1460 was initiated and guided by a 'lawful assembly of citizens', the Estates General. It was emphatically not a result of the spontaneous action of the 'whole people' (Hotman, 1972, p. 443). But while they were eager to deny a right of resistance to what Mornay called that 'many-headed monster' the people, Calvin's French successors insisted that tyranny should not be tolerated. As Beza put it in *The Right of Magistrates* (1574):

> I detest seditions and disorders of all kinds as horrible monstrosities, and I agree that in affliction most of all we should depend on God alone. I admit that prayers united with repentance are proper and necessary remedies to tyranny since it is most often an evil or scourge sent by God for the chastisement of nations. But for all this, I deny that it is illicit for peoples oppressed by notorious tyranny to make use of lawful remedies in addition to repentance and prayers (Beza, 1969, pp. 104–05).

This statement captures Beza's determination to allow resistance while admitting the force of conventional objections to it. It also points the way to the essentially legal and constitutional conception of resistance that characterises late-sixteenth-century Huguenot treatments of this issue. This last point is underlined in a somewhat paradoxical manner by Beza's insistence that while suffering and patience are the only legitimate response to religious persecution, resistance to tyranny – that is, 'confirmed wickedness involving general subversion of the political order and of the fundamental laws of the realm' – is founded on 'human institution' (ibid., pp. 132, 103). In *Vindiciae contra tyrannos* (1579) Mornay made a very similar point, but he grounded his argument on a distinction between two different forms of contract: one between God, princes and their subjects; the other involving only human subjects and sovereigns. The first contract, the object of which is obligatory 'religious piety', is enforced by God alone. The second, designed to secure earthly justice, must be enforced by human agency (Mornay, 1969, p. 181).

Theodore Beza (1519–1605)

Beza, a disciple of Calvin, followed his master from France to Geneva and succeeded him as leader of the Reformed Church in Geneva in 1564. His political ideas are expounded most fully in *Of the Law of Magistrates* (1574).

Key reading: Franklin, 1969b; Skinner, 1978.

Beza and Mornay not only differentiated religious and political abuses of princely power, they also argued that it is necessary to distinguish between usurpation and tyranny. The crucial point is that, since there is no contract between usurpers and their victims, there is no question of the latter being obliged to obey the former: they are not part of the same political community and have no right to exercise political authority. Usurpers can be resisted by *any* individual because they pose a threat to the existence of a civilised community. In this case resistance is necessary to preserve the basis of human life (Franklin, 1969b, p. 34). Mornay's statement of this position was particularly clear and forceful. He argued that tyrants 'without title' are merely invaders. They may therefore be resisted on the grounds of self-defence as recognised in the universal law of nations. Usurpation is also contrary to civil law precisely because it involves rule without title. Resistance to such affronts to the constitutional and legal basis of political authority is not a *right*, for there can be no rights where there is no compact, no relationship based on collective recognition. There is, however, a *duty* to resist usurpers because they threaten the basis of beneficial and orderly human interaction. The usurper

> does violence to that association to which we owe everything we have, because he subverts the foundations of the fatherland to which we are bound – by nature, by the laws, and by our oath. Therefore, if we do not resist, we are traitors to our country, deserters of human society, and contemners of the law (Mornay, 1969, p. 188).

Mornay insisted, however, that the very grounds that make it obligatory for individuals to resist tyrants without title make it illegitimate for them to resist the gross abuse of political authority by legitimately established rulers. He argued that tyrants *with* title are part of a legal and constitutional structure because there is a compact between them and their subjects that establishes the legitimacy of the ruler's claim to power. Since private individuals are not assigned power within this structure, they can have no right or duty to resist tyrannical rulers: 'private persons have no power, discharge no magistracy, and have no dominion … or right of punishment' (ibid., p. 154). Because individuals do not possess the 'sword of magistracy' God cannot require them to use it. But while private individuals have neither a right nor a duty to resist tyrants in their personal capacities as subjects, they are obliged to follow magistrates who resist abuses of power by their princes. Mornay underlined the impotence of private persons within a constitutional structure by noting that where magisterial initiatives are not forthcoming, ordinary subjects face the choice of self-imposed exile or silent suffering. The sole exception that he allowed to this prohibition concerns those extraordinary occasions where individuals receive a special 'call' from God. In such cases they became *God's agents* (not private persons) and are endowed with the sword by Him. Mornay was aware that this exception could be abused, and so he warned of the dangers of self-deception and laid down strict criteria for identifying an authentic call from God (ibid., pp. 155–56).

Phillipe Duplessis-Mornay (1549–1623)

Mornay, a leading military and political figure among French Protestants, is thought to have been the author of the *Vindiciae contra tyrannos* (1579).

Key reading: Franklin, 1969b.

Mornay and Beza ascribe a constitutional role to magistrates in their theories of resistance that rest on related assumptions about the nature of the state, the purpose of sovereignty and the structure within which power is exercised. Both writers maintained that the state exists to further the common good and that legitimate sovereignty must be exercised for the welfare of the subjects and is, indeed, created by them for this purpose. Whatever the mode of succession, the authority of princes depends on the consent of the people, a point that is both signified and confirmed by devices such as coronation oaths, which indicate that there is a 'pact' or covenant between subjects and their sovereign. Like all contractual arrangements, those between subjects and sovereigns stipulate conditions that must be fulfilled and the means by which performance is monitored and, if necessary, enforced. In politics the central obligation is to secure justice by upholding a just system of law. As Mornay put it, law

> is like an instrument, divinely given … . A king who finds obedience
> to the law demeaning is … as ridiculous as a surveyor who considers
> the rule and compass and other instruments of skilled geometers to be
> disgraceful and absurd (ibid., pp. 169–70).

He argued that since sovereignty and law are produced by the community they can only be effectively regulated and upheld through corporate (as opposed to individual and private) means that embody its interests. 'The people' does not refer to the 'entire multitude, that many headed monster', but to 'the people collectively', or, 'those who receive authority from the people, that is, the magistrates below the king who have been elected by the people or established in some other ways' (ibid., p. 149). As representatives of the community, these magistrates are endowed with the exclusive right to resist sovereigns who misuse their power. They alone have responsibility for ensuring that the terms of the compact are upheld and sovereign power directed towards the ends for which it has been created.

A variation of this argument is presented by Beza. He distinguished between lesser magistrates who may resist, but not depose, a tyrant, and the more extensive powers belonging to representative 'estates' or assemblies. These powers are a consequence of the fact that particular sovereigns receive their authority directly from the estates, who have been given this responsibility by the people: 'those who have the power to give … [princes] their authority have no less power to deprive them of it' when the conditions attached to the grant are breached grossly (Beza, 1969, pp. 114, 123). In Mornay's formulation, magistrates and assemblies are described as 'coprotectors' of the kingdom; in normal circumstances they are subject to the sovereign, but when a ruler becomes a tyrant they have a duty to resist him (Mornay, 1969, pp. 191–92). As coprotectors, magistrates and estates possess powers that are independent of the sovereign but are part of the *sovereignty* of the state. They are, as Franklin puts it, 'not isolated' from the structure of the state; they provide the ultimate guarantee of a set of particular controls upon authority that are 'implicit' in the act of election (Franklin, 1969b, p. 37).

Late Huguenot theories of resistance are, therefore, both constitutional and popular. For reasons of safety and efficiency, however, it was thought necessary to use representative assemblies to transform 'the people' from a mass of individuals into a corporate whole. When these ideas were applied to the problem of how tyrants should be resisted, they identified constitutional bodies as the appropriate agencies for checking the abuse of power. In so doing, they gave rise to an understanding of the ongoing exercise of political power that corresponded with assumptions underlying mixed constitutions. Mornay illustrated this point in a contrast between legitimate 'kingdoms' and tyranny:

> [A]s a well-constructed kingdom contains all the advantages of the other
> good regimes, tyranny contains all the evils of the bad ones. A kingdom
> resembles aristocracy in that the best men are invited to the royal coun-
> cil, whereas tyranny resembles oligarchy in inviting the worst and most
> corrupt … A kingdom also resembles constitutional democracy …
> in that there is an assembly of all the orders to which the best men
> are sent as deputies to deliberate the affairs of the commonwealth.
> Tyranny resembles lawless democracy, or mob-rule … because, in so far
> as it cannot prevent assemblies, it bends every effort, uses every device

of electioneering and deception, to insure that the worst of men are sent
to them. Thus does the tyrant affect the posture of a king, and tyranny,
the appearance of a kingdom (Mornay, 1969, pp. 186–87).

Beza and Mornay introduced a number of arguments that played an important role
in the subsequent development of resistance theory. Despite their attachments to the
Huguenot cause their approach was largely secular, or at least non-sectarian, and
could thus be utilised by those who were not concerned solely with the defence of
a Protestant minority (Skinner, 1978, vol. ii, p. 321). Moreover, both these writers
dealt with resistance in distinctly political terms, relating it not only to religious
persecution, but to more widespread injustices that undermine the rationale of the
state. This point was signalled quite clearly by Mornay's emphatic statement that
tyranny concerns the *bilateral* relationship between sovereigns and subjects, not the
trilateral one that embraces God, rulers and subjects. Tyranny is wrong because it
runs counter to the conditions governing membership of a political community,
not because it disrupts humans' fulfilment of their obligations to God. Of course,
Huguenot writers thought justice was a divinely ordained feature of human relationships, and in this sense their theory of resistance cannot be divorced from their
religious views. At the same time, however, their political treatment of resistance
meant that it could provide the basis for later accounts that recognised the right of
individuals to resist. Beza and Mornay avoided this radical conclusion by insisting
that although sovereignty has a popular basis, 'the people' play no role in either the
ordinary administration of the state or the corrective processes that are brought to
bear against tyrants. In addition, while these writers traced sovereignty to a creative
act of the people, their stress on the incorporation of the community into particular
historical institutions meant they did not need to make definitive statements about
the original role of individuals, the nature of the conceptual environment from
which the state emerged, or the relationship between the community's right to resist
and the moral status of those who had created it. Huguenot writers were thus able to
insulate the right to resist from the dangerously popularist potentialities of a theory
that traced this right to popular sovereignty. Features of their approach to resistance
could, however, serve as the foundations of a far more radical account of the implications of popular sovereignty, such as that developed by the English writer John
Locke in the closing decades of the seventeenth century.

Popular sovereignty and resistance: Locke

Locke's *Second Treatise* was written in the early 1680s, but was only published in
1689 following the deposition of James II from the thrones of England, Scotland
and Ireland. In the last chapter of this work, 'On the Dissolution of Government',
Locke produced an account of sovereignty as a form of *trusteeship,* and he argued
that when the terms of this relationship are breached the bonds of civil society are
'dissolved'. For Locke there was no such thing as illegitimate *political* rule; when the
conduct of rulers or the structure of government does not correspond to the requirements of good government, the relationship between subjects and rulers ceases to
be a political one and assumes a non-political form, most commonly that of slavery.
Dissolution frees subjects from their obligations to their sovereign and allows them
to resist demands made by one who no longer has any claim to their allegiance.
Locke regarded resistance as a right possessed by individuals but he also thought
they have a *duty* to resist unjust governors.

   Like his predecessors among the Huguenots, Locke treated resistance as a legitimate response to the exercise of power without, or 'beyond', right. However, he
extended this idea from the conventional categories of usurpation and tyranny to

include certain forms of foreign conquest. In considering this last issue Locke distinguished between cases where conquest is legitimate, that is, where the invader's intention is to punish a breach of his rights or some other serious transgression of the laws of nature, and those instances where invasion constitutes a violation of rights. An invader who acts legitimately is entitled to subject transgressors to despotic rule, but Locke stressed that this is part of a regime of punishment; it should not be regarded as a *political* relationship: they involve subjects and sovereigns, not transgressors and those who punish them. If the conqueror acts unjustly, however, if he attacks those who do not deserve to be punished, they become subject only to his *power,* not to his *authority,* and they do not owe obedience to him (Locke, 1967, pp. 412–13). Any promise of obedience exacted through fear is void, and since the relationship between the conqueror and his victims has no basis in right, the conquered may overthrow their conquerors when the chance arises. As is the case with resistance to a usurper,

> that shaking off a Power, which Force, and not Right hath set over any one, though it hath the Name of *Rebellion,* yet is not an offence before God, but is that, which he allows and countenances, though even Promises and Covenants, when obtained by force, have intervened (ibid., pp. 414–15).

Strictly speaking, conquest and usurpation do not produce political relationships because the power wielded by conquerors and usurpers is not legitimised by the consent of those who are subject to it. The case of tyranny is different because the tyrant misuses power that has been acquired legitimately. Tyranny involves 'the exercise of power beyond right' in ways that are detrimental to the interests of the subject. As Locke put it, '*where-ever Laws end, Tyranny begins,* if the Law be transgressed to another's harm' (ibid., p. 418). Locke allowed that it might occasionally be necessary for a ruler to act extra-legally, but he insisted that this is acceptable only if it is in the interests of the subject. In all other cases, 'the exercise of power beyond right' is tyrannical because it involves a breach of trust on the part of the ruler and runs contrary to the rationale of *political* authority. Tyrants may thus be opposed, as may 'any other Man, who by force invades the right of another' (ibid., pp. 418–19).

Locke's statements on resistance are far less equivocal than those of his French predecessors because they are tied to his idea that rulers hold power in trust for those who are ordinarily subject to them:

> *Who shall be Judge* whether the Prince or the Legislative act contrary to their trust? … *The People shall be Judge*; for who shall be *Judge* whether his Trustee or Deputy acts well, and according to the Trust reposed in him, but he who deputes him, and must, by having deputed him have still a Power to discard him, when he fails in his Trust? (ibid., pp. 444–45).

In addition, while Locke thought that subjects should be prepared to tolerate both 'minor mismanagement' and isolated 'great mistakes', stressed the need to pursue legal avenues of redress, and warned of the human and divine punishment awaiting those who engage in unnecessary resistance, he allowed that subjects have a right to embark upon what might be termed 'anticipatory resistance'. They may resist the impositions of rulers whose actions show they intend to create a system of absolute and arbitrary rule (ibid., pp. 423, 429). Locke responded to the possibility that his position might be seen as a warrant for anarchy by pointing out that 'the people' are usually very slow to respond to significant injustice, and by arguing that unjust sovereigns are the real rebels because their behaviour threatens the peace of the community and involves a disregard for the laws of nature (ibid., pp. 433–34).

As with other theorists considered in this chapter, Locke's treatment of resistance places considerable emphasis on its defensive nature. That is, while allowing that resistance may change both the personnel and structure of government, he offset the radical implications of this position by implying that many acts of resistance aim to restore an existing constitution, rather than create a new form of government (ibid., p. 432). In these respects he treated resistance in relationship to the existing constitutional structures. At the same time, however, his theory highlights the extent to which even constitutional resistance has an extra-political dimension because rulers who abuse their powers cease to be 'true' sovereigns.

This point emerges from Locke's account of the difference between 'dissolution of society' and 'dissolution of government'. The former occurs when foreign invasion reduces subjects to a position of virtual slavery and breaks up the union of society, thus causing the dissolution of political society or government. In addition, however, government may also be dissolved when the bonds of society – the agreement of each person to combine with their fellows – remains intact. Forced alteration of the legislative body, the core of the commonwealth, or the abdication of the supreme executive, dissolves government by stripping those in power of legitimate authority. It leaves the people free to form a new government and/or appoint new officers of state. Since society is not dissolved, this process may be relatively smooth and may involve no significant disruption of the general benefits that the state confers upon its members. While this possibility removes the threatening alternative that confronts the subjects of Hobbes' 'Leviathan', it makes challenges to rulers politically and constitutionally ambivalent. Since political authority no longer exists, resistance takes the form of extraconstitutional responses to the void created by the disappearance of legitimate power. However, these responses come not from isolated individuals in a natural condition, but from 'the people', that is, from members of the collective entity formed by an agreement to pool individual powers and place them in the hands of a sovereign. Seen from this point of view, resistance takes place within a social framework that forms an essential component of the state, albeit one that temporarily lacks the distinctive political quality of voluntary submission and legitimate rule.

The radicalism of Locke's theory of resistance is evident in his argument that 'the people' have the right to judge the actions of their rulers and to determine whether resistance is necessary (ibid., p. 445). The fact that Locke's stipulation is not hedged by a reference to the role of inferior magistrates signals a move beyond the constitutional conception of resistance advanced by earlier French thinkers. Locke argued that if rulers refuse to accept the judgement of the people, the political relationship between them is destroyed: 'Force between either Persons, who have no known Superior on earth, or which permits no Appeal to a Judge on Earth, being properly a state of war, wherein the Appeal lies only to Heaven, and in that state the *injured Party must judge* for himself' (ibid.). Individuals cannot take legislative power into their hands while government still exists, but this power devolves to them when government is dissolved. The dissolution of government thus makes it impossible for resistance to be reserved for those inferior magistrates who play such an important role in French resistance theory. When, 'by the Miscarriages of those in Authority (legislative power) is forfeited ... *it reverts to the Society,* and the People have a Right to act as Supreme, and continue the Legislative in themselves, or erect a new Form, or under the old form place it in new hands, as they think good' (ibid., p. 446).

Conclusion

While aspects of Locke's theory deal with forms of resistance that do not necessarily result in the creation of a new form of government, his belief that the dissolution of government can provide the opportunity to establish a new political structure means that it could be used to justify a revolutionary transformation of the state. For the most part, however, Locke followed his medieval and early-modern predecessors, in considering resistance as a response either to the unjust exercise of power by officeholders, or, in the case of usurpation, to the illegitimate possession of power. While tyrants exercise power 'beyond right', usurpers exercise it 'without right'. Theories permitting resistance to usurpers reflect a widely held assumption that those who seize power illegitimately are unlikely to use it in an acceptable way. They also rest on an understanding of the conditions that must be satisfied by *political* relationships. Political societies are made up of sovereigns and subjects; the former has a right to rule that is accepted by the latter, and may in some cases be explained by reference to ideas of consent. However, the sovereign's legitimacy depends upon the way in which, and the ends for which, power is exercised.

Acts of resistance have important political implications, but they have not always been seen as part of a political process. Theories that see resisters as agents of God, and those that present resistance as a duty individuals owe to God, may be contrasted with those that treat resistance in strictly political terms. In the former case, resistance is external to political relationships: it is applied to them. By contrast, the constitutional theories developed by Huguenot theorists treat resistance in relation to the institutions of government: parts of the constitutional structure are responsible for resisting the improper exercise of political power. Resistance is thus seen as a corrective mechanism designed to ensure the survival of a generally legitimate structure. This feature of resistance theory distinguishes it from the revolutionary theories discussed in the next chapter.

REVOLUTIONARY POLITICAL THOUGHT

14

There is a significant difference between the theories of resistance discussed in the last chapter and the examples of revolutionary political thinking dealt with in this one. While resistance theory focuses on the behaviour of rulers, revolutionary political thought involves a fundamental critique of prevailing political and social structures and the promotion of radically different alternatives to them. As we have seen, many theories of resistance have a constitutional basis, so claims to resist are part of the structure of a state. By contrast, revolutionary change is extra-legal, and as it aims to make fundamental alterations to the state, it assumes the need for a violent challenge to an existing political system and to those who wield power within it.

This chapter begins with a brief account of ancient, medieval and early-modern treatments of revolution. Subsequent sections of the chapter look in some detail at revolutionary political thinking in late-eighteenth-century America and France, and at a range of Marxist theories of revolution and anarchist responses to them. The chapter concludes with an account of an important example of revolutionary thinking set within the context of post-war anti-colonial movements in the second half of the twentieth century.

Ancient, medieval and early-modern theories of revolution: Plato, Aristotle, radical Protestants and Levellers

Revolutions have been a recurring feature of political history, but self-consciously revolutionary theories were not developed until relatively recently. Although Plato and Aristotle discussed revolutions, they had no intention of promoting them. Plato treated revolutions as a consequence of the moral corruption of the population, a process that inaugurated lawless mob rule and ended in tyranny. Aristotle attributed them to the desire of certain sections of the population – especially the rich few and the numerous poor – to press their unjust claims for exclusive power in the state. He also related revolutions to changes in the socio-economic structure of the *polis* (Aristotle, 1958, p. 213). In these circumstances, and in others where the claims of certain sections are completely ignored, there may be a sense in which revolutions can be justified. However, Aristotle's political instincts were conservative so he generally viewed revolutions with a jaundiced eye. His perspective is reflected in the observation that while only the virtuous few really have a claim to seize power, their sense of virtue, and presumably their awareness of the destabilising effects of revolutionary activity, means that they will not press their claims (ibid., p. 204). Polybius and Machiavelli also discussed revolution, but their focus, like that of Plato and Aristotle, was very much on keeping revolutionary action at bay. For these writers, revolution was part of a process of political change associated with the corruption of the state and its degeneration to a less acceptable form.

Revolutionary political theory made its first direct appearance among some radical Protestants during the Reformation. Although mainstream Protestant thinkers only moved very tentatively towards justifying resistance on constitutional grounds (see pp. 243ff), some of their radical co-religionists posed a revolutionary challenge to the existing political order. For example, the unknown author of *To the Assembly of the Common Peasantry,* written at the time of the Peasants Revolt in Germany in 1525, rejected the idea of a hereditary right to rule on the ground that it is incompatible with Christianity. He argued that such 'false' rulers should be deposed and that Christians should establish new forms of political authority compatible with their faith (Anon, 1991). Arguments of this kind assume that individuals are freed from any obligation to unjust, ungodly superiors and are entitled to reconstruct their political institutions according to their own – God-infused – lights.

Religious justification for political revolution also played a role in mid-seventeenth-century England when the long-running conflict between the king and parliament came to a head. While many of those who opposed the king did so because they merely wished to restore the constitutional arrangements that had been undermined by the crown and its agents, others developed distinctly revolutionary positions. In the early stages of the Civil War, members of some Protestant sects thought that the clash between parliament and the king marked the 'last days' in a struggle between the forces of Christ and those of the Antichrist. They looked forward to the millenarian transformation foretold in the Bible which would inaugurate a reign of justice and prosperity presided over by Christ himself or by his saints (Wootton, 1994, pp. 421–22). While religious considerations were almost always central to the political thinking of those engaged in the English Revolution, two sets of developments in the period had more distinctively political implications.

The civil war resulted in the king's execution, the rejection of monarchy and hereditary aristocracy, and the establishment of a republic. Although many proponents of republicanism were conservative in other respects, the change from monarchy to republic was a revolutionary one. The same point may also be made about some of the ideas produced by the Levellers (see p. 145–46). Some Levellers argued for electoral rights on the basis of natural rights rather than the conventional property qualification, and they also claimed that an elected assembly resting ultimately on the sovereignty of the people should have supreme authority in the state. It is significant that these proposals were not presented as an attempt to restore a corrupted constitution but involved a radical departure from the ideas and practices of contemporary government (Foxley, 2015).

From the late 1640s the spectre of Levelling served as a constant, oft-evoked warning of the dangers of radical politics. When their ideas finally began to get a sympathetic airing, tentatively in the early-nineteenth-century writings of William Godwin and more fulsomely in the works of later socialist thinkers, they did so in an environment in which revolutionary political thinking had become self-conscious, unequivocal and relatively common. This development owed much to the French Revolution of 1789, an event that marked the establishment of the modern idea that revolutions were necessary to ensure that a previously excluded and oppressed majority took their rightful place in the state. In some significant cases, revolutionary ideas were underwritten by integrated accounts of the economic, social and political sources of popular oppression.

Natural rights and revolutionary political theory in late-eighteenth-century America and France: Otis, Sièyes and Babeuf

Those who resisted the British parliament's attempts to impose taxes on the North American colonies frequently based their claims on an appeal to historical constitutional principles. This meant that aspects of the American Revolution reflected the old idea that revolutions restore pre-existing and preferred states of affairs. In some respects, however, both the establishment of a republican United States of America and the arguments used to justify rejection of the authority of the British parliament meant that the breach between Britain and its colonies constituted a revolution in the modern, innovatory sense of that term. This possibility was inherent in John Locke's theory of resistance, and in the appeal to rights that were derived from 'nature' rather than from law or custom (see p. 318). In addition, however, debates on the relationship between the parliament at Westminster and the North American colonies pointed to more deep-seated socio-economic grounds for a political rupture between Britain and its colonies.

The first point can be illustrated by the writings of James Otis. Although Otis' position was not overtly revolutionary, he insisted that the colonists were entitled to uphold their natural rights even if this necessitated a fundamental change in their system of government. In arguing this point Otis advanced a straightforward justification for resistance on Lockean grounds: 'whenever the administrators ... deviate from truth, justice and equity, they verge towards tyranny, and ought to be opposed; and if they prove incorrigible, they will be deposed by the people' as they were in England by the Glorious Revolution of 1688–89 (Otis, 1766, pp. 21–22). Subjects' right to resist is a consequence of their natural freedom and of the requirement that legitimate government must be based upon consent. It thus follows that individuals are free to choose the form of government to which they will be subject: 'The form of government is by *nature* and by *right* so far left to *individuals* of each society, that they may alter it from a simple democracy ... to any other form they please. Such alteration may and ought to be made by express consent' (ibid., p. 16).

In addition to affirming the contractual source of government and the right of the people to depose their rulers and establish a new form of government, some defenders of the rights of the American colonists argued that the development of the colonies had undercut the basis of earlier subservience to Britain. These writers argued that since legitimate government is directed towards the 'common good' of society, the control of one society by another cannot be justified if they no longer possessed a common sense of interest. In the 1760s this line of argument was used to de-legitimate British government and provide the foundation for a reconstitution of political authority in North America on the basis of the natural rights of those residing there. The issue of distance played a role in divorcing the interests of the colonists from those of Britain, but this process was also seen as a consequence of the economic and social development of the colonies. They had now become distinct societies, and their interests could no longer be included within the conception of the common good adhered to by political elites in Britain. In this situation a revolutionary breach with Britain was the only appropriate response (Miller, 1994).

The equivocation that marked political debates on the government of North America in the 1760s and 1770s gave way in the 1790s to new and unequivocal revolutionary political theories. As noted above, Thomas Paine rejected monarchy and aristocracy and argued that only representative democracy is compatible with the rights of man. Given the structure of contemporary British government, Paine's position was unmistakeably revolutionary. The same can be said of the Abbé Sièyes' response to the crisis that confronted French government and society in the late 1780s and 1790s. In *What is the Third Estate?* Sièyes argued that the distinction traditionally made between the three estates (the 'third', the 'noble' and the 'clerical') was unsustainable because there was now only *one* estate in France. Sièyes argued that the third estate *was* the 'nation', that is, an equal union of individuals formed by a voluntary engagement. Since the feudal structure from which the nobility had derived its rationale no longer existed, this class had no claim to a distinct political status. There was no place for privileged classes in a union of equals that embodied the 'common will' of the nation (Sièyes, 1963, p. 58).

> ## Emmanuel Joseph Sièyes (1748–1836)
>
> Sièyes was educated at the Sorbonne and ordained in 1772, and prior to the outbreak of the French Revolution he held a number of clerical appointments. Sièyes published *What is the Third Estate?* early in 1789, and was subsequently elected to the Estates-General, where he framed the resolutions that transformed that body into the National Assembly. Having played a prominent role in the politics of the 1790s, Sièyes worked with Napoleon to establish the Consulate, which paved the way for the emergence of the Empire. His role in the condemnation of Louis XVI resulted in him being forced into exile when the Bourbons were restored in 1815.
>
> *Key reading:* Forsyth, 1987; Rubinelli, 2018; Sonenscher, 2015.

In rejecting the political claims of the nobility and the clergy, Sièyes was proposing a revolutionary transformation of French government. The effect of this change was intensified by his claim that 'the nation' should establish a political structure appropriate to the realisation of its interests. This structure, one that maintained and developed citizens' natural and civil rights and assigned political rights in a way that would serve these ends, was to be created by a constituent assembly. While Sièyes thought that there was a role for monarchy in representative government, he did not think of it in traditional terms. For him monarchy was valuable because it avoided the dangers inherent in placing all executive and legislative functions in a single chamber. Consequently, Sièyes proposed that ministers should be chosen by the monarch, but should be answerable to parliament. The king would not be answerable to this body, rather he would be accountable to the constituent assembly from which he derived his power (Forsyth, 1987, pp. 176–79). Monarchs, like the other organs of government, were created by the people and should be answerable to them.

The revolutionary character of Sièyes political thinking was also clearly apparent in his assumption that human beings are entitled to take it upon themselves to recreate their political institutions. In making his case Sièyes appealed to the principles of 'reason' and 'equity' as the basis of a new order embodying immutable standards of truth and justice. This aspiration, which was common among revolutionary figures in contemporary France, was expressed most forcefully by Maximilien Robespierre (a leading member of the radically anti-aristocratic Jacobin group) in a speech to the National Assembly in late 1789: 'Eternal Providence has summoned you alone since the origin of the world to re-establish on earth the empire of justice and liberty.' In Robespierre's view, this task involved the regeneration of institutions and of human nature itself. In the past, human character had been corrupted by the oppressive and unjust influences of non-egalitarian forms of government. It was now necessary to substitute 'all the virtues and miracles of the Republic for all the vices and puerilities of the monarchy' (Tholfsen, 1984, pp. 64, 69–70).

At a later stage in the Revolution, however, Gracchus Babeuf and his followers argued that a merely political revolution was incomplete and precarious (see p. 189). Babeuf maintained that the new constitution of 1794 marked a retreat from the true principles of the revolution because it abandoned universal male suffrage in favour of a relatively high property qualification for voters. He argued for thoroughgoing democracy, and for the use of the power of a democratised state to eliminate the gross inequalities that undermined the formal equality recognised by the French Republic. As Babeuf put it, 'The first and basic prerequisite of human association is the recognition of an implicit right to improve the social and political system in order to promote the happiness of its members. This right is usually unwritten, but it is absolutely inalienable' (Babeuf, 1972, pp. 35–36).

Babeuf's 'conspiracy of the equals' was exposed before action could be taken to realise its objectives, but the idea that the attainment of liberty and equality necessitates both social and political revolution became a key feature of socialist political thought in the nineteenth century. Socialists portrayed existing society as inherently unjust, and they sought to replace inegalitarian and oppressive social and political institutions with a variety of arrangements that would make liberty and equality a reality for all members of society. A number of important nineteenth-century socialist thinkers believed that violent action would be necessary to attain these ends. The most significant examples of this strand of socialist theory were produced by Marxist and anarchist thinkers.

Marxist theories of revolution: Marx and Engels, Kautsky, Lenin, Stalin, Trotsky, Gramsci and Mao Tse-tung

In common with a number of his contemporaries, Marx wished to promote a radical transformation of human society that would make human emancipation a reality rather than a dream. Marx thought that the agrarian and industrial revolutions meant it was now possible to satisfy the material needs of all human beings but he believed that these benefits could only be realised if they were freed from the oppressive inequalities that disfigured all previous and existing social and political structures. Revolutionary Marxists thus called for the abolition of private property and the state, as well as for the communal control of material resources and the establishment of a system of distribution directed towards the fulfilment of human needs.

Marx and his collaborator Engels believed that they had established a scientific basis for understanding both capitalism and the revolutionary process that would destroy it. This theory rested on an analysis of the historical development of European societies that informed their conception of historical materialism. They argued that the capitalist class had emerged from the previous feudal mode of production through successful expropriation of the labour of those who lacked access to capital. Over time, this process had produced a social structure that contained two major classes: the capitalists, or *bourgeoisie,* and the *proletariat,* a property-less class that was obliged to sell its labour power in order to secure a minimal level of material well-being.

The growth of the bourgeoisie as the dominant economic class underwrote its eventual dominance of the modern state. This process was marked by revolutionary outbreaks (in England in the seventeenth century, and France in the late eighteenth century) that transformed the social and political structures of those societies. The English and French revolutions signalled the demise of feudal elites and their displacement by a class that controlled the key productive resource of modern societies, that is, capital. Capitalism had broken free from the constraints imposed on it by feudal society and established political institutions that, in more or less overt ways, ensured that the state had become a 'committee for managing the common affairs of the whole bourgeoisie' (Marx, 1973, p. 69). Marx and Engels' historical account provided the basis for identifying developmental tendencies inherent in the capitalist mode of production. Their analysis focused on the rationale of the capitalist mode of production and its implications for the class structure of modern society and for the development and eventual demise of capitalism itself.

Karl Marx (1818–83) and Friedrich Engels (1820–1895)

Marx was founder (along with his collaborator Friedrich Engels) of the school of political thinking that bears his name. He was born and educated in Germany, but spent the second half of his life in exile in London. There he wrote extensively on economics, sociology and politics and played a vigorous role in the internal politics of various European socialist movements. Marx's political writings include *The German Ideology* (written in 1846 but published posthumously) and *The Communist Manifesto* (1848), both of which were written with Engels. Engels, who was also born in Germany, spent most of his adult life in England, where he managed a succesful branch of his family's extensive textile business. In addition to the works that Engels co-authored with Marx, he also wrote *The Origins of the Family, Private Property and the State* (1884), an influential account of the impact of the rise of capitalism on the family and gender relationships. Both Marx and Engels were heavily involved in European socialist politics from the 1860s.

In *Capital*, Marx provided a critical account of a range of aspects of 'capitalism', the system of social and political relations that was characteristic of the most economically developed states of Europe in the nineteenth century. Much of the economic and social data on which he drew came from recent British sources, but Marx set his account in a broad historical framework and drew on a range of ancient and modern sources to present his case. He argued that by the nineteenth century the belief systems, social relations and political structures that Western European societies had inherited from the medieval world had been transformed beyond recognition. This transformation yielded staggering gains in productivity and great technological advances, but it gave rise to huge discrepancies between property holders (members of the 'bourgeoisie') and the majority of property-less labourers (the 'proletariat') who lived by selling their labour power to capitalists. As capitalism developed, these classes came into increasingly overt hostility, dividing society into two camps. Exploitation, antagonism and immiseration meant that despite the economic resources generated by them, most members of capitalist societies were unable to realise their human potential or to find satisfaction in their relationships with their fellow human beings. In capitalist society, as in those which had preceded it, the dominant class used the power of the state to protect its interests and created complex ideological structures which sought to legitimate its position.

The proletariat, who were called into being in order to satisfy the demands of capital, increasingly experienced conditions of deprivation that would banish any lingering illusions about the disinterestedness of the modern state, help solidify its sense of class identity and common interest and forge it into a revolutionary force. Eventually, the proletariat would take advantage of the fragility of capitalism engendered by increasingly sharp competition between capitalists, mount a successful revolution and seize control of the state. The revolutionaries would use state power to destroy the capitalist system, while utilising its productive potentialities to meet human needs through social relationships that were built upon the voluntary cooperation of free beings.

Although Marxism was only one among a number of nineteenth-century critiques of capitalism from a socialist perspective, it assumed great significance in the twentieth century when it was taken up by leading figures in the October Revolution in 1917 in Russia and by other revolutionaries in China and South America.

Key reading: Avineri, 1968; Carver, 1991; Elster, 1986; Hunt, 2009; McLellan, 1986; Stedman Jones, 2017; Wright, 2015.

In their efforts to maximise the profitability of capital and labour, the capitalist class had developed the productive capacities of society to such an extent that it was now possible to satisfy humanity's fundamental material needs. The growth of capitalism, however, had given rise to a large impoverished class of ruthlessly exploited, property-less workers. Exploitation was facilitated by the erosion of medieval regulations and conventions governing employer-employee relationships, by the increase in population stimulated by economic growth, and by the utilisation of machinery. These developments deprived the working class of traditional forms of protection and weakened their bargaining position in an unregulated labour market; they resulted in fierce competition between workers and a reduction in wages to the lowest level necessary to sustain human life. To these material forms of impoverishment were added those produced by desperate overwork, by the tendency to make the labour of human beings subservient to the superhuman capacities of machines, and by the impoverishment of the human spirit by a system of production that made human activity, the satisfaction of human needs and social interaction the source of misery rather than benefit (ibid., pp. 70–76).

Marx and Engels thought that an understanding of the underlying basis of capitalism was the key to explaining the revolutionary forces that would emerge from it. Foremost among them was a large and increasingly disaffected proletarian class that was deprived of the material benefits of economic and technological development, and subject to the dehumanising conditions of life and labour that were characteristic of the capitalist mode of production. The threat posed to capitalism by this potentially revolutionary proletariat would be augmented by failures in its internal workings. For example, increasingly intense competition between capitalists produced commercial crises that would destroy capital and destabilize the system of which it was an integral part:

> the productive forces at the disposal of society no longer tend to further the development of the conditions of bourgeoisie property; on the contrary, they have become too powerful for these conditions, by which they are fettered, and so soon as they overcome these fetters, they bring disorder into the whole of bourgeois society, endanger the existence of bourgeois property. The conditions of bourgeois society are too narrow to comprise the wealth created by them (ibid., p. 73).

One result of Marx and Engels' analysis was that revolutionary action was given a strongly positive bearing. Revolution had become necessary for the progressive development of human society, and for the universal benefit of humanity. Under capitalism the proletariat had been stripped of all of its particular interests, leaving it with nothing but its humanity. Marx and Engels thus argued that the cause of the proletariat was the cause of humanity, and that its emancipation would entail the emancipation of humanity.

Marx and Engels regarded capitalism as a global rather than a merely national or European phenomenon. As competition between capitalists in the most developed economies of Europe increased, they sought new markets overseas and in some cases set up manufacturing and trading operations there. Since return on capital was the primary object, these developments were undertaken without regard to existing national centres of production and placed severe pressures on the internal economies of European states. They also, however, created demands for new products and transformed and homogenised national cultures.

> In place of the old local and national seclusion and self-sufficiency, we have intercourse in every direction, universal inter-dependence of

nations. And as in material, so also in intellectual production. The intellectual creations of individual nations become common property. National one-sideness and narrow-mindness become more and more impossible, and from the numerous national and local literatures, there arises a world literature (ibid., p. 71).

For those countries and empires that were the objects of the capitalists' search for new markets, transformation was equally profound. Capitalism 'compels all nations to adopt the bourgeois mode of production; it compels them to introduce what it calls civilisation into their midst, *i.e.*, to become bourgeois themselves. In one word it creates a world after its own image' (ibid.). This compulsion was sometimes due solely to the power of European capitalism applied in pre-capitalist societies but it also resulted from the joint action of European capital and European states. Thus on the Indian sub-continent, the combined influences of capitalists, the (British) East India Company (a monopoly created by the government), and the British government's coercion of local rulers and traders destroyed the structure of traditional Indian communities and made their economic activity completely subsidiary to the needs of British capital. Marx and Engels regarded these developments as essential steps in the emergence of global capitalism and preparatory to the revolutionary transformation that would result from it.

> The devastating effects of English industry, when contemplated with regard to India, a country as vast as Europe ... are palpable and con-founding. But we must not forget that they are only the organic results of the whole system of production as it is now constituted. That production rests on the supreme rule of capital. ... The bourgeois period of history has to create the material basis of the new world (Marx, 1973, p. 324).

Because global capitalism was conceived of as a system of malign interdependency, Marx and Engels anticipated that events in distant and undeveloped countries would produce shock waves of crisis in the most advanced economies of the west. Thus in 1853 Marx expected that a large-scale peasant uprising in China, and the resulting disruption of the tea trade and the fall in demand for British goods in China, would induce crises in British manufacturing industries and the agricultural areas that fed their workforces (ibid., p. 330).

By relating revolution to developments taking place within capitalist society, Marx and Engels believed that they were able to specify the conditions under which a proletarian revolution would be possible. The key requirements were the full development of capitalism so that it would form the dominant mode of production on a global, not merely a national scale, and conversion of the proletariat into an effective revolutionary force.

> [I]f these material elements of a complete revolution are not present (namely, on the one hand the existing productive forces, on the other the formation of a revolutionary mass, which revolts not only against separate conditions of society up till then, but against the very 'productive life' till then, the 'total activity' on which it was based), then, as far as practical development is concerned, it is absolutely imma-terial whether the idea of this revolution has been expressed a hundred times already; as the history of communism proves (Marx and Engels, 1968, pp. 29–30).

In their earliest writings Marx and Engels suggested that once these conditions were satisfied a proletarian revolution would become an inevitable 'historical necessity'. The *Communist Manifesto* of 1848 focused on the seizure of state power by the proletariat and the use of this power to establish the conditions necessary for the evolution of a classless, stateless society:

> the first step in the revolution ... is to raise the proletariat to the position of ruling class, to win the battle of democracy.
>
> The proletariat will use its political supremacy to wrest, by degrees, all capital from the bourgeoisie, to centralise all instruments of production in the hands of the state, i.e., of the proletariat organised as the ruling class, and to increase the total productive forces as rapidly as possible ... .
>
> When, in the course of development, class distinctions have disappeared, and all production has been concentrated in the hands of a vast association of the whole nation, the public power will lose its political character ... If the proletariat ... sweeps away by force the old conditions of production, then it will, along with these conditions, have swept away the conditions for the existence of class antagonisms and of classes generally, and will thereby have abolished its own supremacy as a class.
>
> In place of the old bourgeois society, with all its classes and class antagonisms, we shall have an association, in which the free development of each is the condition for the free development of all (Marx, 1973, pp. 86–87).

Marx later refined this account. He argued that the proletariat would not merely seize hold of a ready-made state apparatus, but would need to transform it into a truly democratic system of government. Thus, in his late reflections on the Paris Commune of 1870–71 he made much of 'working', as opposed to the merely 'parliamentary' character of the Commune. The Commune provided a model for genuine government of the nation by the nation: 'The Communal Constitution would have restored to the social body all the forces hitherto absorbed by the State parasite feeding upon, and clogging the freer movements of, society' (Marx and Engels, 1973, vol. ii, p. 222). While earlier revolutionaries had mistakenly attempted to seize control of the existing machinery of government and perfect its operation, the Communards sought to transform it into a vehicle for radical social and political change (ibid., p. 224). The conventional bourgeois state was a class instrument and control of it was not part of a viable revolution. To the contrary, Marx saw revolution as a process that transcended class interests; it was therefore necessary to create a radically democratic structure that would direct political power to the attainment of universal ends.

The global reach of capitalism created an international working class as well as a cosmopolitan bourgeoisie. Marx and Engels saw these two great hostile classes as the primary actors on the international as well as the national stage. As workers throughout the world were increasingly brought under the control of international capitalism, any lingering sense of national solidarity gave way before the growing realisation of the universal subjugation of labour to capital and a growing understanding of the common interests of all workers. In a speech to the International Working Men's Association in 1863 Marx urged it to adopt a common counter-foreign policy to confront the bourgeois regimes of Western Europe. This approach reflected 'the simple laws of morals and justice, which ought to govern the relations of private individuals, as the rules paramount of the intercourse of nations. The fight for such a foreign policy forms part of the struggle for the emancipation of the working classes' (Marx and Engels, 1973, vol. ii, p. 18).

The impact of Marx and Engels' theory was felt most immediately in Germany, where a very large electorally successful Marxist party, the Social Democratic Party (SDP), came into being. In 1891 this party adopted the 'Erfurt Programme', a step that marked its self-definition as a revolutionary rather than a 'reformist' party. In his commentary upon this programme the Czech-born Marxist 'revisionist' Karl Kautsky contrasted 'reformism' (attempts to alleviate the problems of capitalism from within the existing structure) with the revolutionary stance adopted by the SDP (Kautsky, 1971, p. 89). However, while Kautsky embraced Marxist ideas about the inevitability of the attainment of the revolutionary abolition of private property, he argued that the pursuit of this goal might involve a number of stages. Moreover, he insisted that if social reform were to be seen in the context of an ultimately revolutionary struggle, it could form part of a viable socialist programme. It would provide partial and temporary relief for the working classes; it might stimulate economic development, and it might also hasten the onset of the revolution by speeding up the demise of small and increasingly marginalised sectors of capitalism (ibid., p. 184).

Karl Kautsky (1854–1938)

Born in Prague and educated at the University of Vienna, Kautsky gravitated from radical Czech nationalism to socialism in the late 1870s. Originally associated with the Austrian Socialist Party, Kautsky later became a leading member of the German Social Democratic Party. Kautsky's *The Dictatorship of the Proletariat* (1915) signalled a clear rift between his conception of the revolutionary process and that promoted by Lenin, the Russian communist leader.

Key reading: Salvador, 1979.

In making these points Kautsky offered a challenge to contemporary Marxist thinkers who argued that working-class attempts to pursue social and political objectives within the structure of a capitalist society were inherently contradictory. To the contrary, he argued that the organisational and educational gains of involvement in trades union activity could enhance the political effectiveness of the proletariat. This point was of great importance to Kautsky since he believed that an active, politically conscious proletariat could use the parliamentary system to advance its revolutionary aspirations. For example, he maintained that if a party representing the proletariat were to gain control of a state through electoral means, a revolutionary change in society could be brought about by parliamentary action. In an implicit departure from Marx's position on the Paris Commune, Kautsky argued that proletarian participation in electoral politics could transform the character of parliaments and greatly increase the workers' political effectiveness:

> Whenever the proletariat engages in parliamentary activity as a self-conscious class, parliamentarianism begins to change its character. It ceases to be a mere tool in the hands of the bourgeoisie. This very participation … proves to be the most effective means of shaking up the

hitherto indifferent divisions of the proletariat and giving them hope and confidence. It is the most powerful lever that can be utilized to raise the proletariat out of its economic, social and moral degradation (ibid., p. 188).

Ten years after the publication of Kautsky's commentary, this position was challenged implicitly in a manifesto issued by V. I. Lenin, a leading member of the Bolsheviks, which at the time was a relatively insignificant Russian Marxist party. In *What is to be Done?* (1905) Lenin claimed that the revolutionary potential of the proletariat would be fulfilled only if its actions were directed by a theoretically informed elite that focused on the 'political' rather than the 'economic' aspects of the struggle against capitalism. This elite must overthrow the state rather than merely try to extract economic concessions from the capitalist class. Lenin's arguments on this point involved a critique of working-class activism. He claimed that the spontaneous activity of the working classes would only produce a limited 'trade union consciousness'. 'Class political consciousness can be brought to the workers *only from without,* that is, only from outside the economic struggle, from outside the sphere of relations between workers and employers' (Lenin, 1975, vol. i, pp. 152–53). This position was quite at odds with Kautsky's belief that a working-class consciousness could develop throughout the labour movement. Kautsky believed that the scientific details of Marxism would be worked out by intellectuals, but he insisted that there was no need for a socialist, revolutionary consciousness to be imported from outside the economic struggle (Kautsky, 1994).

The conflict between Lenin's and Kautsky's positions came to a head in 1917 as a result of Lenin's attempt to apply his ideas to the revolution that broke out in Russia. After the Bolsheviks seized power in October of that year, Lenin found himself having to relate Marxist ideas about revolution to a situation where the major revolutionary force was a peasantry committed to retaining its recently acquired landholdings, rather than a proletariat committed to transforming society and the state. Lenin's and Kautsky's divergent understanding of the socialist revolution caused an open breach between them in the years 1917–18. In *State and Revolution* (1918) Lenin launched an attack on 'Kautskyism', claiming that Marxists of this stamp 'omit, obscure or distort the revolutionary side of this theory, its revolutionary soul' (Lenin, 1975, vol. ii, p. 240). In opposition to this alleged neutralisation of Marxism, Lenin insisted on the need for a violent revolution that would destroy the apparatus of bourgeois state power, and replace it with a new, but still coercive, set of institutions possessing the power and the will to advance the interests of the oppressed masses (ibid., pp. 243–44). The bourgeois state must be stripped of its distinctive bureaucratic, military and political structures and be replaced by a truly democratic form of administration modelled on the Paris Commune. This new political entity – no longer the 'state proper' – would reflect the will of the previously oppressed majority and pursue its interests. The revolutionary state would thus realise what Lenin claimed was the essence of revolutionary Marxism, namely extension of the pre-revolutionary class struggle into a post-revolutionary 'dictatorship of the proletariat'. This period would inevitably be marked by an

unprecedentedly violent class struggle in unprecedently acute forms, and consequently, during this period the state must essentially be a state that is democratic *in a new way* (for the proletariat and the property-less in general) and dictatorial *in a new way* (against the bourgeoisie) (ibid., p. 262).

Lenin's account of the structure and purpose of this new form of democracy reflected his awareness of the numerical weakness of the revolutionary proletariat in contemporary Russia. It also recognised the extent to which Russia fell short of the level of economic development that Marx regarded as a precondition for the emergence of revolutionary communism. In these circumstances, Lenin identified a leading role in the dictatorship of the proletariat for its revolutionary vanguard, the Communist Party. Rejecting anarchist claims that revolutionary social transformation required a transformation of human nature, Lenin insisted that

> we want the socialist revolution with people as they are now, with people who cannot dispense with subordination ... . The subordination, however, must be to the armed vanguard of all the exploited and working people, ie to the proletariat ... . *We,* the workers shall organise large scale production on the basis of what capitalism has already created, relying on our own experience as workers, establishing strict, iron discipline backed up by the state power of the armed workers ... . This is *our* proletarian task, this is what we can and *must start* with in accomplishing the proletarian revolution (ibid., p. 273).

Lenin linked these draconian measures to the beginning of the post-revolutionary process and set them within the context of utopian visions of the ultimate revival of 'primitive democracy', under which 'the *mass* of the population will rise to taking an *independent* part, not only in voting and elections, *but also in the everyday administration of the state*' (ibid., p. 324). He also envisaged a time when even democracy itself, being a form of rule, would wither away (ibid., p. 303). In the immediate future, however, the process of social revolution must be fostered by the dictatorship of the proletarian vanguard. This body would eliminate the bourgeois class, and impose coercive direction on the entire population.

Lenin's polemics against Kautsky included attacks on his views on the international implications of Marx's theory of revolution, as well as on the internal development of bourgeois states. In *Imperialism, The Highest State of Capitalism* (1916) he catalogued Kautsky's alleged deviations from Marxism and noted his failure to see that the large-scale export of finance (as opposed to industrial) capital from Europe necessarily set the major European powers against one another in a struggle for imperial domination (Lenin, 1975, vol. i, pp. 702–03). As the title of his work makes clear, Lenin saw imperialistic competition between Britain, France, Germany and Russia as an advanced stage of the globalisation of capitalism that Marx had described half a century before.

> Imperialism is capitalism at that stage of development at which the dominance of monopolies and finance capital is established; ... in which the division of the world among the international trusts has begun, in which the division of all territories of the globe among the biggest capitalist powers has been completed (ibid., p. 700).

With the assistance of what Lenin referred to as 'the national committees of the millionaires, known as governments' (ibid., p. 630), the capitalist system had reached its highest state of development. As a result, it was increasingly vulnerable to crises precipitated by economic competition and conflict between its governmental backers. While bourgeois governments might enter into temporary alliances aimed at repressing the proletariat, the international environment was unavoidably volatile, with wars and economic crises merely restoring short-lived equilibrium.

In an essay written in 1916 Lenin noted that the uneven development of capitalism across the globe meant socialist revolutions would occur first in a few of the most advanced capitalist countries and that they would be attacked by the remaining bourgeois states. This situation would necessitate an 'international programme of international revolutionary Social-Democracy' that might involve wars between revolutionary socialist governments and bourgeois states to resist threats to the revolution and assist the liberation of the proletariat (ibid., p. 742). These conflicts were 'the only legitimate and revolutionary war – civil war against the imperialist bourgeoisie' (ibid., p. 744). Lenin equated these developments in international politics with the role played by revolutionary regimes in domestic politics and referred to them in an attack on socialists who flirted with the idea of international disarmament. Such a move would merely play into the hands of the bourgeoisie. In much the same way as the coercive power of the state was to be used by the dictatorship of the proletariat to preserve the immediate gains of socialist revolution against reactionary forces and create the conditions for the transition to communism, armed revolutionary republics would be necessary to preserve the momentum of global revolution.

Lenin's conception of the revolutionary process was strenuously rejected by Kautsky. In *The Dictatorship of the Proletariat* (1918) Kautsky reiterated his earlier arguments about the possibility of non-violent revolution, and confirmed the role that even bourgeois parliamentarianism could play in the organisation of the working class and in fostering consciousness (Kautsky, 1983, pp. 101, 114). He also argued that Lenin's idea of the dictatorship of the proletariat was incompatible with the socialist conception of the nature of revolutionary change. Socialism involved the abolition of 'every form of exploitation', including those proposed by Lenin. Kautsky claimed that Marx had used the term 'dictatorship of the proletariat' to refer to a *state of affairs* that necessarily arose whenever the proletariat attained political power, while Lenin had transformed it into a *form of government* in which a party rules on behalf of a class (ibid., pp. 114, 116). This system of rule was totally incompatible with the transformation to socialism.

> A state of chronic civil war, or its alternative under a dictatorship, the complete apathy and despondency of the masses, renders the construction of a socialist system of production well-nigh impossible. And yet the dictatorship of a minority ... necessarily gives rise to civil war and apathy (ibid., p. 120).

In response to what he regarded as an erroneous and dangerous conception of revolutionary change, Kautsky stressed the need to distinguish between 'social revolution', 'political revolution' and 'civil war'. Civil war, a consequence of Lenin's theory and a goal promoted by Kautsky's German contemporary Rosa Luxemburg and her colleagues in the revolutionary Spartacus League (Luxemburg, 1971, pp. 371–73), would positively hinder the revolutionary process. While Kautsky acknowledged that 'political revolution' might involve some violence, he insisted that except in cases where the bourgeoisie refused to accept the legitimate measures of a democratic parliament, the danger of civil war could be largely avoided by a process of 'social revolution'. That is,

> a profound transformation of the whole structure brought about by the creation of a new mode of production. It is a protracted process which can last for decades ... . The more peaceful the manner in which it is

carried out the more successful it will be. Civil and foreign war are its mortal enemies (Kautsky, 1983, p. 121).

'Social revolution' would thus only be truly revolutionary in its final, long-term stage, not in the immediate or the middle term. Kautsky thought that a cautious approach was in order because the eventual triumph of socialism would depend on the enlightenment of the general population, and this process could not be hurried.

Lenin's political ideas focused on the distinctive problems facing Russian Marxists. They also dealt with a post-revolutionary situation. In some respects, however, the seizure of power by the representatives of the oppressed masses had to be seen as merely the first move in a process that would result in attainment of the final goal of revolutionary Marxism – a communist society. For these reasons, Leninism can be seen as a theory of development as well as a theory of revolutionary politics, a point that also applies to Lenin's successors (Kautsky, 1994). The attainment of communism required the development of Russia's economic infrastructure and the growth of a universal proletarian consciousness. The first of these tasks meant that the Communist Party had to utilise the labour of the peasantry in order to feed the population and to provide surpluses with which to fund industrial and infrastructural developments.

Post-Leninist thought saw the abandonment, or at least the postponement, of the international dimensions of the proletarian revolution. This point was confirmed by Joseph Stalin's adoption of 'socialism in one country', a doctrine that was first developed by Nicolai Bukharin in an attempt to legitimise a process of economic and political development that would utilise Russian resources alone. Having tacitly accepted this doctrine by 1924, Stalin advanced a forceful statement of it in his *Problems of Leninism* (1926). 'Socialism in one country' rested on the

> possibility of the proletariat assuming power and using that power to build a complete socialist society in one country with the sympathy and support of the proletariat of other countries, but without the preliminary victory of the proletarian revolution in other countries (Stalin, 1934, vol. i, p. 300).

This doctrine, to which Stalin sought to annex the posthumous authority of Lenin (McLellan, 1979, p. 123), was seriously at odds with the idea of 'permanent revolution' promoted by his bitter rival, Leon Trotsky.

Joseph Stalin (1879–1953)

Stalin succeeded Lenin as head of the communist government of the Soviet Union and maintained his hold on the country until his death. His real and imagined enemies in the upper ranks of the Communist Party were ruthlessly purged from positions of influence and most were executed; these elite purges were part of a prolonged terror that claimed millions of lives. *Problems of Leninism* (1926) was Stalin's major statement of his version of Marxism.

Key reading: Philip, 2004.

Trotsky has been credited with producing the most 'radical restatement, if not a revision, of the prognosis of Socialist revolution undertaken since Marx [and Engels'] *Communist Manifesto*' (Deutscher, 1954, p. 150). He argued that the peculiar conditions prevailing in Russia – the uneven development that had produced an advanced but geographically and numerically limited group of industrial capitalist enterprises dependent upon an autocratic state; a relatively small but cohesive urban proletariat; a large, amorphous, disgruntled and exceedingly backward peasantry; and a virtually non-existent independent bourgeoisie – made a sustainable revolution very unlikely there. Trotsky therefore looked to the Russian proletariat to establish a system of 'permanent revolution' that would eliminate feudal and bourgeois elements, develop the economic base of society, and foster a socialist consciousness among the bulk of the population. Although the proletariat would initially ally itself with the peasantry, its policies would generate conflict with them and other 'backward' elements in society. Since the proletariat were numerically weak and the revolution could only survive if it had external support, Trotsky's idea of permanent revolution necessarily had an international dimension:

> Without the direct support of the European proletariat the working class of Russia cannot remain in power and convert its temporary domination into a lasting socialist dictatorship (Trotsky, 1969, p. 105).

The circumstances facing Russia in the mid-1920s made socialism in one country the only plausible approach, and Trotsky tacitly acknowledged this. However, he remained a stern critic of the way the revolution was being conducted by his political rivals. He warned that failure to eradicate bureaucracy would lay Russia open to the danger of sliding towards capitalism, and he accused Stalin of creating a system of 'Soviet Bonapartism' that rested on a new form of party aristocracy (McLellan, 1979, p. 139). These tendencies needed to be reversed by a *political* revolution that would restore the proletariat to its proper position in a revolutionary social order. Paradoxically, this critique displayed an attitude towards the political dimensions of revolution that was not markedly different from that which had first appeared in France in the 1790s.

The fact that the Russian Revolution was the first successful seizure of power by a revolutionary Marxist party meant that it provided a focal point to encourage, guide and in some cases direct Marxist revolutionaries in other countries. As a consequence, twentieth-century theorists working within the Marxist tradition have sought to relate their positions both to Marx's views and to the Russian experience. An important feature of post-Leninist theories of revolution has been the attempt to determine the theoretical and tactical implications of the distinctive circumstances of the Russian case, and to gauge the extent to which it was necessary to produce varieties of revolutionary Marxist theory that differ from those developed by Lenin and his Russian successors. This aspect of twentieth-century Marxist thought is apparent in the writings of the two leading figures in non-Russian revolutionary politics, the Italian Antonio Gramsci and Mao Tse-tung, who dominated the Chinese communist movement.

Gramsci's major contributions to revolutionary political thought were his development of the idea of 'hegemony', his analysis of the implications of this idea for the revolution as a process in which politics plays an important role, and his attempt to relate the responses of a revolutionary party to the concrete reality of a given capitalist society. Building on Lenin's insistence that the proletariat needs to weld a range of anti-capitalist elements into an effective revolutionary force, Gramsci developed the idea of hegemony into a general theory. On the one hand, it explains how different classes are able to sustain their dominant position without total reliance on physical coercion. For example, Gramsci argued that in the context of Western democracies, the 'normal' exercise of hegemony … is characterised by the combination of force and consent, which balance each other reciprocally without force predominating excessively over consent. Indeed, the attempt is always made to ensure that force would appear to be based on the consent of the majority expressed by the so-called organs of public opinion – newspapers and associations – which therefore, in certain situations, are artificially multiplied (Gramsci, 1971, p. 80).

On the other hand, however, this theory also plays a crucial role in setting the agenda for revolutionary activity. Gramsci rejected deterministic explanations of revolutionary change, arguing that it is necessary for the hegemony of bourgeois society to be challenged by a proletarian counter-hegemony embodying true social interests. Revolution is a *process* rather than an *event,* one that requires a counter-hegemony forged by the interaction of intellectuals and workers within the framework of a revolutionary party.

Antonio Gramsci (1891–1937)

Gramsci, the leading Marxist theoretician of Italian communism, served as general secretary of the Italian Communist Party and was elected to parliament. He was imprisoned by the fascists in 1926 and remained in prison until his death. Gramsci's most important work, the *Prison Notebooks,* written between 1929 and 1935 and published posthumously, sought to re-emphasise the importance of intellectual and political action within the Marxist tradition.

Key reading: Sassoon, 1987.

Ideological and cultural elements play an important role in Gramsci's analysis of pre-, counter- and post-revolutionary hegemonies. He thus argued that the development of a hegemonic revolutionary force requires the development of a proletarian *culture.* This requirement can only be satisfied if the party interacts with a range of organisations and activities in which the bulk of the working class are engaged.

> First of all, [the party] contains within it the best part of the working class, a vanguard tied directly to non-party proletarian organisations, which the communists frequently lead. Secondly, because of its experience and authority, the party is the only organisation able to centralise the struggle of the proletariat and thus to transform the political organisations of the working class into its own coordinating organs. The party is the highest form of class organisation of the proletariat (Sassoon, 1987, p. 81).

The variety of these interactions, and the fact that they necessarily take place within a fluid environment, means that the party is an evolving entity rather than a rigidly fixed structure. It is charged with a political educational role that requires interaction and participation rather than centralised direction. The need to develop the basis for a proletarian hegemony thus has important implications for both the internal structure of the party and for the ways in which its members interacted in the wider working-class culture.

The idea of hegemony also plays a role in Gramsci's understanding of the post-revolutionary situation. In common with other Marxists, Gramsci believed that the seizure of state power is an important stage in the revolutionary process. He also stressed the need to employ the power of the state to transform the social relations of production, and to develop further the cultural hegemony of the proletariat. This process would result in the creation of a new type of state (ibid., p. 132).

Here, as elsewhere in his theory, Gramsci drew attention to the complex nature of the reality that confronts a revolutionary party. This consideration also plays a role in determining the course of the struggle directed at the seizure of state power by the revolutionary party. In discussing revolutionary tactics Gramsci developed a distinction between a 'war of movement or manoeuvre' and a 'war of position'. The first of these engagements involves a direct attack. According to Gramsci, this is only possible in societies such as tsarist Russia where the state lacks the support of a well-entrenched civil society buttressed by a hegemonic bourgeoisie. In more developed societies a 'war of position' – a long-run process involving a search for favourable positions *vis-à-vis* the dominant bourgeois state and development of a counterhegemonic structure that will eventually undermine it – is more appropriate.

Gramsci's distinction between approaches to revolutionary transformation is underwritten by his identification of two sorts of crises providing different opportunities for aggressive action. *Organic* crises signal a breach between a society's social structure and superstructure resulting from deep-seated dislocations within the ruling hegemony. Crises of this kind open the way for wars of manoeuvre and differ from what Gramsci called *conjectural* crises arising from temporary tensions within a dominant class or from loss of confidence in particular members of the political elite. Conjectural crises frequently produce changes of ruling personnel, but they do not threaten the hegemony of the dominant class. They may, however, provide opportunities to engage in wars of position that promote a counter-hegemony providing the basis for future revolutionary action (Gramsci, 1971, pp. 232–38).

Emphasis on concrete circumstances is an important aspect of Gramsci's theory of revolution, and this idea also plays a central role in Mao's conception of the revolutionary process. Mao was openly disdainful of other intellectuals, and much of his theorising took the form of injunctions formulated for the guidance of the Chinese Communist Party in its prolonged military and political struggles against a range of enemies. Mao maintained that the essence of Marxism, its 'living soul', is 'the concrete analysis of concrete conditions' (Mao, 1967, pp. 93–94). Consequently, while he acknowledged the inspirational and theoretical importance of the Russian Revolution, he warned that the pursuit of communism in China must take account of the distinctive circumstances confronting revolutionaries in that country. Of central importance was the relative strength of the revolutionary forces *vis-à-vis* their various opponents, the extent to which China had been reduced to semi-colonial status by the Western powers and the Japanese, and the unevenness of Chinese political and economic development. The last of these considerations is of cardinal importance for the conventional Marxist model. Where a weakly developed capitalist economy coexists with a largely semi-feudal agrarian economy, a revolution cannot take place under the guidance or control of a classical Marxist proletariat. Of course, this issue had also confronted Russian Marxists, but while they continued to cling to the idea that the revolution must be made by the proletariat, Mao focused on the significant (but theoretically ambiguous) revolutionary potential of the rural masses.

During the various armed conflicts in which the Chinese communists were engaged from the early 1920s, the countryside served as both a major theatre of war and as the source of recruits for the Red Army. This body was led by the Communist Party, but it had originated in revolutionary agrarian responses to both feudal and capitalist exploitation. Mao regarded the Red Army as the major instrument of revolutionary change in China.

> Every Communist must grasp the truth 'Political power grows out of the barrel of a gun.' Our principle is that the Party commands the gun, and the gun must never be allowed to command the Party. Yet, having guns we can create Party organisations ... . We can also create cadres, create schools, create culture, create mass movements ... . All things grow out of the barrel of a gun. According to the Marxist theory of the state, the army is the chief component of state power. Whoever wants to seize and retain state power must have a strong army (ibid., pp. 274–75).

Mao Tse-tung (1893–1976)

Following his conversion to Marxism in 1927, Mao played a prominent role in the military struggle against the nationalist leader Chiang Kai-shek and then against the Japanese. Until his death Mao was the dominant figure in the Chinese Communist Party. His political ideas were presented in a large number of essays and speeches addressing the military and political problems facing the Communist Party in its attempt to seize power and establish a communist society.

Key reading: Leese, 2015; Schram, 1989.

Even at that time Mao stressed the political opportunities that military success would open up, and in his later formulations the emphasis on super-structural elements became more marked. This position was closely related to the belief that a peasantry organised and led by the party would possess great revolutionary potential.

Mao originally regarded the Chinese revolution as *a stage* in the progression to socialism, one that would ultimately result in the creation of a genuine democratic republic. In the early 1950s, however, he argued that the transition to socialism had already begun and was being carried out under the direct control of the party. The fact that Mao now discounted the significance of the backward condition of Chinese society, and implicitly rejected the conventional Marxist view that socialism follows the triumph of democracy, made it necessary for him to reformulate his account of the class characteristics of contemporary Chinese society and the role of the class struggle within it. These issues were addressed in *On the Correct Handling of Contradictions Among the People*. In this work Mao argued that the political victory of the forces of socialism in China meant that the 'people's government' could be the direct force a revolutionary transformation of Chinese society by working to resolve the real but non-antagonistic contradictions that still persisted between the surviving classes in Chinese society. Mao expected that these contradictions would be overcome as society progressed towards socialism. In his later writings Mao portrayed this as a semi-permanent process that would stimulate the revolutionary enthusiasm of both party cadres and the masses (Mao, 1957). He insisted, however, that this stimulation should be controlled by the upper echelons of the party, and he gave increasing prominence to the role played by ideas of personal leadership. Mao's theory of leadership is based on the dictum that 'all correct leadership' is necessarily 'from the masses to the masses'. However, the role he ascribed to the party and the individual leadership in drawing in, refining and then disseminating these ideas means that his political theory echoes some of the key themes of traditional Chinese thought by pointing to a patriarchal mode of government set within a strongly hierarchical system of social and political authority (Deutscher, 1966, p. 112).

Marxist revolutionary politics and female emancipation: Clara Zetkin

In the *Communist Manifesto* Marx and Engels identified the family as one of the traditional institutions which had been effectively destroyed by the economic and social transformation wrought by capitalism. This idea was taken up in *The Origin of the Family*, a later work by Engels. He argued that by destroying the family as an economic unit capitalism had liberated working-class women from traditional patriarchal control and placed them on an equal footing with their male counterparts. In both cases, freedom was purely formal since men and women were now subject to the exploitation, deprivation and alienation which Marxists saw as inescapable consequences of life under capitalism. By the same token, however, proletarian men and women had a common interest in promoting the overthrow of capitalism and preparing the way for the liberation of humanity under communism. Engel's conclusion was essentially gender neutral in the sense that it did not recognise differences between the interests and needs of working-class women and men that had implications for their understanding of what human liberation involved, or give them distinctive roles in socialist revolutionary politics. Men and women thus had a common and exclusive identity as members of the proletariat. In the decades after Engel's death, Clara Zetkin, a leading figure in the German Marxist Social Democratic Party, drew on some of his key ideas to identify a distinctive place for proletarian women in revolutionary politics.

Zetkin's position emerged from her analysis of the ideas of female emancipation pursued by women in different social classes within capitalist societies. For women of the upper class, liberation meant that they and their property were freed from the control of their husbands. Once this goal was achieved they would be able to exercise control over their affairs and enjoy in full the privileges that had been exercised on their behalf by their husbands and fathers. The situation of women of the middle classes was rather different. Male domination of politics had allowed men to monopolise professional and managerial positions and to exclude women from a competition supposedly governed by the principle of 'careers open to talent'. As a result, they were debarred from improving their financial position and from accumulating capital through successfully deploying intellectual and technical talents that could be acquired through education. Since middle-class women's participation in the economy could only be secured by government action to outlaw discrimination against them, women of this class were committed to securing political rights. By contrast, proletarian women were already fully engaged in the labour market, adding to an expanding pool of cheap labour that helped drive down the costs of production. They stood in a position of equality with male members of the working class, free to compete against them for employment on an increasingly competitive labour market.

Clara Zetkin (1857–1933)

Zetkin, who was born in Saxony, Germany, was educated initially by her father, a primary school teacher. She subsequently received advanced education at a teacher training college in Leipzig and worked as a teacher in the city. Early in her career she became associated with the Marxist German Social Democratic Party (SDP) and began a lifetime commitment to its revolutionary agenda. Zetkin played a key role in editing the SDP's women's journal and in resisting attempts by the Party leadership to abolish special organisations for women. She was a founding member of the German Communist Party and sat in the German parliament from 1918 to 1932, when she went into exile in Russia. In journalistic writings and speeches from the 1880s, Zetkin contributed to vigorous Marxist debate on the implications of capitalism for the status of women and the family. She argued for women to have a distinctive gendered role in revolutionary political organisations.

Key reading: Dollard, 2016; Zetkin, 1984.

But while proletarian women had gained their economic independence from their husbands and fathers, they had, as Engels argued, become subservient to capital. Moreover, to the extent that they competed with males, their 'liberation' enhanced the exploitation suffered by all members of their class. 'The slave of the husband became the slave of the employer. … The capitalists, however, are not content just to exploit women per se; they use female labour to exploit male labour even more thoroughly' (Zetkin, 1984, p. 47). Although Zetkin thought that working-class women were the equals of working-class men in an economic sense, she believed that the impact of capitalism on them was far more prejudicial to their interests *as women* than the control exercised in conventional patriarchal relations. 'If during the Age of the Family, a man had the right … to tame his wife occasionally with a whip, capitalism is now taming her with scorpions.' As in the case of men, their formal freedom came at the cost of frustrating their capacity to live a life worthy of human beings. For women, however, that included a capacity to perform gender-specific family roles. '[N]either as a human being or as a woman or wife has she the possibility to develop her individuality. For her task as a wife and a mother, there remains only the breadcrumbs which the capitalist production drops from the table' (Zetkin, 1984, p. 77). Women were thus doubly disadvantaged under capitalism: they suffered as workers and as women. Proletarian labour is an alienating burden rather than a means through which humanity collectively fulfils its material, social and psychological needs. For proletarian women, however, it has the added disadvantage of frustrating the realisation of distinctive aspirations which spring from their role in reproduction and nurturing.

In the short term, Zetkin thought that aspects of women's gender-specific disadvantage could be countered by pursuing the political objectives she had identified with the middle-class women's movement. That would allow proletarian women to organise themselves into trades unions and to seek legislated reductions in working hours to mitigate to some extent the harmful effects of female employment on the wages of their male counterparts. It would also provide opportunities for them to reassume some of the responsibilities as wives and mothers that had been compromised by their recruitment into the capitalist labour force. Zetkin insisted, however, that these responsibilities must be seen in terms of working-class women's place in the revolutionary struggle of the proletariat and in the broader context of that struggle. The Socialist Party should thus promote the cause of socialism among working-class women and not allow them to be distracted by the exclusive causes promoted by non-revolutionary feminism: 'We must not conduct special women's propaganda, but Socialist agitation among women. ... Our task must be to incorporate the modern proletarian woman in our class battle!' (ibid., p. 79). At the same time, however, Zetkin stressed that revolutionary socialism should not lose sight of the distinctive contributions that proletarian women could make to advancing the cause. She thus pointed to their critical role in educating the next generation of working-class children in the principles of revolutionary Marxism, and in supporting and encouraging their husbands to take their place among the class-conscious proletariat and work to secure a communist future (ibid., p. 82). In Zetkin's vision, the radical reconstruction of human life under communism involved a transformation of the family that built on the forms pre-figured in the revolutionary process:

> Once the family as an economic unit will vanish and its place will be taken by the family as a moral unit, the woman will become an equally entitled, equally creative, equally goal-oriented, forward-stepping companion of her husband; her individuality will flourish while at the same time, she will fulfil her task as wife and mother to the highest degree possible (ibid., p. 83).

Revolutionary anarchism and the critique of Marxism: Bakunin and Kropotkin

Social anarchists promoted a vision of a classless, stateless future that was similar to the end-point of revolutionary Marxism. These anarchists were intensely critical of the material and moral implications of capitalism, and they believed that its overthrow would come about through an international revolution carried out by the working classes and the oppressed peasantry. Like other revolutionary socialists, anarchists thought that the French Revolution provided both inspiration and warning. In particular, the events of the early 1790s highlighted the limitations of purely formal conceptions of liberty and equality, a point that was driven home by the unsuccessful outcome of Babeuf's conspiracy (see p. 155).

The primary anarchist target was political authority in general, and in particular that source of supreme authority that was located in the state. Anarchists regarded the impositions of capitalism as part of a generalised system of oppression that was centred in the state and spread into various economic, social and religious outworks. The purpose of anarchist revolution was to destroy the state and those oppressive institutions that were maintained by and gave legitimacy to it.

While leading figures in nineteenth-century social anarchism believed that a revolutionary change was imminent, their views on the cause and nature of revolution varied significantly. Proudhon, for example, relied on social transformation through non-political initiatives, and was not a proponent of violent revolution. He believed that the time was ripe for such a change because injustice in contemporary society had risen to a level where it was stimulating individuals to overcome selfish impulses and develop their capacity for cooperation. In contrast, Bakunin and Kropotkin made the idea of revolution a central component of their anarchism. Although these thinkers regarded the advent of anarchism as a consequence of the deep-seated historical processes coming to fruition in the nineteenth century, neither of them adopted Marx's theory of historical materialism. Bakunin regarded anarchism as the outcome of the development of human consciousness from a condition where authority is a regrettable but necessary evil, to one in which it is both unnecessary and regressive. For example, when explaining the universality of the false idea of a 'supreme being' or God, Bakunin attributed it to 'an error historically necessary in the development of humanity' that had been used to explain apparently inexplicable natural phenomena (Bakunin, 1973, p. 122).

Kropotkin's account of anarchism was framed in evolutionary terms. As we have seen, he regarded mutual aid as a natural and beneficial mode of interaction that accounts for both animal and human development. Kropotkin treated authority, oppression and the state as aberrations in evolutionary processes of intellectual and moral development that would terminate in anarchism. These processes were marked by a series of conflicts between two traditions: the 'Roman' tradition of authoritarian and imperial rule, and a 'popular' tradition of federalism and libertarianism that reflects the influence of the mutual aid principle (Kropotkin, 1903, p. 41). As that principle was the key to human progress it had never been stifled completely, even within capitalist societies. However, the main features of capitalism – its denial of equality and its reliance on a coercive state to maintain a system of economic and social oppression – are incompatible with mutual aid. Progress requires the destruction of both capitalism and the state, and the establishment of a system of free federating communes that will make the ideals of the French Revolution – liberty, equality and fraternity – a reality. Given the coercive capacities of the state and its close relationship with capitalism, it is unlikely that such a radical change can be inaugurated without revolutionary action.

In their accounts of the revolutionary process both Bakunin and Kropotkin ascribed a great deal of importance to people's instinctive sense of justice and their natural aversion to the imposition of authority. These drives mean that revolutions are a consequence of spontaneous outbursts of popular indignation arising from a deep-seated spirit of revolt that has survived the stifling oppression of conventional political structures. An important consequence of this position was that nineteenth-century anarchist thinkers rejected the reliance on a conspiratorial elite that had formed the cornerstone of Blanqui's conception of revolution (see p. 135). They were also hostile to what they saw as the authoritarian aspects of the Marxian tradition of revolutionary socialism, claiming that it would pervert the course of revolution and merely create a new political order. These fears played an important role in the history of late-nineteenth- and early-twentieth-century revolutionary socialism because they gave rise to a series of vigorously contested ideological confrontations between the Marxists and the anarchists. In the course of these debates there emerged a number of important divergences between revolutionary Marxism and revolutionary anarchism.

In the first place, both Bakunin and Kropotkin questioned the scientific standing of Marx's theory. They claimed that Marx's materialism had no empirical basis and that it had been applied in a dogmatic and mechanical manner. In particular, Bakunin resisted the idea that the development of a revolutionary consciousness requires the development of capitalism. According to Bakunin, revolutionary consciousness is instinctive and perpetual, and does not have to await the development of a particular form of oppression. Bakunin linked these shortcomings of Marxist theory to its authoritarian political implications. He argued that true science starts from the facts of human existence and then sets up systems of ideas that explain and order these facts. When this approach is applied to politics, it places a premium on the actual aspirations, feeling and knowledge of the populace – these *are* political facts – and discounts the preconceived ideas of self-appointed intellectual leaders. Unlike Marxism, anarchism rests on

the broad popular method, the method of real and total liberation, accessible to anyone and therefore truly popular. It is the method of the *anarchist* social revolution, which arises spontaneously within the people and destroys everything that opposes the broad flow of popular life so as to create new forms of free social existence out of the depths of the people's existence (Bakunin, 1990, p. 133).

According to Kropotkin, Marxism's scientific standing was compromised by Marx's neglect of empirical data and his failure to take account of the lessons of evolutionary theory (Crowder, 2015; Kropotkin, 1970, p. 152).

Bakunin contrasted his general approach with that found in the writings of Marx and his followers, arguing that a Marxist revolution would liberate humanity because it is rooted in ideas that are divorced from human aspirations, experiences and interests. Since Marxist views of the passage to an ideal social order were not attached to the aspirations of the general population, they would have to be imposed on it. In contrast, the anarchist conception of revolution reflects the popular instinct for liberty, equality and fraternity, and recognises that the realisation of popular aspirations has to come about through the development and application of the consciousness of the population itself. The key insight of anarchism is the

> belief that [as] the masses bear all the elements of their future organisational norms in their own more or less historically evolved instincts, in their everyday needs and their conscious and unconscious desires, we seek that ideal within the people themselves (Bakunin, 1990, p. 135).

Kropotkin made a similar point when he claimed that anarchism owes 'its origins to the constructive creative activity of the people, by which all institutions of communal life were developed in the past' (Kropotkin, 1970, p. 149).

Although much of Bakunin's revolutionary career was devoted to setting up hierarchical revolutionary organisations, he did not think that these bodies would take a leading or directive role in the revolutionary process. For example, he dismissed radical attempts to educate the Russian peasantry. Despite appearances, these well-meant gestures involved elite imposition on the people. Bakunin insisted that the only role that elites can play is to incite 'the people' to independent action and to open their eyes to the possibility of their liberation (Bakunin, 1990, p. 200). In place of this focus on spontaneous organisation 'from below', the Marxists had cast themselves as both instigators and 'managers of all popular movements' (ibid., p. 136). The Marxists' presumption explains why their ideas had so little appeal among the masses in Italy and Spain, where the spirit of revolt was still strong. In other parts of Europe, however, Marx's ideas were at the forefront of socialism and posed a serious threat to the revolutionary process. Marxists saw the revolution as a means of destroying the capitalist order, but they wrongly insisted that

> on the morrow of the revolution a new social organisation must be created not by the free union of popular associations, communes, districts, and provinces from below upward, in conformity with popular needs and instincts, but solely by means of the dictatorial power of this learned minority, which *supposedly* expresses the will of all the people (ibid., p. 136).

Both Bakunin and Kropotkin argued that proletarian dictatorship results in the establishment of a new form of state, one that cannot discern or embody the real interests of the population in whose name it presumes to rule. Even given the best of intentions, and ignoring the inevitable tendency for power to corrupt those who wield it, a proletarian state is still a state. It will thus suffer from all the evils inherent in a form of political and social organisation that is imposed on the population rather than being a genuine expression of its aspirations and interests.

When the Russian revolution was in its early stages the 75-year-old Kropotkin travelled to his native country to participate in this momentous event. Over the course of the next few years, however, he lived through the early stages of a nightmare that had haunted the imaginations of nineteenth-century revolutionary anarchists. Under Lenin's direction, the revolution in Russia proved to be the harbinger of an extreme form of state collectivism instituted by a minute section of the population that was divorced from both the peasantry and industrial workers. An important step in the consolidation of the position of Lenin's revolutionary elite was the elimination of the anarchists, a process that was to be repeated by his successors during the civil war in Spain in the late 1930s.

Decolonisation and revolutionary political theory: Fanon

Given the role that Marx ascribed to imperialism – that is, a strategy to sustain the profitability of capitalism by securing new markets and new areas of investment – it is not surprising that opponents of colonisation have often adopted insights derived from Marx's writings. One example of this has been touched upon in the discussion of Mao's theory. As noted there, Mao maintained that the development of a revolutionary movement in China must take account of the fact that the masses were being exploited by native capitalists *and* external forces who were treating China as an informal annexe of their colonial and imperial possessions (see p. 269). In the wake of the Second World War, the declining influence of the major powers of Western Europe gave a fillip to pre-existing indigenous movements in Africa, the Middle East and South-East Asia. Beginning in the late 1940s, there appeared a number of independence movements committed to expelling colonial powers from these regions. Since these movements had to contend with the coercive power of local and imperial governments, and since the struggle for independence was accompanied by a desire to radically restructure the political, social and economic organisation of the state, the pursuit of independence necessitated the development and propagation of revolutionary programmes. In some states, most notably India, liberation and revolutionary transformation were pursued largely through non-violent means and gave rise to a distinctive set of theories (see pp. 360ff).

Elsewhere, however, decolonisation was thought to necessitate violent revolutionary action. The discussion that follows considers the ideas of Franz Fanon, who was closely involved with the attempt by Algeria to free itself from the political domination of the French state and the subjugation of indigenous Algerian interests to those of a numerous population of French settlers. While Mao treated imperialism as one generalised source of exploitation, Fanon drew particular attention to the malign relationship between settler and indigenous cultures. He argued that the combined effect of direct external and internal domination gave rise to deep and widespread dehumanisation within colonial society that would only be addressed when the colonial power and its settlers were expelled. Full liberation of indigenous peoples also necessitated the restructuring of social, economic and political life within former colonies so that human beings can develop a capacity to enjoy a way of life that is free from *all* forms of domination. Although Fanon's understanding of this goal was informed by his study of Marx's writings, he thought that indigenous cultures contain the seeds from which this way of life can grow. Consequently, he was a stern critic of the tendency towards party and personal control that had played an increasingly prominent role in both the theory and the practice of revolutionary Marxism.

Frantz Fanon (1925–61)

Fanon was born in Martinique and trained in medicine and psychiatry in France before serving in a hospital in Algeria during the uprising against French colonial rule. His experience of this particularly brutal conflict led him to become a spokesman for the Algerians. Fanon's most important political writings, *The Wretched of the Earth* (1961) and *Towards the African Revolution* (1964), examined the requirements for human liberation in colonial and post-colonial settings. To some degree Fanon's political thought was indebted to Marx, but it also incorporated insights into the conditions of human well-being that he had gained during his psychiatric training and practice.

Key reading: Hansen, 1977; Guégan, 2015.

Fanon offered three revisions to conventional Marxist accounts of the revolutionary process. In the first place, he argued that the relationship between the dominant and subordinated classes in colonial society differs significantly from those described by Marx in his accounts of capitalist, or even pre-capitalist, societies. There is no dominant bourgeois and no identifiable proletariat in colonies, nor did they conform to conventional accounts of pre-capitalist modes of production. In pre-capitalist Europe the dominant classes were legitimated by culturally embedded ideas (such as divine right) that reflected a widely accepted belief in the moral unity of humanity. In contrast, colonial societies are characterised by a sharp and unbridgeable distinction between the dominant elites (who come from outside the indigenous culture) and the native population, whom they openly and systematically exploit. The attributes that determine class membership in both capitalist and pre-capitalist societies have no bearing in colonial society:

> In the colonies, the foreigner coming from another country, imposed his rule by means of guns and machines. In defiance of his successful transplantation, in spite of his appropriation, the settler remains a foreigner. It is neither the act of owning factories, nor estates, nor a bank balance which distinguishes the governing class. The governing race is first and foremost those who come from elsewhere, those who are unlike the original inhabitants, 'the others' (Fanon, 1967, p. 31).

Secondly, the alien nature of settler domination, and its reliance on violence, means that the process of liberation necessitates the expulsion of the colonialists and reclamation of the colony and its resources by the indigenous inhabitants. Revolutionary violence is a spontaneous product that develops in reaction to the experience of colonisation, and does not need to be fostered by an elite: 'To wreck the colonial world is ... a mental picture of action which is very clear, very easy to understand and which may be assumed by each one of the individuals which constitute the colonized people' (ibid., p. 31).

Thirdly, because colonies lack a conventional proletariat they can only be liberated through a revolution based on the rural masses. Although Fanon's views on this issue are similar to those adhered to by Mao in the 1930s and 1940s, he did not see the creation of bourgeois democracy as the appropriate goal of revolutionary activity. To the contrary, he believed that freeing a colony from the shackles of colonialism is merely the first step in a continuous process of human liberation that diverges from the conventional Marxist model. Fanon claimed that since ex-colonies lack a genuine bourgeoisie, they tend to veer towards economic stagnation and political repression. To avoid these outcomes it is necessary to use the struggle for national independence as the launching pad for cultural and political revolutions that will inaugurate a form of liberation resembling that which Marx identified with true democracy. For Fanon, however, this goal can be achieved by incorporating traditions of social interaction embedded in the popular culture of the rural areas of the colonised society.

In Fanon's analysis, the exploitation that characterises colonial societies is seen as the most overt manifestation of the dehumanising nature of colonisation. Decolonisation is necessary to shake off this incubus and to establish the conditions needed to create 'new men': 'the "thing" which has been colonized becomes man during the same process by which it frees itself' (ibid., p. 28). Fanon's understanding of revolution as a process has important implications for the way in which it is carried out. Anti-colonial revolutions should aim at total destruction of the relationships of colonial society – 'the last shall be first and the first last' (ibid., p. 28) – and of the ideological superstructure imported by the colonists and adopted by some colonised elites and privileged members of the subordinated classes (ibid., p. 36).

The actions and utterances of indigenous (but largely Westernised) elites tend to develop a momentum among the mass of the population that quickly outstrips the limited (and largely self-interested) intentions of those who occupy leading positions in nationalist political parties. These politicians seek compromises with their colonial overlords to preserve their own positions and that of their urban supporters, and they attempt to use outbreaks of mass violence as instruments in this process. In this situation, Fanon looked to rural populations to provide the revolutionary core of anti-colonialism:

> The starving peasant, outside the class system, is the first among the exploited to discover that only violence pays. For him there is no compromise, no possible coming to terms; colonisation and decolonisation are simply a question of strength. The exploited man sees that his liberation implies the use of all means, and that of force first and foremost (ibid., pp. 47–48).

In his treatment of wars of independence, and also in his strictures on the need to continue the revolutionary process in the post-colonial period, Fanon stressed the positive effect of the process of struggle on the consciousness of the rural masses: the 'mobilisation of the masses ... introduces into each man's consciousness the ideas of a common cause, of national destiny and of collective history' (ibid., p. 73). Fanon thought that these ideas arise from social values that still hold sway in the countryside, but have been abandoned by those who have moved to the cities. Popular attachment to these values is revitalised by the experience of revolution. Revolutionary action is thus seen as a way of expelling the colonial power and purifying the indigenous people's present existence to provide the basis for further development of a collective, revolutionary consciousness within the newly liberated state (ibid., p. 105).

Fanon warned, however, that liberation may be threatened by the persisting political, economic and ideological influence of the former colonial power, and also by potentially exploitative elements in indigenous culture, the 'national bourgeoisie'. Within the context of Western capitalism, the bourgeoisie play an important role, but the 'national bourgeoisie' of the post-colonial world has no claims to dominance other than those springing from its corrupt interaction with self-interested and self-perpetuating military and political elites:

> In under-developed countries ... no true bourgeoisie exists; there is only a sort of little greedy caste, avid and voracious, with the mind of a huckster, only too glad to accept the dividends that the former

colonial power hands out to it. This get-rich-quick middle class shows itself incapable of great ideas or of inventiveness. It ... imperceptibly ... becomes not even a replica of Europe, but its caricature (ibid., p. 141).

The tendency to set up a caricature of Europe extends to the sort of single-party state that is spawned by subversion of the process of national and human liberation. Many post-colonial states subvert democracy while claiming to maintain it, and give a prominent role to an irremovable leader. While presenting themselves as an embodiment of the general interest of the community, these figures pursue particular interests expressed in racial and tribal terms. They use the party machine to manipulate the rural population and reduce it to the status of a passive, marginalised group that is of little more consequence in the independent state than it was in its colonial predecessor (ibid., pp. 115–18).

As an alternative to single-party governments of conventional Third World democracy (see p. 158–61), Fanon promoted mass participation in a grassroots party that is the tool of the people, not of a new governing class. He insisted that this party must not dominate the state administration, and that the latter should be radically decentralised, dynamic and sensitive to the expressed preferences of the local population. While retaining faith in a single revolutionary party, Fanon wished to prevent it from directly dominating the state or forming a source of authoritarian control:

> For the people, the party is not an authority, but an organism thorough which they as the people exercise their authority and express their will. The less there is of confusion and duality of powers, the more the party will play its part of guide and the more surely it will constitute for the people a decisive guarantee (ibid., p. 149).

Fanon regarded the beneficial interaction of locally based systems of administration (a 'bottom-up' party) and the rural population as natural developments of the locally based initiatives that provided the driving force for the first stage of the revolutionary process. Post-colonial societies must capitalise on the experiences of the struggle for independence to further the goals of the revolution, including those focused on the development of the economic and human resources of the countryside. Fanon insisted, however, that the material benefits of national revolution must be set within a framework of human liberation. In pursuing this goal, revolutionaries must build upon a sense of collective interest that incorporates ordinary members of the population so that they become the source of economic and political initiatives. The key to fostering this transformation of human life is to expose the public to an interactive and participatory programme of political education:

> To educate the masses politically does not mean, cannot mean making a political speech. What it means is to try, relentlessly and passionately, to teach the masses that everything depends on them; that if we stagnate it is their responsibility, and that if we go forward it is due to them too, that there is no such thing as a demiurge, that there is no famous man who will take responsibility for everything, but that the demiurge is the people themselves and the magic hands are finally only the hands of the people (ibid., p. 159).

Although Fanon's theory of revolution started with the promotion of struggles for national independence, it is significant that it endorses the ethical goals of Marxism as a means of advancing universal human goals: 'Individual experience, because it is national and because it is a link in the chain of national existence, ceases to be individual, limited and shrunken and is enabled to open out into the truth of the nation and the world' (ibid., p. 161). For Fanon, therefore, the development of national consciousness is a significant but temporary step along the road to universal liberation.

Conclusion

Resistance theorists identify general standards to which rulers are expected to conform. They assume that existing regimes are capable of embodying these standards and believe that they are usually endorsed by both rulers and subjects. In contrast, revolutionary thinkers believe that the realisation of fundamental human aspirations is incompatible with both the values and practice of conventional politics. Individuals and classes who frustrate human progress must be removed from positions of power, and political and/or social relations must be radically restructured so that they can be used to promote the realisation of what are taken to be the true ends of politics.

Revolutionary theories identify fundamental failings in existing political structures, promote more satisfactory alternatives, and seek to determine the tactics necessary to realise revolutionary goals. Revolutions are often seen as a way of creating the preconditions for social change, but some forms of modern revolutionary thinking are distinctive because they emphasise the interdependence of social and political structures. As a result, it is argued that substantive political change requires radical changes in the social structure, particularly in the distribution of material resources that have a bearing on power relationships within society.

The connection between social and political revolution is a notable feature of the Marxist tradition, but this idea has also played an important role in revolutionary anarchism and in anti-colonial theories such as those formulated by Fanon. In addition to seeing revolutions as both social and political events, these writers stress their universal significance. While early American and French revolutionary ideas rested on appeals to the 'rights of man' that were focused on particular states, Marxists, anarchists and theorists of anti-colonial revolution challenge systems of oppression that are seen as global in form and scope.

Fanon's focus on the dispossessed as the framers of its own future and the agent in processes of change links his theory of anti-colonial revolution with the concerns of contemporary historians and political theorists who explore the implications and requirements of a post-colonial world. This condition is characterised in terms of the notion of 'subalternity' that is hostile to the euro-centric cast of both Western liberalism and radical alternatives to it, including those derived from Marxism. By focussing on the dispossessed, 'subaltern studies' seek to identify features of the life of communities that have emerged from colonial control. They are seen as distinct from the ideas that structure Western political and social thinking and are incompatible with them. These ideas include distinctions between public and private and between tradition and modernity that play an important role in many varieties of liberal thinking, and also the notion of class that is associated with Marxism. Features of this approach have significant parallels with the stress upon 'difference' that plays a prominent role in other aspects of contemporary political theory (see pp. 182–83).

Although Fanon's theory of revolutionary anti-colonialism involved a rejection of some Western values and stressed the importance of recovering and extending aspects of indigenous culture, his endorsement of the general goals of Marxism meant that his view of the revolutionary process was both modern and secular. As we shall see in the Epilogue, this aspect of Fanon's position stands in stark contrast to the type of revolutionary doctrine espoused by recent proponents of Islamic revolutionary movements, particularly by the Ayatollah Khomeini, the leading figure in the Iranian Revolution.

THEORIES OF CIVIL DISOBEDIENCE AND NON-VIOLENT RESISTANCE TO POLITICAL AUTHORITY

15

The ideas discussed in this chapter are frequently grouped together as theories of 'civil disobedience' and characterised as forms of 'principled' disobedience. This term draws attention to the fact that these acts of disobedience are directed by a desire to resist political injustice and to produce a change in the exercise of political authority, not – as in the case of conventional law breaking – to gain some personal advantage (Harris, 1989). 'Civil disobedience' is related to, but must be distinguished from, the idea of 'passive resistance', which played a role in medieval political theory. 'Passive resistance' refers to a refusal to obey unjust commands; it generally precludes challenges to rulers, and does not involve a concerted attempt to change their conduct or modify the structures within which they operate. Although the term 'civil disobedience' will be used here, it should be noted that one important proponent of non-violent resistance regarded the idea of civil disobedience as too negative. As we shall see, Mahatma Gandhi preferred to describe his doctrine as one of 'civil resistance'. He did so in order to signal a desire to positively transform politics so that political authority would once again become legitimate.

Three theories of civil disobedience or non-violent resistance are discussed in this chapter. The mid-nineteenth-century American writer Henry Thoreau was largely concerned with preserving the moral integrity of the just individual in the face of governmental injustice. Thoreau's notion of civil disobedience contrasts with Mahatma Gandhi's ideas on non-violent resistance. Gandhi's theory was developed as part of a campaign to expel the British from the Indian subcontinent and to promote a radical restructuring of Indian politics and society. Gandhi's revolutionary use of non-violence differs significantly from that promoted by the Reverend Martin Luther King Jr. in the middle years of the twentieth century in reaction to legally sanctioned discrimination against blacks in the United States. For King, civil disobedience was a way of bringing pressure to bear on liberal-democratic governments to make them act in accordance with the moral, and in some cases legal, standards which they professed. King's objectives reflected the aspirations for black liberation that had been promoted by Douglass and Du Bois (see above p. 73–78) and like these earlier writers he drew attention to the clash between American political values and the attitudes that underwrote ongoing discrimination against African-Americans citizens of the United States.

Moral integrity and civil disobedience: Thoreau

Thoreau's 'Resistance to Civil Government', delivered as a lecture in 1848 and published the following year, is often regarded as the first modern statement of civil disobedience. Thoreau's essay was referred to by Gandhi, and it is widely noted in contemporary treatments of civil disobedience. It seems clear, however, that Thoreau's position differed significantly from that employed by later theorists who treat resistance as a means of prompting reform of democratic institutions. Moreover, unlike both Gandhi and King, Thoreau was not opposed to the use of violence in some circumstances. The act of disobedience that provided the focus of 'Resistance to Civil Government' was non-violent, but in a later work he wrote in support of Captain John Brown, an extremely militant member of the movement to abolish slavery in the United States (Thoreau, 1996, pp. 139–40).

In 'Resistance' Thoreau sought to justify his refusal to pay a poll tax levied by the Commonwealth of Massachusetts, an action that unequivocally breached state law. Thoreau made it quite clear that he had no intention of complying with the law, and as a consequence he was imprisoned. Although he was quite prepared to serve his full sentence he spent only one night in prison because his tax obligations were settled without his approval by a member of his family.

Henry Thoreau (1817–62)

Born in and life-long resident of Concord, Massachusetts, Thoreau was educated at Harvard College. Along with Ralph Waldo Emerson he was a key member of the 'New England Transcendentalist' group, and was an essayist, translator and poet. He was closely identified with the anti-slavery movement in the United States. His most important political essay was first delivered in 1849 as a lecture entitled 'The Relation of the Individual to the State'; it was subsequently published as 'Resistance to Civil Government' and 'Civil Disobedience'.

Key reading: Rosenblum, 1996.

Thoreau's refusal to pay the poll tax stemmed from his abhorrence of US aggression in the Mexican-American war of 1846–48 and the persistence of slavery in the United States. By refusing to pay the tax Thoreau wished to draw attention to the fundamental injustice of imperialist adventures and slavery, and to separate himself from a government that infringed the rights of its neighbours and subjects so grossly. In some passages of 'Resistance to Civil Government' Thoreau indicated that he was motivated by a desire to correct the conduct of federal and state governments. For example, he appealed to his readers to deny the authority of the US government: 'Let your life be a counter-friction to stop the machine' (Thoreau, 1992, p. 233). He also remarked that if actions such as his became widespread they would 'clog' the whole machinery of government: if all just men had to be imprisoned, the state would give up slavery immediately (ibid., p. 235).

However, these largely instrumental explanations of civil disobedience seem incidental to Thoreau's general and more consistently stated position. This argument is laid down in the opening passage of the essay where, having alluded to his preference for anarchism – 'That government is best which governs not at all' (ibid., p. 226) – he pleaded in the short term for 'better government' and urged his fellow citizens to 'make known what kind of government would command [their] respect'. He expected that his gesture of non-compliance with the poll tax law would be 'one step towards obtaining' such a government (ibid., p. 227). Significantly, Thoreau was not talking of a *system* of government, but of citizens' and officeholders' *attitude* to it. For the most part, his appeal focused primarily on *citizens* rather than *governors*, and was meant to encourage the former to signal their commitment to a standard of justice to which they expected officeholders to adhere.

Thoreau thought that ideas of justice had their roots in the uncorrupted consciousness of ordinary human beings, and he insisted that it was this – rather than the demands of governors, or the voice of the majority, or the idea that individuals had a primary obligation to smooth the path of government – that provided the standards for individual moral and collective political responsibility. In response to the question 'must the citizen ever for a moment, or in the least degree, resign his conscience to the legislator?' Thoreau observed that 'we should be men first, and subjects afterwards' (ibid., p. 227). He argued that a state that tolerated slavery or engaged in aggressive wars was acting in disregard of justice and was not worthy of the respect or obedience of its citizens.

It is significant, however, that Thoreau focused primarily on maintaining the moral integrity of upright individuals, not upon reforming the system of government, or even correcting the conduct of those who currently controlled it. Thoreau claimed that association with the present government of the United States involved such 'disgrace' that 'I cannot for an instant recognise that political organisation as *my* government which is the slaves government also' (ibid., p. 229). He justified his act of civil disobedience on the ground that there was a lack of correspondence between the actions of government and the moral stance required by the demands of justice. Consequently, Thoreau argued that his refusal to pay the poll tax should be seen as a 'deliberate and practical denial' of the government's authority. It signalled to other upright individuals that he would not lend himself to the wrong he condemned (ibid., p. 233).

The fact that Thoreau was prepared to suffer imprisonment did not imply acceptance of the penalties of the law and the state that lay behind it. To the contrary, his willingness to be excluded from society was a consequence of his general rejection of the legitimacy of an unjust state:

> Under a government which imprisons any unjustly, the true place for a just man is also a prison. The proper place to-day, the only place which Massachusetts has provided for her free and less desponding spirits, is in her prisons, to be put out and locked out of the State by her own act, as they have already put themselves out by their principles (ibid., p. 235).

Even if those who Thoreau called 'abetters' of the state were to pay a protester's tax and secure his release from prison, this would not undermine the position of the 'just man'. He would still remain separate from the state and would have done nothing to compromise his relationship with it.

Thoreau's notion of resistance thus hinges on the determination of just individuals to separate themselves from an unjust state. He made it clear, however, that civil disobedients are not engaging in actions that are part of a conventional political process. Unlike the casting of a vote, which merely expresses a hope that 'right will prevail' but leaves this up to the majority to determine, an act of civil disobedience removes the individual from the state's moral ambit (ibid., p. 230). Thoreau adhered to a notion of 'democratic individualism', which means that the conscience of individuals cannot be represented through the outcome of electoral processes. Democratic communities are made up of individuals who retain responsibility for their own sense of moral rightness. Civil disobedience is an expression of one's duty to be a good member of such a community (Rosenblum, 1996, pp. xxv–xxvi). For Thoreau, therefore, disobedience is a *human* act based on an appeal to a higher law of justice that lies beyond the reach of the state, but which should be upheld by it. It is emphatically not a tactic to win the state over to a particular point of view: 'I simply wish to refuse allegiance to the State, to withdraw and stand away from it effectually' (Thoreau, 1992, p. 241).

Insofar as this act appeals to other upright individuals, the net effect of a number of such withdrawals may be to create enough 'friction' to 'clog' the machinery of the state. Thoreau insisted, however, that this possibility should not be the factor determining whether civil disobedience is appropriate. To the contrary, he argued that individuals owe allegiance to an authority that is far higher than the state, and must adhere to it even when their action has no discernible effect on the state's conduct. It is not the individual who has to seek the approval of the state, but rather the state that must recognise that it is the individual who is the arbiter of justice: 'There will never be a really free and enlightened State, until the State comes to recognise the individual as a higher and independent power, and treats him accordingly' (ibid., p. 245).

In contemporary political theory the term 'civil disobedience' is frequently used to describe irregular and in some cases illegal actions that bring pressure to bear on the operation of the democratic state. Sit-ins, obstructive demonstrations and the flouting of unjust laws are meant to hinder the operation of government, to draw legislators' and voters' attention to alleged injustice by appealing to the shared sense of justice that underwrites democratic communities. This position differs from Thoreau's. His civil disobedient separates himself from the state and his imprisonment epitomises this separation. Moreover, as noted above, Thoreau regarded the individual as the source of ideas of justice, and argued that the best the state can do is to recognise this and avoid transgressing a standard that is independent of it and cannot be related positively to its existence. Even the most democratic states are only incidentally concerned with justice because their main decision-making mechanism – the will of the majority – leaves justice to chance. Since the individual is the repository of ideas of justice, the state can have no effect on an individual's sense of moral responsibility to a higher power, to a perpetually higher authority. According to Thoreau, *all* political authority is conditional; there is no such thing as an *obligation* to submit to government (Rosenblum, 1996, p. xxv).

This doctrine presents a potentially revolutionary challenge to the conventional democratic state because it sees political obligation as a source of danger to the moral conscience. When such dangers materialise, individuals are under an obligation to sever their ties with the state and to stand up against its unjust measures. Thoreau's individual does not have to justify civil disobedience; rather the state must make itself worthy of the necessarily conditional obedience of the individual. In Thoreau's theory, therefore, the conscience of the upright individual provides a permanent source of challenge to those who exercise political power. If they wish to secure the obedience of those nominally subject to them, they must act in ways that conform to the dictates of their subjects' conscience. For Thoreau, the obligation of subjects to their political superiors is so conditional that one could almost say that those in political authority have to ensure that their actions are worthy of the obedience of those over whom they wish to exercise such authority.

Non-violent resistance and anti-colonialism: Gandhi and 'civil resistance'

Thoreau's essay provided a source of inspiration for Mahatma Gandhi, the leading figure in the Indian independence movement in the first half of the twentieth century. But while Gandhi admired Thoreau's stance, he produced a theory of non-violent resistance to unjust authority that differed in significant respects from that of his American predecessor. Gandhi's goal was a distinctly revolutionary one because he sought the liberation of India and other Third World countries from colonial domination. Non-violent resistance was thus meant to provide the basis for a programme of political action rather than being restricted to expressing the moral integrity of just individuals. In developing his theory Gandhi made it clear that its key idea – 'satyagraha' – differed from Thoreau's notion of civil disobedience.

Gandhi first enunciated this concept in response to specific acts of injustice committed by colonial authorities in the South African state of Natal in the early decades of the twentieth century. Later, however, it was applied more generally to the entire struggle for independence in the Indian subcontinent. Pursuit of this goal necessitated the rejection of various schemes mooted in the 1920s and 1930s for power sharing, for 'dominion' status like that enjoyed by predominantly white settler colonies in Australia, Canada and New Zealand, or for any measures that stopped short of independence from Great Britain. As Gandhi wrote in 1930, it was not a question of determining 'how much power India should or should not enjoy, but ... [of considering] ways and means of framing a scheme of complete independence' (Gandhi, 1986, vol. iii, pp. 103–04).

This demand was based on a general critique of the authority of imperial rulers, and a particular rejection of British rule in India. Gandhi argued that however well-intentioned individual officials might be, the British system of rule was inherently autocratic and unjust. The British policy of 'divide and rule' encouraged communal antagonism between ethnic and religious groups within India and made the need for outside intervention part of a self-fulfilling prophecy (ibid., p. 281). The patronage of their British masters allowed local elites to exploit ruthlessly the rest of the community, and provided an important element in a system of rule that subjugated Indian interests to those of the British. The boasted *pax Britannica*, the guarantor of stability and order, epitomised the illusory benefits of colonial domination:

> It has as much value to India as the slave dwellers have in an estate, whose owner keeps the slaves from fighting one another, protects the estate from foreign inroads and makes the slaves work with a regularity that is just enough to keep the estate going in his, the owner's interest (ibid., p. 595).

Mohandas Karamchand Gandhi (1869–1948)

Gandhi, an Indian-born, English-trained lawyer, originally formulated his concept of non-violent resistance while engaged in a campaign against anti-Indian racial discrimination in the South African colony of Natal. This theory was refined during the course of Gandhi's subsequent involvement in the long struggle to free India from British rule. In the course of this campaign (concluded successfully in 1947) Gandhi acquired the status of a special political and spiritual leader, hence the title 'Mahatma', or 'Great Soul'.

Key reading: Bondurant, 1965; Parekh, 1989.

Although Gandhi developed his ideas on civil resistance in an Indian context, he regarded the independence movement there as part of a widespread struggle against colonialism. In India and elsewhere in the Third World, this struggle was directed in the first instance to liberating these countries from the direct political, economic and moral effects of imperialism. In addition, however, the movement for independence also addressed the deep-seated corruption that disfigured colonial countries and impeded their development into viable, morally acceptable societies. As Gandhi put it in 1928, 'My ambition is much higher than independence. Through the deliverance of India, I seek to deliver the so-called weaker races of the earth from the crushing heels of exploitation in which England is the greatest partner' (ibid.,

p. 255). This goal required alien Western values to be shaken off. In light of the programme that Gandhi developed it is also significant that he believed the struggle for independence would bring Englishmen and other Europeans to an understanding of the evils they had inflicted on their colonies, and that this would encourage them to abandon imperialism throughout the world (ibid., p. 255). This aspiration played a central role in Gandhi's belief that the most effective and morally acceptable form of anti-colonialism should be based on the principle of non-violent resistance.

One reason why Gandhi promoted non-violent resistance was that his experiences in South Africa had convinced him of its practical advantages. In Natal, Gandhi had headed a movement that was in confrontation with the colonial administration and white settlers, and the large indigenous population who were played off against the Indian minority. In these circumstances, violent resistance was bound to fail; if anything it would strengthen the hand of the colonial government in its dealings with the Indian population. Later, in India, the proponents of independence had to contend with an extensive, highly militarised colonial government backed by one of the world's most significant naval and military powers. They also faced a situation where an artificially fragmented society was frequently torn apart by outbreaks of 'communal' violence fuelled by ethnic and religious antagonism. Gandhi regarded violence as being morally as well as practically futile: it debases and dehumanises those who resort to it; it limits their capacity to appeal to the moral sense of others; and it also corrupts the outcome of the struggle for independence.

Identification of a genealogy of proponents of non-violence in both the Indian and Western traditions played an important justificatory role in Gandhi's theory. The Western tradition included figures from the ancient world (Socrates), the Bible (Daniel) and near contemporaries such as Thoreau and the English suffragettes. But while Gandhi regarded this tradition as an important source of inspiration and legitimation, his attitude towards it was in some respects critical. In the course of formulating this criticism Gandhi distinguished a range of attitudes towards non-violence. In the first place he rejected contemporary understandings of 'passive resistance', an idea that he associated with the suffragettes. Gandhi argued that since some suffragettes employed violence they could hardly be described as being engaged in passive resistance. In addition, however, Gandhi rejected the idea of passive resistance because he wanted to establish modes of non-violent action that were strongly active rather than passive. It was important for proponents of independence to act with a full sense of their own personal and collective strength: non-violence was not the refuge of the weak, but a tactic employed by those who were strong in numbers, determination and moral rectitude (ibid., pp. 44–45).

Although at times Gandhi seemed to endorse Thoreau's form of civil disobedience, he eventually rejected both the term itself and the approach it described. In its place he developed a doctrine that he thought could best be conveyed in English by the term 'civil resistance'. Unlike civil disobedience, civil resistance was more than just an expression of moral abhorrence; it entailed active resistance directed not merely against particular injustices, but at a system that was inherently unjust. Resistance was meant to discredit the *status quo* and usher in a distinctive and positive alternative to it. The expulsion of the British had to be seen as part of a process that would forge a new, just order free of the incubus of materialistic and individualistic Western culture. Finally, the use of the term 'civil' underlined the non-violent character of resistance:

> the current phrase was 'passive resistance'. But my way of resistance or the force I had in mind was not passive. It was active, but 'active' might also mean violent. The word 'civil' suggests nothing but non-violence. I, therefore, joined it with resistance (ibid., p. 112).

Gandhi's conception of civil resistance was part of a wider doctrine known as *satyagraha*, which incorporated reinterpretations of a number of precepts that were common currency among Hindus. *Satya*, which refers to the primacy of truth and is usually given an individualistic cast relating to individual self-perfection, was endowed by Gandhi with a strongly social connotation. In *satyagraha* the pursuit of truth became a key element in a programme of radical political and social transformation (Bondurant, 1965, pp. 109–10). In place of the conventional and largely negative meaning of *ahimsa* (non-violence or the avoidance of injury to others), Gandhi envisaged a positive force that was integral to the pursuit of social and political truth and involved a revolutionary challenge to British rule and conventional revolutionary ideas (ibid., p. 112). Finally, Gandhi incorporated in his doctrine the idea of *tapasya* (self-sacrifice), but related this to the realisation of a revolutionary social and political programme.

A central point of this reformulation of conventional Hindu concepts was that non-violence was given a positive rather than a negative connotation, and in particular the concept was extended to incorporate a genuine concern for the well-being of opponents. This feature of Gandhi's position was reflected in his refusal to engage in strike action during the heat of the day, or when Britain was at war with Germany and Japan. It also lay behind his attempt to incorporate conventional means of protest – sit-down demonstrations (*dharna*) and strikes (*hartel*) – into a more extensive process of discovering the truth and having this accepted by opponents (ibid., pp. 118–19).

Moreover, while *satyagraha* was a weapon forged in the face of a hostile and overwhelming military capacity for mass oppression, it was not seen as a weapon of the weak. Rather it was possessed by those who recognised a moral right that was superior to the coercive power held by the colonial authorities. The attractiveness and flexibility of this characteristic of *satyagraha* may be illustrated by its adoption by the Pathans, a tribe from the north-west frontier region with a highly developed militaristic ethos and a long tradition of retributive conduct involving extreme violence. The Pathans are Muslims, so the development of an ethic of non-violent resistance among them involved an appeal to Islamic values, and particularly to the stress on peace in the Koran. It also required a transformation of ideas about strength and courage so that emphasis was placed on the pursuit of peace through moral rather than physical force, and on the necessity for endurance in the face of provocation and injury. Endurance was not a sign of helpless weakness. To the contrary, it rested on a form of courage that was infinitely superior to that exhibited by the perpetrators of violence (Gandhi, 1986, vol. iii, pp. 131–44).

Suffering was a product of strength because it enabled the sufferer to change the conduct of the apparently powerful. Victims who did not physically resist the suffering imposed on them inhibited the actions of their oppressors; their power seemed to be negated. In addition, Gandhi maintained that the victims' suffering sparked a sympathetic response among many of those who had supported imperial rule. This sympathy undermined the feelings of hatred between the parties concerned and thus increased the prospect of arriving at a mutual recognition of fundamental truths about the inherent injustice of the colonial system. This expectation was derived from Gandhi's understanding of the role that *satyagraha* played in identifying truth and gaining general acceptance of it.

Gandhi held that non-violent action was the most appropriate form of resistance because it allowed the search for truth, and hence the realisation of the injustice of colonialism, to be a cooperative endeavour. In the course of this search the participating parties, both oppressors and oppressed, might modify or even abandon pre-existing ideas. The process of resistance began with an invitation to pursue truth, and even when it gave rise to direct action, avenues for dialogue were left open. *Satyagraha* thus required a humble and open-minded desire to search for truth, a sincere effort to understand the position of others and sincere goodwill towards them (Parekh, 1989, pp. 143–44). These requirements flowed from the conclusion that Gandhi had drawn from observing the intractable positions that had emerged in debates between colonial elites and proponents of independence. Violence was often seen as the only way of breaking the impasse but Gandhi maintained that violence was incompatible with the discovery and mutual acceptance of truth: it was non-rational, it assumed that agreement was impossible, it implied a debased view of one's opponents and it created hatred rather than goodwill. In order to avoid these counterproductive outcomes, it was necessary to adopt a view of rationality that recognised the need to appeal both to the heart and to the head of one's opponents, to take account of their legitimate interests, and to ensure that trenchant resistance did not deprive the resisters of sympathy for their misguided opponents. As Parekh neatly puts it, *satyagraha*

> combined the patience and persuasive power of reason with the urgency and energy of violence. It respected and reconciled the integrity of the parties involved, tapped and mobilised their moral and spiritual energies, and paved the way for a better mutual understanding … . [I]t did not replace but complemented reason (ibid., p. 148).

In practice *satyagraha* worked through a number of stages. A clear statement and defence of objectives was followed by popular agitation to convince the authorities of the seriousness of the situation. The resisters then issued an ultimatum, and finally they resorted to direct mass action. At each stage the door to resolution remained open. Gandhi stressed that one should be flexible in one's acceptance of compromise solutions to particular issues because the immediate outcome was secondary to the benefits produced by the general process.

Gandhi's later formulation of *satyagraha* described it as a way of exerting pressure on supporters of colonial rule, one that recognised the extent to which the powerful depended ultimately on the cooperation of their apparently powerless subjects. Non-violent action withdrew cooperation and thus weakened the power of dominant elites (ibid., pp. 153–56). To the extent that this development involved the application of pressure as a form of force, it tended to weaken the exclusively moral character of Gandhi's position. It remained true, however, that this pressure was merely a tactic in a struggle that was seen in moral terms. In addition, the application of pressure awakened the imperial power to the precarious nature of its position and helped minimise violent counter-resistance. It thus increased the prospect of a non-violent transition to independence, something that would be especially hard to achieve in an environment where communal conflict was an ever-present threat to human life and the pursuit of collective goals.

Racial discrimination, civil disobedience and just democracy: King

Gandhi applied the idea of civil resistance to a system of rule that he regarded as fundamentally flawed: non-violent resistance was a means of freeing India (and other colonised countries) from the domination of colonial powers. It was also part of a programme that would result in the creation of a just political order. These features of Gandhi's theory limited its application to Western states. Western governments were already democratic; they possessed mechanisms that regulated the exercise of power and ensured that officeholders would act as the agents of those who elected them. In a sense, the members of a democratic state were both rulers and the ruled.

It is worth recalling, however, that Thoreau's ideas had been developed in a democratic context, and he had denied that the mere existence of democratic government made civil disobedience either unnecessary or illegitimate. Seen from this point of view, Thoreau's defence of principled disobedience formed part of a tradition that has played an important role in the recent history of the United States.

Modern American arguments about civil disobedience treat it (as had Douglass and Du Bois) in relation to values that are seen as fundamental to democratic government in the United States. It is assumed that governments that uphold these values are legitimate and that members of the community are therefore under an obligation to uphold the system of government, and to abide by the laws produced by it. Some of these arguments treat disregard for the law as a tactic designed to exert pressure on conventional political processes. Others, however, are more in sympathy with Thoreau's advocacy of civil disobedience as a way of protesting about fundamental injustices. The difference is that many modern writers are more sanguine than Thoreau about the relationship between democracy and justice. More importantly, they assume that people have positive obligations to democratic systems of government. In recent times the doctrine of civil disobedience has been most closely identified with Dr Martin Luther King Jr.

King was a leading civil rights activist in the late 1950s and early 1960s. Despite the efforts of writers such as Douglass and Du Bois, racial discrimination against blacks remained endemic in American culture and was given prominent public sanction in policies which maintained racial segregation in education, public transport and public facilities in the southern United States. In some cases, segregation was upheld by state and municipal law; in others it was not outlawed by local legislation even when it had been deemed unconstitutional by the US Supreme Court. It is important to recall that these institutionalised forms of racial discrimination were common in political systems that were, nominally at least, fully democratic.

Martin Luther King Jr. (1929–68)

Born into a family of black clerics in Atlanta, Georgia, King overcame his reservations about the overly emotional appeal of fundamentalist Christianity and was ordained. His subsequent career as a pastor in the Baptist Church was combined with an increasingly prominent role in black community politics and in the civil rights movement. King was a member of the National Association for the Advancement of Colored People and was the leading figure in protest activities directed against racial discrimination in the southern United States. His later career also embraced the anti-Vietnam War movement, and he won the Nobel Peace Prize in 1964. He was assassinated by a white extremist in 1968 while campaigning in Memphis. King's 'Letter from Birmingham Jail' presents his views on non-violent civil resistance.

Key reading: Ansbro, 1983; Harris, 1989.

King and his supporters challenged discriminatory practices by launching a range of protests, most notably demonstrations, sit-ins and attempts to gain access to segregated services. Some of these actions were contrary to state laws and local ordinances, and resulted in the imprisonment of protesters. In 1963 King and a number of his supporters were imprisoned by the authorities in Birmingham, Alabama. While serving his prison term King published a 'Letter From Birmingham Jail' in which he both explained and justified civil disobedience. This letter was addressed to members of the local clergy, who had claimed that King's conduct had been 'unwise and untimely'. The idea that gross injustice justified a challenge to both the form of the law, and the way in which it was administered, was central to King's rejection of the accusations made against him.

King identified four steps that characterise a morally legitimate campaign of non-violent civil disobedience: identification of a significant injustice; negotiation to resolve it; self-purification to ensure the moral purity of any future action; and finally, protest action itself. Direct action becomes necessary when those who perpetrate injustice refuse to adjust their conduct and/or the legal regulations that uphold it. Acts of civil disobedience are meant to produce what King regarded as a creative, non-violent tension between the demands of those seeking recognition of civil rights and their segregationist opponents. This tension takes a direct political form, but it also draws in those whose economic interests may be compromised by protest action. King was more open than Gandhi in his recognition that civil disobedience involves coercion, but he denied that this gives it a violent character. To the contrary, Gandhi's ideas had a marked impact on King's views of political action (Ansbro, 1983, pp. 3–7). He insisted that if civil rights activists uphold the necessary connection between the morality of their ends and the morality of the means through which these ends are pursued, they must avoid violent forms of protest. Consequently, King denied that the force generated by civil disobedience is violent: it does not produce physical harm, nor does it deprive people of their legitimate economic and political rights. Rather it opens up the prospect of supporters of injustice being made to suffer as a consequence of actions carried out in response to their own intransigence. Civil disobedience is a response to injustice that conforms to the principles of justice (King, 1989, p. 70).

Both conservative and radical critics rejected King's appeal to non-violence on the grounds that it was inconsistent with the revolutionary character of his aspirations. They also argued that his strategy ignored the intractably hostile nature of the political, social and economic environment in which he worked (Storing, 1989, p. 76). For King, however, non-violent civil disobedience was justified because it was directed at the realisation of values that lay at the heart of American politics. His answer to his critics among the clergy of Birmingham addressed four important implications of this relationship.

First, he attempted to justify the involvement of outsiders like himself in what the Birmingham clergy portrayed as a local issue. These critics implied that what happened in Birmingham concerned only the residents of that city; national campaigns of protest were an unwarranted interference in the affairs of others. In response to this charge, King claimed that particular acts of injustice are matters of *universal* concern: 'the interrelatedness of all communities and states' means that 'injustice anywhere is a threat to justice everywhere'. This threat is partly practical – the unjust will promote injustice elsewhere – but it is also a consequence of the idea that a political community marked by injustice in some of its component parts cannot be regarded as just; justice is an absolute. Consequently, King argued that he should not

> sit idly by in Atlanta [his place of residence] and not be concerned about what happens in Birmingham ... . We are caught in an inescapable network of mutuality, tied in a single garment of destiny. Whatever affects one directly, affects all indirectly. Never again can we afford to live with the narrow, provincial 'outside agitator' idea. Anyone who lives inside the United States can never be considered an outsider anywhere within its bounds (ibid., p. 58).

While this argument established a general obligation to oppose particular injustices, King's second response dealt with the claim that civil disobedience is inappropriate in a democratic environment. This objection rests on the grounds that since democracies contain mechanisms for correcting injustice, and since democratic laws are based on the consent of those who are bound by them, there can be no grounds for wilful disregard of the law (Harris, 1989, pp. 22–23). King insisted that this argument could not be applied in the present context because Alabama was not a truly democratic state. Since blacks were prevented from registering as voters, the legislative body that enacted Alabama's segregation laws could not be said to represent all the inhabitants of the state: 'can any law enacted under such circumstances be considered democratically structured?' (King, 1989, p. 62).

Thirdly, King drew a distinction between 'evading' or 'defying' the law on the one hand, and conscientiously and openly breaking it on the other. Evasion or defiance of the law – for example, when segregationists disregarded federal laws upholding the right to peaceful assembly and protest – is not acceptable because it will result in anarchy. In contrast the lawbreaking of civil disobedients is done 'openly, lovingly, and with a willingness to accept the penalty' (ibid., p. 63). It is intended to awaken the moral consciousness of the community to the injustice of a law or practice, not to perpetuate an injustice by evading just law, or, as in the case of ordinary criminality, gaining a personal advantage.

The distinction between just and unjust law formed the fourth and final strand of King's defence of non-violent civil disobedience. He argued that the laws broken by civil disobedients were unjust and he appealed to St Augustine's dictum that 'an unjust law is no law at all' (ibid., p. 61). For King, as for Augustine, just laws are those that are in harmony with moral and divine law; they 'uplift human personality'. In contrast, 'any law that degrades human personality is unjust' (ibid., p. 62). Unlike Augustine, however, King maintained that unjust laws have no legitimate hold on those to whom they are applied (see p. 22). King, in common with Douglass (see above, pp. 73–75), argued that since the constitution of the United States recognises God-given rights, laws that are incompatible with these rights have no place in the American legal system. Thus from both a constitutional and moral perspective, laws supporting racial segregation are illegitimate and challenges to them are justified by reference to the fundamental principles underlying the American system of government: 'the goal of America is freedom. Abused and scorned though we may be, our destiny is tied up with America's destiny' (ibid., p. 69). From this point of view, it may be said that civil disobedients show their respect for the principles of American democracy by openly challenging unjust laws and willingly accepting the penalties annexed to them. Unjust suffering in the cause of justice was regarded by King as a way of signalling acceptance of the principle of law when appealing to the consciences of other members of the community.

Unlike Thoreau, King does not seem to have regarded civil disobedience as a way of insulating upright individuals from a morally dubious political culture. To the contrary, his account suggests that civil disobedience is justified because it involves an appeal to values that underwrite American democracy. Civil disobedience is a corrective mechanism applied to a potentially just system of government. It should therefore be seen as a civil act, one that is directed towards the moral good of the political community.

Conclusion

Because Thoreau did not develop a theory of non-violence – the issue of non-violence versus violence played no role in his account – his ideas were of very limited use to Gandhi. Indeed, to the extent that Thoreau's notion of civil disobedience emphasised its defensive and reactive features, it was not, as Gandhi himself realised, an appropriate model for his followers to adopt. Gandhi's theory of non-violence reflected his understanding of the necessary connection between political effectiveness and moral veracity. Non-violence was designed to achieve objectives that had conventionally been pursued by violent means, without falling prey to the moral and practical shortcomings of that approach.

The fact that Gandhi saw non-violent resistance as part of a revolutionary programme meant that his position differed significantly from that of both Thoreau and King since neither of them wished to promote a general transformation of their society. Rather they sought to appeal against particular acts that ran contrary to conceptions of justice that they identified with American democracy. King, however, did not question conventional notions of political obligation. By contrast, Thoreau's stance was underwritten by a conception of citizenship that made obligation conditional on a correspondence between the actions of government and the conscience of the individual.

The difference between these positions is apparent in King's remarks on democracy. While King argued that citizens were not obliged to obey Alabama's segregation laws because of the corruption of its electoral machinery, Thoreau denied that it was possible for the conscience of the individual to be represented through democratic procedures. Since King would not have accepted legalised segregation even if it had been endorsed by legitimate democratic procedures, this contrast should not be pushed too far. The fact remains, however, that King's remarks on democracy did not rest on the conception of democratic individualism to which Thoreau adhered. Moreover, while King regarded acts of civil disobedience as part of the practice of democratic politics, Thoreau viewed them primarily as a way of sustaining the moral independence of the individual.

EPILOGUE: POST-MODERNISM AND POST-COLONIALISM

This survey concludes with a discussion of 'post-modernist' and 'post-colonialist' challenges to the history of Western political thought. The prefix 'post' signals that these developments mark a significant shift away from the perspectives that have informed past political thinking in the West.

The post-modernist 'turn' refers to critical perspectives on ideas about the self, society and the state that are seen as central to enlightenment and post-enlightenment political thought, that is, to Western thinking since the mid-seventeenth century. 'Modernist' thinking is identified with the assumption that political reflection has objective and universal foundations and that these should underpin political action and be reflected in political institutions (Bennett, 2006, pp. 211–13). Post-modernist critics regard both liberalism and Marxism as characteristic products of modernity, since, while they offer quite different views of the good life, they approach political thinking in similar ways.

Critics of modernism appeal to a complex of intellectual and cultural developments which they relate to other distinctive features of late-twentieth-century Western societies. The 'post-modern problematic' thus focuses on what Stephen White has described as 'the increasing incredulity towards metanarratives, the growing awareness of new problems wrought by societal rationalisation, the explosion of new informational technologies and the emergence of new social movements' (White, 1991, p. 4). All these phenomena have important political implications, and the first of them has a bearing on the history of political thought.

This point is illustrated in the work of the French thinker Jean-Francois Lyotard. Like other post-modernists, Lyotard associates modernity with a stress on science and rationalism. He argued that this way of thinking has provided the basis for 'grand narratives' that characterised post-enlightenment political thinking:

> Societies which anchor the discourses of truth and justice in the great historical and scientific narratives … can be called modern. The French Jacobins don't speak like Hegel but the just and the good are always found caught up in a great progressive odyssey (Sarup, 1988, p. 132).

Hegel and Marx are seen as archetypical creators of metanarratives reflecting universalistic conceptions promoting large-scale programmes of social and political reconstruction. These programmes are claimed to be inherently oppressive because they rest on unitary conceptions of 'truth'. Post-modernists reject universalism, they adopt an ironic stance towards truth claims, and they promote localised action resting on difference and particularity rather than common identity and universalism. A central element of the post-modern response to the 'discourse of truth' is the attempt to unveil the 'truth' of the unitary, rational, essential self of liberalism as a fictional subject.

While aspects of this critique appear to echo the rejection of universality found in the writings of Burke and Hayek (ibid., p. 133), post-modernist perspectives have underwritten distinctive departures in contemporary political thinking. These include feminist arguments about the significance of difference (see above pp. 70ff), and attempts to seek an understanding of the post-modern condition by exploring the implications of 'globalisation', or forms of interdependence and interpenetration that extend beyond the geographical, cultural and intellectual boundaries of nation states in general, and the Western world in particular (Rengger, 1992, p. 570). Post-modernism has also prompted a reevaluation of the ideas of historically significant thinkers in the Western tradition (Connolly, 1988; Shankman, 1994). William Connolly, for example, argues that the Hegelian state and Marx's idea of community are 'anachronistic'. Both are presented as universally attainable forms of life but neither is realisable in the conditions of late-modern life. Hegel's state would have to contend with complex networks of global state and non-state actors pursuing a wide variety of often incompatible interests. The realisation of Marx's vision of a universal non-state community faces equally intractable challenges to its simultaneous pursuit of human liberation and the socially directed control of production. Connolly argues that imperatives of progress and productivity in the late-modern world are bound to frustrate the realisation of these nineteenth-century projects and to discredit the ideas of truth that are integral to them (Connolly, 1988, pp. 133–34).

While post-modern thinkers question enlightenment metanarratives, 'post-colonialism' focuses on the intellectual implications of the dominant role of Western states in world history since the early-modern period. It is sharply critical of the impact of European states, economies and settlers on indigenous communities and cultures in the Americas, the Indian subcontinent, southeast Asia, Australasia and the Pacific. As the label suggests, *post*-colonialism is concerned particularly with the ongoing implications of long periods of Western control in societies that are now no longer subject to the formal political authority of colonial powers. It is possible, however, to identify post-colonial themes in works going back to the earliest periods of European expansion (Gilroy, 2008). For example, Aquinas did not believe that Europeans had the right to subject non-Christians to their control because they were capable of understanding enough about the requirements of natural law to maintain legitimate forms of political rule. This position was upheld in the first half of the sixteenth century by the Spanish theologian and philosopher Francisco de Vitoria. He defended Amerindians' rights to their property and denied that the Pope or the Emperor had any claims to overturn the rule of their chiefs (Pagden, 1991). At the very height of the French Enlightenment Denis Diderot dismissed European claims to cultural and moral superiority over indigenous Pacific islanders. In one of his dialogues Diderot ridiculed a Catholic priest's confused attempts to uphold conventional Western views on personal morality in the face of the ironically incredulous interrogation of a Melanesian chief. Having been told of Christian prescriptions of sexual conduct and the actual state of domestic and sexual relationships in 'civilised' societies, the chief exclaims,

> What could seem more ridiculous than a precept which forbids any change of our affections, which commands that we show a constancy of which we're not capable, which violates the nature and liberty of male and female alike in chaining them to one another for the whole of their lives?... Believe you me, you have made the plight of man worse than that of an animal. I've no understanding of your great craftsman [the Christian God], but I rejoice in his never having addressed our forefathers, and I hope he will never speak to our children; for he might tell them the same nonsense, and they might commit the folly of believing him (Diderot, 1992, pp. 50–51).

One important strand of contemporary post-colonial thought focuses on the ongoing economic domination of the west and the persistent cultural and material deprivation that results from it. Although post-colonial writers reject the assumptions underlying metanarratives of the transformative role of capitalism in Marx's observations on the impact of British expansionism on Indian industries (see above p. 260), many of them accept his account of the global expansion of capitalism, of its insatiable need to source competitively priced labour and materials and expand its markets. They point out that ex-colonies are still part of the global capitalist economy and remain subject to forms of control and exploitation that are associated in many ways with their experience as colonies of Western states. Moreover, non-European societies that were not colonised politically, continue to remain subject to the capitalist forces that exerted a profound influence on them in the nineteenth and twentieth centuries.

The critical political economy of post-colonialism is distinct from, but not mutually exclusive of, its focus on the ongoing domination of former colonies and dependencies by the culture and values of the west. Edward Said's work has been particularly important in framing this approach. In *Orientalism* Said sought, by reference to the history of Europeans' study of Asia, to explain colonisation and its post-colonial aftermath by the ongoing intrusion of attitudes and ideas that had obscured the diversity of colonised cultures and histories, and displaced them with allegedly universal forms that are really an expression of Western values.

> Orientalism ... is a system of representations framed by a whole set of forces that brought the Orient into Western learning. ... [It] aided and was aided by general cultural pressures that tended to make more rigid the sense of difference between the European and Asiatic parts of the world. My contention is that Orientalism is fundamentally a political doctrine ... which elided the Orient's difference with its weakness (Said, 2003, pp. 202–3, 204).

Post-modern and post-colonial critiques of enlightenment thinking's universalistic claims are set in landscapes marked by particularity and diversity and exhibit ambivalent and in some case hostile relationships with past political thinking in the West. Some post-colonial critiques involve a partial and highly selective re-working of enlightenment metanarratives and the incorporation into them of indigenous perspectives and values. In other cases, however, post-colonial thinking involves an emphatic rejection of these approaches and a far more complete and fundamental shift away from the assumptions and preoccupations of Western traditions of political thought. Two examples of post-colonial political thinking serve to illustrate these different responses to the metanarratives of the past. The first occurs in Frantz Fanon writings on revolution which have also been considered in an earlier chapter (see pp. 276–80). The second example focuses on Ayatollah Khomeini's reaction to early Islamic revolutionary thought in twentieth-century Iran.

As we have seen, Fanon utilised aspects of Marxism in his critique of the impact of colonial settlement. He also explored the psychological ramifications of the attitudes of settlers towards indigenous people and the impact of these on the collective consciousness of these societies and the consciousness of individual indigene. For Fanon, the indigenous subjects of colonial governments were inflicted with a divided and alienating self-consciousness which was similar to that which Du Bois had attributed to the African-American victims of white domination and prejudice in the southern states of the American Republic (see p). Fanon claimed that colonialism involved a 'systematic negation of personality' that robbed the subject people of all 'attributes of humanity'. In the eyes and minds of the settlers, the indigenous population was merely one of the alien forces with which they had to contend:

> Hostile nature, obstinate and fundamentally rebellious, is in fact represented in the colonies by the bush, by mosquitoes, natives and fever, and colonisation is a success when all this indocile nature has finally been tamed. Railways across the bush, the draining of swamps and a native population which is non-existent politically and economically are in fact one and the same thing (Fanon, 1967, p. 201).

Fanon thought the recognition of indigenous practices and values by paternalistic colonial authorities exacerbated the subordination of indigenous peoples rather than providing a pathway to future liberation. It served to reinforce the division between colonists and the undifferentiated native 'other', confirming their exclusion from a society supposedly based on commitment to universalistic ideas of liberty and equality. As discussed above, Fanon's response to this state of affairs was to seek the expulsion of colonists and the destruction of the de-indigenised local elite they had spawned. He saw indigenous revolution as a way of forging a future where full membership of free and equal societies made possible the restoration of the alienated divided consciousness of the culturally, economically and politically dominated subject of colonisation. Fanon thought that the development of un-alienated self-consciousness would only be possible when indigenous values were fused with authentically democratic socialism.

Fanon's focus on the dispossessed as the framers of their own futures and the agents in processes of change links his theory of anti-colonial revolution with later post-colonial theory. The conditions of members of post-colonial society have been characterised in terms of critical ideas of 'subalternity' that are not only hostile to the Euro-centric cast of Western liberalism but also to radical alternatives to it, including those derived from Marxism. By focussing on the dispossessed, 'subaltern studies' seek to identify ideational features of ex-colonial communities that are distinct from Western political and social thinking and radically incompatible with it. These ideas include the distinctions between public and private and between tradition and modernity that play an important role in many varieties of liberal thinking. They also include notions of class and class conflict that are associated with Marxism. As we have seen, this approach has given rise to a distinctive idea of democratic government appropriate to societies seeking to reclaim connection with values that predate the interventions of Europeans in their affairs (see above pp. 158–61). It also has significant parallels with the stress upon 'difference' that plays a prominent role in other aspects of contemporary political theory (see p. 162). As Homi Bhabba has put it, 'The very language of cultural community needs to be rethought from the postcolonial perspective, in a move similar to the language of sexuality, the self and cultural community, effected by feminists in the 1970s and the gay community in the 1980s' (Bhabba, 1994, p. 175).

Although Fanon's theory of revolutionary anti-colonialism involved a rejection of Western cultural, economic and political domination and stressed the importance of recovering and extending aspects of indigenous culture, his endorsement of the general goals of Marxism meant that his views remained attached to some strands of modernism. The same is true of a number of writers who were involved in revolutionary politics in post-war Iran. Their ideas were, however, challenged successfully by a figure who claimed to represent a far more authentic connection with anti-European, Islamic values.

Throughout the twentieth century significant elements in the *Shia* clergy tried to use an appeal to Islamic tradition as the basis for resistance to imperialist influences within Iran. Despite the potentially revolutionary implications of such an appeal, it was, however, accompanied by a thoroughgoing conservatism in religious, economic, social and political matters that blunted its impact. This conservative form of anti-colonialism was challenged by two modernising tendencies within Islam. The first of these was associated with the 'constitutionalists' who sought to create a broadly liberal and constitutional state that nevertheless recognised Islam as the supreme religious and moral authority within the political and social culture of Iran. Islamic constitutionalism thus rested on an unstable combination of Western ideas about the supremacy of constitutionally prescribed representative bodies and traditional Islamic expectations that Islamic clergy should oversee secular authority without being integrated into the political system. Thus the constitutional structure created in 1906–7 specified that '[a]ll laws necessary to strengthen the foundations of the State and the Throne and set in order the affairs of the Realm and the establishment of the Ministries, must be submitted for approval to the National Consultative Assembly'. It also required that 'at no time must any legal enactment of the Sacred National Consultative Assembly ... be at variance with the sacred principles of Islam' and sought to reconcile these requirements by instituting a system that subjected the activities of the assembly to the general supervision of clerical jurists (Lahidji, 1988, pp. 140–1).

The second major modernising element within revolutionary Islam rested on a synthesis of Islamic and socialist principles and was overtly hostile to both conservative and constitutionalist movements. Within this tradition the ideas of Ali Shariati and the Mujahedin were particularly significant. Although Shariati rejected the 'first' (atheistic) and the 'third' (political) aspects of Marx, he accepted Marx's contributions as a social scientist and particularly his identification of laws of historical development. He insisted, however, that adaptation of aspects of Western notions of economic development must be grounded in national cultures and particularly in their religious dimensions. Consequently, he argued that the process of development in Iran necessitated two revolutions: the first to be directed against imperialism and towards revitalisation of the national culture; and the second would involve a process of social transformation that eliminated poverty and laid the basis for a classless society. Shariati's revolutionary doctrine was marked by a strong element of anticlericalism. He claimed that Islam was inherently egalitarian and revolutionary, and castigated the *Shiite* clergy for turning Islamic religion into a rigidly institutionalised doctrine that served the interests of the middle classes and ignored those of the lower classes. The corruption of clerical culture meant that the revolution would have to circumvent the clergy's baneful influence, and Shariati looked to the progressive secular intelligentsia to provide guidance and leadership during it (Abrahamian, 1988, pp. 292–6).

The Mujahedin's position was similar in many respects to that of their predecessor. It espoused a democratic, egalitarian, and socialistic doctrine that drew on Marx's economic analysis and made class struggle a part of the Islamic tradition. The Mujahedin saw God as the first mover of the laws of historical development, and Mohamad as the prophet who provided guidance on their implications. They argued that advancement of the goals of Islam required destruction of the current exploitative social system. In an analysis that was influenced by Fanon's writings, Mohamad Hanifrejad (the chief ideologue of the movement) stressed the extent to which exploitation in countries such as Iran was tied up with its subordination to the interests of imperialist powers. Like Shariati, Hanifrejad was strongly anticlerical. As one of his followers put it, 'the most dangerous of all forms of oppression are laws, and restrictions forcibly imposed on the people in the name of religion' (Omid, 1994, p. 53). The goal of the Islamic revolution was to create a universal society that was classless, indifferent to national boundaries and united by a monotheistic religion. It was claimed that these ends could only be realised through a revolutionary organisation that gave the clergy a moral and inspirational role rather than a directive one.

These images of the post-colonial future of Iran were challenged by the Ayatollah Khomeini, the clerical leader of the successful revolution of the 1970s. Khomeini's theory of Islamic revolution was developed in reaction to Western influences in Iran and to the incorporation of Western doctrines in the works of his predecessors. His position is strongly elitist, clerical and anti-Marxist. The key element of this theory is identification of the right to rule by a supreme religious figure and the reworking of conventional views of juristic pluralism to align them with the unitary theocratic leadership created during the Islamic revolution (ibid., p. 194). As one of the participants in this process put it, 'This revolution is the integration of religion and politics, or better put, it is the refutation of the colonialist idea of "separation of religion from politics"' (ibid., p. 195). Khomeini's approach thus marked a radical shift in Iran revolutionaries' attitude towards Western political thought. While his predecessors sought to utilise critical strands from these traditions, Khomeini's ideas of Islamic revolution demonstrate a radically post-colonial determination to strike a new path that is not in any way reliant on the Western political thinking.

FURTHER READING

The first section lists a range of general surveys of the ideas of ancient and medieval, early-modern and modern political thinkers. The biographical notes in the second section identify a few key secondary works relating to the thinkers and themes dealt with in each chapter of the book. The full details of these works can be found in the Bibliography on pp. 289–305.

Readers will find a range of authoritative essays on historical figures and/or themes in the six volumes of the *Cambridge History of Political Thought*, in *Cambridge Companion* volumes and the online *Stanford Encyclopedia*. The volumes in Bloomsbury's Textual Moments in the History of Political Thought series provide concise targeted readings of key historical texts on censorship (Kemp , 2015), conservatism (Garnett, 2018), democracy (Márquez, 2018b), feminism (Bruce and Smits, 2016), liberalism (Atanassow and Kahan, 2017), patriarchalism (Cuttica and Mahlberg, 2016), revolutions (Hammersley, 2015), and utopianism (Avilés and Davis, 2012). Brown et al. (2002) prints a good range of textual extracts on historical ideas on international relations and provides accessible commentary on them. Bonnie Honig and Anne Phillips' *The Oxford Handbook of Political Theory* is a very useful source for contemporary political ideas. Finally, readers will find that many of the modern editions of historical texts listed in the Bibliography include introductory essays with valuable biographical and contextual material and critical reflections.

1. General Surveys

Ancient and Medieval Periods, c. 400 BC–1500 AD

Barker, 1959; Black, 1991; Berki, 1977; Coleman, 2000a; Boucher, 1998; Burns, 1991; Lewis, 1954; McClelland, 1996; Redhead, 1984; Skinner, 1978; Ullman, 1975.

Early-modern Period, c. 1500–1800

Allen, 1951; Berki, 1977; Burns with Goldie, 1994; Boucher, 1998; Coleman, 2000b; Hampsher-Monk, 1992; Keohane, 1980; McClelland, 1966; Plamenatz, 1966; Redhead, 1984; Skinner, 1978; Skinner 1992a; Tuck, 1992.

Modern Period, c. 1800–

Berki, 1977; Boucher, 1998; Francis and Morrow, 1994; Hampsher-Monk, 1992; McClelland, 1996; Plamenatz, 1966; Redhead, 1984; Shapiro, 2003; Skinner, 1992b.

2. Bibliographical Notes

Chapter 1: Politics and Order. On the Athenian background to Plato's and Aristotle's political ideas, see Farrar (1992) and Jones (1957); Annas (1981) and Mulgan (1977) provide excellent surveys of these ideas. Black (1993) and Burns (1991) are good sources on many aspects of medieval political thought. See Doody (2005) on Augustine and Finnis (1998) on Aquinas, Franklin (1992) for an outline of Bodin's political theory and Baumgold (1988) for that of Hobbes. Brooker (1991) provides a full account of modern totalitarianism while Wokler (1994), Murphy

(1970) and Vincent and Plant (1984) provide good introductions to Rousseau, Kant and Green respectively. Miller (1984) surveys modern anarchism while Singer (1980) provides a useful brief introduction to Marx's thought.

Chapter 2: Politics and Virtue. For classical and medieval themes, see the works identified in relation to chapter 1. See Skinner (1981) for a brief introduction to Machiavelli's thought and Skinner (1978) for an authoritative account of both the Italian and Protestant dimensions of the issues discussed here. Baylor (1991) and Hopfl (1981) provide succinct introductions to aspects of the political ideas of the Protestant Reformation. See Kliengeld (2006) for Kant's ideas on interstate relations.

Chapter 3: Politics and Freedom. See Skinner (1978) on the classical republican tradition and Parry (1978) on Locke, Claeys (1989b) and Philp (1989) on Paine, and Thomas (1985) on Mill. Lokke (2016) and Zizeck (2016) provide succinct introductions to Wollstonecraft and de Gouges respectively. See Lloyd (2016) on Douglass and Gooding-Williams (2008) on Du Bois.

Chapter 4: Politics, Freedom and Sociability. Wood (1991) provides an excellent short introduction to aspects of Hegel's political philosophy, including his conception of freedom. See Shklar (1969) on Rousseau and Vincent and Plant (1984) on Green. Avineri (1968) provides a detailed survey of Marx's ideas, while Crowder (1991) considers a range of statements of classical anarchism.

Chapter 5: Politics, Happiness and Welfare. Miller (1981) surveys Hume's political thought while the French tradition of utilitarianism is discussed in Keohane (1980). Hume (1993) considers the political implications of Bentham's utilitarianism; Thomas (1985) examines Mill's modifications to Bentham's doctrine. For succinct surveys of Bentham's legal, moral, and political philosophy, see Crimmins (2004) and Scholfield (2006). See Hoogensen (2005) on Bentham's views on international relations.

Chapter 6: Rule by a Single Person. See Annas (1981) and Mulgan (1977) for ideas of single-person rule in the ancient world and Black (1993) and Burns (1991) for medieval ideas of kingship. Burns with Goldie (1994) contains a chapter discussing ideas of absolute monarchy in the seventeenth century; see also Schochet (1975) for Filmer's political theory in its seventeenth-century context. Keohane (1980) discusses kingship in early-modern French thought. See Lebrun (1988) and Wilson (2011) for Maistre's political ideas, the introduction to Maurras (1971) for French right-wing thought, and Beiser (1996; 2003) and Morrow (2011) for political romanticism.

Chapter 7: The Rule of the Few. See Annas (1981) and Mulgan (1977) for Plato and Aristotle respectively, and Burns (1991) and Black (1993) for aspects of medieval thought on the rule of the few. Skinner (1992a) and the editor's introduction to Harrington (1992) provide an overview of classical republican views of aristocracy. Burke's political thought is outlined in Macpherson (1980), Garnett (2018) and Hampsher-Monk (2014) and that of Coleridge in Morrow (1990) and Morrow (2018). See Thomas (1985) on Mill, Ansell-Pearson (1994) on Nietzsche, and Parry (1970) on modern elite theory.

Chapter 8: The Rule of the Many. Dunn (1992) contains a series of very useful essays on the history and theory of democracy. For Protagoras see Kierstead (2018) and for Socrates and Plato see Arendt (2005). See Baylor (1991) on radical Protestant thinkers, Skinner (1978) on classical republicans, Wotton (1994) on Levellers, and Claeys (1989b) and Feit (2018) on Paine. James Mill's position is discussed by Macpherson (1975) and Thomas (1979) and Sieyes' in Forsyth (1987) and Rubinelli (2018). See Rosen (1993b) on Bentham, Thomas (1985) on J. S. Mill, and Nicholson (1990) on Green.

Chapter 9: *The Sanctions of Nature.* Mulgan (1977) considers Aristotle's ideas on the laws of nature, while Wood (1988) provides a detailed account of Cicero's use of natural law. See Burns (1991), Black (1993), Copleston (1975) and Finnis (1998) for medieval views. Early-modern theories of natural right are discussed in Tuck (1979), with Baumgold (1988), Haakonseen (1985), Tully (1991) and Tully (1980) offering detailed accounts of Hobbes', Grotius', Pufendorf's and Locke's respective ideas on the laws of nature and natural rights. Lloyd (2016) explores the role of natural law thinking in the work of proponents of black liberation.

Chapter 10: *Mixed Government, Balanced Constitutions and the Separation of Powers.* For classical views of mixed government see Fritz (1954), and on those of Cicero see Wood (1988). Skinner (1978) and the editor's introduction to Harrington (1992) consider classical republican theories. See Hampsher-Monk (1992) on *The Federalist* and Zuckert (2017) on Madison. The introduction to Constant (1980) and Forsyth (1987) consider late-eighteenth- and early-nineteenth-century French views.

Chapter 11: *Absolute Government.* For French theories of absolute government, see the introductions to Seyssel (1981) and Bossuet (1990) and Franklin (1992 and 1994) and Keohane (1980). See Baumgold (1988) on Hobbes, and Schochet (1975) and Cuttica (2016) on Filmer. Tully (1991) provides a brief account of Pufendorf's position. Francis (1980) and Lee (1990) consider aspects of Hobbes' legacy to legal positivism.

Chapter 12: *The Rule of Law and Rule-Bound Orders.* See Mulgan (1977) for Aristotle's views and Burns (1991) for those of medieval thinkers. The introductions to Seyssel (1981) and Hooker (1989) consider two early-modern perspectives on the rule of law, while Miller (1981) considers Hume's theory and Kreiger (1972) examines the role of this idea in eighteenth-century German thought. Gray (1984) and Barry (1979) provide valuable introductions to Hayek's political theory.

Chapter 13: *Resisting Unjust Ruler.* Late medieval and early-modern theories of resistance are discussed in some detail in Skinner (1978). Franklin (1969b) is particularly useful on French theories while Hopfl (1981) provides a succinct survey of Calvin's and Luther's political ideas. See Parry (1978) for a useful introduction to Locke's ideas.

Chapter 14: *Revolutionary Political Thought.* Tholfsen (1984) provides a useful survey of European revolutionary thought in the late eighteenth and early nineteenth centuries. Avineri (1968) and McLellan (1986) provide very good introductions to all aspects of Marx's political ideas, while Deutscher (1966), Adamson (1980), McLellan (1979), Lees (2015) and Wright (2015) consider aspects of the Marxist revolutionary tradition. Revolutionary anarchism is discussed in Cahm (1989); on revolutionary ideas in Africa, with particular reference to Fanon, see Jindaus (1986) and Guégan (2015).

Chapter 15: *Theories of Civil Disobedience and Non-Violent Resistance.* Harris (1989) provides a useful introductory historical and philosophical essay on civil disobedience, together with a range of primary texts. Rosenblum (1996) introduces

Thoreau's political ideas, including those on civil disobedience, while Parekh (1989) examines Gandhi's ideas and offers an evaluation of them. See Ansbro (1983) for an account of King's ideas.

Epilogue. On aspects of post-modernism see Connolly (1988), White (1991), Rengger (1992) and Bennett (2006) and on post-colonialism see Ivison (1997), Gilroy (2008) and Kohn (2017).

BIBLIOGRAPHY

The bibliography contains the primary and secondary works referred to in the main body of the text and other useful references. Primary works are listed by original author even when they appear in anthologies or selections. The dates given here are of the editions consulted; the original date of publication and/or composition are noted in the chronological charts (see pp. 4–7, 9–11).

Primary works

Anon (1991) To the Assembly of the Common Peasantry 1525, in Michael Baylor (ed.) *The Radical Reformation* (Cambridge: Cambridge University Press).

Aquinas, St Thomas (1959) *Selected Political Writings*, ed. A. P. D'Entreves, trans. J. G. Dawson (Oxford: Basil Blackwell).

Aristotle (1958) *The Politics*, ed. and trans. Ernest Barker (Oxford: Clarendon Press).

Aristotle (1975) *Ethica Nicomachea*, ed. and trans. W. D. Ross (Oxford: Oxford University Press).

Augustine (1972) *City of God,* ed. David Knowles (Harmondsworth: Penguin).

Augustine (2001) *Political Writings*, ed. E. M. Atkins and Robert Dodaro (Cambridge: Cambridge University Press).

Austin, John (1995) *The Province of Jurisprudence Determined*, ed. Wilfred E. Rumble (Cambridge: Cambridge University Press).

Babeuf, François-Noel (1972) *The Defence of Gracchus Babeuf*, ed. and trans. John Anthony Scott (New York: Schocken Books).

Bakunin, Michael (1970) *God and the State*, ed. Paul Avrich (New York: Dover).

Bakunin, Michael (1973) *Selected Writings*, ed. Arthur Lehning (London: Jonathan Cape).

Bakunin, Michael (1990) *Statism and Anarchy*, ed. and trans. Marshall S. Shatz (Cambridge: Cambridge University Press).

Beccaria, Cesare (1995) *On Crimes and Punishments and Other Writings*, ed. Richard Bellamy, trans. Richard Davis (Cambridge: Cambridge University Press).

Bentham, Jeremy (1843a) 'Anarchical Fallacies', 'Principles of International Law' in John Bowring (ed.) *The Works of Jeremy Bentham*, 10 vols (Edinburgh: William Tait), vol. 2.

Bentham, Jeremy (1843b) 'Constitutional Code', in John Bowring (ed.) *The Works of Jeremy Bentham*, 10 vols (Edinburgh: William Tait), vol. 9.

Bentham, Jeremy (1952–54) *Economic Writings*, 3 vols (London: Allen & Unwin).

Bentham, Jeremy (1967) *A Fragment on Government with an Introduction to the Principles of Morals and Legislation*, ed. Wilfred Harrison (Oxford: Basil Blackwell).

Bentham, Jeremy (1995) *Colonies, Commerce and Constitutional Law*, ed. Philip Schofield, *Collected Works of Jeremy Bentham* (Oxford: Clarendon Press).

Bernstein, Eduard (1972) *Evolutionary Socialism*, trans. Edith C. Harvey (New York: Schocken Books).

Beza, Theodore (1969) The Right of Magistrates, in J. H. Franklin (ed. and trans.), *Constitutionalism and Resistance in the Sixteenth Century: Three Treatises by Hotman, Beza & Mornay* (New York: Pegasus).

Bodin, Jean (n.d.) *Six Books of the Commonwealth*, ed. and trans. M. J. Tooley (Oxford: Basil Blackwell).

Bodin, Jean (1992) *On Sovereignty. Four chapters from The Six Books of the Commonwealth*, ed. and trans. Julian H. Franklin (Cambridge: Cambridge University Press).

Bosanquet, Bernard (1899) *The Philosophical Theory of the State* (London: Macmillan).

Bossuet, Jacques-Bénigne (1990) *Politics Drawn from the Very Words of Holy Scripture*, ed. and trans. Patrick Riley (Cambridge: Cambridge University Press).

Burke, Edmund (1834) *Works*, 2 vols (London: Holdsworth & Bell).

Burke, Edmund (1969) *Reflections on the Revolution in France*, ed. C. C. O'Brien (Harmondsworth: Penguin).

Calvin, Jean (1950) *Institutes of the Christian Religion*, ed. John T. McNeill, trans. Ford Lewis Battles, 2 vols (Philadelphia, PA: The Westminster Press).

Calvin, Jean (1991) *De Politica Administrione*, in Harro Hopfl (ed.) *Luther and Calvin on Secular Authority* (Cambridge: Cambridge University Press).

Carlyle, Thomas (1980) *Selected Writings*, ed. Alan Shelston (Harmondsworth: Penguin).

Chateaubriand, François (1816) *Monarchy According to the Charter* (London: T. Davison).

Cicero (1970) *De Re Publica and De Legibus*, trans. C. W. Keyes (Cambridge, MA: Harvard University Press).

Cicero (1991) *On Duties*, ed. E. M. Atkins (Cambridge: Cambridge University Press).

Cobbett, William (n.d.) *Cobbett's Political Works*, 6 vols (London: John and James Cobbett).

Cole, G. D. H. (1935) *The Simple Case for Socialism* (London: Victor Gollancz).

Coleridge, S. T. (1990) *Coleridge's Writings. Volume I: On Politics and Society*, ed. John Morrow (London: Macmillan).

Condorcet, Antoine-Nicolas de (1955) *Sketch for a Historical Picture of the Progress of the Human Mind*, trans. June Barraclough, ed. Stuart Hampshire (London: Weidenfeld & Nicolson).

Constant, Benjamin (1988) *Political Writings*, ed. and trans. Biancamaria Fontana (Cambridge: Cambridge University Press).

Diderot, Denis (1992) *Political Writings*, ed. and trans. John Hope Mason and Robert Wokler (Cambridge: Cambridge University Press).

Douglass, Frederick (1996) *The Oxford Douglass Reader*, ed. William L. Andrews (New York: Oxford University Press).

Douglass, Frederick (2000) *Selected Speeches*, ed. Philip S. Foner and Yuval Taylor (Chicago, IL: Chicago Review Press).

Douglass, Frederick (2013) *Great Speeches by Frederick Douglass*, ed. James Daley (New York: Dover).

Du Bois, W. E. B. (1920) *Darkwater. Voices from Within the Veil* (New York: Harcourt, Brace and Howe).

Du Bois, W. E. B. (1966) *Black Reconstruction in America* [1934] (London: Frank Cass).

Du Bois, W. E. B. (1986) *Writings* (New York: Library of America).

Du Bois, W. E. B. (1989) *The Souls of Black People* [1903] (London: Penguin Bks).

Fanon, Frantz (1967) *The Wretched of the Earth*, trans. Constance Farrington (Harmondsworth: Penguin).

Fanon, Frantz (1970a) *A Dying Colonialism*, trans. Haakon Chevalier (Harmondsworth: Penguin).

Fanon, Frantz (1970b) *Toward the African Revolution*, trans. Haakon Chevalier (Harmondsworth: Penguin).

Filmer, Sir Robert (1949) *Patriarcha … and Other Political Works*, ed. Peter Laslett (Oxford: Basil Blackwell).

Galston, William A. (1992) 'Introduction', in J. W. Chapman and William A. Galston (eds) *Virtue, Nomos,* vol. 34 (New York: New York University Press), pp. 1–23.

Gandhi, Mahatma (1986) *The Moral and Political Writings of Mahatma Gandhi*, 3 vols, ed. Raghava Iyer (Oxford: Clarendon Press).

Gewirth, Alan (1981) 'The Basis and Content of Human Rights', in J. Roland Pennock and John W. Chapman (eds) *Human Rights, Nomos XXIII* (New York: New York University Press), pp. 119–47.

Godwin, William (1969) *An Enquiry Concerning Political Justice,* 3 vols, ed. F. E. L. Priestley (Toronto: University of Toronto Press).

Goldman, Emma (1911) 'Anarchism: What It Really Stands For', in Emma Goldman (ed.) *Anarchism and Other Essays*, 2nd edn (New York: Mother Earth), pp. 53–73.

Goodin, Robert E. (1995) *Utilitarianism as a Public Philosophy* (Cambridge: Cambridge University Press).

Gouges, Olympe de (2011) The Rights of Women, in John R. Cole *Between the Queen and the Cabby. Olympe de Gouge's Rights of Women* (Montreal & Kingston: McGill-Queen's University Press), pp. 27–42.

Gramsci, Antonio (1971) *Selections from the Prison Notebooks*, ed. and trans. Quinton Hoare and Geoffrey Nowell Smith (London: Lawrence & Wishart).

Green, T. H. (1986) *Lectures on the Principles of Political Obligation and Other Political Writings*, eds Paul Harris and John Morrow (Cambridge: Cambridge University Press).

Grotius, Hugo (1738) *The Rights of War and Peace in Three Books* (London: W. Innys).

Guicciardini, Francesco (1994) *Dialogue on the Government of Florence*, ed. and trans. Alison Brown (Cambridge: Cambridge University Press).

Gutmann, Amy (1992) 'Communitarian Critics of Liberalism', in Shlomo Avineri and Avner De-Shalit (eds) *Communitarianism and Individualism* (Oxford: Oxford University Press), pp. 120–37.

Hamilton, Alexander, John Jay and James Madison (1942) *The Federalist* (London: J. M. Dent).

Hampshire, Stuart (1978) 'Morality and Pessimism', in Stuart Hampshire (ed.) *Public and Private Morality* (Cambridge: Cambridge University Press), pp. 1–22.

Harrington, James (1992) *The Commonwealth of Oceana and A System of Politics*, ed. J. G. A. Pocock (Cambridge: Cambridge University Press).

Hayek, Friedrich A. (1960) *The Constitution of Liberty* (Chicago, IL: University of Chicago Press).

Hayek, Friedrich A. (1982) *Law, Liberty and Legislation*, 3 vols (London: Routledge).

Hazlitt, William (1819) *Political Essays* (London: William Hone).

Hegel, G. W. F. (1991) *Elements of the Philosophy of Right*, ed. Allen W. Wood, trans. H. B. Nisbet (Cambridge: Cambridge University Press).

Henkin, Louis (1981) 'International Human Rights as "Rights"', in Roland J. Pennock and John W. Chapman (eds) *Human Rights, Nomos XXIII* (New York: New York University Press), pp. 257–80.

Hitler, Adolf (1969) *Mein Kampf*, trans. Ralph Manheim (London: Hutchinson).

Hobbes, Thomas (1960) *Leviathan, or the Matter, Forme, Power of a Commonwealth Ecclesiastical and Civil*, ed. Michael Oakeshott (Oxford: Basil Blackwell).

Hobbes, Thomas (1983) *De Cive*, ed. Howard Warrender (Oxford: Oxford University Press).

Hobhouse, L. T. (1909) *Democracy and Reaction*, 2nd edn (London: T. Fisher Unwin).

Hobhouse, L. T. (1990) *Liberalism and Other Writings*, ed. James Meadowcroft (Cambridge: Cambridge University Press).

Hooker, Richard (1989) *Of the Laws of Ecclesiastical Polity*, ed. Arthur Stephen McGrade (Cambridge: Cambridge University Press).

Hopfl, Harro, ed. (1991) *Luther and Calvin on Secular Authority* (Cambridge: Cambridge University Press).

Hotman, François (1972) *Francogallia*, trans. J. H. M. Salmon (Cambridge: Cambridge University Press).

Hume, David (1962) *Moral and Political Philosophy*, ed. Henry D. Aiken (New York: Hafner).

Hume, David (1987) *Essays. Moral, Political and Literary*, ed. Eugene F. Miller (Indianapolis, IA: Liberty Press).

Hume, David (1994) *Political Essays*, ed. Knud Haakonssen (Cambridge: Cambridge University Press).

Huxley, T. H. (n.d.) 'Struggle for Existence', in Peter Kropotkin (ed.) *Mutual Aid* (Boston, MA: Extending Horizon Books).

Ingram, Attracta (1994) *A Political Theory of Rights* (Oxford: Clarendon Press).

John of Salisbury (1990) *Policraticus*, ed. Cary J. Nederman (Cambridge: Cambridge University Press).

Kant, Immanuel (1971) *Political Writings*, ed. Hans Reiss, trans. H. B. Nisbet (Cambridge: Cambridge University Press).

Kant, Immanuel (1972) *Groundwork of the Metaphysic of Morals*, trans. H. J. Paton (London: Hutchinson).

Kant, Immanuel (1975) 'Conjectural Beginning of Human History', in Lewis White Becker (ed.) *Kant: On History* (Indianapolis, IN: Bobbs-Merrill).

Kant, Immanuel (1996) *Practical Philosophy*, ed. and trans. Mary J. Gregor (Cambridge: Cambridge University Press).

Kautsky, Karl (1971) *The Class Struggle*, ed. Robert C. Tucker, trans. William E. Bohn (New York: W. W. Norton).

Kautsky, Karl (1983) *Selected Political Writings*, ed. and trans. Patrick Goode (London: Macmillan).

King, Martin Luther (1989) 'Letter from Birmingham Jail', in Paul Harris (ed.) *Civil Disobedience* (Latham, MD: University Press of America).

Kropotkin, Peter (1903) *The State: Its Historic Role* (London: Freedom Press).

Kropotkin, Peter (1970) *Revolutionary Pamphlets*, ed. Roger N. Baldwin (New York: Dover).

Kropotkin, Peter (1971) *In French and Russian Prisons* (New York: Shocken Books).

Kropotkin, Peter (n.d.) *Mutual Aid* (Boston, MA: Extending Horizon Books).

Kymlicka, Will (1992) 'Liberal Individualism and Liberal Neutrality', in Shlomo Avineri and Avner De-Shalit (eds) *Communitarianism and Individualism* (Oxford: Oxford University Press), pp. 165–85.

Kymlicka, Will (1995) *Multicultural Citizenship: A Liberal Theory of Minority Rights* (Oxford: Oxford University Press).

Lenin, V. I. (1971) *Selected Works* (Moscow: Progress Publishers).

Lenin, V. I. (1975) *Selected Writings*, 3 vols (Moscow: Progress Publishers).

Locke, John (1967) *Two Treatises of Government*, ed. Peter Laslett (Cambridge: Cambridge University Press).

Loyseau, Charles (1994) *A Treatise of Orders and Plain Dignities*, ed. and trans. Howell A. Lloyd (Cambridge: Cambridge University Press).

Luxemburg, Rosa (1971) 'What does the Spartacus League Want?', in Dick Howard (ed.) *Selected Political Writings of Rosa Luxemburg* (New York: Monthly Review Press).

Macaulay, T. B. (1984) 'Mill's Essay on Government: Utilitarian Logic and Politics', in Jack Lively and John Rees (eds) *Utilitarian Logic and Politics* (Oxford: Clarendon Press), pp. 97–130.

Macedo, Stephen (1992) 'Charting Liberal Virtues', in J. W. Chapman and William Galston (eds) *Virtue, Nomos,* vol. 34 (New York: New York University Press), pp. 204–33.

Machiavelli, Niccoló (1988) *The Prince*, eds Quentin Skinner and Russell Price (Cambridge: Cambridge University Press).

Maistre, Joseph de (1965) *The Works of Joseph de Maistre*, ed. and trans. Jack Lively (New York: Macmillan).

Mao Tse-tung (1957) *On the Correct Handling of Contradictions Among the People* (Peking: Foreign Languages Press).

Mao Tse-tung (1967) *Selected Military Writings* (Peking: Foreign Languages Press).

Marsilius of Padua (1956) *The Defender of the Peace,* 2 vols, trans. Alan Gewirth (New York: Columbia University Press).

Marx, Karl (1973) *The Revolutions of 1848*, ed. David Fernbach (Harmondsworth: Penguin).

Marx, Karl (1975) *Early Writings*, ed. Lucio Colletti, trans. Rodney Livingstone and Gregor Benton (Harmondsworth: Penguin).

Marx, Karl and Friedrich Engels (1968) *The German Ideology*, ed. R. Pascal (New York: International Publishers).

Marx, Karl and Friedrich Engels (1973) *Selected Works,* 3 vols (Moscow: Progress Publishers).

Maurras, Charles (1971a) 'Dictator and King', in J. S. McClelland (ed.) *The French Right from de Maistre to Maurras* (London: Jonathan Cape), pp. 215–380.

Maurras, Charles (1971b) 'Romanticism and Revolution', in J. S. McClelland (ed.) *The French Right from de Maistre to Maurras* (London: Jonathan Cape), pp. 239–63.

Mill, James (1984) 'Essay on Government', in Jack Lively and John Rees (eds) *Utilitarian Logic and Politics* (Oxford: Clarendon Press), pp. 53–130.

Mill, John Stuart (1983) *Utilitarianism, On Liberty and Considerations on Representative Government*, ed. H. B. Acton (London: Dent).

Mill, John Stuart (1859) *On Liberty, with the Subjection of Women and Chapters on Socialism*, ed. Stefan Collini (Cambridge: Cambridge University Press).

Mill, John Stuart (1850) 'The Negro Question', *Fraser's Magazine*, 45, 25–31.

Millett, Kate (1970) *Sexual Politics* (Garden City, NY: Doubleday).

Montesquieu, Charles-Louis (1949) *The Spirit of the Laws,* 2 vols, trans. Thomas Nugent (New York: Hafner).

Montesquieu, Charles-Louis (1977) *The Political Theory of Montesquieu*, ed. Melvin Richter (Cambridge: Cambridge University Press).

Mornay, Phillipe (1969) *Vindiciae contra tyrannos*, ed. and trans. J. F. Franklin, *Constitutionalism and Resistance in the Sixteenth Century: Three Treatises by Hotman, Beza & Mornay* (New York: Pegasus).

Mosca, Gaetano (1939) *The Ruling Class*, trans. Hannah D. Kahn (New York: McGraw-Hill).

Müller, Adam (1955) 'Elements of Politics', in H. S. Reiss (ed.) *Political Thought of German Romantics* (Oxford: Basil Blackwell).

Mussolini, Benito (1935) 'The Doctrine of Fascism', in Benito Mussolini (ed.) *Fascism: Doctrines and Institutions* (Rome: Ardita).

Nietzsche, Friedrich (1967) *Beyond Good and Evil*, trans. Marianne Cowan (Chicago, IL: Henry Regnery).

Nietzsche, Friedrich (1968) *The Will to Power*, trans. Walter Kaufmann and R. J. Hollingdale (New York: Vintage Books).

Novalis (1996) Faith and Love, in Frederick C. Beiser (ed. and trans.), *The Early Political Writings of the German Romantics* (Cambridge: Cambridge University Press).

Nozick, Robert (1974) *Anarchy, State, and Utopia* (Oxford: Basil Blackwell).

Otis, James (1766) *The Rights of the British Colonies Asserted and Proved* (London: J Williams).

Owen, Robert (1991) *A New View of Society and Other Writings*, ed. Gregory Claeys (Harmondsworth: Penguin).

Paine, Thomas (1976) *The Rights of Man*, ed. Henry Collins (Harmondsworth: Penguin).

Paley, William (1803) *The Principles of Moral and Political Philosophy,* 2 vols, 14th edn (London: R. Faulder).

Pareto, Vifredo (1966) *Sociological Writings*, ed. S. E. Finer, trans. Derick Mirfin (London: Pall Mall Press).

Pateman, Carole (1970) *Participation & Democratic Theory* (Cambridge: Cambridge University Press).

Phillips, Anne (1991) *Engendering Democracy* (Cambridge: Polity Press).

Pizan Christine de (1982) *The Book of the City of the Ladies* (New York: Persea Books).

Pizan, Christine de (1994) *The Book of the Body Politic*, ed. and trans. Kate Langdon Forham (Cambridge: Cambridge University Press).

Plato (1960) *The Gorgias*, trans. Walter Hamilton (Harmondsworth: Penguin).

Plato (1970) *The Republic*, trans. M. D. P. Lee (Harmondsworth: Penguin).

Plato (1980) *The Laws*, trans. T. J. Saunders (Harmondsworth: Penguin).

Plato (1991) *Protagoras*, trans. C. C. W. Taylor, revised edn (Oxford: Clarendon Press).

Plato (1994) *Republic*, trans Robin Waterfield (Oxford: Oxford University Press).

Polybius (1979) *The Rise of the Roman Empire*, ed. F. W. Walbank, trans. Ian Scott-Kilvert (Harmondsworth: Penguin).

Proudhon, P.-J. (1923) *General Idea of the Revolution in the Nineteenth Century*, trans. John Beverley Robinson (London: Freedom Press).

Proudhon, P.-J. (1979) *The Principle of Federation*, trans. Richard Vernon (Toronto: University of Toronto Press).

Pufendorf, Samuel (1927) *The Two Books on the Duty of Man and Citizen According to the Natural Law*, trans. Frank Gardner Moore (New York: Oxford University Press).

Pufendorf, Samuel (1934) *On the Law of Nature and Nations, Eight Books*, trans. C. H. Oldfather and W. A. Oldfather (Oxford: Clarendon Press).

Pufendorf, Samuel (1991) *On the Duty of Man and Citizen*, ed. James Tully, trans. Michael Silverthorne (Cambridge: Cambridge University Press).

Rawls, John (1973) *A Theory of Justice* (Oxford: Oxford University Press).

Ritchie, D. G. (1894) *Natural Rights* (London: Allen & Unwin).

Ritchie, D. G. (1902) *Studies in Social and Political Ethics* (London: Swan Sonnenschein).

Rosenberg, Alfred (1971) *Selected Writings*, ed. Robert Pois (London: Jonathan Cape).

Rousseau, Jean-Jacques (1987) *The Basic Political Writings*, trans. Donald A. Cress (Indianapolis, IN: Hackett).

Rousseau, Jean-Jacques (2005a) 'Abstract of Monsieur the Abbé de Saint-Pierre's Plan for Perpetual Peace', in Jean-Jacques Rousseau (ed.) *The Plan for Perpetual Peace, On the Government of Poland, and Other Writings on History and Politics, The Collected Writings of Rousseau*, vol 11, ed. Christopher Kelly, trans. Christopher Kelly and Judith Bush (Hanover, NH: Dartmouth College Press), pp. 27–49.

Rousseau, Jean-Jacques (2005b) 'Polysnody By the Abbé de Saint Pierre', in Jean-Jacques Rousseau (ed.) *The Plan for Perpetual Peace, on the Government of Poland, and Other Writings on History and Politics, The Collected Writings of Rousseau*, vol 11, ed. Christopher Kelly, trans. Christopher Kelly and Judith Bush (Hanover, NH: Dartmouth College Press), pp. 77–99.

Said, Edward (2003) *Orientalism [1978]* (London: Penguin).

Saint-Pierre, Charles (1714) *A Project for Settling an Everlasting Peace in Europe* (London: J Watts).

Sandel, Michael (1992) 'The Procedural Republic and the Unencumbered Self', in Shlomo Avineri and Avner De-Shalit (eds) *Communitarianism and Individualism* (Oxford: Oxford University Press), pp. 12–28.

Sattler, Michael (1991) *The Schleitheim Articles*, in Michael B. Baylor (ed.) *The Radical Reformation* (Cambridge: Cambridge University Press), pp. 172–80.

Schlegel, F. (1964) *Die Entwicklung Der Philosophie In Zwolf Buchern*, in *Philoso-phische Vorlesungen* (ed.) Jean-Jacques Ansttett, *Kritsche Friedrich-Schlegel-Ausgabe*, vol. 13 (Munich: F. Schoningh).

Schumpeter, Joseph, A. (1954) *Capitalism, Socialism, and Democracy* (London: George Allen & Unwin).

Seyssel, Claude de (1981) *The Monarchy of France*, ed. Donald A. Kelly, trans. J. H. Hexter (New Haven, CT: Yale University Press).

Sidgwick, Henry (1891) *The Elements of Politics* (London: Macmillan).

Sièyes, Emanuel Joseph (1963) *What is the Third Estate?*, ed. S. E. Finer, trans. M. Blondel (London: Pall Mall Press).

Siltanen, Janet and Michelle Stanworth (1984) 'The Politics of Private Woman and Public Man', in Janet Siltanen and Michelle Stanworth (eds) *Women and the Public Sphere* (London: Hutchinson), pp. 185–208.

Stalin, Joseph (1934) *Leninism*, 2 vols (Moscow and Leningrad: Co-operative Publishing Society).

Stirner, Max (1995) *The Ego and Its Own*, ed. David Leopold (Cambridge: Cambridge University Press).

Suàrez, Francisco (1856–78) *De Opere Sex Dierum, in Suàrez, Opera Omnia*, 27 vols, ed. Carolus Berton (Paris: Apud Ludovicum Vives), vol. iii.

Taylor, Charles (1992) 'Atomism', in Shlomo Avineri and Avner De-Shalit (eds) *Communitarianism and Individualism* (Oxford: Oxford University Press), pp. 29–50.

Taylor, Harriet (1993) *The Enfranchisement of Women*, in Marie Mulvey Roberts and Tamae Mizuta (eds) *The Disenfranchised. The Fight for the Suffrage* (London, Routledge/Thoemmes Press; Tokyo: Kinokuniya).

Thompson, Willam and Anna Wheeler (1970) *Appeal of One Half of The Human Race, Women, Against the Pretensions of the Other Half, Men*, in Marie Mulvey Roberts and Tamae Mizuta (eds) *The Reformers. Socialist Feminism* (New York: Burt Franklin).

Thompson, Willam and Anna Wheeler (1993) *Appeal of One Half of The Human Race, Women, Against the Pretensions of the Other Half, Men*, in Marie Mulvey Roberts and Tamae Mizuta (eds) *The Reformers. Socialist Feminism* (London: Routledge/Thoemmes Press; Tokyo: Kinokuniya).

Thoreau, Henry D. (1992) *Walden and Resistance to Civil Government*, ed. William Rossi (New York: W. W. Norton).

Thoreau, Henry D. (1996) *Political Writings*, ed. Nancy L. Rosenblum (Cambridge: Cambridge University Press).

Tocqueville, Alexis de (1945) *Democracy in America*, 2 vols, trans. Henry Reeve (New York: Vintage Books).

Trotsky, Leon (1969) *The Permanent Revolution and Results and Prospects*, 3rd edn (New York: Labour Publications).

Tucker, Benjamin (1970) 'State Socialism and Libertarianism', in Irving L. Horowitz (ed.) *The Anarchists* (New York: Dell), pp. 169–82.

Walzer, Michael (1992) 'Membership', in Shlomo Avineri and Avner De-Shalit (eds) *Communitarianism and Individualism* (Oxford: Oxford University Press), pp. 65–84.

Warren, Josiah (1970) 'True Civilisation and Personal Liberty', in Irving L. Horowitz (ed.) *The Anarchists* (New York: Dell), pp. 321–9.

Webb, Beatrice (1948) *Our Partnership* (London: Longman).

Webb, Sidney (1889) 'Historic', in G. Bernard Shaw (ed.) *Fabian Essays in Socialism* (London: The Fabian Society), pp. 30–61.

Weber, Max (1994) *Political Writings*, eds Peter Lassman and Ronald Spiers (Cambridge: Cambridge University Press).

William of Ockham (1992) *A Short Discourse on the Tyrannical Government of Things Divine and Human, but Especially over the Empire*, ed. A. S. McGrade, trans. John Killkullen (Cambridge: Cambridge University Press).

Wollstonecraft, Mary (1790) *A Vindication of the Rights of Men* (London: J. Johnson).

Wollstonecraft, Mary (1983) *A Vindication of the Rights of Women*, ed. Miriam Brody (Harmondsworth: Penguin).

Wollstonecraft, Mary (1995) *A Vindication of the Rights of Men and A Vindication of the Rights of Women*, ed. Sylvana Tomaselli (Cambridge: Cambridge University Press).

Woodhouse, A. S. P. (ed.) (1951) *Puritanism and Liberty* (London: Dent).

Young, Iris Marion (1990a) *Justice and the Politics of Difference* (Princeton, NJ: Princeton University Press).

Young, Iris Marion (1990b) 'Polity and Group Difference: A Critique of Universal Citizenship', in Cass R. Sunstein (ed.) *Feminism & Political Theory* (Chicago, IL: University of Chicago Press), pp. 117–42.

Zetkin, Clara (1984) *Selected Writings*, ed. Philip S. Foner (New York: International Publishers).

Secondary works

Abrahamian, Ervand (1988) 'Ali Shari'ati: Ideologue of the Iranian Revolution', in Edmund Burke III and Ira M. Lapidas (eds) *Islam Politics and Social Movements* (Berkeley, CA: University of California Press), pp. 289–97.

Adams, Tracy (2014) *Christian de Pizan and the fight for France* (University Park, PA: Pennsylvania University Press).

Adamson, W. L. (1980) *Hegemony and Revolution: A Study of Gramsci's Political and Cultural Theory* (Berkeley, CA: University of California Press).

Akhavi, Shahrough (1990) *Religion and Politics in Contemporary Iran* (Albany, NY: University of New York Press).

Allen, J. W. (1951) *A History of Political Thought in the Sixteenth Century* (London: Methuen).

Anderson, Olive (1991) 'The Feminism of T. H. Green: A Late Victorian Success Story?', *History of Political Thought*, 12, 671–694.

Annas, Julia (1981) *An Introduction to Plato's Republic* (Oxford: Clarendon Press).

Ansbro, John J. (1983) *Martin Luther King Jr: The Making of a Mind* (New York: Orbis Books).

Ansell-Pearson, Keith (1994) *An Introduction to Nietzsche as Political Thinker* (Cambridge: Cambridge University Press).

Atanassow, Ewa (2017) 'Tocqueville's New Liberalism', in Ewa Atanassow and Alan S. Kahan (eds) *Liberal Moments* (London: Bloomsbury), pp. 51–57.

Avilés, Maguel and Davis, J. C. (eds) (2012) *Utopian Moments* (London: Bloomsbury).

Avineri, Shlomo (1968) *The Social and Political Thought of Karl Marx* (Cambridge: Cambridge University Press).

Avineri, Shlomo (1972) *Hegel's Theory of the Modern State* (Cambridge: Cambridge University Press).

Avineri, Shlomo and Avner De-Shalit (eds) (1992) *Communitarianism and Individualism* (Oxford: Oxford University Press).

Avrich, Paul (1988) *Anarchist Portraits* (Princeton, NJ: Princeton University Press).

Baker, Keith Michael (1975) *Condorcet: From Natural Philosophy to Social Mathematics* (Chicago, IL: University of Chicago Press).

Balfour, Lawrie (2011) *Democracies Reconstruction* (New York: Oxford University Press).

Balfour, Lawrie (2010) 'Darkwaters' Democratic Vision', *Political Theory*, 38(4), 537–63.

Balot, Ryan K. and Tong, Zhichao (2018) 'The Puzzle of Leadership in Toquevellie's Democracy in America', in Xavier Márquez (ed.) *Democratic Moments* (London: Bloomsbury), pp.113–22.

Barker, Ernest (1959) *The Political Thought of Plato and Aristotle* (New York: Dover).

Barnes, Jonathan (ed.) (1995) *The Cambridge Companion to Aristotle* (Cambridge: Cambridge University Press).

Barrow, Robin (1991) *Utilitarianism: A Contemporary Statement* (Aldershot: Edward Elgar).

Barry, Norman (1979) *Hayek's Social and Economic Philosophy* (London: Macmillan).

Bathory, P. D. (1981) *Political Theory as Public Confession: The Social and Political Thought of Augustine of Hippo* (New Brunswick, NJ: Transaction Books).

Baumgold, Deborah (1988) *Hobbes' Political Theory* (Cambridge: Cambridge University Press).

Bax, Ernest Belfort (1911) *The Last Episode of the French Revolution* (London: Grant Richards).

Beale, Derek (2006) 'Philosophical Kingship and Enlightened Despotism', in Mark Goldie and Robert Wokler (eds) *The Cambridge History of Eighteenth-Century Political Thought* (Cambridge: Cambridge University Press), pp. 497–524.

Beetham, David (1991) *The Legitimation of Power* (London: Macmillan).

Bell, Duncan (2016) *Reordering the World: Essays on Liberalism and Empire* (Princeton, NJ: Princeton University Press).

Beiser, F. C. (1996) 'Introduction', *The Early Political Thought of the German Romantics*, ed. and trans. F. C. Beiser (Cambridge: Cambridge University Press).

Beiser, F. C. (2003) *Romantic Imperative: The Concept of Early German Romanticism* (Cambridge, MA: Harvard University Press).

Beiser, F. C. (ed.) (1993) *The Cambridge Companion to Hegel* (Cambridge: Cambridge University Press).

Beiser, Frederick C. (1992) *Enlightenment, Revolution & Romanticism. The Genesis of Modern German Thought* (Cambridge, MA: Harvard University Press).

Bennett, Jane (2006) 'Modernity and its Critics', in John Dryzek, Bonnie Honig and Anne Phillips (eds) *The Oxford Handbook of Political Theory* (Oxford: Oxford University Press), pp. 211–24.

Berki, R. N. (1977) *A History of Political Thought: A Short Introduction* (London: Dent).

Bernstein, Samuel (1972) *Auguste Blanqui and the Art of Insurrection* (London: Lawrence & Wishart).

Bhabba, Homi (1994) *The Location of Culture* (London: Routledge).

Black, Anthony (1992) *Political Thought in Europe 1250–1450* (Cambridge: Cambridge University Press).

Blight, David W. (2018) *Frederick Douglass. Prophet of Freedom* (New York: Simon and Schuster).

Bondurant, Joan V. (1965) *Conquest of Violence. The Gandhian Philosophy of Conflict*, 2nd edn (Berkeley, CA: University of California Press).

Bottomore, T. B. (1966) *Elites and Society* (Harmondsworth: Penguin).

Boucher, David (1998) *Political Theories of International Relations* (Oxford: Oxford University Press).

Brooker, Paul (1985) 'The Nazi *Fuehrerprinzip*: A Weberian Analysis', *Political Science*, 37(1), 50–71.

Brooker, Paul (1991) *The Faces of Fraternalism: Nazi Germany, Fascist Italy and Imperial Japan* (Oxford: Clarendon Press).

Brown, Chris, Nardin, Terry and Rengger, N. (2002) *International Relations in Political Thought: Texts from the Ancient Greeks to the First World War* (Cambridge: Cambridge University Press).

Bruce, Susan and Smits, Katherine (eds) (2016) *Feminist Moments* (London: Bloomsbury).

Burgess, Glen (1992) *The Politics of the Ancient Constitution. An Introduction to English Political Theory, 1603–1642* (London: Macmillan).

Burgess, Glen (2013) 'Bodin in the English Revoution', in Howell A. Lloyd ed. *The Reception of Bodin* (Leyden: Brill), pp. 387–408.

Burns, J. H. (ed.) (1991) *The Cambridge History of Medieval Political Thought c. 350–c.1450* (Cambridge: Cambridge University Press).

Burns, J. H. with Mark Goldie (eds) (1994) *The Cambridge History of Political Thought 1450–1700* (Cambridge: Cambridge University Press).

Cahm, C. (1989) *Kropotkin and the Rise of Revolutionary Anarchism* (Cambridge: Cambridge University Press).

Canning, J. P. (1991) 'Law, Sovereignty and Corporation Theory, 1300–1450', in Burns (ed.) *The Cambridge History of Medieval Political Thought*, pp. 454–77.

Capaldi, Nicholas (2017) 'John Stuart Mill', in Ewa Atanassow and Alan S. Kahan (eds) *Liberal Moments* (London: Bloomsbury), pp. 69–75.

Carroll, John (1974) *Break-out from the Crystal Palace: The Anarcho-psychological Critique; Stirner, Nietzsche, Dostoevsky* (London: Routledge).

Carver, Terrell (ed.) (1991) *The Cambridge Companion to Karl Marx* (Cambridge: Cambridge University Press).

Chapman, J. W. and Galston, William (eds) (1992) *Virtue, Nomos,* vol. 34 (New York: New York University Press).

Chappell, V. C. (1994) *The Cambridge Companion to Locke* (Cambridge: Cambridge University Press).

Claeys, Gregory (1989a) *Citizens and Saints. Politics and Anti-politics in Early British Socialism* (Cambridge: Cambridge University Press).

Claeys, Gregory (1989b) *Thomas Paine* (Boston, MA: Unwin, Hyman).

Cohen, Joshua (1989) 'Deliberation and Democratic Deliberation', in Alan Hamlin and Philip Pettit (eds) *The Good Polity: Normative Analysis of the State* (Oxford: Basil Blackwell), pp. 17–34.

Cole, John R. (2011) *Between the Queen and the Cabby. Olympe de Gouge's Rights of Women* (Montreal & Kingston: McGill-Queen's University Press).

Coleman, Janet (2000a) *A History of Political Thought from Ancient Greece to Early Christianity* (Oxford: Basil Blackwell).

Coleman, Janet (2000b) *A History of Political Thought: From the Middle Ages to the Renaissance* (Oxford: Basil Blackwell).

Collini, Stefan (1977) 'Liberalism and the Legacy of Mill', *Historical Journal*, 20, 337–54.

Collini, Stefan (1979) *Liberalism and Sociology: L. T. Hobhouse and Political Argument in England, 1880–1914* (Cambridge: Cambridge University Press).

Connolly, William E. (1988) *Political Theory & Modernity* (Oxford: Basil Blackwell).

Coole, Diana H. (1988) *Women in Political Theory. From Ancient Misogyny to Contemporary Feminism* (Brighton: Wheatsheaf).

Copleston, F. C. (1975) *Aquinas* (Harmondsworth: Penguin).

Cross, R. C. and Woozley, A. D. (1971) *Plato's Republic: A Philosophical Commentary* (London: Macmillan).

Crowder, George (1991) *Classical Anarchism* (Oxford: Clarendon Press).

Crowder, George (2015) 'Revolution and Evolution: Kropotkin's Anarchism', in Rachel Hammersley (ed.) *Revolutionary Moments* (London: Bloomsbury).

Cullen, D. E. (1993) *Freedom in Rousseau's Political Philosophy* (DeKalb, IL: Northern Illinois University Press).

Cuttica, Cesare (2016) 'Filmer's Patriarcha (1680): Absolute Power, Political Patriarchalism and Patriotic Language', in Cesare Cuttica and Gaby Mahlberg (eds) *Patriarchal Moments* (London: Bloomsbury), pp. 65–72.

Cuttica, Cesare and Mahlberg, Gaby (eds) (2016) *Patriarchal Moments* (London: Bloomsbury).

Davis, J. C. (1994) 'Utopianism', in J. H. Burns with Mark Goldie (eds) *The Cambridge History of Political Thought, 1450–1700* (Cambridge: Cambridge University Press), pp. 329–46.

Davis, J. C. (1981) 'Pocock's Harrington: Grace, Nature and Art in the Classical Republicanism of James Harrington', *Historical Journal*, 24, 683–97.

Deane, Herbert (1963) *The Political and Social Ideas of Saint Augustine* (New York: Columbia University Press).

Detwiler, Bruce (1990) *Nietzsche and the Politics of Aristocratic Radicalism* (Chicago, IL: University of Chicago Press).

Deutscher, Isaac (1954) *The Prophet Armed: Trotsky, 1879–1921* (New York: Oxford University Press).

Deutscher, Isaac (1966) 'Maoism – its Origins and Outlook', in Isaac Deutscher (ed.) *Ironies of History: Essays on Contemporary Communism* (Oxford: Oxford University Press), pp. 88–120.

Dietz, Mary (ed.) (1990) *Thomas Hobbes and Political Theory* (Lawrence, KS: University of Kansas Press).

Dinwiddy, J. R. (1993) 'Early-Nineteenth-Century Reactions to Benthamism', in Bhikhu Parekh (ed.) *Jeremy Bentham: Critical Assessments* (London: Routledge) vol. 1, pp. 255–76.

Dollard, Catherine (2016) 'German Maternalist Socialism: Clara Zetkin and the 1896 Social Democratic Party Congress', in Susan Bruce and Katherine Smits (eds) (2016) *Feminist Moments* (London: Bloomsbury), pp. 91–98.

Donaldson, P. S. (1988) *Machiavelli and the Mystery of State* (Cambridge: Cambridge University Press).

Doody, John et al. (2005) *Augustine and Politics* (Lanham, MD: Lexington Books).

Drolet, Michael (2003) *Tocqueville, Democracy, and Social Reform* (New York: Palgrave Macmillan).

Dunbabin, Jean (1991) 'Government', in Burns (ed.) *The Cambridge History of Medieval Political Thought, c.350–c.1450* (Cambridge: Cambridge University Press), pp. 477–519.

Dunn, John (1984a) *The Politics of Socialism* (Cambridge: Cambridge University Press).

Dunn, John (1984b) *Locke* (Oxford: Oxford University Press).

Dunn, John (ed.) (1992) *Democracy. The Unfinished Journey, 508 BC to AD 1993* (Oxford: Oxford University Press).

Dwan, David and Insole, Christopher (eds) (2012) *The Cambridge Companion to Edward Burke* (Cambridge: Cambridge University Press).

Dyck, Ian (ed.) (1988) *Citizen of the World: Essays on Thomas Paine* (New York: St Martin's Press).

Elster, Jon (1986) *An Introduction to Karl Marx* (Cambridge: Cambridge University Press).

Farrar, Cynthia (1992) 'Ancient Greek Political Theory as a Response to Democracy', in John Dunn (ed.) *Democracy. The Unfinished Journey,508 BC to AD 1993* (Oxford: Oxford University Press), pp. 17–40.

Ferejohn, John (2000) 'Instituting Deliberative Democracy', in Ian Shapiro and Stephen Macedo (eds) *Designing Democratic Institutions* (New York: New York University Press), pp. 75–104.

Fidler, David P. (1999) 'Desperately Clinging to Grotian and Kantian Sheep: Rousseau's Attempted Escape from the State of War', in Clark, Ian and Neuman, Iver B. (eds) *Classical Theories of International Relations* (Basingstoke: Macmillan), pp. 120–41.

Fiet, Mario (2018) 'Thomas Paine and Democratic Contempt', in Xavier Márquez (ed.) *Democratic Moments* (London: Bloomsbury), pp. 81–88.

Finnis, John (1980) *Natural Law and Natural Rights* (Oxford: Clarendon Press).

Finnis, John (1998) *Aquinas* (Oxford: Clarendon Press).

Fontana, Biancamaria (1992) 'Democracy and the French Revolution', in John Dunn (ed.) *Democracy. The Unfinished Journey, 508 BC to AD 1993* (Oxford: Oxford University Press), pp. 107–24.

Forbes, Duncan (1975) *Hume's Philosophical Politics* (Cambridge: Cambridge University Press).

Forsyth, Murray (1987) *Reason and Revolution. The Political Thought of the Abbé Sièyes* (Leicester: Leicester University Press).

Foxley, Rachel (2015) 'From Native Rights to Natural Equality: The Agreement of the People (1647)', in Rachel Hammersley (ed.) *Revolutionary Moments* (London: Bloomsbury), pp. 11–18.

Francis, Mark (1980) 'The Nineteenth-Century Theory of Sovereignty and Thomas Hobbes', *History of Political Thought*, 1, 517–40.

Francis, Mark and Morrow, John (1994) *A History of English Political Thought in the Nineteenth Century* (London: Duckworth).

Franklin, J. H. (ed. and trans.) (1969a) *Constitutionalism and Resistance in the Sixteenth Century: Three Treatises by Hotman, Beza & Mornay* (New York: Pegasus).

Franklin, J. H. (1969b) 'Introduction', in Franklin (ed.) *Constitutionalism and Resistance in the Sixteenth Century: Three Treatises by Hotman, Beza & Mornay* (New York: Pegasus).

Franklin, J. H. (1973) *Jean Bodin and the Rise of Absolutism* (Cambridge: Cambridge University Press).

Franklin, J. H. (1992) 'Introduction', in Jean Bodin *On Sovereignty. Four chapters from The Six Books of the Commonwealth*, ed. and trans. Julian H. Franklin (Cambridge: Cambridge University Press).

Franklin, J. H. (1994) 'Sovereignty and the mixed constitution: Bodin and his critics', in J. H. Burns with Mark Goldie (eds.) *The Cambridge History of Political Thought 1470–1700* (Cambridge: Cambridge University Press), pp. 299–328.

Fritz, Kurt von (1954) *The Theory of the Mixed Constitution in Antiquity* (New York: Columbia University Press).

Garnett, Mark (2018) 'Edmund Burke (1729–1997)', in Mark Garnett (ed.) *Conservative Moments* (London: Bloomsbury).

Garnett, Mark (ed.) (2018) *Conservative Moments* (London: Bloomsbury).

Gay, Peter (1953) *The Dilemma of Democratic Socialism: Edward Bernstein's Challenge to Marx* (New York: Columbia University Press).

Gewirth, Alan (1954) '*Introduction*', *Marsilius of Padua, The Defender of the Peace*, 2 vols, trans. Alan Gewirth (New York: Columbia University Press).

Gilby, Thomas (1958) *Principality and Polity: Aquinas and the Rise of State Theory in the West* (London: Longman).

Gilroy, Paul (2008) 'Multiculturalism and Post-colonial Theory', in Bonnie Honig and Anne Phillips (eds) *The Oxford Handbook of Political Theory* (Oxford: Oxford University Press).

Gooding-Williams, Robert (2009) *In the Shadow of Du Bois. Afro Modern Political Thought in America* (Cambridge, MA: Harvard University Press).

Grant, R. W. (1987) *John Locke's Liberalism* (Chicago, IL: University of Chicago Press).

Gray, John (1983) *Mill on Liberty: A Defence* (London: Routledge & Kegan Paul).

Gray, John (1984) *Hayek on Liberty* (Oxford: Basil Blackwell).

Green, Martin (1986) *The Origins of Nonviolence: Tolstoy and Gandhi in their Historical Setting* (University Park, PA: Pennsylvania University Press).

Guégan, Xavier (2015) 'Frantz Fanon's The Wretched of the Earth: Embodying Anti-Colonial Action', in Rachel Hammersley (ed.) *Revolutionary Moments* (London: Bloomsbury), pp. 165–74.

Gunn, J. A. W. (1983) *Beyond Liberty and Property. The Process of Self-Recognition in Eighteenth-Century Political Thought* (Kingston and Montreal: McGill-Queen's University Press).

Gutmann, Amy and Thompson, Dennis (1996) *Democracy and Disagreement* (Cambridge, MA: Harvard University Press).

Haakonssen, Knud (1981) *The Science of a Legislator: The Natural Jurisprudence of David Hume & Adam Smith* (Cambridge: Cambridge University Press).

Haakonssen, Knud (1985) 'Hugo Grotius and the History of Political Thought', *Political Theory*, 13, 239–65.

Haakonssen, Knud (1993) 'The Structure of Hume's Political Theory', in David Fate Norton (ed.) *The Cambridge Companion to Hume* (Cambridge: Cambridge University Press), pp. 182–221.

Halévy, Elie (1972) *The Growth of Philosophical Radicalism* (London: Faber).

Hall, Edith (2016) 'Citizens But Second Class: Women in Aristotle's Politics', in Cesare Cuttica and Gaby Mahlberg (eds) *Patriarchal Moments* (London: Bloomsbury), pp. 35–42.

Hammersley, Rachel (ed.) (2015) *Revolutionary Moments* (London: Bloomsbury).

Hampsher-Monk, Iain (1987) *The Political Philosophy of Edmund Burke* (London: Longman).

Hampsher-Monk, Iain (1992) *A History of Modern Political Thought. Major Political Thinkers from Hobbes to Marx* (Oxford: Basil Blackwell).

Hampsher-Monk, Iain (2014) 'Introduction', in Iain Hampsher-Monk (ed.) Edmund Burke, *Revolutionary Writings* (Cambridge: Cambridge University Press).

Hampson, Norman (1991) *Saint-Just* (Oxford: Basil Blackwell).

Hansen, Emmanuel (1977) *Frantz Fanon: Social and Political Thought* (Columbus, OH: Ohio State University Press).

Harding, Neil (1992) 'The Marxist Leninist Detour', in John Dunn (ed.) *Democracy. The Unfinished Journey, 508 BC to AD 1993* (Oxford: Oxford University Press), pp. 155–88.

Harris, Paul (ed.) (1989) *Civil Disobedience* (Latham, MD: University Press of America).

Hart, H. L. A. (1982) *Essays on Bentham. Jurisprudence and Political Theory* (Oxford: Clarendon Press).

Havelock, Eric A. (1964) *The Liberal Temper in Greek Politics* (New Haven, CT: Yale University Press).

Hillerbrand, Hans, J. (ed.) (1968) *The Protestant Reformation* (New York: Harper & Row).

Hont, Istvan (2015) *Politics and Commercial Society: Jean-Jacques Rousseau and Adam Smith* (Cambridge, MA: Harvard University Press).

Hoogensen, G. (2005) *International Relations, Security, and Jeremy Bentham* (London: Routledge).

Hopfl, Harro (1982) *The Christian Polity of John Calvin* (Cambridge: Cambridge University Press).

Hopfl, Harro (1991) 'Introduction', in Harro Hopfl (ed.) *Luther and Calvin on Secular Authority* (Cambridge: Cambridge University Press).

Horowitz, Irving, L. (1954) *Claude Helvetius: Philosopher of Democracy and Enlightenment* (New York: Paine-Whitman).

Horton, John (1992) *Political Obligation* (London: Macmillan).

Hume, L. J. (1993) 'Bentham as Social and Political Theorist', in Bhikhu Parekh (ed.) *Jeremy Bentham: Critical Assessments* (London: Routledge), vol. 3, pp. 482–500.

Hunt, Tristram (2009) *The Frock-coated Communist: The Revolutionary Life of Frederick Engels* (London: Allen Lane).

Ivison, Duncan (1997) 'Postcolonialism and Political Theory', in Andrew Vincent (ed.) *Political Theory: Tradition and Diversity* (Cambridge: Cambridge University Press), pp. 154–71.

Jinadu, L. A. (1986) *Fanon: In Search of the African Revolution* (London: KPI).

Jones, A. H. M. (1957) *Athenian Democracy* (Oxford: Basil Blackwell).

Jose, Jim (2016) 'Giving Voice to Feminist Political Theory: The Radical Discourse of Anna Doyle Wheeler and William Thompson' in Suan Bruce and Katherine Smits (eds) (2016) *Feminist Moments* (London: Bloomsbury), pp. 59–66.

Kautsky, John H. (1994) *Karl Kautsky: Marxism, Revolution and Democracy* (New Brunswick, NJ: Transaction Publishers).

Kemp, Geoff (ed.) (2015) *Censorship Moments* (London: Bloomsbury).

Keohane, Nannerl O. (1980) *Philosophy and the State in France: The Renaissance to the Enlightenment* (Princeton, NJ: Princeton University Press).

Keyt, David (1991) *A Companion to Aristotle's Politics* (Oxford: Basil Blackwell).

Khilnani, Sunil (1992) 'India's Democratic Career', in John Dunn (ed.) *Democracy. The Unfinished Journey, 508 BC to AD 1993* (Oxford: Oxford University Press), pp. 189–205.

Kierstead, James (2018) 'Protagoras' Cooperative Know-how', in Xavier Márquez (ed.) *Democratic Moments* (London: Bloomsbury), pp. 18–23.

King, Preston (1974) *The Ideology of Order: A Comparative Analysis of Jean Bodin and Thomas Hobbes* (London: George Allen & Unwin).

Kleingeld, Pauline (2006) 'Kant's Theory of Peace', in Peter Guyer (ed.) *The Cambridge Companion to Kant and Modern Philosophy* (Cambridge: Cambridge University Press), pp. 477–504.

Klosko, George (1986) *The Development of Plato's Political Theory* (London: Methuen).

Kohn, Margaret (2017) 'Colonialism', *Stanford Encyclopaedia of Philosophy* https://plato.stanford.edu/entries/colonialism/ accessed 18/07/2018.

Kraut, Richard (ed.) (1992) *The Cambridge Companion to Plato* (Cambridge: Cambridge University Press).

Krieger, Leonard (1972) *The German Idea of Freedom* (Chicago, IL: University of Chicago Press).

Kukathas, Chandran (1989) *Hayek and Modern Liberalism* (Oxford: Clarendon Press).

Lahidji, Abdol Karim (1988) 'Constitutionalism and Clerical Authority', in Said Amir Arjomand (ed.) *Authority and Political Culture in Shi'ism* (Albany, NY: State University of New York Press), pp. 133–58.

Laslett, Peter (1949) 'Introduction', in Sir Robert Filmer (ed.) *Patriarcha … and Other Political Works*, ed. Peter Laslett (Oxford: Basil Blackwell).

Lebrun, R. A. (1988) *Joseph de Maistre: An Intellectual Militant* (Kingston and Montreal: Queens-McGill University Press).

Lederman, S. (2016) 'Philosophy, Politics and Participatory Democracy in Hannah Arendt's Political Thought', *History of Political Thought,* 37(3), 480–508.

Lee, K. (1990) *The Legal-Rational State: A Comparison of Hobbes, Bentham and Kelsen* (Aldershot: Avebury).

Leese, Daniel (2015) 'Between Socialist Futures: Mao Zedong on the 'Ten Major Relationships', in Rachel Hammersley (ed.) *Revolutionary Moments* (London: Bloomsbury), pp. 159–66.

Leopold, David (1995) 'Introduction', in David Leopold (ed.) *Max Stirner, The Ego and Its Own* (Cambridge: Cambridge University Press).

Lewis, Ewart (1954) *Medieval Political Ideas*, 2 vols (London: Routledge & Kegan Paul).

Lichtheim, George (1968) *The Origins of Socialism* (London: Weidenfeld & Nicolson).

Lively, Jack and John Rees (eds) (1984) *Utilitarian Logic and Politics* (Oxford: Clarendon Press).

Lively, Jack (1965) *The Social and Political Thought of Alexis de Tocqueville* (Oxford: Clarendon Press).

Lloyd, Howel, A. (2017) *John Bodin, 'this pre-eminent man of France': An intellectual biography* (Oxford: Oxford University Press).

Lloyd, Howell A. (1994) 'Constitutionalism', in J. H. Burns with Mark Goldie (eds.) *The Cambridge History of Political Thought 1450–1700* (Cambridge: Cambridge University Press), pp. 254–97.

Lloyd, Vincent (2016) *Black Natural Law* (New York: Oxford University Press).

Lokke, Kari (2016) 'Radical Spirituality and Reason', in Susan Bruce and Kathy Smits (eds) *Mary Wollstonecraft's A Vindication of the Rights of Women Feminist Moments* (London: Bloomsbury), pp.51–58.

Lyons, David (1973) *In the Interests of the Governed. A Study of Bentham's Philosophy of Utility and Law* (Oxford: Clarendon Press).

Macpherson, C. B. (1965) *The Real World of Democracy* (Toronto: CBC).

Macpherson, C. B. (1977) *The Life and Times of Liberal-Democracy* (Oxford: Oxford University Press).

Macpherson, C. B. (1980) *Burke* (Oxford: Oxford University Press).

Maier, Charles S. (1992) 'Democracy Since the French Revolution', in John Dunn (ed.) *Democracy. The Unfinished Journey 508 BC to AD 1993* (Oxford: Oxford University Press), pp. 125–44.

Mansbridge, Jane J. (1980) *Beyond Adversary Democracy* (New York: Basic Books).

Markus, R. A. (1970) *Saeculum: History and Society in the Theology of Saint Augustine* (Cambridge: Cambridge University Press).

Markus, R. A. (1991) 'The Latin Fathers', in J. H. Burns (ed.) *The Cambridge History of Medieval Political Thought, c.350–c.1450* (Cambridge: Cambridge University Press), pp. 92–122.

Márquez, Xavier (2018a) 'Max Weber's Charismatic Democracy', in Xavier Márquez (ed.) *Democratic Moments* (London: Bloomsbury), pp. 145–52.

Márquez, Xavier (ed.) (2018b) *Democratic Moments* (London: Bloomsbury).

Masters, R. (1968) *The Political Philosophy of Rousseau* (Princeton, NJ: Princeton University Press).

McClelland, J. S. (1996) *A History of Western Political Theory* (London: Routledge).

McGrade, Arthur Stephen (1989), 'Introduction', in Richard Hooker, *Of the Laws of Ecclesiastical Polity*, ed. Arthur Stephen McGrade (Cambridge: Cambridge University Press), pp. xiii–xxxx.

McLellan, David (1979) *Marxism After Marx: An Introduction* (London: Macmillan).

McLellan, David (1986) *Karl Marx* (London: Fontana).

Miller, David (1981) *Hume's Political Thought* (Oxford: Clarendon Press).

Miller, David (1984) *Anarchism* (London: J. M. Dent).

Miller, Peter N. (1994) *Defining the Common Good. Empire, Religion and Philosophy in Eighteenth-Century Britain* (Cambridge: Cambridge University Press).

Monoson, Susan Sara (2000) *Plato's Democratic Entanglements: Athenian Politics and the Practice of Philosophy* (Princeton, NJ: Princeton University Press).

Morrow, John (2006) *Thomas Carlyle* (London: Continuum).

Morrow, John (2011) 'Romanticism and Political Thought in the Early Nineteenth Century', in Gareth Stedman Jones and Gregory Claeys (eds) *The Cambridge History of Nineteenth-Century Political Thought* (Cambridge: Cambridge University Press), pp. 39–76.

Morrow, John (2017) 'T. H. Green', in Ewa Atanassow and Alan S. Kahan (eds) *Liberal Moments* (London: Bloomsbury), pp. 83–90.

Mulgan, R. G. (1977) *Aristotle's Political Theory* (Oxford: Clarendon Press).

Mulgan, Tim (2007) *Understanding Utilitarianism* (Stocksfield: Acumen).

Murphy, Jeffrie G. (1970) *Kant: The Philosophy & Right* (London: Macmillan).

Nederman, Cary J. (1990) 'Introduction', *in John of Salisbury, Policraticus*, ed. Cary J. Nederman (Cambridge: Cambridge University Press).

Nelson, Janet (1991) 'Kingship and Empire', in J. H. Burns (ed.) *The Cambridge History of Political Thought, c.350–c.1700* (Cambridge: Cambridge University Press), pp. 211–50.

Neumann, F. (1944) *Behemoth: The Structure and Practice of National Socialism, 1933–1944* (London: Victor Gollancz).

Nicholson, Peter (1990) *The Political Philosophy of the British Idealists* (Cambridge: Cambridge University Press).

Nursey-Bray, Paul (1983) 'Consensus and Community: The Theory of African One-party Democracy', in Graeme Duncan (ed.) *Democratic Theory and Practice* (Cambridge: Cambridge University Press), pp. 96–114.

Okin, Susan Mollor (1992) *Women in Western Political Thought* (Princeton, NJ: Princeton University Press).

Omid, Homa (1994) *Islam and the Post-Revolutionary State in Iran* (London: Macmillan).

Orend, Brian (2000) *War and International Justice: A Kantian Perspective* (Waterloo: Wilfred Laurier University Press).

Parekh, Bhikhu (1989) *Gandhi's Political Philosophy. A Critical Examination* (London: Macmillan).

Parekh, Bhikhu (ed.) (1973) *Bentham's Political Thought* (London: Croom Helm).

Parekh, Bhikhu (ed.) (1993) *Jeremy Bentham: Critical Assessments*, 4 vols (London: Routledge).

Parry, Geraint (1970) *Political Elites* (London: George Allen & Unwin).

Paterson, R. W. K. (1971) *The Nihilistic Egoist: Max Stirner* (London: Hull University Press).

Pennington, K. (1991) 'Law, legislative authority and theories of government, 1150–1450', in J. H. Burns (ed.) *The Cambridge History of Medieval Political Thought c.350–c.1700* (Cambridge: Cambridge University Press), pp. 424–53.

Pennock, J. Roland (1981) 'Rights, Natural Rights, and Human Rights – A General Overview', in Pennock, J. and John W. Chapman (1981) *Human Rights, Nomos xxiii* (New York: New York University Press), pp. 1–28.

Pettit, Philip (1997) 'Republican Political Theory', in Andrew Vincent (ed.) *Political Theory: Tradition and Diversity* (Cambridge: Cambridge University Press), pp. 112–31.

Philip, John (2004) *Stalin* (London: Collins).

Philp, Mark (1986) *Godwin's Political Justice* (London: Duckworth).

Philp, Mark (1989) *Paine* (Oxford: Oxford University Press).

Pitts, Jennifer (2003) 'Legislator of the World? A Rereading of Bentham on Colonies', *Political Theory*, 31(2), 200–34.

Plamenatz, John (1963) *Man and Society: A Critical Examination of Some Important Social and Political Theories from Machiavelli to Marx*, 2 vols (London: Longmans).

Plummer, Alfred (1971) *Bronterre* (London: Allen & Unwin).

Pocock, J. G. A. (1957) *The Ancient Constitution and the Feudal Law* (Cambridge: Cambridge University Press).

Pocock, J. G. A. (1975) *The Machiavellian Moment* (Princeton, NJ: Princeton University Press).

Pocock, J. G. A. (1985) *Virtue, Commerce and History* (Cambridge: Cambridge University Press).

Quillet, Jeannine (1991) 'Community, Counsel and Representation', in J. H. Burns (ed.) *The Cambridge History of Medieval Political Thought c.350–c.1700* (Cambridge: Cambridge University Press), pp. 520–72.

Redhead, Brian (1984) *Political Thought from Plato to Nato* (London: Ariel).

Reed, Adolph (1997) *W. E. B. Du Bois and American Political Thought: Fabianism and the Color Line* (New York: Oxford University Press).

Reeve, C. D. C. (1988) *Philosopher-Kings: The Argument of Plato's Republic* (Princeton, NJ: Princeton University Press).

Reiss, Hans (1971), 'Introduction', in *Immanuel Kant, Political Writings*, ed. Hans Reiss, trans. H. B. Nisbet (Cambridge: Cambridge University Press).

Rengger, N. J. (1992) 'No Time Like the Present? Postmodernism and Political Theory', *Political Studies*, 40(3), 561–70.

Richter, Melvin (ed.) (1977) *The Political Theory of Montesquieu* (Cambridge: Cambridge University Press).

Rosen, Allan D. (1993a) *Kant's Theory of Justice* (Ithaca, NY: Cornell University Press).

Rosen, F. (1993b) 'Jeremy Bentham and Democratic Theory', in Bhikhu Parekh (ed.) *Jeremy Bentham: Critical Assessments* (London: Routledge), vol. 3, pp. 573–92.

Rosenblum, Nancy L. (1996) 'Introduction', in Henry D. Thoreau *Political Writings*, ed. Nancy L. Rosenblum (Cambridge: Cambridge University Press).

Rowen, Herbert H. (1980) *The King's State: Proprietary Dynasticism in Early Modern France* (New Brunswick, NJ: Rutgers University Press).

Rubinelli, Lucia (2018) 'Of Postmen and Democracy: Siéyes Theory of Representation', in Xavier Márquez (ed.) *Democratic Moments* (London: Bloomsbury), pp. 97–104.

Salvador, Massimo (1979) *Karl Kautsky and the Socialist Revolution, 1880–1938*, trans. Jon Rothschild (London: New Left Books).

Sartori, G. (1965) *Democratic Theory* (New York: Praeger).

Sassoon, Anne Showstack (1987) *Gramsci's Politics*, 2nd edn (London: Hutchinson).

Schneewind, J. B. (1977) *Sidgwick's Ethics and Victorian Moral Philosophy* (Oxford: Clarendon Press).

Schochet, Gordon J. (1975) *Patriarchalism in Political Thought: The Authoritarian Family and Political Speculation and Attitudes Especially in Seventeenth-Century England* (Oxford: Basil Blackwell).

Schofield, T. P. (1993) '"Economy as Applied to Office" and the Development of Bentham's Democratic Thought', in Bhikhu Parekh (ed.) *Jeremy Bentham: Critical Assessments* (London: Routledge), vol. 3, pp. 868–78.

Scholfield, Philip (2006) *Utility and Democracy: The Political Thought of Jeremy Bentham* (Oxford: Oxford University Press).

Schram, Stuart (1989) *The Thought of Mao Tse-Tung* (Cambridge: Cambridge University Press).

Scott, Jonathan (1988) *Algernon Sidney and the English Republic 1623–1677* (Cambridge: Cambridge University Press).

Shankman, Steven (ed.) (1994) *Plato and Postmodernism* (Glenside, PA: Aldine Press).

Shapiro, Ian (2003) *The Moral Foundations of Politics* (New Haven, CT: Yale University Press).

Shklar, J. N. (1969) *Men and Citizens: A Study of Rousseau's Social Theory* (Cambridge: Cambridge University Press).

Shulman, Alix Katz (1971) *To the Barricades: The Anarchist Life of Emma Goldman* (New York: Crowell).

Siedentop, Larry (1994) *Tocqueville* (Oxford: Oxford University Press).

Sigmund, Paul E. (1971) *Natural Law in Political Thought* (Cambridge, MA: Winthrop).

Simhony, Avital and Weinstein, David (eds) (2001) *The New Liberalism: Reconciling Liberty and Community* (Cambridge: Cambridge University Press).

Sinclair, R. K. (1988) *Democracy and Participation in Athens* (Cambridge: Cambridge University Press).

Singer, Peter (1980) *Marx* (Oxford: Oxford University Press).

Singer, Peter (1983) *Hegel* (Oxford: Oxford University Press).

Skinner, Quentin (1978) *The Foundations of Modern Political Thought*, 2 vols (Cambridge: Cambridge University Press).

Skinner, Quentin (1981) *Machiavelli* (Oxford: Oxford University Press).

Skinner, Quentin (1992) 'The Italian City Republics', in John Dunn (ed.) *Democracy. The Unfinished Journey, 508 BC to AD 1993* (Oxford: Oxford University Press), pp. 57–70.

Skinner, Quentin (1996) *Reason and Rhetoric in the Philosophy of Hobbes* (Cambridge: Cambridge University Press).

Skinner, Quentin et al. (1992) *Great Political Thinkers* (Oxford: Oxford University Press).

Smits, Katherine (2008) 'John Stuart Mill on the Antipodes: Settler Violence against Indigenous Peoples and the Legitimacy of Colonial Rule, *Australian Journal of Politics and History*, 54(1), 1–15.

Sonenscher, Michael (2015) 'Revolution, Reform and the Political Thought of Emmanuel-Joseph Sieyés', in Rachel Hammersley (ed.) *Revolutionary Moments* (London: Bloomsbury), pp. 67–76.

Spinner-Halev, Jeff (2006) 'Multiculturalism and Its Critics', in John Dryzek, Bonnie Honig and Anne Phillips (eds) *The Oxford Handbook of Political Theory* (Oxford: Oxford University Press), pp. 546–63.

Stedman Jones, Gareth (2017) *Karl Marx* (London: Allen Lane).

Storing, Herbert J. (1989) 'The Case Against Civil Disobedience', in Paul Harris (ed.) *Civil Disobedience* (Latham, MD: University Press of America), pp. 73–90.

Ten, C. L. (1999) *Mill's Moral, Political and Legal Philosophy* (Aldershot: Ashgate).

Tholfsen, Trygve R. (1984) *Ideology and Revolution in Modern Europe. An Essay in the History of Ideas* (New York: Columbia University Press).

Thomas, William (1979) *The Philosophic Radicals: Nine Studies in Theory and Practice, 1817–1841* (Oxford: Clarendon Press).

Thomas, William (1985) *Mill* (Oxford: Oxford University Press).

Tooley, M. J. (n.d.) 'Introduction', in Jean Bodin (ed.) *Six Books of the Commonwealth*, ed. and trans. M. J. Tooley (Oxford: Basil Blackwell).

Tuck, Richard (1979) *Natural Rights Theories: Their Origin and Development* (Cambridge: Cambridge University Press).

Tuck, Richard (1984) 'Thomas Hobbes: The Sceptical State', in Brian Redhead (ed.) *Political Thought from Plato to Nato* (London: Ariel).

Tuck, Richard (1989) *Hobbes* (Oxford: Oxford University Press).

Tuck, Richard (1993) *Philosophy and Government 1572–1651* (Cambridge: Cambridge University Press).

Tudor, H. and Tudor, J. M. (eds) (1988) *Marxism and Social Democracy* (Cambridge: Cambridge University Press).

Tully, James (1980) *A Discourse on Property: John Locke and His Adversaries* (Cambridge: Cambridge University Press).

Tully, James (1991) 'Introduction', in James Tully (ed.) *Samuel Pufendorf, On the Duty of Man and Citizen according to Natural Law* (Cambridge: Cambridge University Press).

Ullmann, Walter (1975) *Medieval Political Thought* (Harmondsworth: Penguin).

Vanden Bossche, Chris (1991) *Carlyle and the Search for Authority* (Columbus, OH: University of Ohio Press).

Vincent, Andrew (1997) *Political Theory: Tradition and Diversity* (Cambridge: Cambridge University Press).

Vincent, Andrew and Plant, Raymond (1984) *Philosophy, Politics and Citizenship: The Life and Thought of the British Idealists* (Oxford: Basil Blackwell).

Whatmore, Richard (2015) 'Rousseau and Revolution', in Rachel Hammersley (ed.) *Revolutionary Moments* (London: Bloomsbury), pp. 45–52.

Whelan, Frederick G. (1985) *Order and Artifice in Hume's Political Philosophy* (Princeton, NJ: Princeton University Press).

White, N. P. (1979) *A Companion to Plato's Republic* (Indianapolis, IN: Hackett).

White, Stephen, Gardner, John and Schopflin, George (1982) *Communist Political Systems* (London: Macmillan).

Williams, H. L. (ed.) (1992) *Essays on Kant's Political Philosophy* (Chicago, IL: University of Chicago Press).

Wilson, Bee (2011) 'Counter Revolutionary Thought', in Gareth Stedman Jones and Gregory Claeys (ed.) *The Cambridge History of Nineteenth-Century Political Thought* (Cambridge: Cambridge University Press), pp. 9–38.

Wilson, Brett, D. (2016) 'Nothing Pleases Like an Intire Subjection: Mary Astell Reflects on the Politics of Marriage', in Cesare Cuttica and Gaby Mahlberg (eds) *Patriarchal Moments* (London: Bloomsbury), pp. 89–96.

Wokler, Robert (1994) *Rousseau* (Oxford: Oxford University Press).

Wood, Allen W. (1991) 'Introduction', in G. W. F. Hegel, *Elements of the Philosophy of Right*, ed. Allen W. Wood, trans. H. B. Nisbet (Cambridge: Cambridge University Press).

Wood, Allen W. (2006) 'The supreme principle of morality', in Peter Guyer (ed.) *The Cambridge Companion to Kant and Modern Philosophy* (Cambridge: Cambridge University Press), pp. 342–80.

Wood, Ellen Meiskins and Wood, Neal (1978) *Class Ideology and Ancient Political Theory: Socrates, Plato and Aristotle in Social Context* (Oxford: Basil Blackwell).

Wood, Gordon S. (1992) 'Democracy and the American Revolution', in John Dunn (ed.) *Democracy. The Unfinished Journey, 508 BC to AD 1993* (Oxford: Oxford University Press), pp. 91–106.

Wood, Neal (1988) *Cicero's Social and Political Thought* (Berkeley, CA: University of California Press).

Woodcock, George (1965) *Pierre-Joseph Proudhon: A Biography* (London: Routledge & Kegan Paul).

Wootton, David (1992) 'The Levellers', in John Dunn (ed.) *Democracy. The Unfinished Journey, 508 BC to AD 1993* (Oxford: Oxford University Press) pp. 71–90.

Wootton, David (1994) 'Leveller Democracy and the Puritan Revolution', in J. H. Burns and Mark Goldie (eds) *The Cambridge History of Political Thought*, pp. 412–42.

Wright, Julian (2015) 'A Lesson in Revolution: Karl Mark and Friedrich Engels, *The Communist Manifesto*, in Rachel Hammersley (ed.) *Revolutionary Moments* (London: Bloomsbury), pp. 109–16.

Zizek, Joseph (2016) 'Justice and Gender in Revolution: Olympe de Gouges Speaks for Women', in Susan Bruce and Kathy Smits (eds) *Feminist Moments* (London: Bloomsbury), pp. 43–50.

Zuckert, Michael P. (2017) 'James Madison', in Ewa Atanassow and Alan S. Kahan (eds) *Liberal Moments* (London: Bloomsbury), pp. 43–50.

NAME INDEX

Note: **bold** type indicates biographical information is available in Thinker boxes.

SUBJECT INDEX

Marxism   38–40, 91, 140, 159, 258, 263–66, 269, 270, 273–76, 279–80, 293, 295, 296
Marxist revolutionary theories   257ff
    alienation in   87, 271
    bourgeoisie in   156, 257–65, 26–63, 265
    capitalism in   9, 90, 92, 159–60, 257ff, 271–74, 276, 278, 295
    class(es) in   257ff
    destruction of state in   265, 267
    dictatorship of the proletariat in   16–59, 262–67, 275
    Gramsci on   267–69
    historical materialism in   257, 273
    international relations in   259–60
    Kautsky on   262–66
    Lenin on   263–65
    Mao on   269–71
    Paris Commune in   156, 261, 262–63
    parliamentary politics in   262–63
    permanent revolution and   266–67
    post-revolutionary state in   156–57, 159, 262–67, 275
    process of change in   257, 273
    proletarian class   257ff, 272, 277
    roles of elites in   155–59
    rural masses in   269–70, 277–78
    socialism -in- one- country and   266–67
    Stalin on   266–67
    stateless society in   261
    Trotsky on   266–67
    true democracy in   331
monarchy 27, 37, 51, 62, 66, 113ff
    absolute   36–37, 117–21
    constitutional   85
    descending power in 115, 117
    early modern theories of   103–06
    hereditary   119, 120, 122
    Holy Scriptures and   119–20
    medieval theories of   100–03
    Paine's critique of   66–67
multiculturalism   182–83

Natal   285
natural law(s)   26, 51, 65, 74, 91, 101, 120, 167ff
    absolute government and   205ff
    divine source of   24, 167, 171–72
    human law and   117, 167, 172–73
    international relations and   30, 127, 173–74, 176
    natural inclinations and   172
    natural rights and   174ff
    property and   167, 170, 173, 175, 177
    reason and   167, 169, 170–72, 174–75, 178
    Roman Republic and   170
    rulers and   170, 172–74
    social life and   172, 174–75, 178, 185, 203–04, 212

natural right(s)   8, 25, 36, 66, 80, 95, 132, 162, 167–68, 174–79
    consent and   177–78
    French Revolution and   178–79
    natural freedom and   179–80
    property as   117
    rejections of   132, 181–82
    slavery and   74, 249
    utility and   181–82
    women and   71–72
nature   167ff
    state of   25, 26–30, 31–32, 64–66, 80–81, 167, 174–78, 180, 210, 212–14
Negritude Movement, the   160
non-violent resistance   281, 284ff
    anti-colonialism and   284–86
    civil resistance and   286
    Hindu ideas and   287–88
    imperialism and   286
    Islam and   287
    political action and   284–85
    reason and   288
    suffering and   287
    tradition of   286–87
    truth and   287–88

order   12, 17ff, 42, 45, 48, 52, 74, 89, 91, 99, 139, 158, 165, 198–99, 205ff, 238, 246, 253, 256, 267, 274–75, 286, 288
    spontaneous   92

pains and pleasures   232–34
Paris Commune, the   155–56, 261–63
party/parties   124, 138, 159, 278
    revolutionary   262ff, 276, 278–79
peace (internal)   21–23, 29–30, 51–52, 62–63, 115–16, 120, 173, 175, 208–11, 214, 218, 224, 237, 238, 240, 251, 287
peace (international)   25, 50, 54, 81–82, 86, 92, 133–34, 154
    perpetual   56–59, 105–06
Peasants Revolt, the (1525)   242, 254
perfection (moral)   15, 43, 45, 48, 51–52, 55–60, 108, 115, 287
philosopher king(s)   113–14, 164
political obligation   218, 235–36, 239, 244, 284, 292
polity   20, 143–44, 187–88
Pope(s)   242, 294
post-colonial(ism)   295–98
postmodern(ism)   293–95
powers, balance of   151, 185, 197
powers, separation of   185–86, 198–202, 203
presidents   124–25, 199
progress   12, 32, 56, 60–61, 68–69, 76–78, 81, 89, 92, 107–08, 125, 132–33, 136, 152, 158, 181, 232, 259, 274, 293–94

property   31, 32, 38–39, 44, 59, 73, 75, 77, 79, 86–89,
   94, 103, 109, 117, 128, 131–33, 144, 147, 149,
   167–170, 173, 175, 177, 183, 186–88, 192, 195,
   197, 206, 209, 211, 217, 228–9, 257–60, 263,
   271, 294
Protestant(ism)   2, 8, 17, 24, 41, 50, 53–55, 60, 71, 96–97,
   145, 204–05, 217, 226, 241ff
punishment   98, 100–01, 103, 178, 211–12, 214, 218,
   238, 242, 247
Putney Debates, the   146

reason   2, 29, 42, 44, 55, 57, 71, 74, 81, 88–89, 98, 102,
   116, 146, 169, 170–72, 174–5, 178, 210, 214, 215,
   218, 222–24, 226, 229, 242–43, 256, 288
reason of state   196
relativism   42
representation (political)   104, 124, 126, 145, 218, 238,
   242, 247
republic(s)   4, 125, 131, 145, 197, 225, 229, 265
   American   75–77, 148–49, 155, 199–200, 295
   Aristocratic   141, 196–98
   Florentine   52–53, 130–31, 194–95
   French   39, 244–45
   Italian   145, 198
   Roman   1, 4, 62–63, 170, 188, 189–92, 195–97
   popular   23, 58, 63–64, 145, 195–96, 240
   Venetian   117, 119, 130–31, 141, 194, 198,
   Weimar   125
resistance   2, 8, 13, 66, 173, 217, 235ff
   anticipatory   250–51
   Christians and   237–38, 240ff
   constitutionalism and   237, 239, 240–41, 246–48,
      251–52
   contract with God and   246
   contract with rulers and   244, 247–48, 255
   duty of   239, 240, 243, 243–49, 252, 283
   foreign conquest and   249–50
   Huguenot theories of   243ff
   officeholders ('magistrates') and   243ff
   passive   281, 286
   popular right of   242, 244–45, 248–51
   self-defence and   246
   tyranny and   238–9, 243, 246–50, 253, 255
   usurpation and   239, 246–47, 250, 252
   see also non-violent resistance
revolution(s)   2, 8, 9, 13, 20, 36, 38–39, 41, 56, 64, 67,
   76, 82, 87–88, 93, 109, 120, 139–40, 155ff, 188, 253ff
   Algerian   276
   American   147–50, 186, 200, 254–55
   ancient views of   188, 253
   Bolsheviks and   140–41
   Chinese   269–71
   English   145, 254, 257
   French   67, 70–71, 73, 122–23, 132–34, 147–50,
      154–55, 157, 179, 180, 186, 200–01, 265–67

Glorious, of   168–89, 220, 255
Islamic   296–97
Levellers and   254
natural rights and   255–56
process of   257–61
Protestant Reformation and   253–54
Russian   140–41, 155–56, 158–60
see also anarchist revolutionary theories;
Islamic revolutionary theories;
Marxist revolutionary theories; anti-colonial revolutionary
   theories
rhetoric   18, 20, 42
right(s)   9, 26–29, 32–36, 41, 51, 58–59, 62, 64–65, 68–70,
   89, 96, 135, 146–48, 150–53, 163, 180–84, 191–93, 195,
   201, 203–04, 207ff, 224, 282
   abstract   71, 83–84, 181
   active   167–68
   actual   90
   civil   66, 71, 74, 179, 289, 290
   Declaration of the Rights of Men and Citizens   70,
      148, 179
   duties and   167, 175, 191, 201
   equality/inequality and   36, 49, 75, 80–81, 93, 103, 136,
      148, 152, 154–55, 160, 162–63, 179, 182, 256–57,
      273–75, 296
   liberty and   25, 59, 64ff, 74–77, 95, 208, 118, 154–55,
      160, 167–68, 178–79, 191, 198–201, 231–33
   passive   167–68
   women's,   70–72, 162–63
   see also natural right(s)
Romantics, German   121–22, 133
Russia   39, 89, 91–92, 122, 140–41, 155, 158, 159, 232,
   234, 258, 263–67, 269, 275–76

scepticism   26, 28, 98–99, 226–27
Senate   199
   Harrington's   198
   Holy Roman   240
   Roman   189, 191–92
   Venetian   195
Singapore   161
single-person rule   12, 23, 37, 113ff, 128, 201,
   222
slavery in the United States   62, 72–78, 137, 155, 157–58,
   249, 251, 282–83
sociability   22–23, 25, 31–32, 79ff, 109, 123, 153,
   174–75, 213–14, 277
social contract
socialism   109–10, 136, 154ff
   democratic   296
   feminism and   179–80
   national socialism   12, 37–38, 88–93
   revolutionary   38–39, 140, 157, 236, 257ff
   see also Marxism, revolution(s)
Sophists, the   41–42, 48